"Dreams and visions are infused into men for their advantage and instruction..."

Artemidoros at Daldus
- Oneirocritica
Second Century A.D.

"Dreams are weird and stupid and they scare me"

- Rose Walker
April 1990.

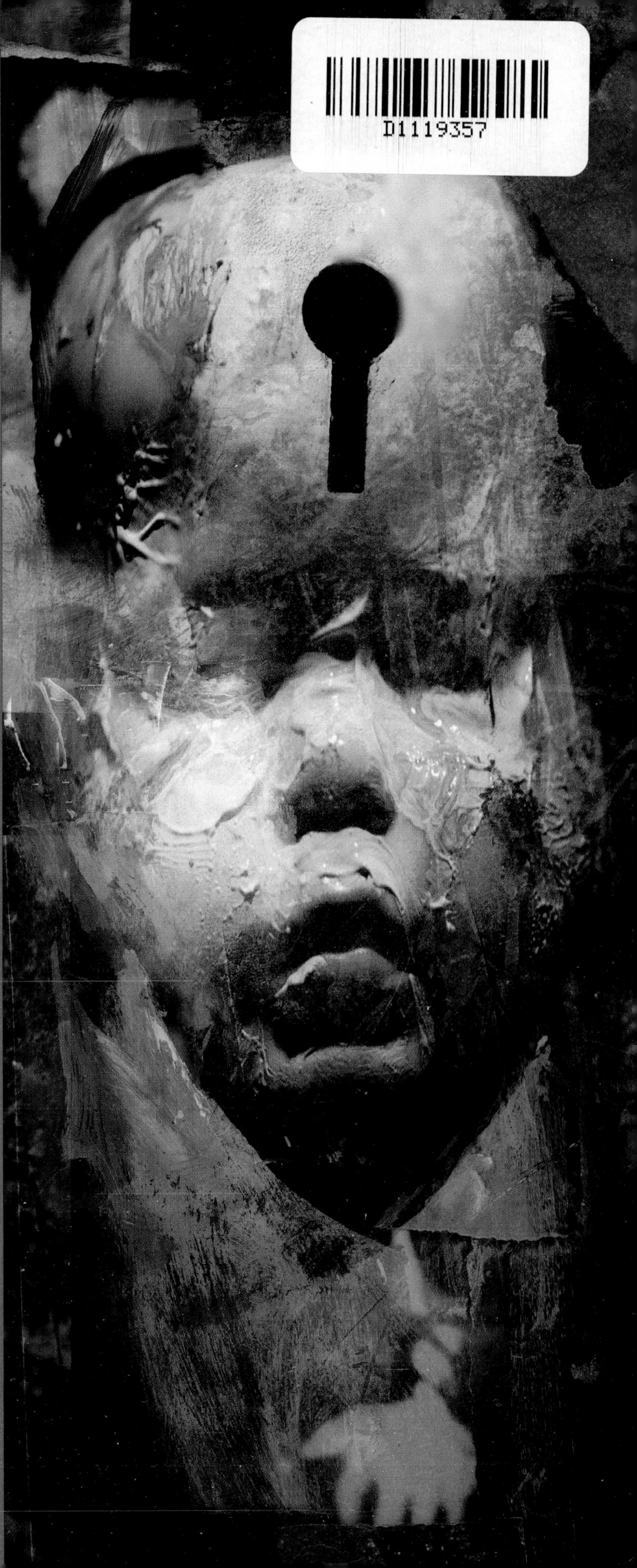

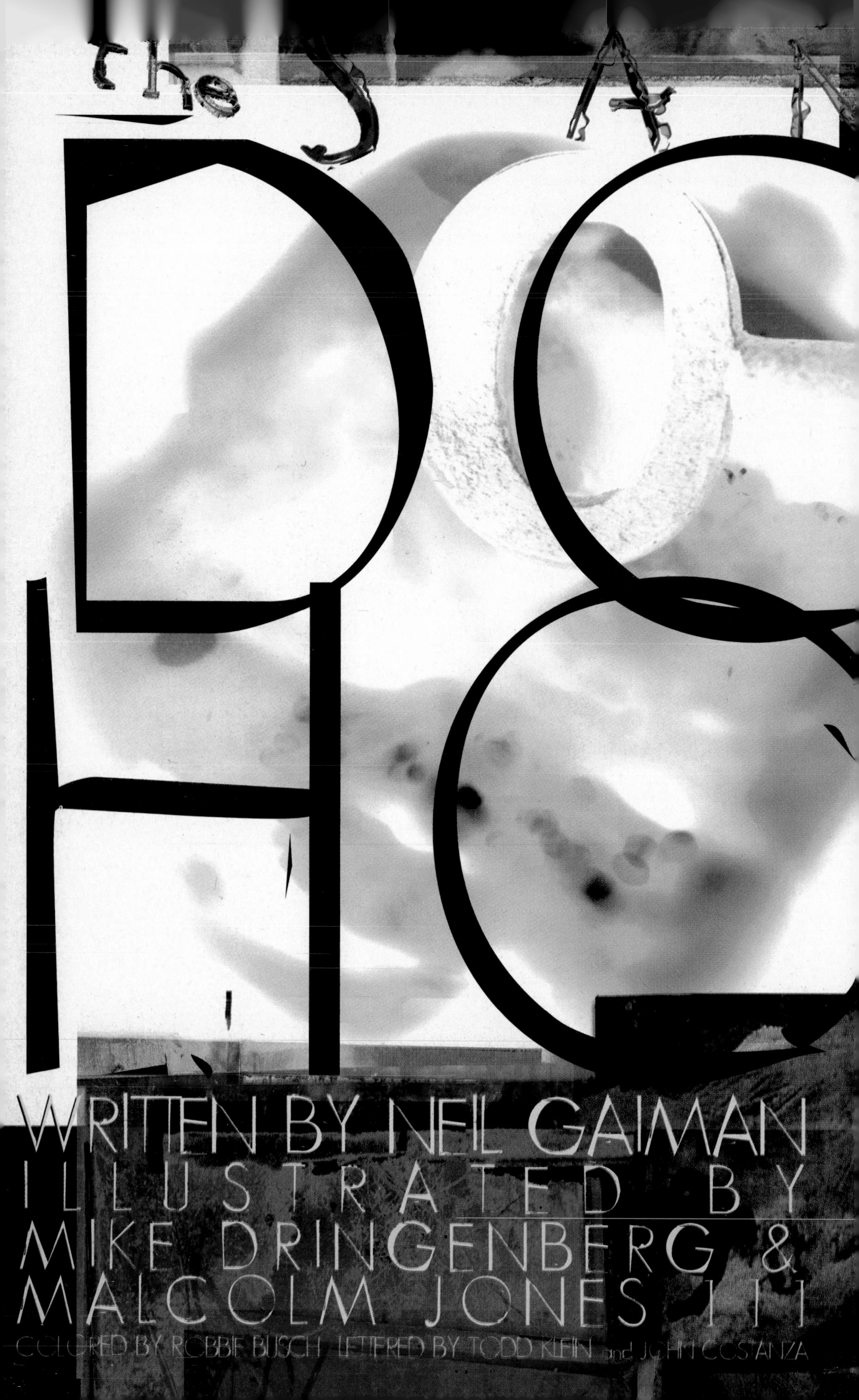
the
WRITTEN BY NEIL GAIMAN
ILLUSTRATED BY
MIKE DRINGENBERG &
MALCOLM JONES III
COLORED BY ROBBIE BUSCH LETTERED BY TODD KLEIN and JOHN COSTANZA

GAIMAN

DOLL'S HOUSE

DEDICATION

From Neil Gaiman:
For Pete Atkins, Nick Vince,
Anne and Kate Bobby.
For no particular reason
From Mike Dringenberg:
To GiGi, Paula and Eric
From Malcolm Jones III:
To Malcolm Campbell

INTRODUCTION BY CLIVE BARKER
WITH CHRIS BACHALO
MICHAEL ZULLI &
STEVE PARKHOUSE
COVERS AND DESIGN BY DAVE McKEAN

The Sandman: The Doll's House

Published by DC Comics.

Originally published in single magazine form as THE SANDMAN 9-16.

DC Comics, 1700 Broadway, New York, NY 10019
A division of Warner Bros. - An AOL Time Warner Company
Printed in Canada.
ISBN: 0-930289-59-5
Eleventh Printing.
Cover and publication design by Dave McKean.

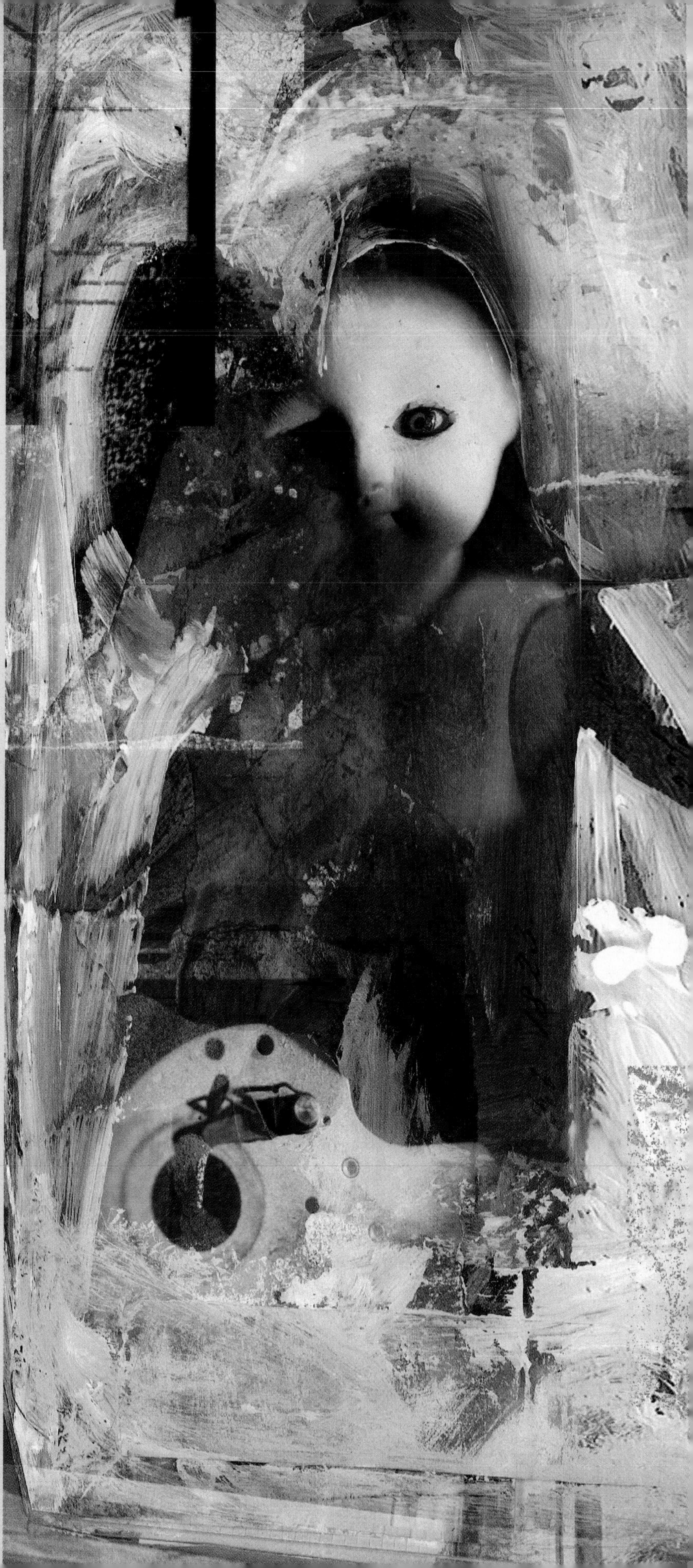

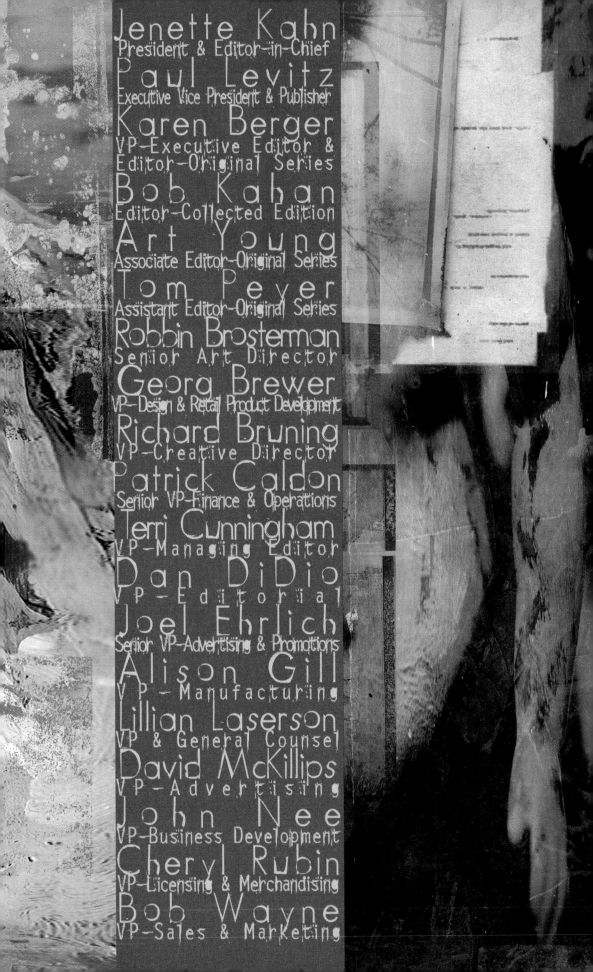

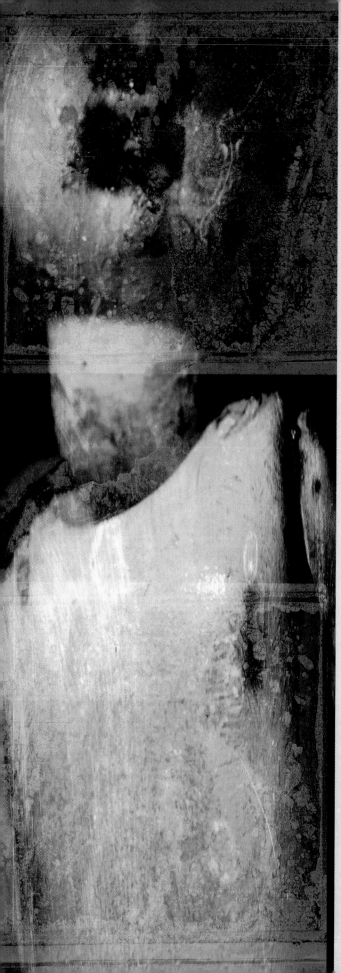

INTRODUCTION

May we open this celebration of the work in your hand by defining two kinds of fantastic fiction? One, the kind most often seen in horror novels and movies, offers up a reality that resembles our own, then postulates a second invading reality, which has to be accommodated or exiled by the status quo it is attempting to overtake. Sometimes, as in any exorcism movie — and most horror movies are that, by other names — the alien thorn is successfully removed from the suppurating flank of the real. On other occasions the visitor becomes part of the fabric of "everyday" life. Superman is, after all, an alien lifeform. He's simply the acceptable face of invading realities.

The second kind of fantastique is far more delirious. In these narratives, the whole world is haunted and mysterious. There is no solid status quo, only a series of relative realities, personal to each of the characters, any or all of which are frail, and subject to eruptions from other states and conditions. One of the finest writers in this second mode is Edgar Allan Poe, in whose fevered stories landscape, character — even architecture — become a function of the tormented, sexual anxious psyche of the author; in which anything is possible because the tales occur within the teller's skull.

Is it perhaps freedom from critical and academic scrutiny that has made the medium of the comic book so rich an earth in which to nurture this second kind of fiction? In movies it is the art-house product (Fellini leads the pack) that dares to let go of naturalism. But in recent years the most successful comic book creators are those who have strayed furthest from the security of the river bank, into the fury of white waters.

For instance, Mr. Gaiman. In a relatively short time his imaginings have made him the crowd's darling,

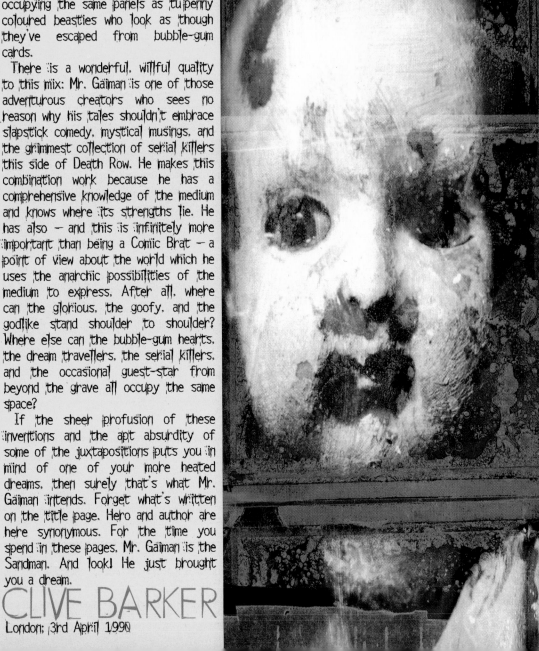

but his stories are perfectly cavalier in their re-ordering of realities. He doesn't tell straightforward, read-it-and-forget-it tales; he doesn't supply pat moral solutions. Instead he constructs stories like some demented cook might make a wedding cake, building layer upon layer, hiding all kinds of sweet and sour in the mix. The characters who populate these tales are long past questioning the plausibility of the outrages Mr. Gaiman visits upon normality. They were born into this maelstrom and know no other reality. There are creatures that dream of dreams; and others who dream about the dream-pretenders. Here are dimension-hopping entities who have a Napoleonic sense of their own destiny, occupying the same panels as tu'penny coloured beasties who look as though they've escaped from bubble-gum cards.

There is a wonderful, willful quality to this mix: Mr. Gaiman is one of those adventurous creators who sees no reason why his tales shouldn't embrace slapstick comedy, mystical musings, and the grimmest collection of serial killers this side of Death Row. He makes this combination work because he has a comprehensive knowledge of the medium and knows where its strengths lie. He has also — and this is infinitely more important than being a Comic Brat — a point of view about the world which he uses the anarchic possibilities of the medium to express. After all, where can the glorious, the goofy, and the godlike stand shoulder to shoulder? Where else can the bubble-gum hearts, the dream travellers, the serial killers, and the occasional guest-star from beyond the grave all occupy the same space?

If the sheer profusion of these inventions and the apt absurdity of some of the juxtapositions puts you in mind of one of your more heated dreams, then surely that's what Mr. Gaiman intends. Forget what's written on the title page. Hero and author are here synonymous. For the time you spend in these pages, Mr. Gaiman is the Sandman. And look! He just brought you a dream.

CLIVE BARKER

London; 3rd April 1990

In the beginning...

But of course we never see the beginning. We come in in the middle, after the lights have gone down, and try to make some sense of the story so far. Whisper to our neighbours "Who's he? Who's she? Have they met each other before?"
We get by.

In this case, let us imagine our neighbour to be tall, robed perhaps in old, monkish garments, his face hidden in the shadows of his cowl. He smells of age and dust, not unpleasantly, and in his hands he holds a book. As he opens the book (leather bound, undoubtedly, and every word in it traced meticulously by hand) we hear the *clink* of metal, and realise the book is chained to his wrist.

Never mind. We have seen stranger things in dreams; and fictions are merely frozen dreams, linked images with some semblance of structure. They are not to be trusted, no more than the people who create them.

Are we dreaming?

Possibly.

But the man in the robe is talking. His voice is the rustling of old parchments in a library, late at night, when the people have gone home and the books begin to read themselves. We strain to listen: the story so far...

***

"It was not enough that Roderick Burgess was an evil man, but he was a vain one, and presumptuous. He was not content with riches, or with the leadership of the Order of Ancient Mysteries (although the Order was in no wise Ancient, having been founded only sixteen years earlier, at the turn of the century, by Burgess himself): he desired notoriety among his peers, and he craved physical immortality.

"The year was 1916. In the world outside the Great War dragged on, and in "Fawney Rig," his Sussex house, Roderick Burgess conceived a plan. He would capture Death, bind the Reaper.

"With an invocation from a stolen grimoire he performed a Rite of Summoning. I suspect he was in truth surprised when his invocation bore fruit, when a figure took shape in the circle in the basement of his manor house.

"It was *not* Death.

"The Man in the circle was dressed in black, His head hidden by a helm carved of bone, and glass, and metal. Fires danced in the velvet darkness of His robe; around His neck hung a precious stone, a ruby; and by His side was a leathern pouch, drawn tight at the top by cords.

"Did Burgess know, then, what he had got? Did he guess at the forces that had already weakened Morpheus, the Lord of Dreams; that Burgess's Chant of Summoning had proved the final straw to Someone——*Something*——already tried almost beyond endurance?

"I doubt it. And if he knew he did not care.

"Burgess stripped the near-lifeless form of clothes and accoutrements, imprisoned his unwilling guest in an airless glass cage inside the circle, and left Him there.

"King Dream was caught and caged.

"The impact of this was felt around the world: children fell asleep and did not wake up. Their lives were canceled——Unity Kinkaid was one of these, fifteen years old and lost in a world of dreams. *Sleepy Sickness*, the disease was called, and many thousands fell victim to it.

"There were four of them who knew the truth about the Man in the cage: Roderick Burgess himself; his young son Alexander; Ruthven Sykes; Burgess's aide; and Ethel Cripps, Burgess's young mistress.

"All Roderick Burgess truly wanted was to live forever.

"In November of 1930 things began to go wrong for him. A scandal eventuated——Burgess was sued by the children of an elderly woman who had left her not-inconsiderable estate to his Order. The court case brought chaos and scandal to the Order of Ancient Mysteries.

It was then that Ethel Cripps and Ruthven Sykes absconded together, secretly, taking with them over £200,000. They took other things: a Ruby, a Helmet, a Pouch...

"The lovers fled to San Francisco, where the Helmet was given to a demon. Sykes needed protection, and the demon took the Helmet in exchange for an amulet——an eye on a chain. The Amulet kept Sykes safe from anything that could have harmed him, for the next six years. If Ethel Cripps had not left him——and taken with her both the Amulet and the Ruby——it would have protected him for longer.

"Ruthven Sykes's death was messy, and unpleasant, and somewhere Roderick Burgess was smiling.

"Burgess lived another eleven years, and then he died, still raging at his prisoner, still pleading for Life Eternal. His place was taken by his son, Alexander. Down in the cellar, in a glass cage surrounded by a chalk circle, His pale skin and His eyes burning like distant stars, the Captive waited. He had all the time in the world.

"Alexander Burgess was not the man his father was. In his hands the Order of Ancient Mysteries dried up, withered: the body was dead, but the shadow lived on.

"Over seventy years after the circle was drawn on the floor of 'Fawney Rig,' it was broken. Morpheus escaped. It was as simple as that. The Endless have time. They can wait. He could have waited until every stone of the house was dust. He had been waiting in the darkness for a human lifetime, and now He was free.

"When He escaped, the people who had fallen asleep all those years before awoke to themselves again——people whose lives had been stolen, torn from childhood to old age with nothing in between.

"In a dream Morpheus summoned Alexander Burgess, and condemned him to Eternal Waking. Listen: as Alex awakes from each dream, heart pounding, cold sweat sticking to his elderly skin, he finds himself in another nightmare, worse than the last. Somewhere, even now, he is lost in his mind, praying that somebody, somehow, will wake him up. And in his dreams every second lasts forever..."

The dark figure pauses. We try to make out the features of his face, to tease something definite from the shadows beneath his hood. No use. Perhaps there is nothing there at all.

"Dream, who is the younger brother of Death, traveled back to His realm. Picture Him, weakened, lacking His tools, returning to His castle.

"Morpheus, Dream —— call Him what you will —— is not the only entity living —— living is, of course, a misprecision —— in the Dream Place. There are others. Many others. The lost and the bodiless, archetypes and ghosts and...others. They are His servants, His creatures, while they live in His realm; and He is their lord.

"He found His castle destroyed, His servants scattered. He began the process of restoration. But to restore He needed things stolen from Him by the Burgesses, many years before.

"The Dream Lord summoned to Him the Fates, the Triple Goddess —— Maiden and Mother and Crone —— asked Her what had become of His tools: the Pouch, inexhaustibly filled with the Sands of Dream; the Helmet, His symbol of office in other Realms; the Ruby, which He had created out of His substance, and into which He had put so much of His power, a long, long time ago."

He hears our unspoken question.

"How long ago?

"Have you ever wondered what the planet Earth dreamed of, in the early days, when it was cooling from a molten state, long before a thin crust had formed on its surface —— let alone an atmosphere? It was then. Long ago.

The Dreamlord had come to rely on the Ruby for even the simplest manipulations of the Dreamworld. Tools can be the subtlest of traps.

"He asked the Hecatae where His tools had gone, and She gave Him answers, of a sort.

"The Pouch was lost for years, finally purchased by an Englishman, John Constantine. The Helmet was in Hell, taken there by a demon. The Ruby had passed from Ethel Cripps to her son, John Dee."

A page turns. We have time to wonder, perhaps, where we are. And we wonder what else is written in our neighbour's book. The irrational conviction comes over us that our name is in there —— every detail of our life, everything, no matter how petty or discreditable; all our past, all our future. Do you want to know how you're going to die?

He resumes talking.

"The Pouch had been taken from Constantine by an old lover, a woman called Rachel. She had opened it, and had discovered the joys and delights of Dream Sand. It never ran out. It was always there for her. And she lay in bed, eating it, breathing it, rubbing it into her skin, adrift in perfect dreams.

"Rachel no longer ate or slept. But still she dreamed.

"With Constantine's aid, the Dream Lord found the woman, and the Pouch. And, at Constantine's request, He granted the shattered thing a dream to take with her into death."

Another page turns. Are the pages made of paper? We find ourselves wondering whether human skin, dried and stretched, would make that same dry rustling, if bound into book form...

"To Hell He travelled then, the Pouch by His side. And in Hell He met Lord Lucifer —— once the most beautiful, and the proudest of the angels, now the Lord of the World Below, Master of Lies, Commander of the Triumvirate of Hell.

"The demon that possessed the Helmet was Choronzon, one of Beelzebub's creatures, and the Dream Lord was forced to battle Choronzon for possession of the Helmet.

"The battle was won, Morpheus regained His Helm, earning the enmity of Lucifer for His pains.

"They say we are known by our enemies. If this is so, then Morpheus is to be highly regarded.

"With the Helm regained, the compact was over, and the power of the Amulet that kept Ethel Cripps (now Ethel Dee, and old as sin) alive was withdrawn. She died, and the Amulet passed to her son, John."

Somehow we know her son, without being told. Mad as seaspray, crazy as a coot, the skin of his body stretched tightly over his fleshless bones. John Dee, self-styled *Doctor Destiny* (but shouldn't that name belong to another? to someone like our neighbour, with his robe, and his book?), dreamless dream maker, last owner of the Dream Lord's Ruby.

"Dee escaped the prison he had been held in for many years, crawled out into the night, seeking the Ruby.

"At the same time, the Dream King sought the jewel. He was not to know that Dee had tampered with its fabric.

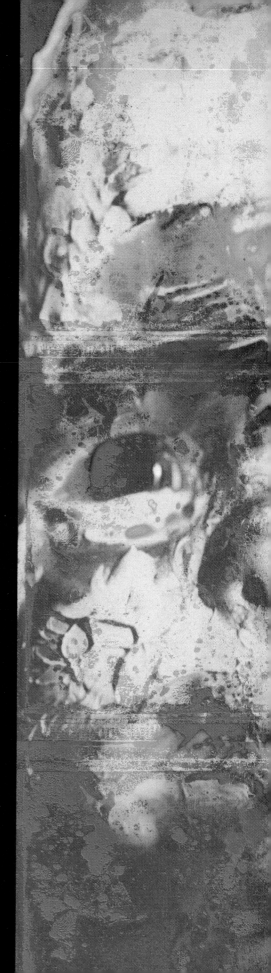

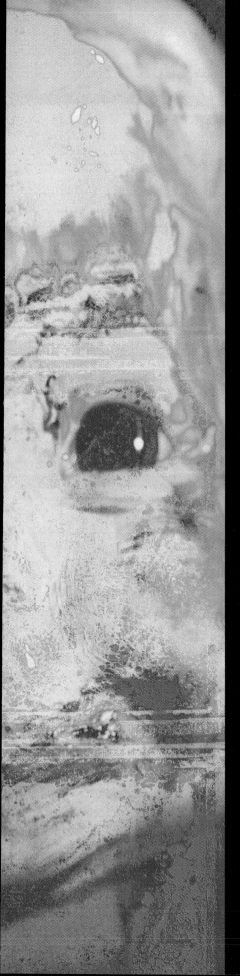

"Eventually, in a warehouse that held a treasure trove of lost artifacts, Morpheus found His Ruby again. But He found it warped and changed: instead of focusing and enhancing His energies it began to absorb them.

"It left Him weak and —— literally —— drained. Dee took the Ruby from the Dream Lord's hand, and set it to destroy the minds of the weak and the sleeping. He amused himself in His own way, while He waited."

We realise we have no desire to know how Dee amused himself.

"Morpheus lay on the cold warehouse floor, helpless and less than fully conscious; He could feel, far away, the disruptions in the dream time, the distortion and the pain. It took him more than a day to regain any strength.

"And then, incarnate, He walked the mile to where the Ruby waited with its master, whispering its message of pain and madness to the world.

"Morpheus strove with Dee in dreams for control of the Ruby, for mastery. But He strove in vain: the Ruby was sapping His essence.

"It is perfectly conceivable that Dee could have drawn all of Morpheus into the jewel and left Him a ghost frozen in crystal, His power all at the madman's disposal. Perfectly conceivable..."

Our neighbour stops reading, raises his head. Under the hood there are only shadows, but we feel that he is looking at us; and perhaps there are no true eyes beneath the cowl. This seems strangely as it should be, and it scarcely disturbs us.

"If there is a moral to this part of the story, and I distrust morals in the same way that I distrust beginnings, it is simply this: know that with which you deal.

"Dee thought that by destroying the Ruby he was administering the coup de grâce. But the Dream Lord is of the Endless, the race that are not Gods (for Gods die, when their believers are gone, but the Endless will be here when the last God has gone beyond the Realm of Death, and into non-existence), and shattering the Ruby did not destroy its Creator.

"Instead it liberated Him. More, perhaps, than that. It freed all the energies He had placed in the Ruby over the aeons.

"Lord Morpheus took Dee back to his place of imprisonment, and He left him there."

* * *

We are still listening to the story, waiting for some kind of conclusion, when our neighbour closes his book. The cold chains that bind blind Destiny to His book chink quietly.

The story is, of course, far from finished. But we know we will get no more of it from this source and, discomforted, we take our leave. The mists are rising, and it is time to be getting back.

We come in in the middle, watch for a time, leave before the lights go up. If there are no beginnings, then there can be no endings.

We are alone in the darkness. Every answer prompts another question, and things are happening all the time.

That's all you need to know for the time being. Trust me.

'The story so far.' Maybe it's all we can ever hope for...

NEIL GAIMAN

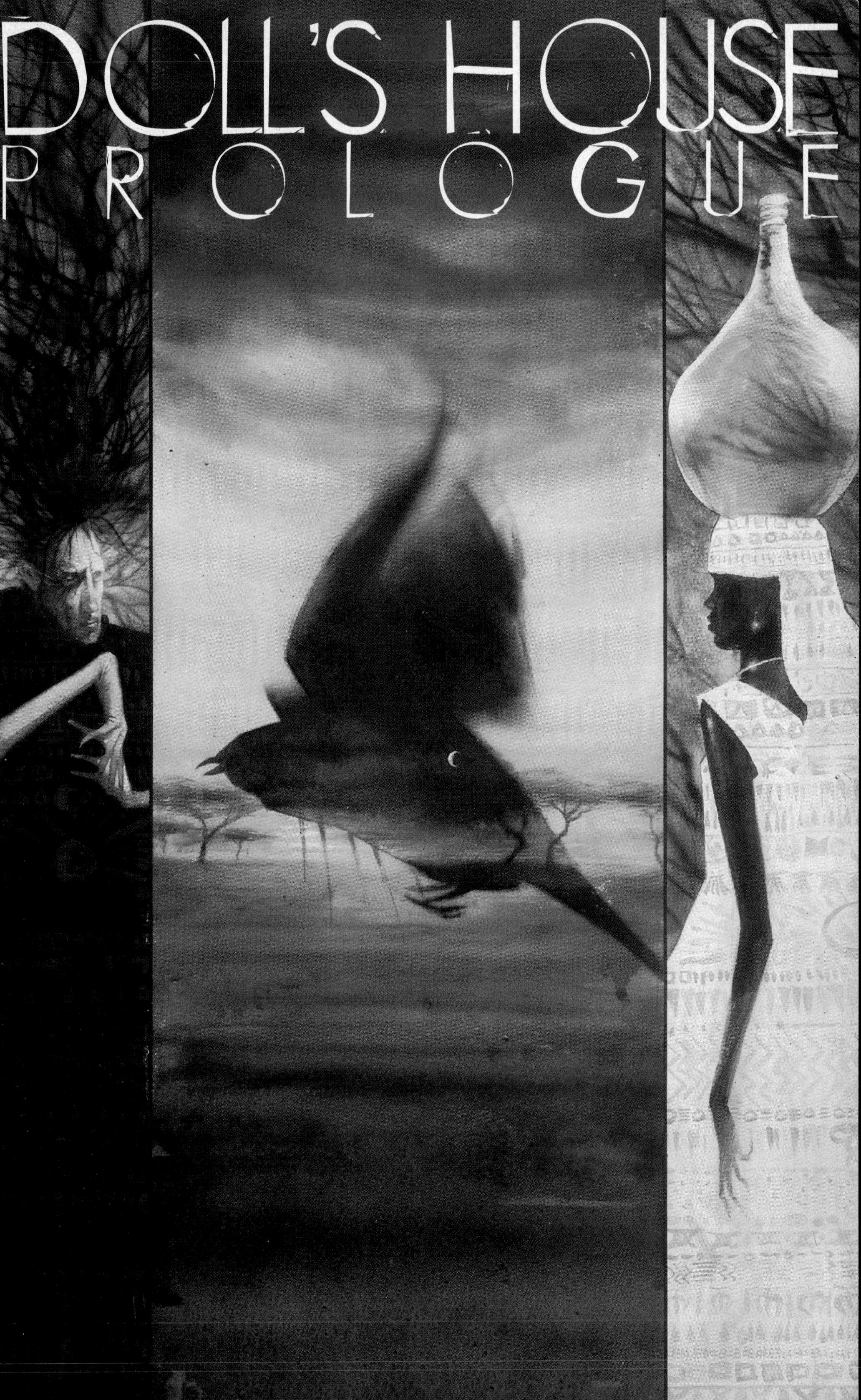
DOLL'S HOUSE
PROLOGUE

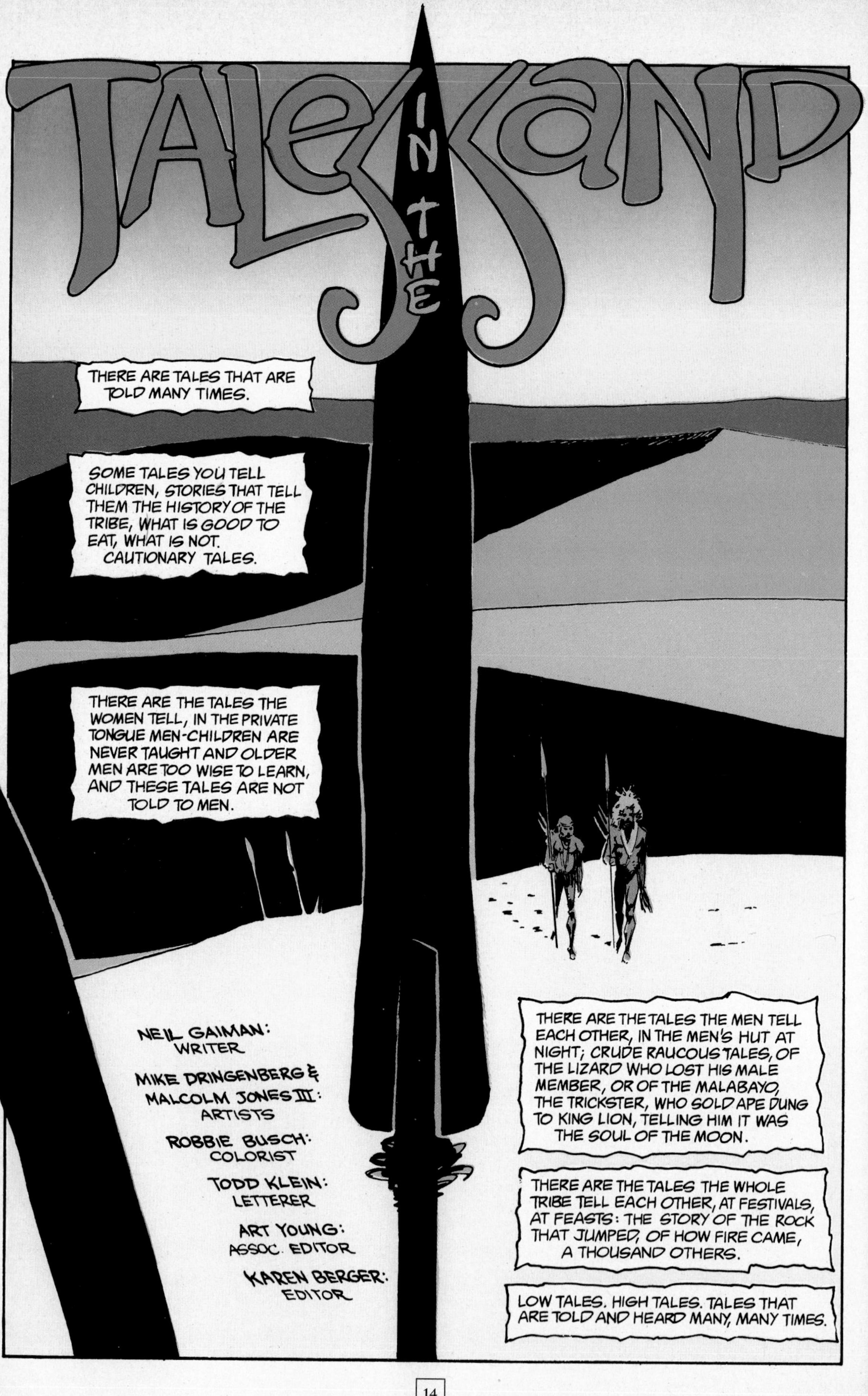

TALES IN THE SAND
THERE ARE TALES THAT ARE TOLD MANY TIMES.
SOME TALES YOU TELL CHILDREN, STORIES THAT TELL THEM THE HISTORY OF THE TRIBE, WHAT IS GOOD TO EAT, WHAT IS NOT. CAUTIONARY TALES.
THERE ARE THE TALES THE WOMEN TELL, IN THE PRIVATE TONGUE MEN-CHILDREN ARE NEVER TAUGHT AND OLDER MEN ARE TOO WISE TO LEARN, AND THESE TALES ARE NOT TOLD TO MEN.
NEIL GAIMAN: WRITER
MIKE DRINGENBERG & MALCOLM JONES III: ARTISTS
ROBBIE BUSCH: COLORIST
TODD KLEIN: LETTERER
ART YOUNG: ASSOC. EDITOR
KAREN BERGER: EDITOR
THERE ARE THE TALES THE MEN TELL EACH OTHER, IN THE MEN'S HUT AT NIGHT; CRUDE RAUCOUS TALES, OF THE LIZARD WHO LOST HIS MALE MEMBER, OR OF THE MALABAYO, THE TRICKSTER, WHO SOLD APE DUNG TO KING LION, TELLING HIM IT WAS THE SOUL OF THE MOON.
THERE ARE THE TALES THE WHOLE TRIBE TELL EACH OTHER, AT FESTIVALS, AT FEASTS: THE STORY OF THE ROCK THAT JUMPED, OF HOW FIRE CAME, A THOUSAND OTHERS.
LOW TALES. HIGH TALES. TALES THAT ARE TOLD AND HEARD MANY, MANY TIMES.

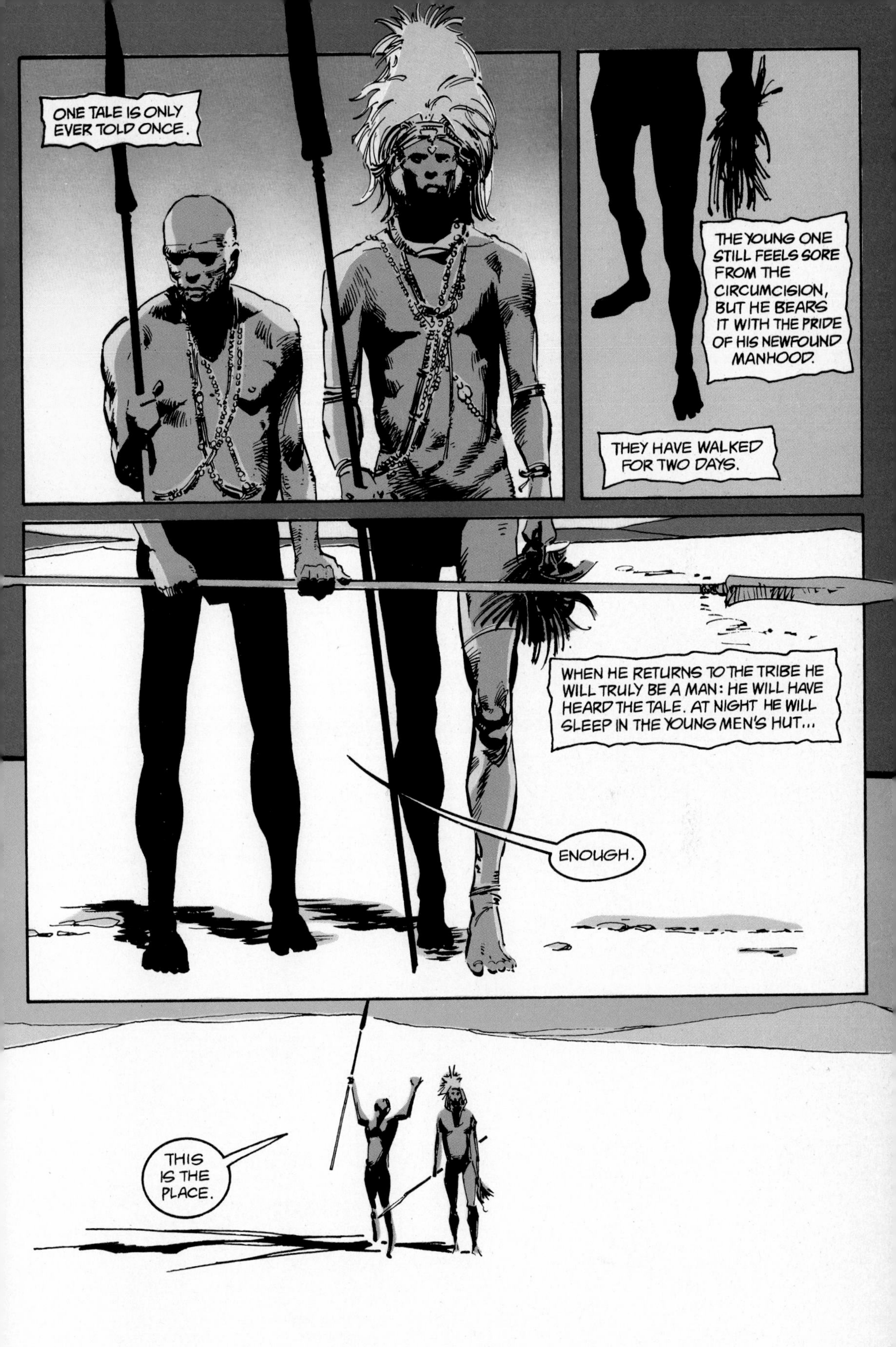
ONE TALE IS ONLY EVER TOLD ONCE.
THE YOUNG ONE STILL FEELS SORE FROM THE CIRCUMCISION, BUT HE BEARS IT WITH THE PRIDE OF HIS NEWFOUND MANHOOD.
THEY HAVE WALKED FOR TWO DAYS.
WHEN HE RETURNS TO THE TRIBE HE WILL TRULY BE A MAN: HE WILL HAVE HEARD THE TALE. AT NIGHT HE WILL SLEEP IN THE YOUNG MEN'S HUT...
ENOUGH.
THIS IS THE PLACE.

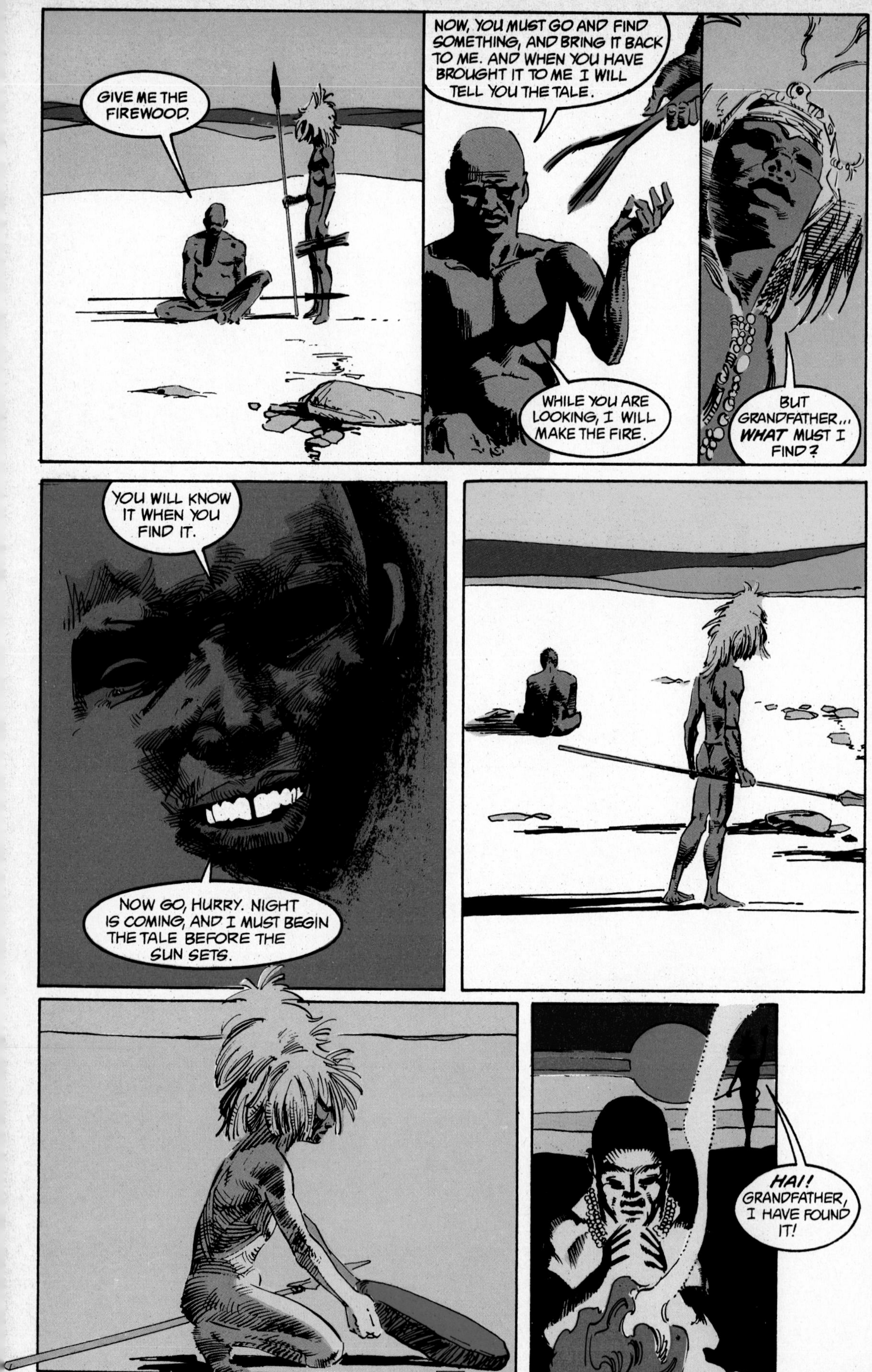

GIVE ME THE FIREWOOD.
NOW, YOU MUST GO AND FIND SOMETHING, AND BRING IT BACK TO ME. AND WHEN YOU HAVE BROUGHT IT TO ME I WILL TELL YOU THE TALE.
WHILE YOU ARE LOOKING, I WILL MAKE THE FIRE.
BUT GRANDFATHER... *WHAT* MUST I FIND?
YOU WILL KNOW IT WHEN YOU FIND IT.
NOW GO, HURRY. NIGHT IS COMING, AND I MUST BEGIN THE TALE BEFORE THE SUN SETS.
HAI! GRANDFATHER, I HAVE FOUND IT!

BUT WHAT IS IT?

GIVE IT TO ME.

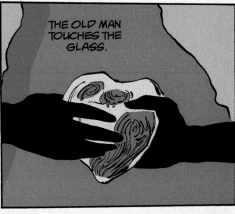

THE OLD MAN TOUCHES THE GLASS.

HE REMEMBERS, FLEETINGLY, THE TIME HIS MOTHER'S BROTHER TOOK HIM OUT TO THIS PLACE, SENT HIM TO FIND A SIMILAR SHARD...

AND THEN HE BEGINS TO TELL THE TALE.

THIS GLASS WAS ONCE PART OF A CITY. IF YOU LOOK AROUND IN THIS PLACE YOU WILL FIND OTHER SHARDS LIKE IT.

IT IS FORBIDDEN TO TAKE THEM FROM THIS PLACE.

I WILL TELL YOU OF THAT CITY, AND OF HOW IT WAS LOST TO US...

AND ONE DAY, IF YOU LIVE LONG ENOUGH, YOU WILL BRING ONE OTHER OUT HERE, AND TELL HIM THE TALE.

FOR THIS IS THE WAY IT HAS ALWAYS BEEN. EACH OF US HEARS THE TALE ONCE, IN THIS PLACE. AND EACH OF US TELLS THE STORY ONCE IN THIS PLACE...

...IF GRANDMOTHER DEATH SPARES US LONG ENOUGH TO TELL IT...

LISTEN.

THIS PLACE WAS NO DESERT THEN. FERTILE IT WAS, WITH MANY FRUIT TREES, AND FAT, SLOW ANIMALS EVERYWHERE, SO THAT HUNTING WAS EASY.

IF YOU SIMPLY CLOSED YOUR EYES AND THREW YOUR SPEAR, WHY, THERE WOULD BE SOMETHING GOOD TO EAT ON THE END OF IT.

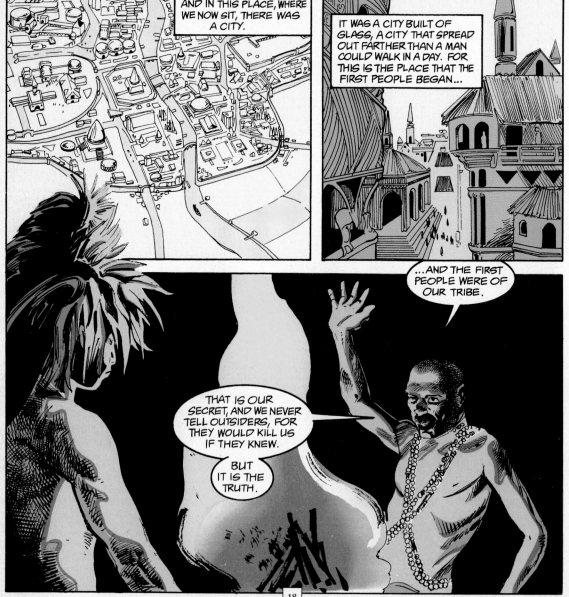

AND IN THIS PLACE, WHERE WE NOW SIT, THERE WAS A CITY.

IT WAS A CITY BUILT OF GLASS, A CITY THAT SPREAD OUT FARTHER THAN A MAN COULD WALK IN A DAY. FOR THIS IS THE PLACE THAT THE FIRST PEOPLE BEGAN...

...AND THE FIRST PEOPLE WERE OF OUR TRIBE.

THAT IS OUR SECRET, AND WE NEVER TELL OUTSIDERS, FOR THEY WOULD KILL US IF THEY KNEW.

BUT IT IS THE TRUTH.

AND IN THAT CITY THERE RULED A QUEEN. SHE WAS CALLED NADA.

BY THE TIME SHE REACHED HER SIXTEENTH YEAR SHE WAS THE MOST BEAUTIFUL WOMAN THE SUN HAD EVER SEEN IN HIS TRAVELS ACROSS THE SKY.

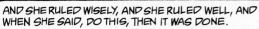

AND SHE RULED WISELY, AND SHE RULED WELL, AND WHEN SHE SAID, DO THIS, THEN IT WAS DONE.

BUT SHE HAD NO MAN.

FOR WHEN THE WOMEN OF THE TRIBE WOULD SAY TO HER THAT SHE SHOULD TAKE A HUSBAND, SHE WOULD TURN FROM THEM AND SAY,

WHERE, THEN, IS THE MAN FOR ME?

...AND THE WOMEN WOULD ALL FALL SILENT.

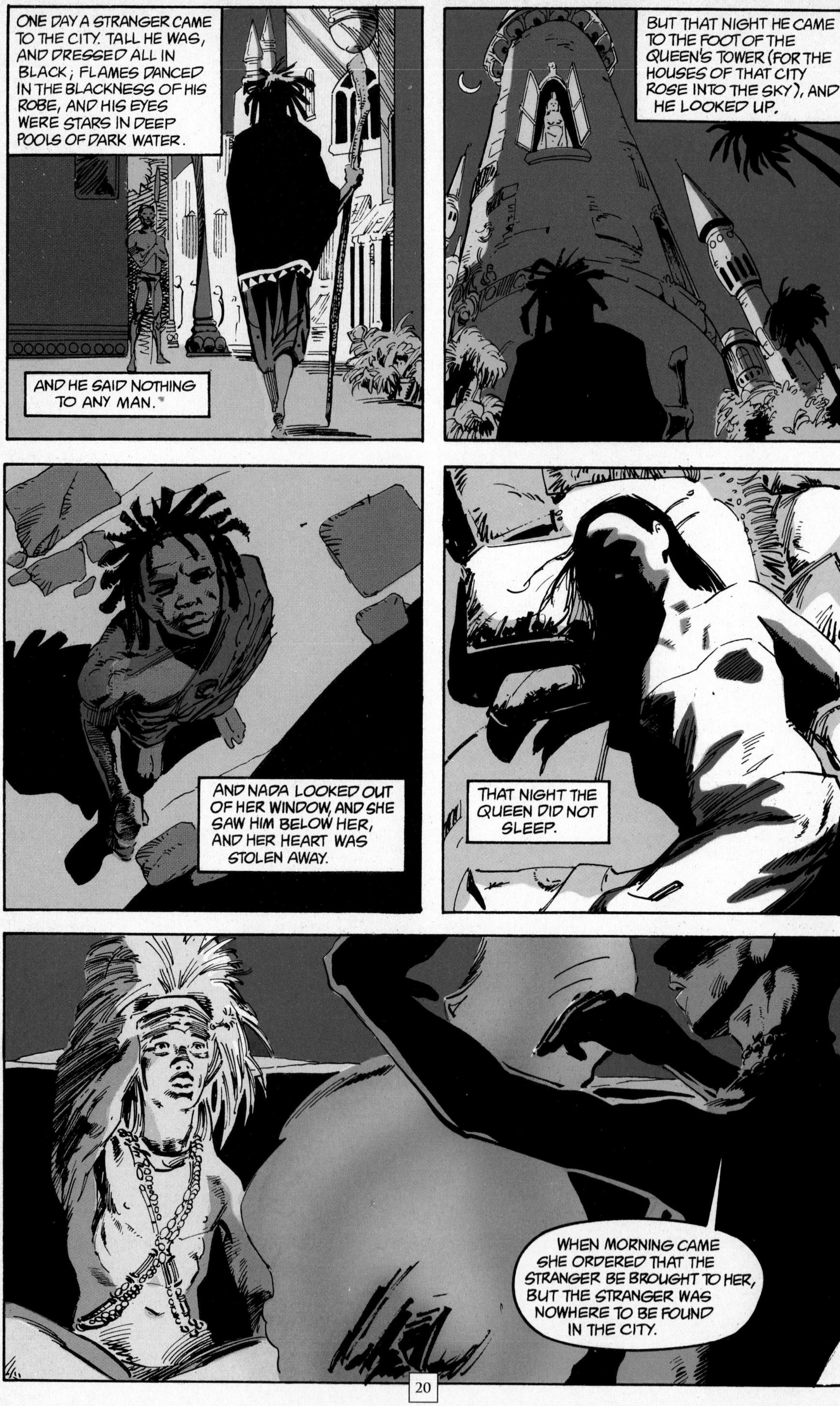
ONE DAY A STRANGER CAME TO THE CITY. TALL HE WAS, AND DRESSED ALL IN BLACK; FLAMES DANCED IN THE BLACKNESS OF HIS ROBE, AND HIS EYES WERE STARS IN DEEP POOLS OF DARK WATER.
AND HE SAID NOTHING TO ANY MAN.
BUT THAT NIGHT HE CAME TO THE FOOT OF THE QUEEN'S TOWER (FOR THE HOUSES OF THAT CITY ROSE INTO THE SKY), AND HE LOOKED UP.
AND NADA LOOKED OUT OF HER WINDOW, AND SHE SAW HIM BELOW HER, AND HER HEART WAS STOLEN AWAY.
THAT NIGHT THE QUEEN DID NOT SLEEP.
WHEN MORNING CAME SHE ORDERED THAT THE STRANGER BE BROUGHT TO HER, BUT THE STRANGER WAS NOWHERE TO BE FOUND IN THE CITY.

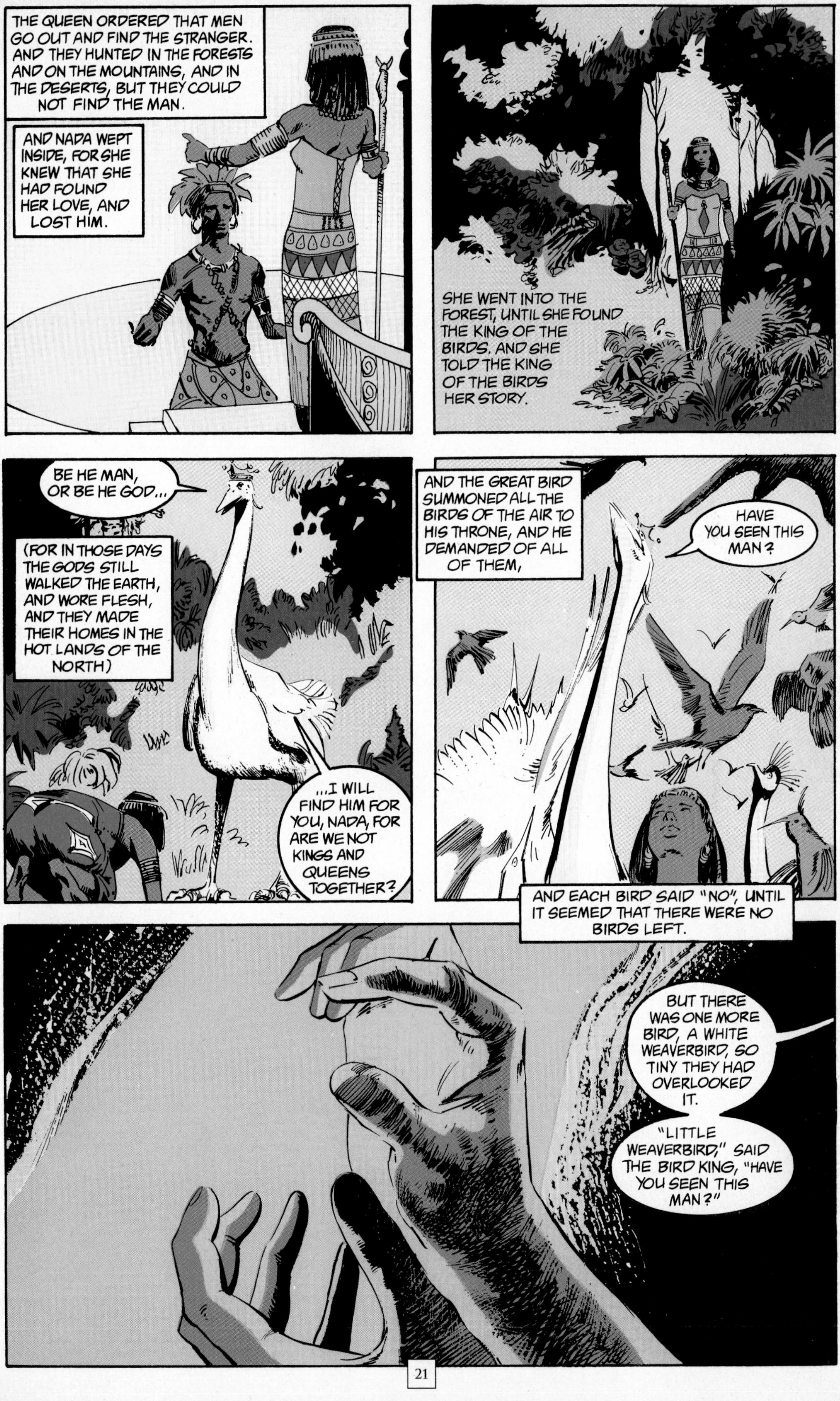
THE QUEEN ORDERED THAT MEN GO OUT AND FIND THE STRANGER. AND THEY HUNTED IN THE FORESTS AND ON THE MOUNTAINS, AND IN THE DESERTS, BUT THEY COULD NOT FIND THE MAN.
AND NADA WEPT INSIDE, FOR SHE KNEW THAT SHE HAD FOUND HER LOVE, AND LOST HIM.
SHE WENT INTO THE FOREST, UNTIL SHE FOUND THE KING OF THE BIRDS. AND SHE TOLD THE KING OF THE BIRDS HER STORY.
BE HE MAN, OR BE HE GOD...
(FOR IN THOSE DAYS THE GODS STILL WALKED THE EARTH, AND WORE FLESH, AND THEY MADE THEIR HOMES IN THE HOT LANDS OF THE NORTH)
...I WILL FIND HIM FOR YOU, NADA, FOR ARE WE NOT KINGS AND QUEENS TOGETHER?
AND THE GREAT BIRD SUMMONED ALL THE BIRDS OF THE AIR TO HIS THRONE, AND HE DEMANDED OF ALL OF THEM,
HAVE YOU SEEN THIS MAN?
AND EACH BIRD SAID "NO", UNTIL IT SEEMED THAT THERE WERE NO BIRDS LEFT.
BUT THERE WAS ONE MORE BIRD, A WHITE WEAVERBIRD, SO TINY THEY HAD OVERLOOKED IT.
"LITTLE WEAVERBIRD," SAID THE BIRD KING, "HAVE YOU SEEN THIS MAN?"

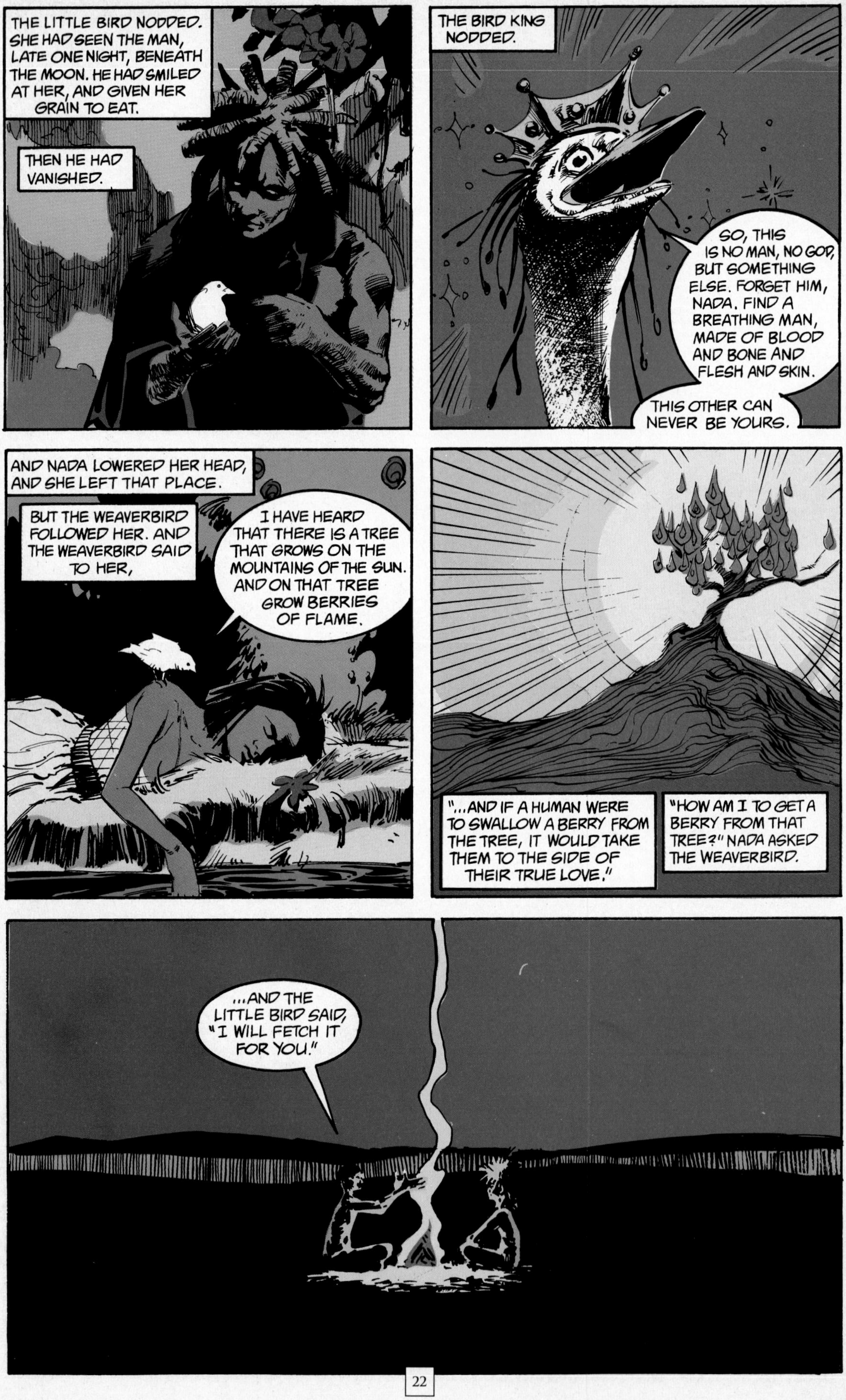

THE LITTLE BIRD NODDED. SHE HAD SEEN THE MAN, LATE ONE NIGHT, BENEATH THE MOON. HE HAD SMILED AT HER, AND GIVEN HER GRAIN TO EAT.
THEN HE HAD VANISHED.
THE BIRD KING NODDED.
SO, THIS IS NO MAN, NO GOD, BUT SOMETHING ELSE. FORGET HIM, NADA. FIND A BREATHING MAN, MADE OF BLOOD AND BONE AND FLESH AND SKIN.
THIS OTHER CAN NEVER BE YOURS.
AND NADA LOWERED HER HEAD, AND SHE LEFT THAT PLACE.
BUT THE WEAVERBIRD FOLLOWED HER. AND THE WEAVERBIRD SAID TO HER,
I HAVE HEARD THAT THERE IS A TREE THAT GROWS ON THE MOUNTAINS OF THE SUN. AND ON THAT TREE GROW BERRIES OF FLAME.
"...AND IF A HUMAN WERE TO SWALLOW A BERRY FROM THE TREE, IT WOULD TAKE THEM TO THE SIDE OF THEIR TRUE LOVE."
"HOW AM I TO GET A BERRY FROM THAT TREE?" NADA ASKED THE WEAVERBIRD.
...AND THE LITTLE BIRD SAID, "I WILL FETCH IT FOR YOU."

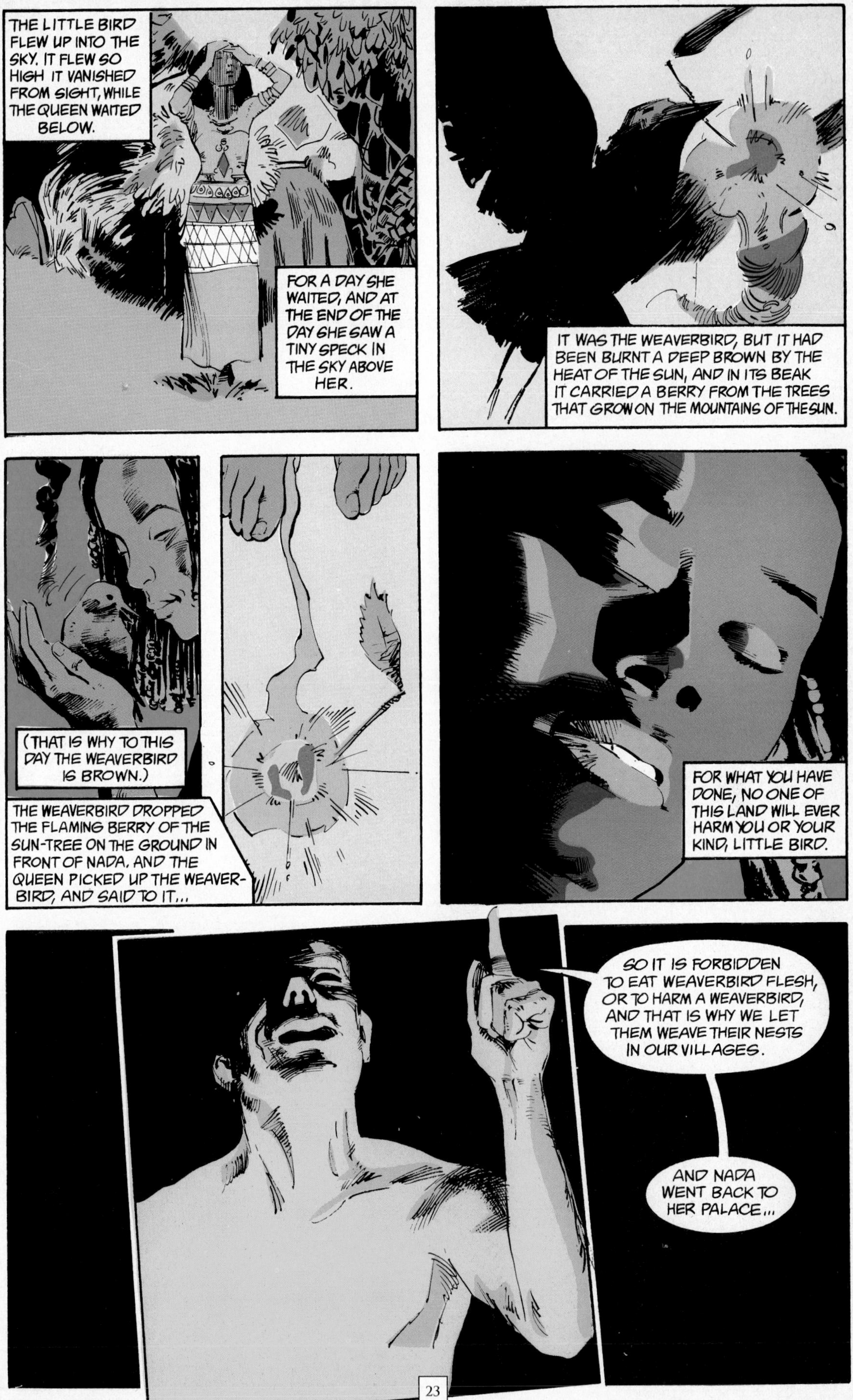
THE LITTLE BIRD FLEW UP INTO THE SKY. IT FLEW SO HIGH IT VANISHED FROM SIGHT, WHILE THE QUEEN WAITED BELOW.
FOR A DAY SHE WAITED, AND AT THE END OF THE DAY SHE SAW A TINY SPECK IN THE SKY ABOVE HER.
IT WAS THE WEAVERBIRD, BUT IT HAD BEEN BURNT A DEEP BROWN BY THE HEAT OF THE SUN, AND IN ITS BEAK IT CARRIED A BERRY FROM THE TREES THAT GROW ON THE MOUNTAINS OF THE SUN.
(THAT IS WHY TO THIS DAY THE WEAVERBIRD IS BROWN.)
THE WEAVERBIRD DROPPED THE FLAMING BERRY OF THE SUN-TREE ON THE GROUND IN FRONT OF NADA, AND THE QUEEN PICKED UP THE WEAVER-BIRD, AND SAID TO IT...
FOR WHAT YOU HAVE DONE, NO ONE OF THIS LAND WILL EVER HARM YOU OR YOUR KIND, LITTLE BIRD.
SO IT IS FORBIDDEN TO EAT WEAVERBIRD FLESH, OR TO HARM A WEAVERBIRD, AND THAT IS WHY WE LET THEM WEAVE THEIR NESTS IN OUR VILLAGES.
AND NADA WENT BACK TO HER PALACE...

AND SHE WENT TO HER ROOM, AND SHE SWALLOWED THE FIRE-BERRY, THOUGH IT SEARED HER THROAT. AND SHE FELL DOWN, AS IF IN A DEEP SLEEP...

...AND HER SOUL WAS PULLED OUT OF HER, AND HER SPIRIT WENT WALKING.

IT SEEMED TO HER THAT SHE WAS IN A DARKENED WORLD.

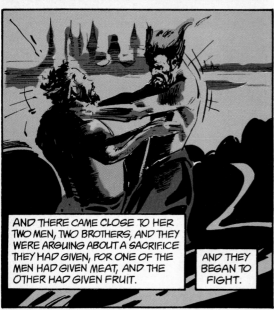

AND THERE CAME CLOSE TO HER TWO MEN, TWO BROTHERS, AND THEY WERE ARGUING ABOUT A SACRIFICE THEY HAD GIVEN, FOR ONE OF THE MEN HAD GIVEN MEAT, AND THE OTHER HAD GIVEN FRUIT.

AND THEY BEGAN TO FIGHT.

PRESENTLY ONE BROTHER KILLED THE OTHER, AND WALKED ON DOWN THE ROAD.

THEN SHE SAID TO THE BROTHER WHO WAS DEAD,

WHAT IS THIS PLACE?

"THIS IS THE DREAMWORLD, LADY," HE TOLD HER. "THIS IS THE REALM OF SLEEP AND DREAM, RULED BY KAI'CKUL, THE LORD OF DREAMS.

"THAT HOUSE IS HIS HOUSE."

SHE WALKED UP TO THE HOUSE, AND WENT IN TO IT. THE GUARDIANS LET HER PASS, BECAUSE THEY COULD FEEL THE FLAMING BERRY INSIDE HER.

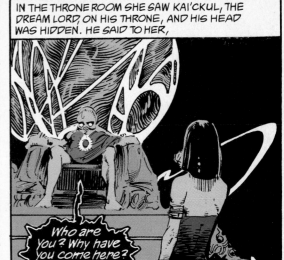

IN THE THRONE ROOM SHE SAW KAI'CKUL, THE DREAM LORD, ON HIS THRONE, AND HIS HEAD WAS HIDDEN. HE SAID TO HER,

Who are you? Why have you come here?

I SEEK A STRANGER, FOR I LOVE HIM. FLAMES DANCE IN THE BLACKNESS OF HIS ROBE, AND HIS EYES ARE STARS IN POOLS OF DEEP WATER.

HE CAME TO MY TOWER ONE NIGHT, AND LOOKED UP AT ME, BUT HE SAID NOTHING.

AT THIS, KAI'CKUL REMOVED HIS HELMET, AND SHE SAW BEFORE HER THE STRANGER WHO HAD STOOD BENEATH HER HOUSE IN THE CITY OF GLASS.

AND HER HEART SANK WITHIN HER, FOR SHE HAD CONFESSED HER LOVE TO ONE OF THE ENDLESS, WHO ARE NOT GODS, AND WILL NEVER DIE LIKE GODS.

AND IN THE TWIN STARS OF HIS EYES SHE SAW HE LOVED HER TOO.

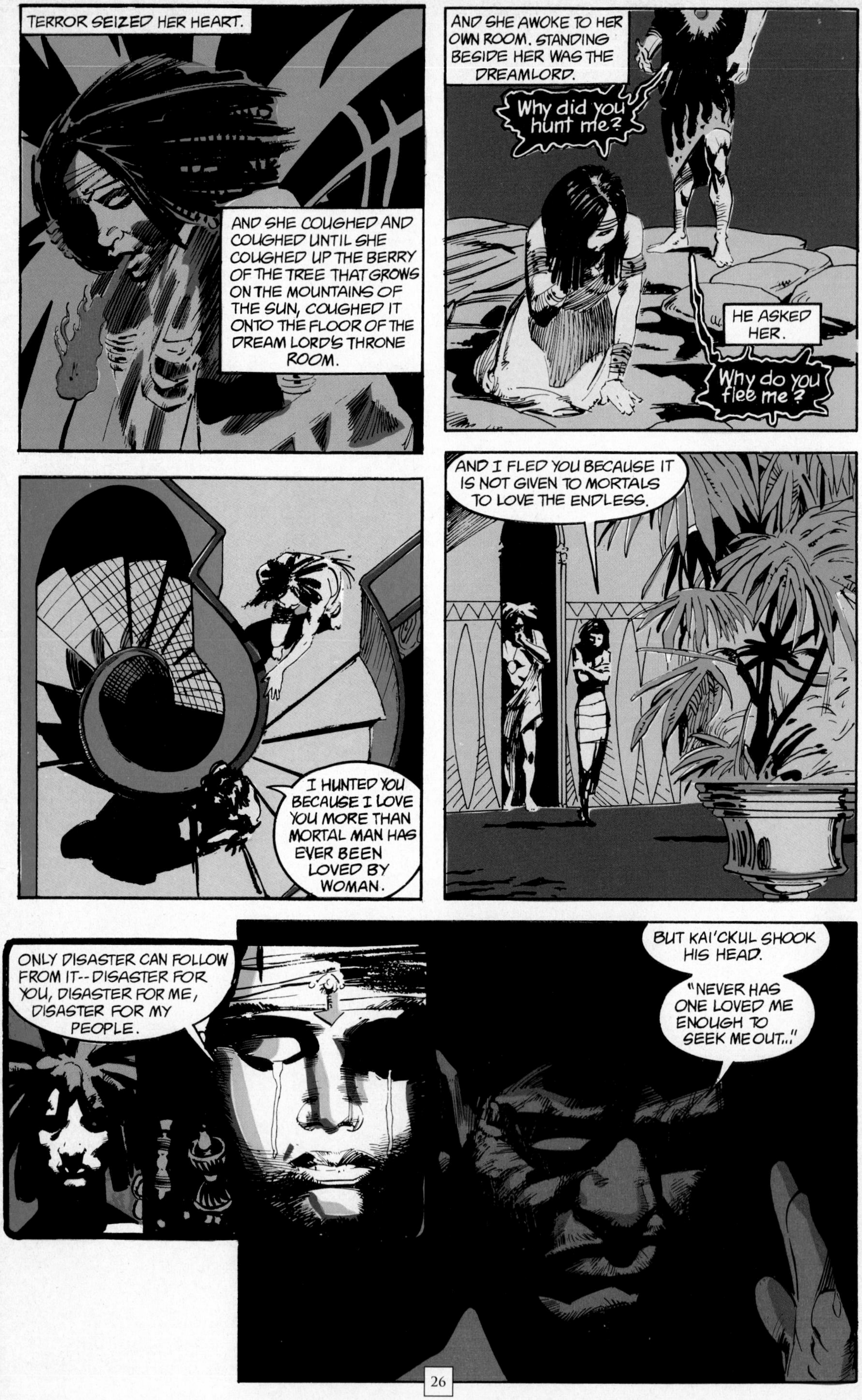
TERROR SEIZED HER HEART.
AND SHE COUGHED AND COUGHED UNTIL SHE COUGHED UP THE BERRY OF THE TREE THAT GROWS ON THE MOUNTAINS OF THE SUN, COUGHED IT ONTO THE FLOOR OF THE DREAM LORD'S THRONE ROOM.
AND SHE AWOKE TO HER OWN ROOM. STANDING BESIDE HER WAS THE DREAMLORD.
Why did you hunt me?
HE ASKED HER.
Why do you flee me?
I HUNTED YOU BECAUSE I LOVE YOU MORE THAN MORTAL MAN HAS EVER BEEN LOVED BY WOMAN.
AND I FLED YOU BECAUSE IT IS NOT GIVEN TO MORTALS TO LOVE THE ENDLESS.
ONLY DISASTER CAN FOLLOW FROM IT--DISASTER FOR YOU, DISASTER FOR ME, DISASTER FOR MY PEOPLE.
BUT KAI'CKUL SHOOK HIS HEAD.
"NEVER HAS ONE LOVED ME ENOUGH TO SEEK ME OUT..."

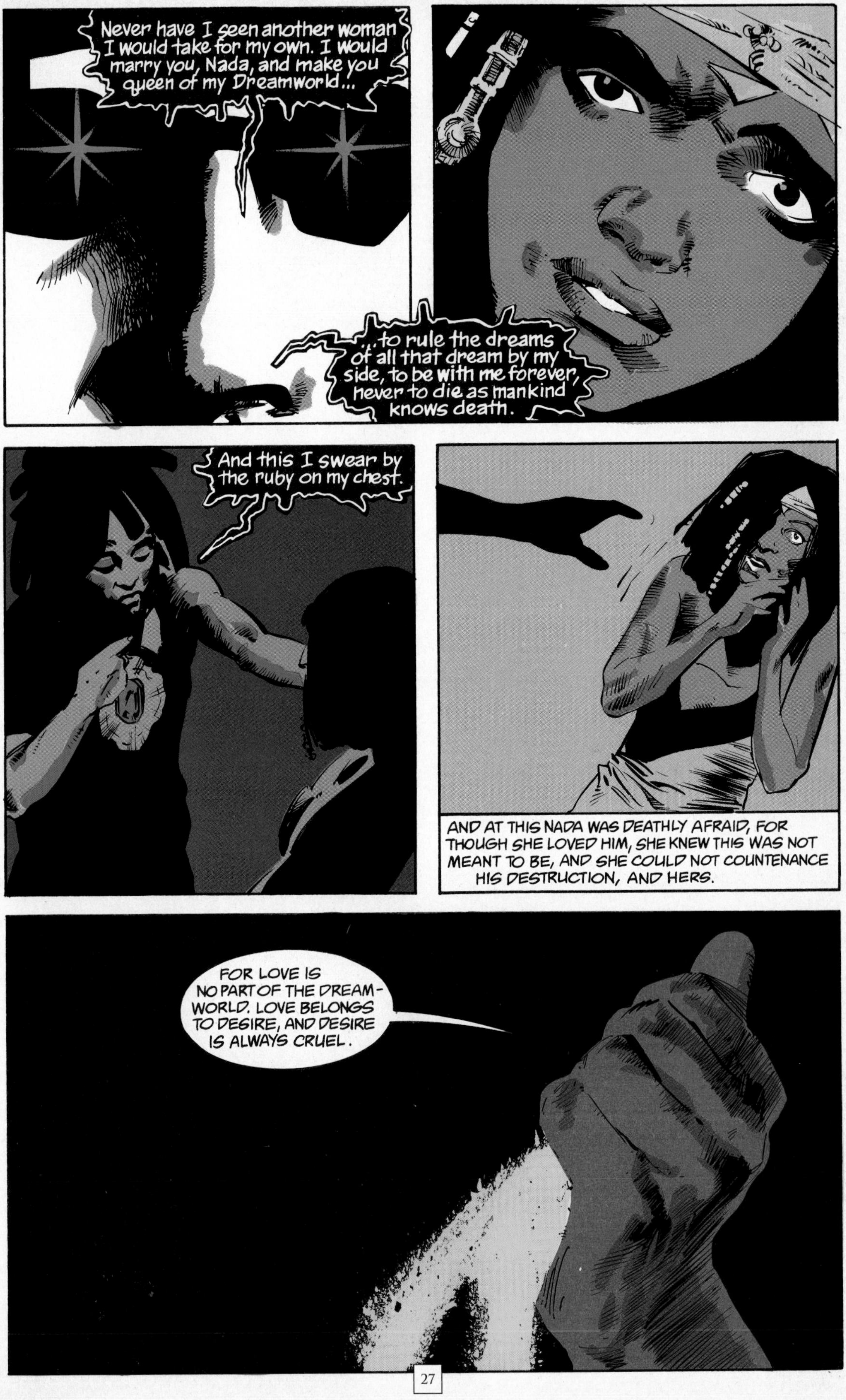
Never have I seen another woman I would take for my own. I would marry you, Nada, and make you queen of my Dreamworld...
...to rule the dreams of all that dream by my side, to be with me forever, never to die as mankind knows death.
And this I swear by the ruby on my chest.
AND AT THIS NADA WAS DEATHLY AFRAID, FOR THOUGH SHE LOVED HIM, SHE KNEW THIS WAS NOT MEANT TO BE, AND SHE COULD NOT COUNTENANCE HIS DESTRUCTION, AND HERS.
FOR LOVE IS NO PART OF THE DREAM-WORLD. LOVE BELONGS TO DESIRE, AND DESIRE IS ALWAYS CRUEL.

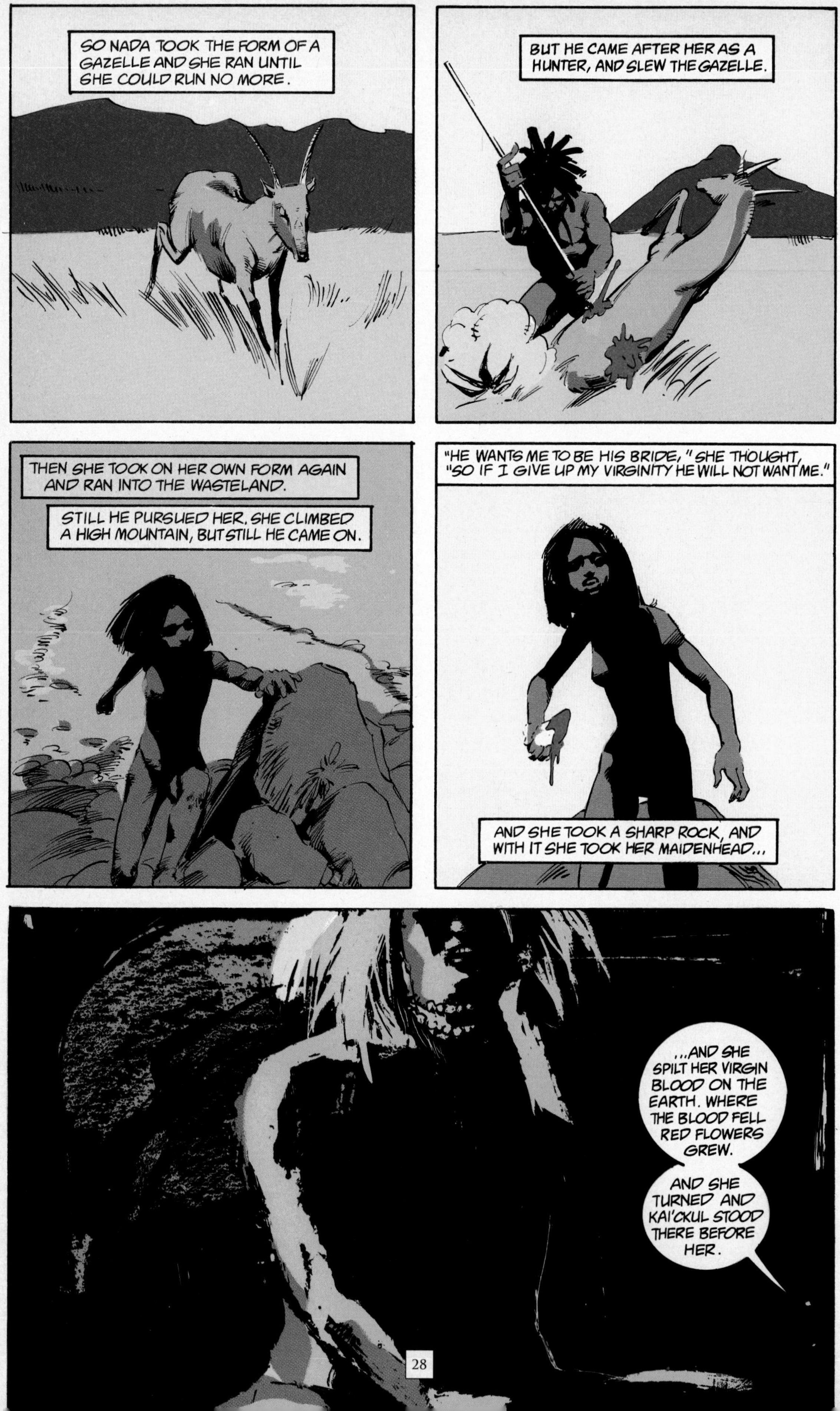
SO NADA TOOK THE FORM OF A GAZELLE AND SHE RAN UNTIL SHE COULD RUN NO MORE.
BUT HE CAME AFTER HER AS A HUNTER, AND SLEW THE GAZELLE.
THEN SHE TOOK ON HER OWN FORM AGAIN AND RAN INTO THE WASTELAND.
STILL HE PURSUED HER. SHE CLIMBED A HIGH MOUNTAIN, BUT STILL HE CAME ON.
"HE WANTS ME TO BE HIS BRIDE," SHE THOUGHT, "SO IF I GIVE UP MY VIRGINITY HE WILL NOT WANT ME."
AND SHE TOOK A SHARP ROCK, AND WITH IT SHE TOOK HER MAIDENHEAD...
...AND SHE SPILT HER VIRGIN BLOOD ON THE EARTH. WHERE THE BLOOD FELL RED FLOWERS GREW.
AND SHE TURNED AND KAI'CKUL STOOD THERE BEFORE HER.

YOU KNOW I AM NOW NO VIRGIN?

...SHE SAID, EXPECTING HIM TO LEAVE HER BE.

I am no mortal man, and I love you as no mortal man could love...

What matters your body to me?

AND HE TOUCHED HER SEX WITH HIS HAND, AND AT HIS TOUCH SHE WAS HEALED, AND THE PAIN LEFT HER, AND THE WOUND WAS HEALED, THOUGH HER MAIDENHEAD WAS NOT RESTORED.

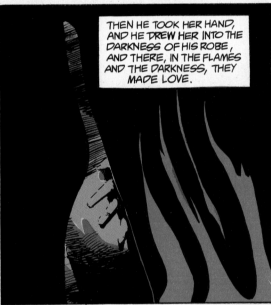

THEN HE TOOK HER HAND, AND HE DREW HER INTO THE DARKNESS OF HIS ROBE, AND THERE, IN THE FLAMES AND THE DARKNESS, THEY MADE LOVE.

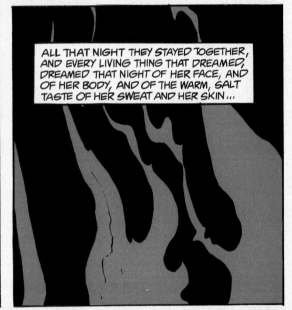

ALL THAT NIGHT THEY STAYED TOGETHER, AND EVERY LIVING THING THAT DREAMED, DREAMED THAT NIGHT OF HER FACE, AND OF HER BODY, AND OF THE WARM, SALT TASTE OF HER SWEAT AND HER SKIN...

AND EVERY LIVING THING THAT COULD DREAM DREAMED OF LOVE.

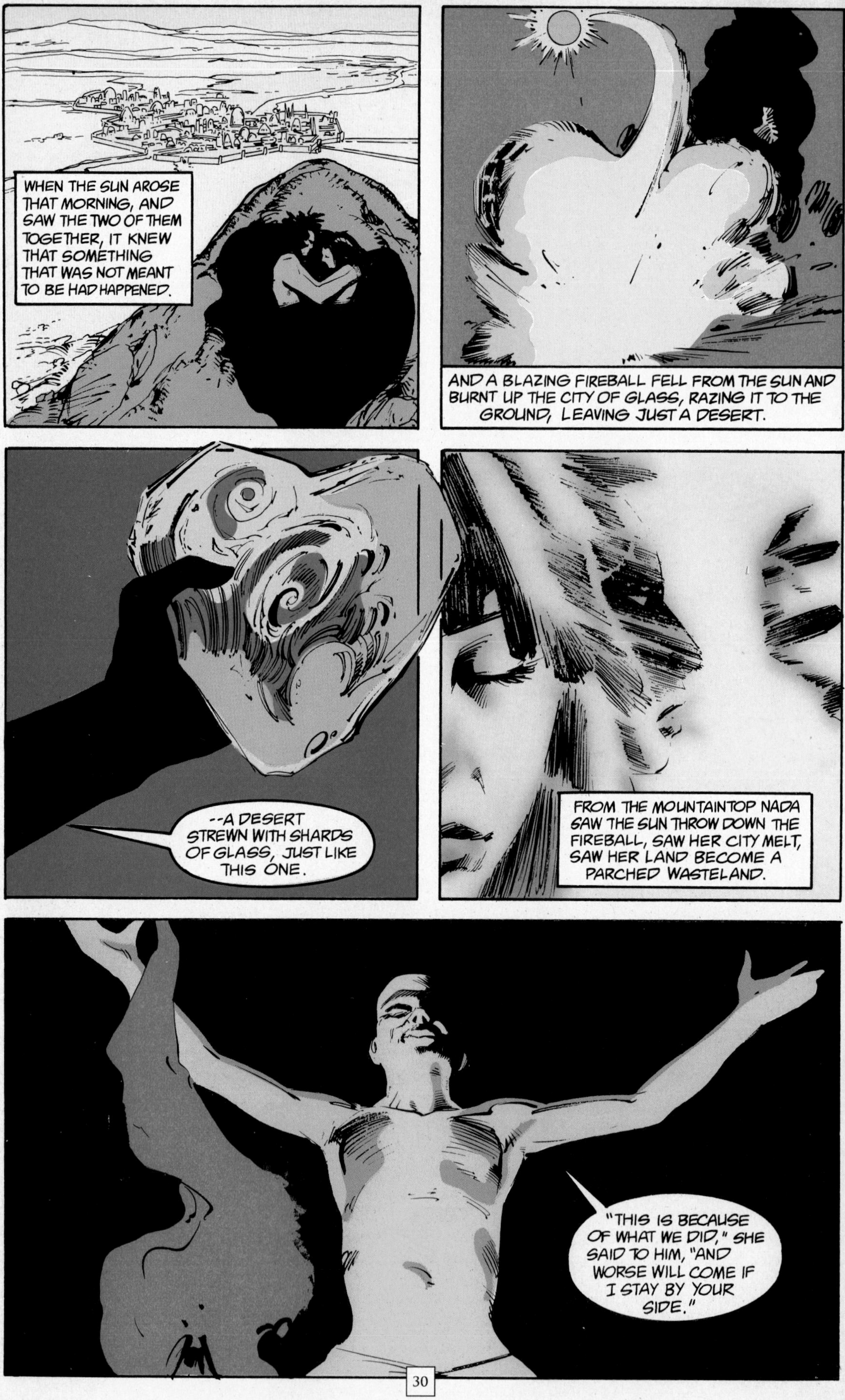

WHEN THE SUN AROSE THAT MORNING, AND SAW THE TWO OF THEM TOGETHER, IT KNEW THAT SOMETHING THAT WAS NOT MEANT TO BE HAD HAPPENED.
AND A BLAZING FIREBALL FELL FROM THE SUN AND BURNT UP THE CITY OF GLASS, RAZING IT TO THE GROUND, LEAVING JUST A DESERT.
--A DESERT STREWN WITH SHARDS OF GLASS, JUST LIKE THIS ONE.
FROM THE MOUNTAINTOP NADA SAW THE SUN THROW DOWN THE FIREBALL, SAW HER CITY MELT, SAW HER LAND BECOME A PARCHED WASTELAND.
"THIS IS BECAUSE OF WHAT WE DID," SHE SAID TO HIM, "AND WORSE WILL COME IF I STAY BY YOUR SIDE."

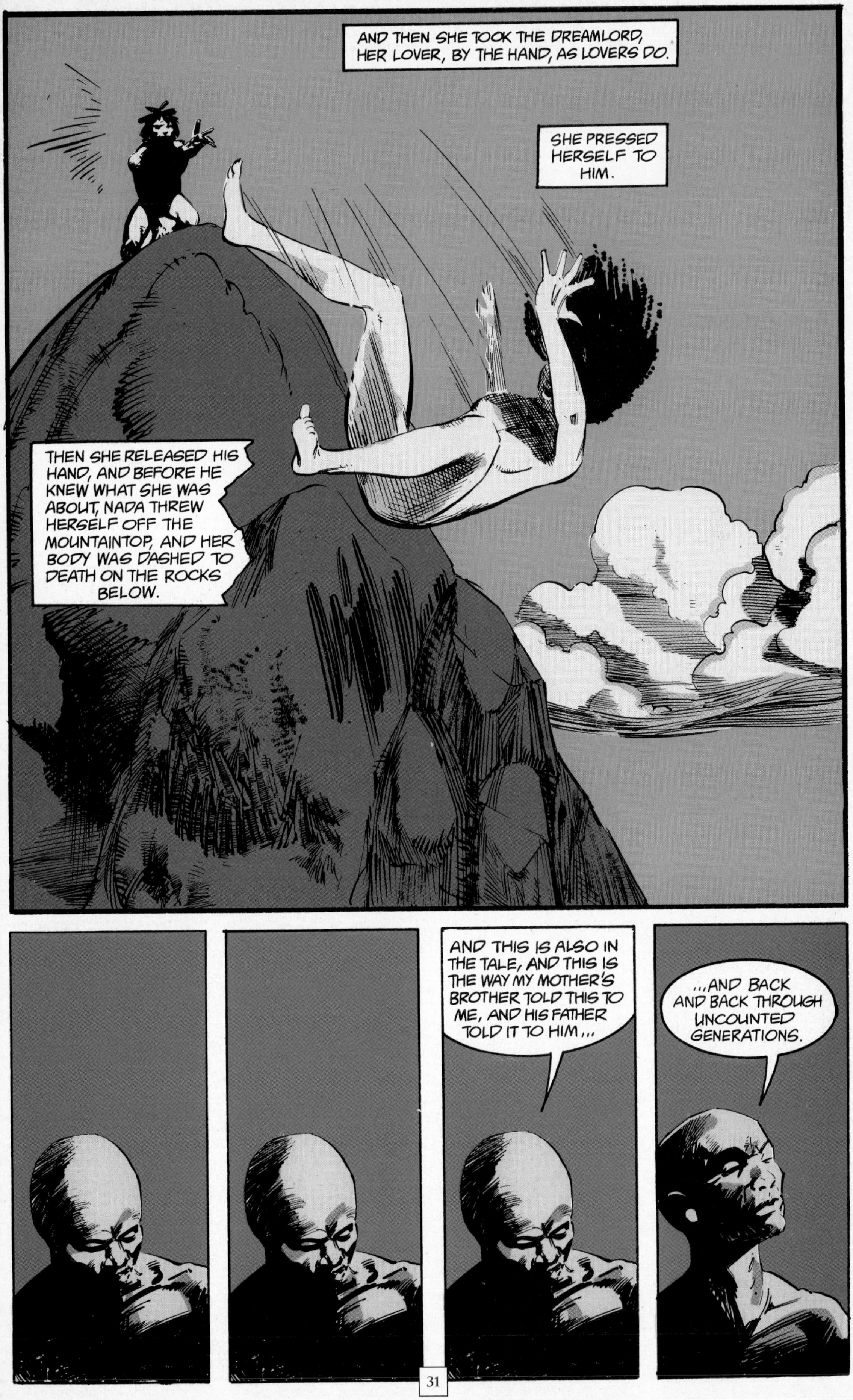
AND THEN SHE TOOK THE DREAMLORD, HER LOVER, BY THE HAND, AS LOVERS DO.
SHE PRESSED HERSELF TO HIM.
THEN SHE RELEASED HIS HAND, AND BEFORE HE KNEW WHAT SHE WAS ABOUT, NADA THREW HERSELF OFF THE MOUNTAINTOP, AND HER BODY WAS DASHED TO DEATH ON THE ROCKS BELOW.
AND THIS IS ALSO IN THE TALE, AND THIS IS THE WAY MY MOTHER'S BROTHER TOLD THIS TO ME, AND HIS FATHER TOLD IT TO HIM...
...AND BACK AND BACK THROUGH UNCOUNTED GENERATIONS.

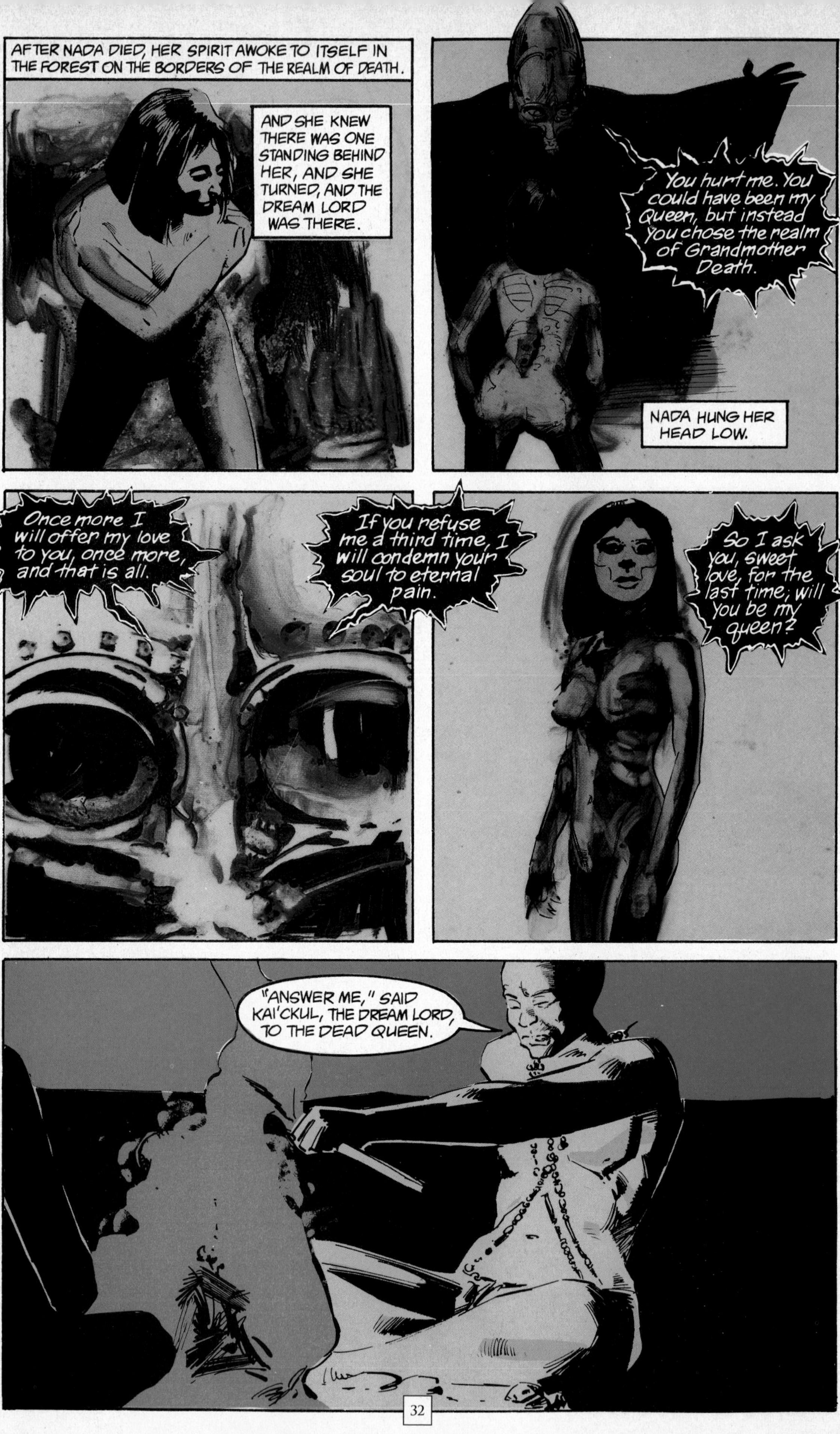
AFTER NADA DIED, HER SPIRIT AWOKE TO ITSELF IN THE FOREST ON THE BORDERS OF THE REALM OF DEATH.
AND SHE KNEW THERE WAS ONE STANDING BEHIND HER, AND SHE TURNED, AND THE DREAM LORD WAS THERE.
You hurt me. You could have been my Queen, but instead you chose the realm of Grandmother Death.
NADA HUNG HER HEAD LOW.
Once more I will offer my love to you, once more, and that is all.
If you refuse me a third time, I will condemn your soul to eternal pain.
So I ask you, sweet love, for the last time; will you be my queen?
"ANSWER ME," SAID KAI'CKUL, THE DREAM LORD, TO THE DEAD QUEEN.

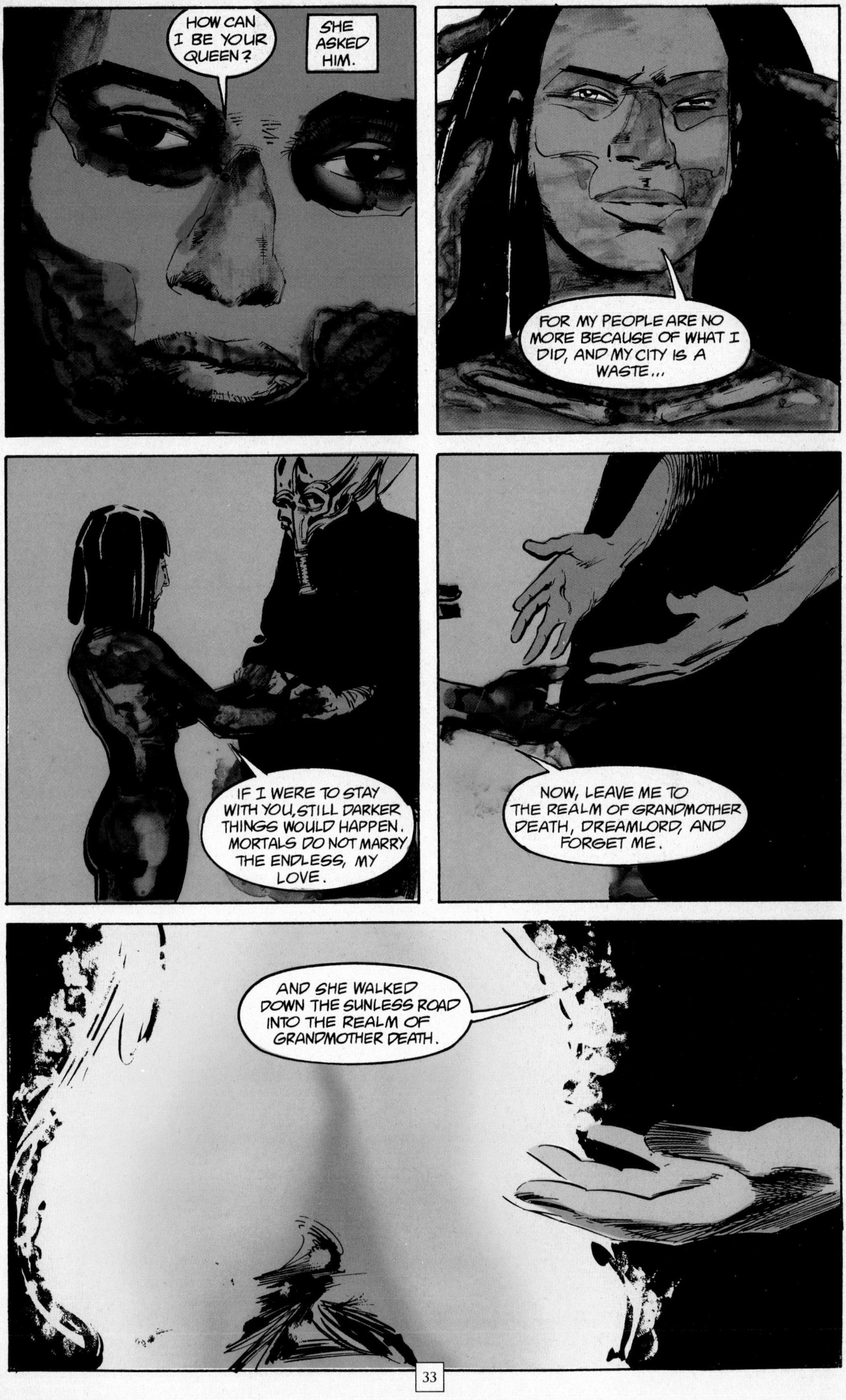
HOW CAN I BE YOUR QUEEN?
SHE ASKED HIM.
FOR MY PEOPLE ARE NO MORE BECAUSE OF WHAT I DID, AND MY CITY IS A WASTE...
IF I WERE TO STAY WITH YOU, STILL DARKER THINGS WOULD HAPPEN. MORTALS DO NOT MARRY THE ENDLESS, MY LOVE.
NOW, LEAVE ME TO THE REALM OF GRANDMOTHER DEATH, DREAMLORD, AND FORGET ME.
AND SHE WALKED DOWN THE SUNLESS ROAD INTO THE REALM OF GRANDMOTHER DEATH.

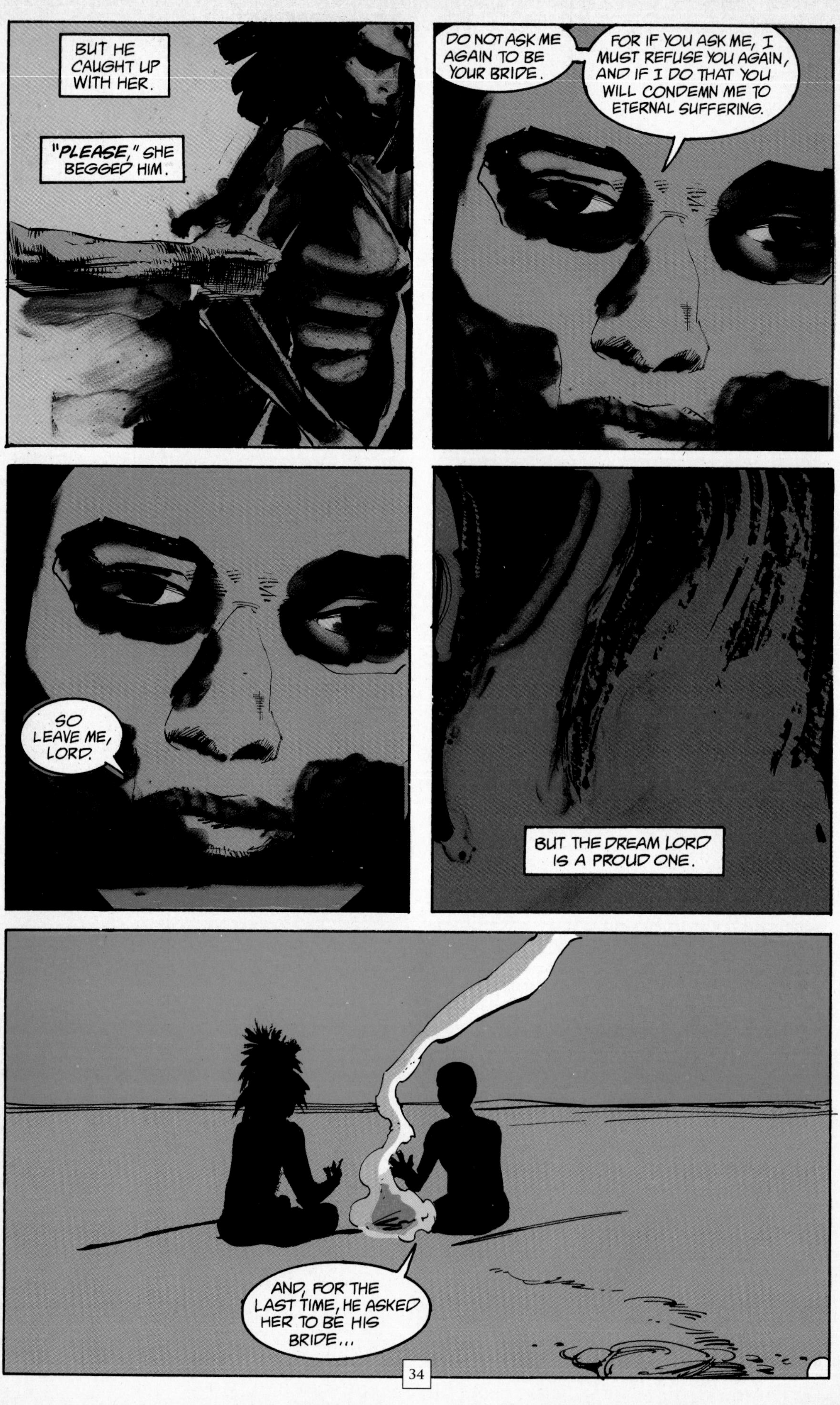
BUT HE CAUGHT UP WITH HER.
"PLEASE," SHE BEGGED HIM.
DO NOT ASK ME AGAIN TO BE YOUR BRIDE.
FOR IF YOU ASK ME, I MUST REFUSE YOU AGAIN, AND IF I DO THAT YOU WILL CONDEMN ME TO ETERNAL SUFFERING.
SO LEAVE ME, LORD.
BUT THE DREAM LORD IS A PROUD ONE.
AND, FOR THE LAST TIME, HE ASKED HER TO BE HIS BRIDE...

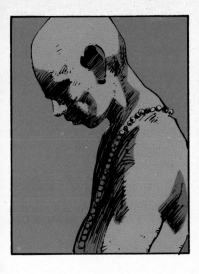

WHAT HAPPENED THEN?

THAT IS THE STORY. THAT *IS* ALL THERE IS.

THAT IS THE WAY MY UNCLE TOLD IT TO ME, THE WAY HIS FATHER TOLD IT TO HIM, THE WAY YOU, TOO, MUST TELL IT, IN YOUR TURN.

BUT--THAT'S NOT A REAL STORY. IT DOESN'T *END* PROPERLY!

WHAT DID NADA *SAY* WHEN KAI'CKUL ASKED HER FOR THE LAST TIME?

WHAT *HAPPENED*?

...SHE SAID *NO*. WHAT ELSE *COULD* SHE SAY?

35

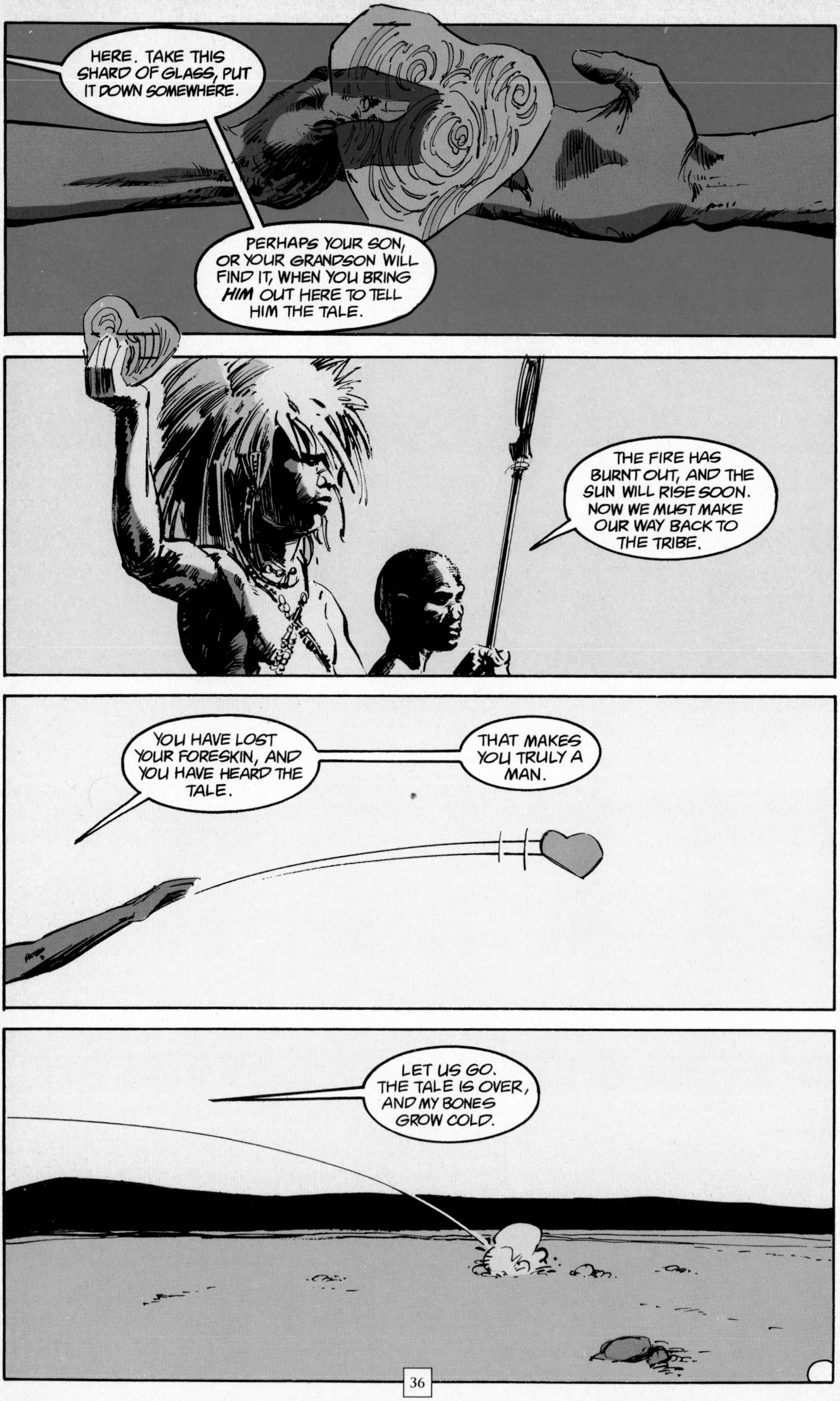
HERE. TAKE THIS SHARD OF GLASS, PUT IT DOWN SOMEWHERE.
PERHAPS YOUR SON, OR YOUR GRANDSON WILL FIND IT, WHEN YOU BRING HIM OUT HERE TO TELL HIM THE TALE.
THE FIRE HAS BURNT OUT, AND THE SUN WILL RISE SOON. NOW WE MUST MAKE OUR WAY BACK TO THE TRIBE.
YOU HAVE LOST YOUR FORESKIN, AND YOU HAVE HEARD THE TALE.
THAT MAKES YOU TRULY A MAN.
LET US GO. THE TALE IS OVER, AND MY BONES GROW COLD.

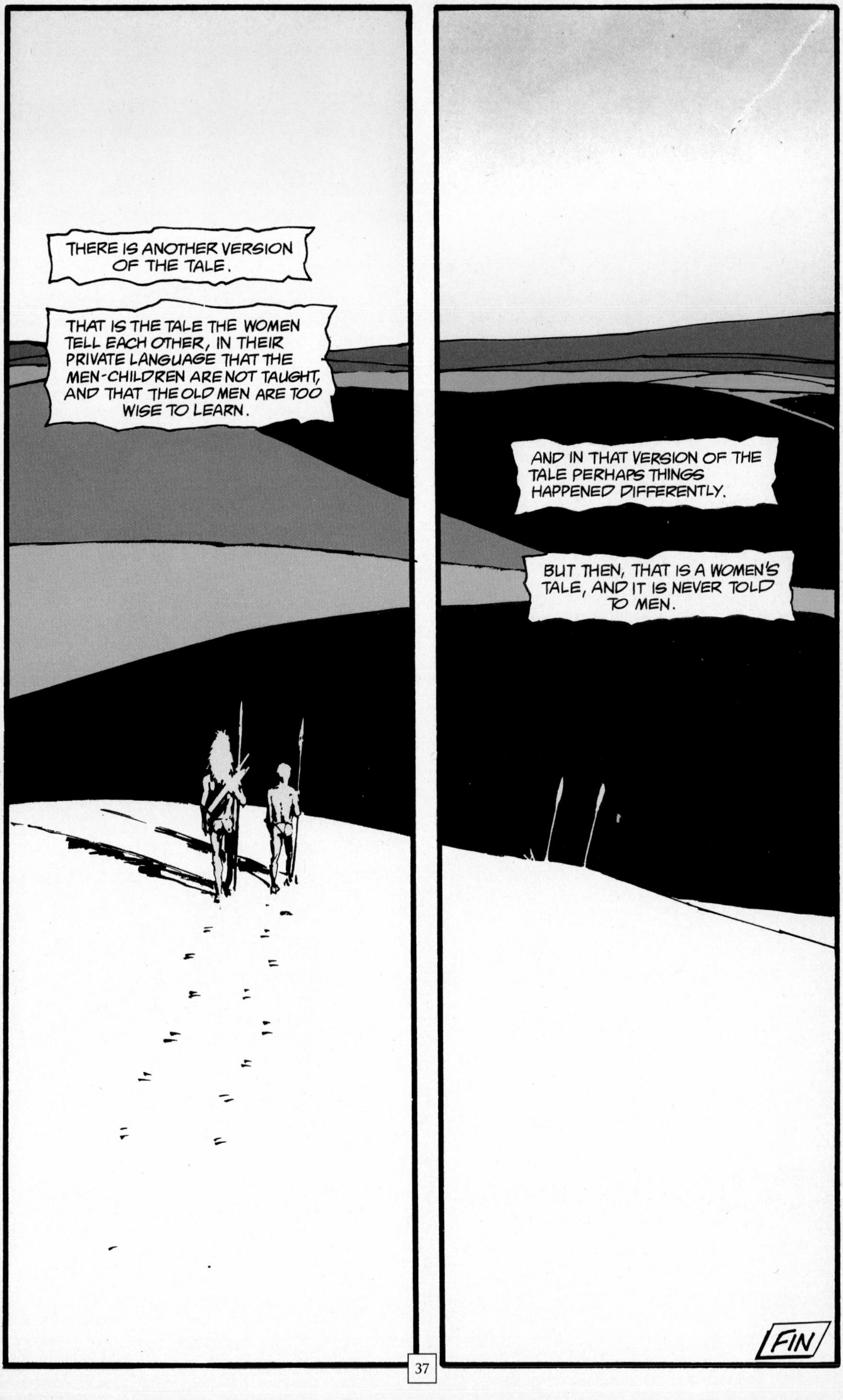
THERE IS ANOTHER VERSION OF THE TALE.
THAT IS THE TALE THE WOMEN TELL EACH OTHER, IN THEIR PRIVATE LANGUAGE THAT THE MEN-CHILDREN ARE NOT TAUGHT, AND THAT THE OLD MEN ARE TOO WISE TO LEARN.
AND IN THAT VERSION OF THE TALE PERHAPS THINGS HAPPENED DIFFERENTLY.
BUT THEN, THAT IS A WOMEN'S TALE, AND IT IS NEVER TOLD TO MEN.
FIN

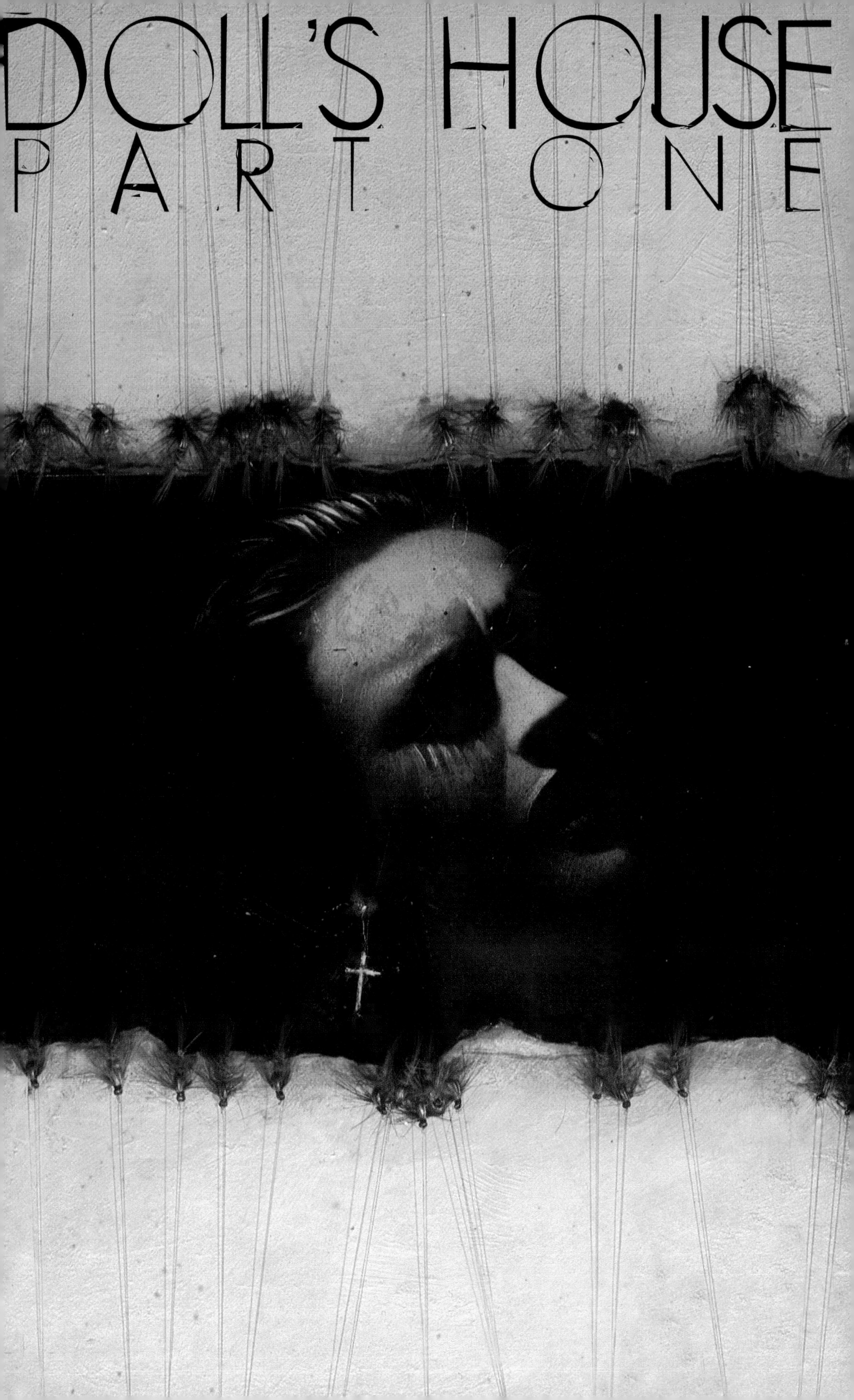
DOLL'S HOUSE
PART ONE

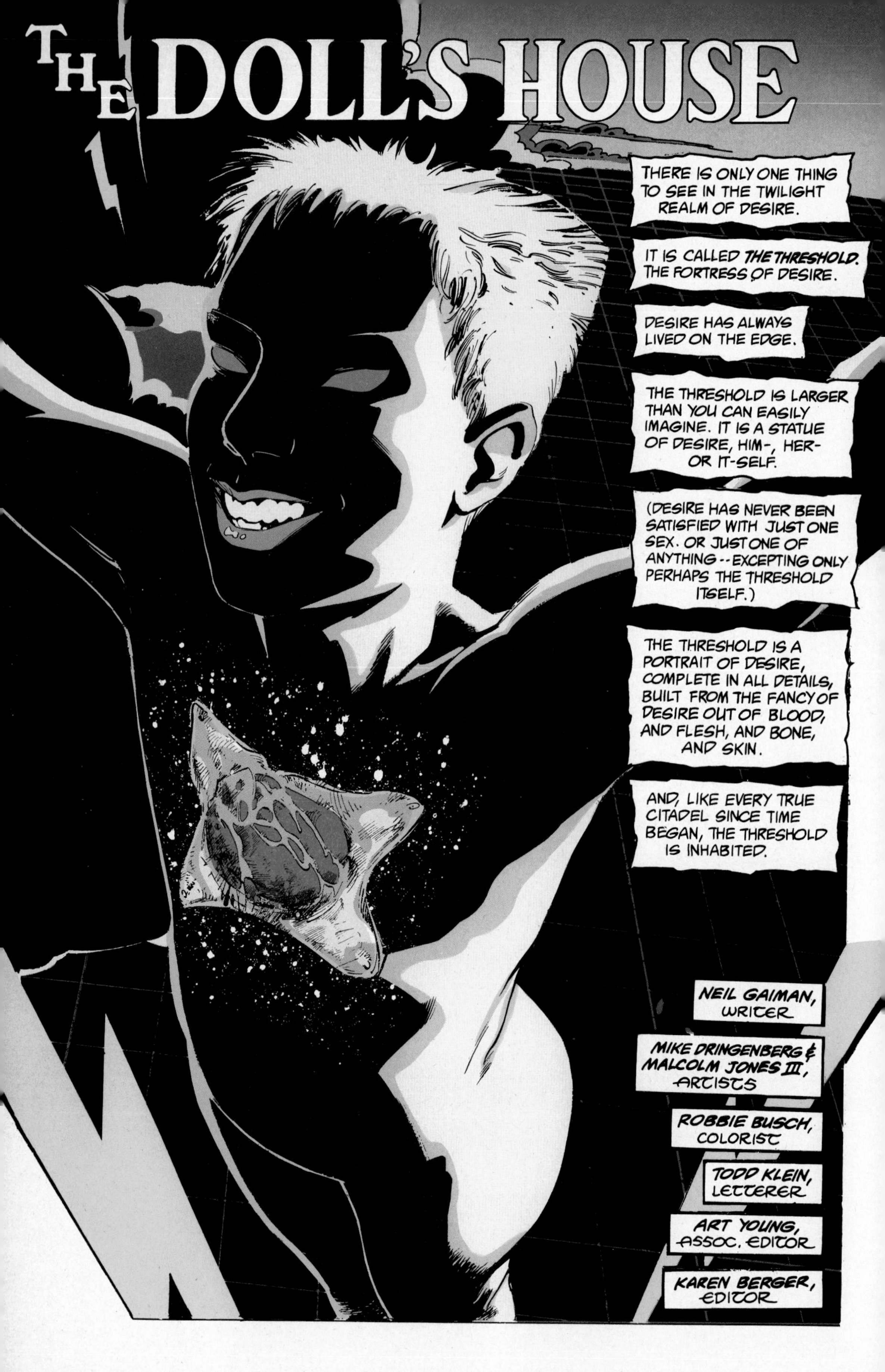
THE DOLL'S HOUSE
THERE IS ONLY ONE THING TO SEE IN THE TWILIGHT REALM OF DESIRE.
IT IS CALLED THE THRESHOLD. THE FORTRESS OF DESIRE.
DESIRE HAS ALWAYS LIVED ON THE EDGE.
THE THRESHOLD IS LARGER THAN YOU CAN EASILY IMAGINE. IT IS A STATUE OF DESIRE, HIM-, HER- OR IT-SELF.
(DESIRE HAS NEVER BEEN SATISFIED WITH JUST ONE SEX. OR JUST ONE OF ANYTHING--EXCEPTING ONLY PERHAPS THE THRESHOLD ITSELF.)
THE THRESHOLD IS A PORTRAIT OF DESIRE, COMPLETE IN ALL DETAILS, BUILT FROM THE FANCY OF DESIRE OUT OF BLOOD, AND FLESH, AND BONE, AND SKIN.
AND, LIKE EVERY TRUE CITADEL SINCE TIME BEGAN, THE THRESHOLD IS INHABITED.
NEIL GAIMAN, WRITER
MIKE DRINGENBERG & MALCOLM JONES III, ARTISTS
ROBBIE BUSCH, COLORIST
TODD KLEIN, LETTERER
ART YOUNG, ASSOC. EDITOR
KAREN BERGER, EDITOR

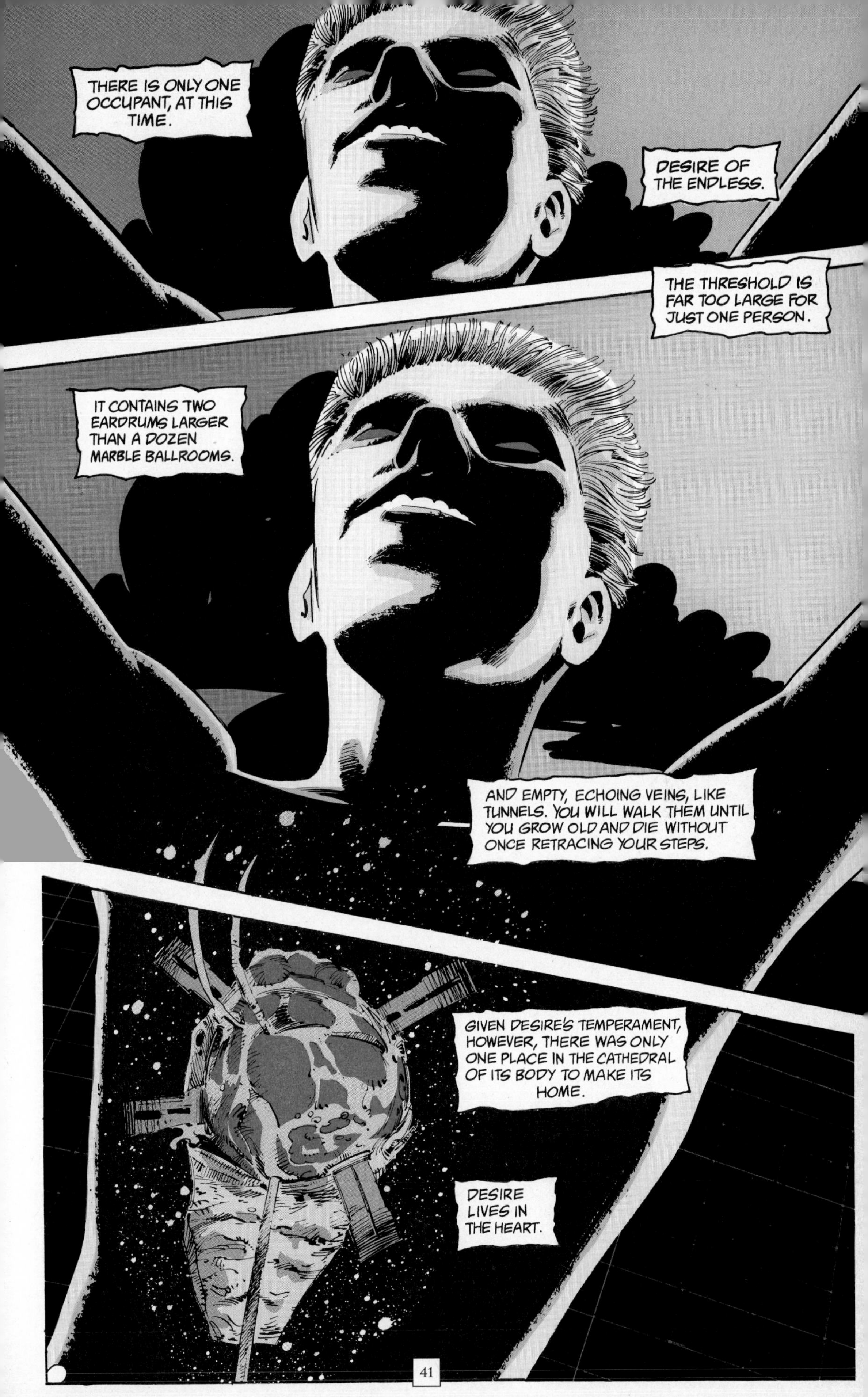
THERE IS ONLY ONE OCCUPANT, AT THIS TIME.
DESIRE OF THE ENDLESS.
THE THRESHOLD IS FAR TOO LARGE FOR JUST ONE PERSON.
IT CONTAINS TWO EARDRUMS LARGER THAN A DOZEN MARBLE BALLROOMS.
AND EMPTY, ECHOING VEINS, LIKE TUNNELS. YOU WILL WALK THEM UNTIL YOU GROW OLD AND DIE WITHOUT ONCE RETRACING YOUR STEPS.
GIVEN DESIRE'S TEMPERAMENT, HOWEVER, THERE WAS ONLY ONE PLACE IN THE CATHEDRAL OF ITS BODY TO MAKE ITS HOME.
DESIRE LIVES IN THE HEART.

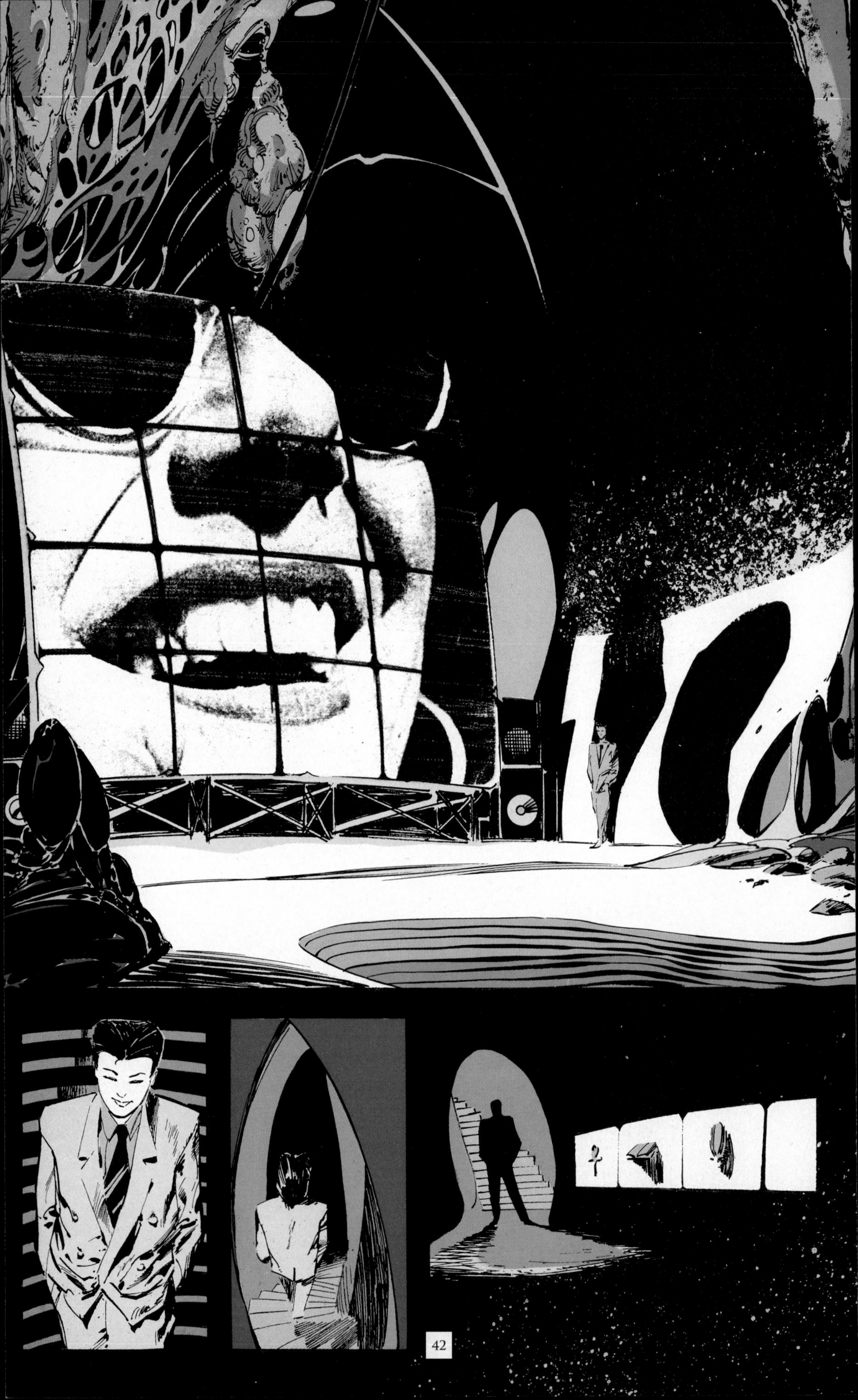

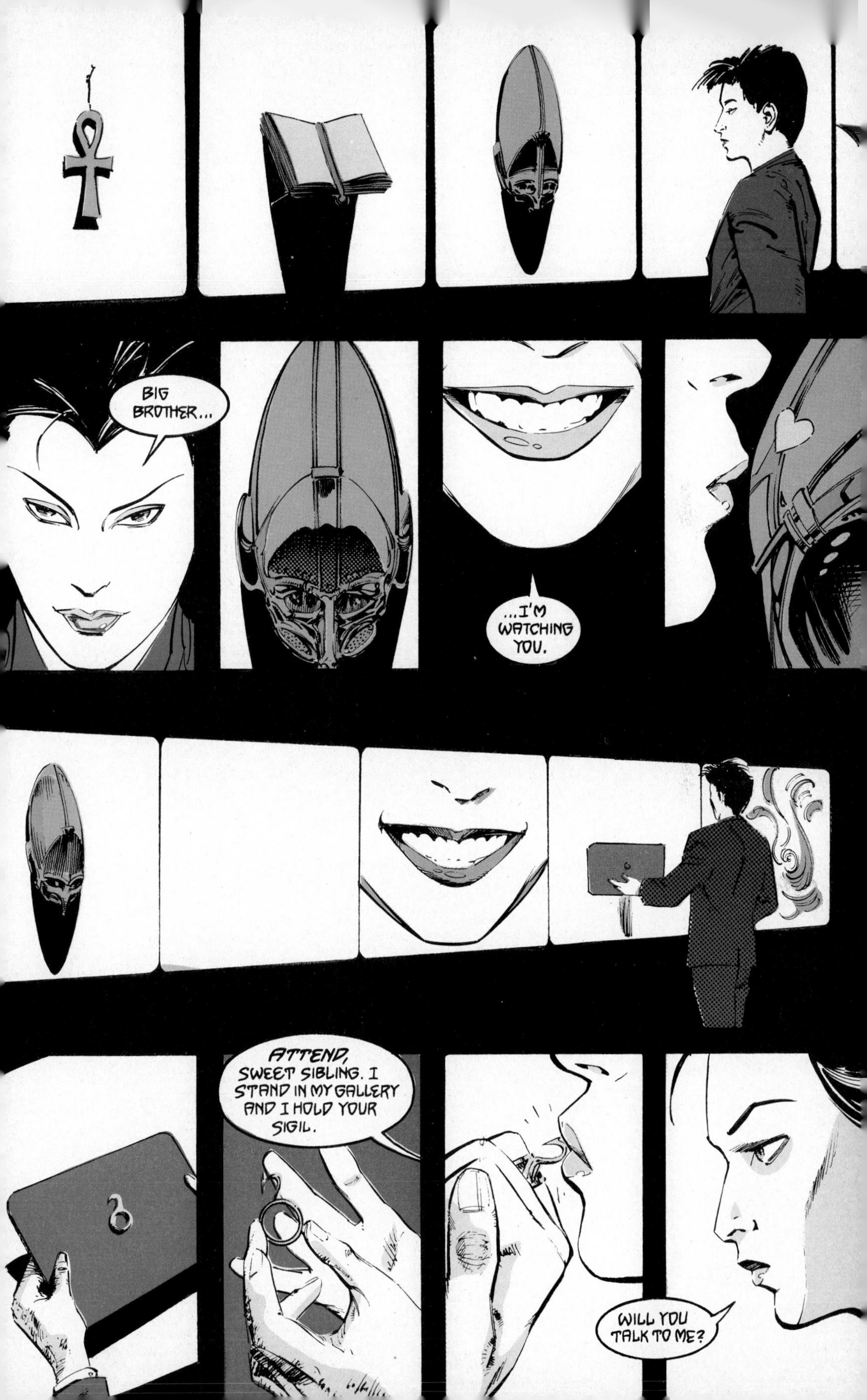
BIG BROTHER...
...I'M WATCHING YOU.
ATTEND, SWEET SIBLING. I STAND IN MY GALLERY AND I HOLD YOUR SIGIL.
WILL YOU TALK TO ME?

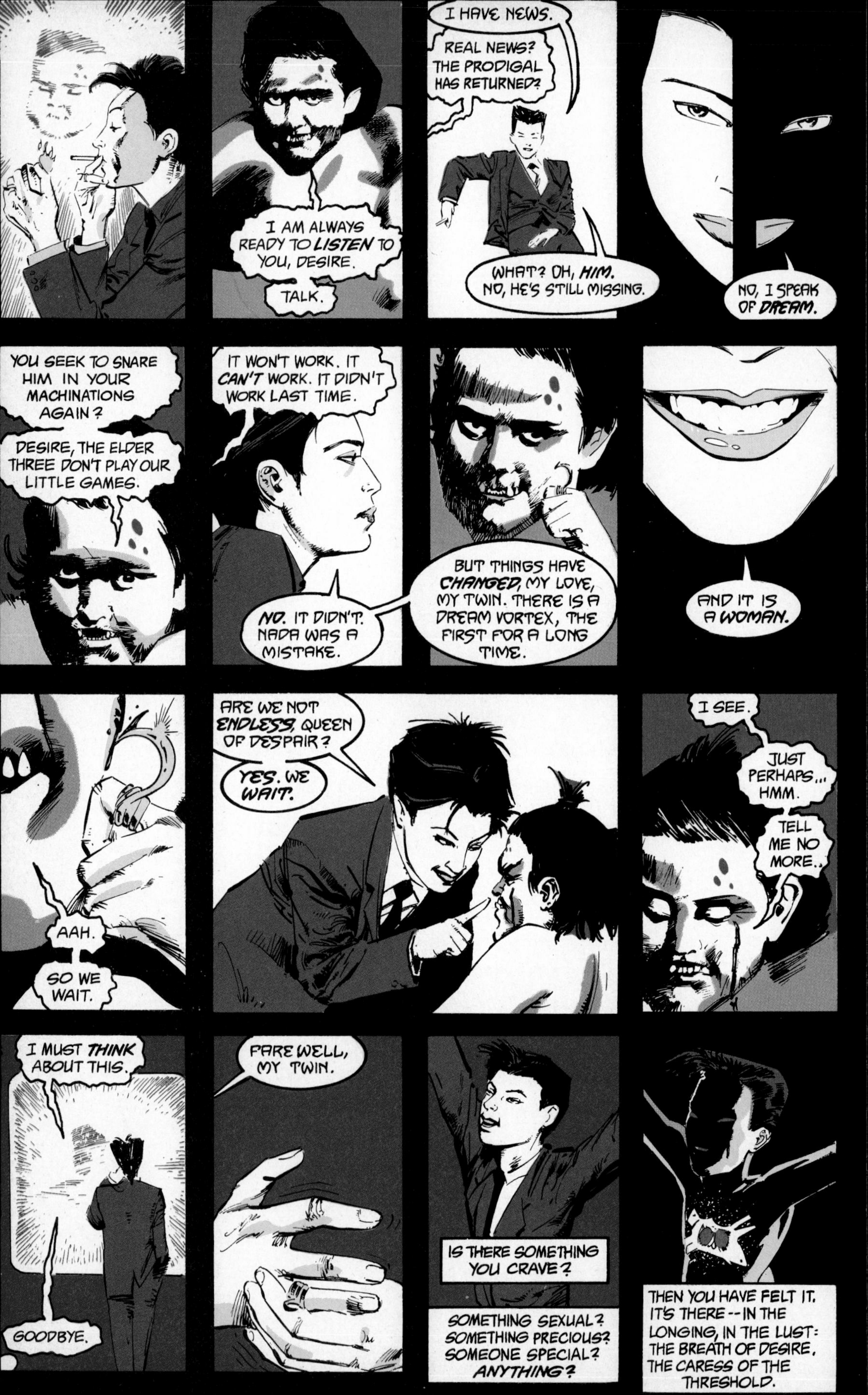

I AM ALWAYS READY TO LISTEN TO YOU, DESIRE.
TALK.
I HAVE NEWS.
REAL NEWS? THE PRODIGAL HAS RETURNED?
WHAT? OH, HIM. NO, HE'S STILL MISSING.
NO, I SPEAK OF DREAM.
YOU SEEK TO SNARE HIM IN YOUR MACHINATIONS AGAIN?
DESIRE, THE ELDER THREE DON'T PLAY OUR LITTLE GAMES.
IT WON'T WORK. IT CAN'T WORK. IT DIDN'T WORK LAST TIME.
NO. IT DIDN'T. NADA WAS A MISTAKE.
BUT THINGS HAVE CHANGED, MY LOVE, MY TWIN. THERE IS A DREAM VORTEX, THE FIRST FOR A LONG TIME.
AND IT IS A WOMAN.
AAH.
SO WE WAIT.
ARE WE NOT ENDLESS, QUEEN OF DESPAIR?
YES. WE WAIT.
I SEE.
JUST PERHAPS... HMM.
TELL ME NO MORE...
I MUST THINK ABOUT THIS.
GOODBYE.
FARE WELL, MY TWIN.
IS THERE SOMETHING YOU CRAVE?
SOMETHING SEXUAL? SOMETHING PRECIOUS? SOMEONE SPECIAL? ANYTHING?
THEN YOU HAVE FELT IT. IT'S THERE -- IN THE LONGING, IN THE LUST: THE BREATH OF DESIRE, THE CARESS OF THE THRESHOLD.

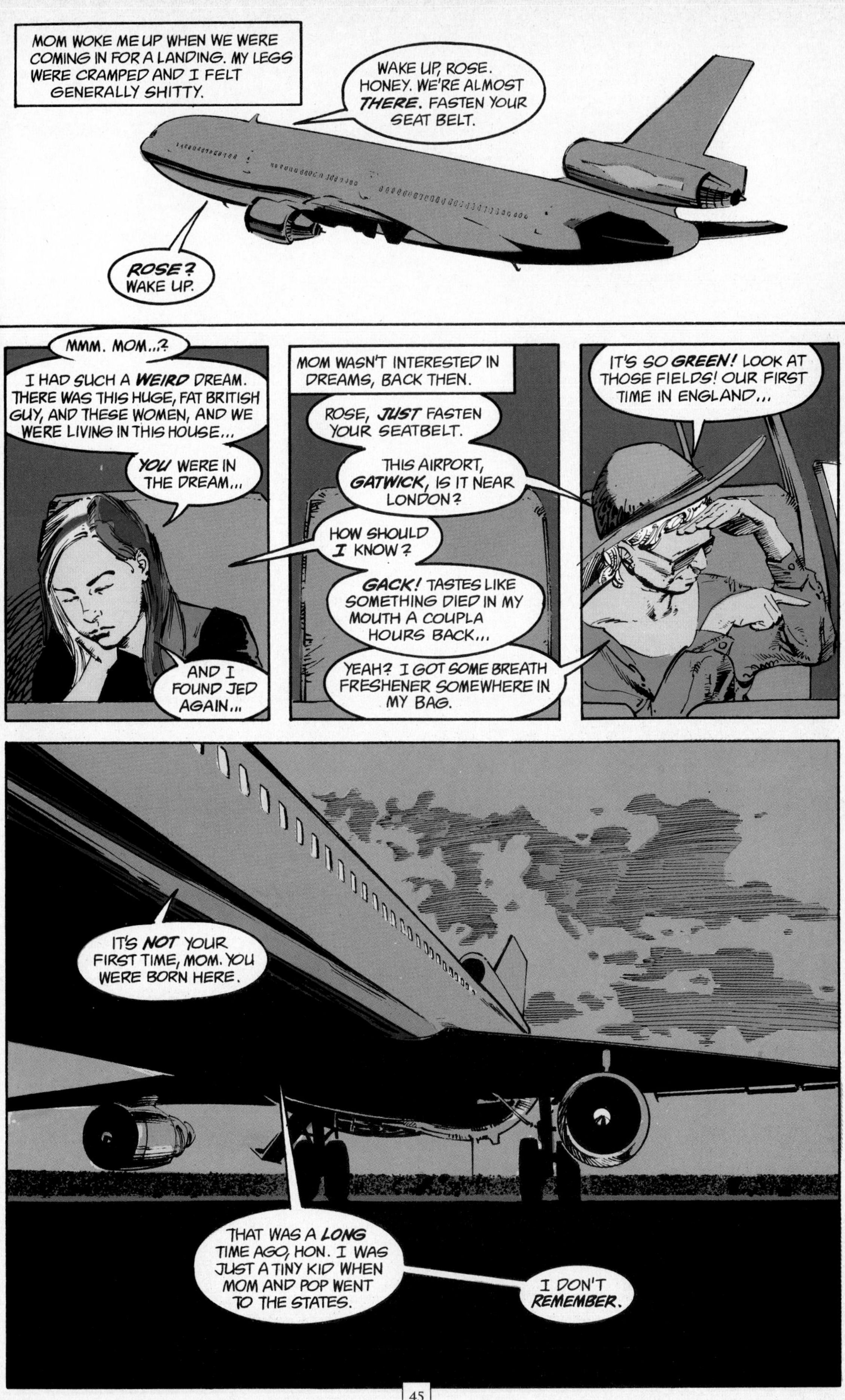

MOM WOKE ME UP WHEN WE WERE COMING IN FOR A LANDING. MY LEGS WERE CRAMPED AND I FELT GENERALLY SHITTY.
WAKE UP, ROSE. HONEY. WE'RE ALMOST THERE. FASTEN YOUR SEAT BELT.
ROSE? WAKE UP.
MMM. MOM...?
I HAD SUCH A WEIRD DREAM. THERE WAS THIS HUGE, FAT BRITISH GUY, AND THESE WOMEN, AND WE WERE LIVING IN THIS HOUSE...
YOU WERE IN THE DREAM...
AND I FOUND JED AGAIN...
MOM WASN'T INTERESTED IN DREAMS, BACK THEN.
ROSE, JUST FASTEN YOUR SEATBELT.
THIS AIRPORT, GATWICK, IS IT NEAR LONDON?
HOW SHOULD I KNOW?
GACK! TASTES LIKE SOMETHING DIED IN MY MOUTH A COUPLA HOURS BACK...
YEAH? I GOT SOME BREATH FRESHENER SOMEWHERE IN MY BAG.
IT'S SO GREEN! LOOK AT THOSE FIELDS! OUR FIRST TIME IN ENGLAND...
IT'S NOT YOUR FIRST TIME, MOM. YOU WERE BORN HERE.
THAT WAS A LONG TIME AGO, HON. I WAS JUST A TINY KID WHEN MOM AND POP WENT TO THE STATES.
I DON'T REMEMBER.

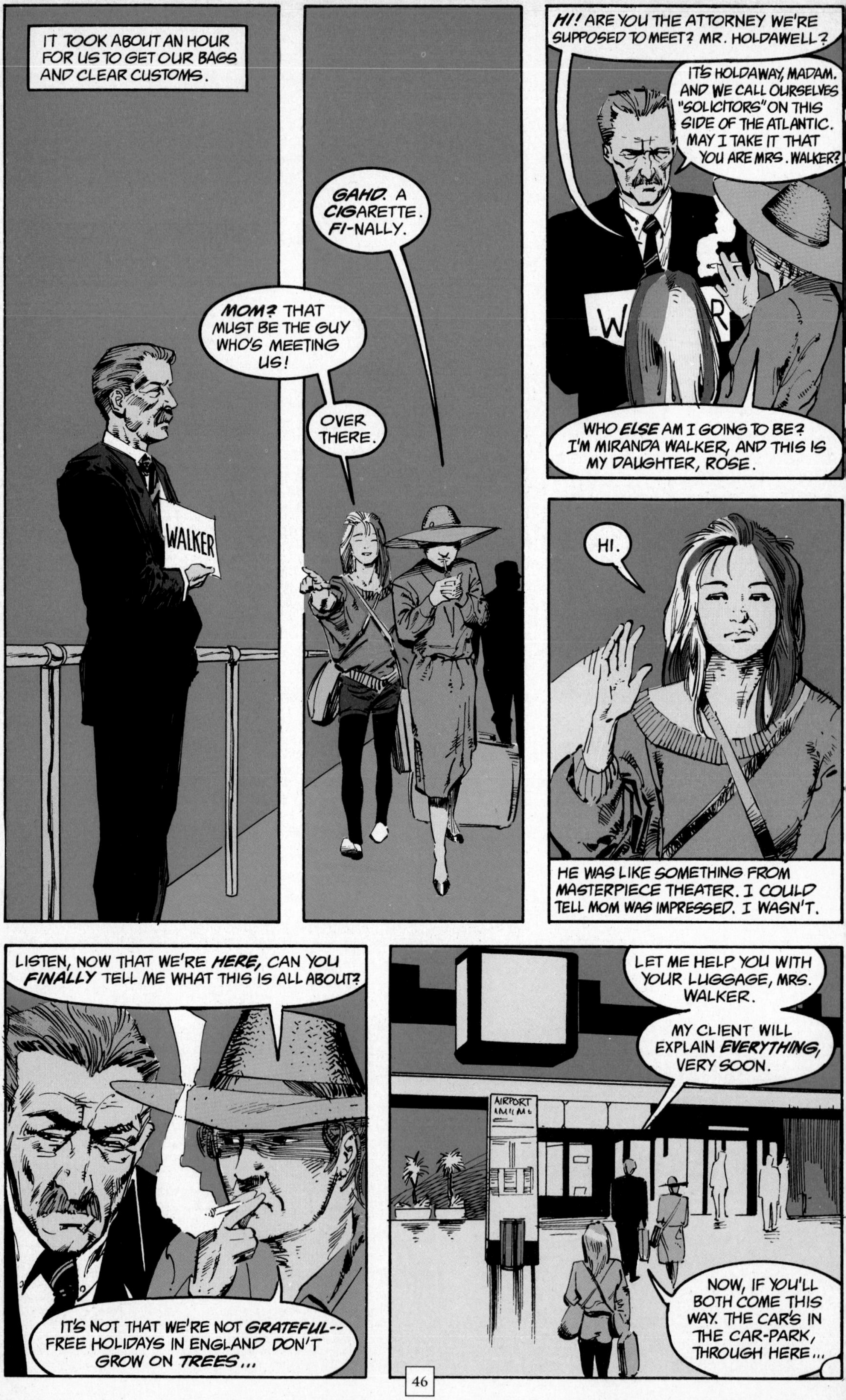

IT TOOK ABOUT AN HOUR FOR US TO GET OUR BAGS AND CLEAR CUSTOMS.
WALKER
GAHD. A CIGARETTE. FI-NALLY.
MOM? THAT MUST BE THE GUY WHO'S MEETING US!
OVER THERE.
HI! ARE YOU THE ATTORNEY WE'RE SUPPOSED TO MEET? MR. HOLDAWELL?
IT'S HOLDAWAY, MADAM. AND WE CALL OURSELVES "SOLICITORS" ON THIS SIDE OF THE ATLANTIC. MAY I TAKE IT THAT YOU ARE MRS. WALKER?
WHO ELSE AM I GOING TO BE? I'M MIRANDA WALKER, AND THIS IS MY DAUGHTER, ROSE.
HI.
HE WAS LIKE SOMETHING FROM MASTERPIECE THEATER. I COULD TELL MOM WAS IMPRESSED. I WASN'T.
LISTEN, NOW THAT WE'RE HERE, CAN YOU FINALLY TELL ME WHAT THIS IS ALL ABOUT?
IT'S NOT THAT WE'RE NOT GRATEFUL-- FREE HOLIDAYS IN ENGLAND DON'T GROW ON TREES...
LET ME HELP YOU WITH YOUR LUGGAGE, MRS. WALKER.
MY CLIENT WILL EXPLAIN EVERYTHING, VERY SOON.
AIRPORT
NOW, IF YOU'LL BOTH COME THIS WAY. THE CAR'S IN THE CAR-PARK, THROUGH HERE...

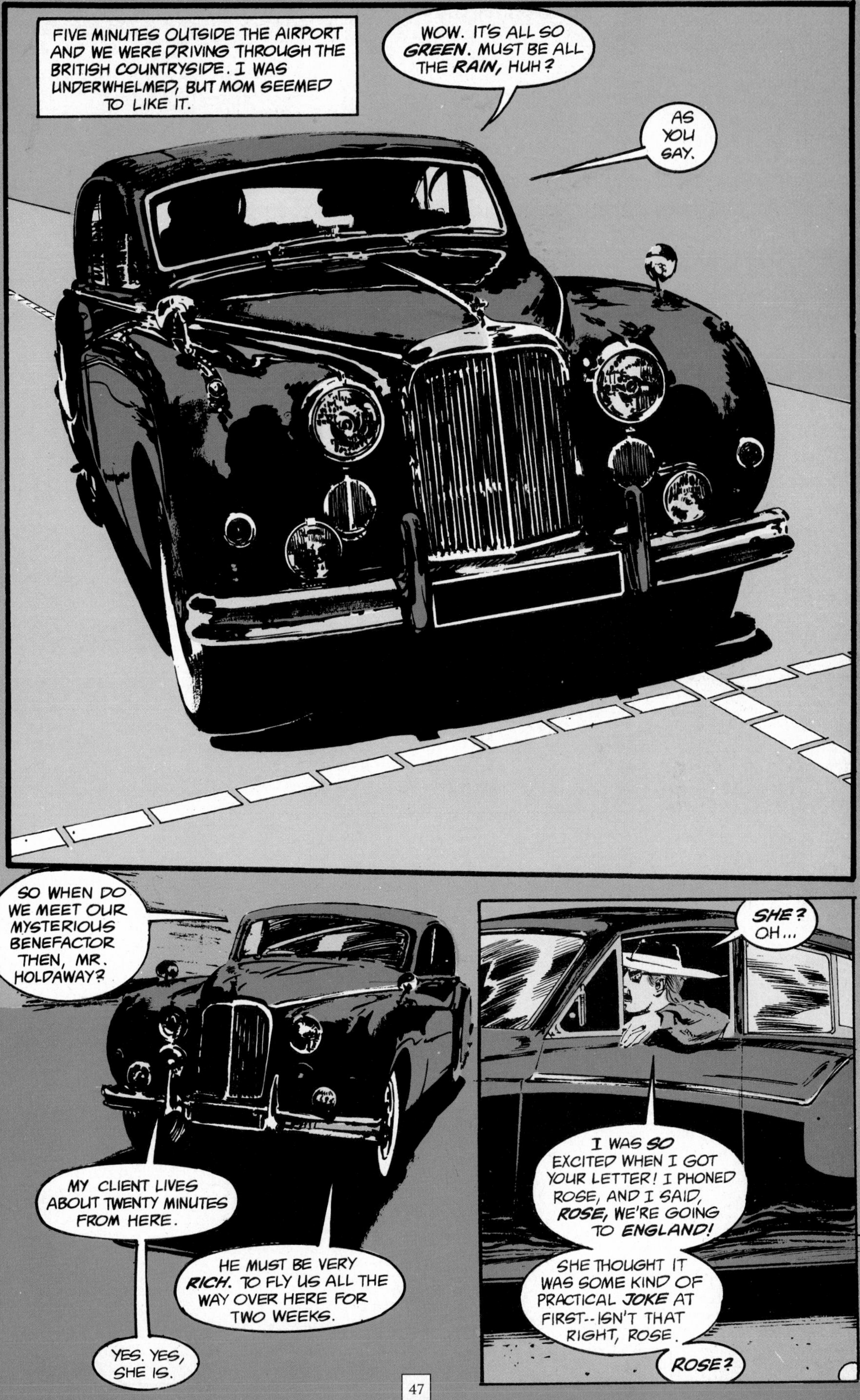
FIVE MINUTES OUTSIDE THE AIRPORT AND WE WERE DRIVING THROUGH THE BRITISH COUNTRYSIDE. I WAS UNDERWHELMED, BUT MOM SEEMED TO LIKE IT.
WOW. IT'S ALL SO GREEN. MUST BE ALL THE RAIN, HUH?
AS YOU SAY.
SO WHEN DO WE MEET OUR MYSTERIOUS BENEFACTOR THEN, MR. HOLDAWAY?
MY CLIENT LIVES ABOUT TWENTY MINUTES FROM HERE.
HE MUST BE VERY RICH. TO FLY US ALL THE WAY OVER HERE FOR TWO WEEKS.
YES. YES, SHE IS.
SHE? OH...
I WAS SO EXCITED WHEN I GOT YOUR LETTER! I PHONED ROSE, AND I SAID, ROSE, WE'RE GOING TO ENGLAND!
SHE THOUGHT IT WAS SOME KIND OF PRACTICAL JOKE AT FIRST--ISN'T THAT RIGHT, ROSE.
ROSE?

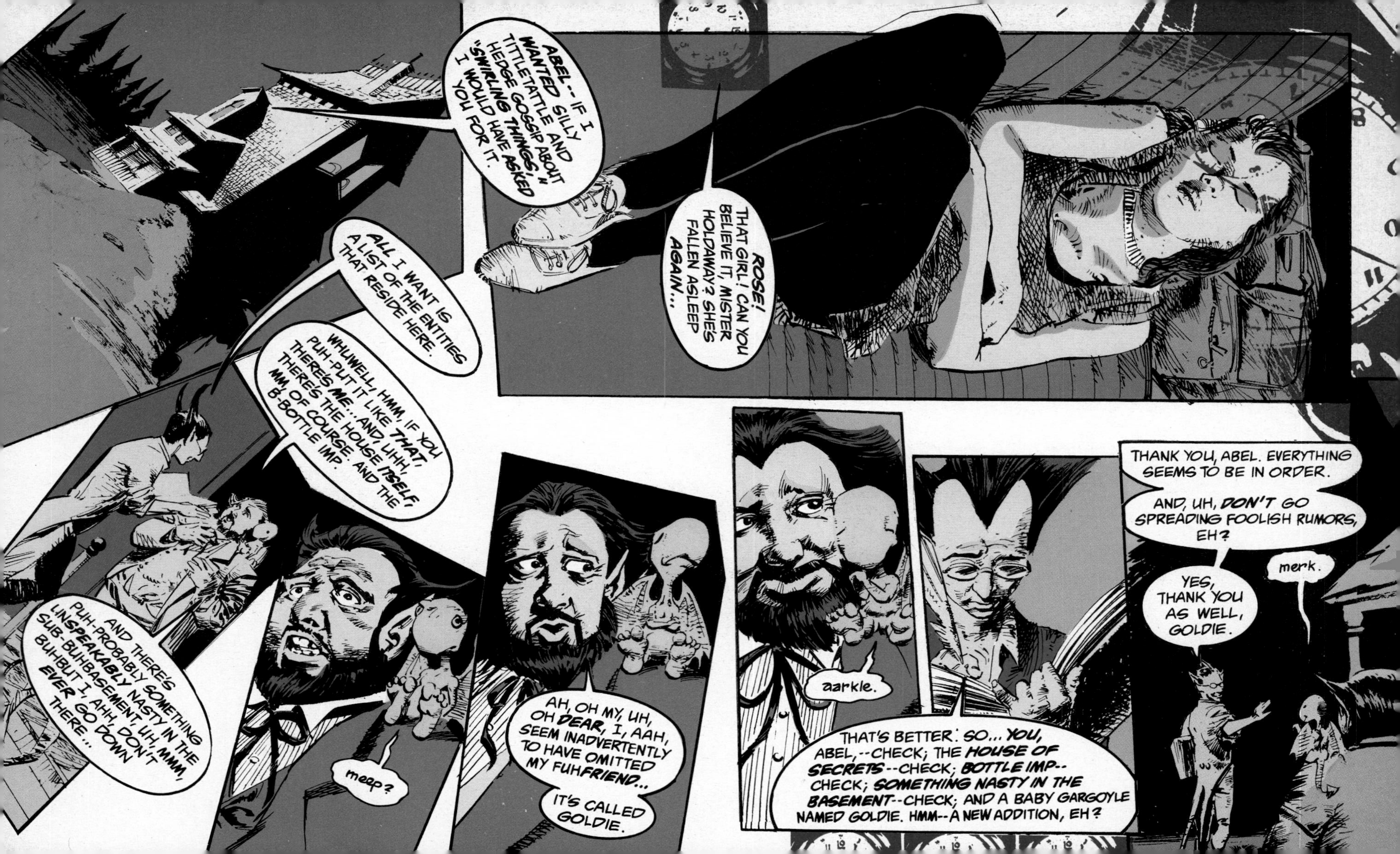

ROSE! THAT GIRL! CAN YOU BELIEVE IT, MISTER HOLDAWAY? SHE'S FALLEN ASLEEP AGAIN...
ABEL-- IF I WANTED SILLY TITTLETATTLE AND HEDGE GOSSIP ABOUT "SWIRLING THINGS," I WOULD HAVE ASKED YOU FOR IT.
ALL I WANT IS A LIST OF THE ENTITIES THAT RESIDE HERE.
WHUWELL, HMM, IF YOU PUH-PUT IT LIKE THAT, THERE'S ME... AND, UHH, THERE'S THE HOUSE ITSELF, MM, OF COURSE. AND THE B-BOTTLE IMP.
AND THERE'S PUH-PROBABLY SOMETHING UNSPEAKABLY NASTY IN THE SUB-BUHBASEMENT, UH, MMM, BUHBUT I, AHH, DON'T EVER GO DOWN THERE...
meep?
AH, OH MY, UH, OH DEAR, I, AAH, SEEM INADVERTENTLY TO HAVE OMITTED MY FUHFRIEND...
IT'S CALLED GOLDIE.
aarkle.
THAT'S BETTER. SO... YOU, ABEL, --CHECK; THE HOUSE OF SECRETS--CHECK; BOTTLE IMP--CHECK; SOMETHING NASTY IN THE BASEMENT--CHECK; AND A BABY GARGOYLE NAMED GOLDIE. HMM--A NEW ADDITION, EH?
THANK YOU, ABEL. EVERYTHING SEEMS TO BE IN ORDER.
AND, UH, DON'T GO SPREADING FOOLISH RUMORS, EH?
YES, THANK YOU AS WELL, GOLDIE.
merk.

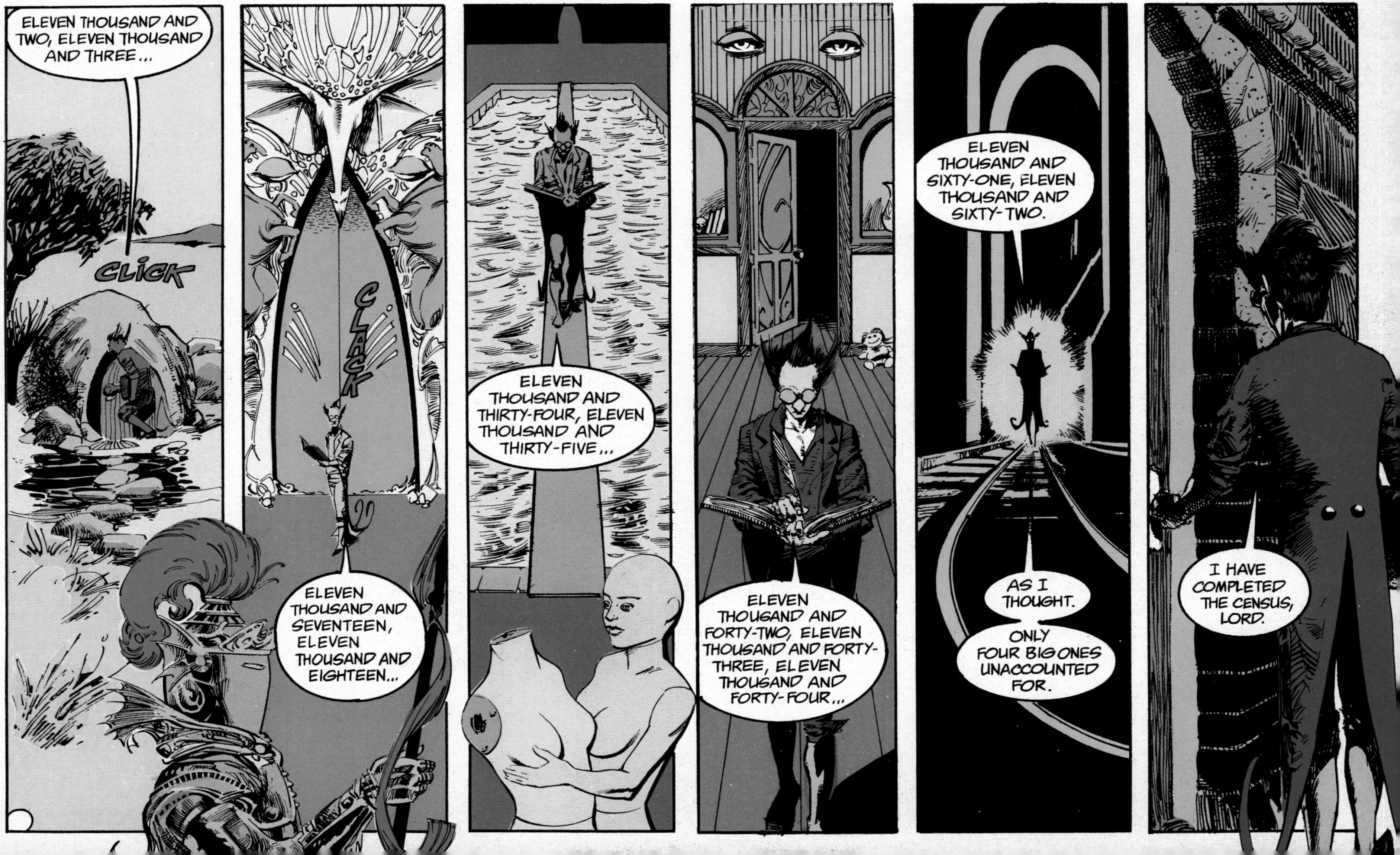
ELEVEN THOUSAND AND TWO, ELEVEN THOUSAND AND THREE...
CLICK
CLACK
ELEVEN THOUSAND AND SEVENTEEN, ELEVEN THOUSAND AND EIGHTEEN...
ELEVEN THOUSAND AND THIRTY-FOUR, ELEVEN THOUSAND AND THIRTY-FIVE...
ELEVEN THOUSAND AND FORTY-TWO, ELEVEN THOUSAND AND FORTY-THREE, ELEVEN THOUSAND AND FORTY-FOUR...
ELEVEN THOUSAND AND SIXTY-ONE, ELEVEN THOUSAND AND SIXTY-TWO.
AS I THOUGHT.
ONLY FOUR BIG ONES UNACCOUNTED FOR.
I HAVE COMPLETED THE CENSUS, LORD.

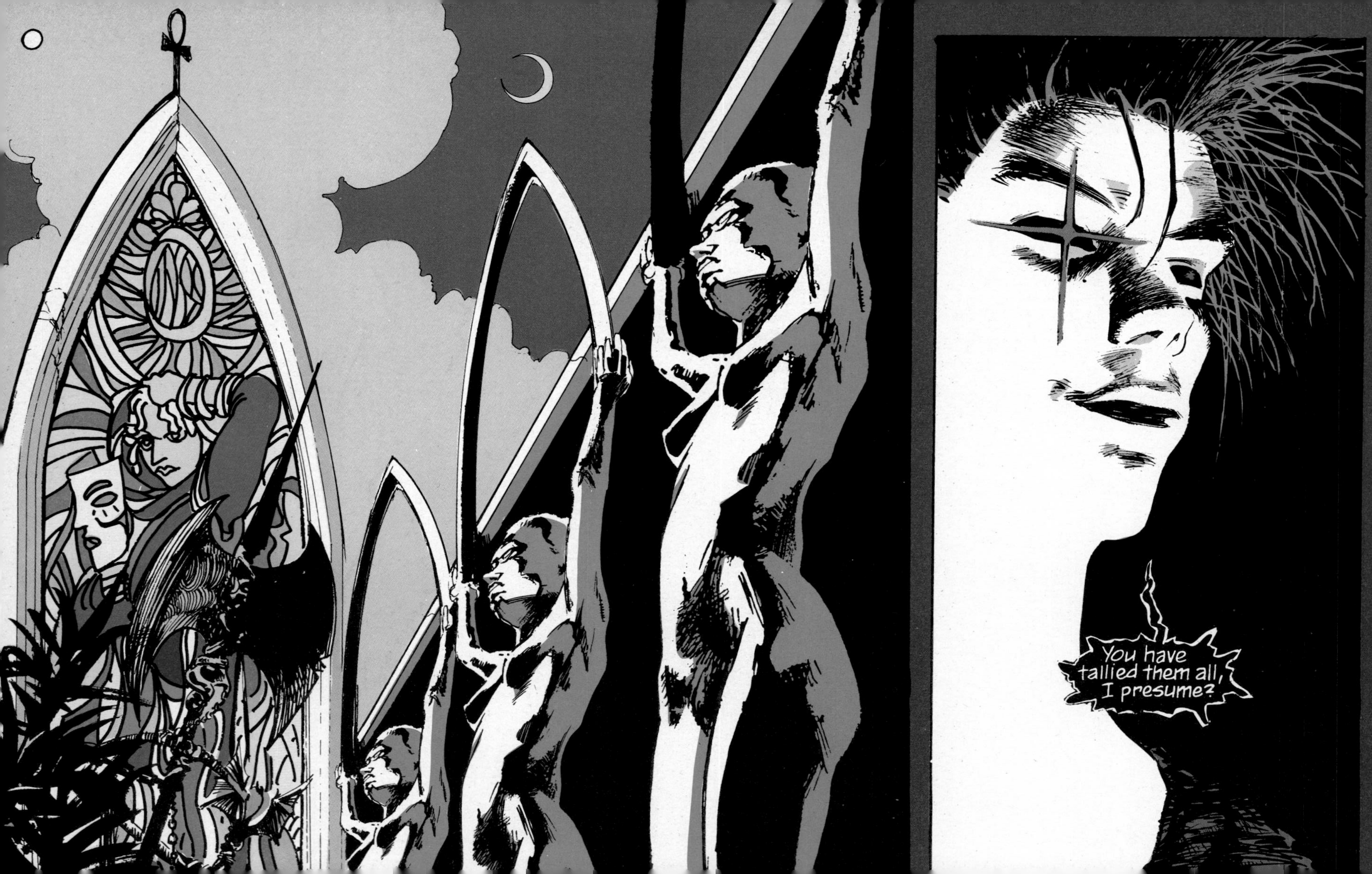
You have tallied them all, I presume?

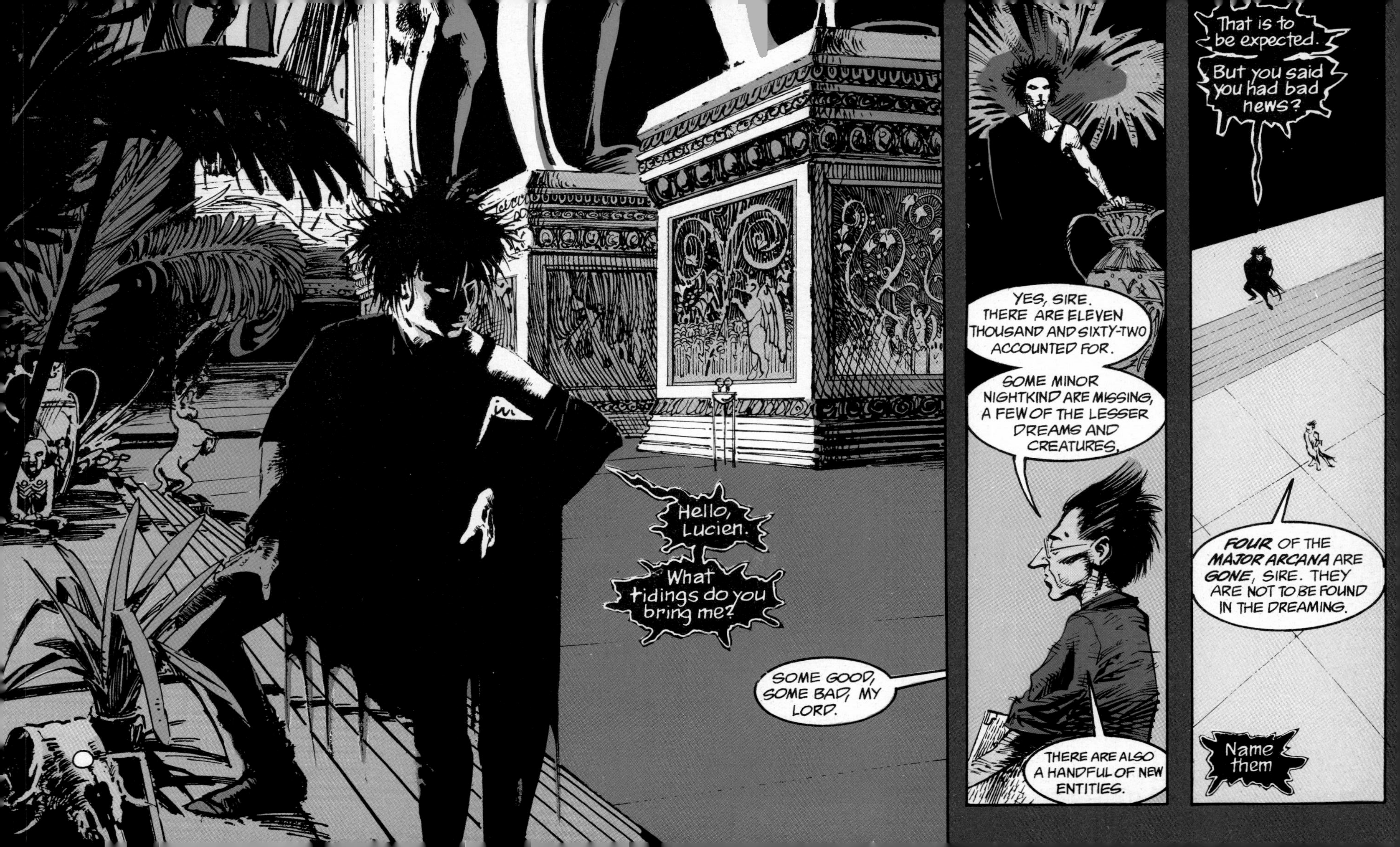

Hello, Lucien.
What tidings do you bring me?
SOME GOOD, SOME BAD, MY LORD.
YES, SIRE. THERE ARE ELEVEN THOUSAND AND SIXTY-TWO ACCOUNTED FOR.
SOME MINOR NIGHTKIND ARE MISSING, A FEW OF THE LESSER DREAMS AND CREATURES,
THERE ARE ALSO A HANDFUL OF NEW ENTITIES.
That is to be expected.
But you said you had bad news?
FOUR OF THE MAJOR ARCANA ARE GONE, SIRE. THEY ARE NOT TO BE FOUND IN THE DREAMING.
Name them

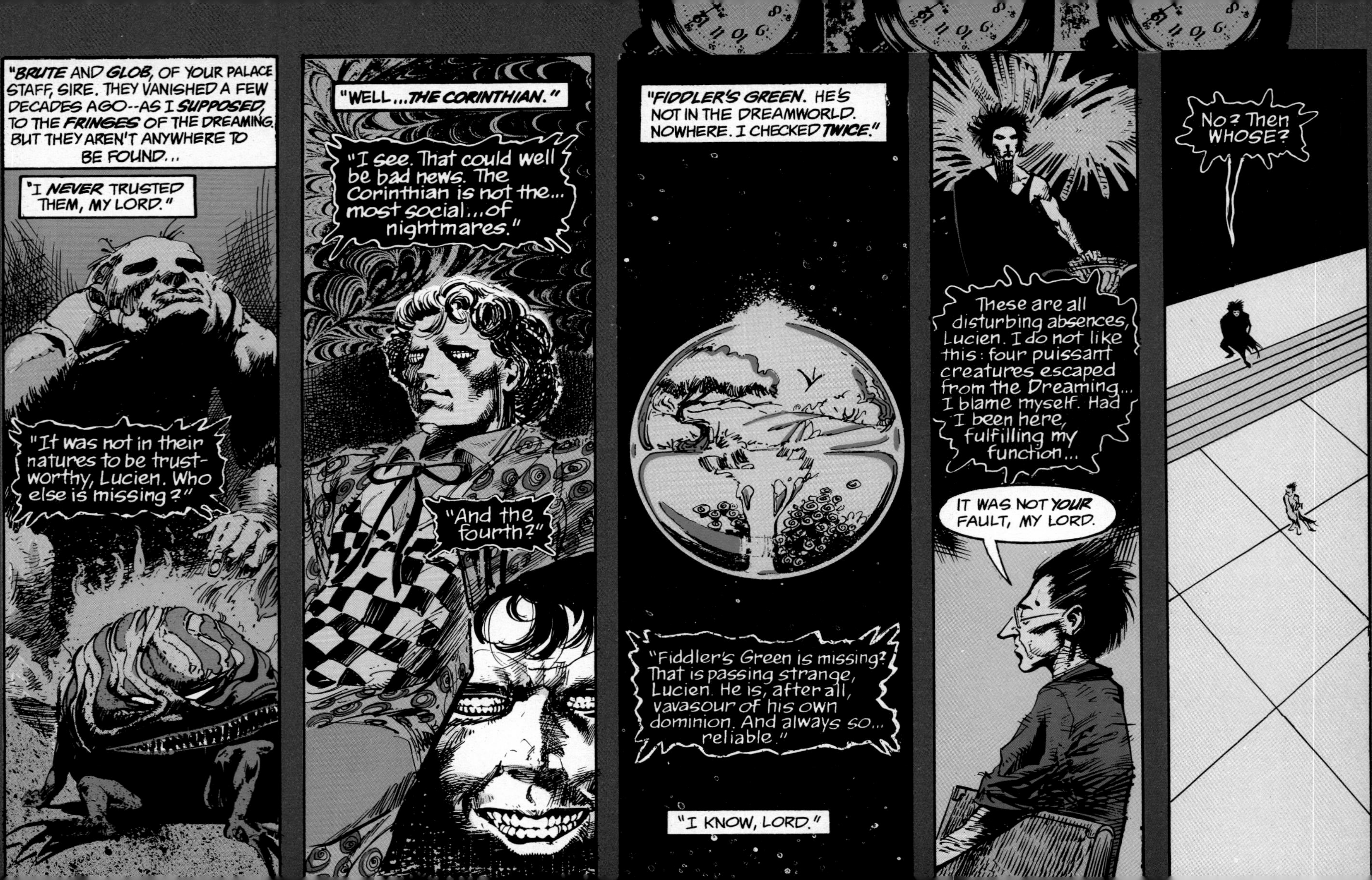
"BRUTE AND GLOB, OF YOUR PALACE STAFF, SIRE. THEY VANISHED A FEW DECADES AGO--AS I SUPPOSED, TO THE FRINGES OF THE DREAMING. BUT THEY AREN'T ANYWHERE TO BE FOUND...
"I NEVER TRUSTED THEM, MY LORD."
"It was not in their natures to be trustworthy, Lucien. Who else is missing?"
"WELL... THE CORINTHIAN."
"I see. That could well be bad news. The Corinthian is not the... most social... of nightmares."
"And the fourth?"
"FIDDLER'S GREEN. HE'S NOT IN THE DREAMWORLD. NOWHERE. I CHECKED TWICE."
"Fiddler's Green is missing? That is passing strange, Lucien. He is, after all, vavasour of his own dominion. And always so... reliable."
"I KNOW, LORD."
These are all disturbing absences, Lucien. I do not like this: four puissant creatures escaped from the Dreaming... I blame myself. Had I been here, fulfilling my function...
IT WAS NOT YOUR FAULT, MY LORD.
No? Then WHOSE?

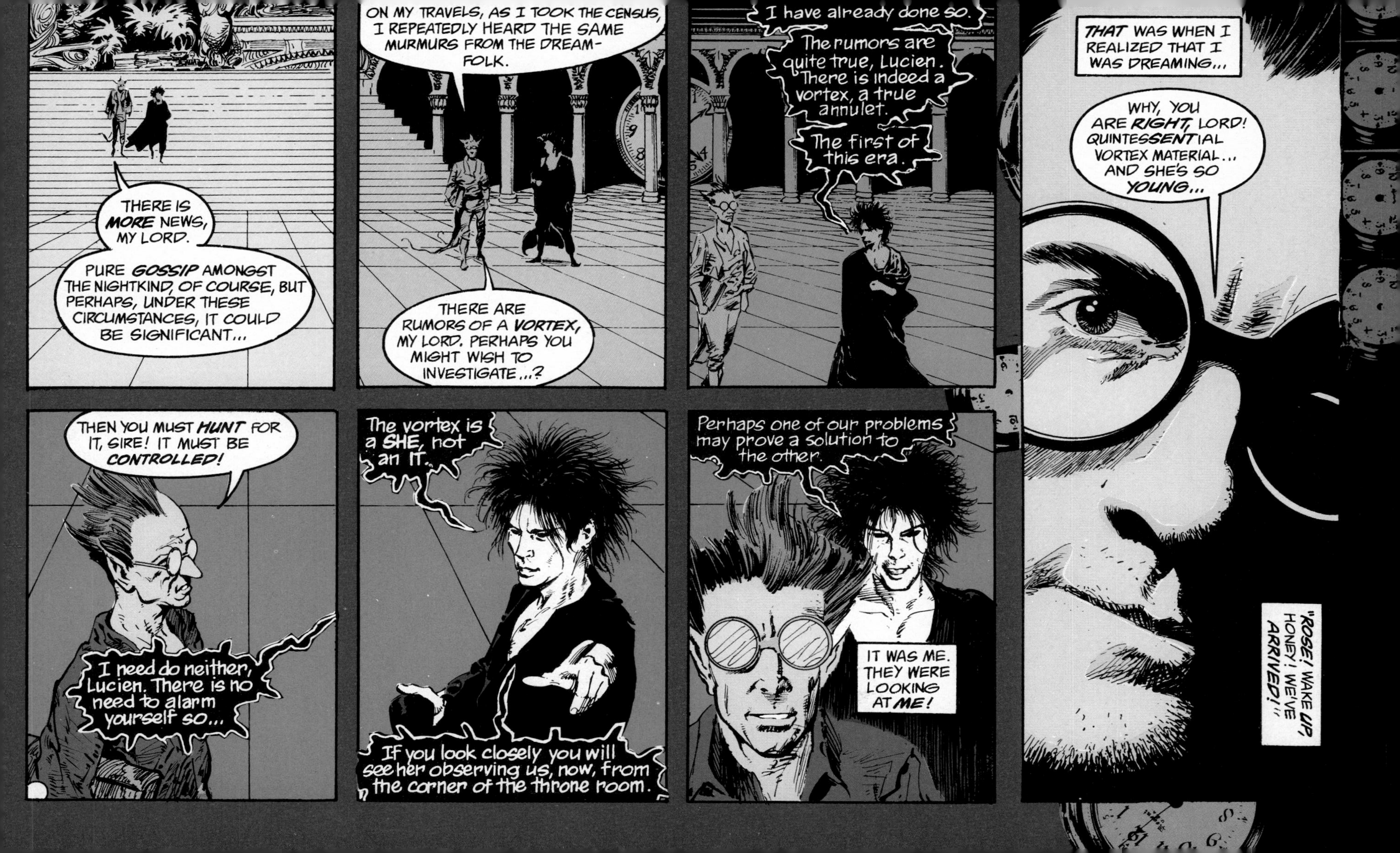
THERE IS MORE NEWS, MY LORD.
PURE GOSSIP AMONGST THE NIGHTKIND, OF COURSE, BUT PERHAPS, UNDER THESE CIRCUMSTANCES, IT COULD BE SIGNIFICANT...
THEN YOU MUST HUNT FOR IT, SIRE! IT MUST BE CONTROLLED!
I need do neither, Lucien. There is no need to alarm yourself so...
ON MY TRAVELS, AS I TOOK THE CENSUS, I REPEATEDLY HEARD THE SAME MURMURS FROM THE DREAM-FOLK.
THERE ARE RUMORS OF A VORTEX, MY LORD. PERHAPS YOU MIGHT WISH TO INVESTIGATE...?
The vortex is a SHE, not an IT.
If you look closely you will see her observing us, now, from the corner of the throne room.
I have already done so.
The rumors are quite true, Lucien. There is indeed a vortex, a true annulet.
The first of this era.
Perhaps one of our problems may prove a solution to the other.
IT WAS ME. THEY WERE LOOKING AT ME!
THAT WAS WHEN I REALIZED THAT I WAS DREAMING...
WHY, YOU ARE RIGHT, LORD! QUINTESSENTIAL VORTEX MATERIAL... AND SHE'S SO YOUNG...
"ROSE! WAKE UP, HONEY! WE'VE ARRIVED!"

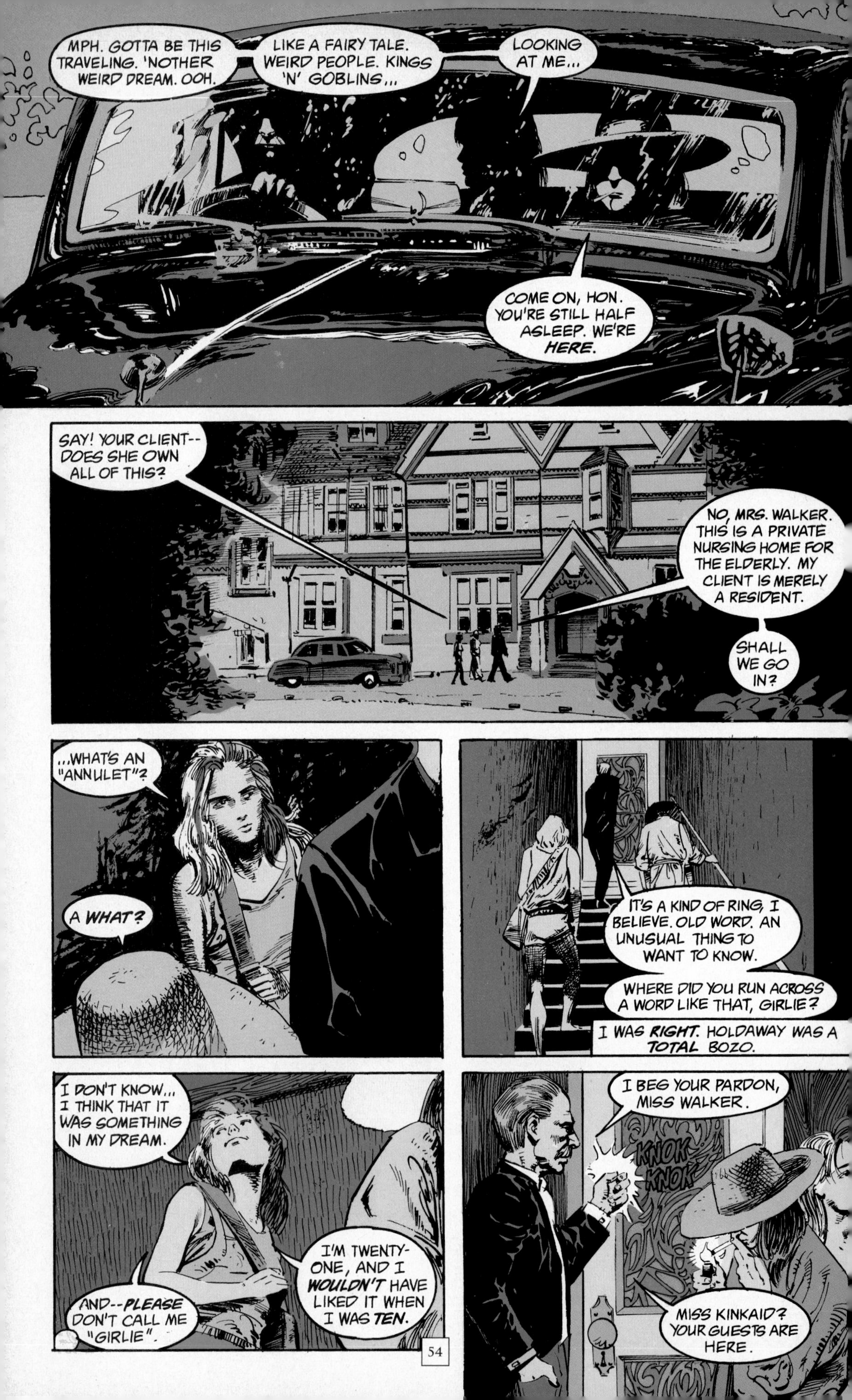
MPH. GOTTA BE THIS TRAVELING. 'NOTHER WEIRD DREAM. OOH.
LIKE A FAIRY TALE. WEIRD PEOPLE. KINGS 'N' GOBLINS...
LOOKING AT ME...
COME ON, HON. YOU'RE STILL HALF ASLEEP. WE'RE HERE.
SAY! YOUR CLIENT-- DOES SHE OWN ALL OF THIS?
NO, MRS. WALKER. THIS IS A PRIVATE NURSING HOME FOR THE ELDERLY. MY CLIENT IS MERELY A RESIDENT.
SHALL WE GO IN?
...WHAT'S AN "ANNULET"?
A WHAT?
IT'S A KIND OF RING, I BELIEVE. OLD WORD. AN UNUSUAL THING TO WANT TO KNOW.
WHERE DID YOU RUN ACROSS A WORD LIKE THAT, GIRLIE?
I WAS RIGHT. HOLDAWAY WAS A TOTAL BOZO.
I DON'T KNOW... I THINK THAT IT WAS SOMETHING IN MY DREAM.
I'M TWENTY-ONE, AND I WOULDN'T HAVE LIKED IT WHEN I WAS TEN.
AND--PLEASE DON'T CALL ME "GIRLIE".
I BEG YOUR PARDON, MISS WALKER.
KNOK KNOK
MISS KINKAID? YOUR GUESTS ARE HERE.

PLEASE COME IN! IT ISN'T LOCKED.

I DON'T KNOW WHAT I WAS EXPECTING. NOT HER. SHE LOOKED LOST, AND FRAGILE, LIKE A LITTLE CHINA DOLL.

AND WEIRDLY FAMILIAR, AND I DIDN'T KNOW WHY.

YES. OH *YES.*

PLEASE, BOTH OF YOU, SIT NEXT TO ME.

HELLO. YOU'RE MIRANDA WALKER. AND YOU MUST BE ROSE. COME OVER HERE, DARLING. BOTH OF YOU. LET ME LOOK AT YOU.

I'M *UNITY.* UNITY KINKAID.

THIS...THIS IS MY ROOM. I THOUGHT BRIEFLY ABOUT MOVING OUT, BUT THE BEDFORD SQUARE HOUSE WAS *SOLD* A LONG TIME AGO, AND I'VE LIVED HERE SO *LONG.*

OVER THIRTY YEARS, THEY *TELL* ME.

THAT'S ALL I HAVE LEFT OF THE OLD HOUSE. HOLDAWAYS HELD ONTO IT WHEN THE FURNITURE WAS SOLD, ALONG WITH A FEW PERSONAL POSSESSIONS.

I'M *SORRY* ABOUT ALL THIS RIGMAROLE. IT WAS MY OWN FAULT.

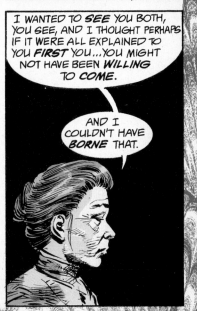

I WANTED TO *SEE* YOU BOTH, YOU SEE, AND I THOUGHT PERHAPS IF IT WERE ALL EXPLAINED TO YOU *FIRST* YOU...YOU MIGHT NOT HAVE BEEN *WILLING* TO *COME.*

AND I COULDN'T HAVE *BORNE* THAT.

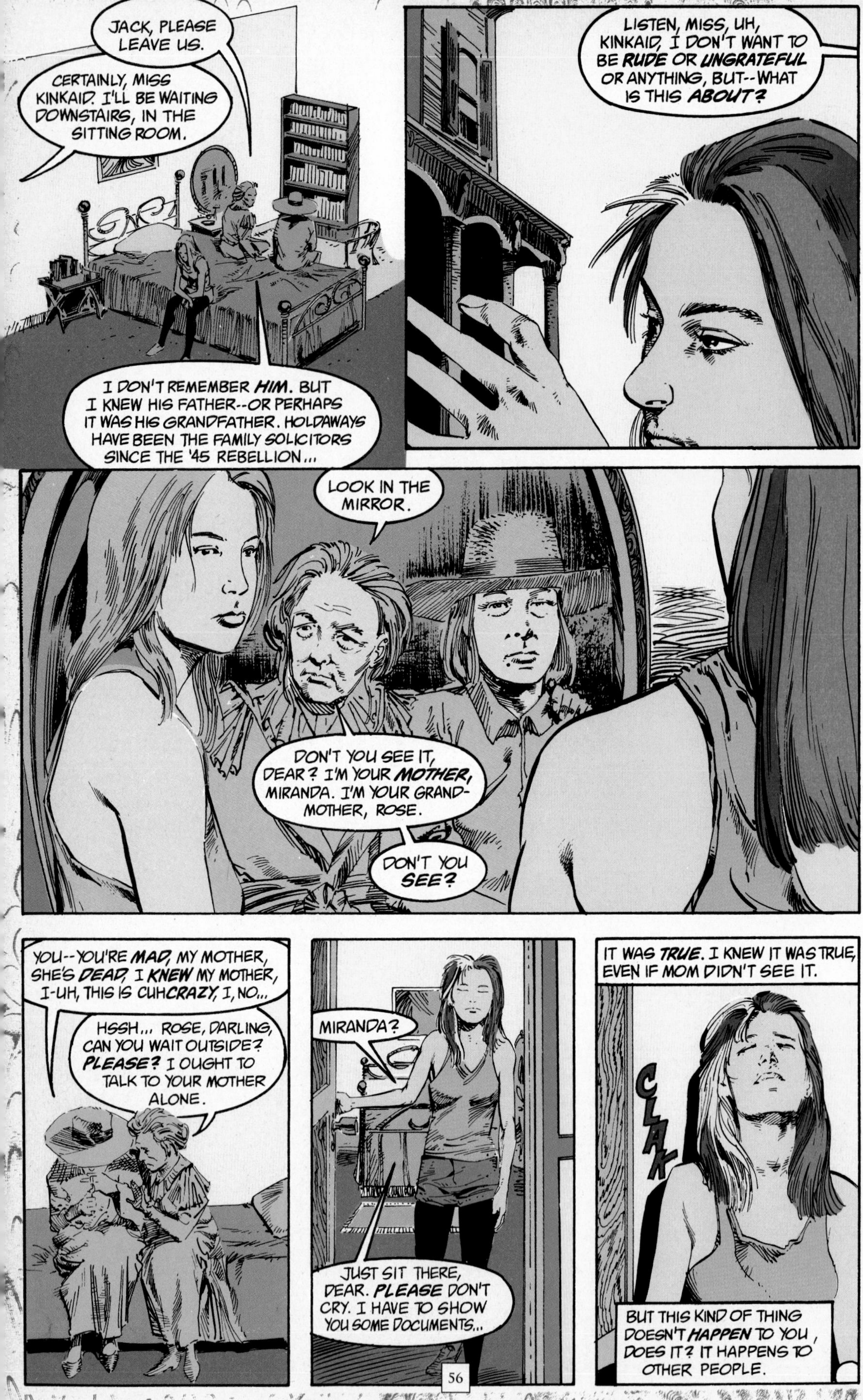

JACK, PLEASE LEAVE US.
CERTAINLY, MISS KINKAID. I'LL BE WAITING DOWNSTAIRS, IN THE SITTING ROOM.
I DON'T REMEMBER HIM. BUT I KNEW HIS FATHER--OR PERHAPS IT WAS HIS GRANDFATHER. HOLDAWAYS HAVE BEEN THE FAMILY SOLICITORS SINCE THE '45 REBELLION...
LISTEN, MISS, UH, KINKAID, I DON'T WANT TO BE RUDE OR UNGRATEFUL OR ANYTHING, BUT--WHAT IS THIS ABOUT?
LOOK IN THE MIRROR.
DON'T YOU SEE IT, DEAR? I'M YOUR MOTHER, MIRANDA. I'M YOUR GRAND-MOTHER, ROSE.
DON'T YOU SEE?
YOU--YOU'RE MAD, MY MOTHER, SHE'S DEAD, I KNEW MY MOTHER, I-UH, THIS IS CUHCRAZY, I, NO...
HSSH... ROSE, DARLING, CAN YOU WAIT OUTSIDE? PLEASE? I OUGHT TO TALK TO YOUR MOTHER ALONE.
MIRANDA?
JUST SIT THERE, DEAR. PLEASE DON'T CRY. I HAVE TO SHOW YOU SOME DOCUMENTS...
IT WAS TRUE. I KNEW IT WAS TRUE, EVEN IF MOM DIDN'T SEE IT.
CLAK
BUT THIS KIND OF THING DOESN'T HAPPEN TO YOU, DOES IT? IT HAPPENS TO OTHER PEOPLE.

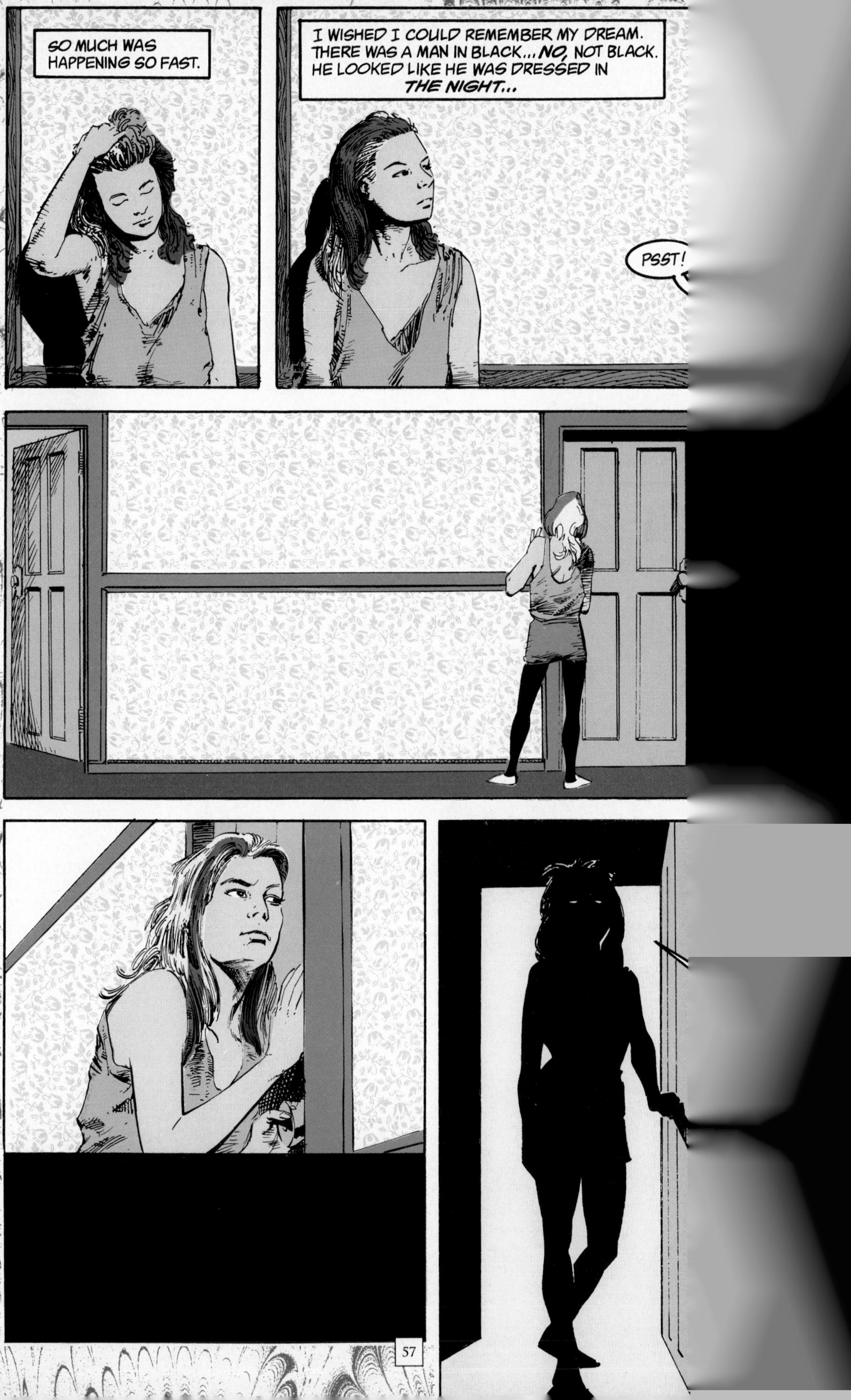
SO MUCH WAS HAPPENING SO FAST.
I WISHED I COULD REMEMBER MY DREAM. THERE WAS A MAN IN BLACK... NO, NOT BLACK. HE LOOKED LIKE HE WAS DRESSED IN THE NIGHT...
PSST!

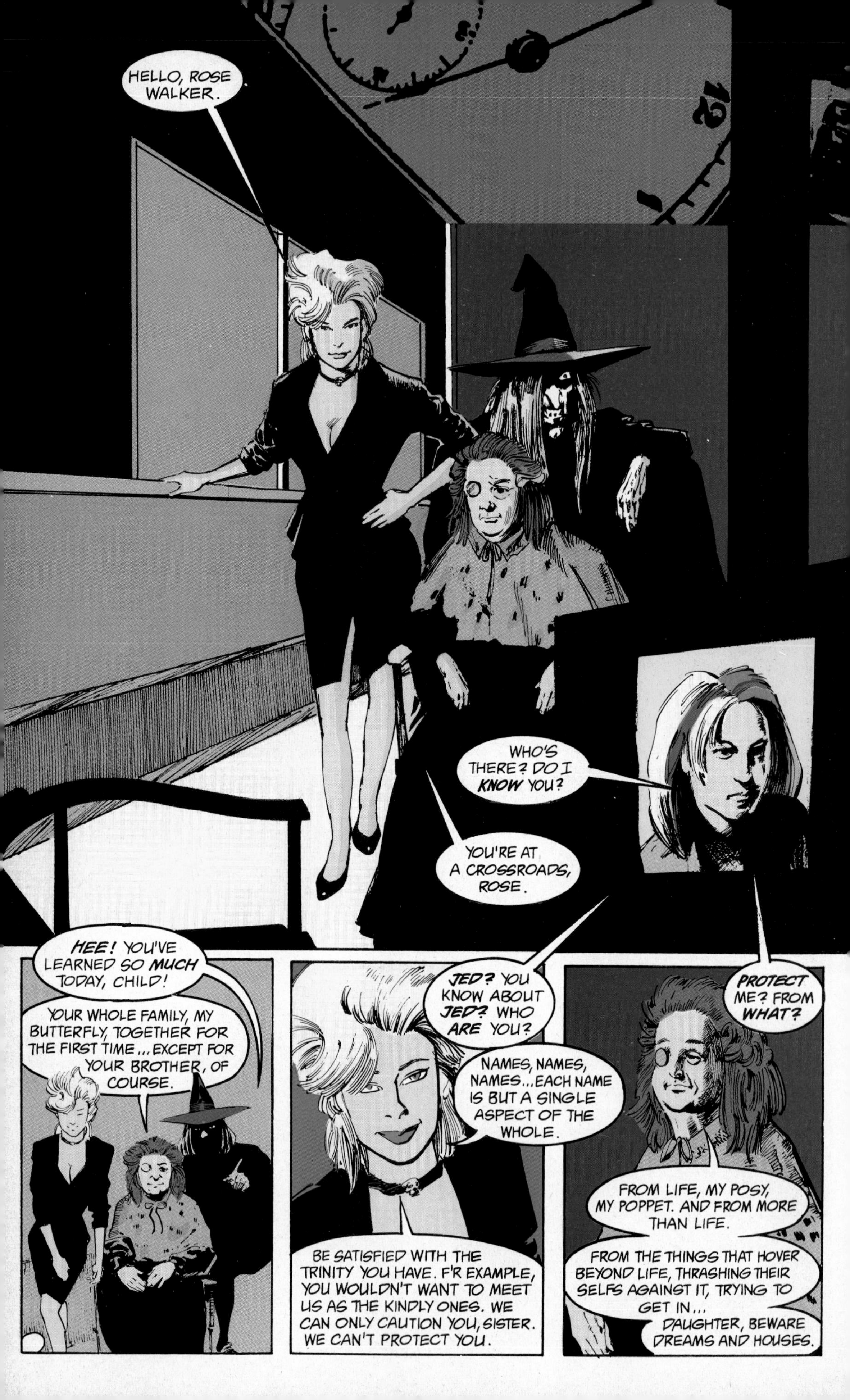
HELLO, ROSE WALKER.
WHO'S THERE? DO I KNOW YOU?
YOU'RE AT A CROSSROADS, ROSE.
HEE! YOU'VE LEARNED SO MUCH TODAY, CHILD!
YOUR WHOLE FAMILY, MY BUTTERFLY, TOGETHER FOR THE FIRST TIME... EXCEPT FOR YOUR BROTHER, OF COURSE.
JED? YOU KNOW ABOUT JED? WHO ARE YOU?
NAMES, NAMES, NAMES... EACH NAME IS BUT A SINGLE ASPECT OF THE WHOLE.
BE SATISFIED WITH THE TRINITY YOU HAVE. F'R EXAMPLE, YOU WOULDN'T WANT TO MEET US AS THE KINDLY ONES. WE CAN ONLY CAUTION YOU, SISTER. WE CAN'T PROTECT YOU.
PROTECT ME? FROM WHAT?
FROM LIFE, MY POSY, MY POPPET. AND FROM MORE THAN LIFE.
FROM THE THINGS THAT HOVER BEYOND LIFE, THRASHING THEIR SELFS AGAINST IT, TRYING TO GET IN...
DAUGHTER, BEWARE DREAMS AND HOUSES.

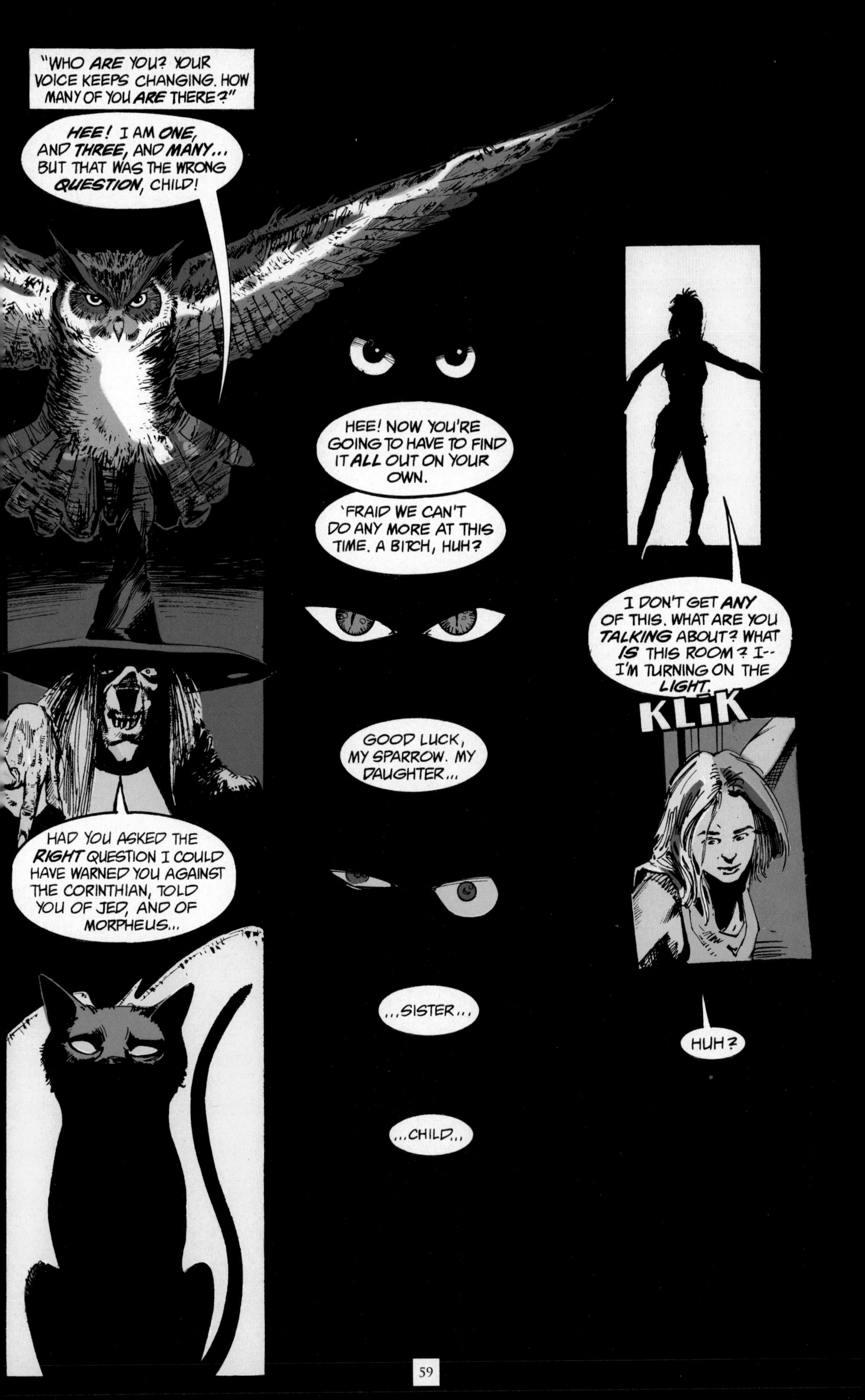
"WHO ARE YOU? YOUR VOICE KEEPS CHANGING. HOW MANY OF YOU ARE THERE?"
HEE! I AM ONE, AND THREE, AND MANY... BUT THAT WAS THE WRONG QUESTION, CHILD!
HAD YOU ASKED THE RIGHT QUESTION I COULD HAVE WARNED YOU AGAINST THE CORINTHIAN, TOLD YOU OF JED, AND OF MORPHEUS...
HEE! NOW YOU'RE GOING TO HAVE TO FIND IT ALL OUT ON YOUR OWN.
'FRAID WE CAN'T DO ANY MORE AT THIS TIME. A BITCH, HUH?
GOOD LUCK, MY SPARROW. MY DAUGHTER...
...SISTER...
...CHILD...
I DON'T GET ANY OF THIS. WHAT ARE YOU TALKING ABOUT? WHAT IS THIS ROOM? I-- I'M TURNING ON THE LIGHT.
KLIK
HUH?

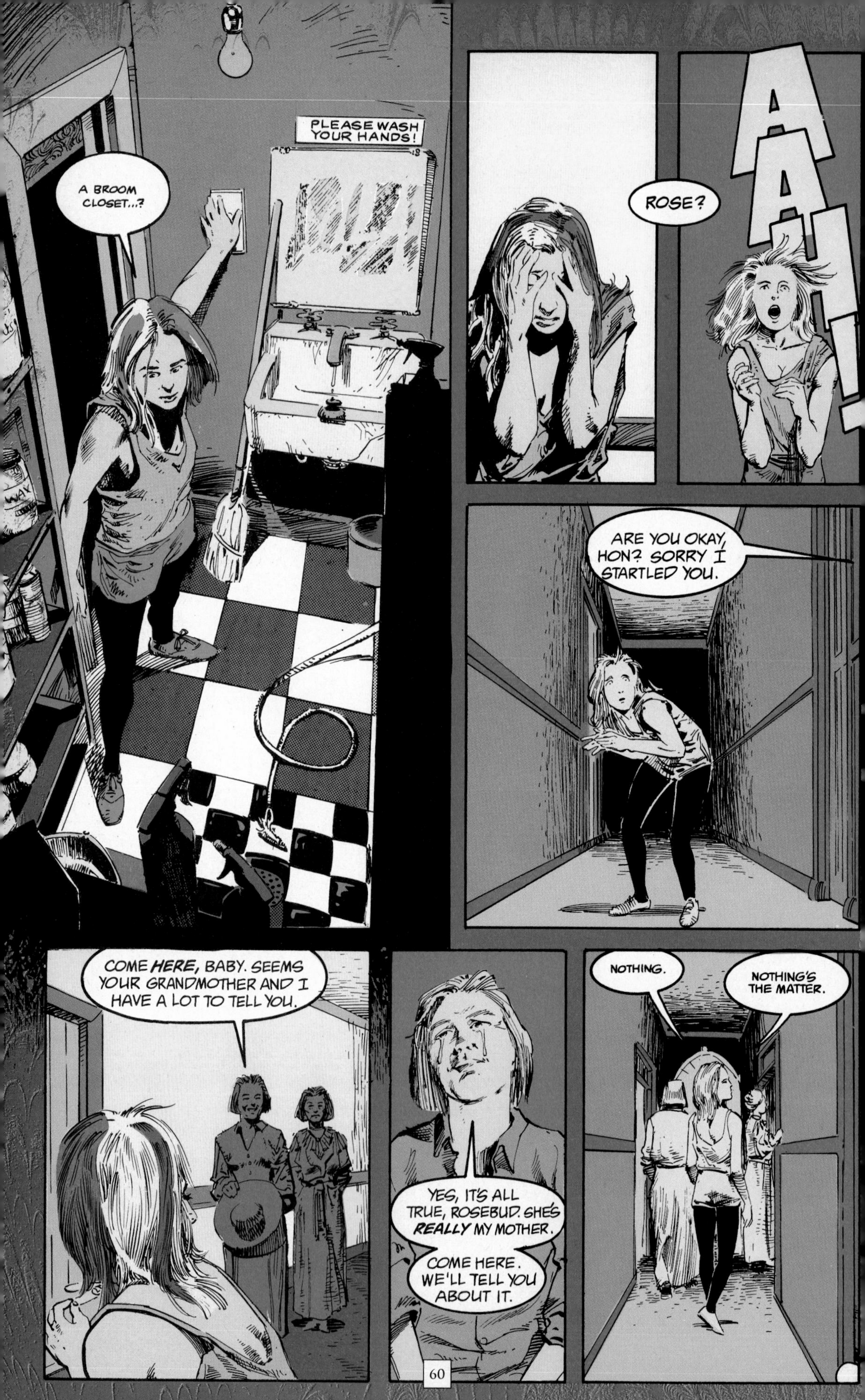
PLEASE WASH YOUR HANDS!
A BROOM CLOSET...?
ROSE?
AAAH!!
ARE YOU OKAY, HON? SORRY I STARTLED YOU.
COME *HERE*, BABY. SEEMS YOUR GRANDMOTHER AND I HAVE A LOT TO TELL YOU.
YES, IT'S ALL TRUE, ROSEBUD. SHE'S *REALLY* MY MOTHER.
COME HERE. WE'LL TELL YOU ABOUT IT.
NOTHING.
NOTHING'S THE MATTER.

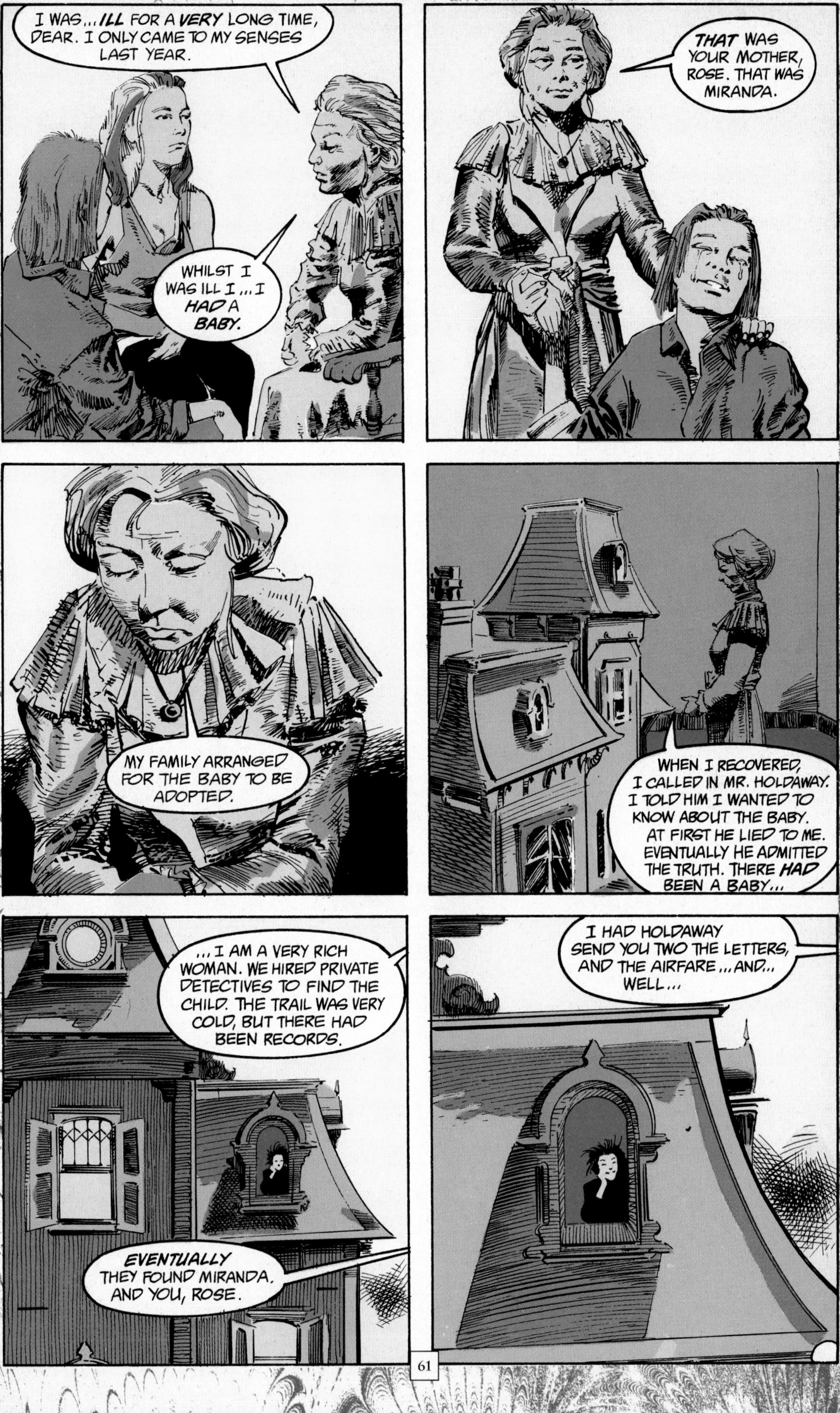
I WAS... ILL FOR A VERY LONG TIME, DEAR. I ONLY CAME TO MY SENSES LAST YEAR.
WHILST I WAS ILL I... I HAD A BABY.
THAT WAS YOUR MOTHER, ROSE. THAT WAS MIRANDA.
MY FAMILY ARRANGED FOR THE BABY TO BE ADOPTED.
WHEN I RECOVERED, I CALLED IN MR. HOLDAWAY. I TOLD HIM I WANTED TO KNOW ABOUT THE BABY. AT FIRST HE LIED TO ME. EVENTUALLY HE ADMITTED THE TRUTH. THERE HAD BEEN A BABY...
...I AM A VERY RICH WOMAN. WE HIRED PRIVATE DETECTIVES TO FIND THE CHILD. THE TRAIL WAS VERY COLD, BUT THERE HAD BEEN RECORDS.
EVENTUALLY THEY FOUND MIRANDA, AND YOU, ROSE.
I HAD HOLDAWAY SEND YOU TWO THE LETTERS, AND THE AIRFARE... AND... WELL...

...HERE YOU ARE.

THE WHOLE FAMILY. TOGETHER FOR THE FIRST TIME.

NOT JED, THOUGH. I *WONDERED*-- HAD MOM *TOLD* HER ABOUT JED?

I'M ALMOST NINETY, ROSE. BUT I'VE ONLY REALLY *LIVED* FOR ABOUT SEVENTEEN YEARS. IN A FUNNY WAY, I'M YOUNGER THAN *YOU*...

I...I SHOULD *GIVE* YOU SOMETHING, SHOULDN'T I? HERE. SOMETHING FOR YOU. A *RING*.

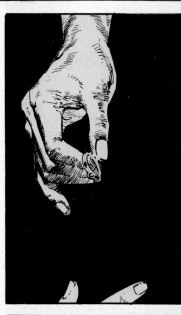

THE ANNULET...?

WHAT?

IT'S ALL COMING TRUE, ISN'T IT? MY DREAMS...

WHAT ARE YOU *TALKING* ABOUT, ROSEBUD?

WHAT'S *HAPPENING* TO ME, MOM? THE WOMAN IN THE HALL CLOSET. SHE KNEW ABOUT *JED*. SHE SAID I SHOULD BEWARE OF THE CORINTHIAN...

WHAT'S *"THE CORINTHIAN"*?

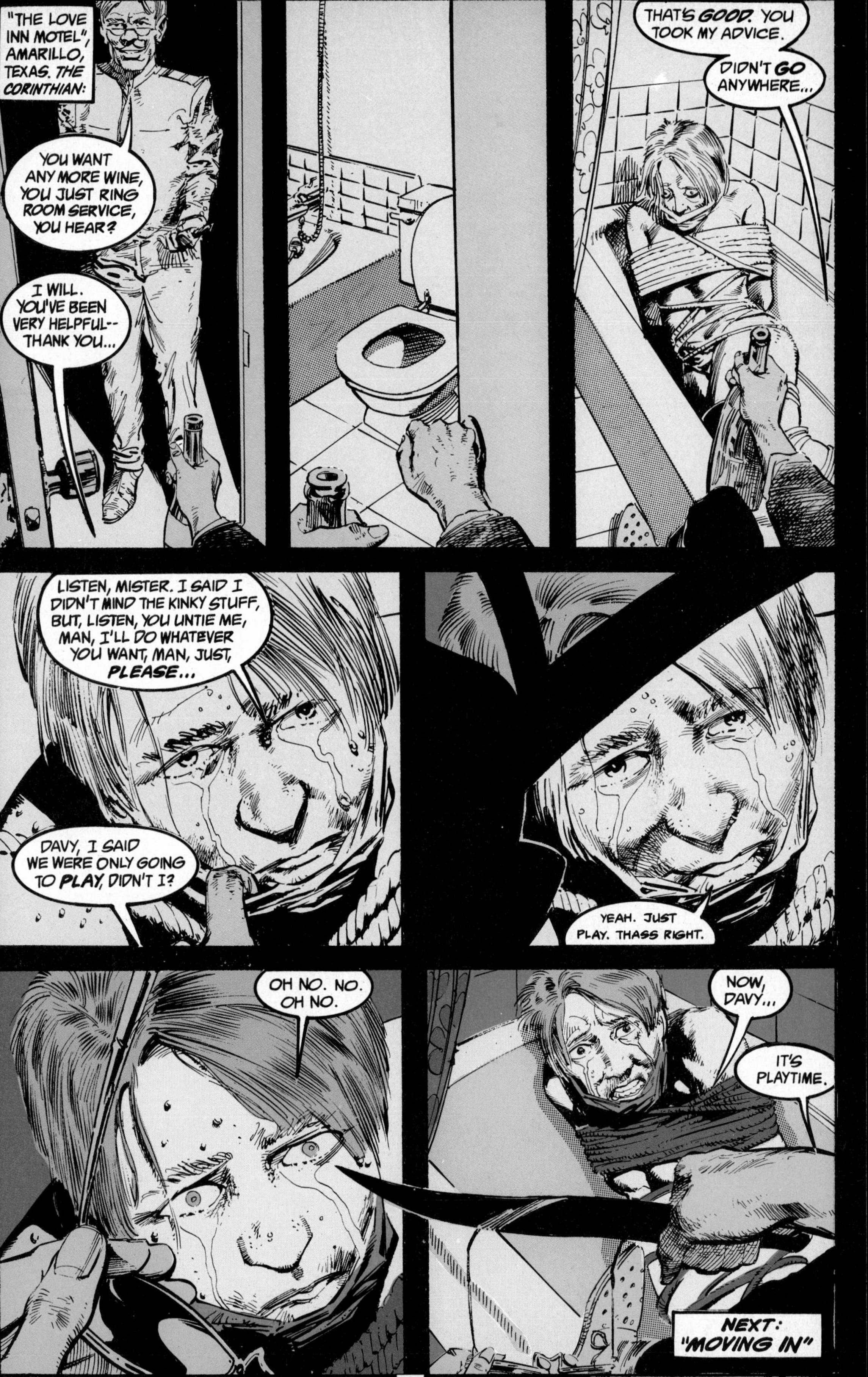
"THE LOVE INN MOTEL", AMARILLO, TEXAS. THE CORINTHIAN:
YOU WANT ANY MORE WINE, YOU JUST RING ROOM SERVICE, YOU HEAR?
I WILL. YOU'VE BEEN VERY HELPFUL-- THANK YOU...
THAT'S GOOD. YOU TOOK MY ADVICE.
DIDN'T GO ANYWHERE...
LISTEN, MISTER. I SAID I DIDN'T MIND THE KINKY STUFF, BUT, LISTEN, YOU UNTIE ME, MAN, I'LL DO WHATEVER YOU WANT, MAN, JUST, PLEASE...
DAVY, I SAID WE WERE ONLY GOING TO PLAY, DIDN'T I?
YEAH. JUST PLAY. THASS RIGHT.
OH NO. NO. OH NO.
NOW, DAVY...
IT'S PLAYTIME.
NEXT: "MOVING IN"

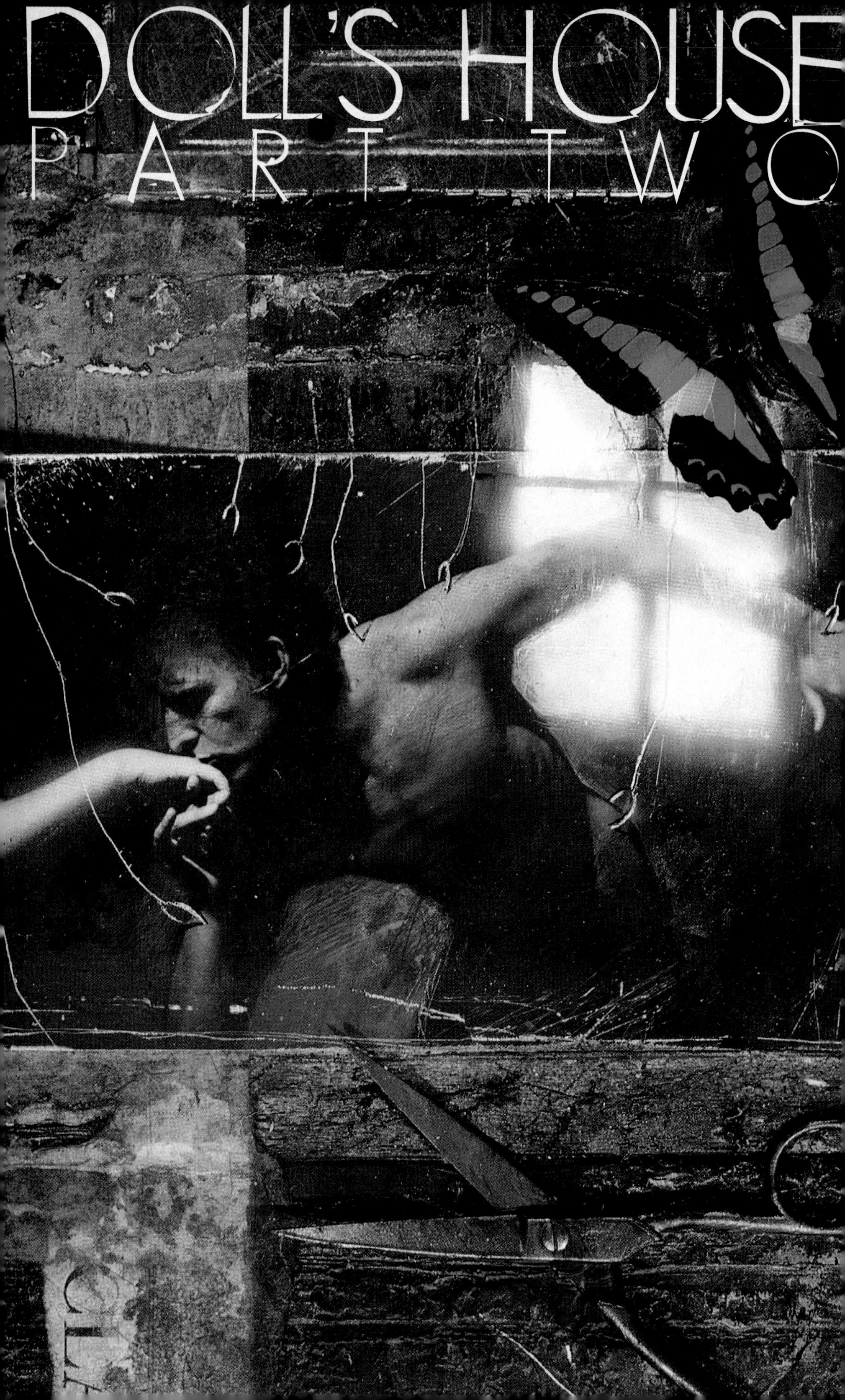
DOLL'S HOUSE
PART TWO

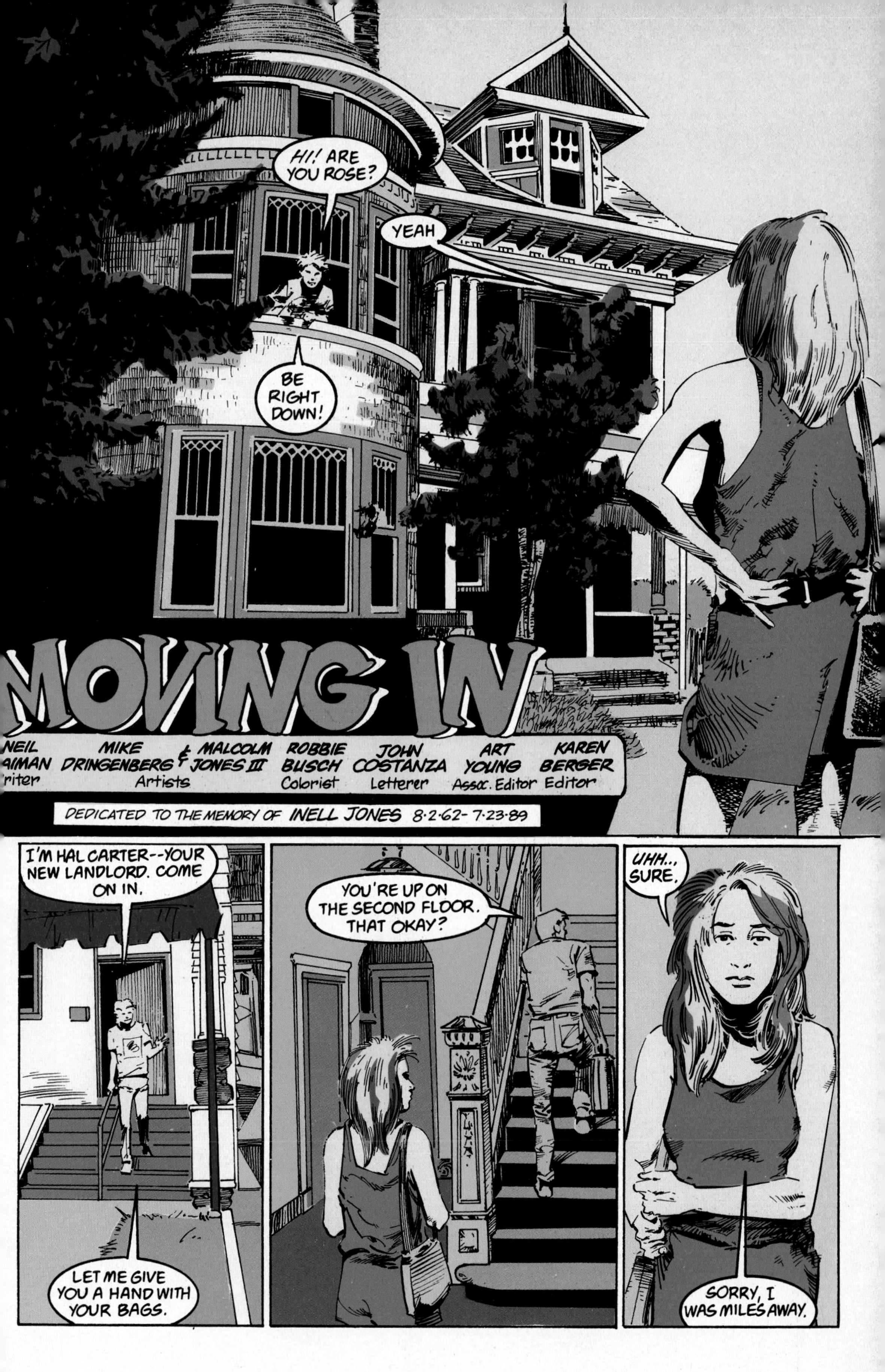

HI! ARE YOU ROSE?
YEAH
BE RIGHT DOWN!
MOVING IN
NEIL AIMAN riter
MIKE DRINGENBERG & MALCOLM JONES III Artists
ROBBIE BUSCH Colorist
JOHN COSTANZA Letterer
ART YOUNG Assoc. Editor
KAREN BERGER Editor
DEDICATED TO THE MEMORY OF INELL JONES 8·2·62-7·23·89
I'M HAL CARTER--YOUR NEW LANDLORD. COME ON IN.
LET ME GIVE YOU A HAND WITH YOUR BAGS.
YOU'RE UP ON THE SECOND FLOOR. THAT OKAY?
UHH... SURE.
SORRY, I WAS MILES AWAY.

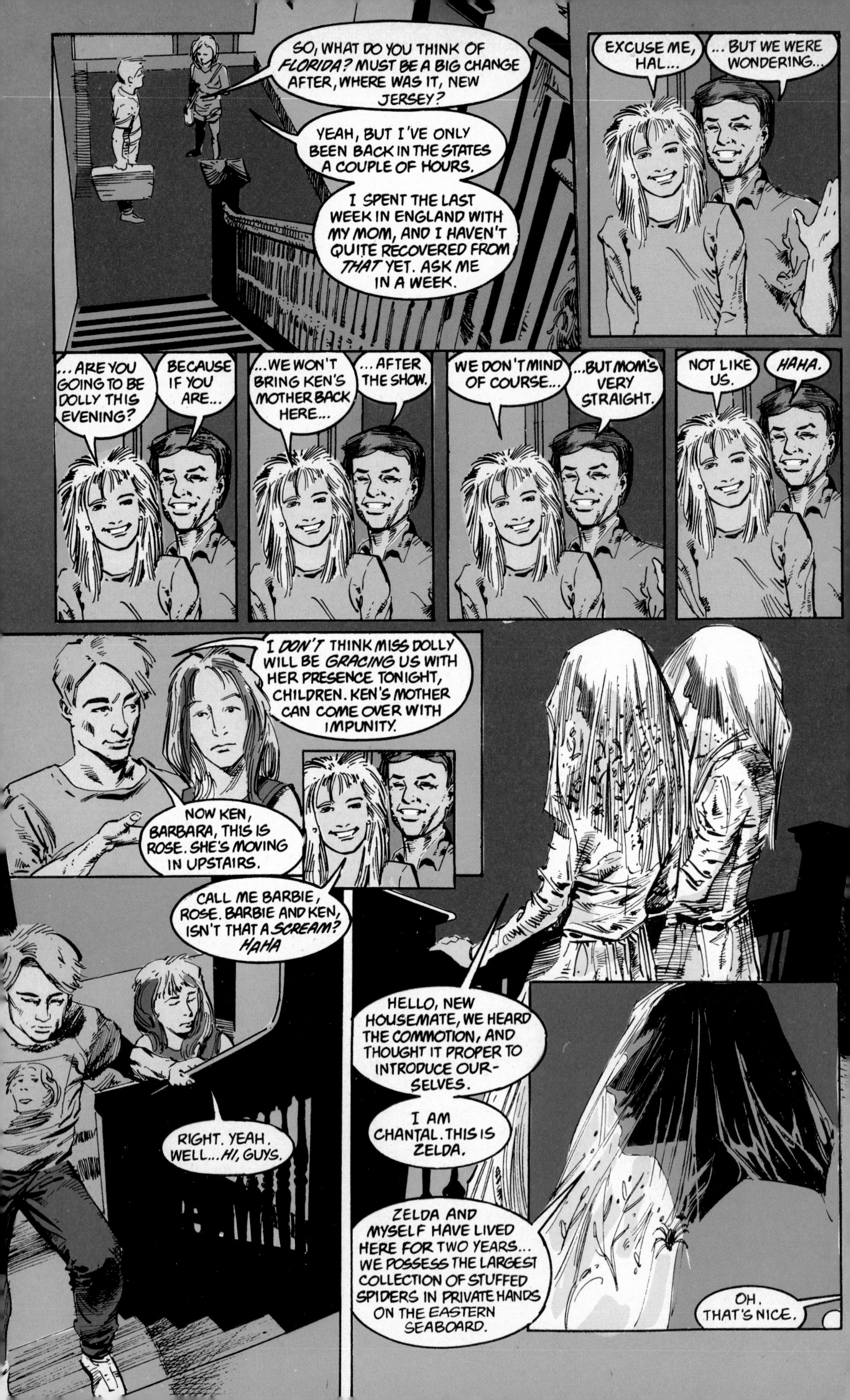
SO, WHAT DO YOU THINK OF FLORIDA? MUST BE A BIG CHANGE AFTER, WHERE WAS IT, NEW JERSEY?
YEAH, BUT I'VE ONLY BEEN BACK IN THE STATES A COUPLE OF HOURS.
I SPENT THE LAST WEEK IN ENGLAND WITH MY MOM, AND I HAVEN'T QUITE RECOVERED FROM THAT YET. ASK ME IN A WEEK.
EXCUSE ME, HAL...
... BUT WE WERE WONDERING...
...ARE YOU GOING TO BE DOLLY THIS EVENING?
BECAUSE IF YOU ARE...
...WE WON'T BRING KEN'S MOTHER BACK HERE...
...AFTER THE SHOW.
WE DON'T MIND OF COURSE...
...BUT MOM'S VERY STRAIGHT.
NOT LIKE US.
HAHA.
I DON'T THINK MISS DOLLY WILL BE GRACING US WITH HER PRESENCE TONIGHT, CHILDREN. KEN'S MOTHER CAN COME OVER WITH IMPUNITY.
NOW KEN, BARBARA, THIS IS ROSE. SHE'S MOVING IN UPSTAIRS.
CALL ME BARBIE, ROSE. BARBIE AND KEN, ISN'T THAT A SCREAM? HAHA
RIGHT. YEAH. WELL...HI, GUYS.
HELLO, NEW HOUSEMATE, WE HEARD THE COMMOTION, AND THOUGHT IT PROPER TO INTRODUCE OUR-SELVES.
I AM CHANTAL. THIS IS ZELDA.
ZELDA AND MYSELF HAVE LIVED HERE FOR TWO YEARS... WE POSSESS THE LARGEST COLLECTION OF STUFFED SPIDERS IN PRIVATE HANDS ON THE EASTERN SEABOARD.
OH. THAT'S NICE.

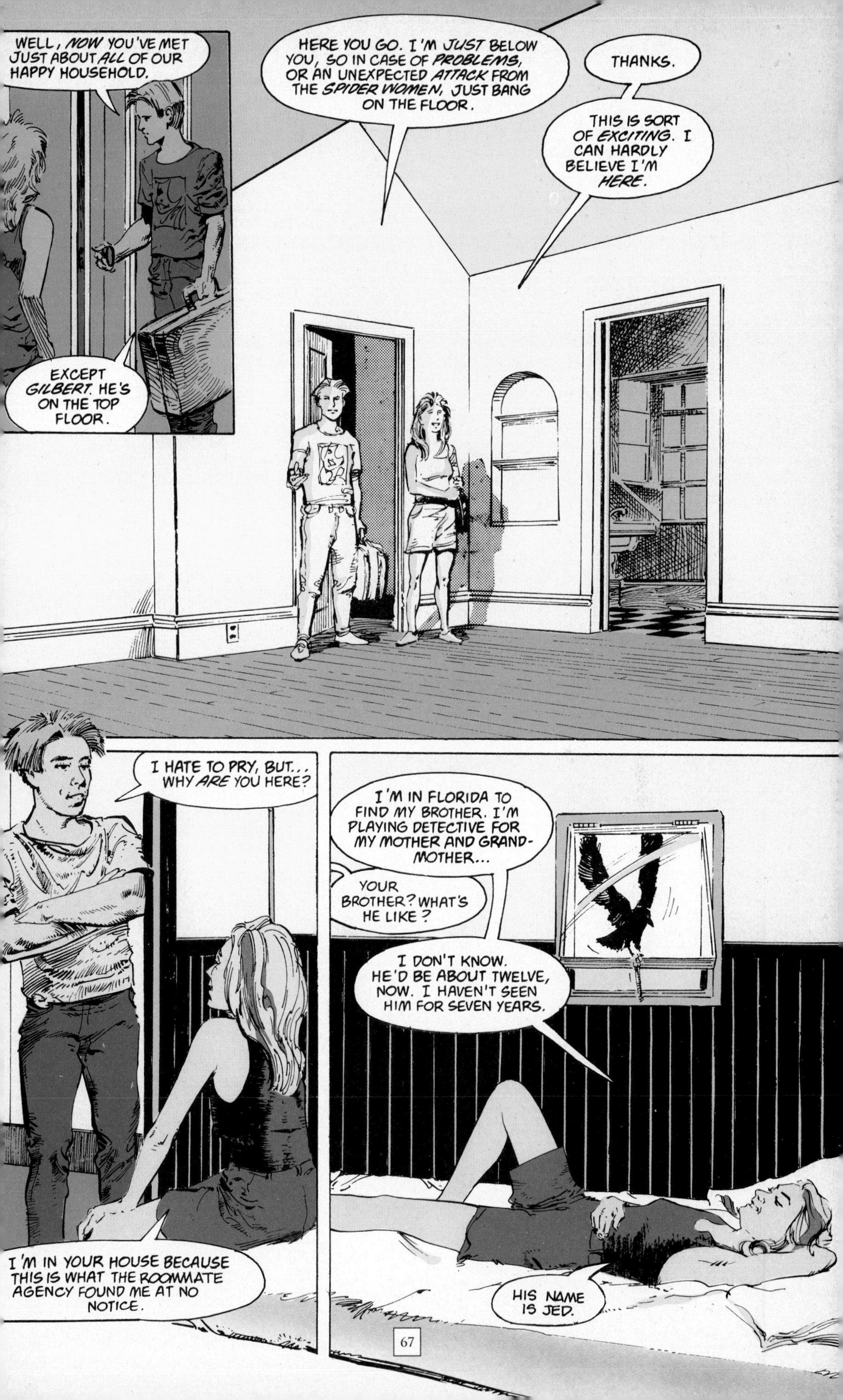
WELL, NOW YOU'VE MET JUST ABOUT ALL OF OUR HAPPY HOUSEHOLD.
EXCEPT GILBERT. HE'S ON THE TOP FLOOR.
HERE YOU GO. I'M JUST BELOW YOU, SO IN CASE OF PROBLEMS, OR AN UNEXPECTED ATTACK FROM THE SPIDER WOMEN, JUST BANG ON THE FLOOR.
THANKS.
THIS IS SORT OF EXCITING. I CAN HARDLY BELIEVE I'M HERE.
I HATE TO PRY, BUT... WHY ARE YOU HERE?
I'M IN YOUR HOUSE BECAUSE THIS IS WHAT THE ROOMMATE AGENCY FOUND ME AT NO NOTICE.
I'M IN FLORIDA TO FIND MY BROTHER. I'M PLAYING DETECTIVE FOR MY MOTHER AND GRAND-MOTHER...
YOUR BROTHER? WHAT'S HE LIKE?
I DON'T KNOW. HE'D BE ABOUT TWELVE, NOW. I HAVEN'T SEEN HIM FOR SEVEN YEARS.
HIS NAME IS JED.

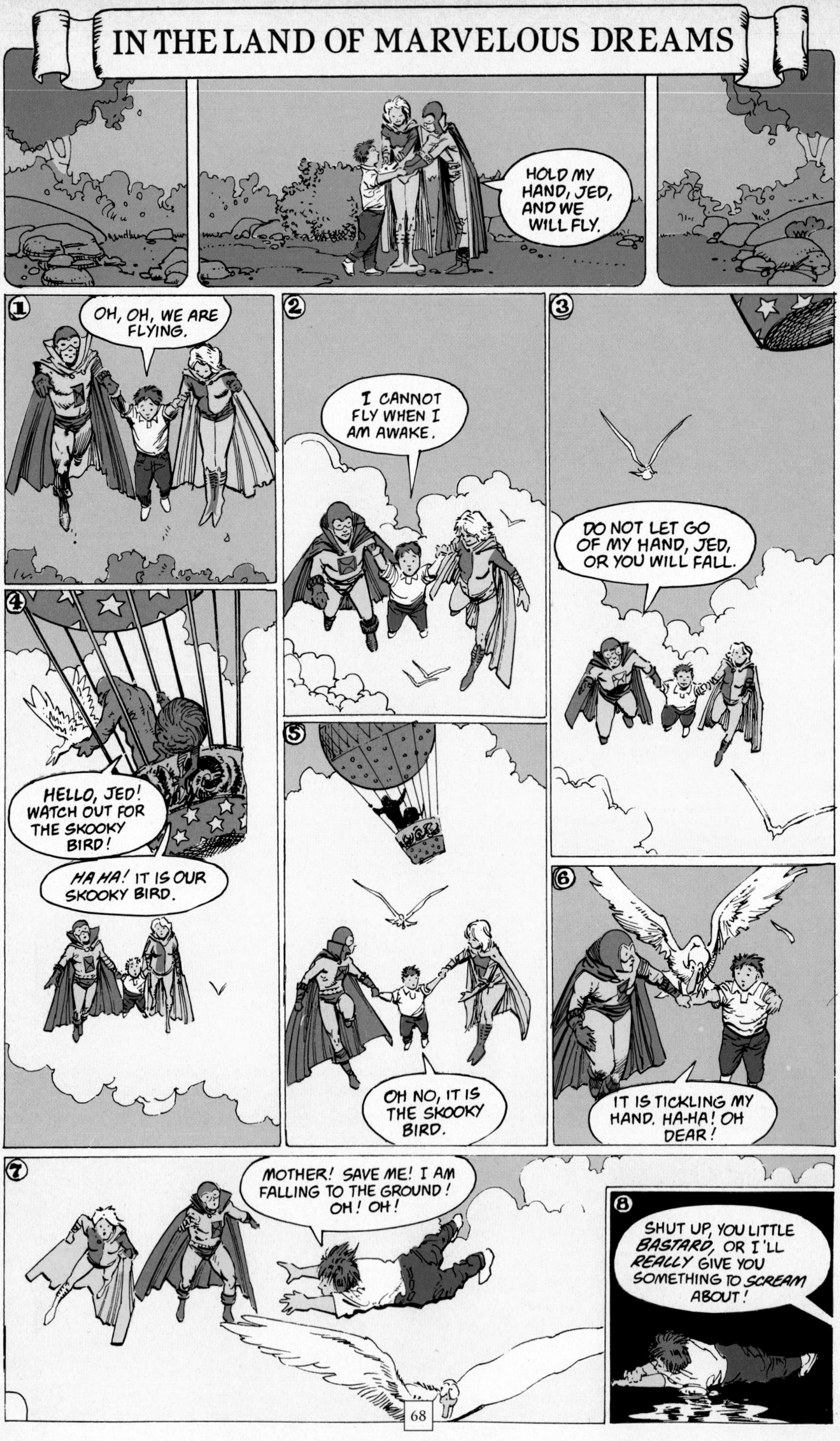
IN THE LAND OF MARVELOUS DREAMS
HOLD MY HAND, JED, AND WE WILL FLY.
1
OH, OH, WE ARE FLYING.
2
I CANNOT FLY WHEN I AM AWAKE.
3
DO NOT LET GO OF MY HAND, JED, OR YOU WILL FALL.
4
HELLO, JED! WATCH OUT FOR THE SKOOKY BIRD!
HA HA! IT IS OUR SKOOKY BIRD.
5
OH NO, IT IS THE SKOOKY BIRD.
6
IT IS TICKLING MY HAND. HA-HA! OH DEAR!
7
MOTHER! SAVE ME! I AM FALLING TO THE GROUND! OH! OH!
8
SHUT UP, YOU LITTLE BASTARD, OR I'LL REALLY GIVE YOU SOMETHING TO SCREAM ABOUT!

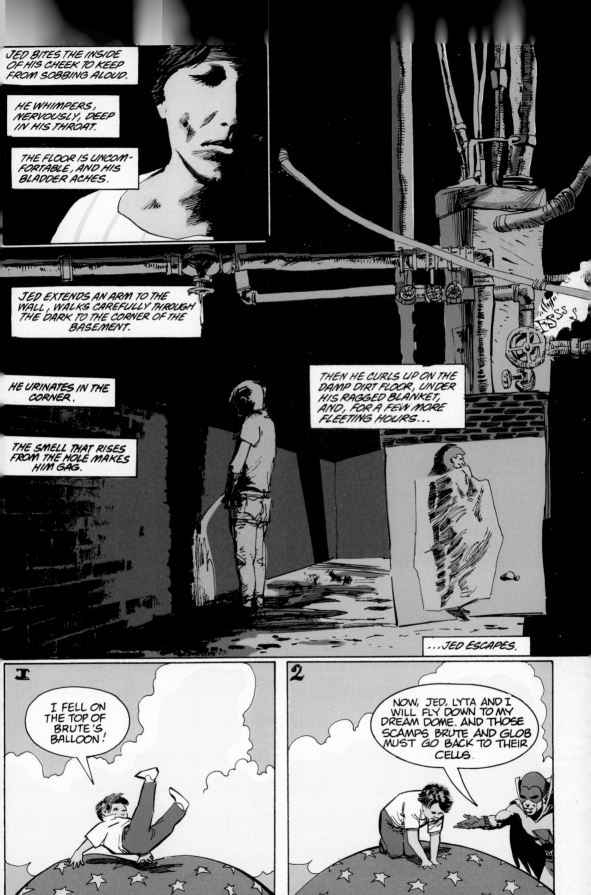

JED BITES THE INSIDE OF HIS CHEEK TO KEEP FROM SOBBING ALOUD.

HE WHIMPERS, NERVOUSLY, DEEP IN HIS THROAT.

THE FLOOR IS UNCOMFORTABLE, AND HIS BLADDER ACHES.

JED EXTENDS AN ARM TO THE WALL, WALKS CAREFULLY THROUGH THE DARK TO THE CORNER OF THE BASEMENT.

HE URINATES IN THE CORNER.

THE SMELL THAT RISES FROM THE HOLE MAKES HIM GAG.

THEN HE CURLS UP ON THE DAMP DIRT FLOOR, UNDER HIS RAGGED BLANKET, AND, FOR A FEW MORE FLEETING HOURS...

...JED ESCAPES.

1

I FELL ON THE TOP OF BRUTE'S BALLOON!

2

NOW, JED, LYTA AND I WILL FLY DOWN TO MY DREAM DOME. AND THOSE SCAMPS BRUTE AND GLOB MUST GO BACK TO THEIR CELLS.

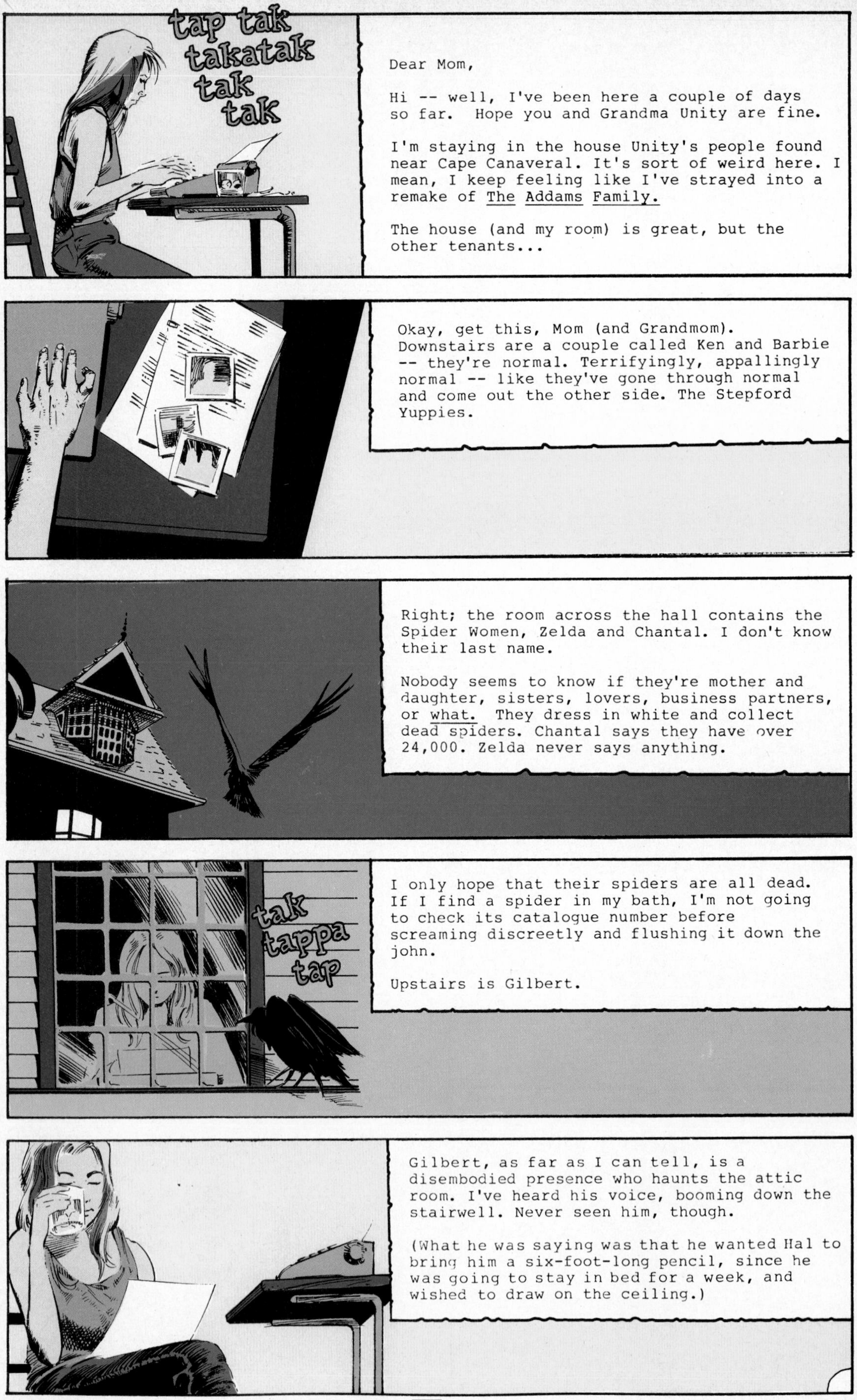
tap tak takatak tak tak
Dear Mom,
Hi -- well, I've been here a couple of days so far. Hope you and Grandma Unity are fine.
I'm staying in the house Unity's people found near Cape Canaveral. It's sort of weird here. I mean, I keep feeling like I've strayed into a remake of The Addams Family.
The house (and my room) is great, but the other tenants...
Okay, get this, Mom (and Grandmom). Downstairs are a couple called Ken and Barbie -- they're normal. Terrifyingly, appallingly normal -- like they've gone through normal and come out the other side. The Stepford Yuppies.
Right; the room across the hall contains the Spider Women, Zelda and Chantal. I don't know their last name.
Nobody seems to know if they're mother and daughter, sisters, lovers, business partners, or what. They dress in white and collect dead spiders. Chantal says they have over 24,000. Zelda never says anything.
I only hope that their spiders are all dead. If I find a spider in my bath, I'm not going to check its catalogue number before screaming discreetly and flushing it down the john.
Upstairs is Gilbert.
tak tappa tap
Gilbert, as far as I can tell, is a disembodied presence who haunts the attic room. I've heard his voice, booming down the stairwell. Never seen him, though.
(What he was saying was that he wanted Hal to bring him a six-foot-long pencil, since he was going to stay in bed for a week, and wished to draw on the ceiling.)

tak... tak

Weird, huh? And he sounds British to me, Unity. Fruit loops from the mother country.

At least Hal, our landlord, is normal.

BAM

HUH?

THAT *MAN!* THE *GALL* OF THAT IF-HE'S-SO-CLEVER-WHAT-*IS*-HE-DOING-DIRECTING-A-DRAG-SHOW-NO-TALENT *MAN!*

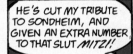

HE'S *CUT* MY TRIBUTE TO *SONDHEIM,* AND GIVEN AN EXTRA NUMBER TO THAT SLUT *MITZI!*

I TOLD HIM, DOUGLAS, I DON'T CARE *WHO* YOU'RE SCREWING...

BUT IF *"BROADWAY BABY"* GOES, THEN SO DO *I*!

THE CURE

BOYS DON'T CRY

ASSHOLE!

SLAM!

tap tak takatak tak tak

Well, relatively normal, anyway.

Oh -- another tenant showed up when I did. He -- or she -- is a big raven (I think), who's been hanging round outside my window. Hal says I ought to charge him rent on my window-ledge.

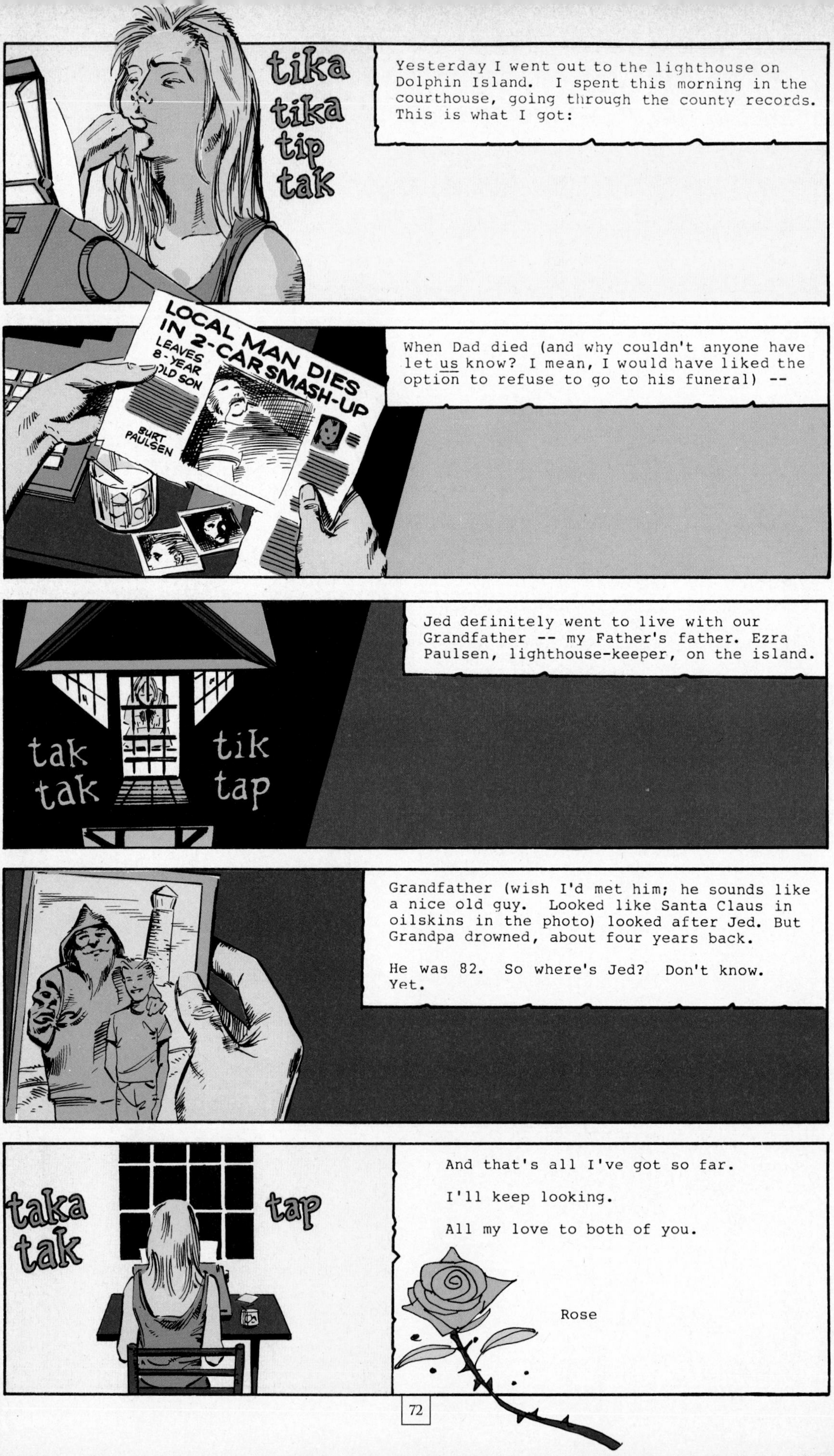
tika
tika
tip
tak
Yesterday I went out to the lighthouse on Dolphin Island. I spent this morning in the courthouse, going through the county records. This is what I got:
LOCAL MAN DIES IN 2-CAR SMASH-UP
LEAVES 8-YEAR OLD SON
BURT PAULSEN
When Dad died (and why couldn't anyone have let us know? I mean, I would have liked the option to refuse to go to his funeral) --
tak
tak
tik
tap
Jed definitely went to live with our Grandfather -- my Father's father. Ezra Paulsen, lighthouse-keeper, on the island.
Grandfather (wish I'd met him; he sounds like a nice old guy. Looked like Santa Claus in oilskins in the photo) looked after Jed. But Grandpa drowned, about four years back.
He was 82. So where's Jed? Don't know. Yet.
taka
tak
tap
And that's all I've got so far.
I'll keep looking.
All my love to both of you.
Rose

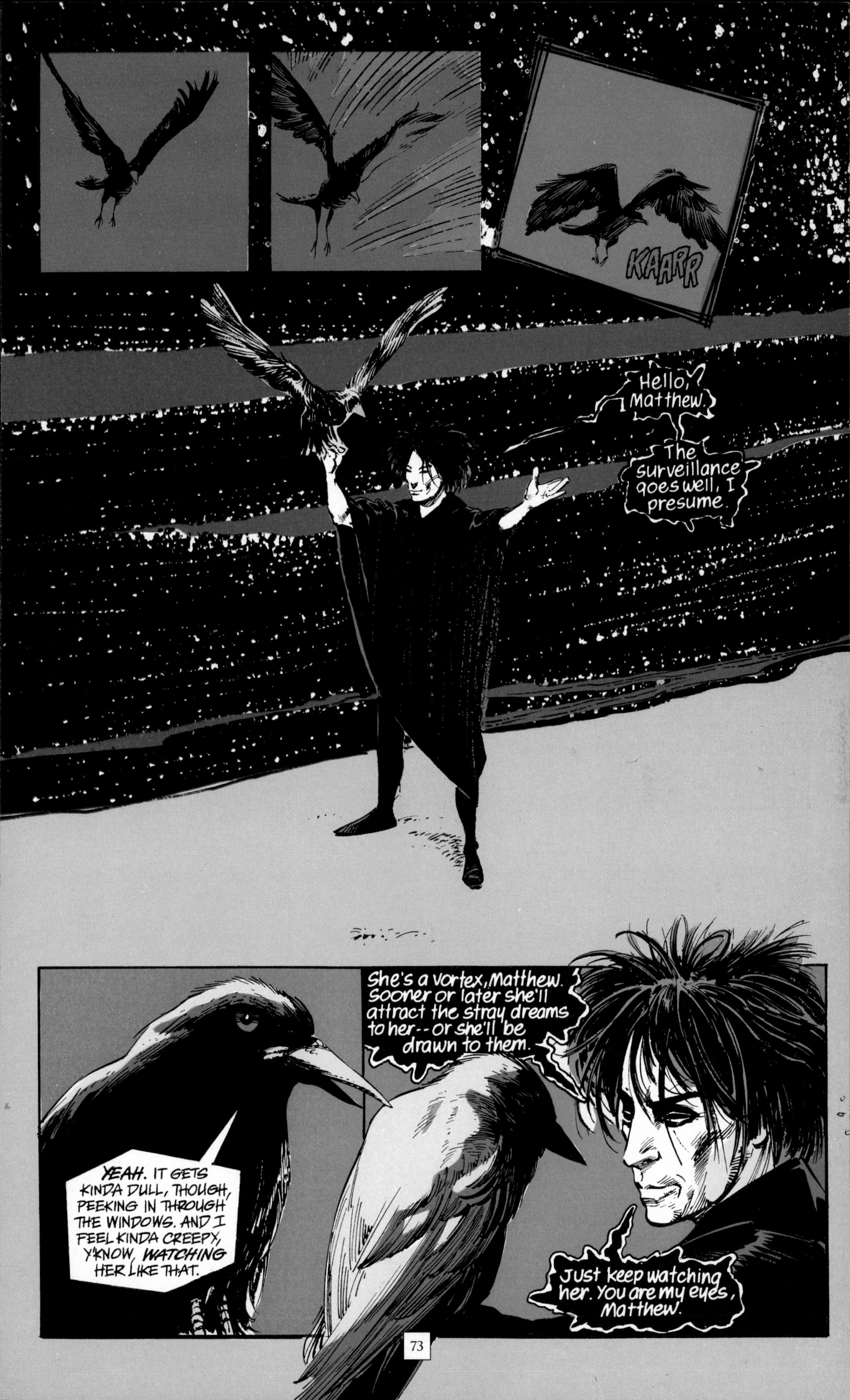
KAARR
Hello, Matthew.
The surveillance goes well, I presume.
YEAH. IT GETS KINDA DULL, THOUGH, PEEKING IN THROUGH THE WINDOWS. AND I FEEL KINDA CREEPY, Y'KNOW, WATCHING HER LIKE THAT.
She's a vortex, Matthew. Sooner or later she'll attract the stray dreams to her--or she'll be drawn to them.
Just keep watching her. You are my eyes, Matthew.

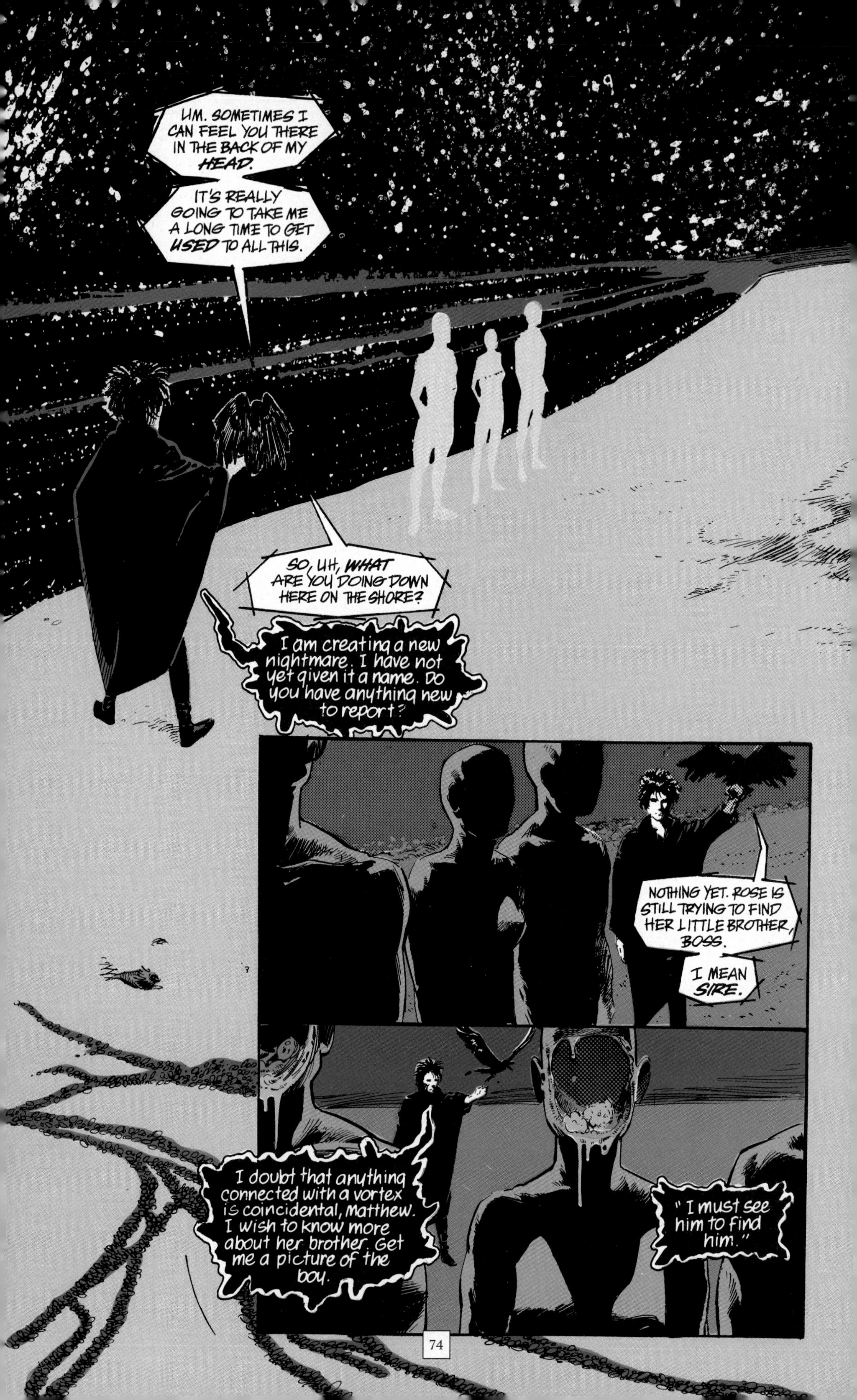
UM. SOMETIMES I CAN FEEL YOU THERE IN THE BACK OF MY HEAD.
IT'S REALLY GOING TO TAKE ME A LONG TIME TO GET USED TO ALL THIS.
SO, UH, WHAT ARE YOU DOING DOWN HERE ON THE SHORE?
I am creating a new nightmare. I have not yet given it a name. Do you have anything new to report?
NOTHING YET. ROSE IS STILL TRYING TO FIND HER LITTLE BROTHER, BOSS.
I MEAN SIRE.
I doubt that anything connected with a vortex is coincidental, Matthew. I wish to know more about her brother. Get me a picture of the boy.
"I must see him to find him."

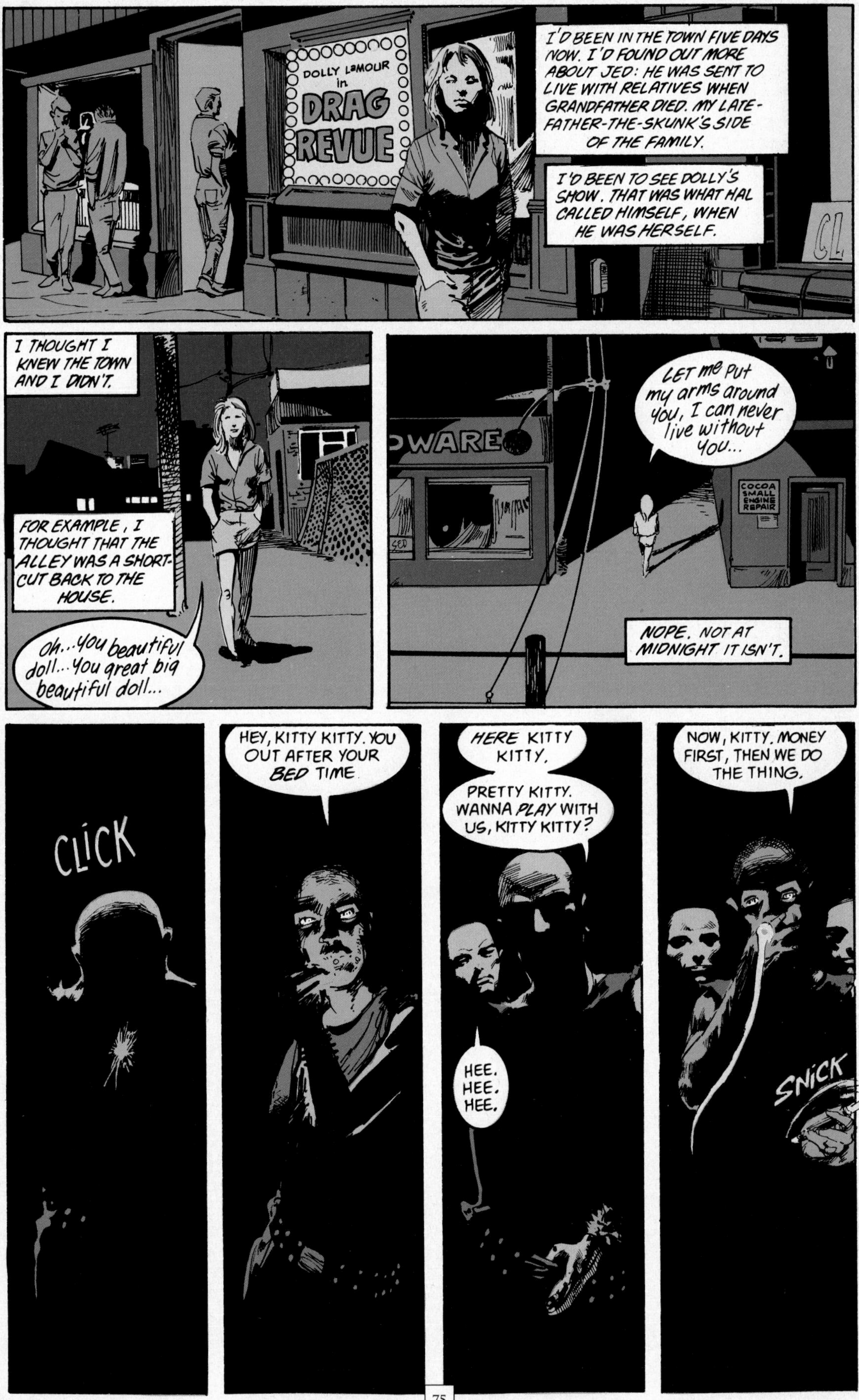
I'D BEEN IN THE TOWN FIVE DAYS NOW. I'D FOUND OUT MORE ABOUT JED: HE WAS SENT TO LIVE WITH RELATIVES WHEN GRANDFATHER DIED. MY LATE-FATHER-THE-SKUNK'S SIDE OF THE FAMILY.
I'D BEEN TO SEE DOLLY'S SHOW. THAT WAS WHAT HAL CALLED HIMSELF, WHEN HE WAS HERSELF.
DOLLY LaMOUR in DRAG REVUE
I THOUGHT I KNEW THE TOWN AND I DIDN'T.
FOR EXAMPLE, I THOUGHT THAT THE ALLEY WAS A SHORT-CUT BACK TO THE HOUSE.
Oh...You beautiful doll...You great big beautiful doll...
LET ME PUT MY ARMS AROUND YOU, I CAN NEVER LIVE WITHOUT YOU...
COCOA SMALL ENGINE REPAIR
NOPE. NOT AT MIDNIGHT IT ISN'T.
CLICK
HEY, KITTY KITTY. YOU OUT AFTER YOUR BED TIME.
HERE KITTY KITTY.
PRETTY KITTY. WANNA PLAY WITH US, KITTY KITTY?
HEE. HEE. HEE.
NOW, KITTY. MONEY FIRST, THEN WE DO THE THING.
SNICK

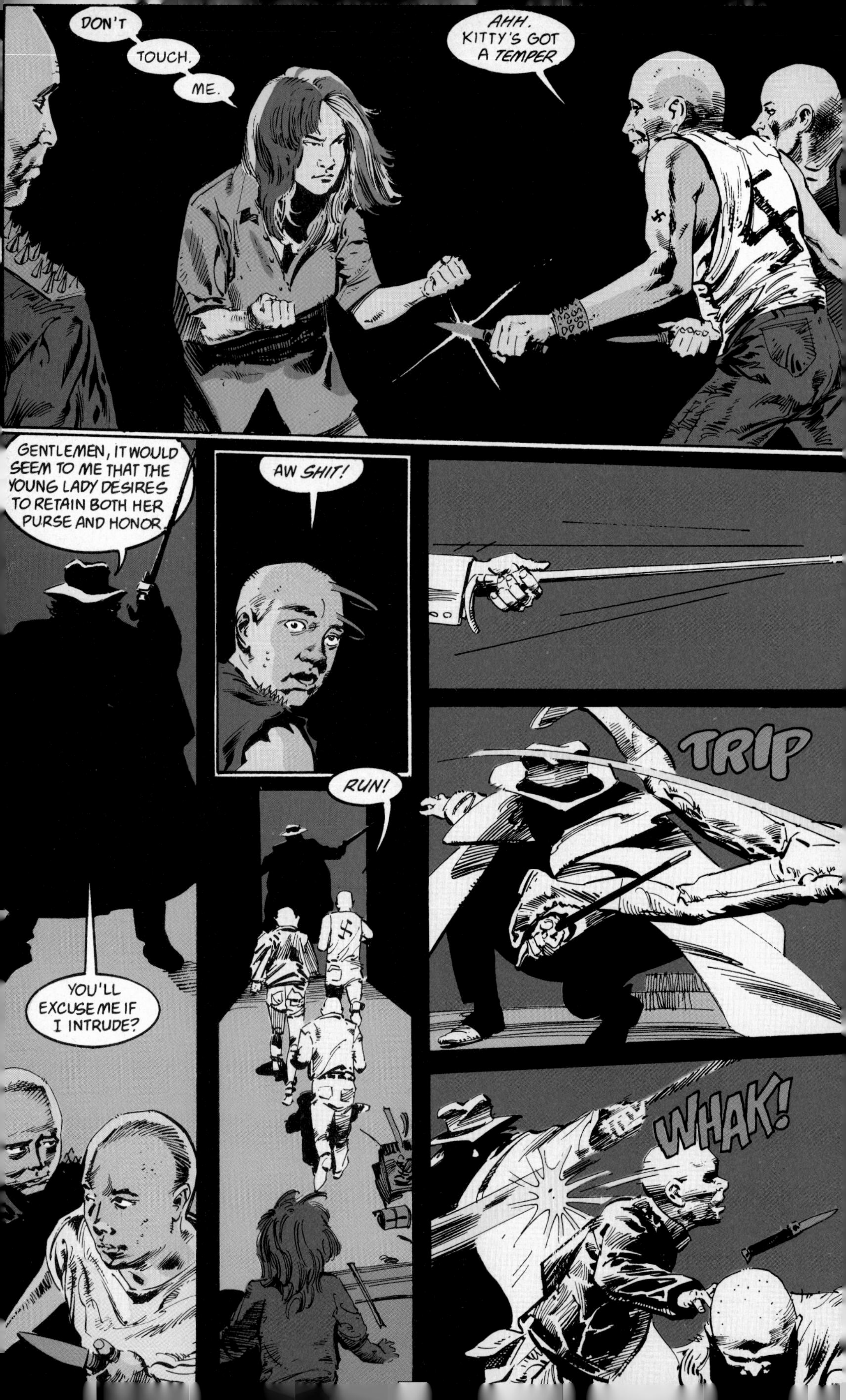
DON'T
TOUCH.
ME.
AHH. KITTY'S GOT A *TEMPER*
GENTLEMEN, IT WOULD SEEM TO ME THAT THE YOUNG LADY DESIRES TO RETAIN BOTH HER PURSE AND HONOR.
YOU'LL EXCUSE ME IF I INTRUDE?
AW *SHIT!*
RUN!
TRIP
WHAK!

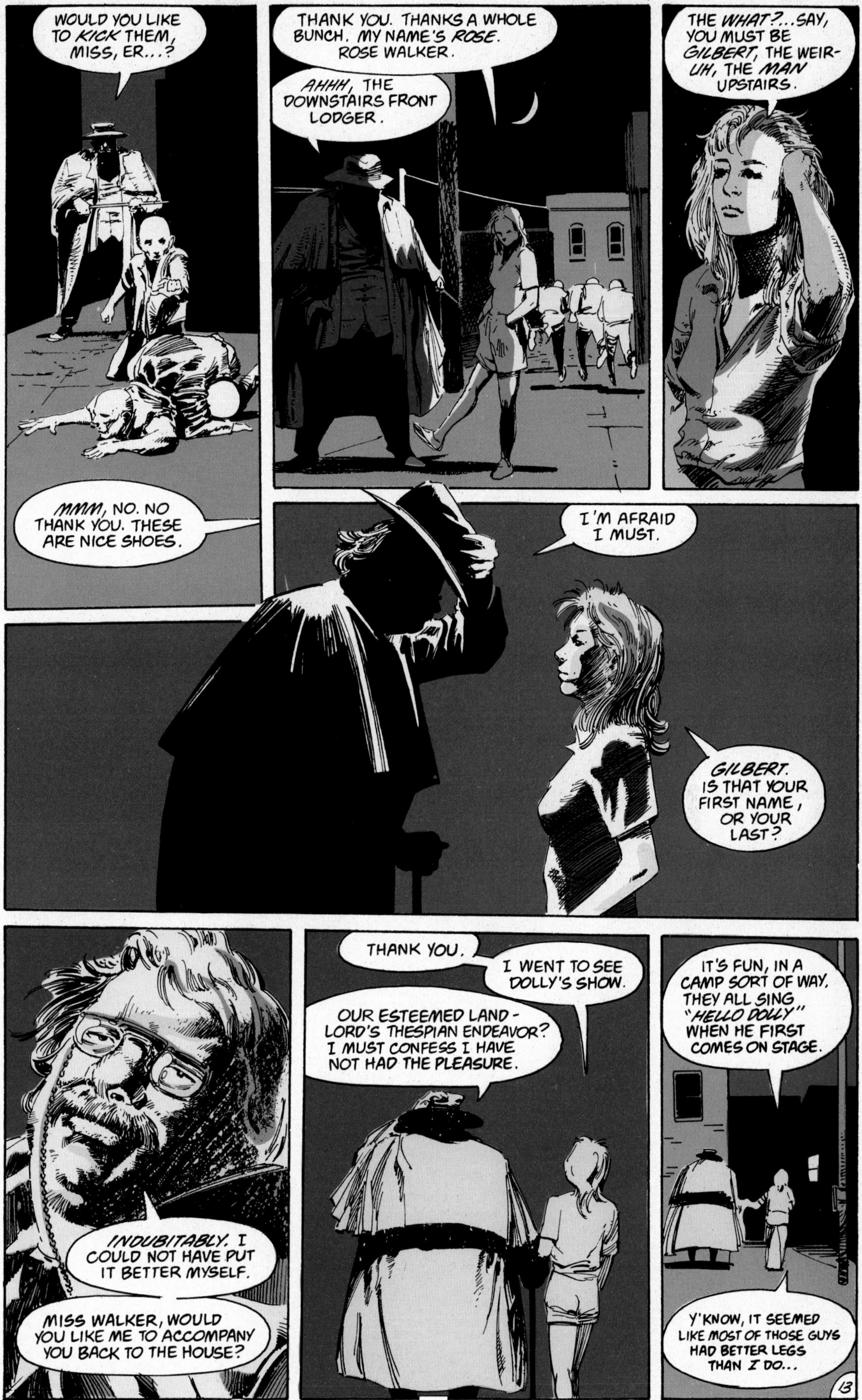
WOULD YOU LIKE TO *KICK* THEM, MISS, ER...?
THANK YOU. THANKS A WHOLE BUNCH. MY NAME'S *ROSE*. ROSE WALKER.
AHHH, THE DOWNSTAIRS FRONT LODGER.
THE *WHAT?*...SAY, YOU MUST BE *GILBERT*, THE WEIR- *UH*, THE *MAN* UPSTAIRS.
MMM, NO. NO THANK YOU. THESE ARE NICE SHOES.
I'M AFRAID I MUST.
GILBERT. IS THAT YOUR FIRST NAME, OR YOUR LAST?
INDUBITABLY. I COULD NOT HAVE PUT IT BETTER MYSELF.
MISS WALKER, WOULD YOU LIKE ME TO ACCOMPANY YOU BACK TO THE HOUSE?
THANK YOU.
I WENT TO SEE DOLLY'S SHOW.
OUR ESTEEMED LAND-LORD'S THESPIAN ENDEAVOR? I MUST CONFESS I HAVE NOT HAD THE PLEASURE.
IT'S FUN, IN A CAMP SORT OF WAY. THEY ALL SING *"HELLO DOLLY"* WHEN HE FIRST COMES ON STAGE.
Y'KNOW, IT SEEMED LIKE MOST OF THOSE GUYS HAD BETTER LEGS THAN *I* DO...
13

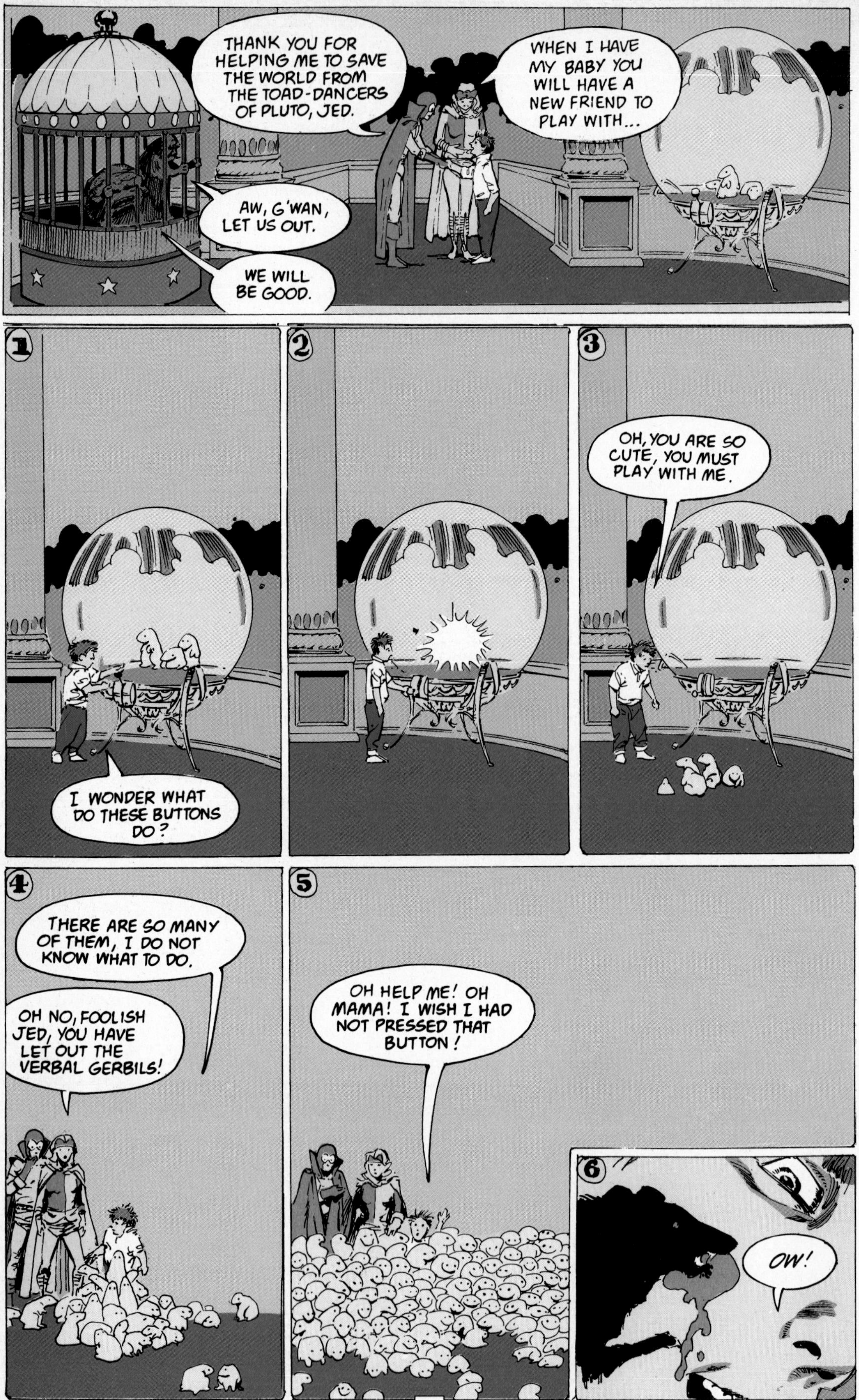
THANK YOU FOR HELPING ME TO SAVE THE WORLD FROM THE TOAD-DANCERS OF PLUTO, JED.
WHEN I HAVE MY BABY YOU WILL HAVE A NEW FRIEND TO PLAY WITH...
AW, G'WAN, LET US OUT.
WE WILL BE GOOD.
1
I WONDER WHAT DO THESE BUTTONS DO?
2
3
OH, YOU ARE SO CUTE, YOU MUST PLAY WITH ME.
4
THERE ARE SO MANY OF THEM, I DO NOT KNOW WHAT TO DO.
OH NO, FOOLISH JED, YOU HAVE LET OUT THE VERBAL GERBILS!
5
OH HELP ME! OH MAMA! I WISH I HAD NOT PRESSED THAT BUTTON!
6
OW!

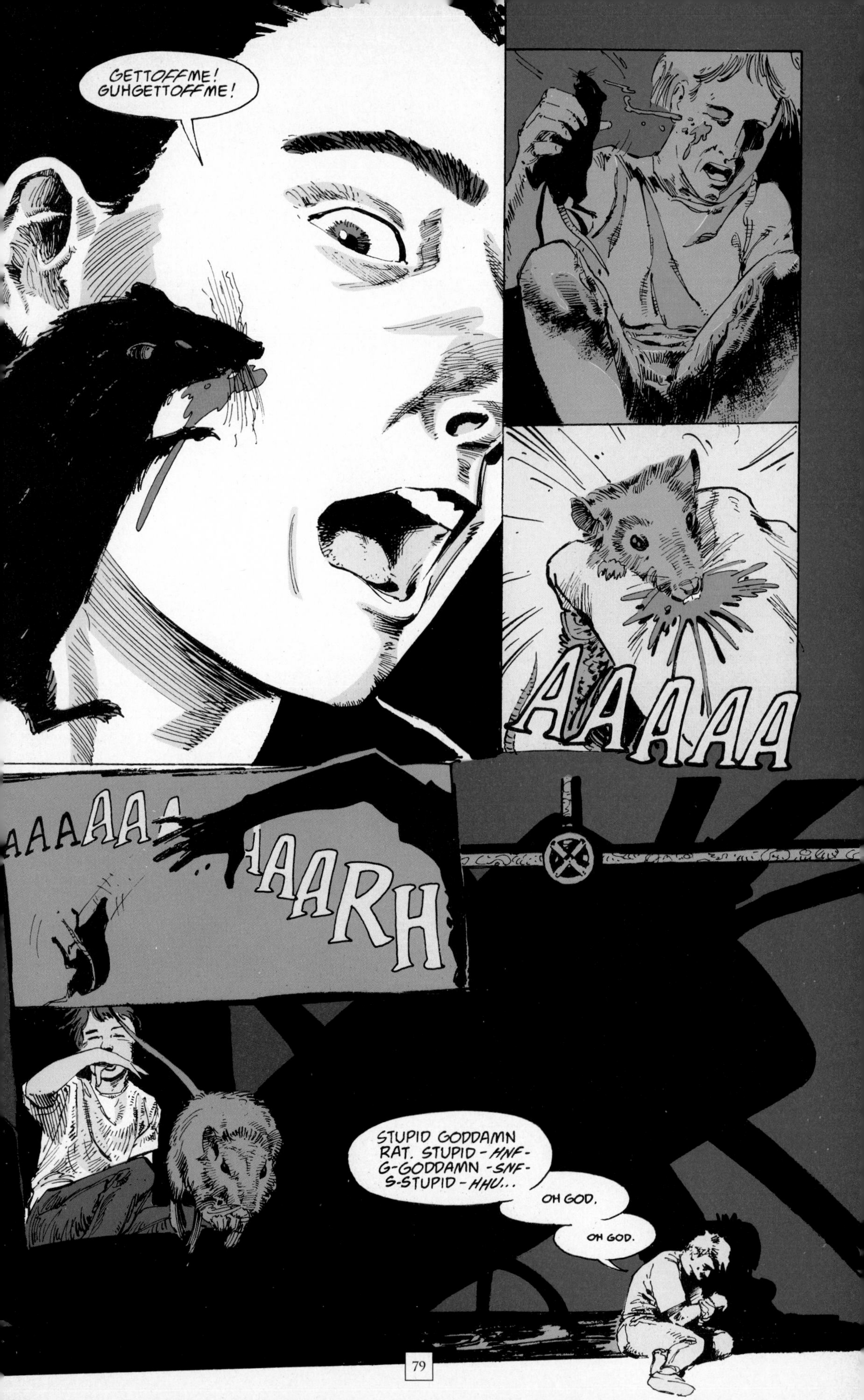
GETTOFFME! GUHGETTOFFME!
AAAAA
AAAAAAAAARH
STUPID GODDAMN RAT. STUPID -HNF- G-GODDAMN -SNF- S-STUPID -HHU...
OH GOD.
OH GOD.

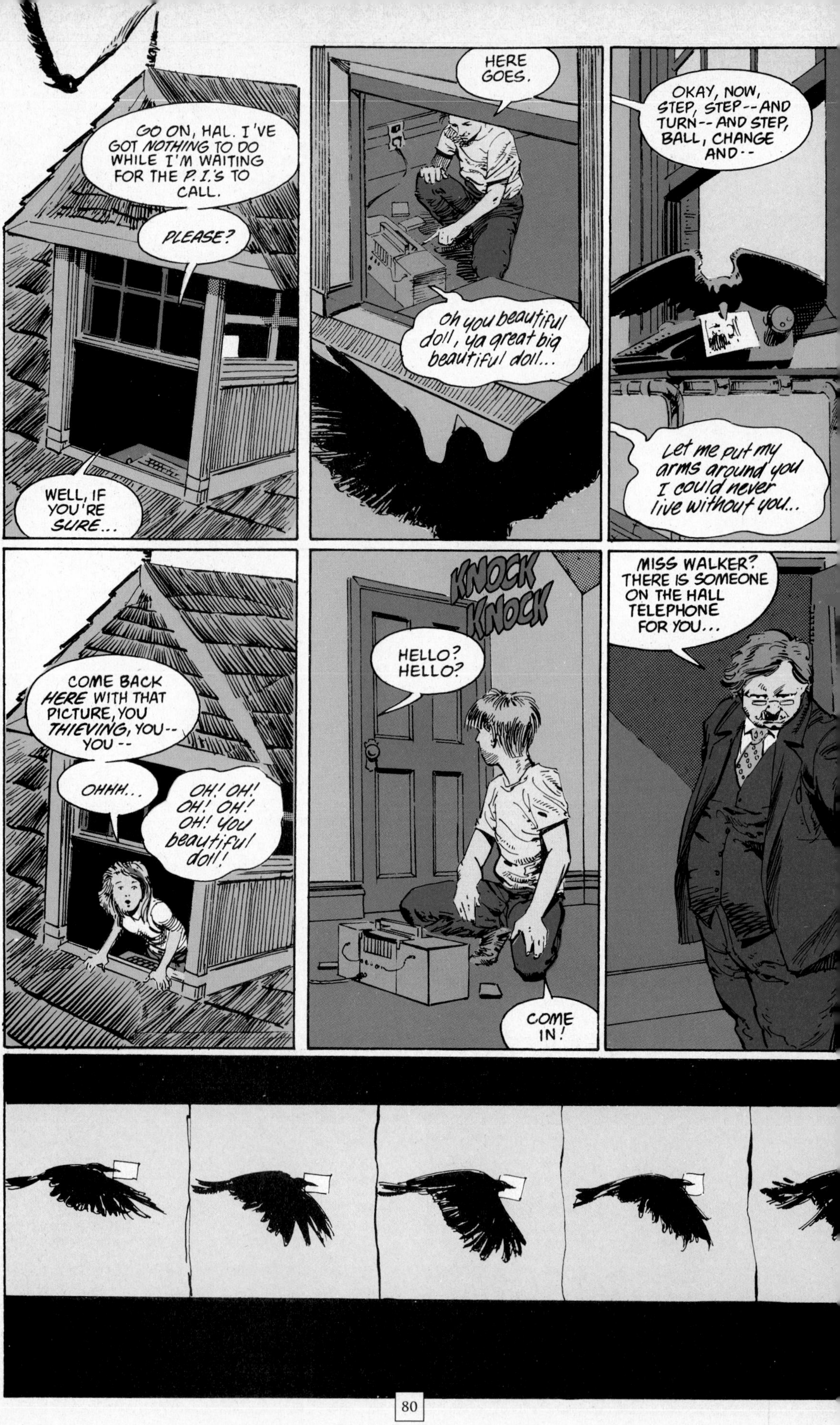
GO ON, HAL. I'VE GOT NOTHING TO DO WHILE I'M WAITING FOR THE P.I.'S TO CALL.
PLEASE?
WELL, IF YOU'RE SURE...
HERE GOES.
Oh you beautiful doll, ya great big beautiful doll...
OKAY, NOW, STEP, STEP--AND TURN--AND STEP, BALL, CHANGE AND--
Let me put my arms around you I could never live without you...
COME BACK HERE WITH THAT PICTURE, YOU THIEVING, YOU--YOU--
OHHH...
OH! OH! OH! OH! OH! You beautiful doll!
KNOCK KNOCK
HELLO? HELLO?
COME IN!
MISS WALKER? THERE IS SOMEONE ON THE HALL TELEPHONE FOR YOU...

HEY! STOP THAT!

...beautiful doll, if you ever leave me how my heart would ache...

I want to hug you but I fear you'd break...

GAAANGWAY!

WELL? WHAT'S THE NEWS, THEN?

AM I TO INFER, SIR, THAT YOU ARE PRESUMING THAT I MIGHT ACTUALLY HAVE INQUIRED AS TO THE NATURE OF SOMEONE ELSE'S TELEPHONE CALL?

GILBERT...

HOOM.

WELL, I BELIEVE THE CALL COMES FROM THE PRIVATE DETECTIVES MISS WALKER HAD HIRED TO FIND HER BROTHER...

SUCCESSFULLY.

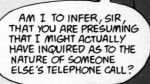

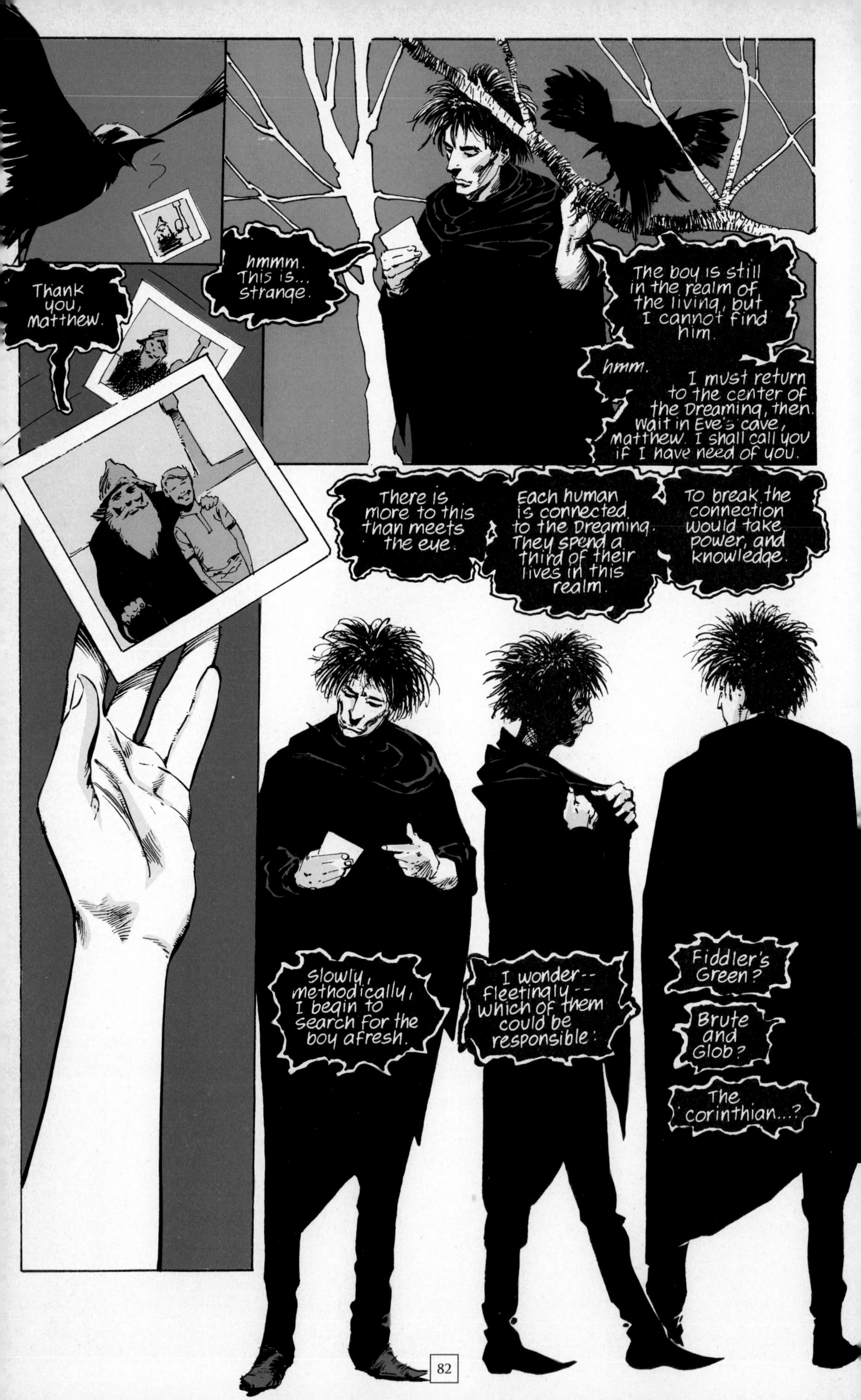
Thank you, Matthew.
hmmm. This is... strange.
The boy is still in the realm of the living, but I cannot find him.
hmm. I must return to the center of the Dreaming, then. Wait in Eve's cave, Matthew. I shall call you if I have need of you.
There is more to this than meets the eye.
Each human is connected to the Dreaming. They spend a third of their lives in this realm.
To break the connection would take power, and knowledge.
Slowly, methodically, I begin to search for the boy afresh.
I wonder-- fleetingly-- which of them could be responsible:
Fiddler's Green?
Brute and Glob?
The Corinthian...?

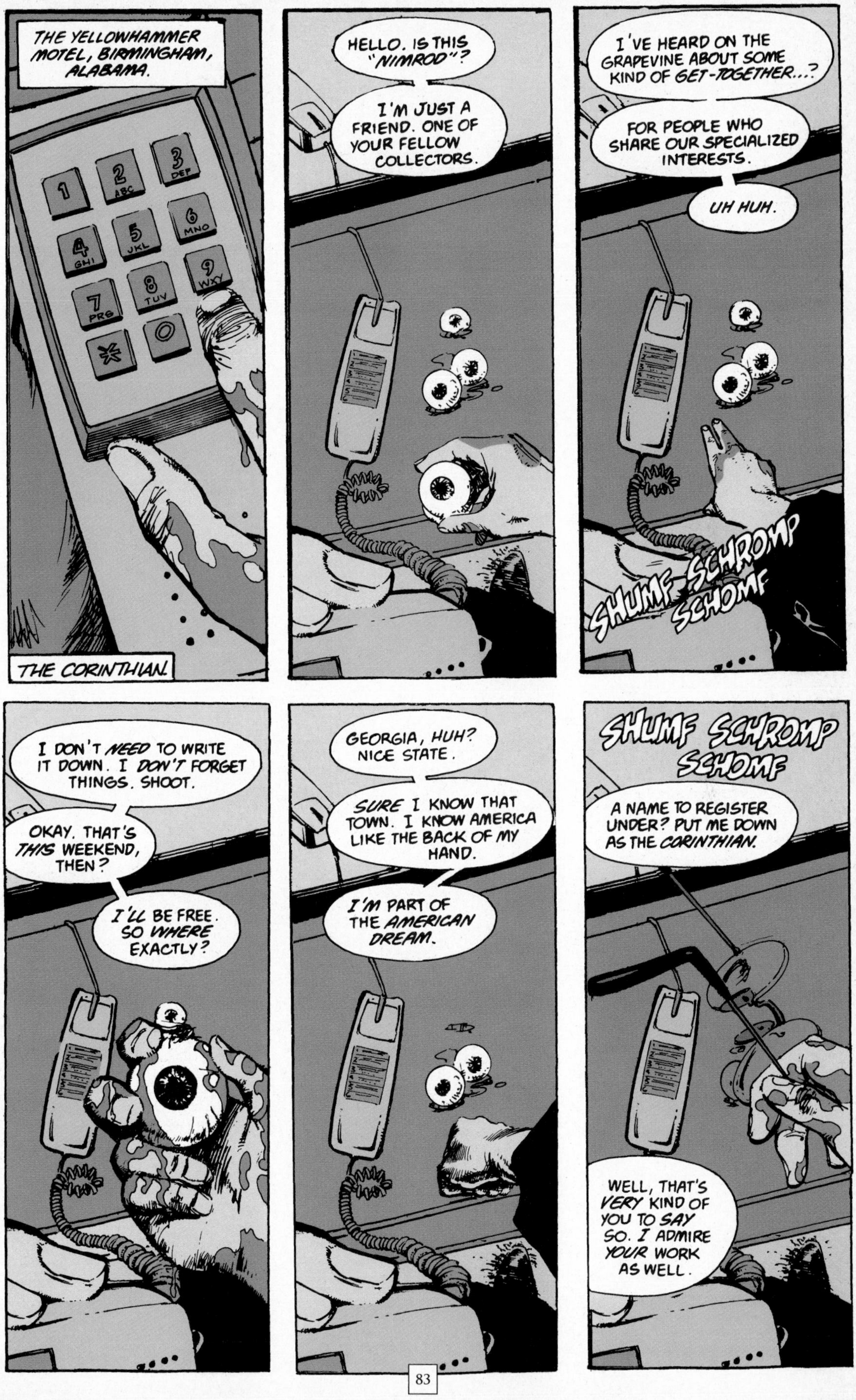
THE YELLOWHAMMER MOTEL, BIRMINGHAM, ALABAMA.
THE CORINTHIAN.
HELLO. IS THIS "NIMROD"?
I'M JUST A FRIEND. ONE OF YOUR FELLOW COLLECTORS.
I'VE HEARD ON THE GRAPEVINE ABOUT SOME KIND OF GET-TOGETHER...?
FOR PEOPLE WHO SHARE OUR SPECIALIZED INTERESTS.
UH HUH.
SHUMF SCHROMP SCHOMF
I DON'T NEED TO WRITE IT DOWN. I DON'T FORGET THINGS. SHOOT.
OKAY. THAT'S THIS WEEKEND, THEN?
I'LL BE FREE. SO WHERE EXACTLY?
GEORGIA, HUH? NICE STATE.
SURE I KNOW THAT TOWN. I KNOW AMERICA LIKE THE BACK OF MY HAND.
I'M PART OF THE AMERICAN DREAM.
SHUMF SCHROMP SCHOMF
A NAME TO REGISTER UNDER? PUT ME DOWN AS THE CORINTHIAN.
WELL, THAT'S VERY KIND OF YOU TO SAY SO. I ADMIRE YOUR WORK AS WELL.

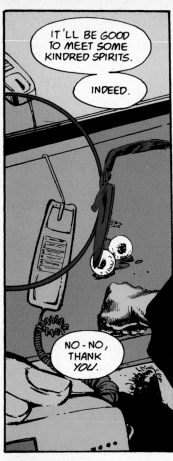

IT'LL BE GOOD TO MEET SOME KINDRED SPIRITS.

INDEED.

NO-NO, THANK YOU.

G'BYE, BOYS.

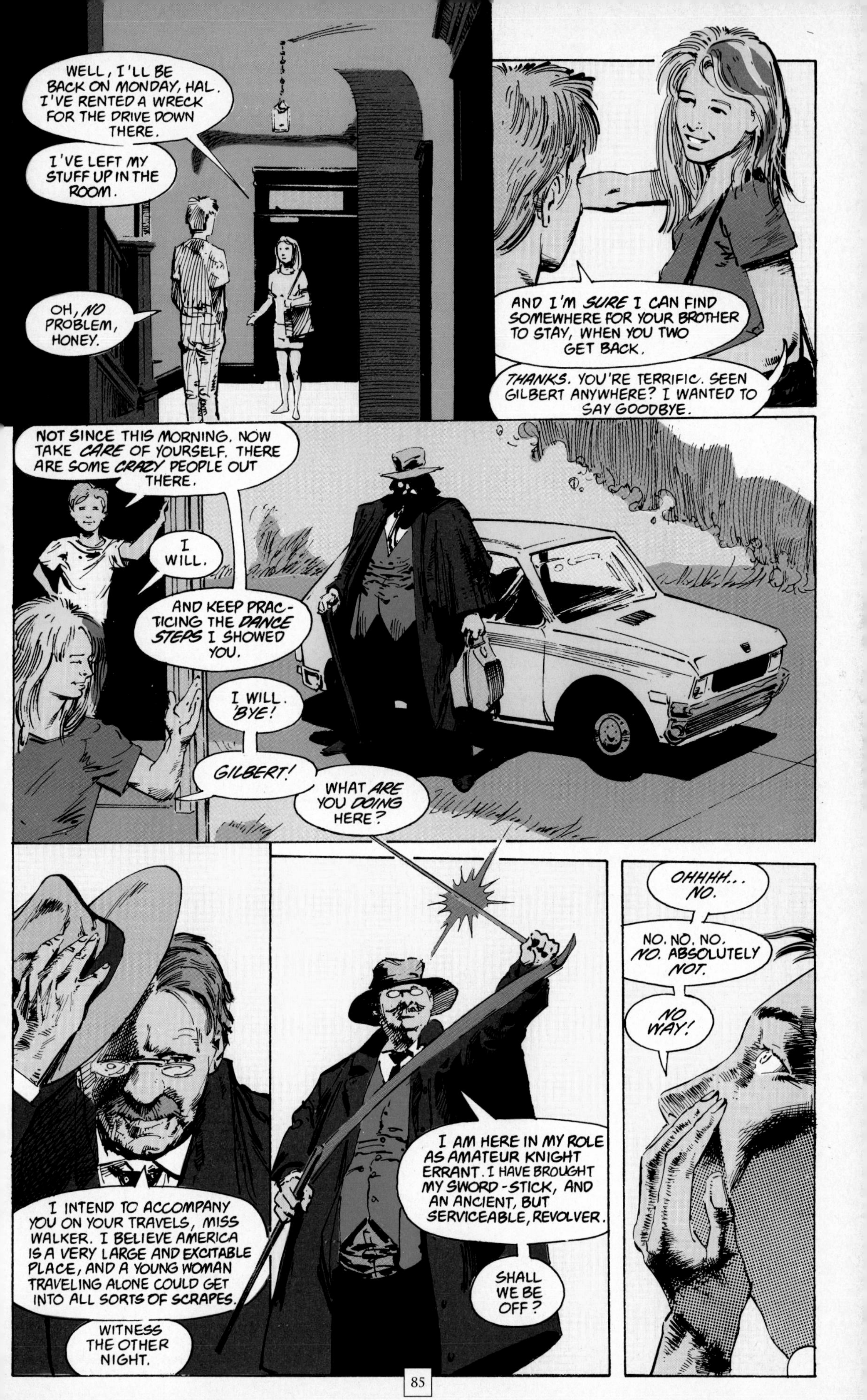
WELL, I'LL BE BACK ON MONDAY, HAL. I'VE RENTED A WRECK FOR THE DRIVE DOWN THERE.
I'VE LEFT MY STUFF UP IN THE ROOM.
OH, NO PROBLEM, HONEY.
AND I'M SURE I CAN FIND SOMEWHERE FOR YOUR BROTHER TO STAY, WHEN YOU TWO GET BACK.
THANKS. YOU'RE TERRIFIC. SEEN GILBERT ANYWHERE? I WANTED TO SAY GOODBYE.
NOT SINCE THIS MORNING. NOW TAKE CARE OF YOURSELF. THERE ARE SOME CRAZY PEOPLE OUT THERE.
I WILL.
AND KEEP PRACTICING THE DANCE STEPS I SHOWED YOU.
I WILL. 'BYE!
GILBERT!
WHAT ARE YOU DOING HERE?
I INTEND TO ACCOMPANY YOU ON YOUR TRAVELS, MISS WALKER. I BELIEVE AMERICA IS A VERY LARGE AND EXCITABLE PLACE, AND A YOUNG WOMAN TRAVELING ALONE COULD GET INTO ALL SORTS OF SCRAPES.
WITNESS THE OTHER NIGHT.
I AM HERE IN MY ROLE AS AMATEUR KNIGHT ERRANT. I HAVE BROUGHT MY SWORD-STICK, AND AN ANCIENT, BUT SERVICEABLE, REVOLVER.
SHALL WE BE OFF?
OHHHH... NO.
NO. NO. NO. NO. ABSOLUTELY NOT.
NO WAY!

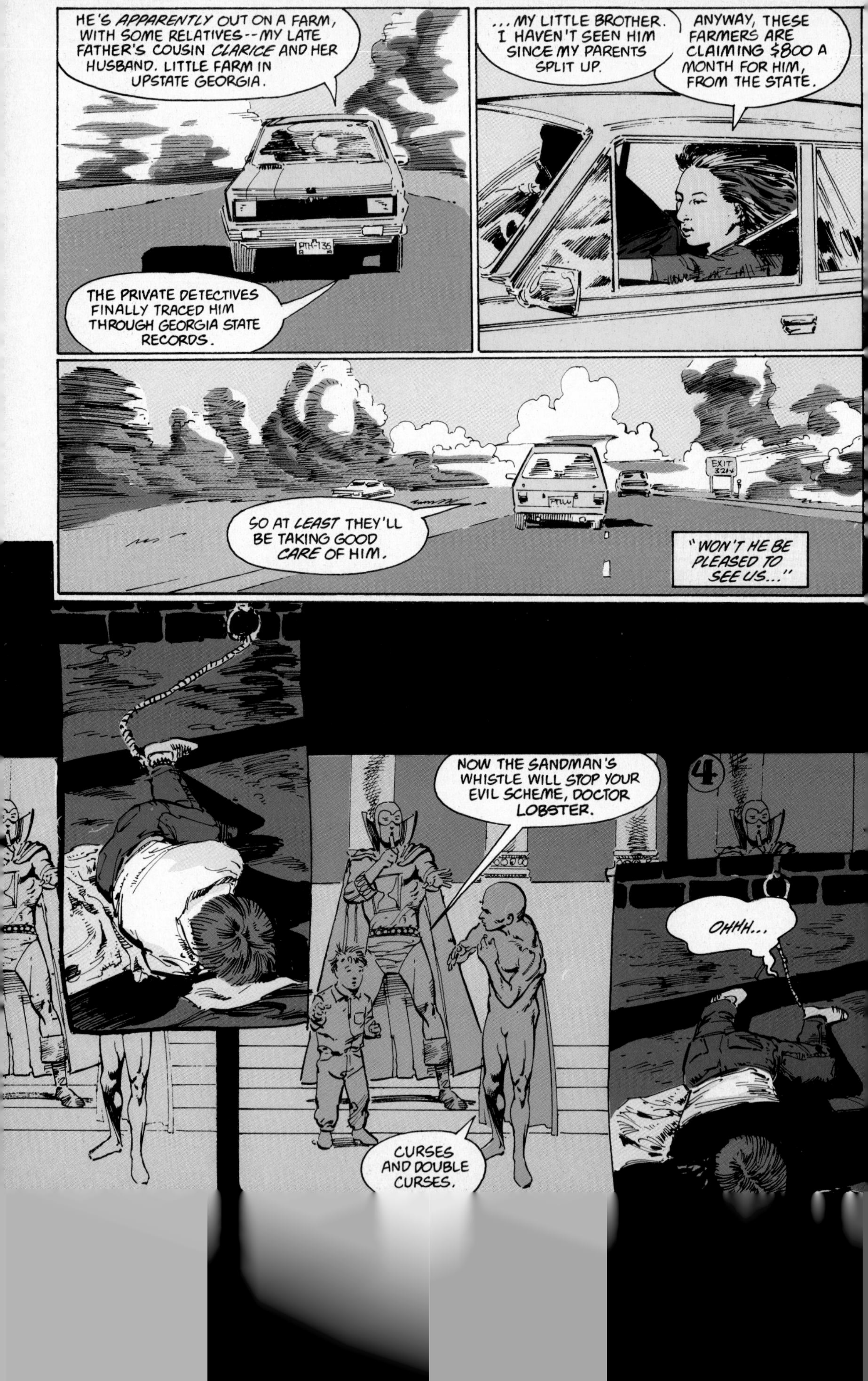
HE'S APPARENTLY OUT ON A FARM, WITH SOME RELATIVES--MY LATE FATHER'S COUSIN CLARICE AND HER HUSBAND. LITTLE FARM IN UPSTATE GEORGIA.
THE PRIVATE DETECTIVES FINALLY TRACED HIM THROUGH GEORGIA STATE RECORDS.
...MY LITTLE BROTHER. I HAVEN'T SEEN HIM SINCE MY PARENTS SPLIT UP.
ANYWAY, THESE FARMERS ARE CLAIMING $800 A MONTH FOR HIM, FROM THE STATE.
SO AT LEAST THEY'LL BE TAKING GOOD CARE OF HIM.
"WON'T HE BE PLEASED TO SEE US..."
NOW THE SANDMAN'S WHISTLE WILL STOP YOUR EVIL SCHEME, DOCTOR LOBSTER.
CURSES AND DOUBLE CURSES.
OHHH...

Found him.

HOW DARE THEY?

HOW DARE THEY?

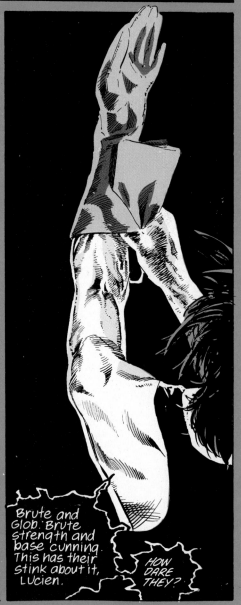

Brute and Glob. Brute strength and base cunning. This has their stink about it, LUCIEN.

HOW DARE THEY?

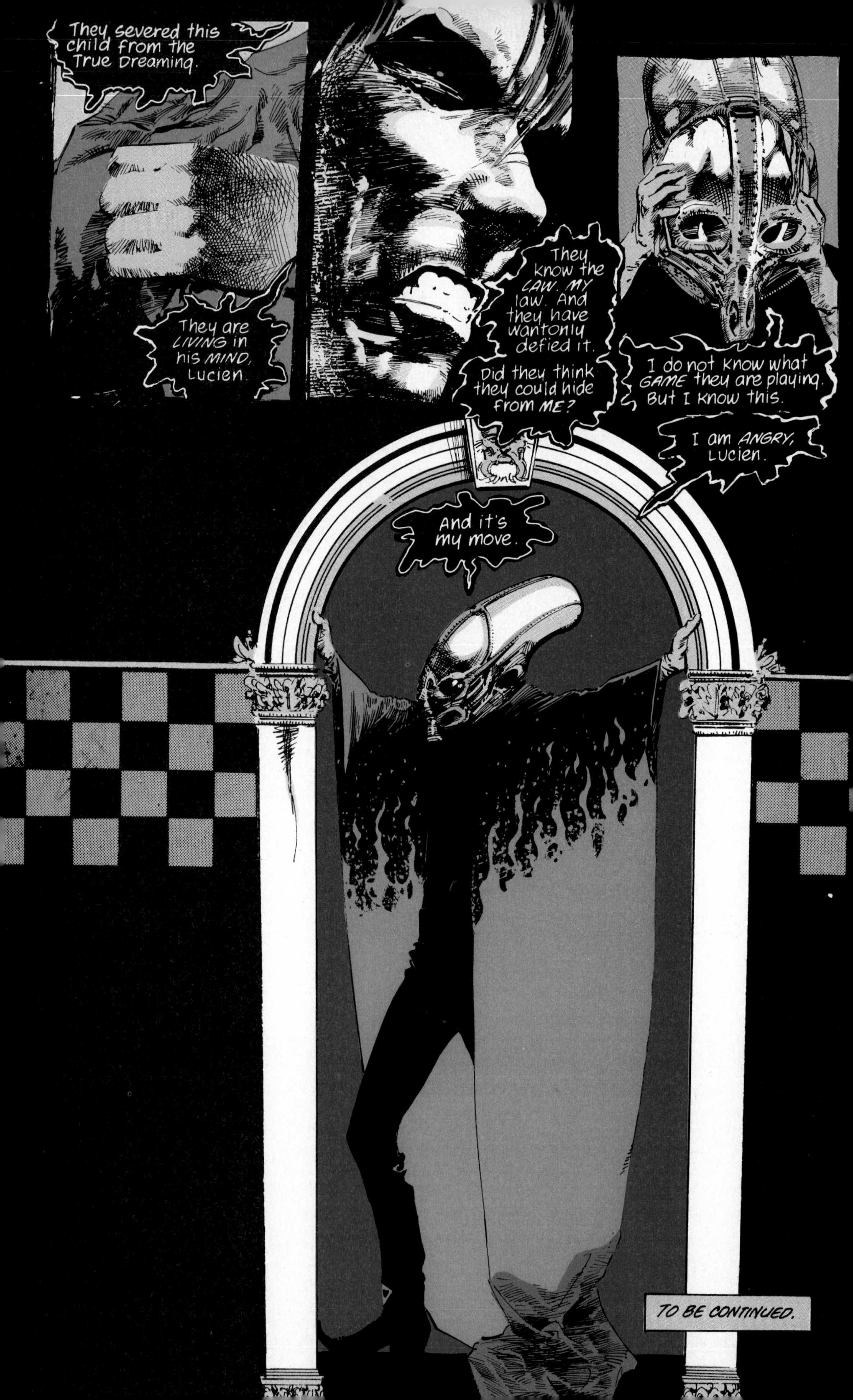
They severed this child from the True Dreaming.
They are LIVING in his MIND, Lucien.
They know the LAW. MY law. And they have wantonly defied it.
Did they think they could hide from ME?
I do not know what GAME they are playing. But I know this.
I am ANGRY, Lucien.
And it's my move.
TO BE CONTINUED.

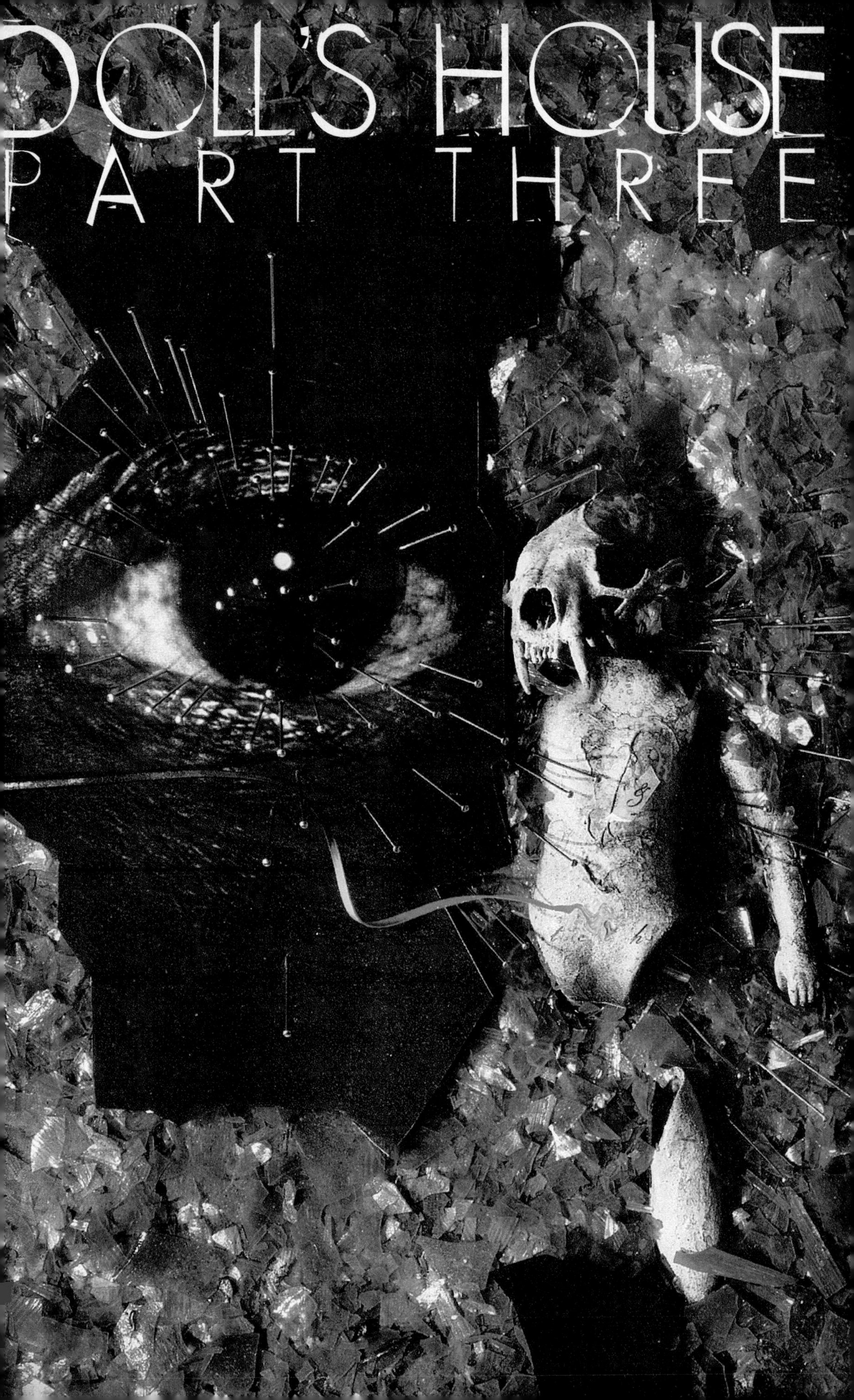
DOLL'S HOUSE
PART THREE

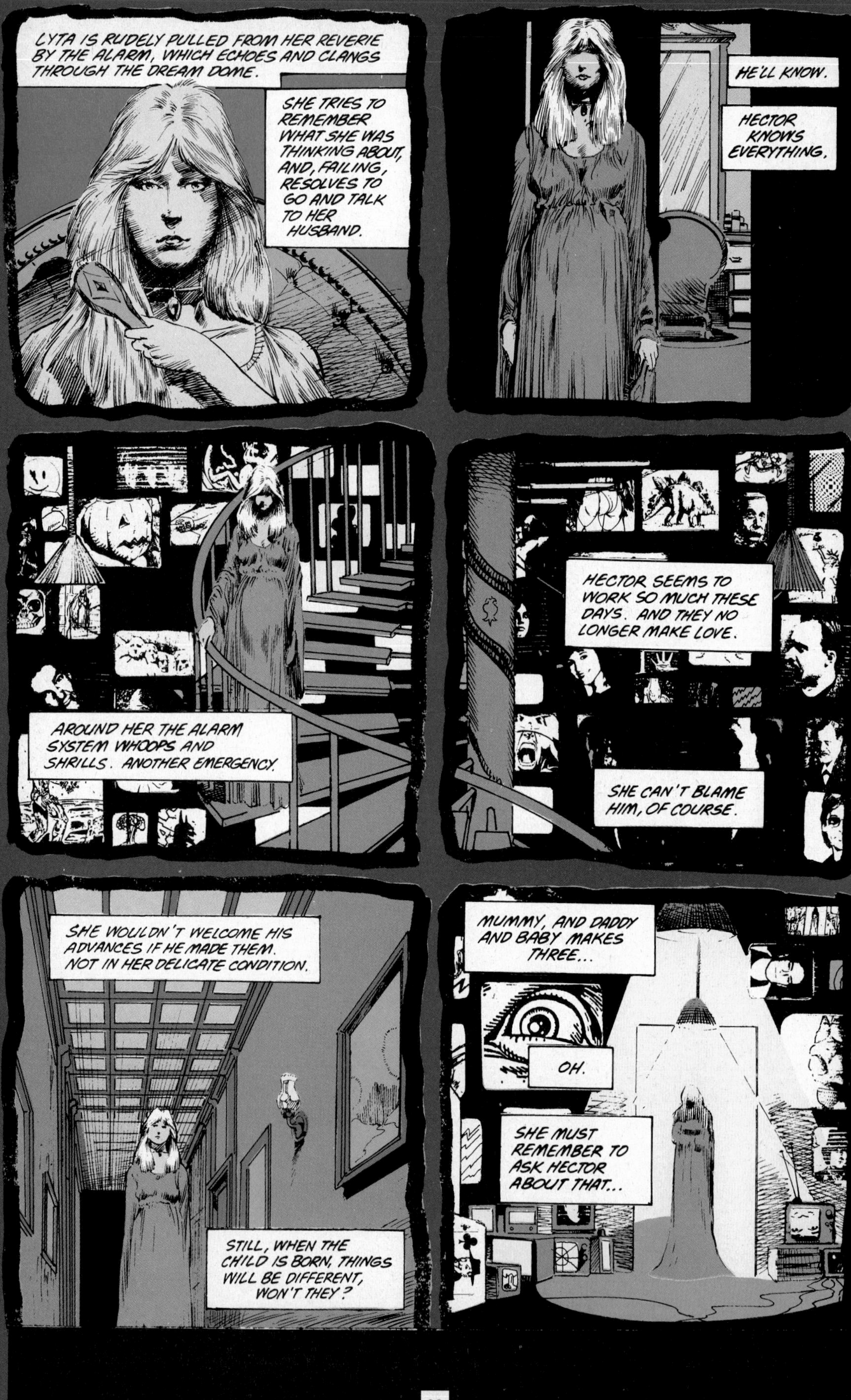
LYTA IS RUDELY PULLED FROM HER REVERIE BY THE ALARM, WHICH ECHOES AND CLANGS THROUGH THE DREAM DOME.
SHE TRIES TO REMEMBER WHAT SHE WAS THINKING ABOUT, AND, FAILING, RESOLVES TO GO AND TALK TO HER HUSBAND.
HE'LL KNOW.
HECTOR KNOWS EVERYTHING.
AROUND HER THE ALARM SYSTEM WHOOPS AND SHRILLS. ANOTHER EMERGENCY.
HECTOR SEEMS TO WORK SO MUCH THESE DAYS. AND THEY NO LONGER MAKE LOVE.
SHE CAN'T BLAME HIM, OF COURSE.
SHE WOULDN'T WELCOME HIS ADVANCES IF HE MADE THEM. NOT IN HER DELICATE CONDITION.
STILL, WHEN THE CHILD IS BORN, THINGS WILL BE DIFFERENT, WON'T THEY?
MUMMY, AND DADDY AND BABY MAKES THREE...
OH.
SHE MUST REMEMBER TO ASK HECTOR ABOUT THAT...

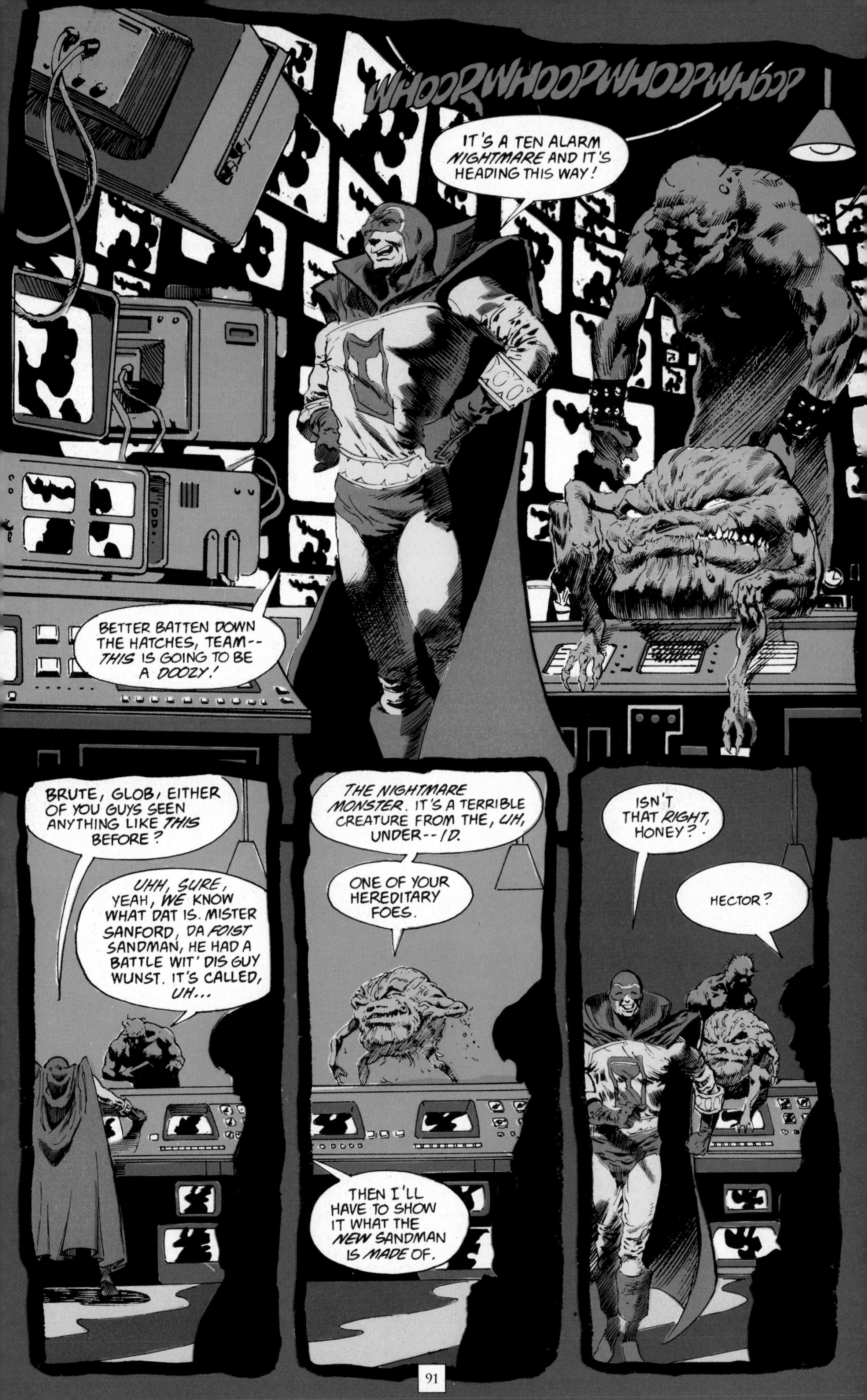
WHOOPWHOOPWHOOPWHOOP
IT'S A TEN ALARM NIGHTMARE AND IT'S HEADING THIS WAY!
BETTER BATTEN DOWN THE HATCHES, TEAM-- THIS IS GOING TO BE A DOOZY!
BRUTE, GLOB, EITHER OF YOU GUYS SEEN ANYTHING LIKE THIS BEFORE?
UHH, SURE, YEAH, WE KNOW WHAT DAT IS. MISTER SANFORD, DA FOIST SANDMAN, HE HAD A BATTLE WIT' DIS GUY WUNST. IT'S CALLED, UH...
THE NIGHTMARE MONSTER. IT'S A TERRIBLE CREATURE FROM THE, UH, UNDER--ID.
ONE OF YOUR HEREDITARY FOES.
THEN I'LL HAVE TO SHOW IT WHAT THE NEW SANDMAN IS MADE OF.
ISN'T THAT RIGHT, HONEY?
HECTOR?

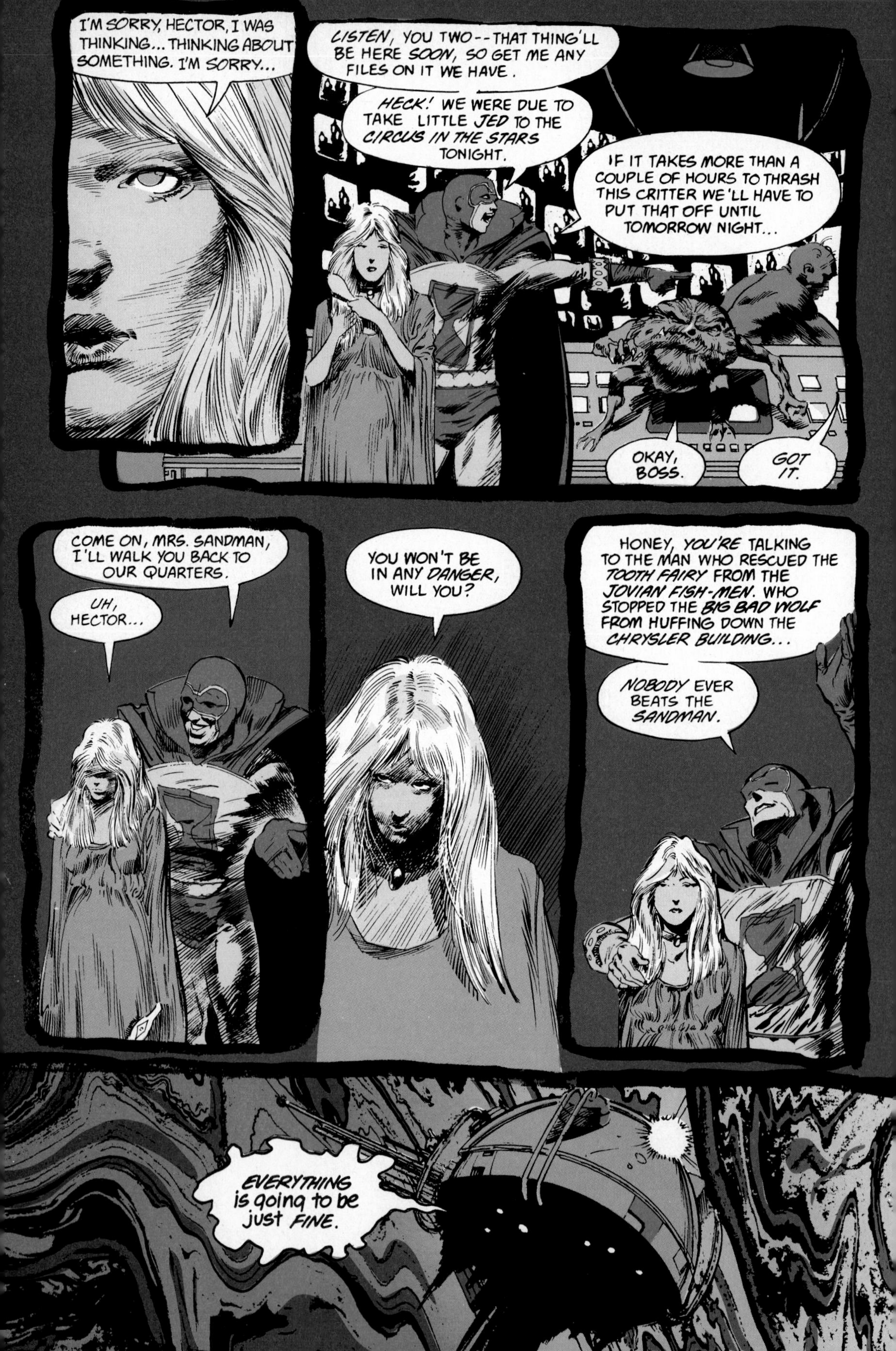
I'M SORRY, HECTOR, I WAS THINKING... THINKING ABOUT SOMETHING. I'M SORRY...
LISTEN, YOU TWO--THAT THING'LL BE HERE SOON, SO GET ME ANY FILES ON IT WE HAVE.
HECK! WE WERE DUE TO TAKE LITTLE JED TO THE CIRCUS IN THE STARS TONIGHT.
IF IT TAKES MORE THAN A COUPLE OF HOURS TO THRASH THIS CRITTER WE'LL HAVE TO PUT THAT OFF UNTIL TOMORROW NIGHT...
OKAY, BOSS.
GOT IT.
COME ON, MRS. SANDMAN, I'LL WALK YOU BACK TO OUR QUARTERS.
UH, HECTOR...
YOU WON'T BE IN ANY DANGER, WILL YOU?
HONEY, YOU'RE TALKING TO THE MAN WHO RESCUED THE TOOTH FAIRY FROM THE JOVIAN FISH-MEN. WHO STOPPED THE BIG BAD WOLF FROM HUFFING DOWN THE CHRYSLER BUILDING...
NOBODY EVER BEATS THE SANDMAN.
EVERYTHING is going to be just FINE.

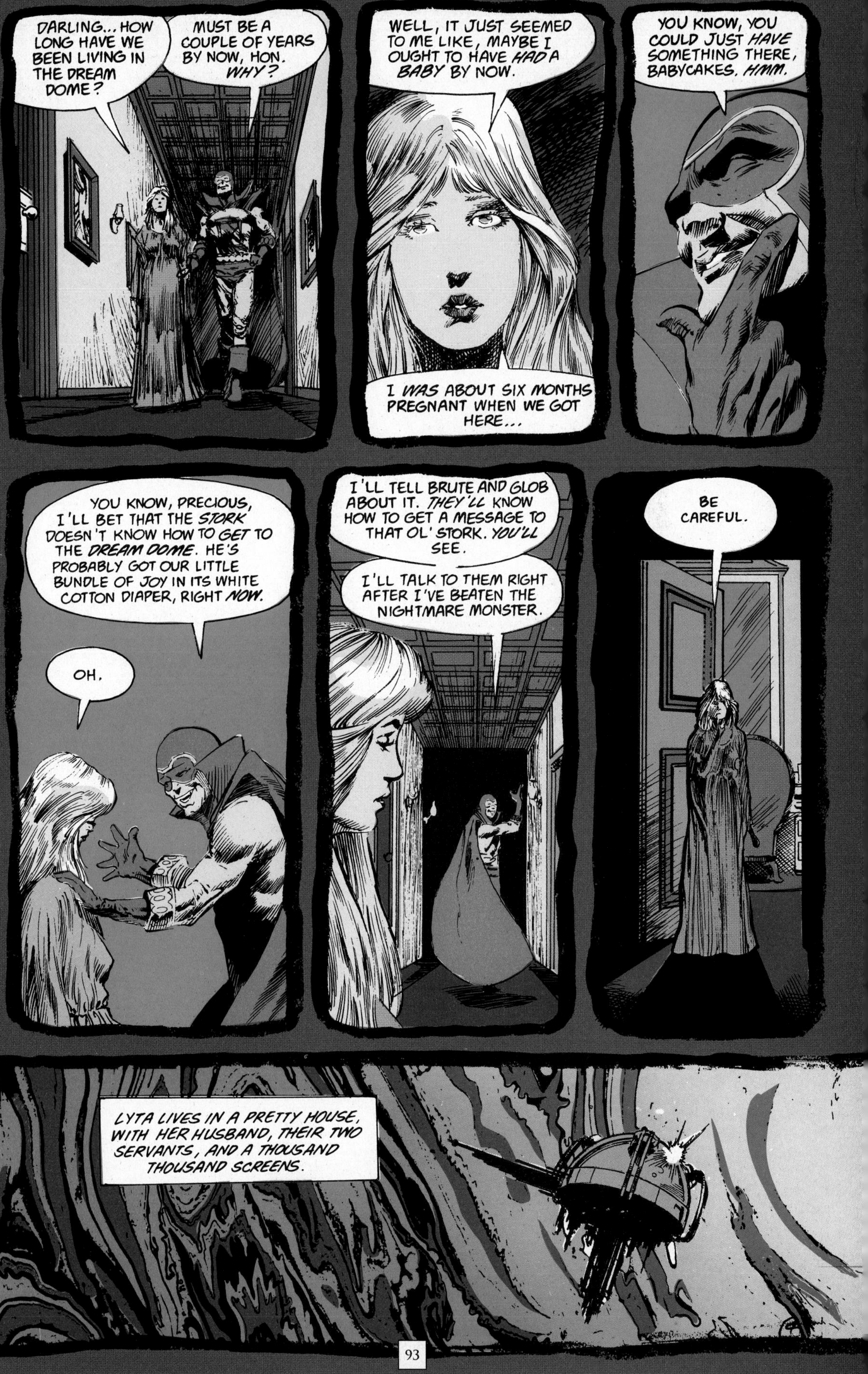
DARLING... HOW LONG HAVE WE BEEN LIVING IN THE DREAM DOME?
MUST BE A COUPLE OF YEARS BY NOW, HON. WHY?
WELL, IT JUST SEEMED TO ME LIKE, MAYBE I OUGHT TO HAVE HAD A BABY BY NOW.
I WAS ABOUT SIX MONTHS PREGNANT WHEN WE GOT HERE...
YOU KNOW, YOU COULD JUST HAVE SOMETHING THERE, BABYCAKES. HMM.
YOU KNOW, PRECIOUS, I'LL BET THAT THE STORK DOESN'T KNOW HOW TO GET TO THE DREAM DOME. HE'S PROBABLY GOT OUR LITTLE BUNDLE OF JOY IN ITS WHITE COTTON DIAPER, RIGHT NOW.
OH.
I'LL TELL BRUTE AND GLOB ABOUT IT. THEY'LL KNOW HOW TO GET A MESSAGE TO THAT OL' STORK. YOU'LL SEE.
I'LL TALK TO THEM RIGHT AFTER I'VE BEATEN THE NIGHTMARE MONSTER.
BE CAREFUL.
LYTA LIVES IN A PRETTY HOUSE, WITH HER HUSBAND, THEIR TWO SERVANTS, AND A THOUSAND THOUSAND SCREENS.

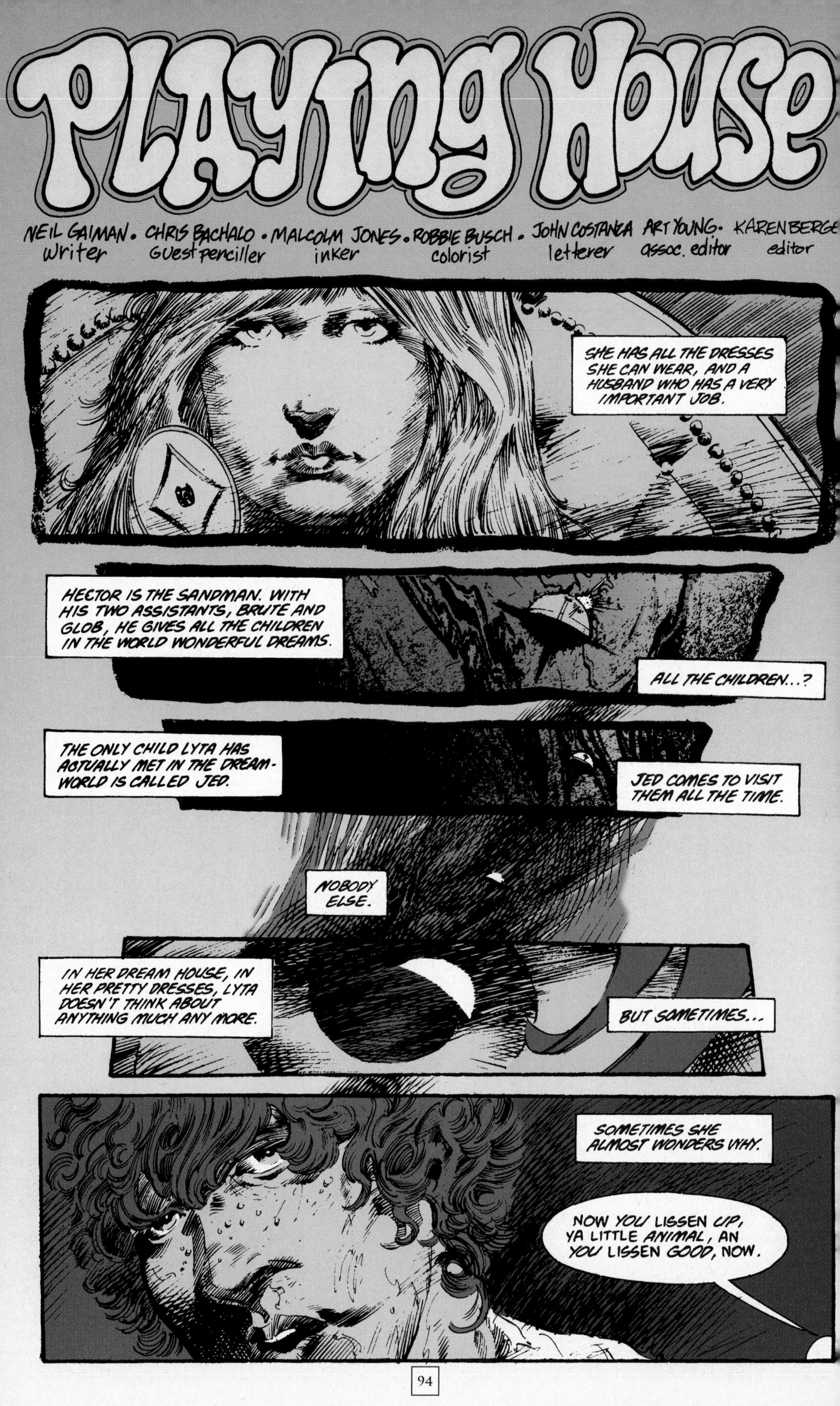
PLAYING HOUSE
NEIL GAIMAN • CHRIS BACHALO • MALCOLM JONES • ROBBIE BUSCH • JOHN COSTANZA ART YOUNG • KAREN BERGER
writer Guest penciller inker colorist letterer assoc. editor editor
SHE HAS ALL THE DRESSES SHE CAN WEAR, AND A HUSBAND WHO HAS A VERY IMPORTANT JOB.
HECTOR IS THE SANDMAN. WITH HIS TWO ASSISTANTS, BRUTE AND GLOB, HE GIVES ALL THE CHILDREN IN THE WORLD WONDERFUL DREAMS.
ALL THE CHILDREN...?
THE ONLY CHILD LYTA HAS ACTUALLY MET IN THE DREAM-WORLD IS CALLED JED.
JED COMES TO VISIT THEM ALL THE TIME.
NOBODY ELSE.
IN HER DREAM HOUSE, IN HER PRETTY DRESSES, LYTA DOESN'T THINK ABOUT ANYTHING MUCH ANY MORE.
BUT SOMETIMES...
SOMETIMES SHE ALMOST WONDERS WHY.
NOW YOU LISSEN UP, YA LITTLE ANIMAL, AN YOU LISSEN GOOD, NOW.

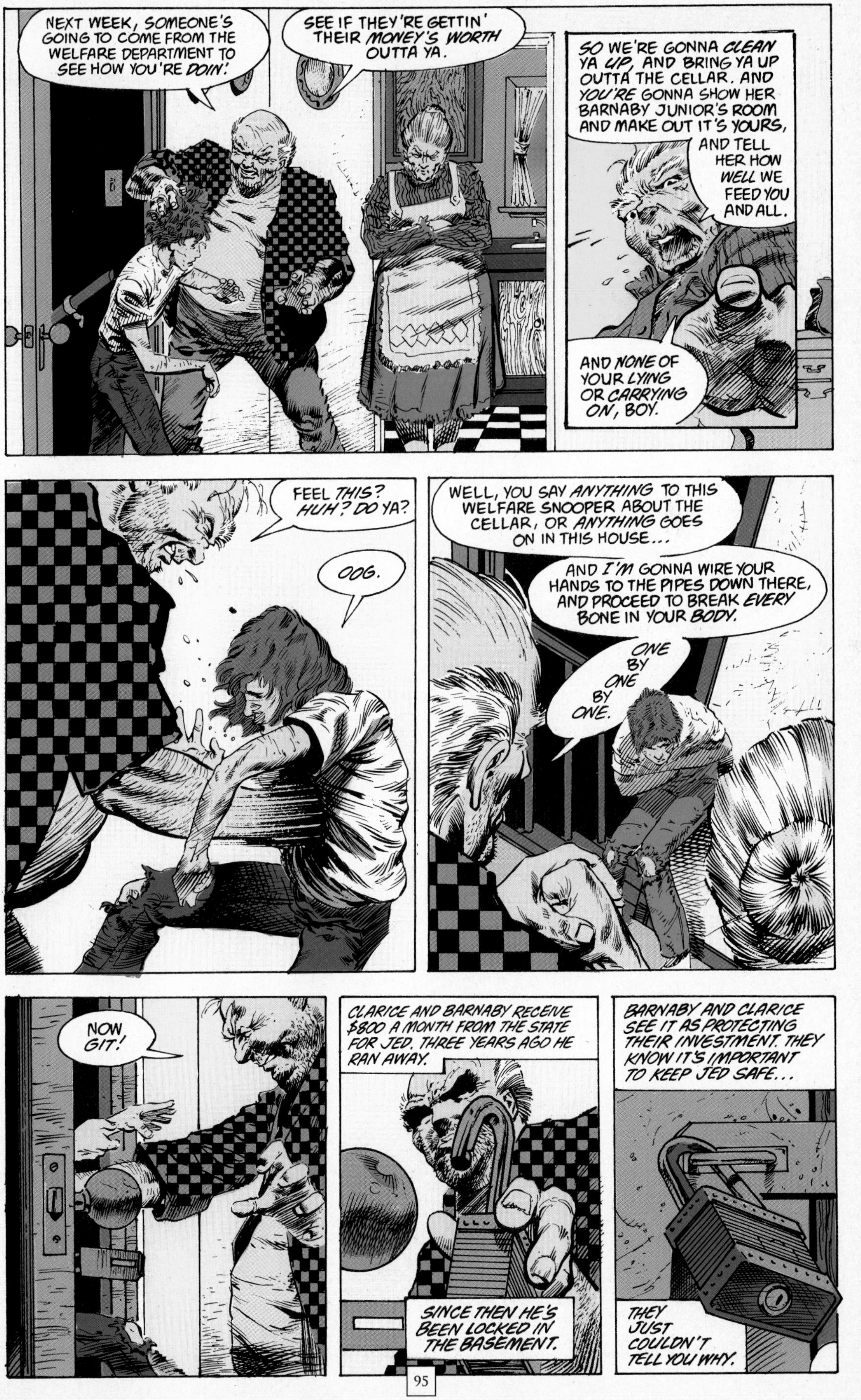
NEXT WEEK, SOMEONE'S GOING TO COME FROM THE WELFARE DEPARTMENT TO SEE HOW YOU'RE DOIN'.
SEE IF THEY'RE GETTIN' THEIR MONEY'S WORTH OUTTA YA.
SO WE'RE GONNA CLEAN YA UP, AND BRING YA UP OUTTA THE CELLAR. AND YOU'RE GONNA SHOW HER BARNABY JUNIOR'S ROOM AND MAKE OUT IT'S YOURS,
AND TELL HER HOW WELL WE FEED YOU AND ALL.
AND NONE OF YOUR LYING OR CARRYING ON, BOY.
FEEL THIS? HUH? DO YA?
OOG.
WELL, YOU SAY ANYTHING TO THIS WELFARE SNOOPER ABOUT THE CELLAR, OR ANYTHING GOES ON IN THIS HOUSE...
AND I'M GONNA WIRE YOUR HANDS TO THE PIPES DOWN THERE, AND PROCEED TO BREAK EVERY BONE IN YOUR BODY.
ONE BY ONE BY ONE.
NOW GIT!
CLARICE AND BARNABY RECEIVE $800 A MONTH FROM THE STATE FOR JED. THREE YEARS AGO HE RAN AWAY.
SINCE THEN HE'S BEEN LOCKED IN THE BASEMENT.
BARNABY AND CLARICE SEE IT AS PROTECTING THEIR INVESTMENT. THEY KNOW IT'S IMPORTANT TO KEEP JED SAFE...
THEY JUST COULDN'T TELL YOU WHY.

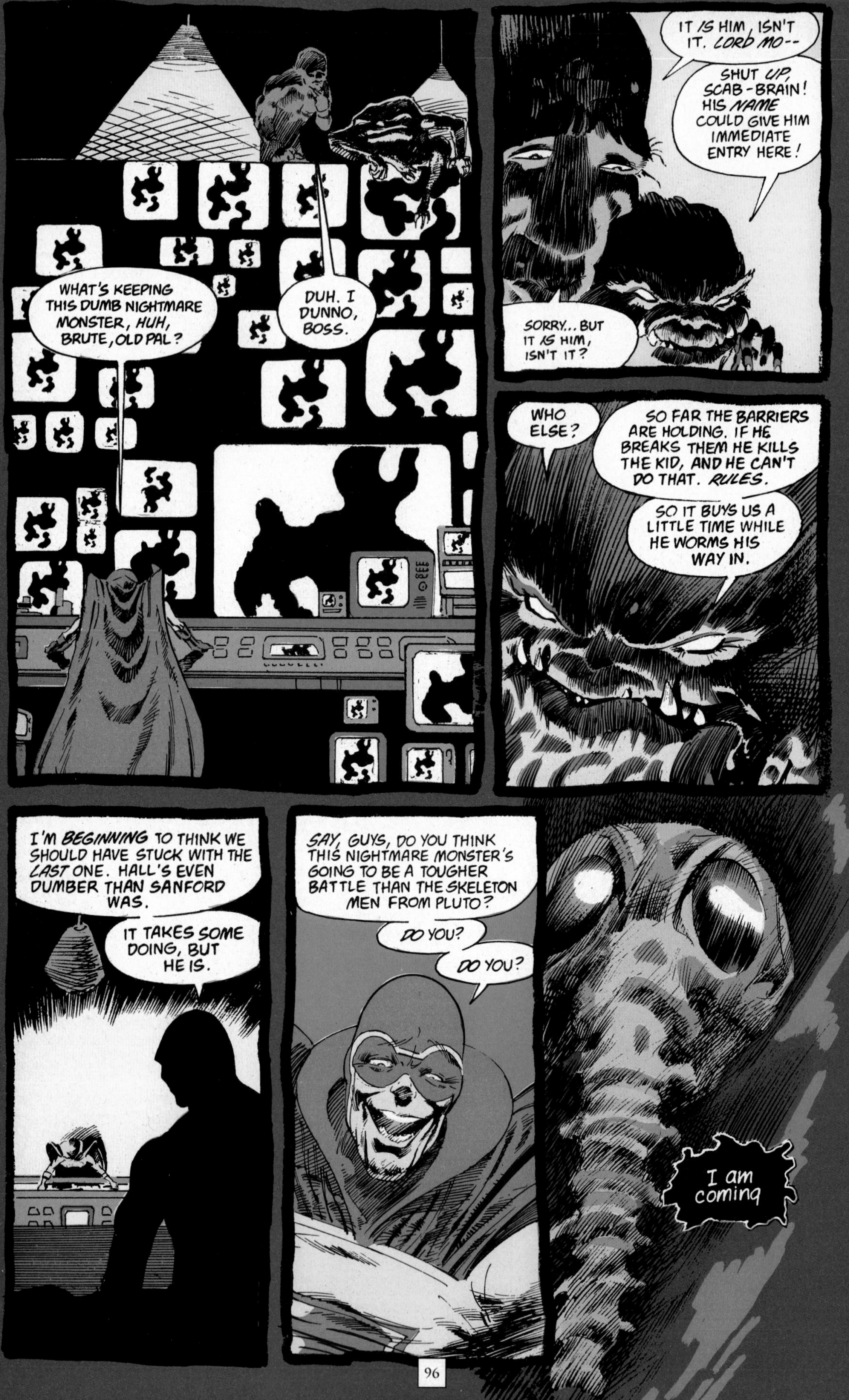

WHAT'S KEEPING THIS DUMB NIGHTMARE MONSTER, HUH, BRUTE, OLD PAL?
DUH. I DUNNO, BOSS.
IT IS HIM, ISN'T IT. LORD MO--
SHUT UP, SCAB-BRAIN! HIS NAME COULD GIVE HIM IMMEDIATE ENTRY HERE!
SORRY... BUT IT IS HIM, ISN'T IT?
WHO ELSE?
SO FAR THE BARRIERS ARE HOLDING. IF HE BREAKS THEM HE KILLS THE KID, AND HE CAN'T DO THAT. RULES.
SO IT BUYS US A LITTLE TIME WHILE HE WORMS HIS WAY IN.
I'M BEGINNING TO THINK WE SHOULD HAVE STUCK WITH THE LAST ONE. HALL'S EVEN DUMBER THAN SANFORD WAS.
IT TAKES SOME DOING, BUT HE IS.
SAY, GUYS, DO YOU THINK THIS NIGHTMARE MONSTER'S GOING TO BE A TOUGHER BATTLE THAN THE SKELETON MEN FROM PLUTO?
DO YOU?
DO YOU?
I am coming

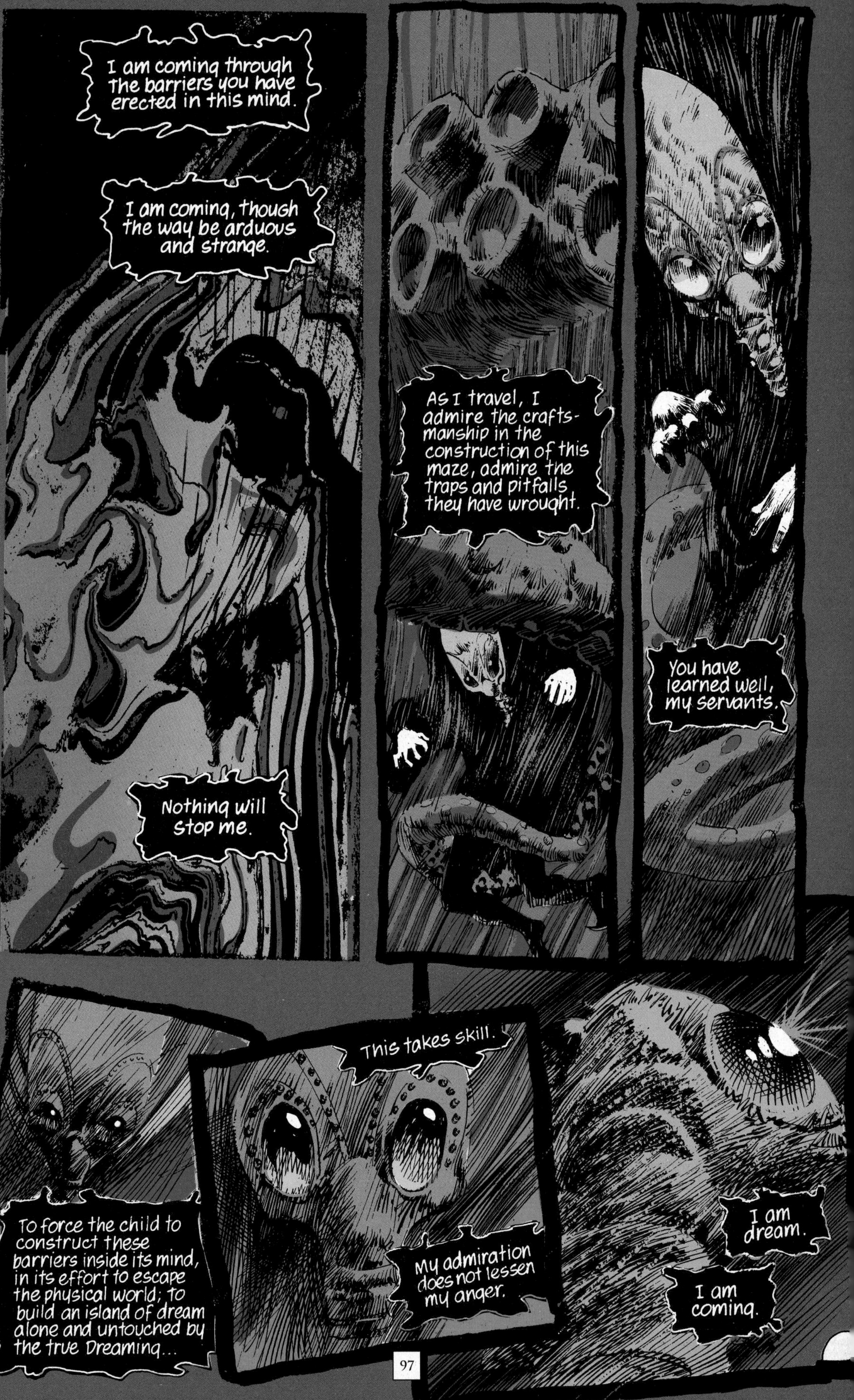
I am coming through the barriers you have erected in this mind.
I am coming, though the way be arduous and strange.
Nothing will stop me.
As I travel, I admire the crafts-manship in the construction of this maze, admire the traps and pitfalls they have wrought.
You have learned well, my servants.
To force the child to construct these barriers inside its mind, in its effort to escape the physical world; to build an island of dream alone and untouched by the true Dreaming...
This takes skill.
My admiration does not lessen my anger.
I am dream.
I am coming.

LIVING IN A DREAM HOUSE, WITH A DREAM HUSBAND AND...

LYTA LOSES HER TRAIN OF THOUGHT, AND COMMENCES ABSENTLY TO BRUSH HER HAIR.

IS THIS WHAT SHE WANTS?

IS THIS WHAT SHE WANTED?

SHE ALWAYS WANTED TO BE WITH HECTOR. EVEN WHEN THEY WERE CHILDREN, WHEN SHE WAS A STRONG RICH KID AND HE WAS A HERO BRAT...

BUT SHE MUST HAVE WANTED MORE THAN THAT.

MUSTN'T SHE?

BUT HECTOR'S DREAMS CAME FIRST. THEY ALWAYS DID. LYTA AND HECTOR DID SO MUCH TOGETHER...

THEY CAME OUT OF THE CLOSET ON THE COSTUME STUFF TOGETHER. WHEN THEY WERE AT UCLA.

WHY DID SHE DO THAT? BECOME A CHEAP COPY OF HER VANISHED MOTHER?

IT ALL SEEMS LIKE A DREAM NOW. SO HARD TO HOLD ON TO. NOTHING'S TANGIBLE ANYMORE.

THERE WERE THE NIGHTMARE TIMES WHEN SHE THOUGHT HECTOR WAS DEAD.

WELL, TO BE FAIR, HE WAS DEAD...

AND SHE WAS PREGNANT WITH HIS CHILD.

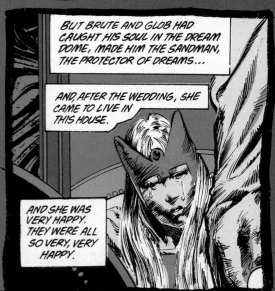

BUT BRUTE AND GLOB HAD CAUGHT HIS SOUL IN THE DREAM DOME, MADE HIM THE SANDMAN, THE PROTECTOR OF DREAMS...

AND, AFTER THE WEDDING, SHE CAME TO LIVE IN THIS HOUSE.

AND SHE WAS VERY HAPPY. THEY WERE ALL SO VERY, VERY HAPPY.

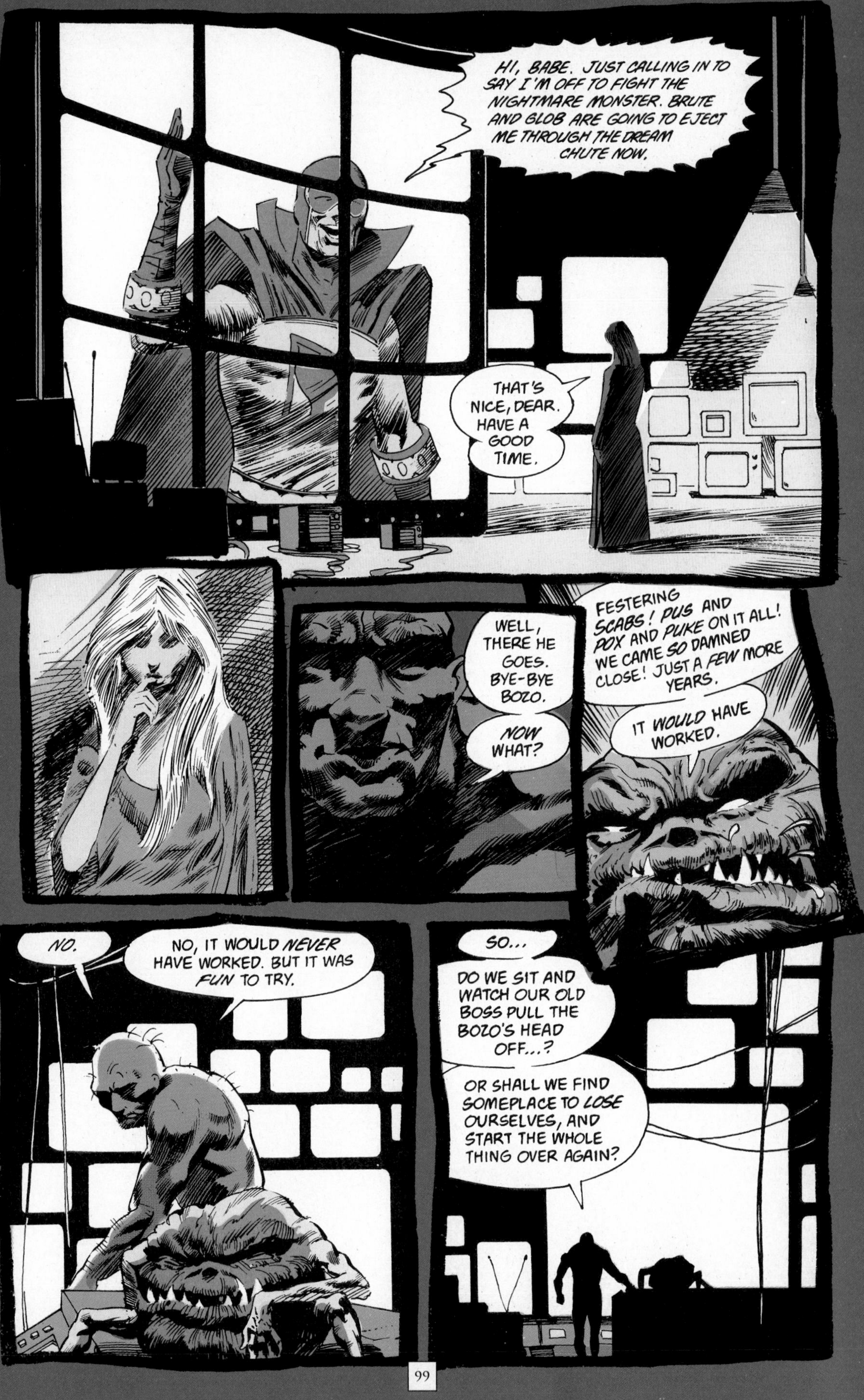
HI, BABE. JUST CALLING IN TO SAY I'M OFF TO FIGHT THE NIGHTMARE MONSTER. BRUTE AND GLOB ARE GOING TO EJECT ME THROUGH THE DREAM CHUTE NOW.
THAT'S NICE, DEAR. HAVE A GOOD TIME.
WELL, THERE HE GOES. BYE-BYE BOZO.
NOW WHAT?
FESTERING SCABS! PUS AND POX AND PUKE ON IT ALL! WE CAME SO DAMNED CLOSE! JUST A FEW MORE YEARS.
IT WOULD HAVE WORKED.
NO.
NO, IT WOULD NEVER HAVE WORKED. BUT IT WAS FUN TO TRY.
SO...
DO WE SIT AND WATCH OUR OLD BOSS PULL THE BOZO'S HEAD OFF...?
OR SHALL WE FIND SOMEPLACE TO LOSE OURSELVES, AND START THE WHOLE THING OVER AGAIN?

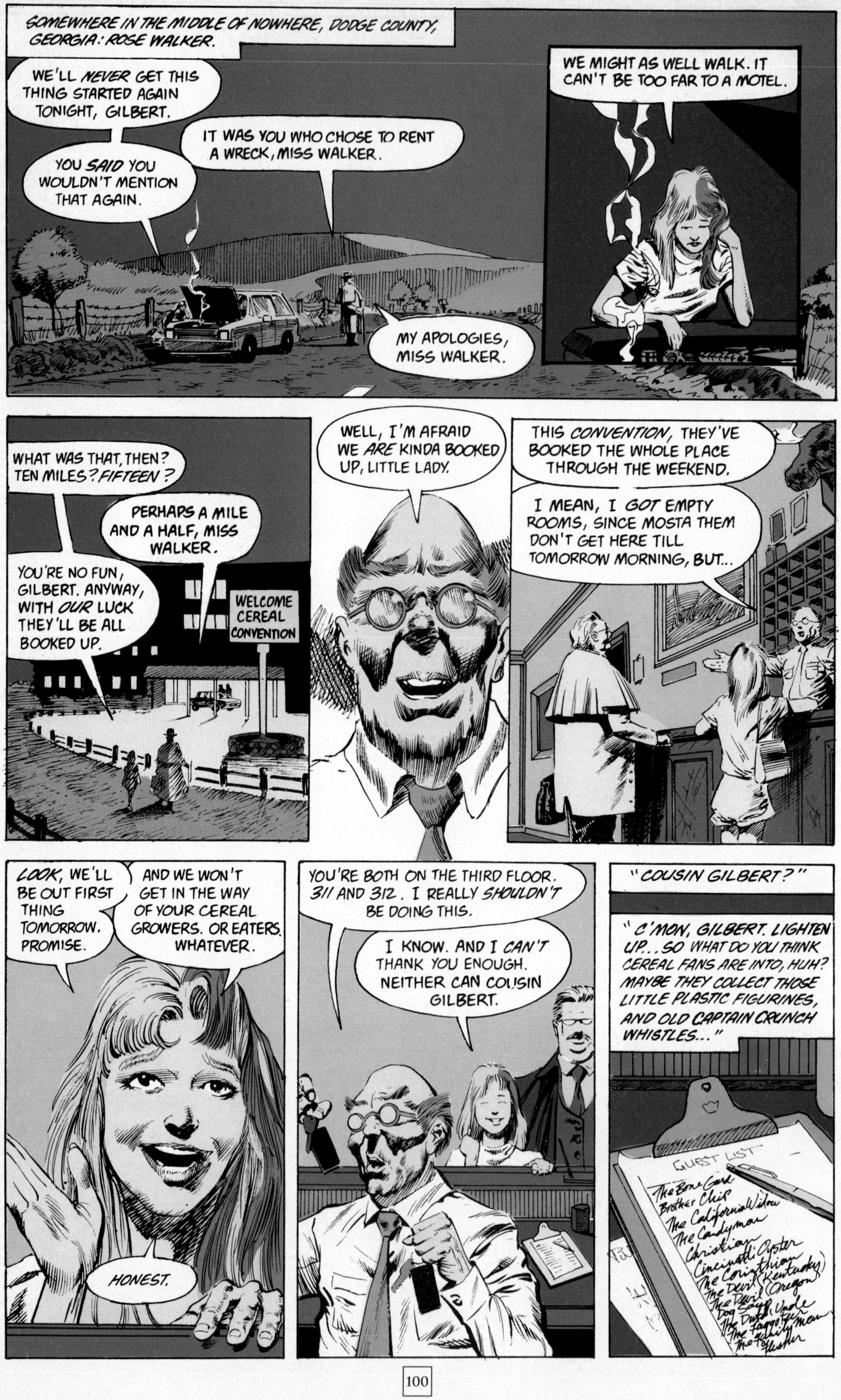
SOMEWHERE IN THE MIDDLE OF NOWHERE, DODGE COUNTY, GEORGIA: ROSE WALKER.
WE'LL NEVER GET THIS THING STARTED AGAIN TONIGHT, GILBERT.
IT WAS YOU WHO CHOSE TO RENT A WRECK, MISS WALKER.
YOU SAID YOU WOULDN'T MENTION THAT AGAIN.
MY APOLOGIES, MISS WALKER.
WE MIGHT AS WELL WALK. IT CAN'T BE TOO FAR TO A MOTEL.
WHAT WAS THAT, THEN? TEN MILES? FIFTEEN?
PERHAPS A MILE AND A HALF, MISS WALKER.
YOU'RE NO FUN, GILBERT. ANYWAY, WITH OUR LUCK THEY'LL BE ALL BOOKED UP.
WELCOME CEREAL CONVENTION
WELL, I'M AFRAID WE ARE KINDA BOOKED UP, LITTLE LADY.
THIS CONVENTION, THEY'VE BOOKED THE WHOLE PLACE THROUGH THE WEEKEND.
I MEAN, I GOT EMPTY ROOMS, SINCE MOSTA THEM DON'T GET HERE TILL TOMORROW MORNING, BUT...
LOOK, WE'LL BE OUT FIRST THING TOMORROW. PROMISE.
AND WE WON'T GET IN THE WAY OF YOUR CEREAL GROWERS. OR EATERS. WHATEVER.
HONEST.
YOU'RE BOTH ON THE THIRD FLOOR. 311 AND 312. I REALLY SHOULDN'T BE DOING THIS.
I KNOW. AND I CAN'T THANK YOU ENOUGH. NEITHER CAN COUSIN GILBERT.
"COUSIN GILBERT?"
"C'MON, GILBERT. LIGHTEN UP... SO WHAT DO YOU THINK CEREAL FANS ARE INTO, HUH? MAYBE THEY COLLECT THOSE LITTLE PLASTIC FIGURINES, AND OLD CAPTAIN CRUNCH WHISTLES..."
GUEST LIST
The Bone Gard
Brother Chip
The California Widow
The Candyman
Christian
Cincinatti Oyster
The Corinthian
The Devil (Kentucky)
The Devil (Oregon)

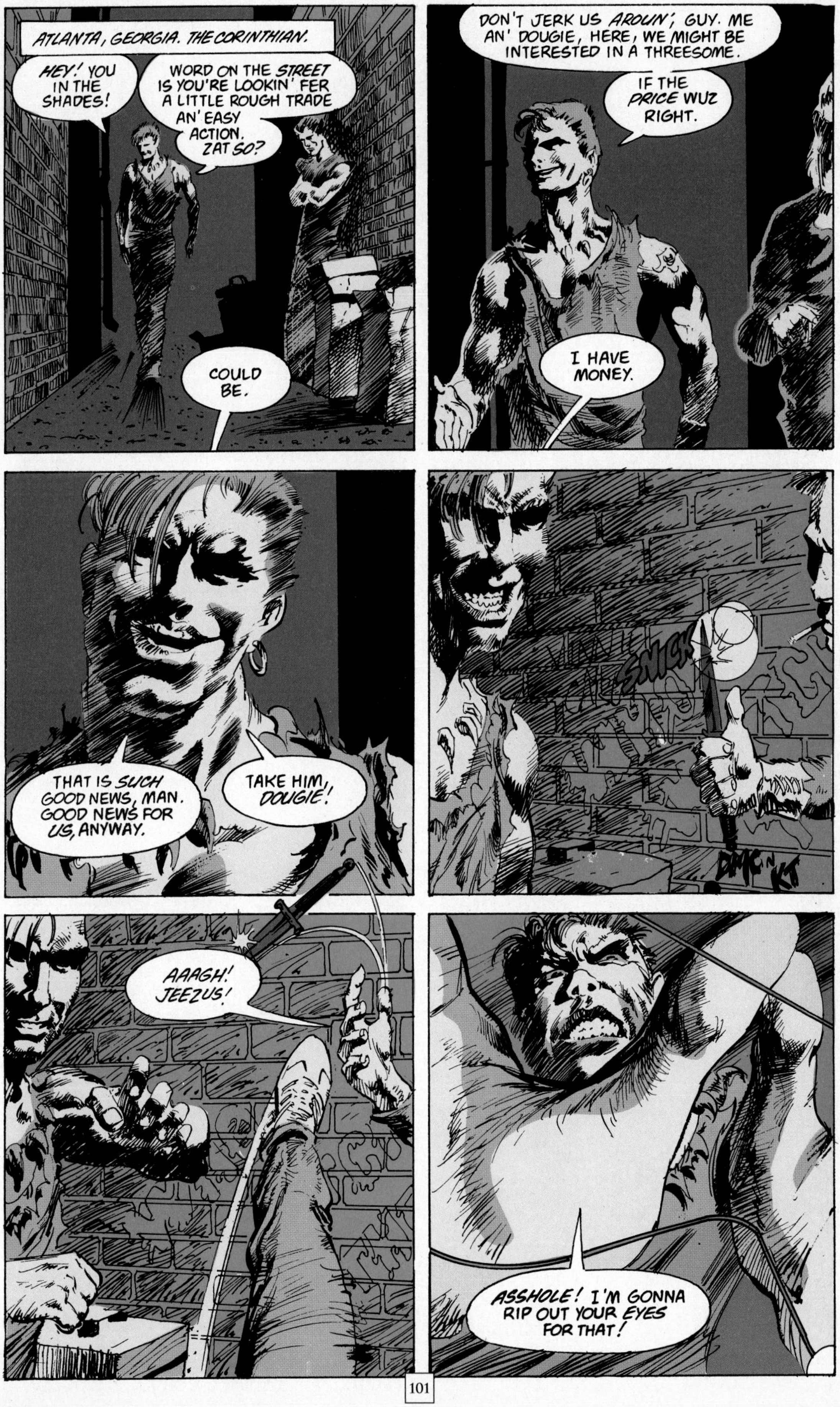

ATLANTA, GEORGIA. THE CORINTHIAN.
HEY! YOU IN THE SHADES!
WORD ON THE STREET IS YOU'RE LOOKIN' FER A LITTLE ROUGH TRADE AN' EASY ACTION. ZAT SO?
COULD BE.
DON'T JERK US AROUN', GUY. ME AN' DOUGIE, HERE, WE MIGHT BE INTERESTED IN A THREESOME.
IF THE PRICE WUZ RIGHT.
I HAVE MONEY.
THAT IS SUCH GOOD NEWS, MAN. GOOD NEWS FOR US, ANYWAY.
TAKE HIM, DOUGIE!
SNICK
AAAGH! JEEZUS!
ASSHOLE! I'M GONNA RIP OUT YOUR EYES FOR THAT!

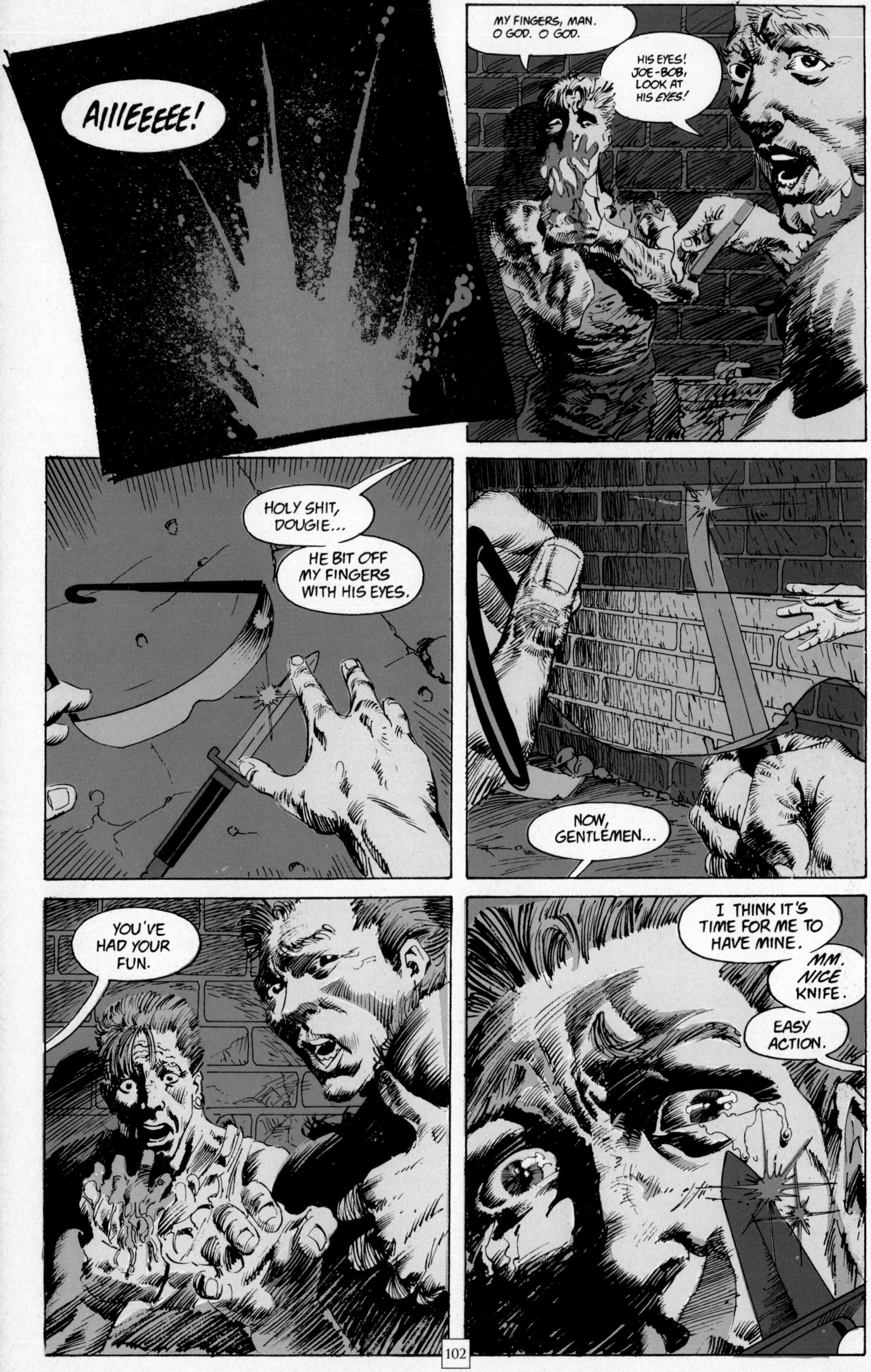

AIIIEEEEE!
MY FINGERS, MAN. O GOD. O GOD.
HIS EYES! JOE-BOB, LOOK AT HIS EYES!
HOLY SHIT, DOUGIE...
HE BIT OFF MY FINGERS WITH HIS EYES.
NOW, GENTLEMEN...
YOU'VE HAD YOUR FUN.
I THINK IT'S TIME FOR ME TO HAVE MINE.
MM. NICE KNIFE.
EASY ACTION.

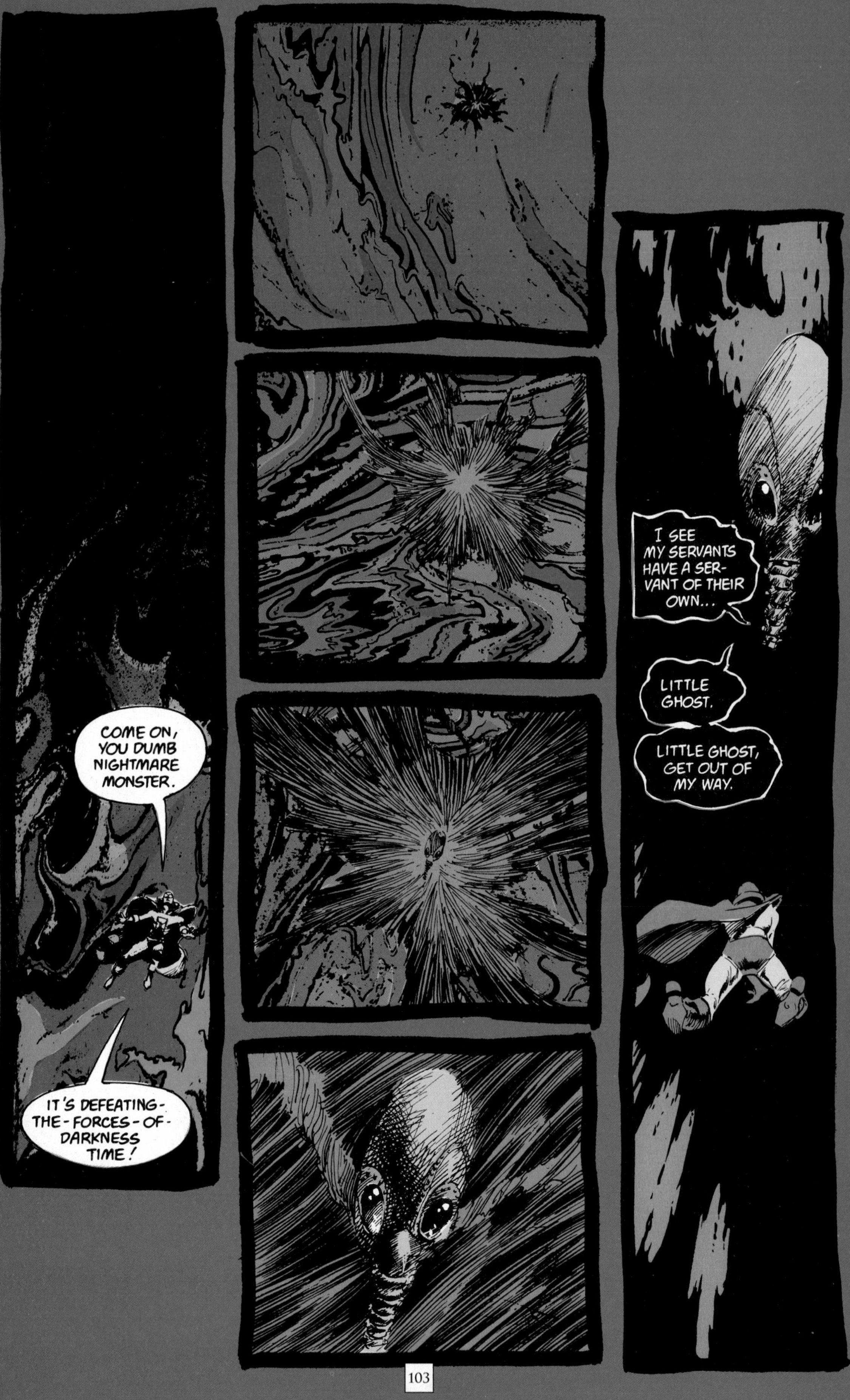
COME ON, YOU DUMB NIGHTMARE MONSTER.
IT'S DEFEATING-THE-FORCES-OF-DARKNESS TIME!
I SEE MY SERVANTS HAVE A SER-VANT OF THEIR OWN...
LITTLE GHOST.
LITTLE GHOST, GET OUT OF MY WAY.

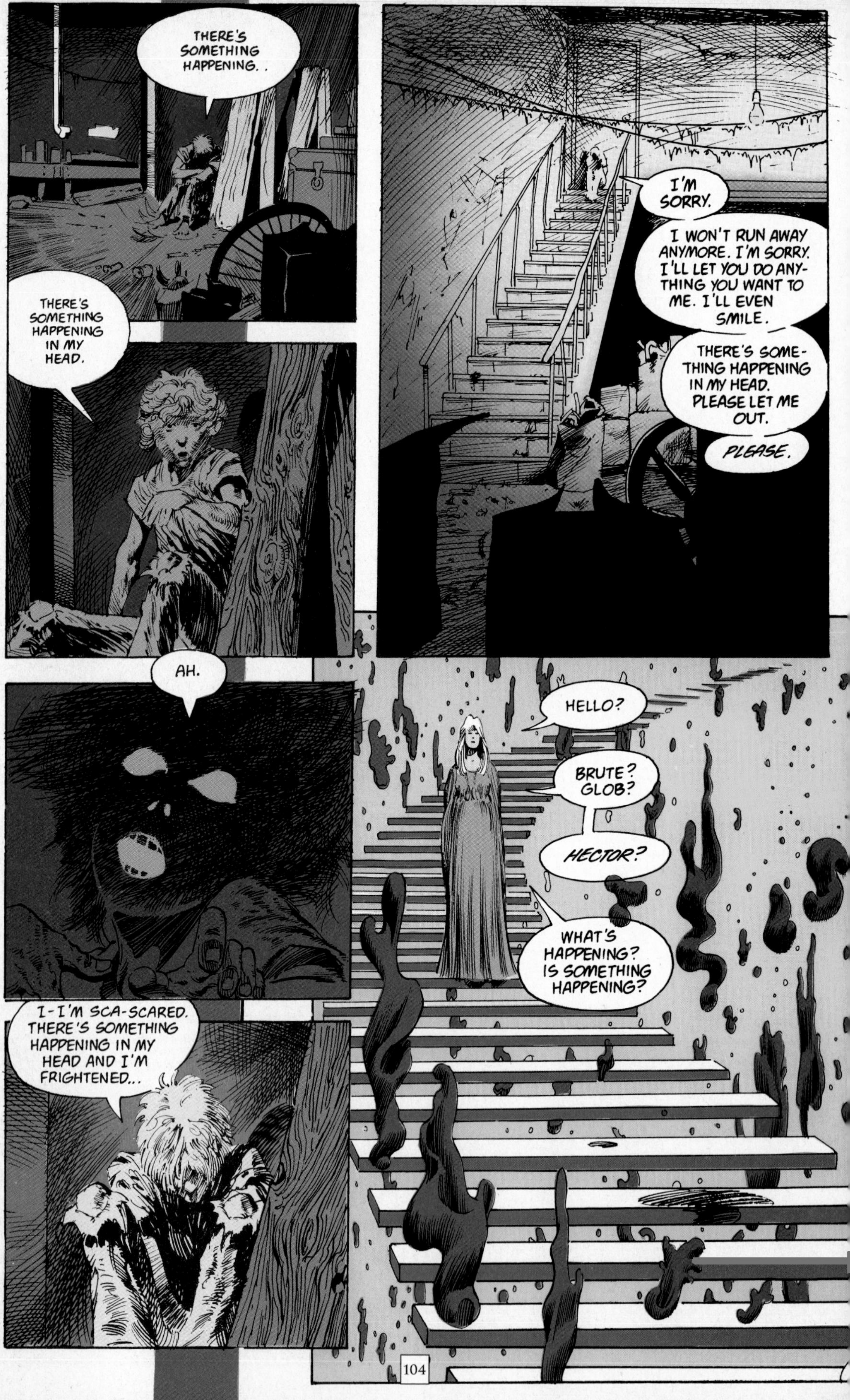
THERE'S SOMETHING HAPPENING. .
I'M SORRY.
I WON'T RUN AWAY ANYMORE. I'M SORRY. I'LL LET YOU DO ANYTHING YOU WANT TO ME. I'LL EVEN SMILE.
THERE'S SOMETHING HAPPENING IN MY HEAD.
THERE'S SOMETHING HAPPENING IN MY HEAD. PLEASE LET ME OUT.
PLEASE.
AH.
HELLO?
BRUTE? GLOB?
HECTOR?
WHAT'S HAPPENING? IS SOMETHING HAPPENING?
I-I'M SCA-SCARED. THERE'S SOMETHING HAPPENING IN MY HEAD AND I'M FRIGHTENED...

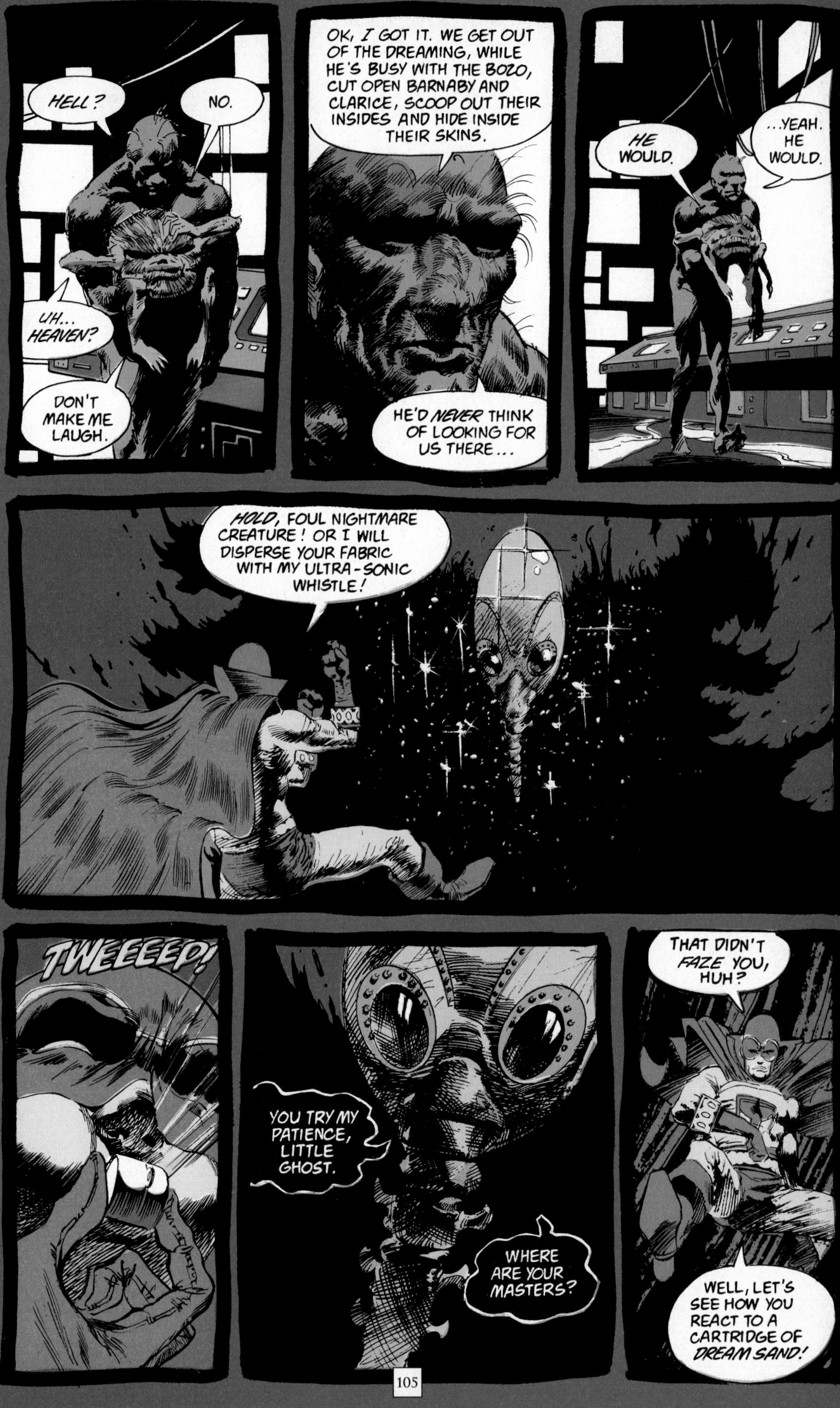
HELL?
NO.
UH... HEAVEN?
DON'T MAKE ME LAUGH.
OK, I GOT IT. WE GET OUT OF THE DREAMING, WHILE HE'S BUSY WITH THE BOZO, CUT OPEN BARNABY AND CLARICE, SCOOP OUT THEIR INSIDES AND HIDE INSIDE THEIR SKINS.
HE'D NEVER THINK OF LOOKING FOR US THERE...
HE WOULD.
...YEAH. HE WOULD.
HOLD, FOUL NIGHTMARE CREATURE! OR I WILL DISPERSE YOUR FABRIC WITH MY ULTRA-SONIC WHISTLE!
TWEEEEP!
YOU TRY MY PATIENCE, LITTLE GHOST.
WHERE ARE YOUR MASTERS?
THAT DIDN'T FAZE YOU, HUH?
WELL, LET'S SEE HOW YOU REACT TO A CARTRIDGE OF DREAM SAND!

I CAN FEEL THEM, HIDING IN THAT PLACE. GET OUT OF MY WAY.

MONSTER, YOU SHALL NEVER GET PAST *ME*.

AND WHO ARE YOU...?

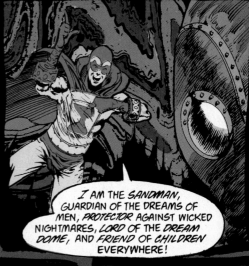

I AM THE *SANDMAN*, GUARDIAN OF THE DREAMS OF MEN, *PROTECTOR* AGAINST WICKED NIGHTMARES, *LORD* OF THE *DREAM DOME*, AND *FRIEND OF CHILDREN* EVERYWHERE!

YOU ARE *WHAT?*

HRR.

HRR.

HRRRAAHH.

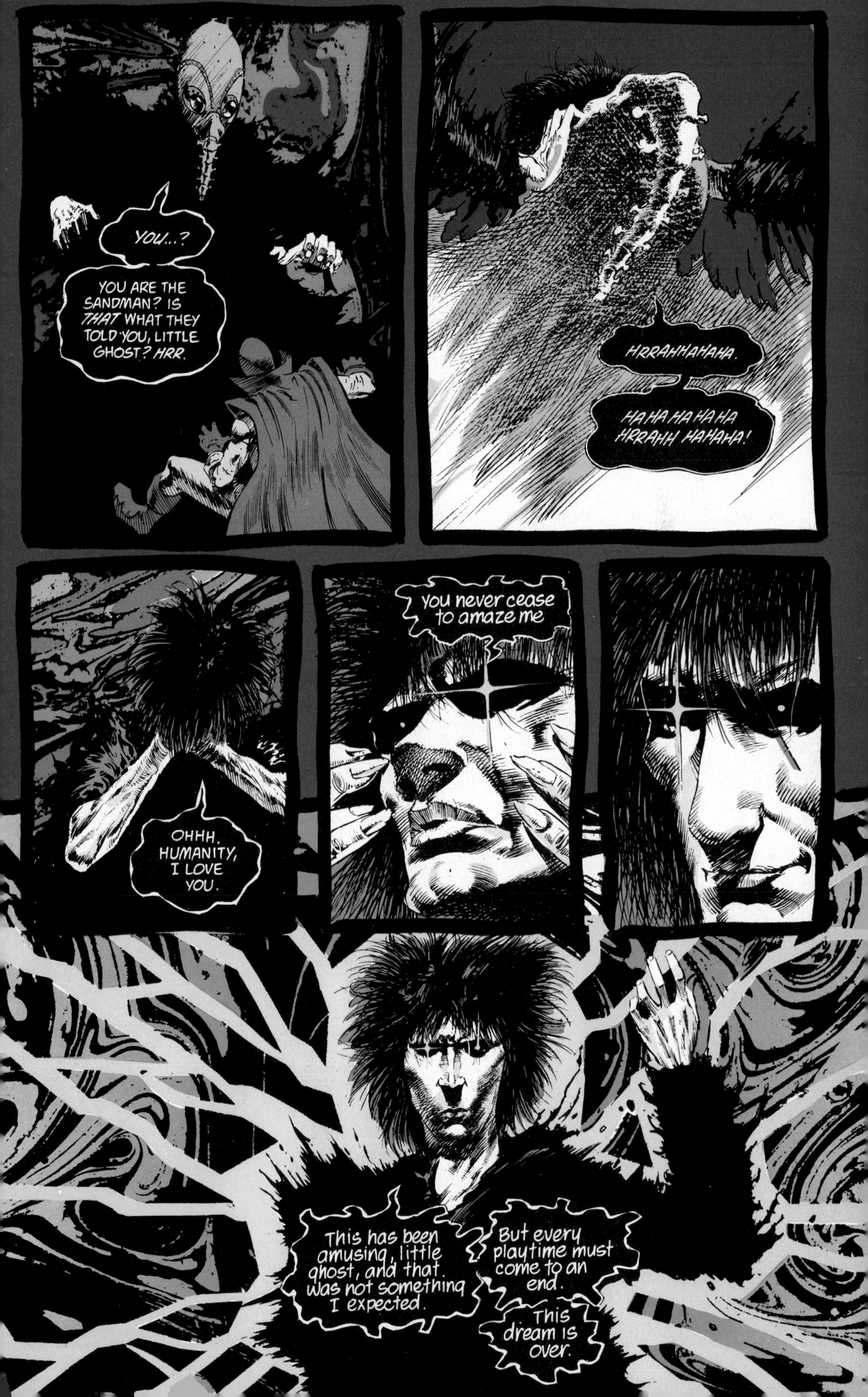
YOU...?
YOU ARE THE SANDMAN? IS THAT WHAT THEY TOLD YOU, LITTLE GHOST? HRR.
HRRAHHAHAHA.
HA HA HA HA HA HRRAHH HAHAHA!
OHHH. HUMANITY, I LOVE YOU.
you never cease to amaze me
This has been amusing, little ghost, and that was not something I expected.
But every playtime must come to an end.
This dream is over.

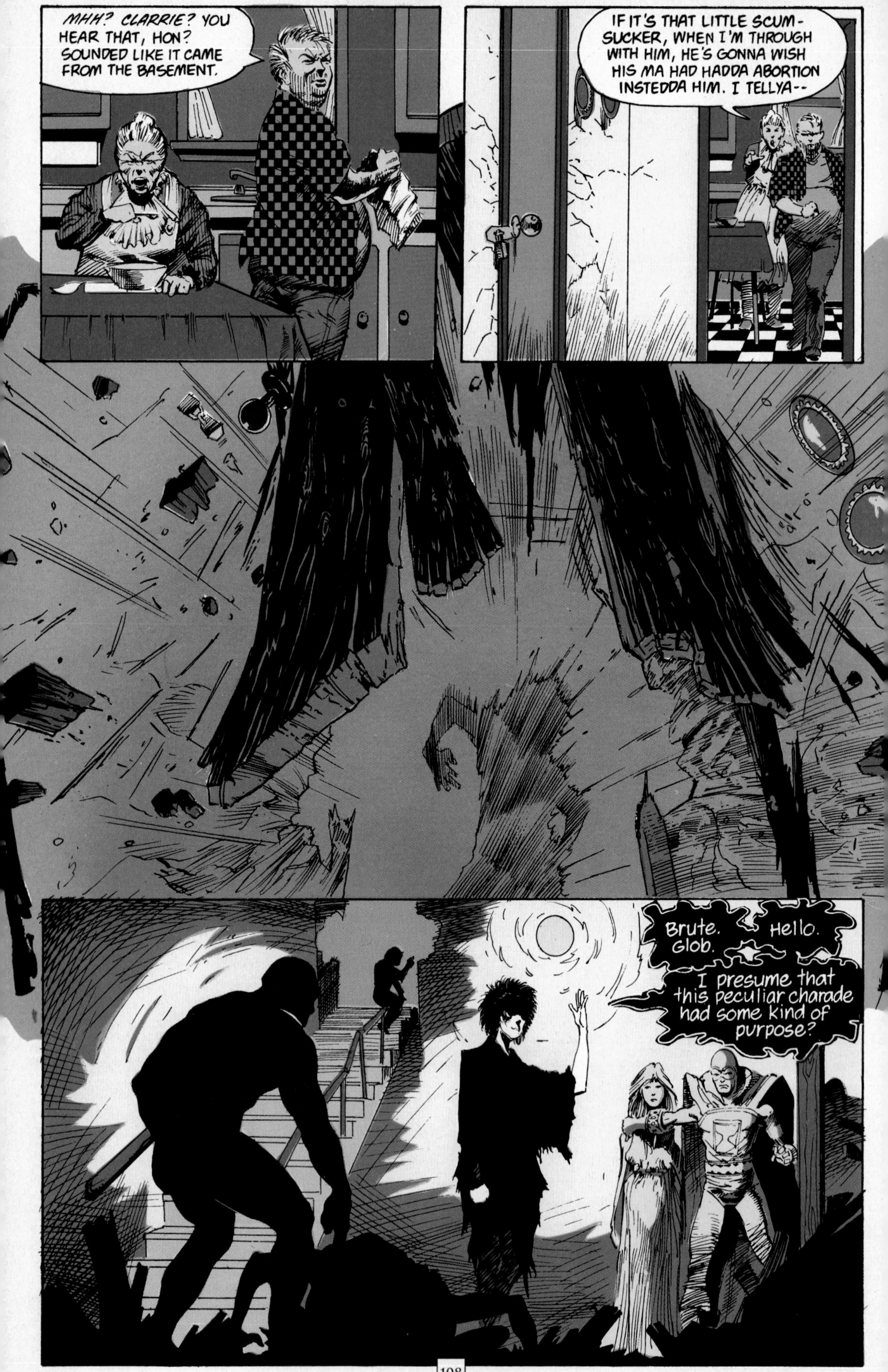
MHH? CLARRIE? YOU HEAR THAT, HON? SOUNDED LIKE IT CAME FROM THE BASEMENT.
IF IT'S THAT LITTLE SCUM-SUCKER, WHEN I'M THROUGH WITH HIM, HE'S GONNA WISH HIS MA HAD HADDA ABORTION INSTEDDA HIM. I TELLYA--
Brute. Glob.
Hello.
I presume that this peculiar charade had some kind of purpose?

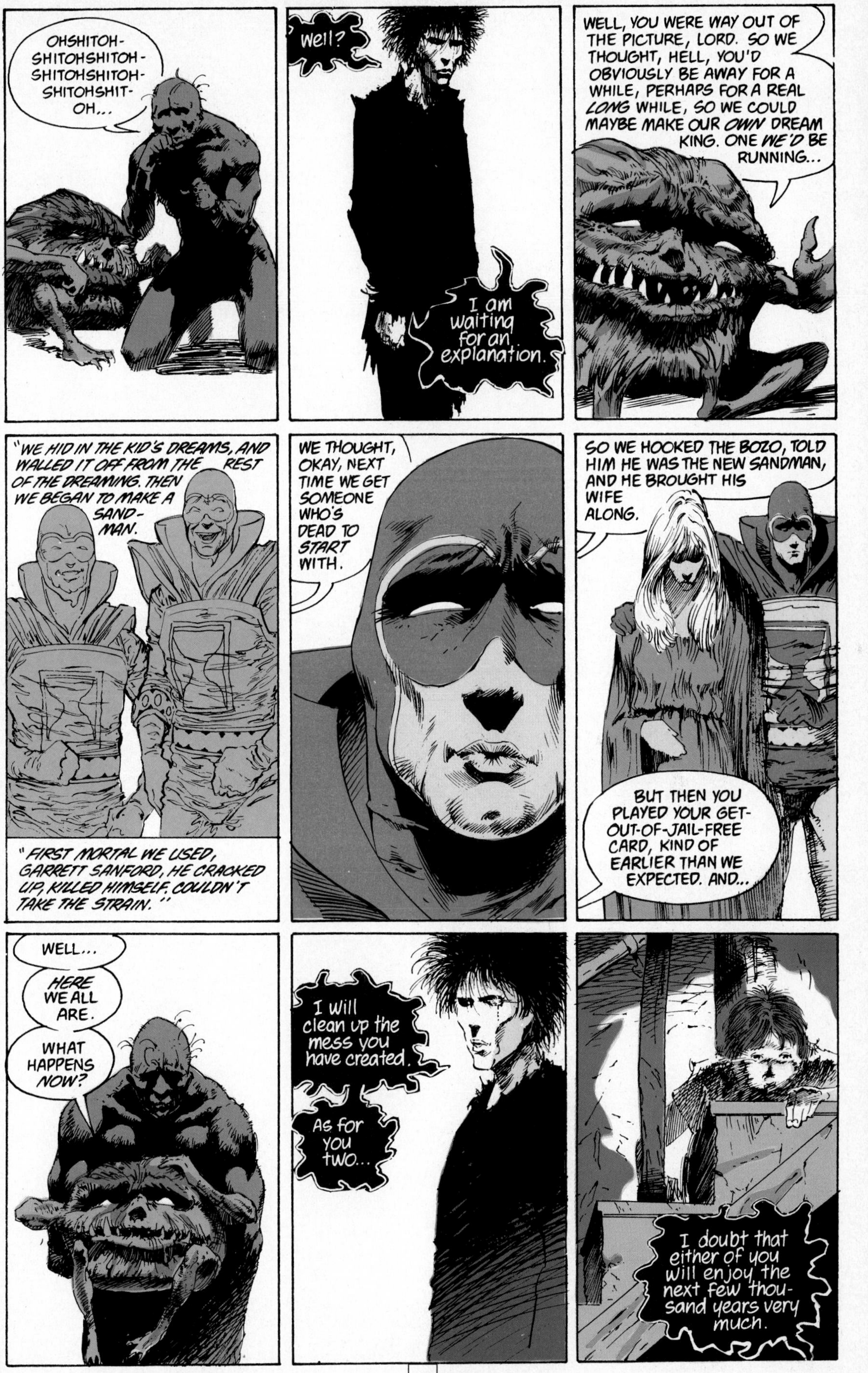
OHSHITOH-SHITOHSHITOH-SHITOHSHITOH-SHITOHSHIT-OH...
Well?
I am waiting for an explanation.
WELL, YOU WERE WAY OUT OF THE PICTURE, LORD. SO WE THOUGHT, HELL, YOU'D OBVIOUSLY BE AWAY FOR A WHILE, PERHAPS FOR A REAL LONG WHILE, SO WE COULD MAYBE MAKE OUR OWN DREAM KING. ONE WE'D BE RUNNING...
"WE HID IN THE KID'S DREAMS, AND WALLED IT OFF FROM THE REST OF THE DREAMING. THEN WE BEGAN TO MAKE A SANDMAN.
"FIRST MORTAL WE USED, GARRETT SANFORD, HE CRACKED UP, KILLED HIMSELF. COULDN'T TAKE THE STRAIN."
WE THOUGHT, OKAY, NEXT TIME WE GET SOMEONE WHO'S DEAD TO START WITH.
SO WE HOOKED THE BOZO, TOLD HIM HE WAS THE NEW SANDMAN, AND HE BROUGHT HIS WIFE ALONG.
BUT THEN YOU PLAYED YOUR GET-OUT-OF-JAIL-FREE CARD, KIND OF EARLIER THAN WE EXPECTED. AND...
WELL...
HERE WE ALL ARE.
WHAT HAPPENS NOW?
I will clean up the mess you have created.
As for you two...
I doubt that either of you will enjoy the next few thousand years very much.

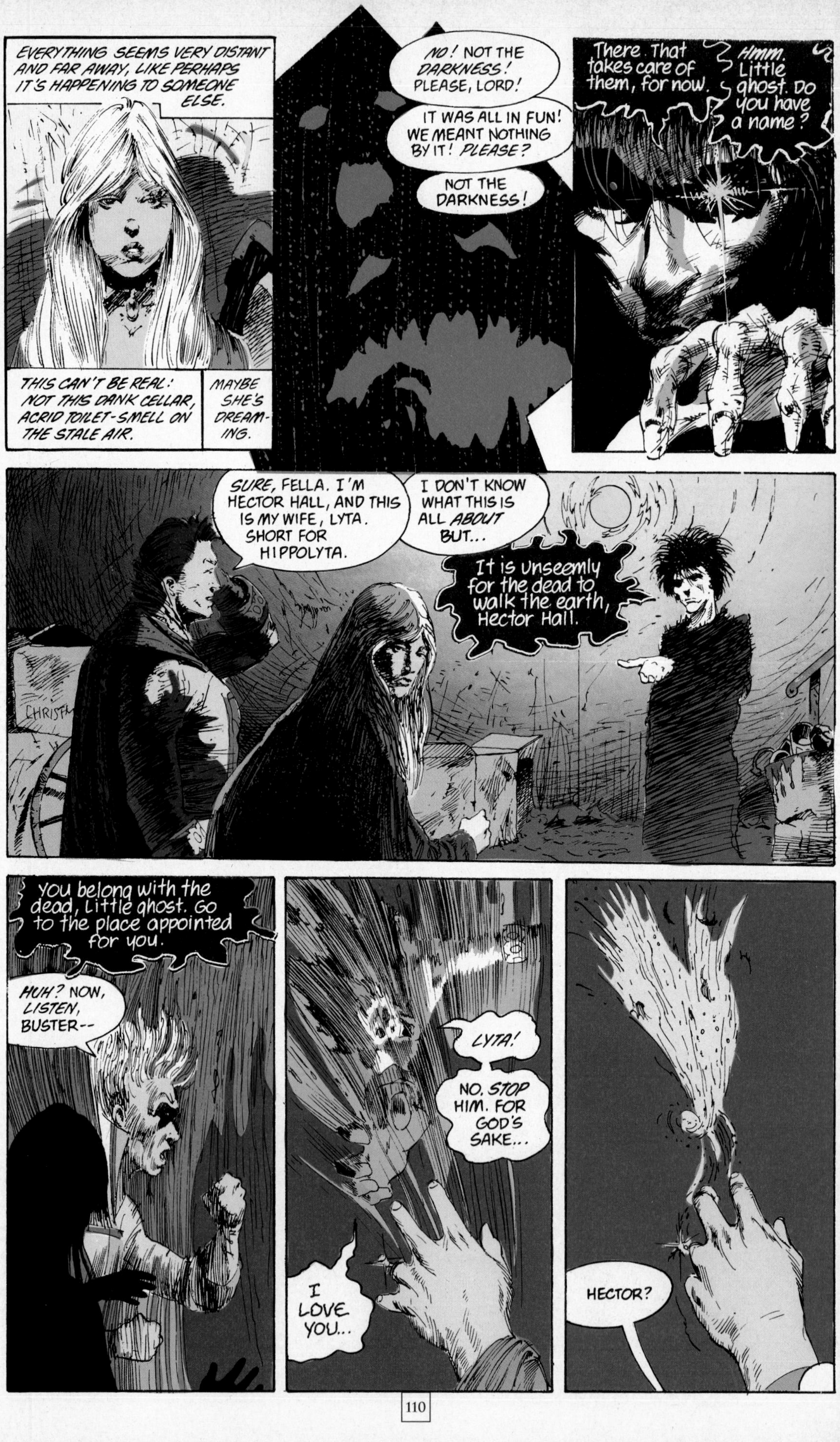
EVERYTHING SEEMS VERY DISTANT AND FAR AWAY, LIKE PERHAPS IT'S HAPPENING TO SOMEONE ELSE.
THIS CAN'T BE REAL: NOT THIS DANK CELLAR, ACRID TOILET-SMELL ON THE STALE AIR.
MAYBE SHE'S DREAMING.
NO! NOT THE DARKNESS! PLEASE, LORD!
IT WAS ALL IN FUN! WE MEANT NOTHING BY IT! PLEASE?
NOT THE DARKNESS!
There. That takes care of them, for now.
Hmm. Little ghost. Do you have a name?
SURE, FELLA. I'M HECTOR HALL, AND THIS IS MY WIFE, LYTA. SHORT FOR HIPPOLYTA.
I DON'T KNOW WHAT THIS IS ALL ABOUT BUT...
It is unseemly for the dead to walk the earth, Hector Hall.
CHRISTM
You belong with the dead, little ghost. Go to the place appointed for you.
HUH? NOW, LISTEN, BUSTER--
LYTA!
NO. STOP HIM. FOR GOD'S SAKE...
I LOVE YOU...
HECTOR?

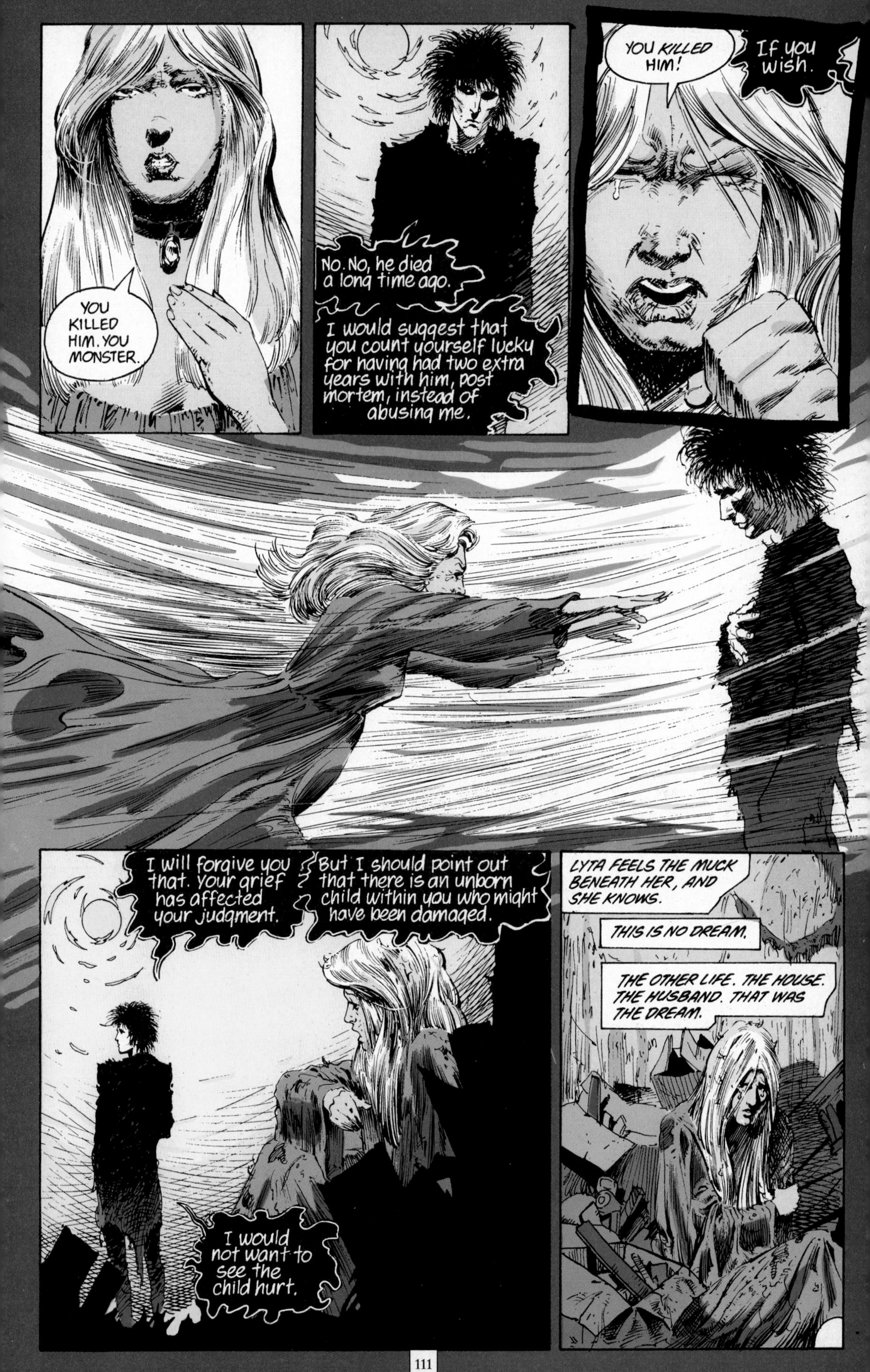
YOU KILLED HIM. YOU MONSTER.
No. No, he died a long time ago.
I would suggest that you count yourself lucky for having had two extra years with him, post mortem, instead of abusing me.
YOU KILLED HIM!
If you wish.
I will forgive you that. Your grief has affected your judgment.
But I should point out that there is an unborn child within you who might have been damaged.
I would not want to see the child hurt.
LYTA FEELS THE MUCK BENEATH HER, AND SHE KNOWS.
THIS IS NO DREAM.
THE OTHER LIFE. THE HOUSE. THE HUSBAND. THAT WAS THE DREAM.

SO. WHAT ARE YOU GOING TO DO TO ME?

Nothing.

NOTHING? YOU KILLED HECTOR. YOU DESTROYED OUR HOME. YOU'VE RUINED MY LIFE.

YOU CALL THAT NOTHING?

Exactly Nothing.

You are free to go. Build yourself a new life, Hippolyta Hall.

Oh. I almost forgot. The child-- the child you have carried so long in dreams. That child is mine.

Take good care of it. One day I will come for it.

BUT, BUT, YOU CAN'T, MY BABY...

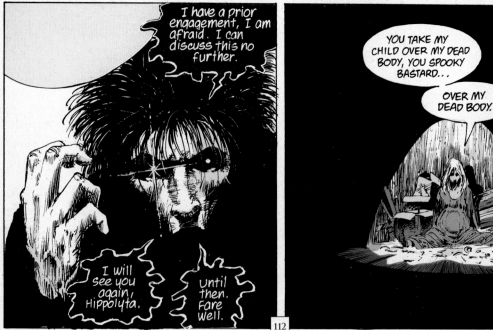

I have a prior engagement, I am afraid. I can discuss this no further.

YOU TAKE MY CHILD OVER MY DEAD BODY, YOU SPOOKY BASTARD...

OVER MY DEAD BODY.

I will see you again, Hippolyta.

Until then. Fare Well.

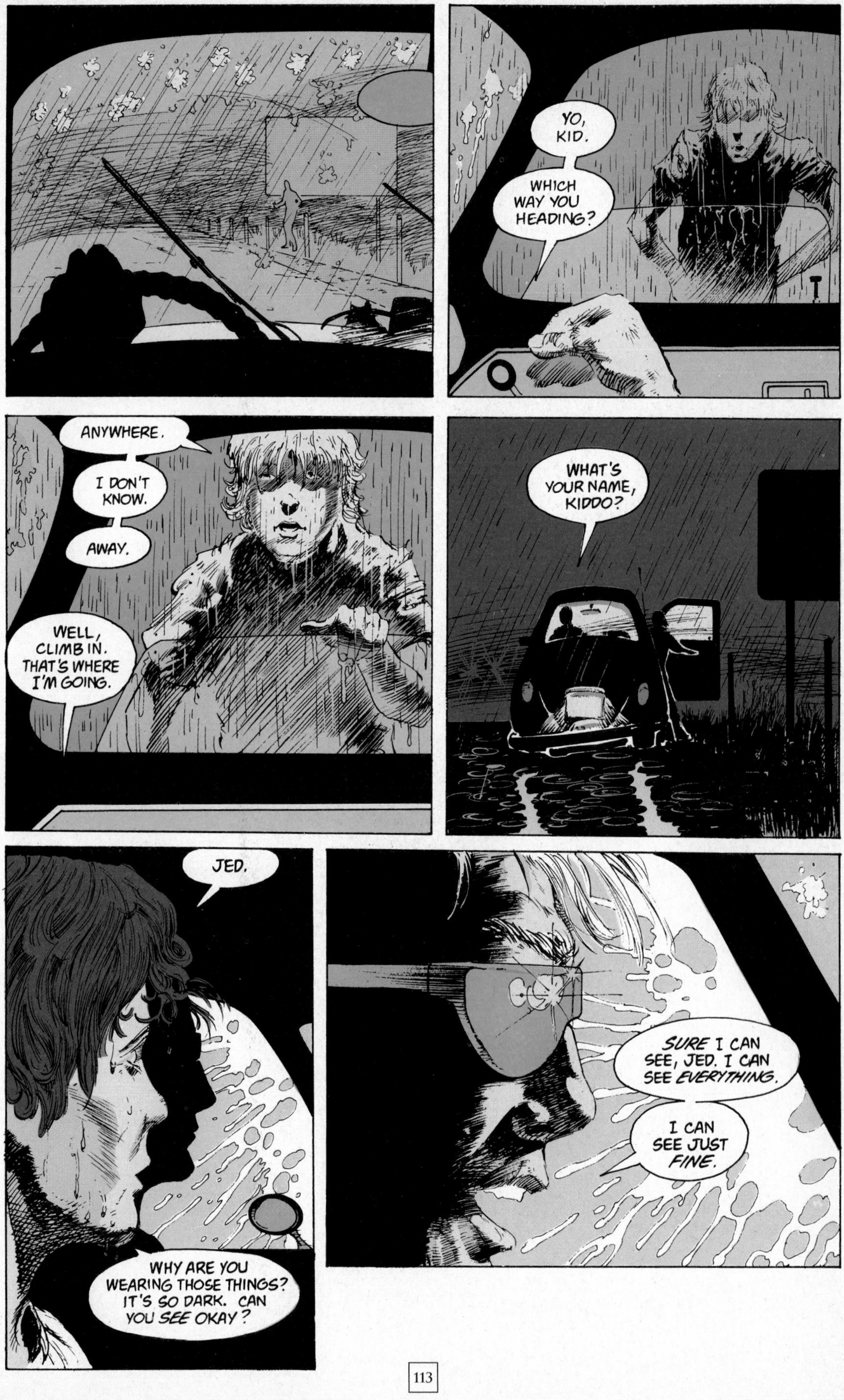

YO, KID.
WHICH WAY YOU HEADING?
ANYWHERE.
I DON'T KNOW.
AWAY.
WELL, CLIMB IN. THAT'S WHERE I'M GOING.
WHAT'S YOUR NAME, KIDDO?
JED.
WHY ARE YOU WEARING THOSE THINGS? IT'S SO DARK. CAN YOU *SEE* OKAY?
SURE I CAN SEE, JED. I CAN SEE *EVERYTHING*.
I CAN SEE JUST *FINE*.

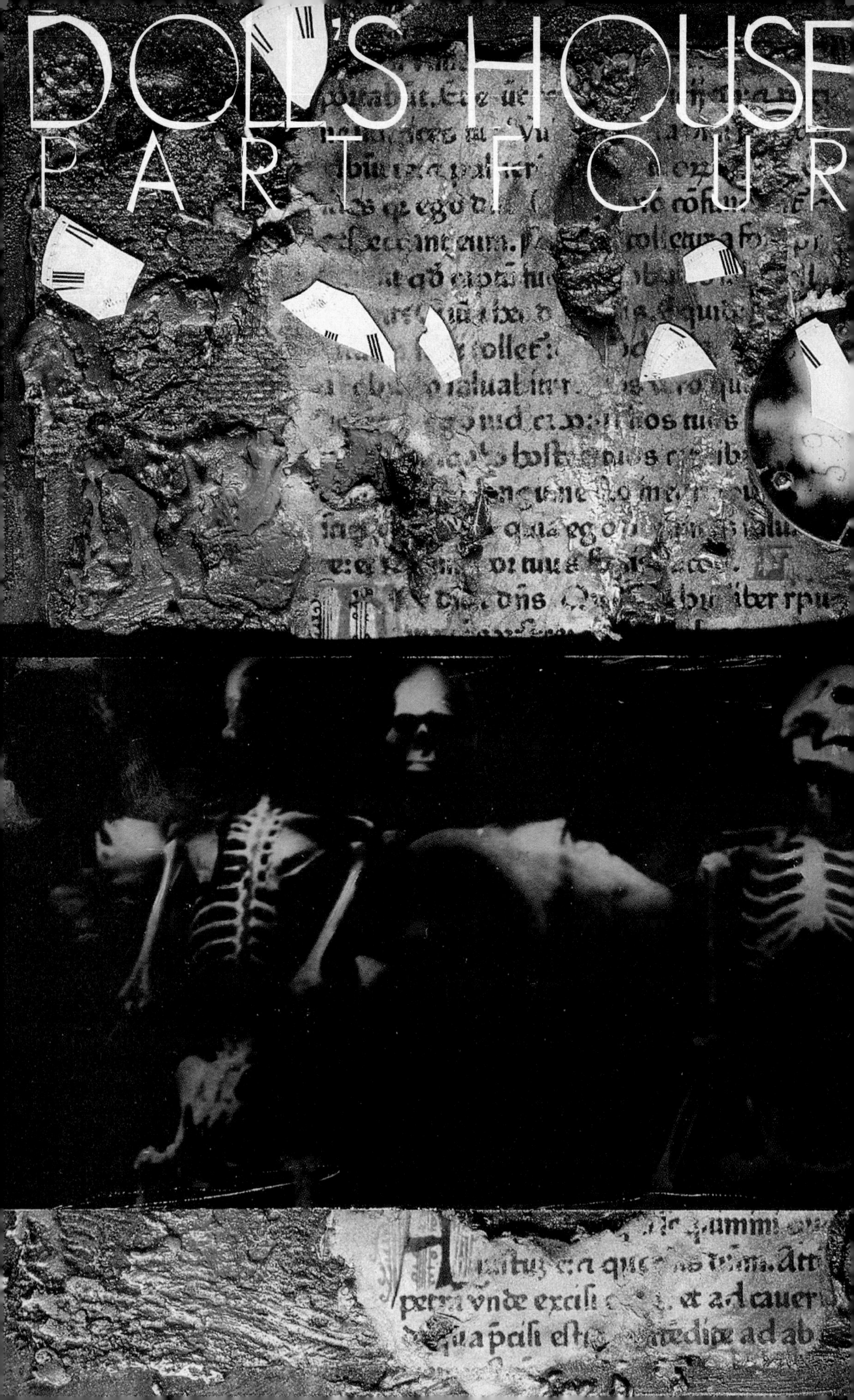
DOLL'S HOUSE
PART FOUR

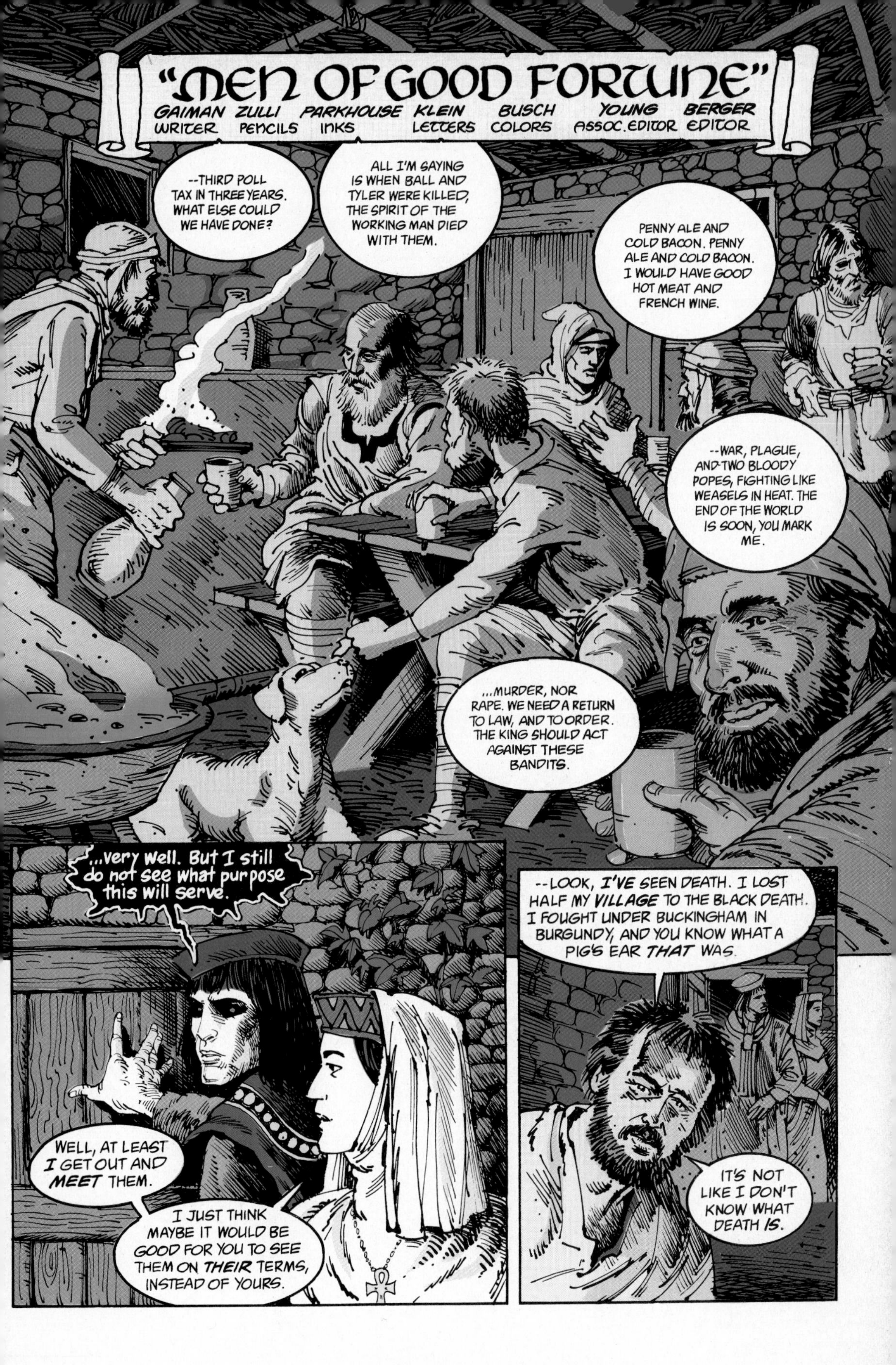

"MEN OF GOOD FORTUNE"
GAIMAN WRITER ZULLI PENCILS PARKHOUSE INKS KLEIN LETTERS BUSCH COLORS YOUNG ASSOC. EDITOR BERGER EDITOR
--THIRD POLL TAX IN THREE YEARS. WHAT ELSE COULD WE HAVE DONE?
ALL I'M SAYING IS WHEN BALL AND TYLER WERE KILLED, THE SPIRIT OF THE WORKING MAN DIED WITH THEM.
PENNY ALE AND COLD BACON. PENNY ALE AND COLD BACON. I WOULD HAVE GOOD HOT MEAT AND FRENCH WINE.
--WAR, PLAGUE, AND TWO BLOODY POPES, FIGHTING LIKE WEASELS IN HEAT. THE END OF THE WORLD IS SOON, YOU MARK ME.
...MURDER, NOR RAPE. WE NEED A RETURN TO LAW, AND TO ORDER. THE KING SHOULD ACT AGAINST THESE BANDITS.
...very well. But I still do not see what purpose this will serve.
WELL, AT LEAST I GET OUT AND MEET THEM.
I JUST THINK MAYBE IT WOULD BE GOOD FOR YOU TO SEE THEM ON THEIR TERMS, INSTEAD OF YOURS.
--LOOK, I'VE SEEN DEATH. I LOST HALF MY VILLAGE TO THE BLACK DEATH. I FOUGHT UNDER BUCKINGHAM IN BURGUNDY, AND YOU KNOW WHAT A PIG'S EAR THAT WAS.
IT'S NOT LIKE I DON'T KNOW WHAT DEATH IS.

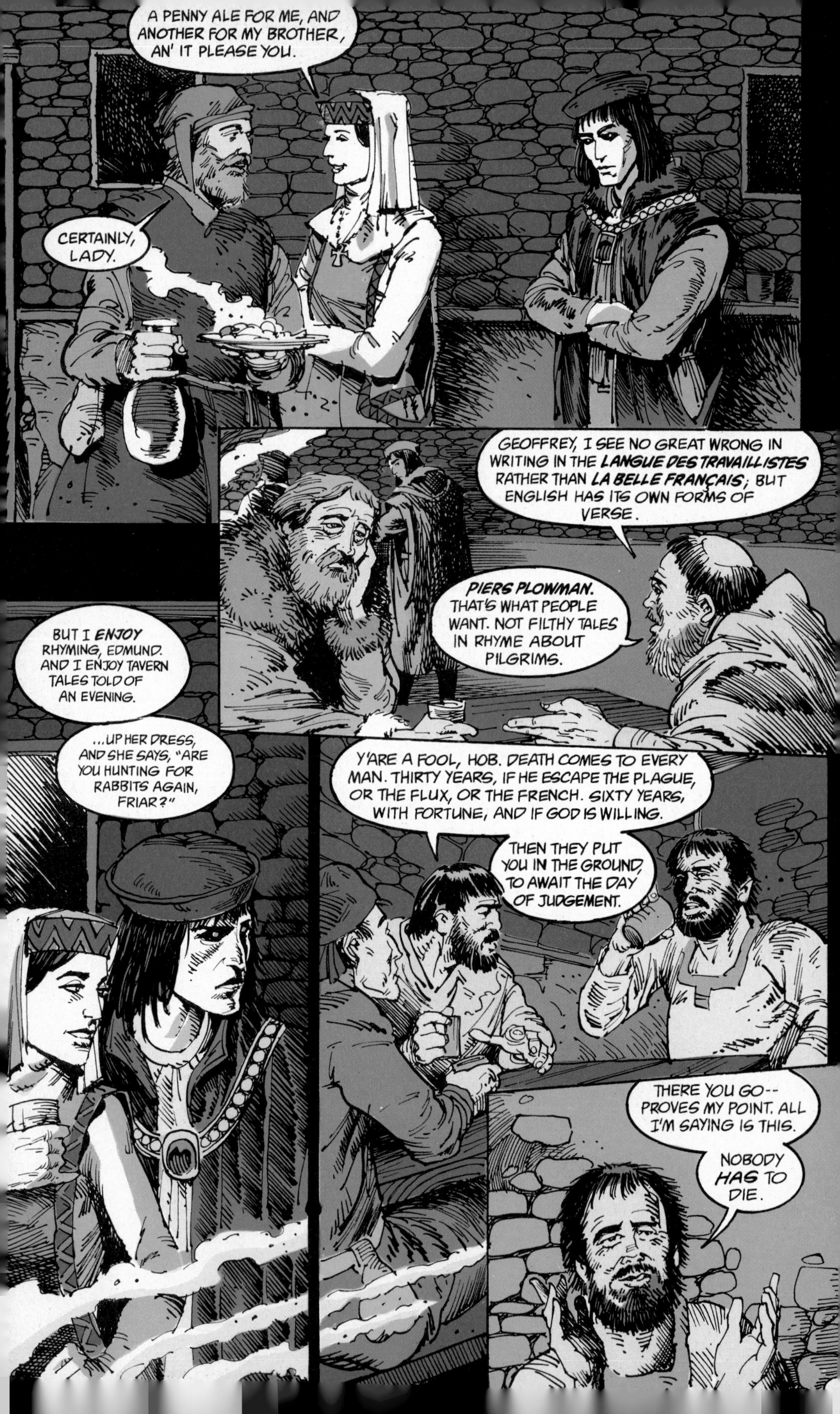
A PENNY ALE FOR ME, AND ANOTHER FOR MY BROTHER, AN' IT PLEASE YOU.
CERTAINLY, LADY.
GEOFFREY, I SEE NO GREAT WRONG IN WRITING IN THE LANGUE DES TRAVAILLISTES RATHER THAN LA BELLE FRANÇAIS; BUT ENGLISH HAS ITS OWN FORMS OF VERSE.
PIERS PLOWMAN. THAT'S WHAT PEOPLE WANT. NOT FILTHY TALES IN RHYME ABOUT PILGRIMS.
BUT I ENJOY RHYMING, EDMUND. AND I ENJOY TAVERN TALES TOLD OF AN EVENING.
...UP HER DRESS, AND SHE SAYS, "ARE YOU HUNTING FOR RABBITS AGAIN, FRIAR?"
Y'ARE A FOOL, HOB. DEATH COMES TO EVERY MAN. THIRTY YEARS, IF HE ESCAPE THE PLAGUE, OR THE FLUX, OR THE FRENCH. SIXTY YEARS, WITH FORTUNE, AND IF GOD IS WILLING.
THEN THEY PUT YOU IN THE GROUND, TO AWAIT THE DAY OF JUDGEMENT.
THERE YOU GO-- PROVES MY POINT. ALL I'M SAYING IS THIS.
NOBODY HAS TO DIE.

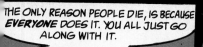

THE ONLY REASON PEOPLE DIE, IS BECAUSE *EVERYONE* DOES IT. YOU ALL JUST GO ALONG WITH IT.

IT'S *RUBBISH,* DEATH. IT'S *STUPID.* I DON'T WANT NOTHING TO DO WITH IT.

A delegation of faerie came to me, last night. They are talking about abandoning this plane for ever.

SHUSH. LISTEN TO THE PEOPLE.

I MEAN, WHAT'S IT *GOOD* FOR, EH?

THINK ABOUT IT.

I MADE MY MIND UP ARSE DEEP IN BURGUNDY MUD. "HOB GADLING," I TOLD MYSELF, EVERY MAN AND WOMAN DIES, THEY SAY--"

--EXCEPT THE WANDERING JEW, AHASUERUS, WHO DENIED OUR LORD.

YEAH. FAIR ENOUGH. EVERYONE DIES, I THOUGHT (EXCEPT FOR MAYBE THE WANDERING JEW), BUT WHY THE HELL SHOULD *I*? I MIGHT GET LUCKY.

THERE'S ALWAYS A FIRST TIME.

NO, IT'S RUBBISH, DEATH IS. I MEAN, THERE'S SO MUCH TO DO. SO MANY THINGS TO SEE. PEOPLE TO DRINK WITH. WOMEN TO SWIVE.

YOU LOT MAY DIE. I EXPECT YOU *WILL,* 'COS YOU'RE STUPID. NOT ME, THOUGH.

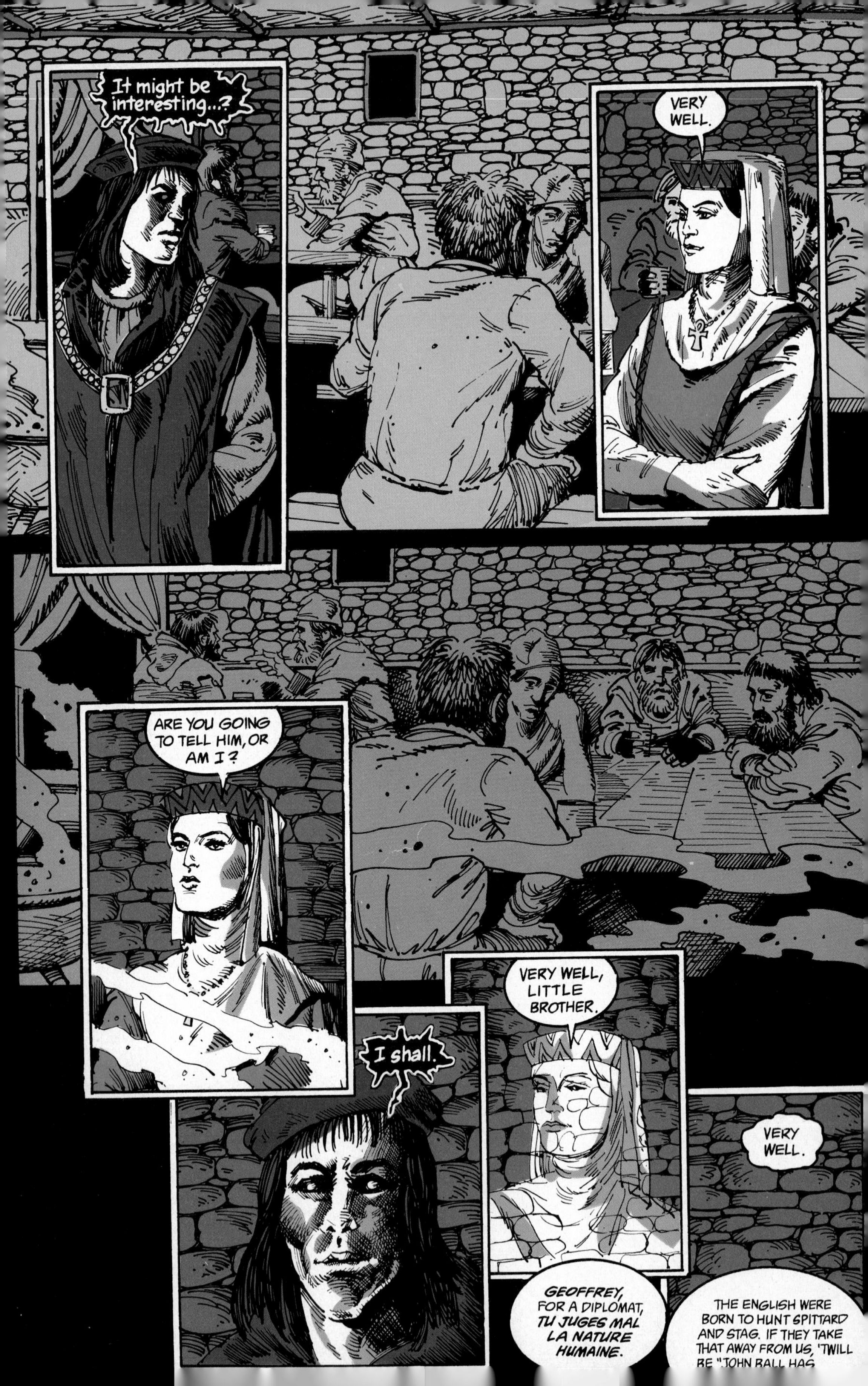
It might be interesting...?
VERY WELL.
ARE YOU GOING TO TELL HIM, OR AM I?
I shall.
VERY WELL, LITTLE BROTHER.
VERY WELL.
GEOFFREY, FOR A DIPLOMAT, *TU JUGES MAL LA NATURE HUMAINE.*
THE ENGLISH WERE BORN TO HUNT SPITTARD AND STAG. IF THEY TAKE THAT AWAY FROM US, 'TWILL BE "JOHN BALL HAS

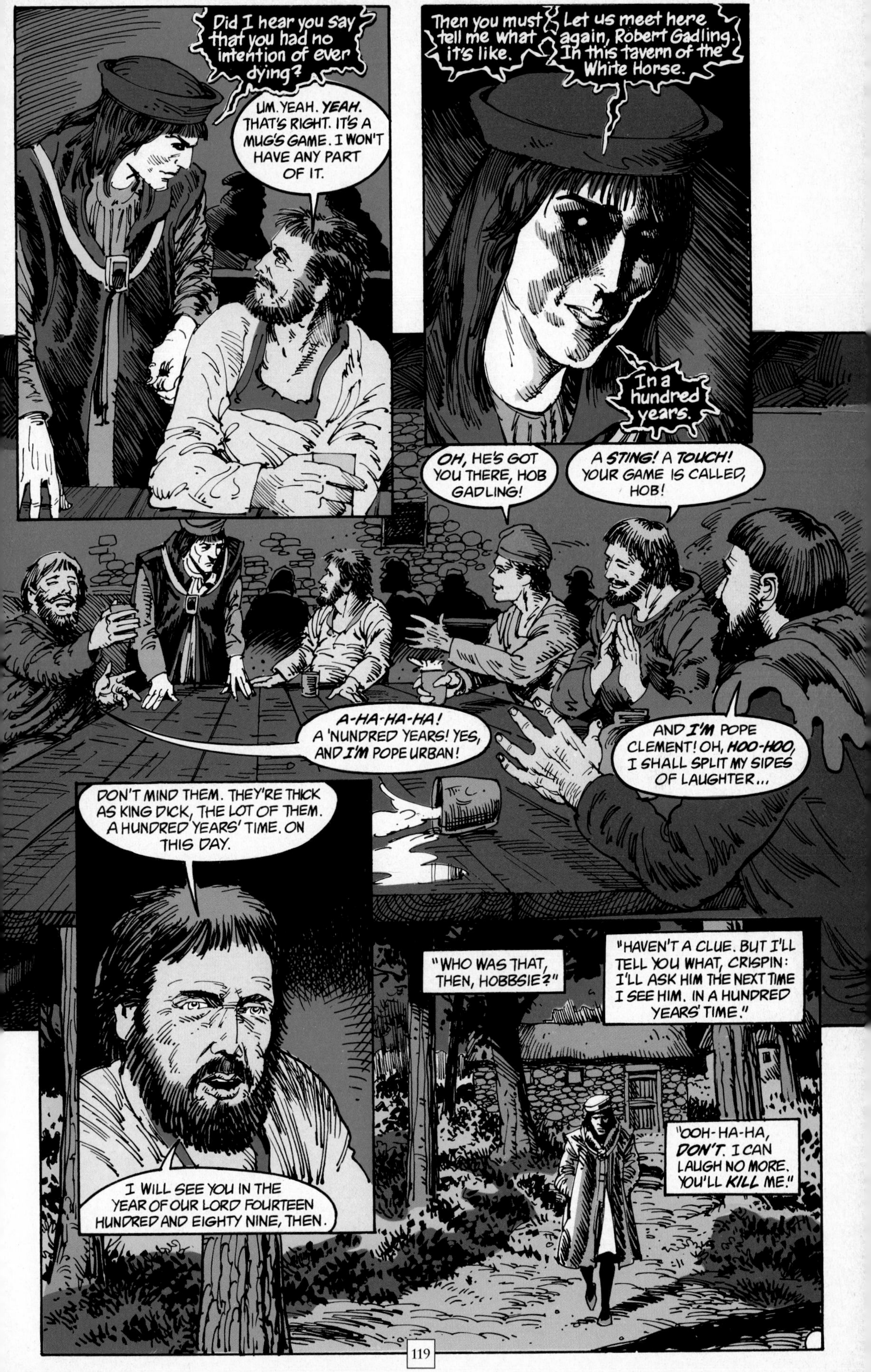
Did I hear you say that you had no intention of ever dying?
UM. YEAH. YEAH. THAT'S RIGHT. IT'S A MUG'S GAME. I WON'T HAVE ANY PART OF IT.
Then you must tell me what it's like.
Let us meet here again, Robert Gadling. In this tavern of the White Horse.
In a hundred years.
OH, HE'S GOT YOU THERE, HOB GADLING!
A STING! A TOUCH! YOUR GAME IS CALLED, HOB!
A-HA-HA-HA! A 'NUNDRED YEARS! YES, AND I'M POPE URBAN!
AND I'M POPE CLEMENT! OH, HOO-HOO, I SHALL SPLIT MY SIDES OF LAUGHTER...
DON'T MIND THEM. THEY'RE THICK AS KING DICK, THE LOT OF THEM. A HUNDRED YEARS' TIME. ON THIS DAY.
I WILL SEE YOU IN THE YEAR OF OUR LORD FOURTEEN HUNDRED AND EIGHTY NINE, THEN.
"WHO WAS THAT, THEN, HOBBSIE?"
"HAVEN'T A CLUE. BUT I'LL TELL YOU WHAT, CRISPIN: I'LL ASK HIM THE NEXT TIME I SEE HIM. IN A HUNDRED YEARS' TIME."
"OOH-HA-HA, DON'T. I CAN LAUGH NO MORE. YOU'LL KILL ME."

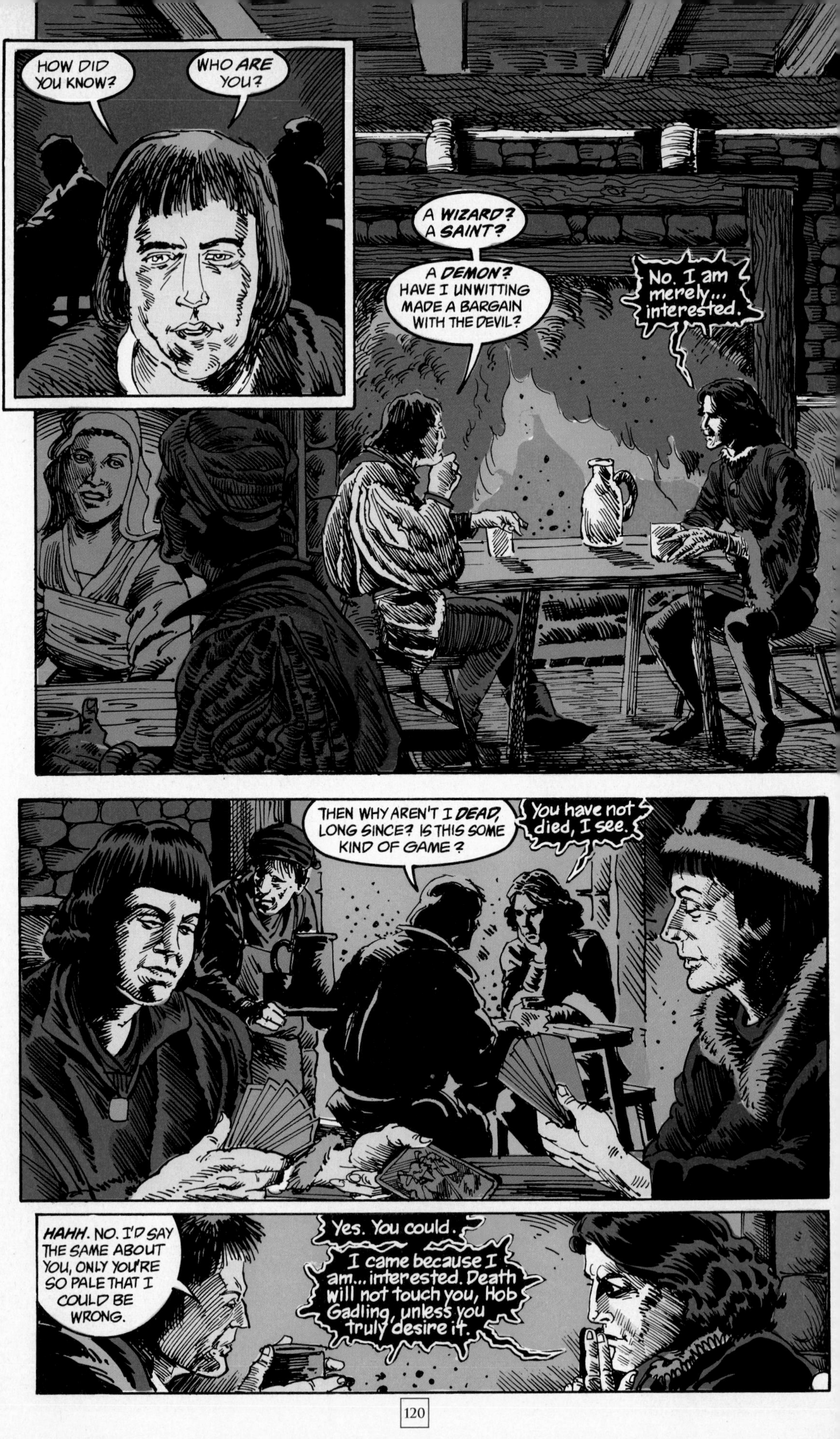
HOW DID YOU KNOW?
WHO ARE YOU?
A WIZARD? A SAINT?
A DEMON? HAVE I UNWITTING MADE A BARGAIN WITH THE DEVIL?
No. I am merely... interested.
THEN WHY AREN'T I DEAD, LONG SINCE? IS THIS SOME KIND OF GAME?
You have not died, I see.
HAHH. NO. I'D SAY THE SAME ABOUT YOU, ONLY YOU'RE SO PALE THAT I COULD BE WRONG.
Yes. You could.
I came because I am... interested. Death will not touch you, Hob Gadling, unless you truly desire it.

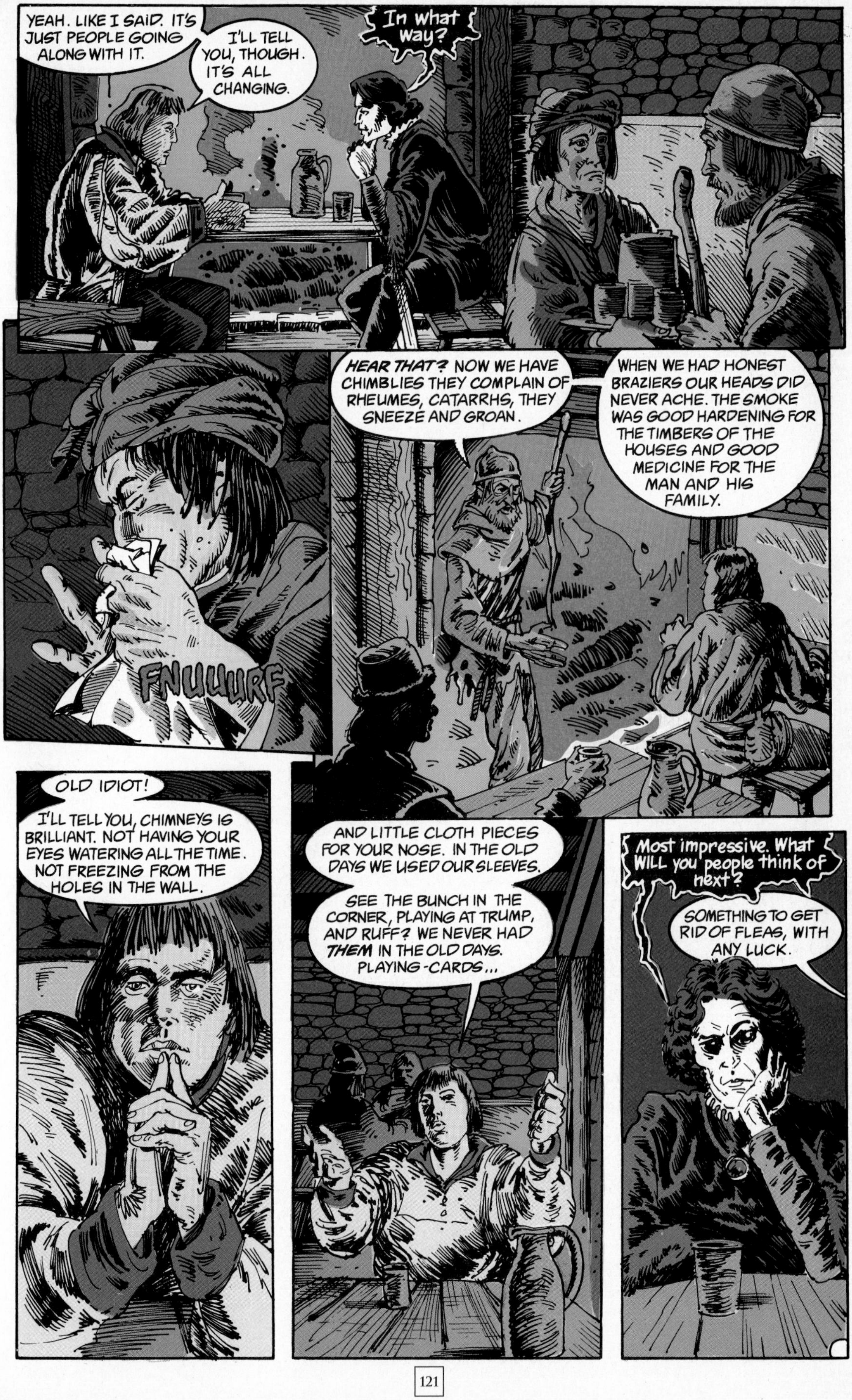
YEAH. LIKE I SAID. IT'S JUST PEOPLE GOING ALONG WITH IT.
I'LL TELL YOU, THOUGH. IT'S ALL CHANGING.
In what way?
HEAR THAT? NOW WE HAVE CHIMBLIES THEY COMPLAIN OF RHEUMES, CATARRHS, THEY SNEEZE AND GROAN.
WHEN WE HAD HONEST BRAZIERS OUR HEADS DID NEVER ACHE. THE SMOKE WAS GOOD HARDENING FOR THE TIMBERS OF THE HOUSES AND GOOD MEDICINE FOR THE MAN AND HIS FAMILY.
FNUUUURF
OLD IDIOT!
I'LL TELL YOU, CHIMNEYS IS BRILLIANT. NOT HAVING YOUR EYES WATERING ALL THE TIME. NOT FREEZING FROM THE HOLES IN THE WALL.
AND LITTLE CLOTH PIECES FOR YOUR NOSE. IN THE OLD DAYS WE USED OUR SLEEVES.
SEE THE BUNCH IN THE CORNER, PLAYING AT TRUMP, AND RUFF? WE NEVER HAD THEM IN THE OLD DAYS. PLAYING-CARDS...
Most impressive. What WILL you people think of next?
SOMETHING TO GET RID OF FLEAS, WITH ANY LUCK.

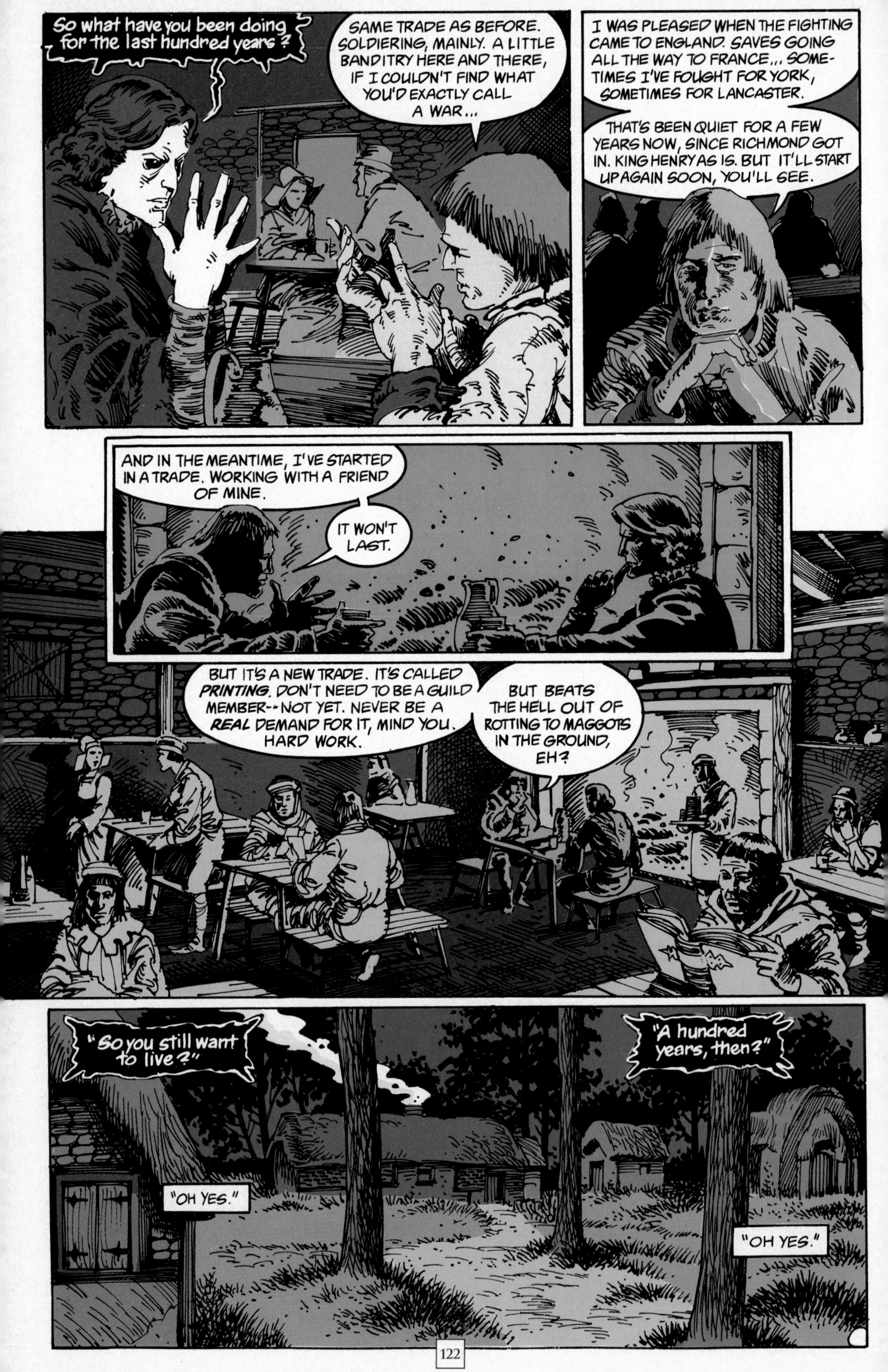
So what have you been doing for the last hundred years?
SAME TRADE AS BEFORE. SOLDIERING, MAINLY. A LITTLE BANDITRY HERE AND THERE, IF I COULDN'T FIND WHAT YOU'D EXACTLY CALL A WAR...
I WAS PLEASED WHEN THE FIGHTING CAME TO ENGLAND. SAVES GOING ALL THE WAY TO FRANCE... SOMETIMES I'VE FOUGHT FOR YORK, SOMETIMES FOR LANCASTER.
THAT'S BEEN QUIET FOR A FEW YEARS NOW, SINCE RICHMOND GOT IN. KING HENRY AS IS. BUT IT'LL START UP AGAIN SOON, YOU'LL SEE.
AND IN THE MEANTIME, I'VE STARTED IN A TRADE. WORKING WITH A FRIEND OF MINE.
IT WON'T LAST.
BUT IT'S A NEW TRADE. IT'S CALLED *PRINTING*. DON'T NEED TO BE A GUILD MEMBER--NOT YET. NEVER BE A *REAL* DEMAND FOR IT, MIND YOU. HARD WORK.
BUT BEATS THE HELL OUT OF ROTTING TO MAGGOTS IN THE GROUND, EH?
"So you still want to live?"
"OH YES."
"A hundred years, then?"
"OH YES."

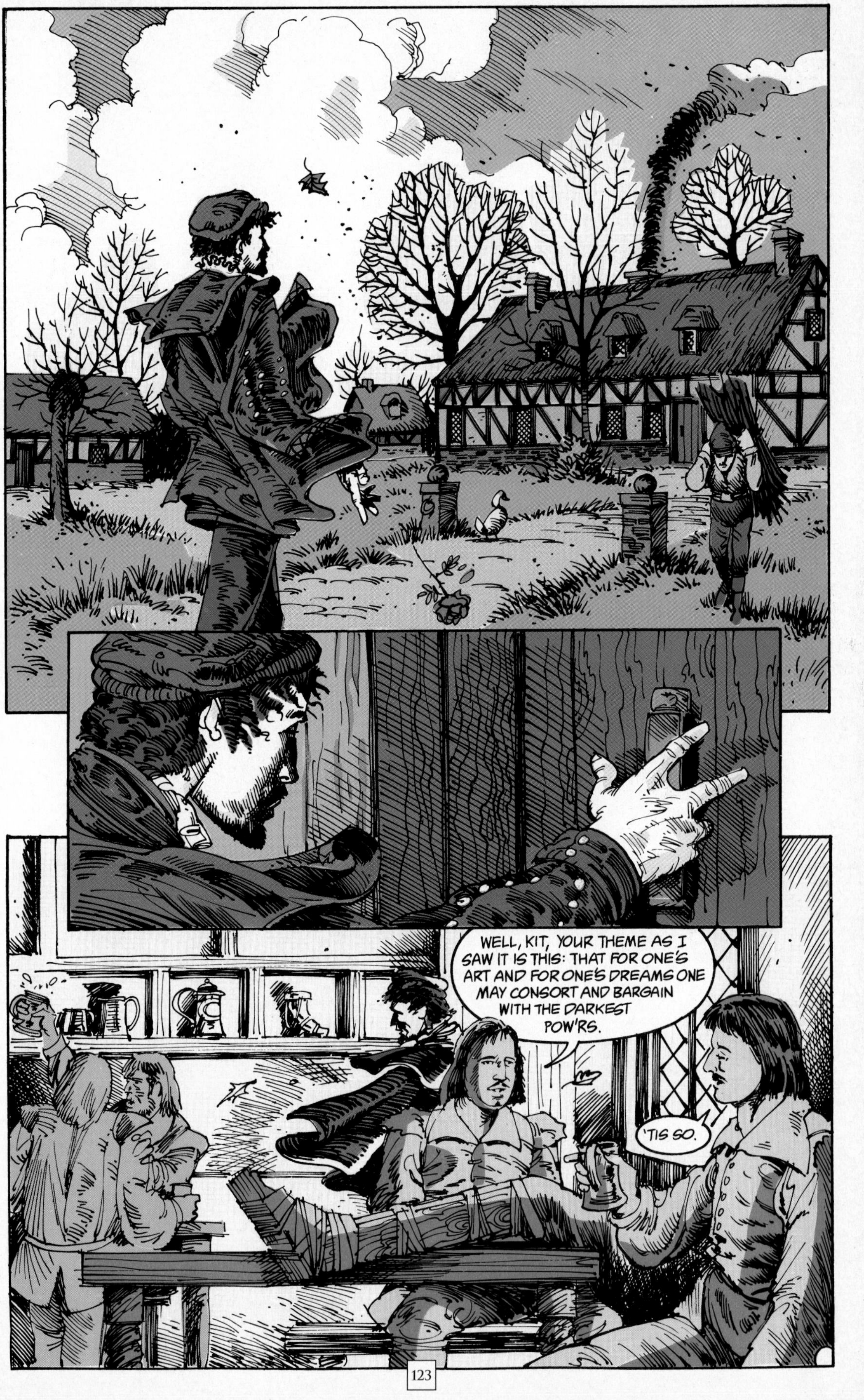
WELL, KIT, YOUR THEME AS I SAW IT IS THIS: THAT FOR ONE'S ART AND FOR ONE'S DREAMS ONE MAY CONSORT AND BARGAIN WITH THE DARKEST POW'RS.
'TIS SO.

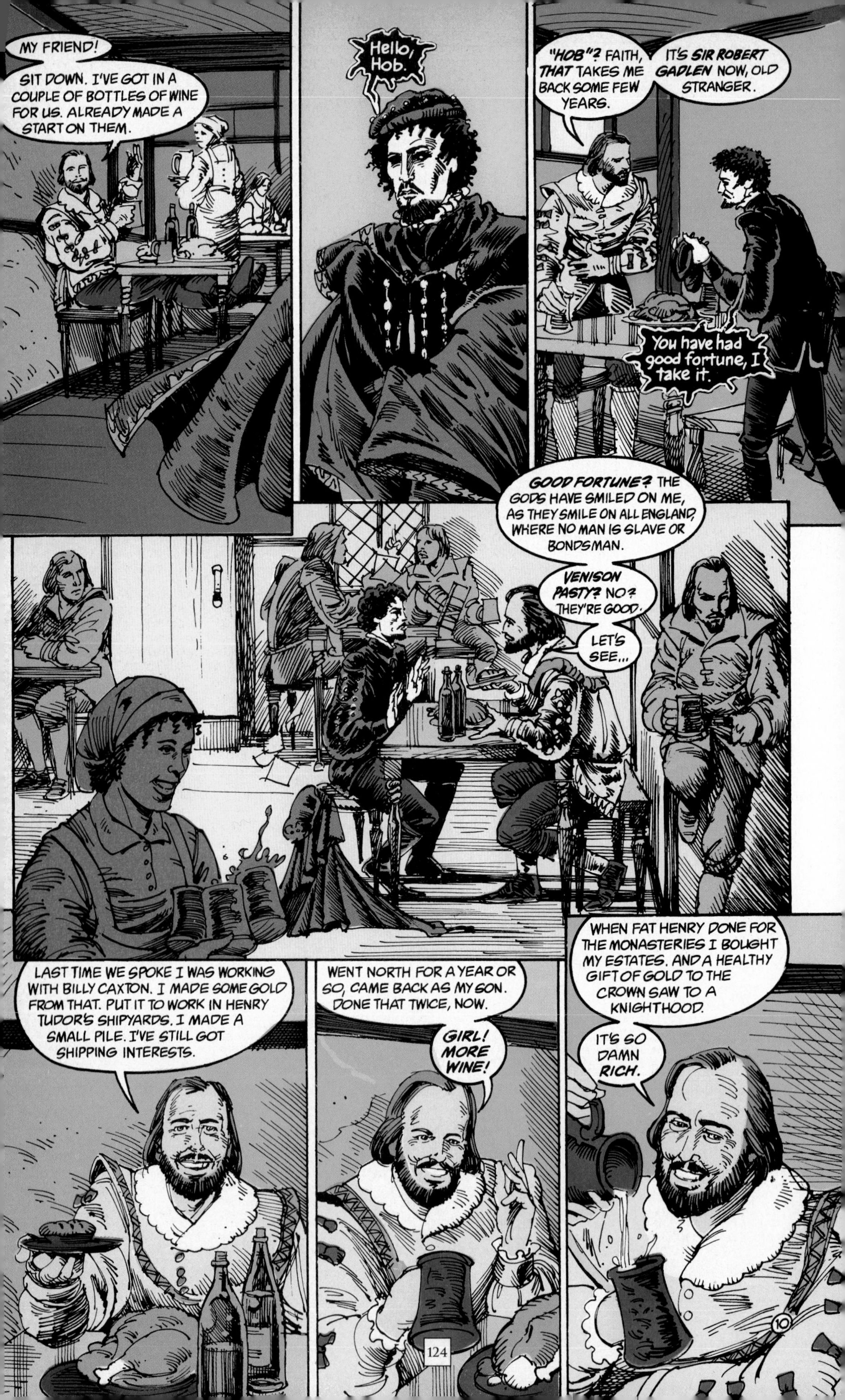
MY FRIEND!
SIT DOWN. I'VE GOT IN A COUPLE OF BOTTLES OF WINE FOR US. ALREADY MADE A START ON THEM.
Hello, Hob.
"HOB"? FAITH, THAT TAKES ME BACK SOME FEW YEARS.
IT'S SIR ROBERT GADLEN NOW, OLD STRANGER.
You have had good fortune, I take it.
GOOD FORTUNE? THE GODS HAVE SMILED ON ME, AS THEY SMILE ON ALL ENGLAND, WHERE NO MAN IS SLAVE OR BONDSMAN.
VENISON PASTY? NO? THEY'RE GOOD.
LET'S SEE...
LAST TIME WE SPOKE I WAS WORKING WITH BILLY CAXTON. I MADE SOME GOLD FROM THAT. PUT IT TO WORK IN HENRY TUDOR'S SHIPYARDS. I MADE A SMALL PILE. I'VE STILL GOT SHIPPING INTERESTS.
WENT NORTH FOR A YEAR OR SO, CAME BACK AS MY SON. DONE THAT TWICE, NOW.
GIRL! MORE WINE!
WHEN FAT HENRY DONE FOR THE MONASTERIES I BOUGHT MY ESTATES. AND A HEALTHY GIFT OF GOLD TO THE CROWN SAW TO A KNIGHTHOOD.
IT'S SO DAMN RICH.
10

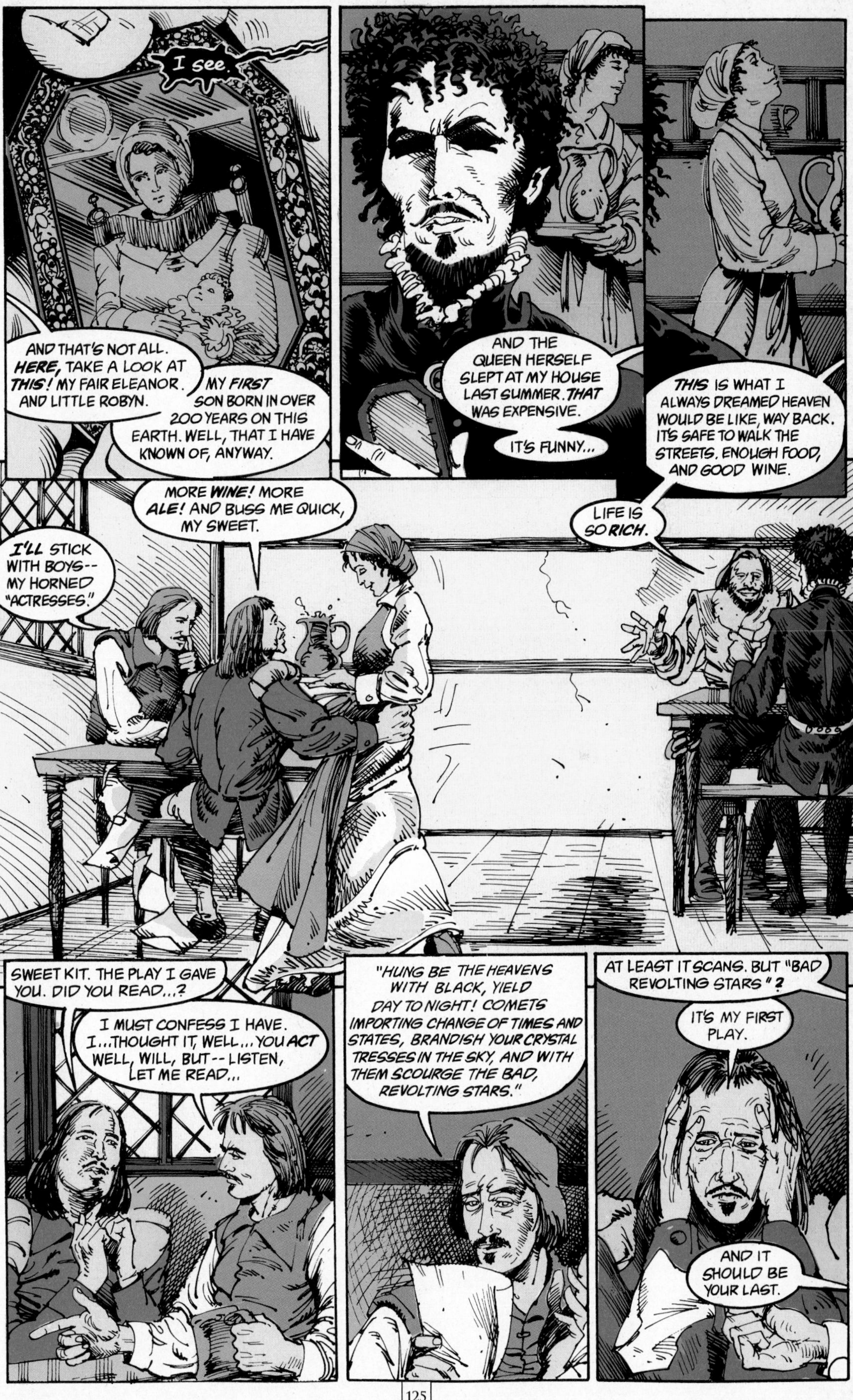
I see.
AND THAT'S NOT ALL. HERE, TAKE A LOOK AT THIS! MY FAIR ELEANOR. AND LITTLE ROBYN.
MY FIRST SON BORN IN OVER 200 YEARS ON THIS EARTH. WELL, THAT I HAVE KNOWN OF, ANYWAY.
AND THE QUEEN HERSELF SLEPT AT MY HOUSE LAST SUMMER. THAT WAS EXPENSIVE.
IT'S FUNNY...
THIS IS WHAT I ALWAYS DREAMED HEAVEN WOULD BE LIKE, WAY BACK. IT'S SAFE TO WALK THE STREETS. ENOUGH FOOD, AND GOOD WINE.
LIFE IS SO RICH.
MORE WINE! MORE ALE! AND BUSS ME QUICK, MY SWEET.
I'LL STICK WITH BOYS-- MY HORNED "ACTRESSES."
SWEET KIT. THE PLAY I GAVE YOU. DID YOU READ...?
I MUST CONFESS I HAVE. I...THOUGHT IT, WELL... YOU ACT WELL, WILL, BUT-- LISTEN, LET ME READ...
"HUNG BE THE HEAVENS WITH BLACK, YIELD DAY TO NIGHT! COMETS IMPORTING CHANGE OF TIMES AND STATES, BRANDISH YOUR CRYSTAL TRESSES IN THE SKY, AND WITH THEM SCOURGE THE BAD, REVOLTING STARS."
AT LEAST IT SCANS. BUT "BAD REVOLTING STARS"?
IT'S MY FIRST PLAY.
AND IT SHOULD BE YOUR LAST.

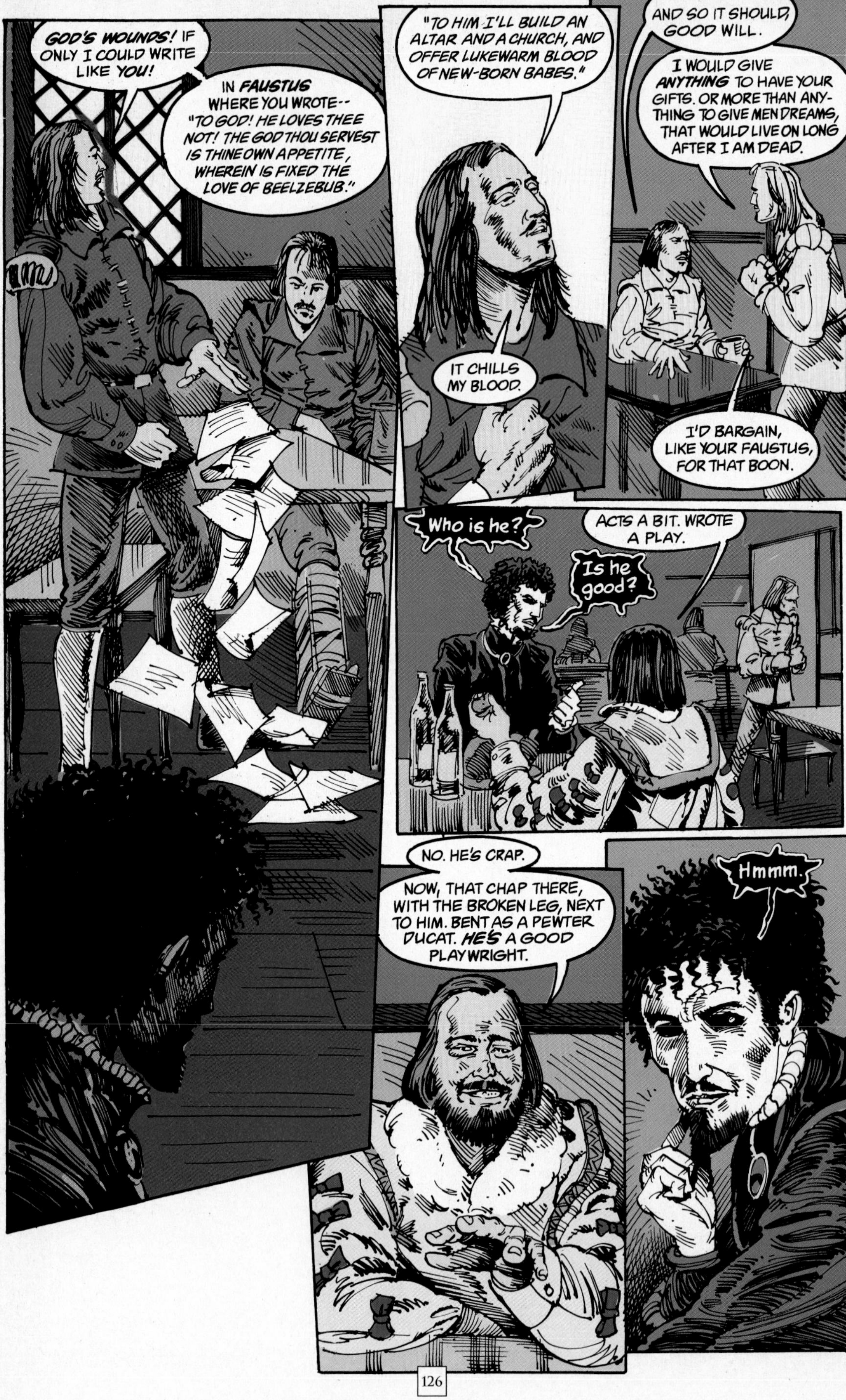

GOD'S WOUNDS! IF ONLY I COULD WRITE LIKE YOU!
IN FAUSTUS WHERE YOU WROTE-- "TO GOD! HE LOVES THEE NOT! THE GOD THOU SERVEST IS THINE OWN APPETITE, WHEREIN IS FIXED THE LOVE OF BEELZEBUB."
"TO HIM I'LL BUILD AN ALTAR AND A CHURCH, AND OFFER LUKEWARM BLOOD OF NEW-BORN BABES."
IT CHILLS MY BLOOD.
AND SO IT SHOULD, GOOD WILL.
I WOULD GIVE ANYTHING TO HAVE YOUR GIFTS. OR MORE THAN ANYTHING TO GIVE MEN DREAMS, THAT WOULD LIVE ON LONG AFTER I AM DEAD.
I'D BARGAIN, LIKE YOUR FAUSTUS, FOR THAT BOON.
Who is he?
ACTS A BIT. WROTE A PLAY.
Is he good?
NO. HE'S CRAP.
NOW, THAT CHAP THERE, WITH THE BROKEN LEG, NEXT TO HIM. BENT AS A PEWTER DUCAT. HE'S A GOOD PLAYWRIGHT.
Hmmm.

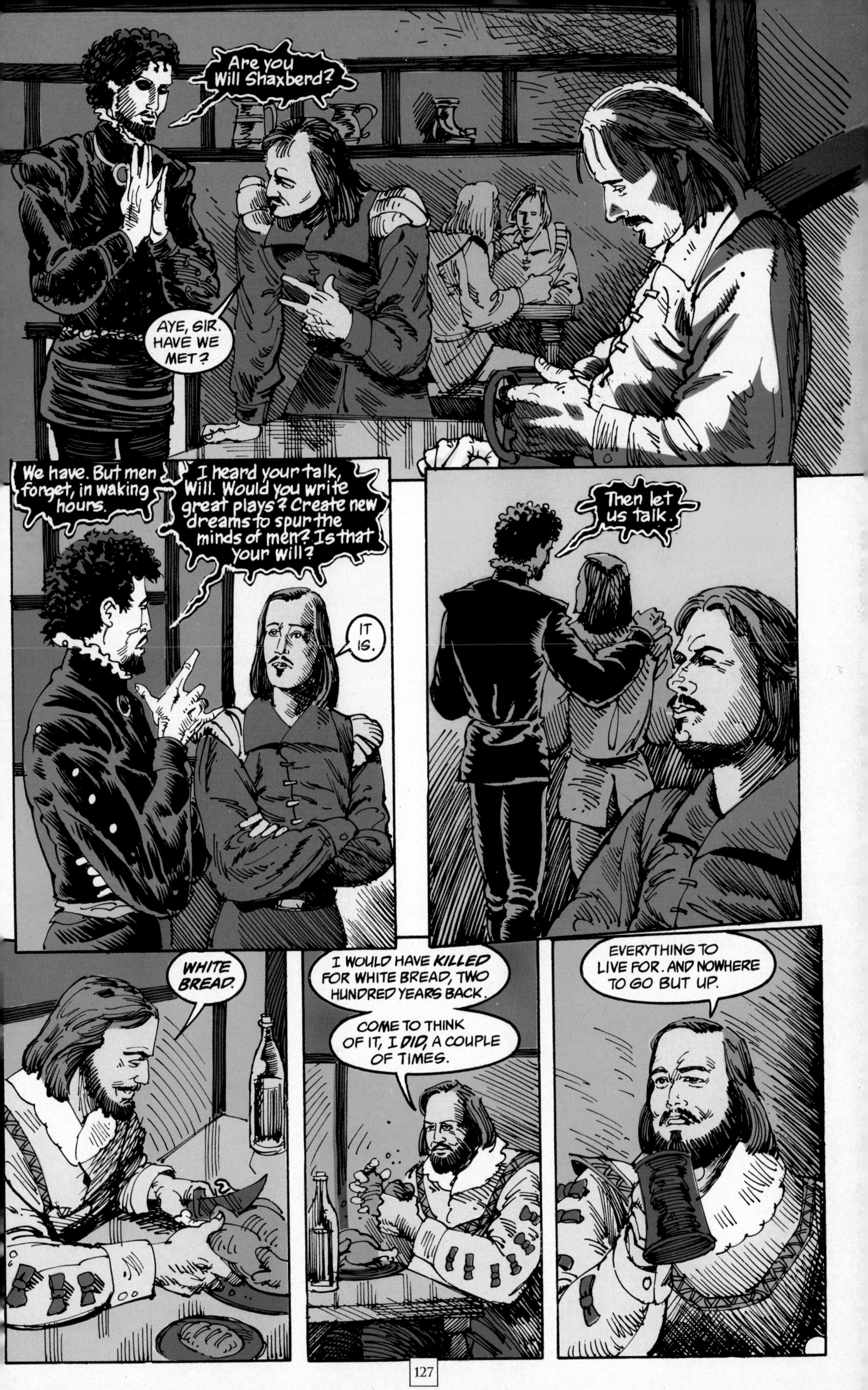
Are you Will Shaxberd?
AYE, SIR. HAVE WE MET?
We have. But men forget, in waking hours.
I heard your talk, Will. Would you write great plays? Create new dreams to spur the minds of men? Is that your will?
IT IS.
Then let us talk.
WHITE BREAD.
I WOULD HAVE KILLED FOR WHITE BREAD, TWO HUNDRED YEARS BACK.
COME TO THINK OF IT, I DID, A COUPLE OF TIMES.
EVERYTHING TO LIVE FOR. AND NOWHERE TO GO BUT UP.

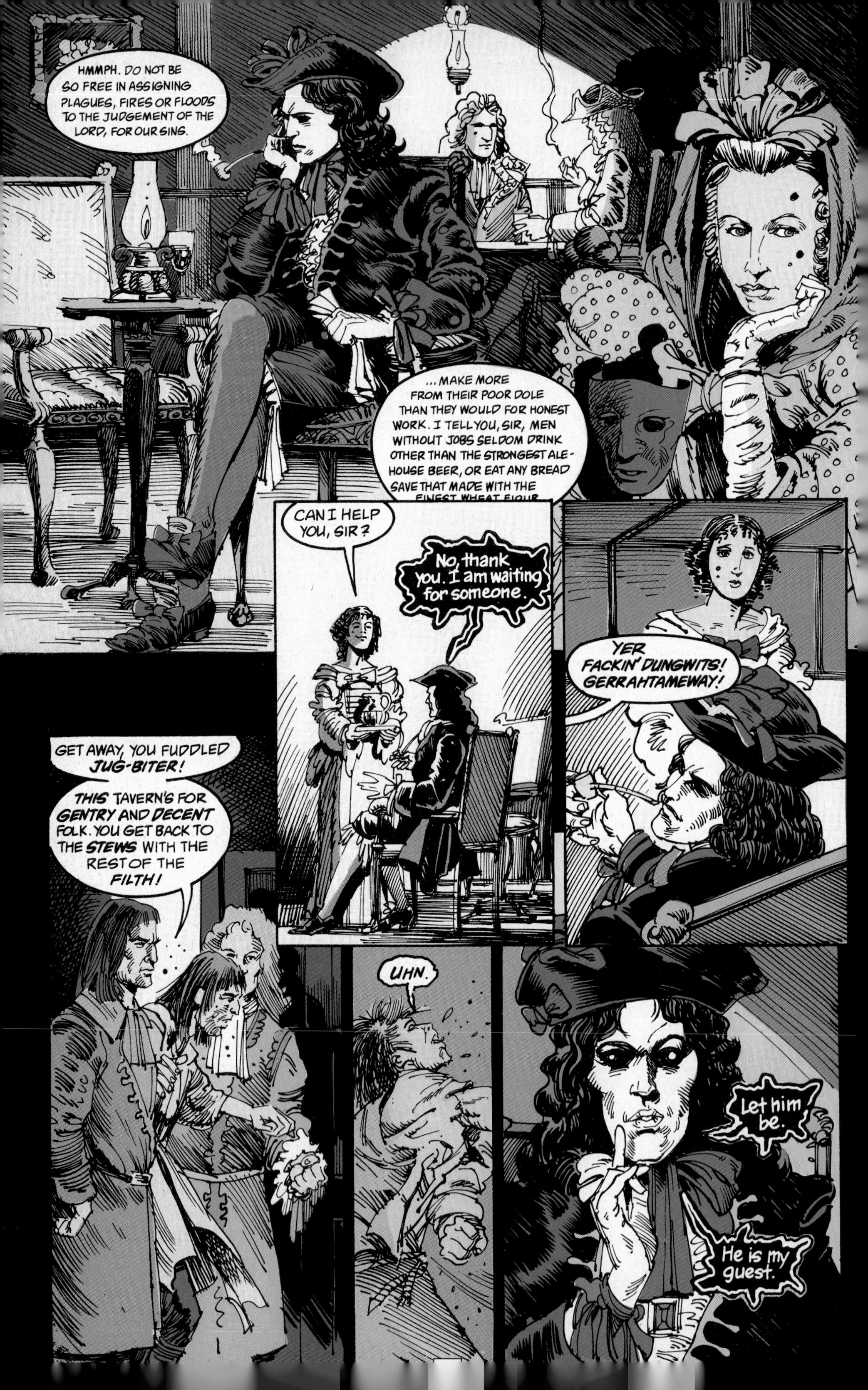

HMMPH. DO NOT BE SO FREE IN ASSIGNING PLAGUES, FIRES OR FLOODS TO THE JUDGEMENT OF THE LORD, FOR OUR SINS.
...MAKE MORE FROM THEIR POOR DOLE THAN THEY WOULD FOR HONEST WORK. I TELL YOU, SIR, MEN WITHOUT JOBS SELDOM DRINK OTHER THAN THE STRONGEST ALE-HOUSE BEER, OR EAT ANY BREAD SAVE THAT MADE WITH THE
CAN I HELP YOU, SIR?
No, thank you. I am waiting for someone.
YER FACKIN' DUNGWITS! GERRAHTAMEWAY!
GET AWAY, YOU FUDDLED JUG-BITER!
THIS TAVERN'S FOR GENTRY AND DECENT FOLK. YOU GET BACK TO THE STEWS WITH THE REST OF THE FILTH!
UHN.
Let him be.
He is my guest.

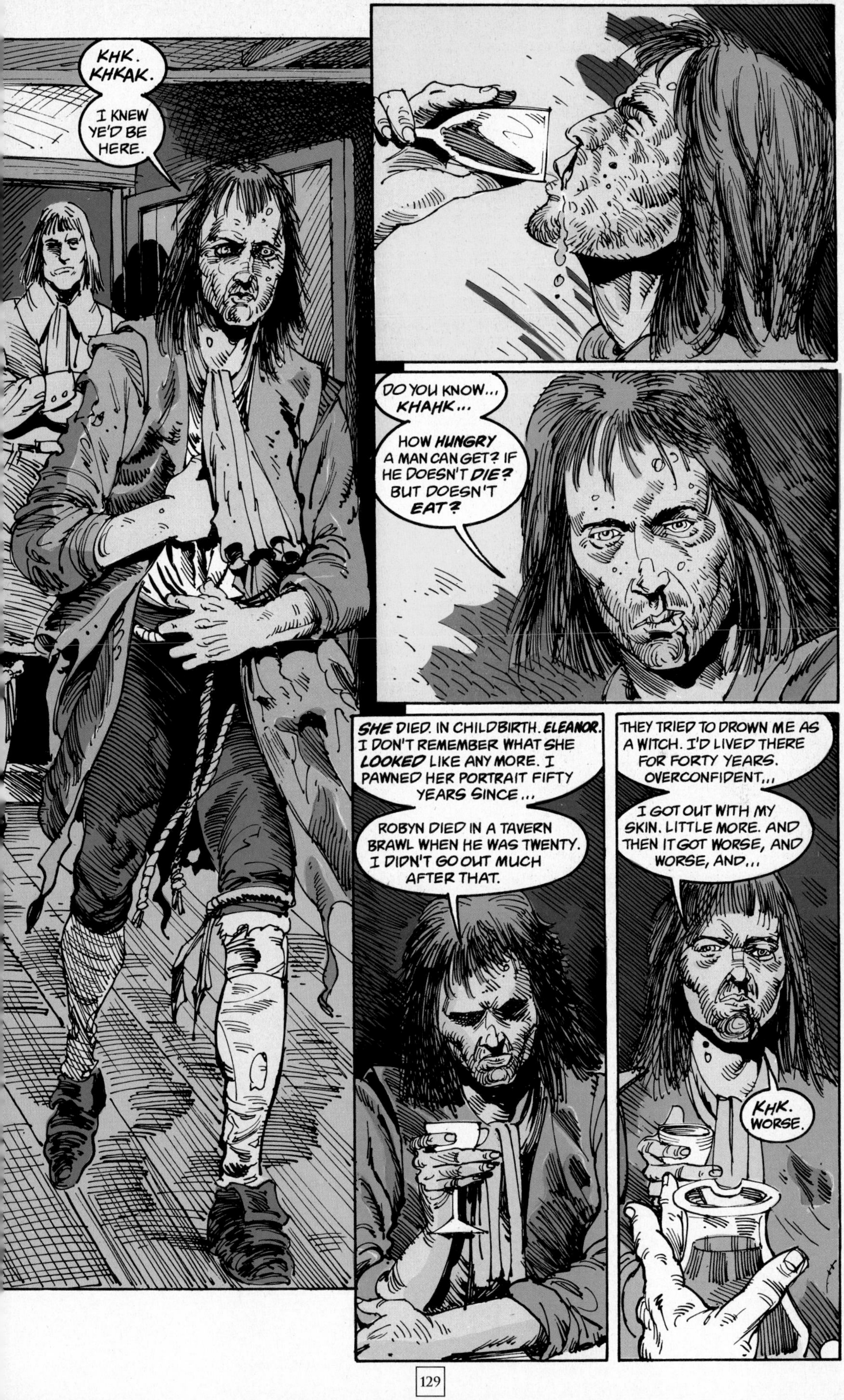
KHK. KHKAK.
I KNEW YE'D BE HERE.
DO YOU KNOW... KHAHK...
HOW HUNGRY A MAN CAN GET? IF HE DOESN'T DIE? BUT DOESN'T EAT?
SHE DIED. IN CHILDBIRTH. ELEANOR. I DON'T REMEMBER WHAT SHE LOOKED LIKE ANY MORE. I PAWNED HER PORTRAIT FIFTY YEARS SINCE...
ROBYN DIED IN A TAVERN BRAWL WHEN HE WAS TWENTY. I DIDN'T GO OUT MUCH AFTER THAT.
THEY TRIED TO DROWN ME AS A WITCH. I'D LIVED THERE FOR FORTY YEARS. OVERCONFIDENT...
I GOT OUT WITH MY SKIN. LITTLE MORE. AND THEN IT GOT WORSE, AND WORSE, AND...
KHK. WORSE.

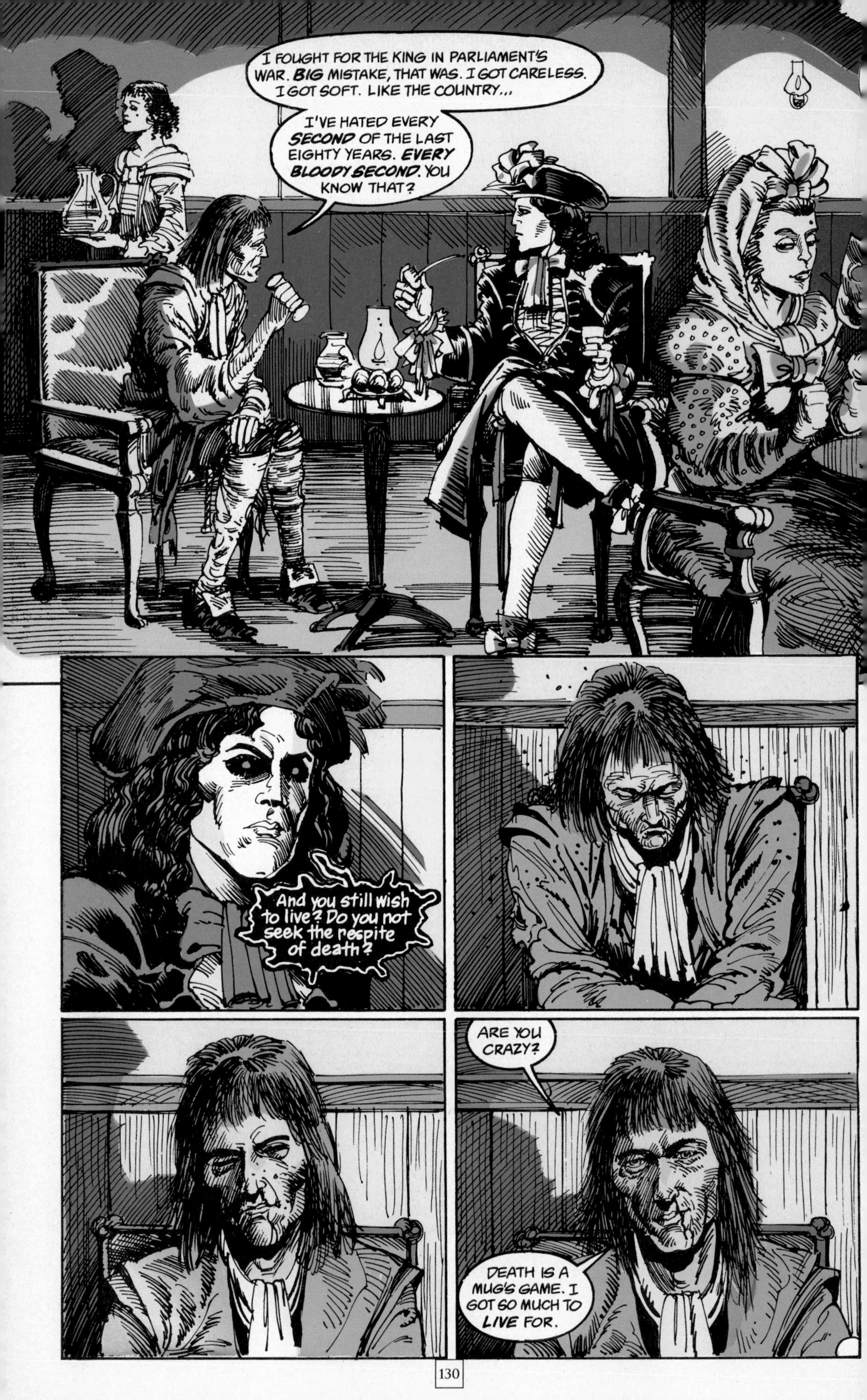
I FOUGHT FOR THE KING IN PARLIAMENT'S WAR. BIG MISTAKE, THAT WAS. I GOT CARELESS. I GOT SOFT. LIKE THE COUNTRY...
I'VE HATED EVERY SECOND OF THE LAST EIGHTY YEARS. EVERY BLOODY SECOND. YOU KNOW THAT?
And you still wish to live? Do you not seek the respite of death?
ARE YOU CRAZY?
DEATH IS A MUG'S GAME. I GOT SO MUCH TO LIVE FOR.

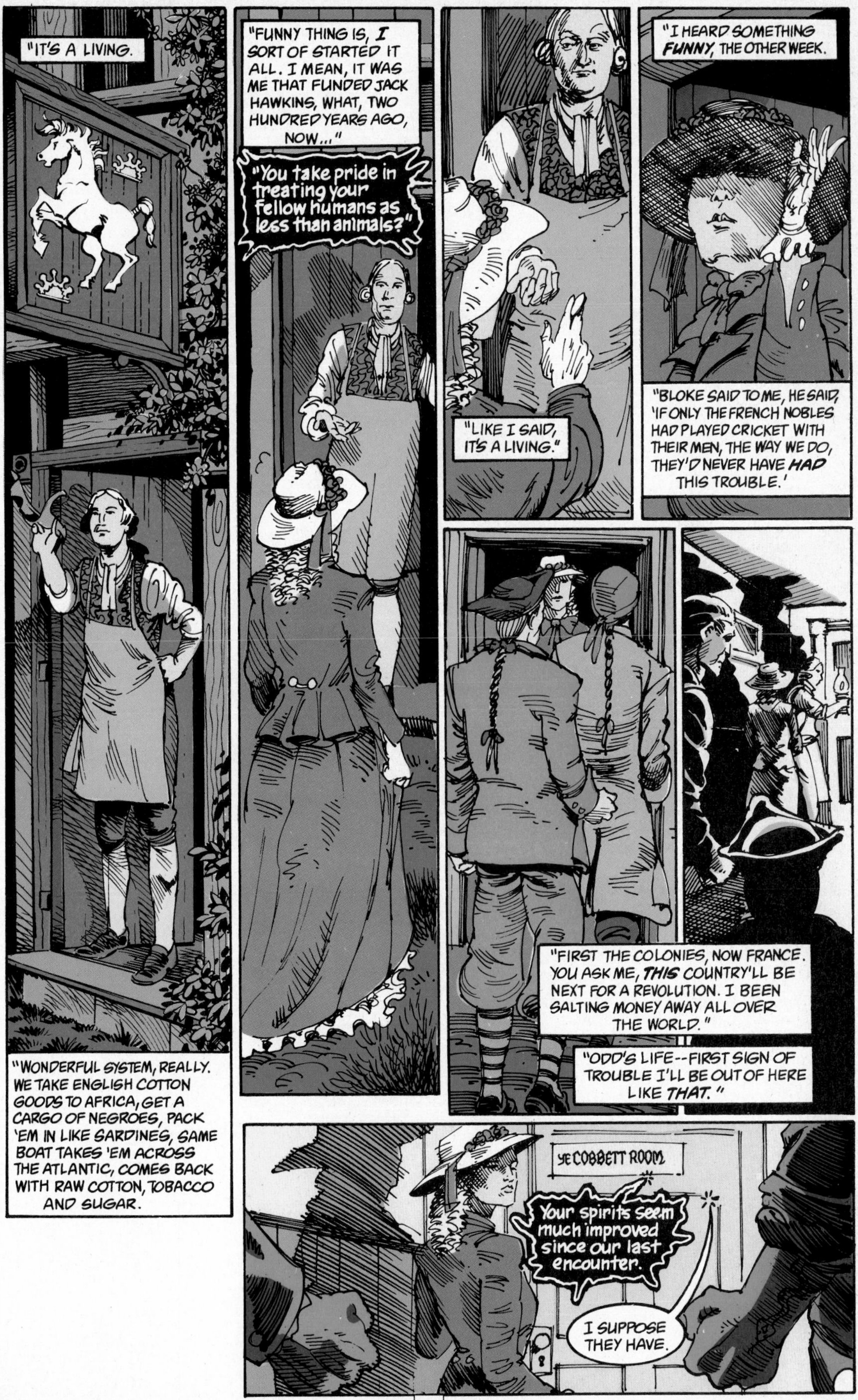

"IT'S A LIVING.
"WONDERFUL SYSTEM, REALLY. WE TAKE ENGLISH COTTON GOODS TO AFRICA, GET A CARGO OF NEGROES, PACK 'EM IN LIKE SARDINES, SAME BOAT TAKES 'EM ACROSS THE ATLANTIC, COMES BACK WITH RAW COTTON, TOBACCO AND SUGAR.
"FUNNY THING IS, I SORT OF STARTED IT ALL. I MEAN, IT WAS ME THAT FUNDED JACK HAWKINS, WHAT, TWO HUNDRED YEARS AGO, NOW..."
"You take pride in treating your fellow humans as less than animals?"
"LIKE I SAID, IT'S A LIVING."
"I HEARD SOMETHING FUNNY, THE OTHER WEEK.
"BLOKE SAID TO ME, HE SAID, 'IF ONLY THE FRENCH NOBLES HAD PLAYED CRICKET WITH THEIR MEN, THE WAY WE DO, THEY'D NEVER HAVE HAD THIS TROUBLE.'
"FIRST THE COLONIES, NOW FRANCE. YOU ASK ME, THIS COUNTRY'LL BE NEXT FOR A REVOLUTION. I BEEN SALTING MONEY AWAY ALL OVER THE WORLD."
"ODD'S LIFE--FIRST SIGN OF TROUBLE I'LL BE OUT OF HERE LIKE THAT."
YE COBBETT ROOM
Your spirits seem much improved since our last encounter.
I SUPPOSE THEY HAVE.

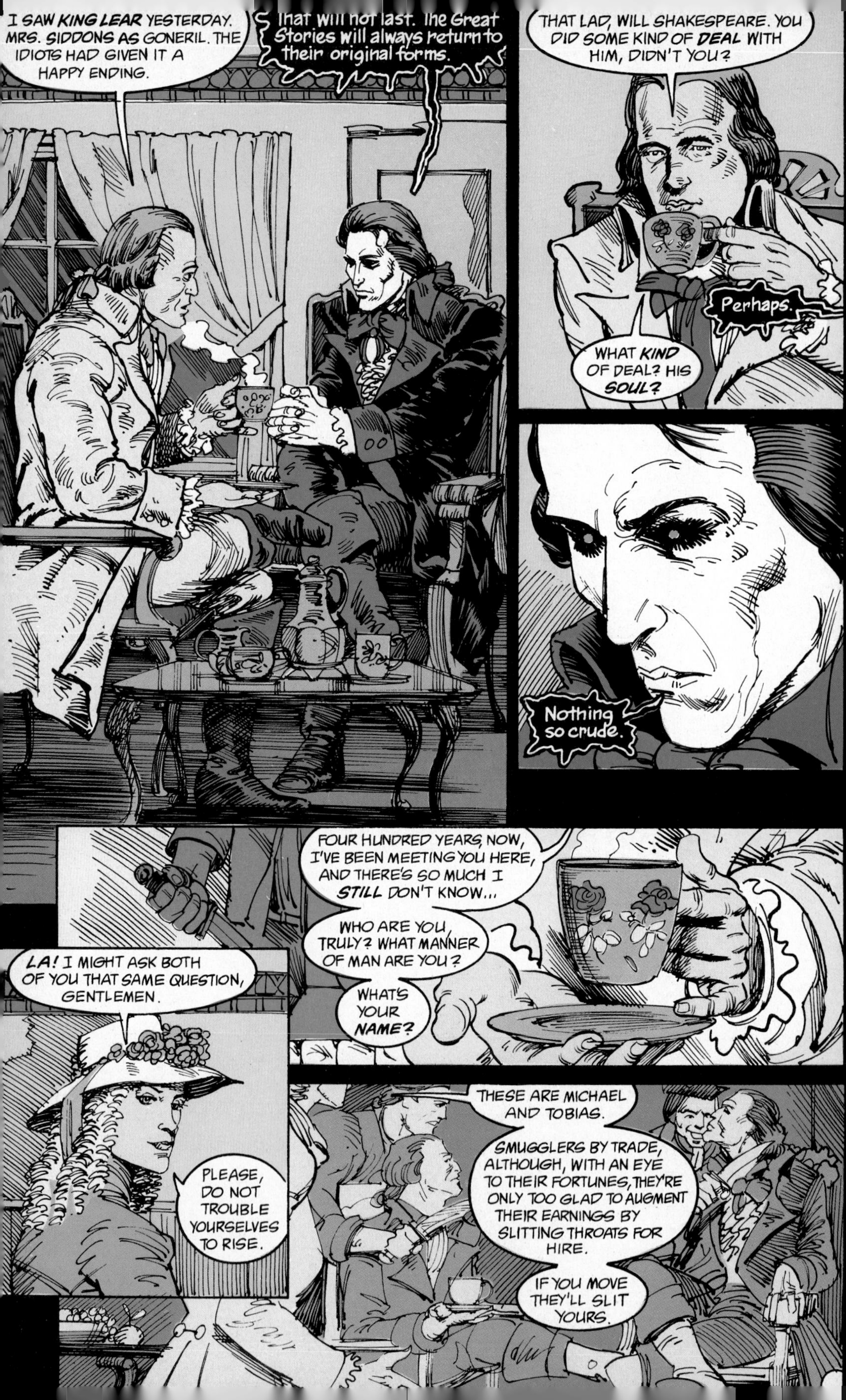
I SAW KING LEAR YESTERDAY. MRS. SIDDONS AS GONERIL. THE IDIOTS HAD GIVEN IT A HAPPY ENDING.
That will not last. The Great Stories will always return to their original forms.
THAT LAD, WILL SHAKESPEARE. YOU DID SOME KIND OF DEAL WITH HIM, DIDN'T YOU?
Perhaps.
WHAT KIND OF DEAL? HIS SOUL?
Nothing so crude.
FOUR HUNDRED YEARS, NOW, I'VE BEEN MEETING YOU HERE, AND THERE'S SO MUCH I STILL DON'T KNOW...
WHO ARE YOU, TRULY? WHAT MANNER OF MAN ARE YOU?
WHAT'S YOUR NAME?
LA! I MIGHT ASK BOTH OF YOU THAT SAME QUESTION, GENTLEMEN.
PLEASE, DO NOT TROUBLE YOURSELVES TO RISE.
THESE ARE MICHAEL AND TOBIAS.
SMUGGLERS BY TRADE, ALTHOUGH, WITH AN EYE TO THEIR FORTUNES, THEY'RE ONLY TOO GLAD TO AUGMENT THEIR EARNINGS BY SLITTING THROATS FOR HIRE.
IF YOU MOVE THEY'LL SLIT YOURS.

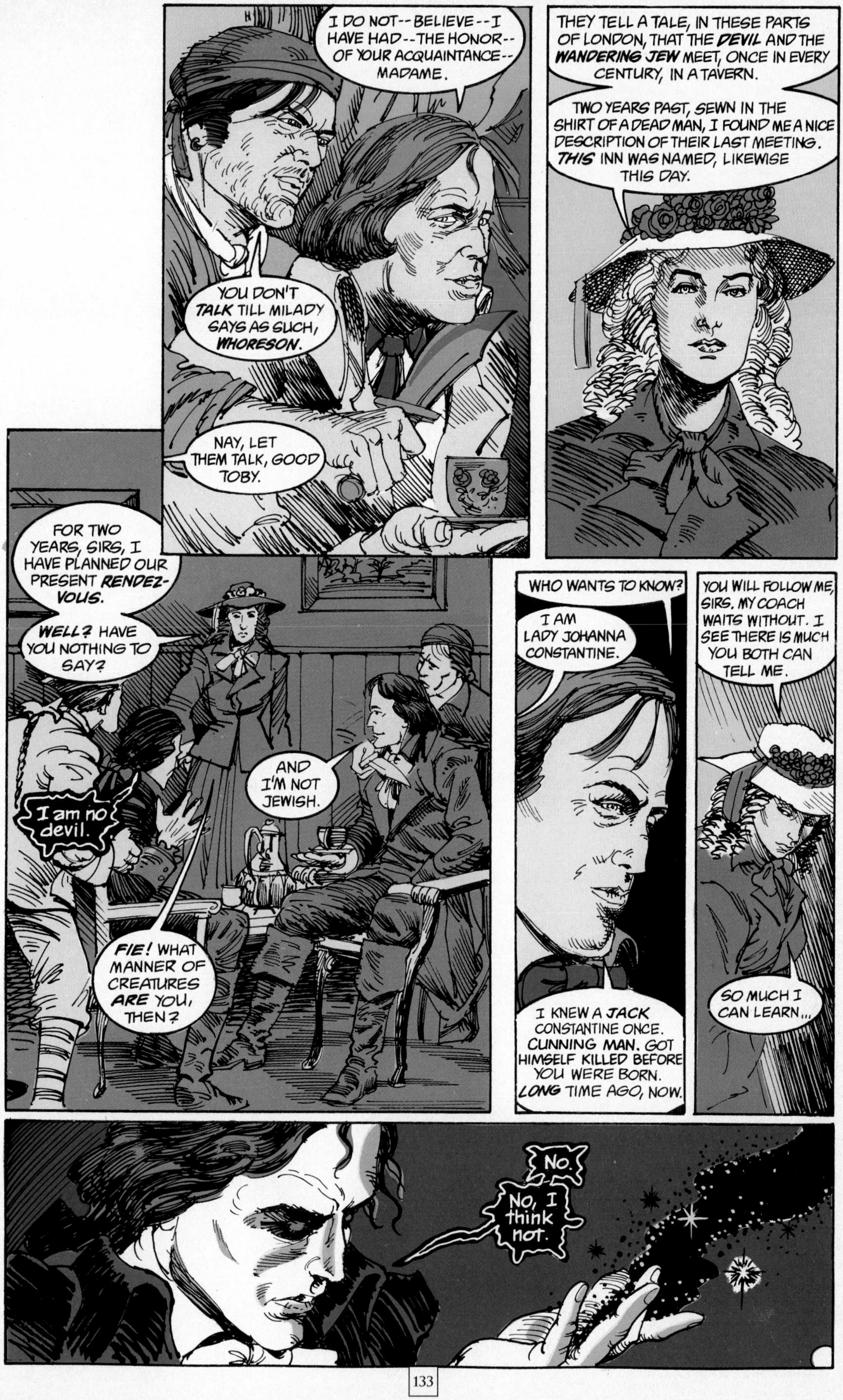

I DO NOT--BELIEVE--I HAVE HAD--THE HONOR--OF YOUR ACQUAINTANCE--MADAME.
YOU DON'T TALK TILL MILADY SAYS AS SUCH, WHORESON.
NAY, LET THEM TALK, GOOD TOBY.
THEY TELL A TALE, IN THESE PARTS OF LONDON, THAT THE DEVIL AND THE WANDERING JEW MEET, ONCE IN EVERY CENTURY, IN A TAVERN.
TWO YEARS PAST, SEWN IN THE SHIRT OF A DEAD MAN, I FOUND ME A NICE DESCRIPTION OF THEIR LAST MEETING. THIS INN WAS NAMED, LIKEWISE THIS DAY.
FOR TWO YEARS, SIRS, I HAVE PLANNED OUR PRESENT RENDEZ-VOUS.
WELL? HAVE YOU NOTHING TO SAY?
AND I'M NOT JEWISH.
I am no devil.
FIE! WHAT MANNER OF CREATURES ARE YOU, THEN?
WHO WANTS TO KNOW?
I AM LADY JOHANNA CONSTANTINE.
I KNEW A JACK CONSTANTINE ONCE. CUNNING MAN. GOT HIMSELF KILLED BEFORE YOU WERE BORN. LONG TIME AGO, NOW.
YOU WILL FOLLOW ME, SIRS. MY COACH WAITS WITHOUT. I SEE THERE IS MUCH YOU BOTH CAN TELL ME.
SO MUCH I CAN LEARN...
No.
No, I think not.

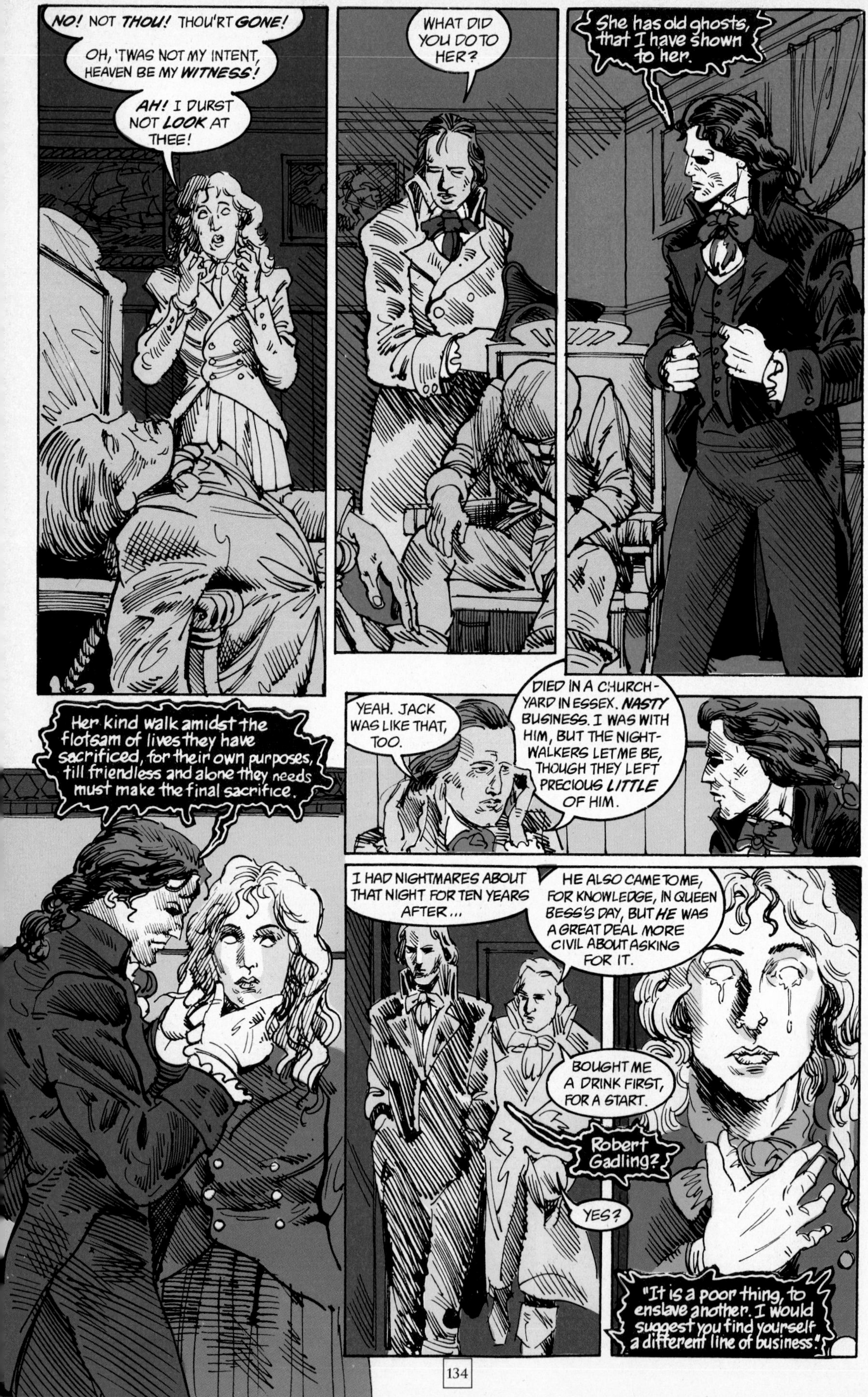

NO! NOT THOU! THOU'RT GONE!
OH, 'TWAS NOT MY INTENT, HEAVEN BE MY WITNESS!
AH! I DURST NOT LOOK AT THEE!
WHAT DID YOU DO TO HER?
She has old ghosts, that I have shown to her.
Her kind walk amidst the flotsam of lives they have sacrificed, for their own purposes, till friendless and alone they needs must make the final sacrifice.
YEAH. JACK WAS LIKE THAT, TOO.
DIED IN A CHURCHYARD IN ESSEX. NASTY BUSINESS. I WAS WITH HIM, BUT THE NIGHT-WALKERS LET ME BE, THOUGH THEY LEFT PRECIOUS LITTLE OF HIM.
I HAD NIGHTMARES ABOUT THAT NIGHT FOR TEN YEARS AFTER...
HE ALSO CAME TO ME, FOR KNOWLEDGE, IN QUEEN BESS'S DAY, BUT HE WAS A GREAT DEAL MORE CIVIL ABOUT ASKING FOR IT.
BOUGHT ME A DRINK FIRST, FOR A START.
Robert Gadling?
YES?
"It is a poor thing, to enslave another. I would suggest you find yourself a different line of business."

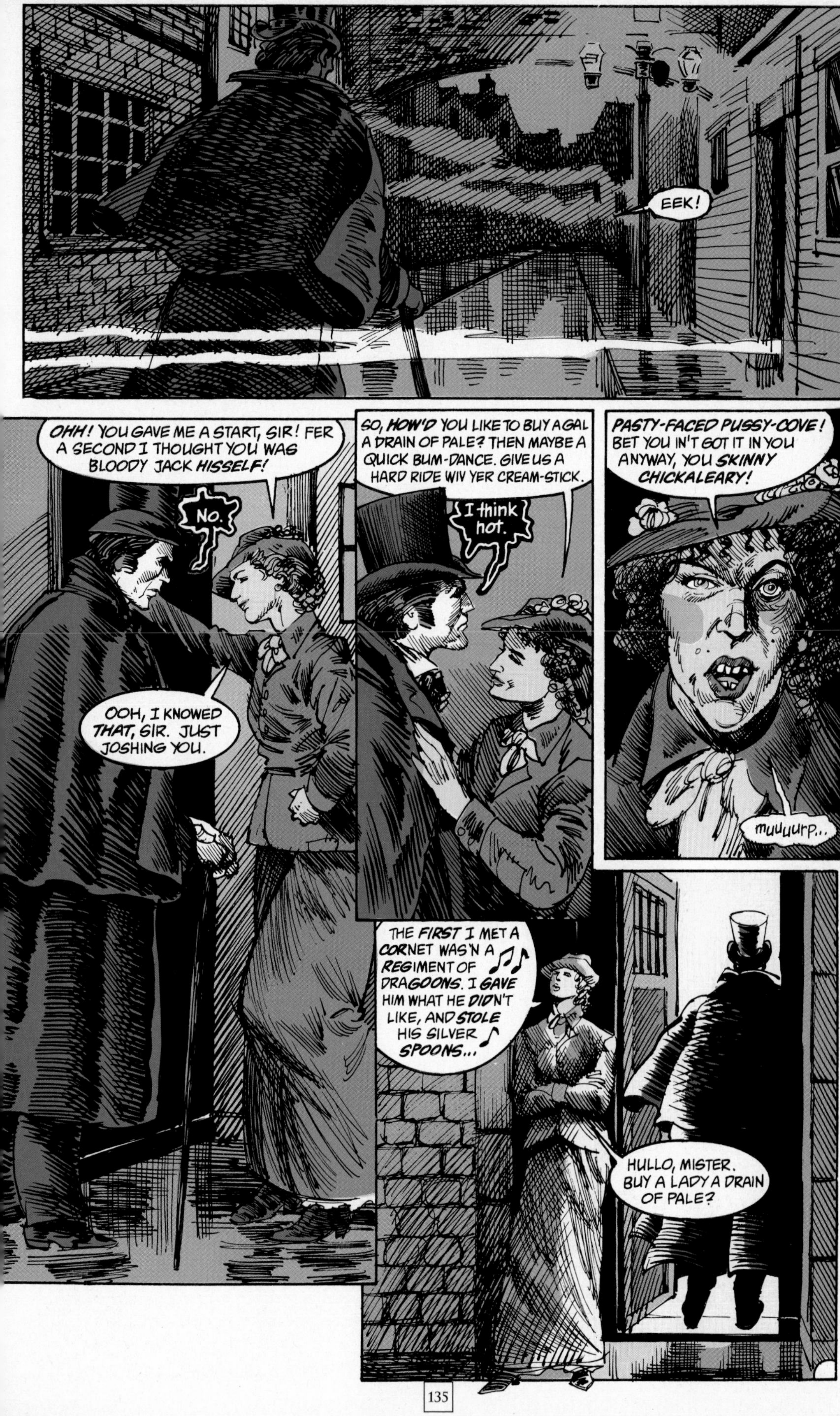

EEK!
OHH! YOU GAVE ME A START, SIR! FER A SECOND I THOUGHT YOU WAS BLOODY JACK HISSELF!
No.
OOH, I KNOWED THAT, SIR. JUST JOSHING YOU.
SO, HOW'D YOU LIKE TO BUY A GAL A DRAIN OF PALE? THEN MAYBE A QUICK BUM-DANCE. GIVE US A HARD RIDE WIV YER CREAM-STICK.
I think not.
PASTY-FACED PUSSY-COVE! BET YOU IN'T GOT IT IN YOU ANYWAY, YOU SKINNY CHICKALEARY!
muuuurp...
THE FIRST I MET A CORNET WAS'N A REGIMENT OF DRAGOONS. I GAVE HIM WHAT HE DIDN'T LIKE, AND STOLE HIS SILVER SPOONS...
HULLO, MISTER. BUY A LADY A DRAIN OF PALE?

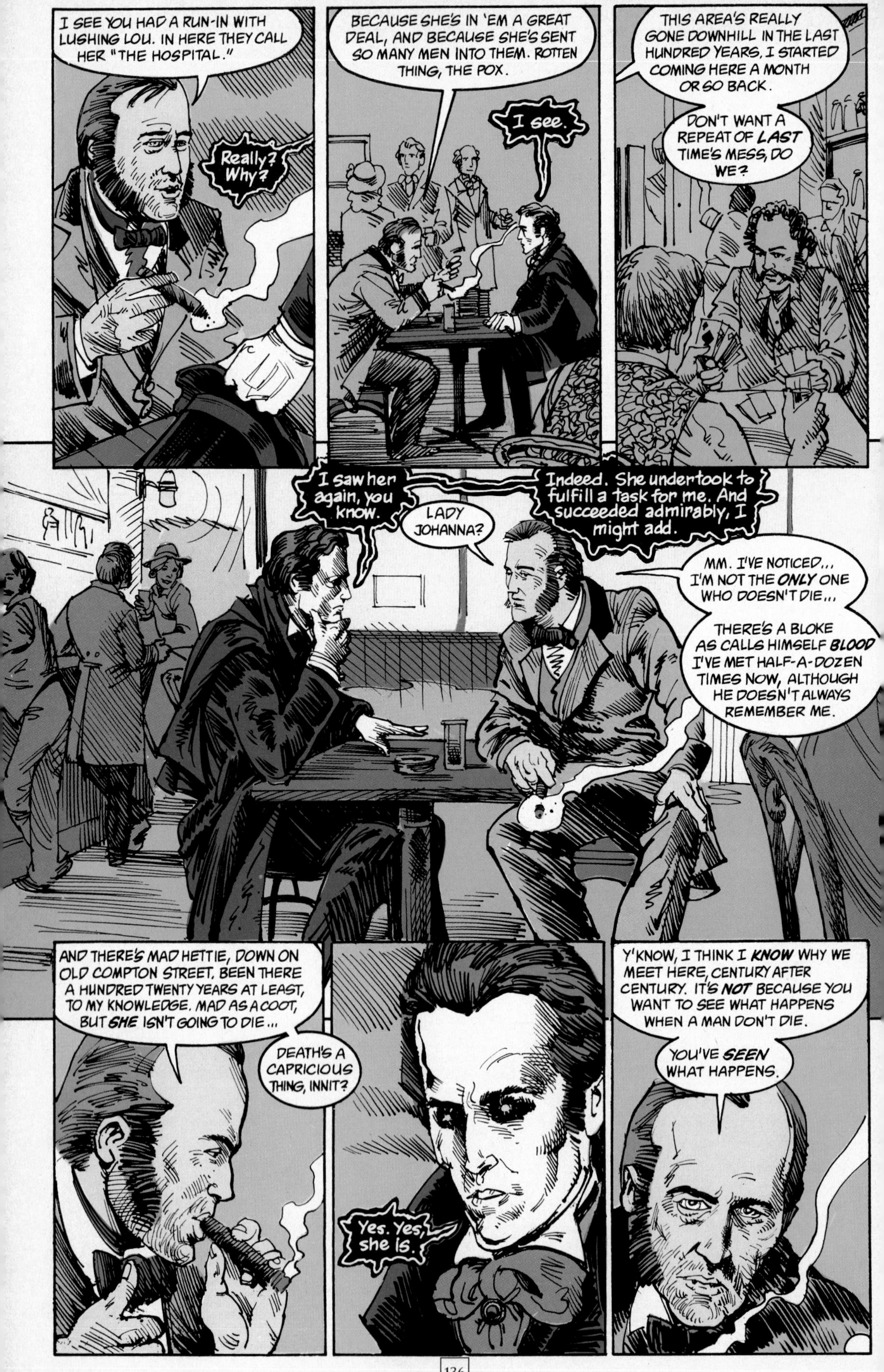
I SEE YOU HAD A RUN-IN WITH LUSHING LOU. IN HERE THEY CALL HER "THE HOSPITAL."
Really? Why?
BECAUSE SHE'S IN 'EM A GREAT DEAL, AND BECAUSE SHE'S SENT SO MANY MEN INTO THEM. ROTTEN THING, THE POX.
I see.
THIS AREA'S REALLY GONE DOWNHILL IN THE LAST HUNDRED YEARS, I STARTED COMING HERE A MONTH OR SO BACK.
DON'T WANT A REPEAT OF LAST TIME'S MESS, DO WE?
I saw her again, you know.
LADY JOHANNA?
Indeed. She undertook to fulfill a task for me. And succeeded admirably, I might add.
MM. I'VE NOTICED... I'M NOT THE ONLY ONE WHO DOESN'T DIE...
THERE'S A BLOKE AS CALLS HIMSELF BLOOD I'VE MET HALF-A-DOZEN TIMES NOW, ALTHOUGH HE DOESN'T ALWAYS REMEMBER ME.
AND THERE'S MAD HETTIE, DOWN ON OLD COMPTON STREET. BEEN THERE A HUNDRED TWENTY YEARS AT LEAST, TO MY KNOWLEDGE. MAD AS A COOT, BUT SHE ISN'T GOING TO DIE...
DEATH'S A CAPRICIOUS THING, INNIT?
Yes. Yes, she is.
Y'KNOW, I THINK I KNOW WHY WE MEET HERE, CENTURY AFTER CENTURY. IT'S NOT BECAUSE YOU WANT TO SEE WHAT HAPPENS WHEN A MAN DON'T DIE.
YOU'VE SEEN WHAT HAPPENS.

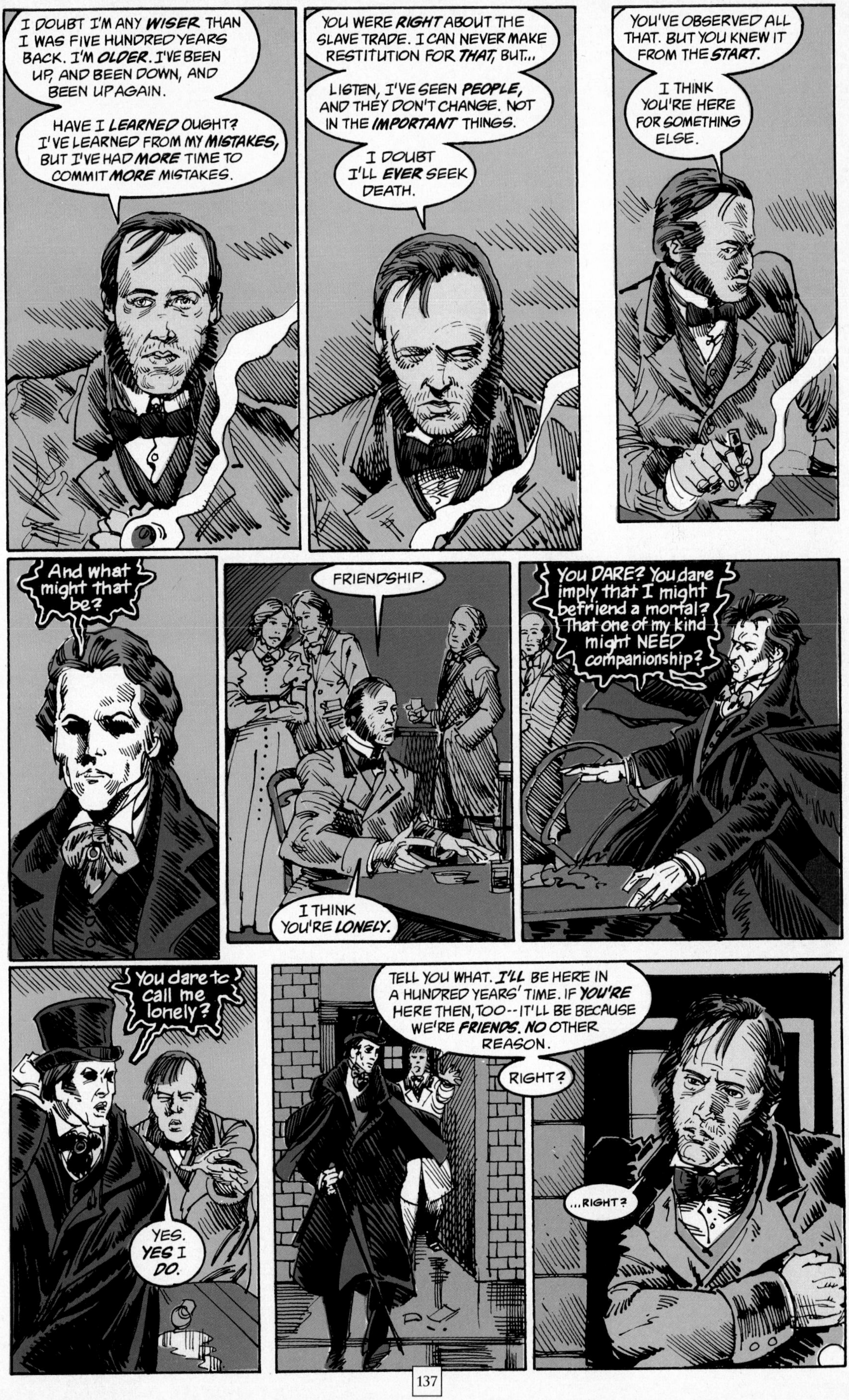
I DOUBT I'M ANY WISER THAN I WAS FIVE HUNDRED YEARS BACK. I'M OLDER. I'VE BEEN UP, AND BEEN DOWN, AND BEEN UP AGAIN.
HAVE I LEARNED OUGHT? I'VE LEARNED FROM MY MISTAKES, BUT I'VE HAD MORE TIME TO COMMIT MORE MISTAKES.
YOU WERE RIGHT ABOUT THE SLAVE TRADE. I CAN NEVER MAKE RESTITUTION FOR THAT, BUT...
LISTEN, I'VE SEEN PEOPLE, AND THEY DON'T CHANGE. NOT IN THE IMPORTANT THINGS.
I DOUBT I'LL EVER SEEK DEATH.
YOU'VE OBSERVED ALL THAT. BUT YOU KNEW IT FROM THE START.
I THINK YOU'RE HERE FOR SOMETHING ELSE.
And what might that be?
FRIENDSHIP.
I THINK YOU'RE LONELY.
You DARE? You dare imply that I might befriend a mortal? That one of my kind might NEED companionship?
You dare to call me lonely?
YES. YES I DO.
TELL YOU WHAT. I'LL BE HERE IN A HUNDRED YEARS' TIME. IF YOU'RE HERE THEN, TOO--IT'LL BE BECAUSE WE'RE FRIENDS. NO OTHER REASON.
RIGHT?
...RIGHT?

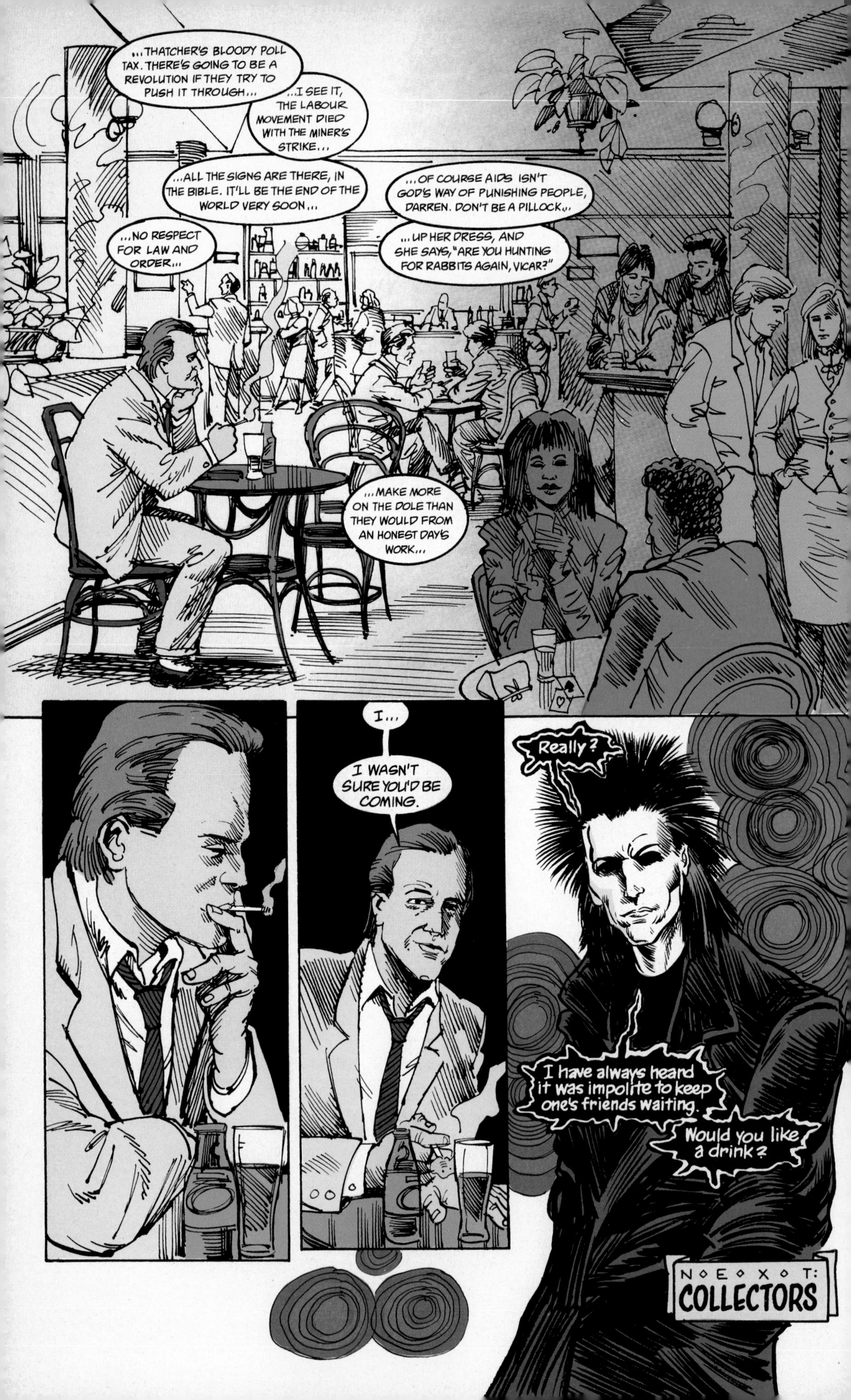
...THATCHER'S BLOODY POLL TAX. THERE'S GOING TO BE A REVOLUTION IF THEY TRY TO PUSH IT THROUGH...
...I SEE IT, THE LABOUR MOVEMENT DIED WITH THE MINER'S STRIKE...
...ALL THE SIGNS ARE THERE, IN THE BIBLE. IT'LL BE THE END OF THE WORLD VERY SOON...
...OF COURSE AIDS ISN'T GOD'S WAY OF PUNISHING PEOPLE, DARREN. DON'T BE A PILLOCK...
...NO RESPECT FOR LAW AND ORDER...
...UP HER DRESS, AND SHE SAYS, "ARE YOU HUNTING FOR RABBITS AGAIN, VICAR?"
...MAKE MORE ON THE DOLE THAN THEY WOULD FROM AN HONEST DAY'S WORK...
I...
I WASN'T SURE YOU'D BE COMING.
Really?
I have always heard it was impolite to keep one's friends waiting.
Would you like a drink?
NEXT: COLLECTORS

DOLL'S HOUSE
PART FIVE

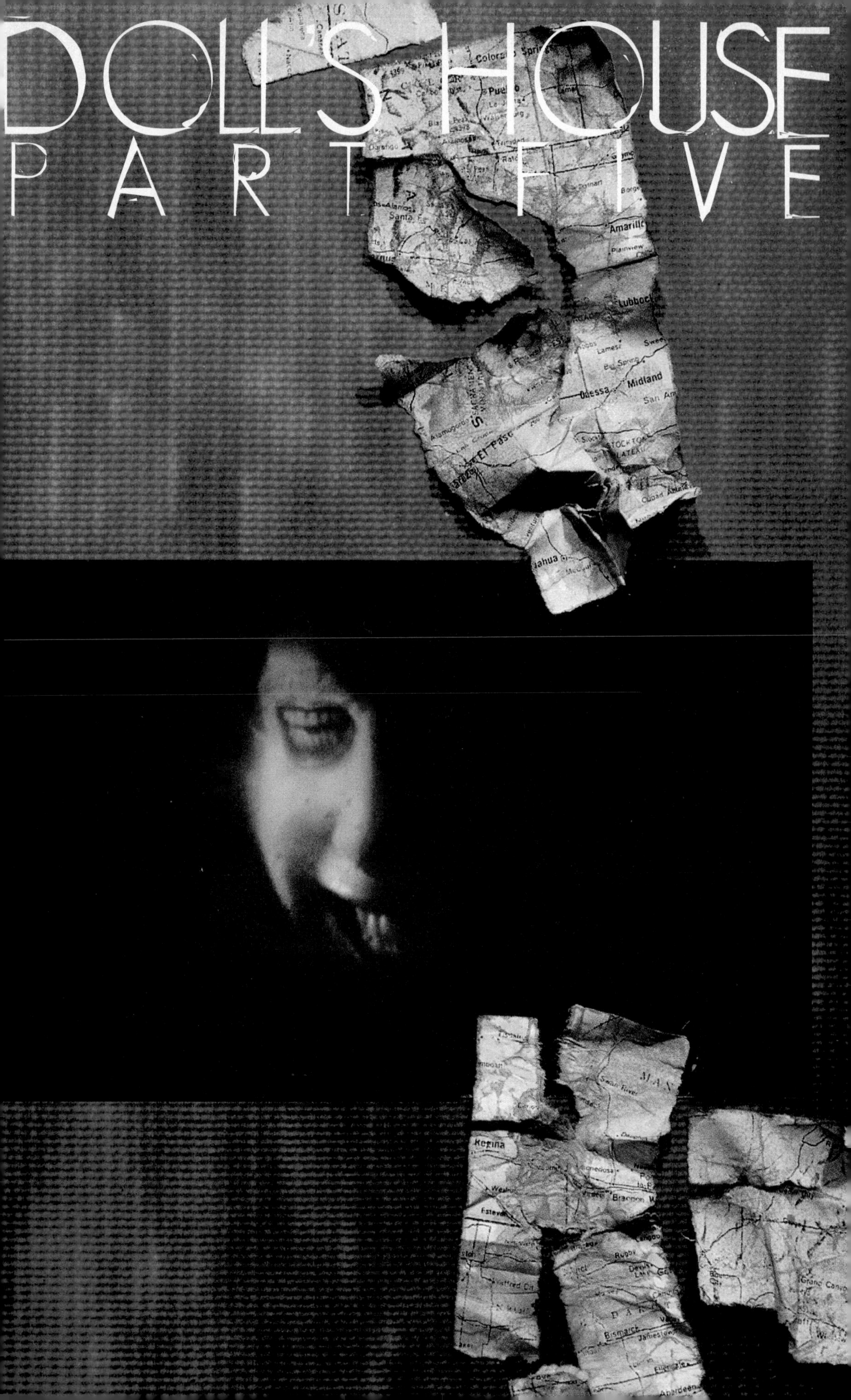
Pueblo
Amarillo
Lubbock
Midland
Odessa
El Paso
Regina
Bismarck

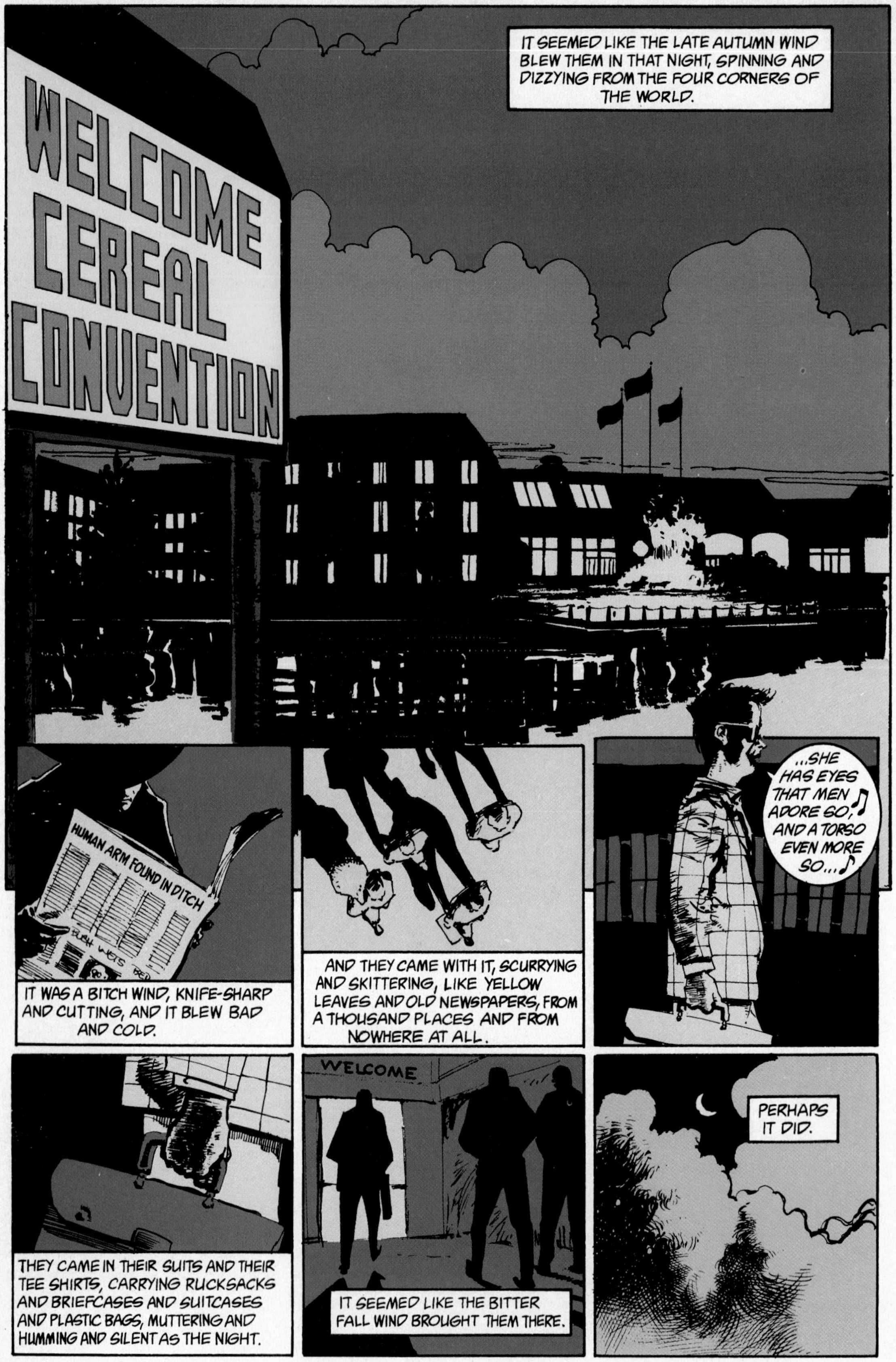
WELCOME CEREAL CONVENTION
IT SEEMED LIKE THE LATE AUTUMN WIND BLEW THEM IN THAT NIGHT, SPINNING AND DIZZYING FROM THE FOUR CORNERS OF THE WORLD.
HUMAN ARM FOUND IN DITCH
IT WAS A BITCH WIND, KNIFE-SHARP AND CUTTING, AND IT BLEW BAD AND COLD.
AND THEY CAME WITH IT, SCURRYING AND SKITTERING, LIKE YELLOW LEAVES AND OLD NEWSPAPERS, FROM A THOUSAND PLACES AND FROM NOWHERE AT ALL.
...SHE HAS EYES THAT MEN ADORE SO, AND A TORSO EVEN MORE SO...
THEY CAME IN THEIR SUITS AND THEIR TEE SHIRTS, CARRYING RUCKSACKS AND BRIEFCASES AND SUITCASES AND PLASTIC BAGS, MUTTERING AND HUMMING AND SILENT AS THE NIGHT.
WELCOME
IT SEEMED LIKE THE BITTER FALL WIND BROUGHT THEM THERE.
PERHAPS IT DID.

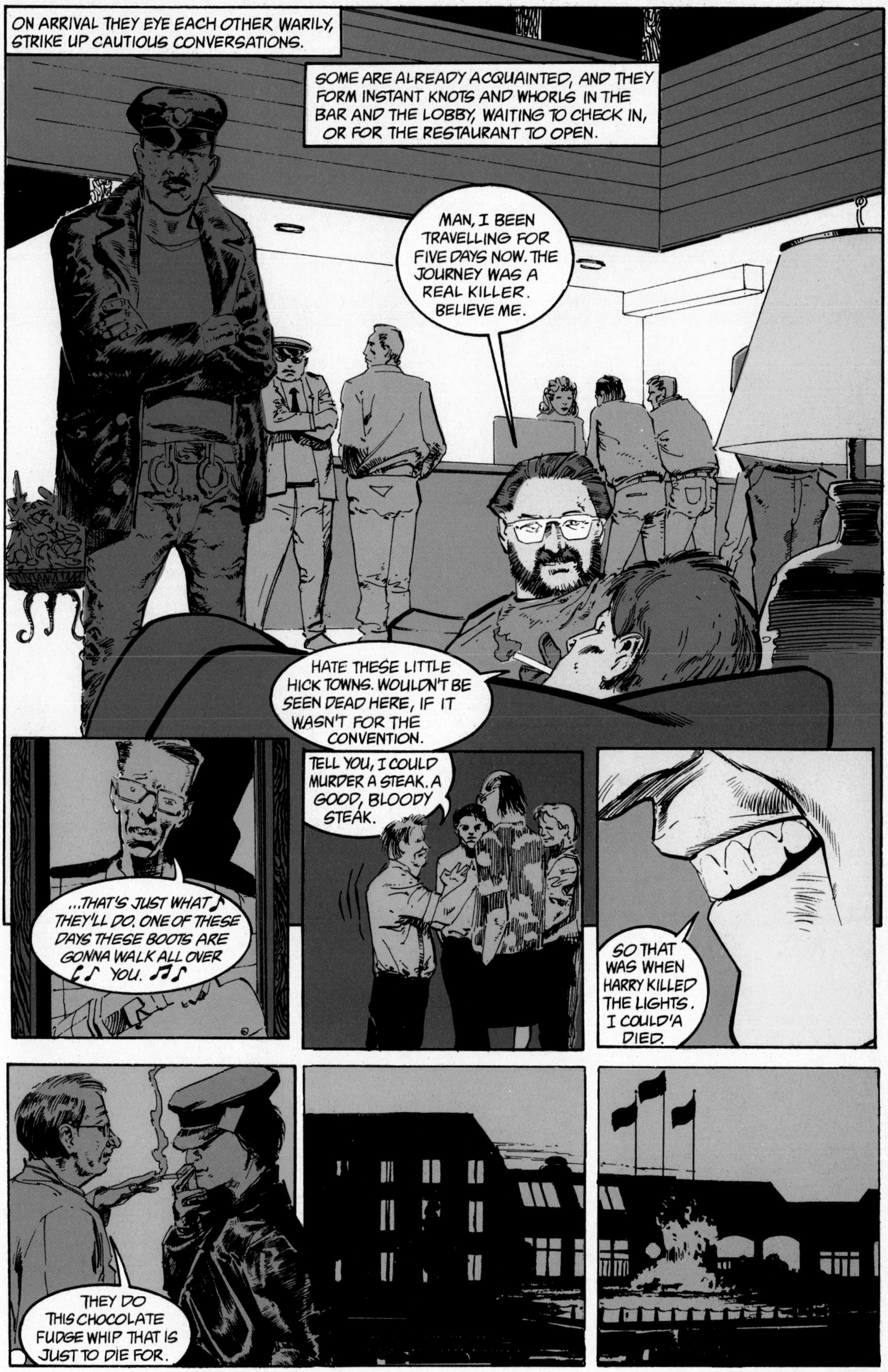

ON ARRIVAL THEY EYE EACH OTHER WARILY, STRIKE UP CAUTIOUS CONVERSATIONS.
SOME ARE ALREADY ACQUAINTED, AND THEY FORM INSTANT KNOTS AND WHORLS IN THE BAR AND THE LOBBY, WAITING TO CHECK IN, OR FOR THE RESTAURANT TO OPEN.
MAN, I BEEN TRAVELLING FOR FIVE DAYS NOW. THE JOURNEY WAS A REAL KILLER. BELIEVE ME.
HATE THESE LITTLE HICK TOWNS. WOULDN'T BE SEEN DEAD HERE, IF IT WASN'T FOR THE CONVENTION.
...THAT'S JUST WHAT THEY'LL DO. ONE OF THESE DAYS THESE BOOTS ARE GONNA WALK ALL OVER YOU.
TELL YOU, I COULD MURDER A STEAK. A GOOD, BLOODY STEAK.
SO THAT WAS WHEN HARRY KILLED THE LIGHTS. I COULD'A DIED.
THEY DO THIS CHOCOLATE FUDGE WHIP THAT IS JUST TO DIE FOR.

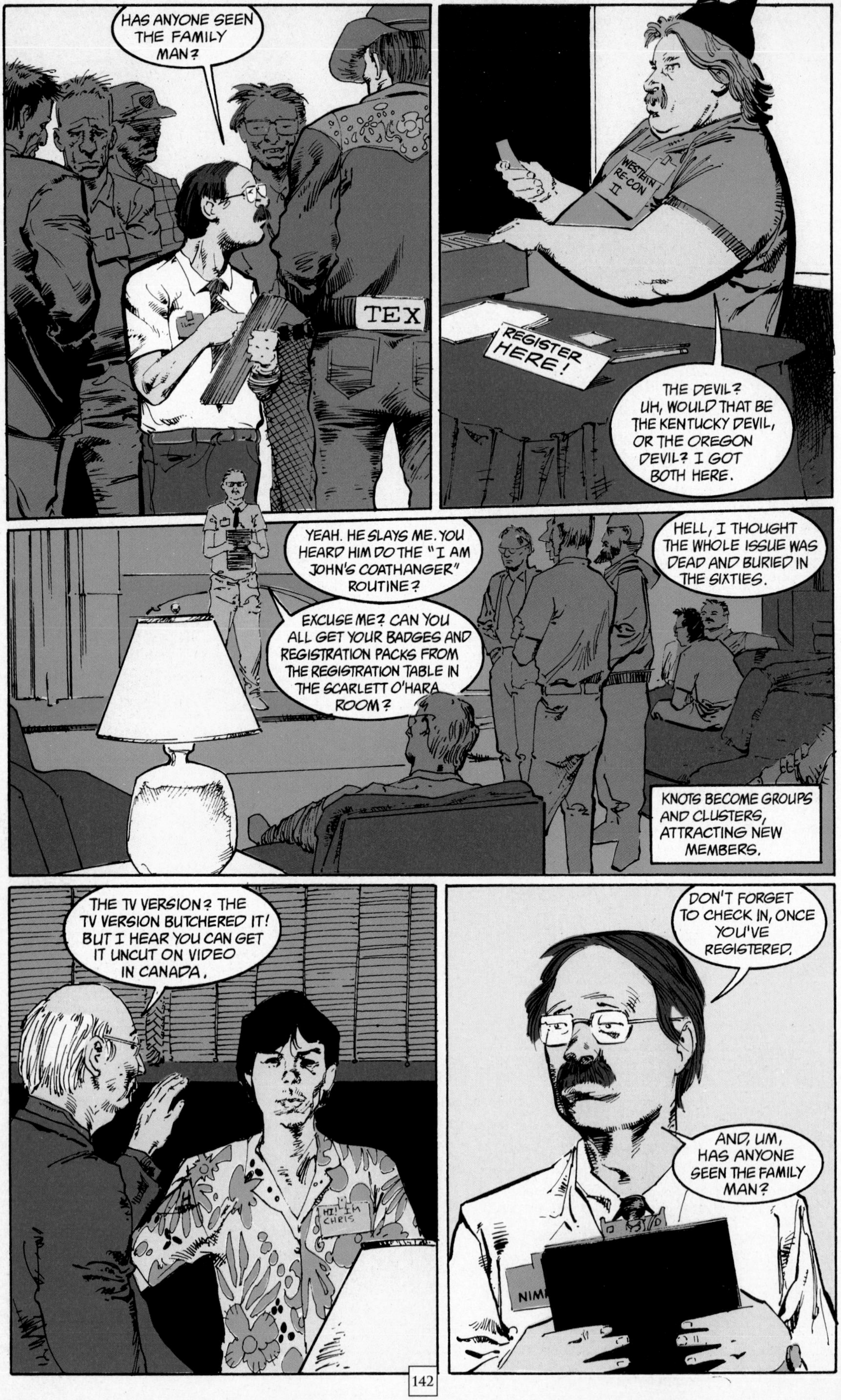
HAS ANYONE SEEN THE FAMILY MAN?
TEX
WESTERN RE-CON II
REGISTER HERE!
THE DEVIL? UH, WOULD THAT BE THE KENTUCKY DEVIL, OR THE OREGON DEVIL? I GOT BOTH HERE.
YEAH. HE SLAYS ME. YOU HEARD HIM DO THE "I AM JOHN'S COATHANGER" ROUTINE?
HELL, I THOUGHT THE WHOLE ISSUE WAS DEAD AND BURIED IN THE SIXTIES.
EXCUSE ME? CAN YOU ALL GET YOUR BADGES AND REGISTRATION PACKS FROM THE REGISTRATION TABLE IN THE SCARLETT O'HARA ROOM?
KNOTS BECOME GROUPS AND CLUSTERS, ATTRACTING NEW MEMBERS.
THE TV VERSION? THE TV VERSION BUTCHERED IT! BUT I HEAR YOU CAN GET IT UNCUT ON VIDEO IN CANADA.
HI! I'M CHRIS
DON'T FORGET TO CHECK IN, ONCE YOU'VE REGISTERED.
AND, UM, HAS ANYONE SEEN THE FAMILY MAN?

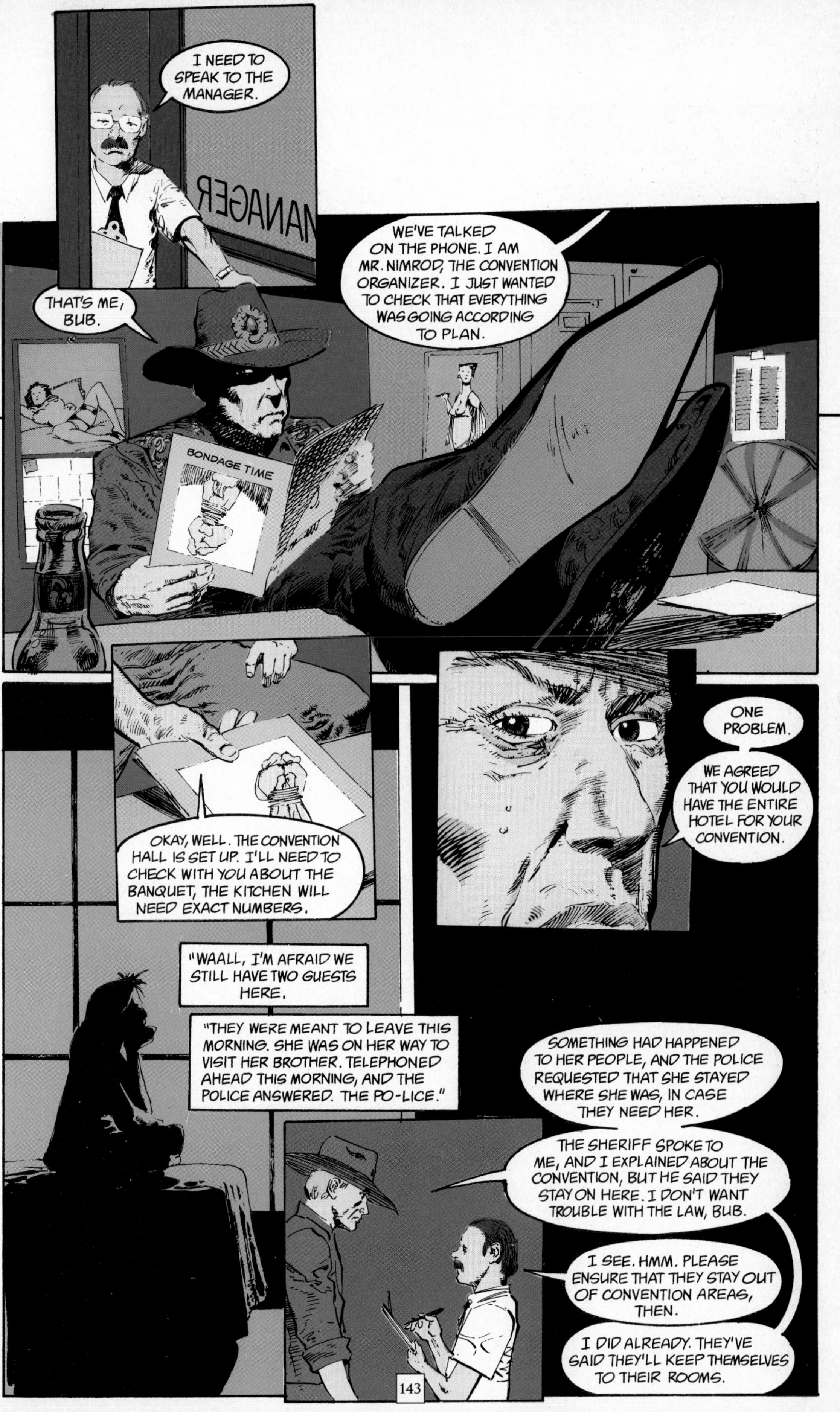

I NEED TO SPEAK TO THE MANAGER.
MANAGER
THAT'S ME, BUB.
WE'VE TALKED ON THE PHONE. I AM MR. NIMROD, THE CONVENTION ORGANIZER. I JUST WANTED TO CHECK THAT EVERYTHING WAS GOING ACCORDING TO PLAN.
BONDAGE TIME
OKAY, WELL. THE CONVENTION HALL IS SET UP. I'LL NEED TO CHECK WITH YOU ABOUT THE BANQUET, THE KITCHEN WILL NEED EXACT NUMBERS.
ONE PROBLEM.
WE AGREED THAT YOU WOULD HAVE THE ENTIRE HOTEL FOR YOUR CONVENTION.
"WAALL, I'M AFRAID WE STILL HAVE TWO GUESTS HERE.
"THEY WERE MEANT TO LEAVE THIS MORNING. SHE WAS ON HER WAY TO VISIT HER BROTHER. TELEPHONED AHEAD THIS MORNING, AND THE POLICE ANSWERED. THE PO-LICE."
SOMETHING HAD HAPPENED TO HER PEOPLE, AND THE POLICE REQUESTED THAT SHE STAYED WHERE SHE WAS, IN CASE THEY NEED HER.
THE SHERIFF SPOKE TO ME, AND I EXPLAINED ABOUT THE CONVENTION, BUT HE SAID THEY STAY ON HERE. I DON'T WANT TROUBLE WITH THE LAW, BUB.
I SEE. HMM. PLEASE ENSURE THAT THEY STAY OUT OF CONVENTION AREAS, THEN.
I DID ALREADY. THEY'VE SAID THEY'LL KEEP THEMSELVES TO THEIR ROOMS.

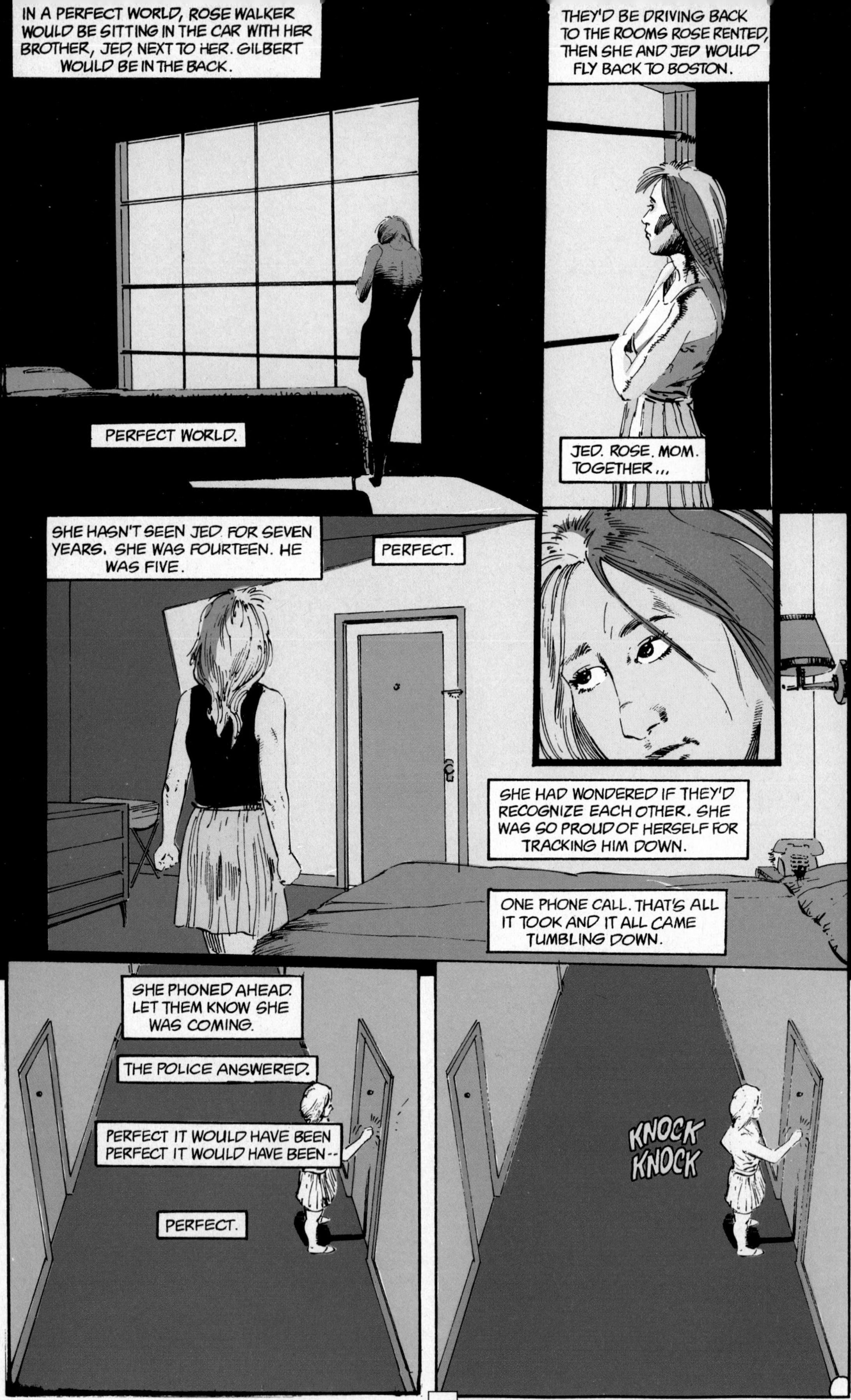
IN A PERFECT WORLD, ROSE WALKER WOULD BE SITTING IN THE CAR WITH HER BROTHER, JED, NEXT TO HER. GILBERT WOULD BE IN THE BACK.
PERFECT WORLD.
THEY'D BE DRIVING BACK TO THE ROOMS ROSE RENTED, THEN SHE AND JED WOULD FLY BACK TO BOSTON.
JED. ROSE. MOM. TOGETHER...
SHE HASN'T SEEN JED FOR SEVEN YEARS. SHE WAS FOURTEEN. HE WAS FIVE.
PERFECT.
SHE HAD WONDERED IF THEY'D RECOGNIZE EACH OTHER. SHE WAS SO PROUD OF HERSELF FOR TRACKING HIM DOWN.
ONE PHONE CALL. THAT'S ALL IT TOOK AND IT ALL CAME TUMBLING DOWN.
SHE PHONED AHEAD. LET THEM KNOW SHE WAS COMING.
THE POLICE ANSWERED.
PERFECT IT WOULD HAVE BEEN PERFECT IT WOULD HAVE BEEN--
PERFECT.
KNOCK KNOCK

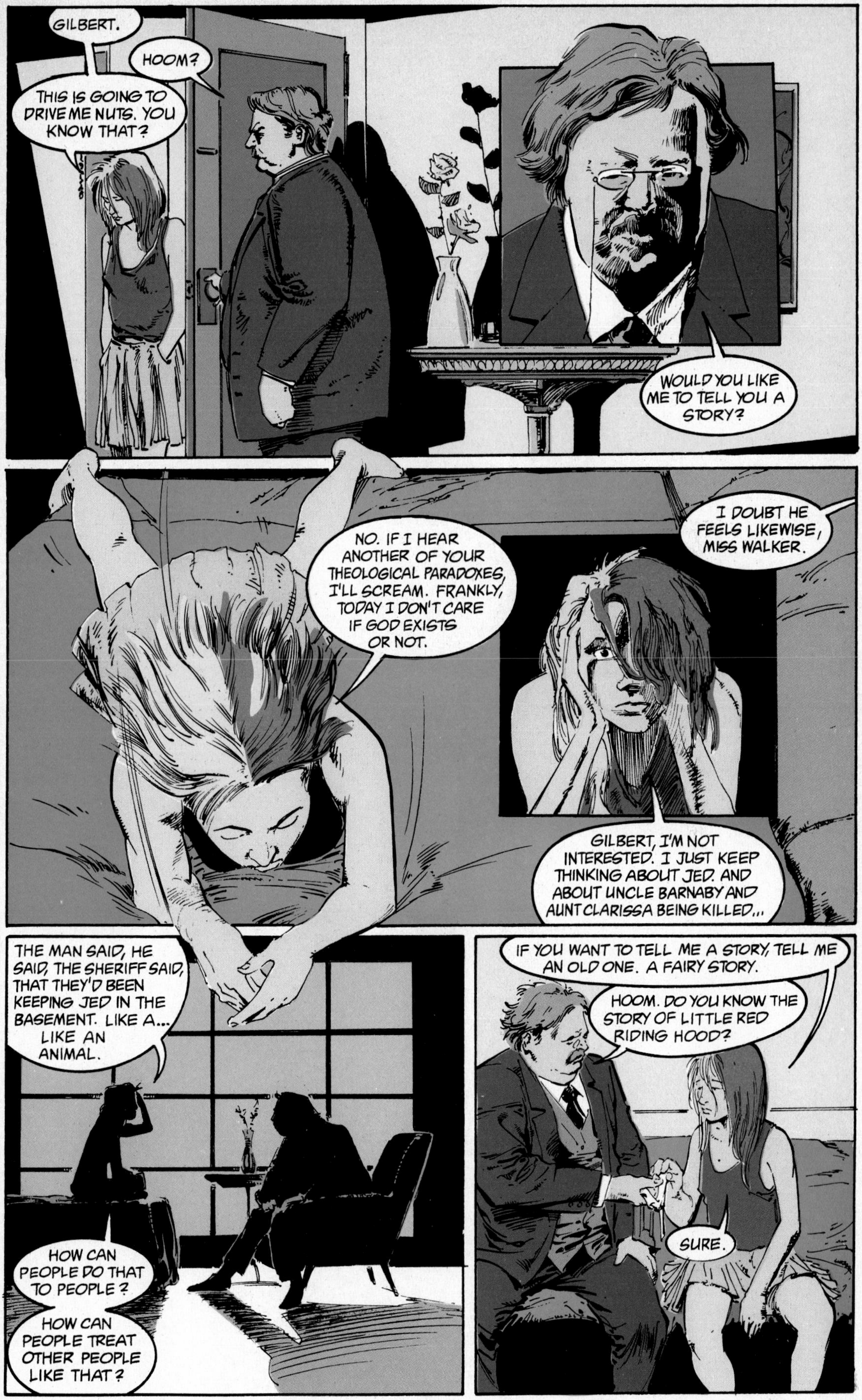
GILBERT.
HOOM?
THIS IS GOING TO DRIVE ME NUTS. YOU KNOW THAT?
WOULD YOU LIKE ME TO TELL YOU A STORY?
NO. IF I HEAR ANOTHER OF YOUR THEOLOGICAL PARADOXES, I'LL SCREAM. FRANKLY, TODAY I DON'T CARE IF GOD EXISTS OR NOT.
I DOUBT HE FEELS LIKEWISE, MISS WALKER.
GILBERT, I'M NOT INTERESTED. I JUST KEEP THINKING ABOUT JED. AND ABOUT UNCLE BARNABY AND AUNT CLARISSA BEING KILLED...
THE MAN SAID, HE SAID, THE SHERIFF SAID, THAT THEY'D BEEN KEEPING JED IN THE BASEMENT. LIKE A... LIKE AN ANIMAL.
HOW CAN PEOPLE DO THAT TO PEOPLE?
HOW CAN PEOPLE TREAT OTHER PEOPLE LIKE THAT?
IF YOU WANT TO TELL ME A STORY, TELL ME AN OLD ONE. A FAIRY STORY.
HOOM. DO YOU KNOW THE STORY OF LITTLE RED RIDING HOOD?
SURE.

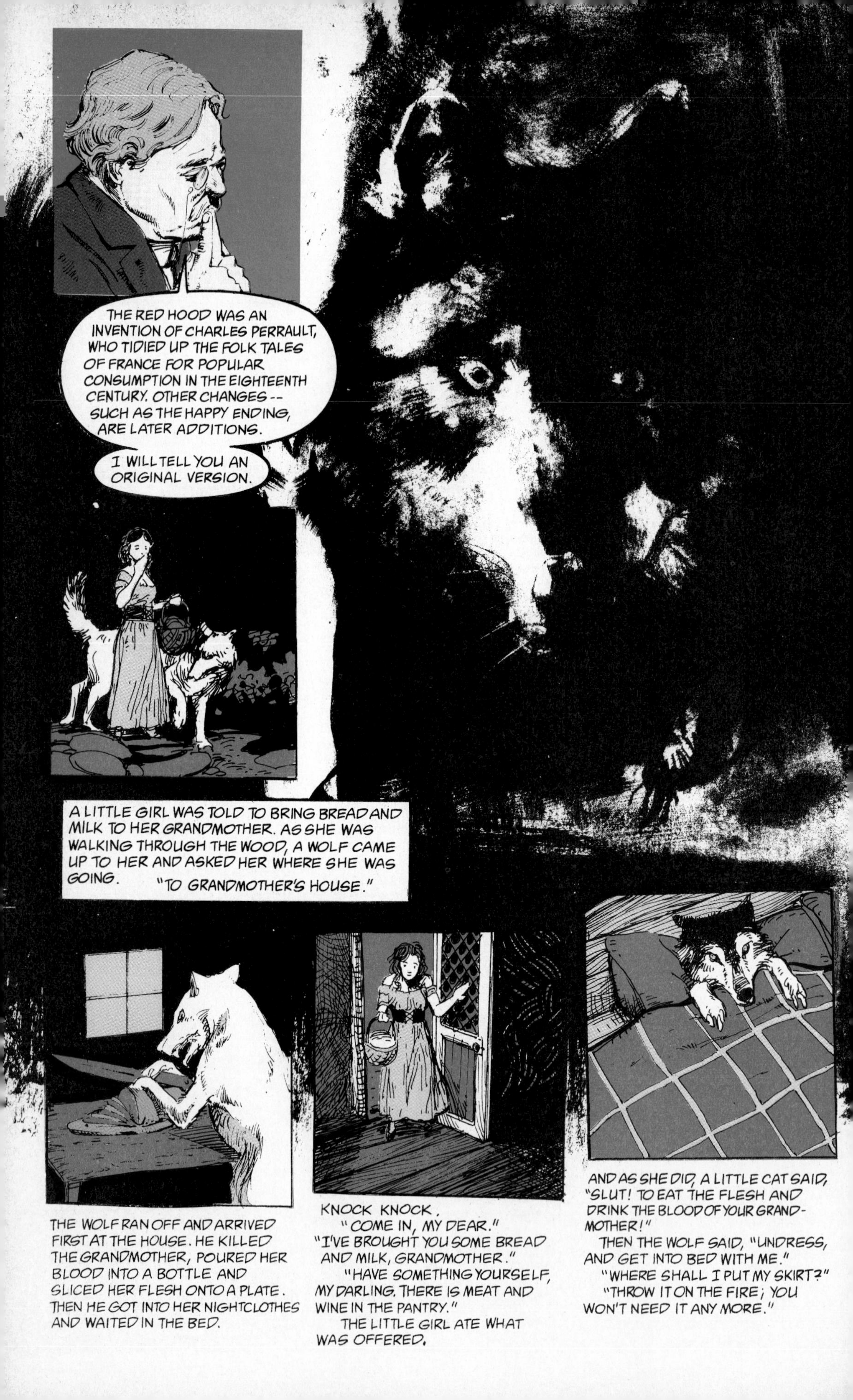
THE RED HOOD WAS AN INVENTION OF CHARLES PERRAULT, WHO TIDIED UP THE FOLK TALES OF FRANCE FOR POPULAR CONSUMPTION IN THE EIGHTEENTH CENTURY. OTHER CHANGES -- SUCH AS THE HAPPY ENDING, ARE LATER ADDITIONS.
I WILL TELL YOU AN ORIGINAL VERSION.
A LITTLE GIRL WAS TOLD TO BRING BREAD AND MILK TO HER GRANDMOTHER. AS SHE WAS WALKING THROUGH THE WOOD, A WOLF CAME UP TO HER AND ASKED HER WHERE SHE WAS GOING. "TO GRANDMOTHER'S HOUSE."
THE WOLF RAN OFF AND ARRIVED FIRST AT THE HOUSE. HE KILLED THE GRANDMOTHER, POURED HER BLOOD INTO A BOTTLE AND SLICED HER FLESH ONTO A PLATE. THEN HE GOT INTO HER NIGHTCLOTHES AND WAITED IN THE BED.
KNOCK KNOCK. "COME IN, MY DEAR." "I'VE BROUGHT YOU SOME BREAD AND MILK, GRANDMOTHER." "HAVE SOMETHING YOURSELF, MY DARLING. THERE IS MEAT AND WINE IN THE PANTRY." THE LITTLE GIRL ATE WHAT WAS OFFERED.
AND AS SHE DID, A LITTLE CAT SAID, "SLUT! TO EAT THE FLESH AND DRINK THE BLOOD OF YOUR GRANDMOTHER!" THEN THE WOLF SAID, "UNDRESS, AND GET INTO BED WITH ME." "WHERE SHALL I PUT MY SKIRT?" "THROW IT ON THE FIRE; YOU WON'T NEED IT ANY MORE."

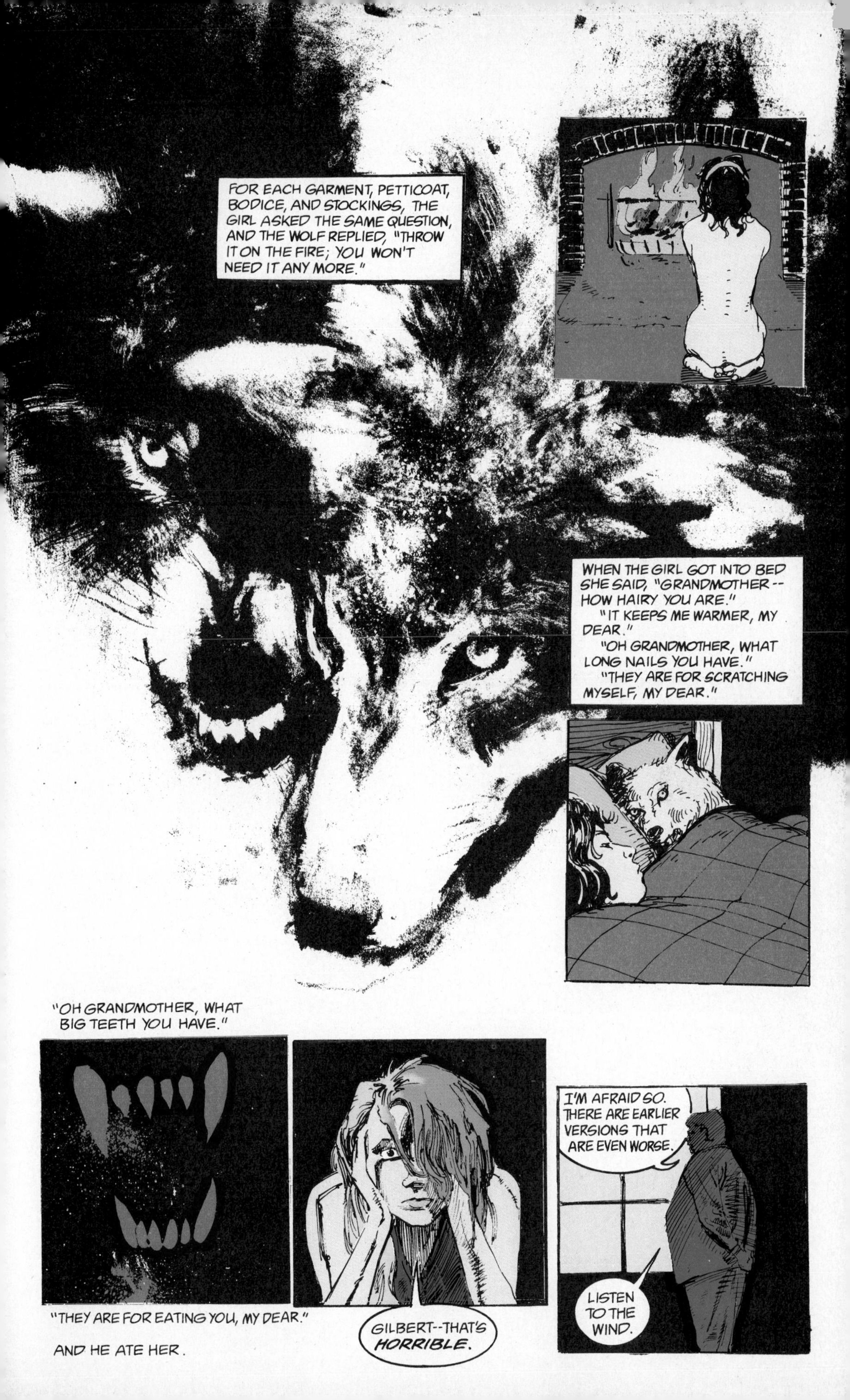

FOR EACH GARMENT, PETTICOAT, BODICE, AND STOCKINGS, THE GIRL ASKED THE SAME QUESTION, AND THE WOLF REPLIED, "THROW IT ON THE FIRE; YOU WON'T NEED IT ANY MORE."
WHEN THE GIRL GOT INTO BED SHE SAID, "GRANDMOTHER -- HOW HAIRY YOU ARE."
"IT KEEPS ME WARMER, MY DEAR."
"OH GRANDMOTHER, WHAT LONG NAILS YOU HAVE."
"THEY ARE FOR SCRATCHING MYSELF, MY DEAR."
"OH GRANDMOTHER, WHAT BIG TEETH YOU HAVE."
"THEY ARE FOR EATING YOU, MY DEAR."
AND HE ATE HER.
GILBERT--THAT'S *HORRIBLE*.
I'M AFRAID SO. THERE ARE EARLIER VERSIONS THAT ARE EVEN WORSE.
LISTEN TO THE WIND.

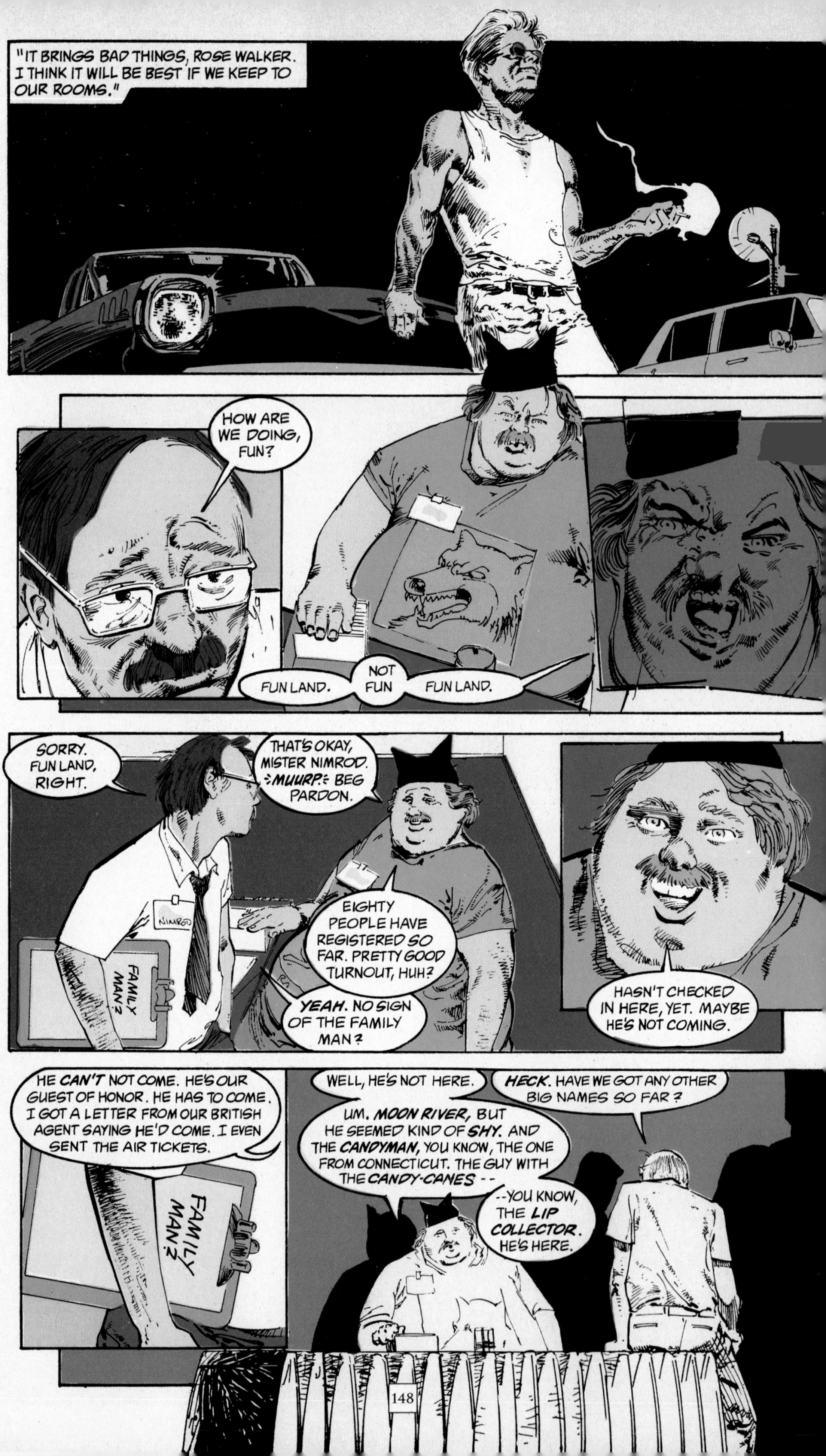
"IT BRINGS BAD THINGS, ROSE WALKER. I THINK IT WILL BE BEST IF WE KEEP TO OUR ROOMS."
HOW ARE WE DOING, FUN?
FUN LAND.
NOT FUN
FUN LAND.
SORRY. FUN LAND, RIGHT.
THAT'S OKAY, MISTER NIMROD. ⁚MUURP⁚ BEG PARDON.
NIMROD
FAMILY MAN?
EIGHTY PEOPLE HAVE REGISTERED SO FAR. PRETTY GOOD TURNOUT, HUH?
YEAH. NO SIGN OF THE FAMILY MAN?
HASN'T CHECKED IN HERE, YET. MAYBE HE'S NOT COMING.
HE CAN'T NOT COME. HE'S OUR GUEST OF HONOR. HE HAS TO COME. I GOT A LETTER FROM OUR BRITISH AGENT SAYING HE'D COME. I EVEN SENT THE AIR TICKETS.
FAMILY MAN?
WELL, HE'S NOT HERE.
HECK. HAVE WE GOT ANY OTHER BIG NAMES SO FAR?
UM. MOON RIVER, BUT HE SEEMED KIND OF SHY. AND THE CANDYMAN, YOU KNOW, THE ONE FROM CONNECTICUT. THE GUY WITH THE CANDY-CANES --
--YOU KNOW, THE LIP COLLECTOR. HE'S HERE.

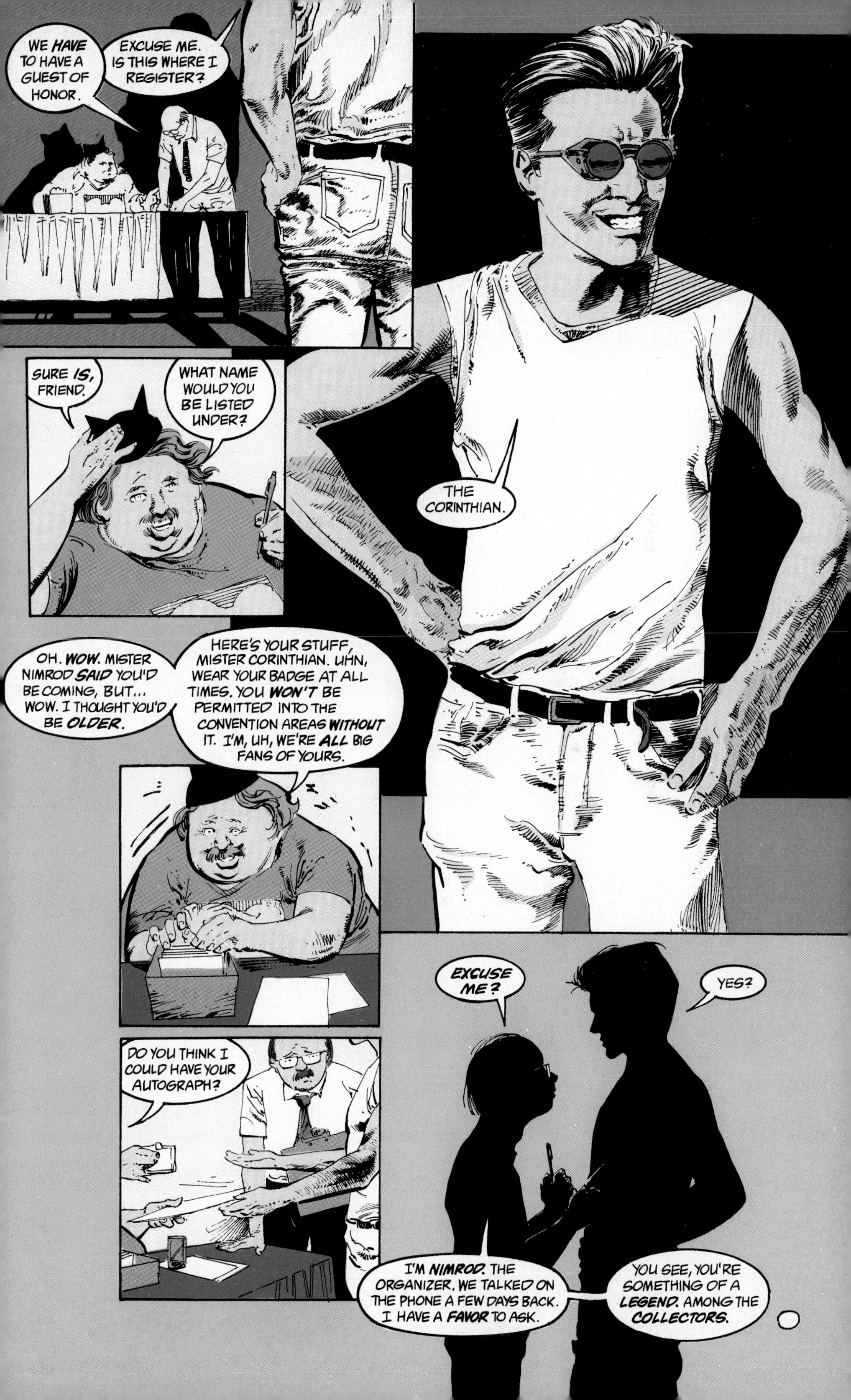
WE HAVE TO HAVE A GUEST OF HONOR.
EXCUSE ME. IS THIS WHERE I REGISTER?
SURE IS, FRIEND.
WHAT NAME WOULD YOU BE LISTED UNDER?
THE CORINTHIAN.
OH. WOW. MISTER NIMROD SAID YOU'D BE COMING, BUT... WOW. I THOUGHT YOU'D BE OLDER.
HERE'S YOUR STUFF, MISTER CORINTHIAN. UHN, WEAR YOUR BADGE AT ALL TIMES. YOU WON'T BE PERMITTED INTO THE CONVENTION AREAS WITHOUT IT. I'M, UH, WE'RE ALL BIG FANS OF YOURS.
DO YOU THINK I COULD HAVE YOUR AUTOGRAPH?
EXCUSE ME?
YES?
I'M NIMROD. THE ORGANIZER. WE TALKED ON THE PHONE A FEW DAYS BACK. I HAVE A FAVOR TO ASK.
YOU SEE, YOU'RE SOMETHING OF A LEGEND. AMONG THE COLLECTORS.

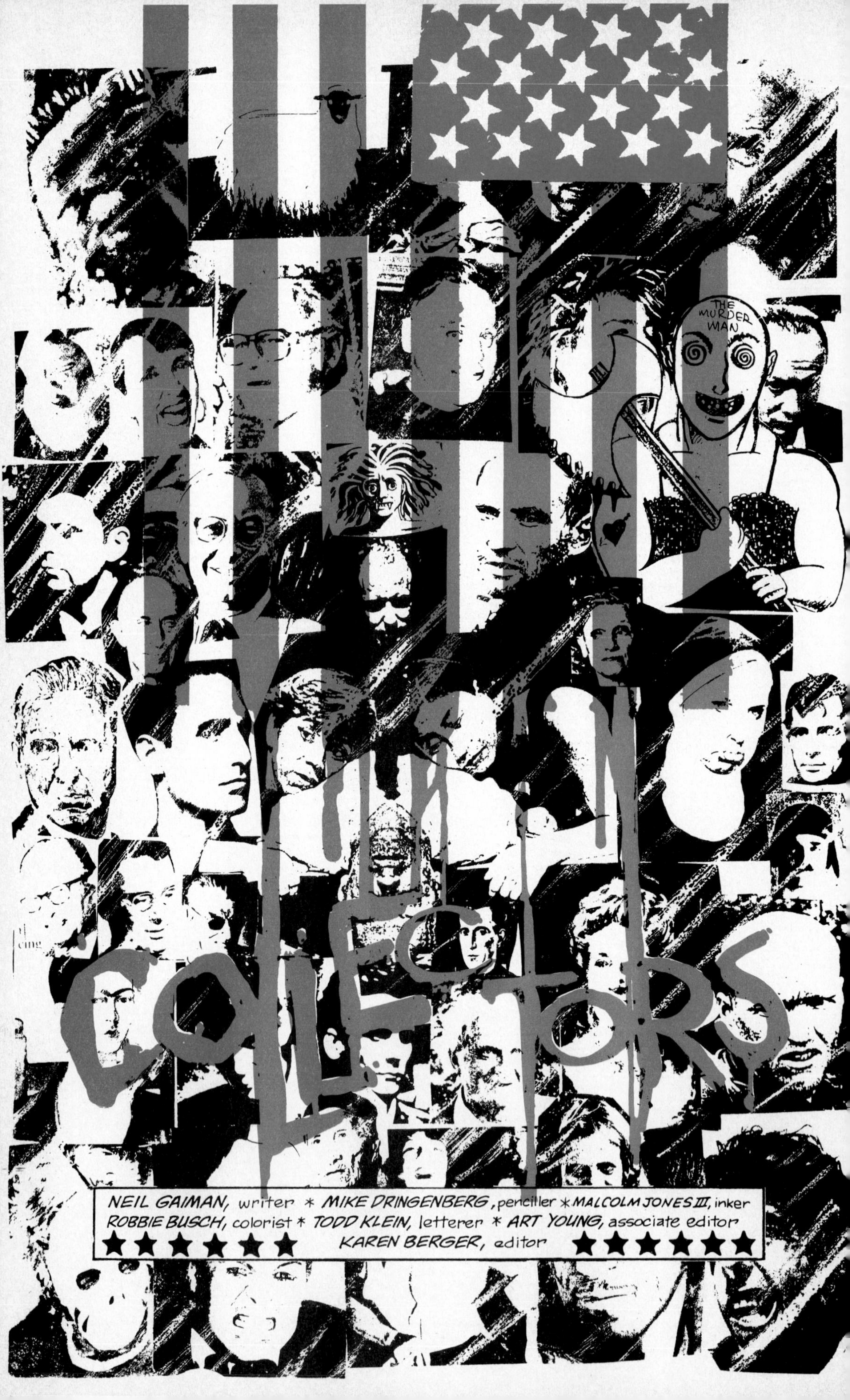
THE MURDER MAN
COLLECTORS
NEIL GAIMAN, writer * MIKE DRINGENBERG, penciller * MALCOLM JONES III, inker
ROBBIE BUSCH, colorist * TODD KLEIN, letterer * ART YOUNG, associate editor
KAREN BERGER, editor

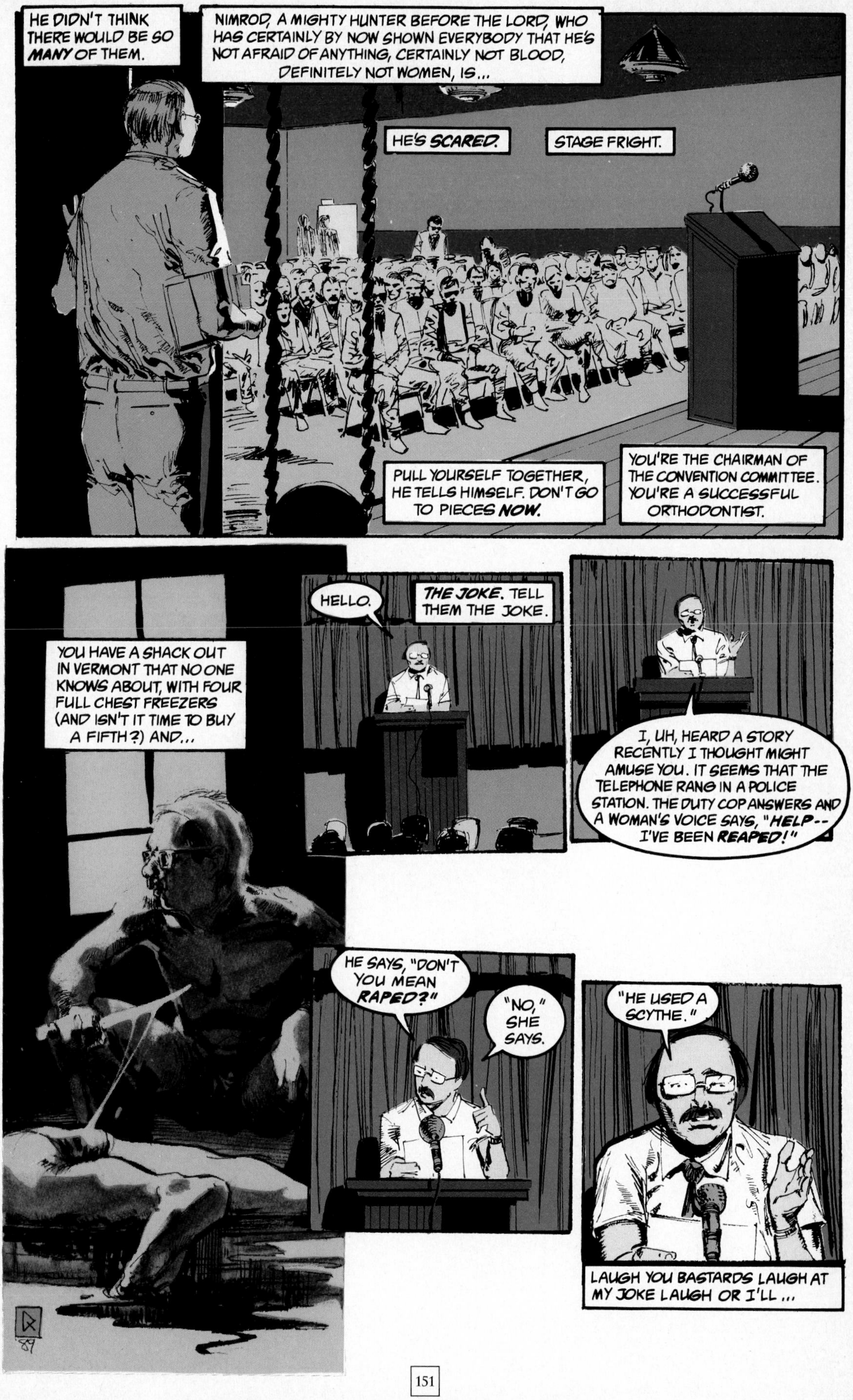
HE DIDN'T THINK THERE WOULD BE SO MANY OF THEM.
NIMROD, A MIGHTY HUNTER BEFORE THE LORD, WHO HAS CERTAINLY BY NOW SHOWN EVERYBODY THAT HE'S NOT AFRAID OF ANYTHING, CERTAINLY NOT BLOOD, DEFINITELY NOT WOMEN, IS...
HE'S SCARED.
STAGE FRIGHT.
PULL YOURSELF TOGETHER, HE TELLS HIMSELF. DON'T GO TO PIECES NOW.
YOU'RE THE CHAIRMAN OF THE CONVENTION COMMITTEE. YOU'RE A SUCCESSFUL ORTHODONTIST.
YOU HAVE A SHACK OUT IN VERMONT THAT NO ONE KNOWS ABOUT, WITH FOUR FULL CHEST FREEZERS (AND ISN'T IT TIME TO BUY A FIFTH?) AND...
HELLO.
THE JOKE. TELL THEM THE JOKE.
I, UH, HEARD A STORY RECENTLY I THOUGHT MIGHT AMUSE YOU. IT SEEMS THAT THE TELEPHONE RANG IN A POLICE STATION. THE DUTY COP ANSWERS AND A WOMAN'S VOICE SAYS, "HELP-- I'VE BEEN REAPED!"
HE SAYS, "DON'T YOU MEAN RAPED?"
"NO," SHE SAYS.
"HE USED A SCYTHE."
LAUGH YOU BASTARDS LAUGH AT MY JOKE LAUGH OR I'LL...
'89

HA HA HA HA HA HA HA HA HA HA HA

IT'S *REALLY GOOD* TO SEE SO MANY OF US HERE. *SO MANY.* THIS IS THE FIRST OF THESE CONS, AND IF YOU WANT TO SEE ANOTHER, A FEW RULES WE MUST ADHERE TO.

FIRSTLY, USE YOUR PREFERRED SOBRIQUET. NO CIVILIAN NAMES. *SECONDLY,* WE DON'T SHIT WHERE WE EAT.

YOU *ALL* KNOW THAT, PARTICULARLY *NOW,* AND *HERE,* WHEN SO MANY OF US WOULD BE AT RISK.

NOBODY DOES *ANY* COLLECTING UNTIL THE CONVENTION'S OVER AND YOU'RE AT *LEAST* TWO HUNDRED MILES AWAY.

AW...

THIRDLY, ON A MORE UNFORTUNATE NOTE, THE FAMILY MAN HAS NOT BEEN ABLE TO MAKE IT. HE'S AN OLD MAN...

BUT EVERY *CLOUD* HAS A SILVER LINING.

I'D LIKE TO PRESENT OUR *NEW* GUEST OF HONOR-- A LEGEND IN HIS OWN LIFETIME, AN INSPIRATION TO US ALL, I KNOW TO ME PERSONALLY... ONE OF THE *FIRST,* AND ONE OF THE *BEST.*

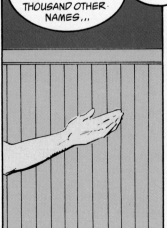

THEY'VE CALLED HIM *THE EYE GUY,* AND THE *DARK ANGEL,* AND *THE SHADES* AND MAYBE A THOUSAND OTHER NAMES...

BUT *WE'VE* ALWAYS KNOWN IT WAS ONE MAN.

GENTLEMEN. LADIES. OUR GUEST OF HONOR.

THE CORINTHIAN.

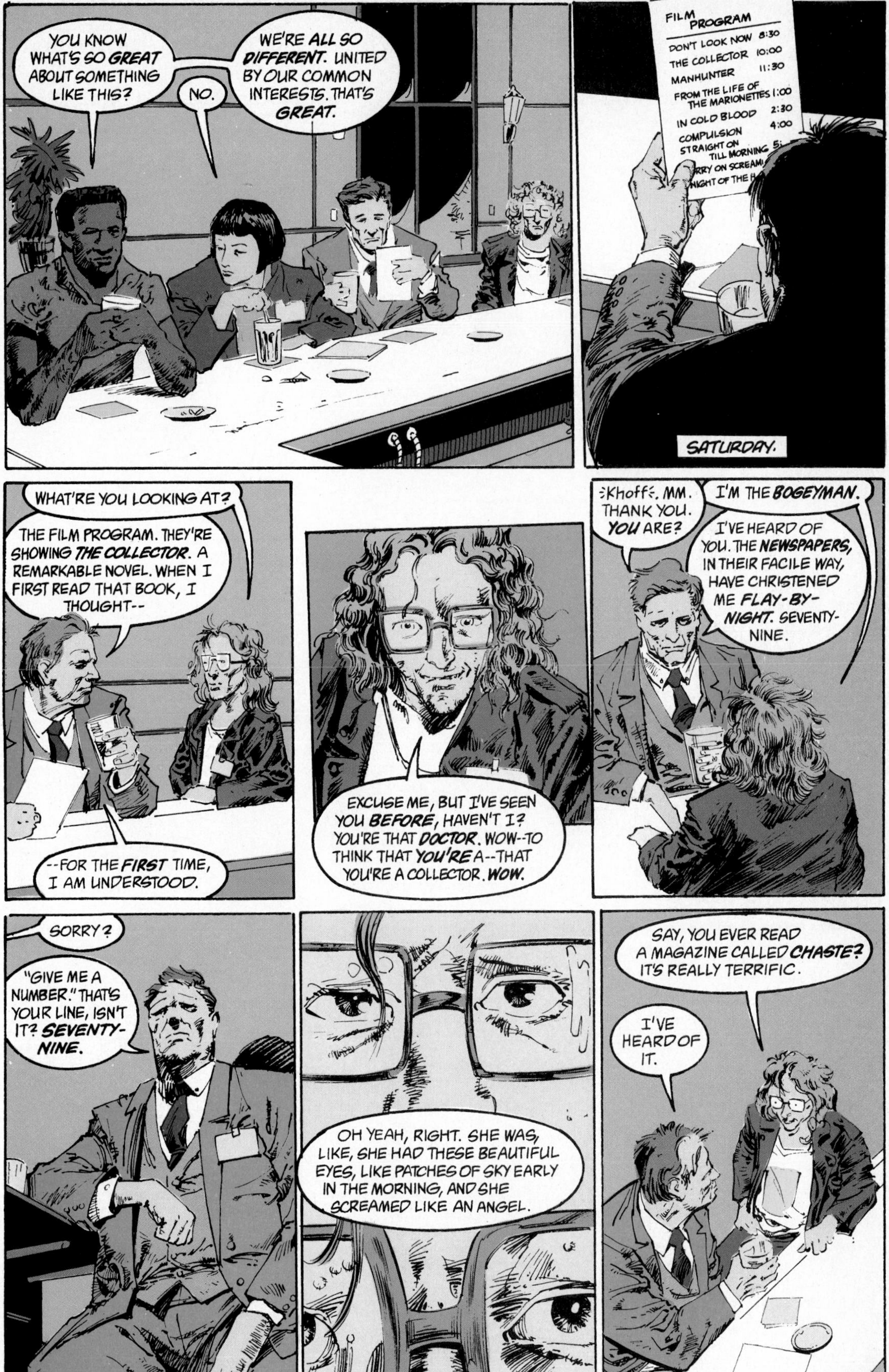
YOU KNOW WHAT'S SO GREAT ABOUT SOMETHING LIKE THIS?
NO.
WE'RE ALL SO DIFFERENT. UNITED BY OUR COMMON INTERESTS. THAT'S GREAT.
FILM PROGRAM
DON'T LOOK NOW 8:30
THE COLLECTOR 10:00
MANHUNTER 11:30
FROM THE LIFE OF THE MARIONETTES 1:00
IN COLD BLOOD 2:30
COMPULSION 4:00
STRAIGHT ON TILL MORNING
SATURDAY.
WHAT'RE YOU LOOKING AT?
THE FILM PROGRAM. THEY'RE SHOWING THE COLLECTOR. A REMARKABLE NOVEL. WHEN I FIRST READ THAT BOOK, I THOUGHT--
--FOR THE FIRST TIME, I AM UNDERSTOOD.
EXCUSE ME, BUT I'VE SEEN YOU BEFORE, HAVEN'T I? YOU'RE THAT DOCTOR. WOW--TO THINK THAT YOU'RE A--THAT YOU'RE A COLLECTOR. WOW.
:Khoff:. MM. THANK YOU. YOU ARE?
I'M THE BOGEYMAN.
I'VE HEARD OF YOU. THE NEWSPAPERS, IN THEIR FACILE WAY, HAVE CHRISTENED ME FLAY-BY-NIGHT. SEVENTY-NINE.
SORRY?
"GIVE ME A NUMBER." THAT'S YOUR LINE, ISN'T IT? SEVENTY-NINE.
OH YEAH, RIGHT. SHE WAS, LIKE, SHE HAD THESE BEAUTIFUL EYES, LIKE PATCHES OF SKY EARLY IN THE MORNING, AND SHE SCREAMED LIKE AN ANGEL.
SAY, YOU EVER READ A MAGAZINE CALLED CHASTE? IT'S REALLY TERRIFIC.
I'VE HEARD OF IT.

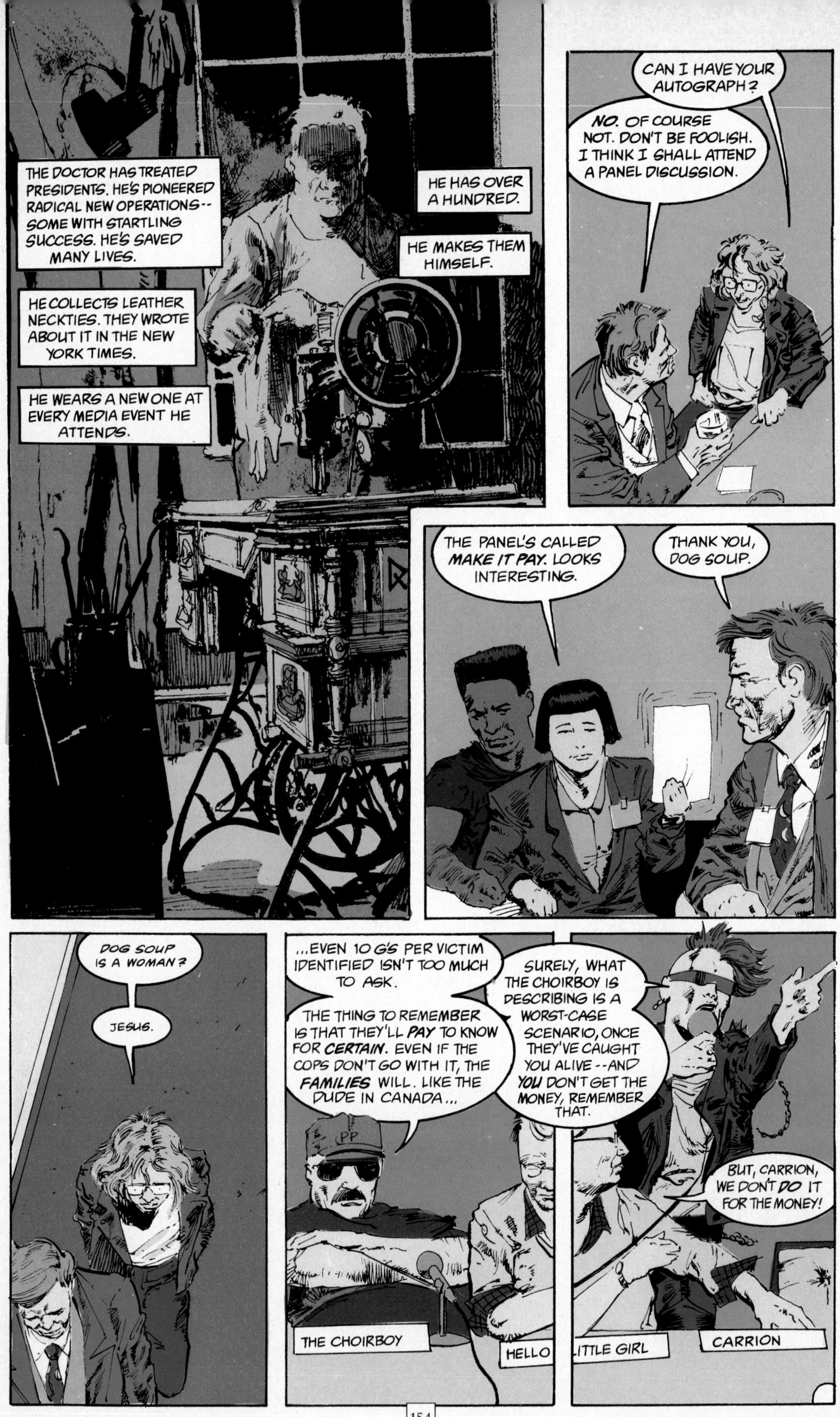

THE DOCTOR HAS TREATED PRESIDENTS. HE'S PIONEERED RADICAL NEW OPERATIONS -- SOME WITH STARTLING SUCCESS. HE'S SAVED MANY LIVES.
HE HAS OVER A HUNDRED.
HE MAKES THEM HIMSELF.
HE COLLECTS LEATHER NECKTIES. THEY WROTE ABOUT IT IN THE NEW YORK TIMES.
HE WEARS A NEW ONE AT EVERY MEDIA EVENT HE ATTENDS.
CAN I HAVE YOUR AUTOGRAPH?
NO. OF COURSE NOT. DON'T BE FOOLISH. I THINK I SHALL ATTEND A PANEL DISCUSSION.
THE PANEL'S CALLED MAKE IT PAY. LOOKS INTERESTING.
THANK YOU, DOG SOUP.
DOG SOUP IS A WOMAN?
JESUS.
...EVEN 10 G'S PER VICTIM IDENTIFIED ISN'T TOO MUCH TO ASK.
THE THING TO REMEMBER IS THAT THEY'LL PAY TO KNOW FOR CERTAIN. EVEN IF THE COPS DON'T GO WITH IT, THE FAMILIES WILL. LIKE THE DUDE IN CANADA...
SURELY, WHAT THE CHOIRBOY IS DESCRIBING IS A WORST-CASE SCENARIO, ONCE THEY'VE CAUGHT YOU ALIVE -- AND YOU DON'T GET THE MONEY, REMEMBER THAT.
BUT, CARRION, WE DON'T DO IT FOR THE MONEY!
PP
THE CHOIRBOY
HELLO LITTLE GIRL
CARRION

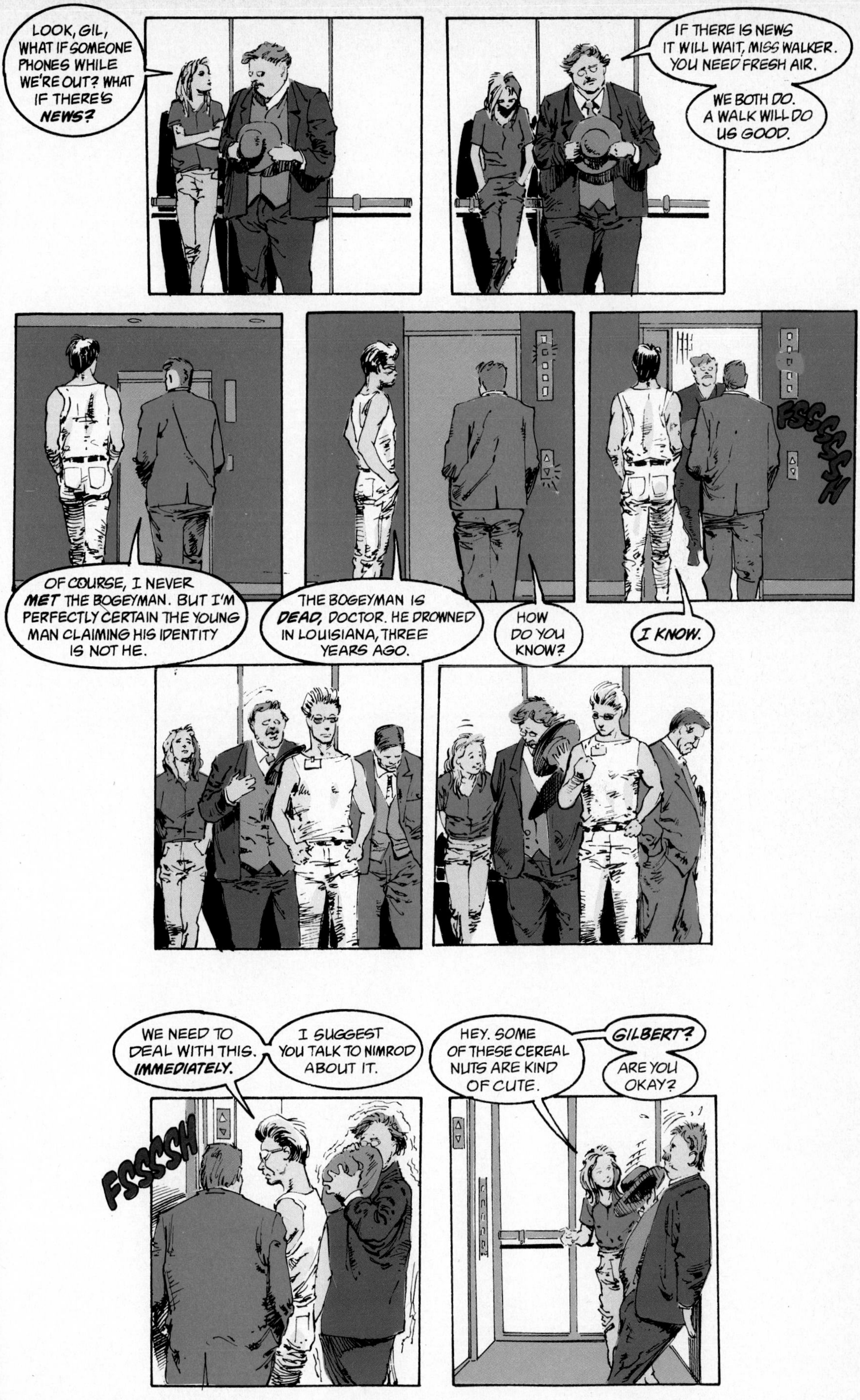
LOOK, GIL, WHAT IF SOMEONE PHONES WHILE WE'RE OUT? WHAT IF THERE'S NEWS?
IF THERE IS NEWS IT WILL WAIT, MISS WALKER. YOU NEED FRESH AIR.
WE BOTH DO. A WALK WILL DO US GOOD.
OF COURSE, I NEVER MET THE BOGEYMAN. BUT I'M PERFECTLY CERTAIN THE YOUNG MAN CLAIMING HIS IDENTITY IS NOT HE.
THE BOGEYMAN IS DEAD, DOCTOR. HE DROWNED IN LOUISIANA, THREE YEARS AGO.
HOW DO YOU KNOW?
FSSSSSH
I KNOW.
WE NEED TO DEAL WITH THIS. IMMEDIATELY.
I SUGGEST YOU TALK TO NIMROD ABOUT IT.
FSSSSH
HEY. SOME OF THESE CEREAL NUTS ARE KIND OF CUTE.
GILBERT?
ARE YOU OKAY?

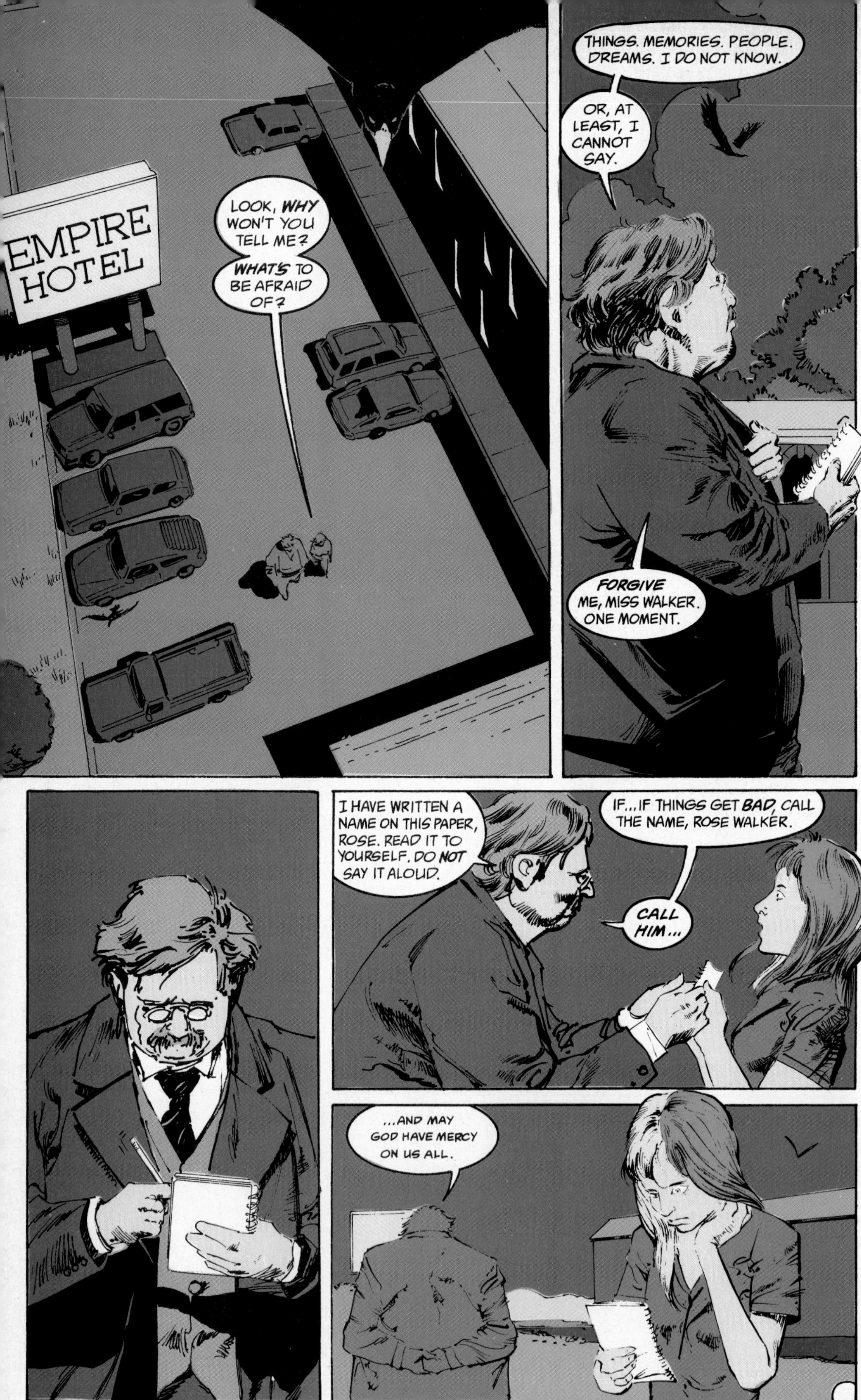
EMPIRE HOTEL
LOOK, WHY WON'T YOU TELL ME? WHAT'S TO BE AFRAID OF?
THINGS. MEMORIES. PEOPLE. DREAMS. I DO NOT KNOW.
OR, AT LEAST, I CANNOT SAY.
FORGIVE ME, MISS WALKER. ONE MOMENT.
I HAVE WRITTEN A NAME ON THIS PAPER, ROSE. READ IT TO YOURSELF. DO NOT SAY IT ALOUD.
IF... IF THINGS GET BAD, CALL THE NAME, ROSE WALKER.
CALL HIM...
...AND MAY GOD HAVE MERCY ON US ALL.

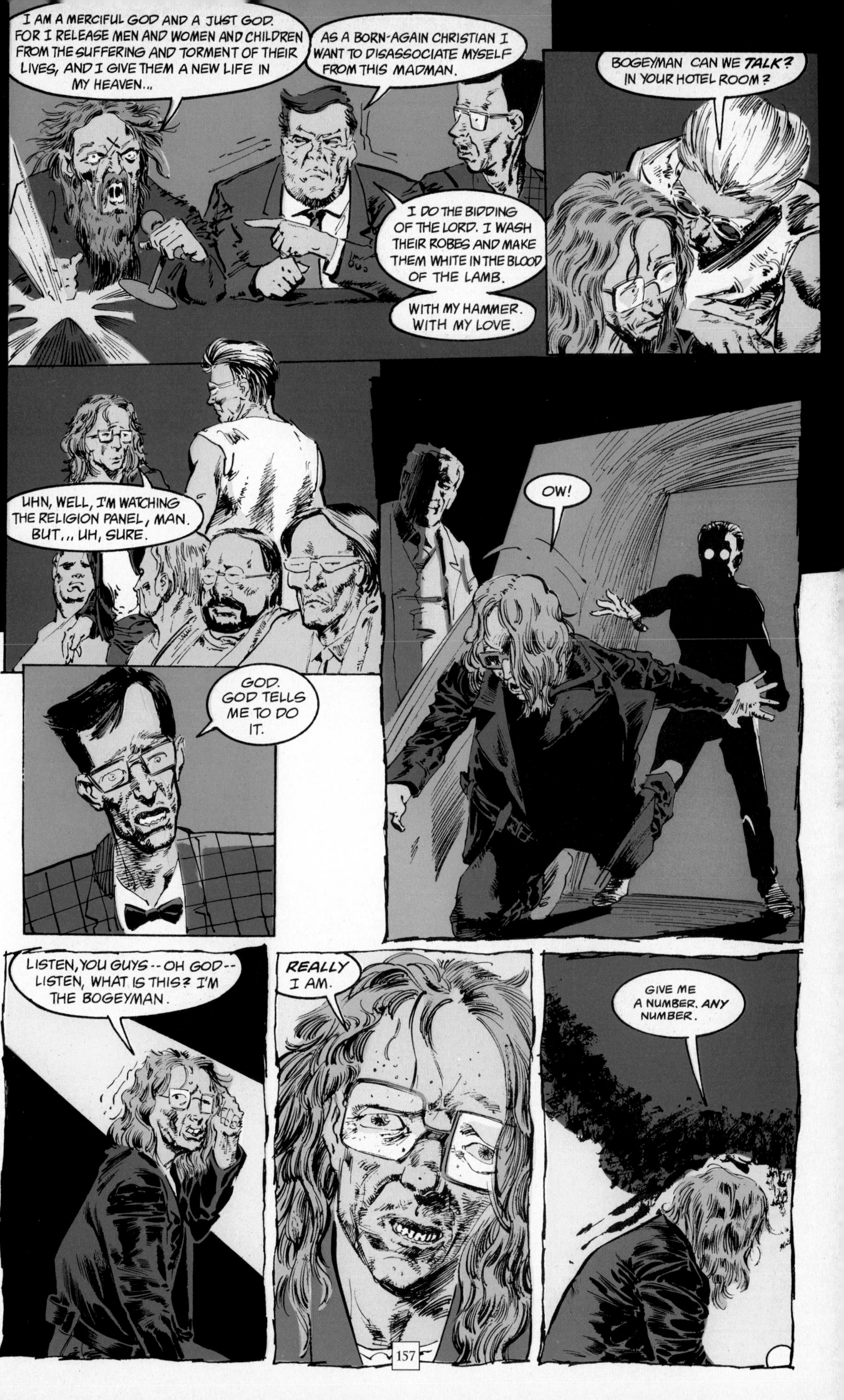

I AM A MERCIFUL GOD AND A JUST GOD. FOR I RELEASE MEN AND WOMEN AND CHILDREN FROM THE SUFFERING AND TORMENT OF THEIR LIVES, AND I GIVE THEM A NEW LIFE IN MY HEAVEN...
AS A BORN-AGAIN CHRISTIAN I WANT TO DISASSOCIATE MYSELF FROM THIS MADMAN.
I DO THE BIDDING OF THE LORD. I WASH THEIR ROBES AND MAKE THEM WHITE IN THE BLOOD OF THE LAMB.
WITH MY HAMMER. WITH MY LOVE.
BOGEYMAN CAN WE TALK? IN YOUR HOTEL ROOM?
UHN, WELL, I'M WATCHING THE RELIGION PANEL, MAN. BUT... UH, SURE.
GOD. GOD TELLS ME TO DO IT.
OW!
LISTEN, YOU GUYS -- OH GOD -- LISTEN, WHAT IS THIS? I'M THE BOGEYMAN.
REALLY I AM.
GIVE ME A NUMBER. ANY NUMBER.

YOUR NAME IS PHILIP SITZ. YOU'RE THE EDITOR, WRITER, WHATEVER, OF *CHASTE* MAGAZINE.

YOUR NUMBER'S UP, PHILIP. YOU AREN'T ONE OF US.

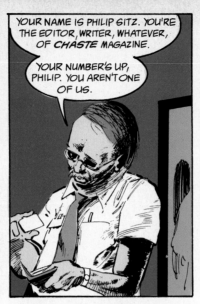

NO--NO, I *AM*. I UNDERSTAND IT. FEMALES ARE INSECTS CREATED FOR MALE PLEASURE. *STRENGTH*. *ENERGY*. *LUST*.

THE WILLINGNESS TO SACRIFICE ANOTHER'S *LIFE* FOR ONE'S *OWN* GRATIFICATION...

I UNDERSTAND IT. THAT'S WHY I *HAD* TO GET HERE. TO SEE YOU ALL. TO *LEARN*.

BIG MISTAKE, PHILIP.

BIG MISTAKE.

"WE DON'T SHIT WHERE WE EAT," MR. NIMROD?

EXCEPT WHEN WE HAVE TO, DOCTOR. NEEDS MUST, WHEN THE DEVIL DRIVES.

DO YOU *ALWAYS* DRIVE LIKE THAT?

SURE.

I WAS NERVOUS, WITH HIM ON MY LAP. WE *SHOULD* HAVE PUT HIM IN THE *TRUNK*.

I HAVE SOMETHING IN THE TRUNK ALREADY.

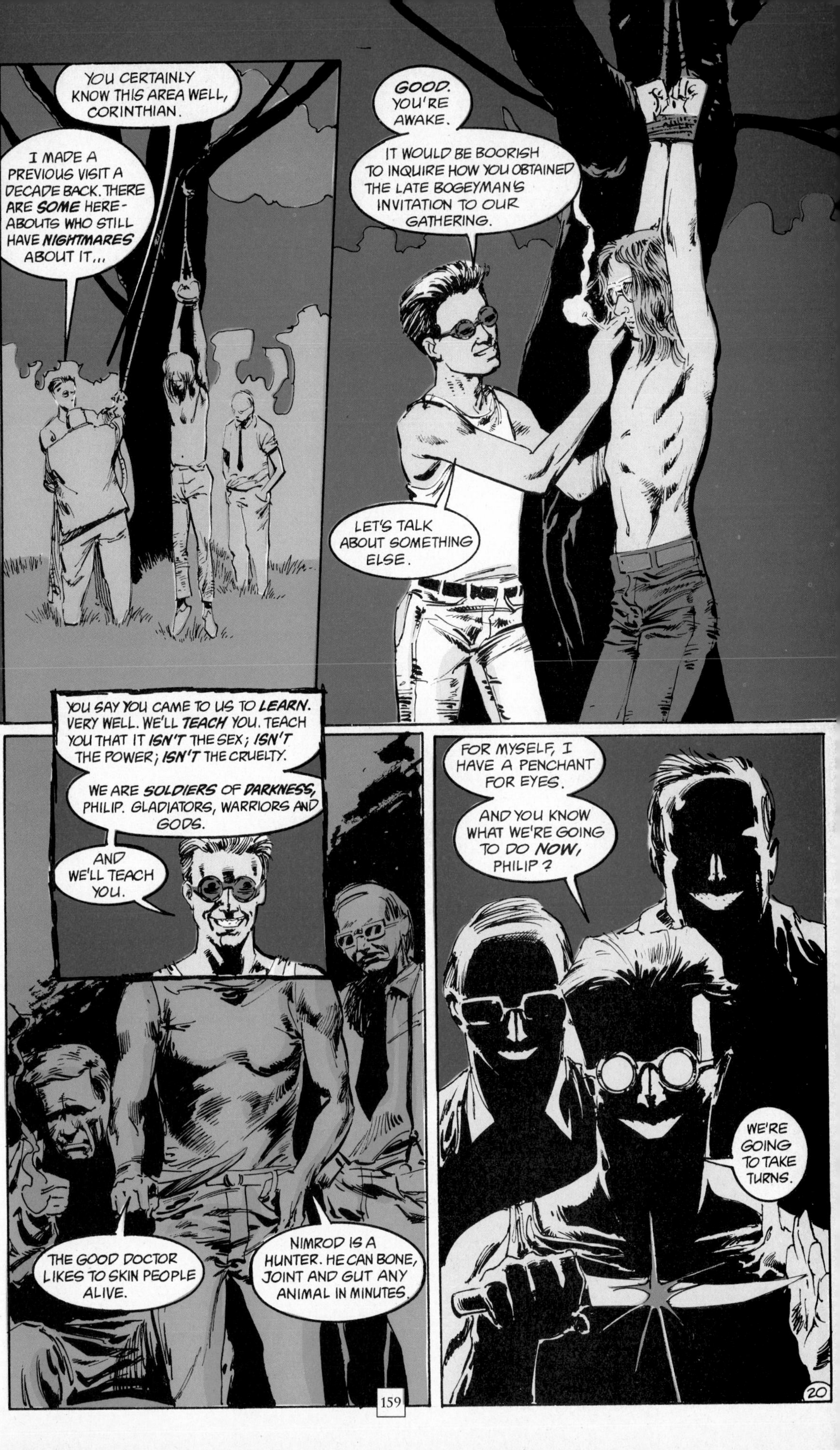
YOU CERTAINLY KNOW THIS AREA WELL, CORINTHIAN.
I MADE A PREVIOUS VISIT A DECADE BACK. THERE ARE **SOME** HERE-ABOUTS WHO STILL HAVE **NIGHTMARES** ABOUT IT...
GOOD. YOU'RE AWAKE.
IT WOULD BE BOORISH TO INQUIRE HOW YOU OBTAINED THE LATE BOGEYMAN'S INVITATION TO OUR GATHERING.
LET'S TALK ABOUT SOMETHING ELSE.
YOU SAY YOU CAME TO US TO **LEARN**. VERY WELL. WE'LL **TEACH** YOU. TEACH YOU THAT IT **ISN'T** THE SEX; **ISN'T** THE POWER; **ISN'T** THE CRUELTY.
WE ARE **SOLDIERS** OF **DARKNESS**, PHILIP. GLADIATORS, WARRIORS AND GODS.
AND WE'LL TEACH YOU.
THE GOOD DOCTOR LIKES TO SKIN PEOPLE ALIVE.
NIMROD IS A HUNTER. HE CAN BONE, JOINT AND GUT ANY ANIMAL IN MINUTES.
FOR MYSELF, I HAVE A PENCHANT FOR EYES.
AND YOU KNOW WHAT WE'RE GOING TO DO **NOW**, PHILIP?
WE'RE GOING TO TAKE TURNS.
20

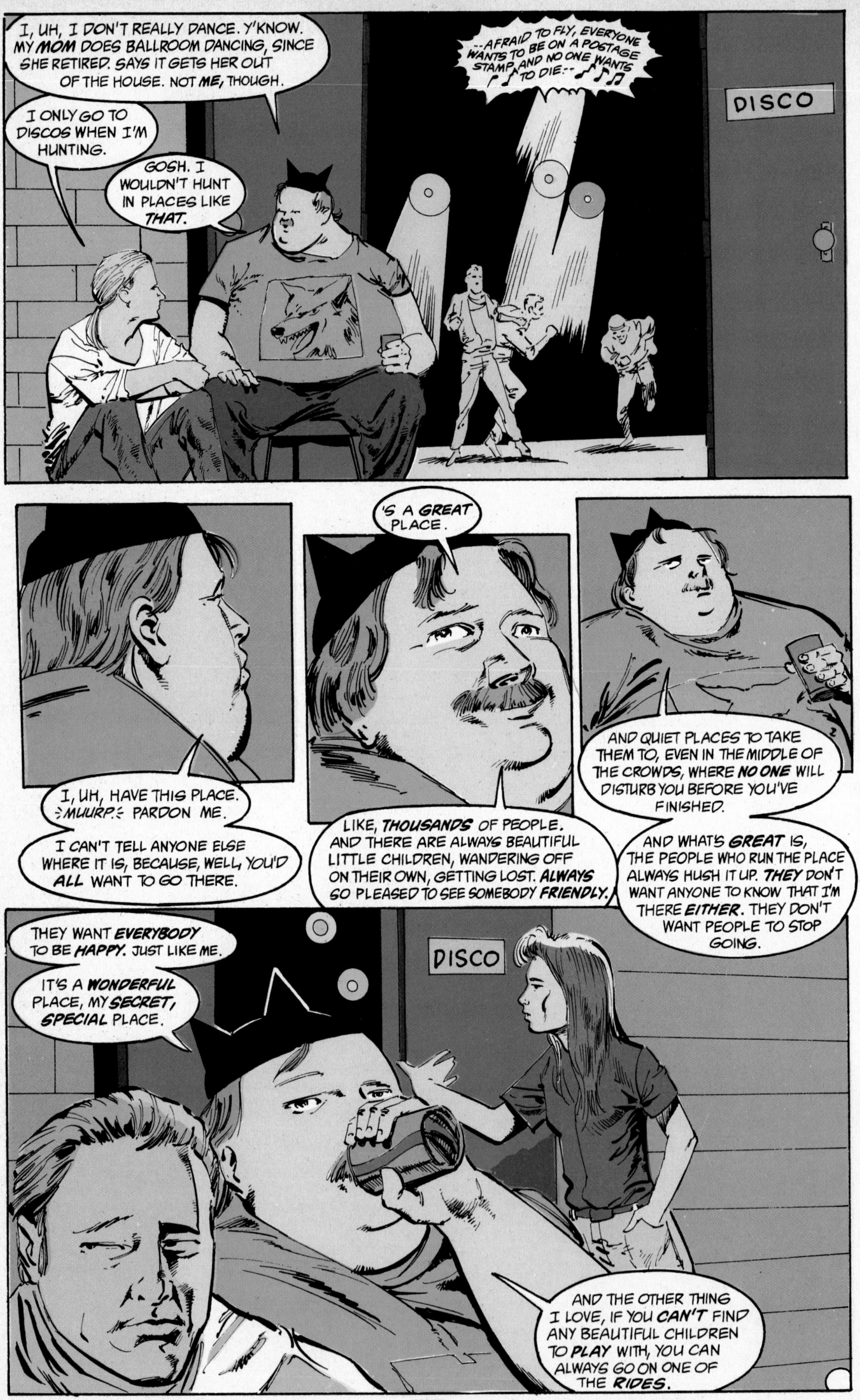
I, UH, I DON'T REALLY DANCE. Y'KNOW. MY MOM DOES BALLROOM DANCING, SINCE SHE RETIRED. SAYS IT GETS HER OUT OF THE HOUSE. NOT ME, THOUGH.
--AFRAID TO FLY, EVERYONE WANTS TO BE ON A POSTAGE STAMP AND NO ONE WANTS TO DIE--
DISCO
I ONLY GO TO DISCOS WHEN I'M HUNTING.
GOSH. I WOULDN'T HUNT IN PLACES LIKE THAT.
I, UH, HAVE THIS PLACE. MUURP. PARDON ME.
I CAN'T TELL ANYONE ELSE WHERE IT IS, BECAUSE, WELL, YOU'D ALL WANT TO GO THERE.
'S A GREAT PLACE.
LIKE, THOUSANDS OF PEOPLE. AND THERE ARE ALWAYS BEAUTIFUL LITTLE CHILDREN, WANDERING OFF ON THEIR OWN, GETTING LOST. ALWAYS SO PLEASED TO SEE SOMEBODY FRIENDLY.
AND QUIET PLACES TO TAKE THEM TO, EVEN IN THE MIDDLE OF THE CROWDS, WHERE NO ONE WILL DISTURB YOU BEFORE YOU'VE FINISHED.
AND WHAT'S GREAT IS, THE PEOPLE WHO RUN THE PLACE ALWAYS HUSH IT UP. THEY DON'T WANT ANYONE TO KNOW THAT I'M THERE EITHER. THEY DON'T WANT PEOPLE TO STOP GOING.
THEY WANT EVERYBODY TO BE HAPPY. JUST LIKE ME.
IT'S A WONDERFUL PLACE, MY SECRET, SPECIAL PLACE.
DISCO
AND THE OTHER THING I LOVE, IF YOU CAN'T FIND ANY BEAUTIFUL CHILDREN TO PLAY WITH, YOU CAN ALWAYS GO ON ONE OF THE RIDES.

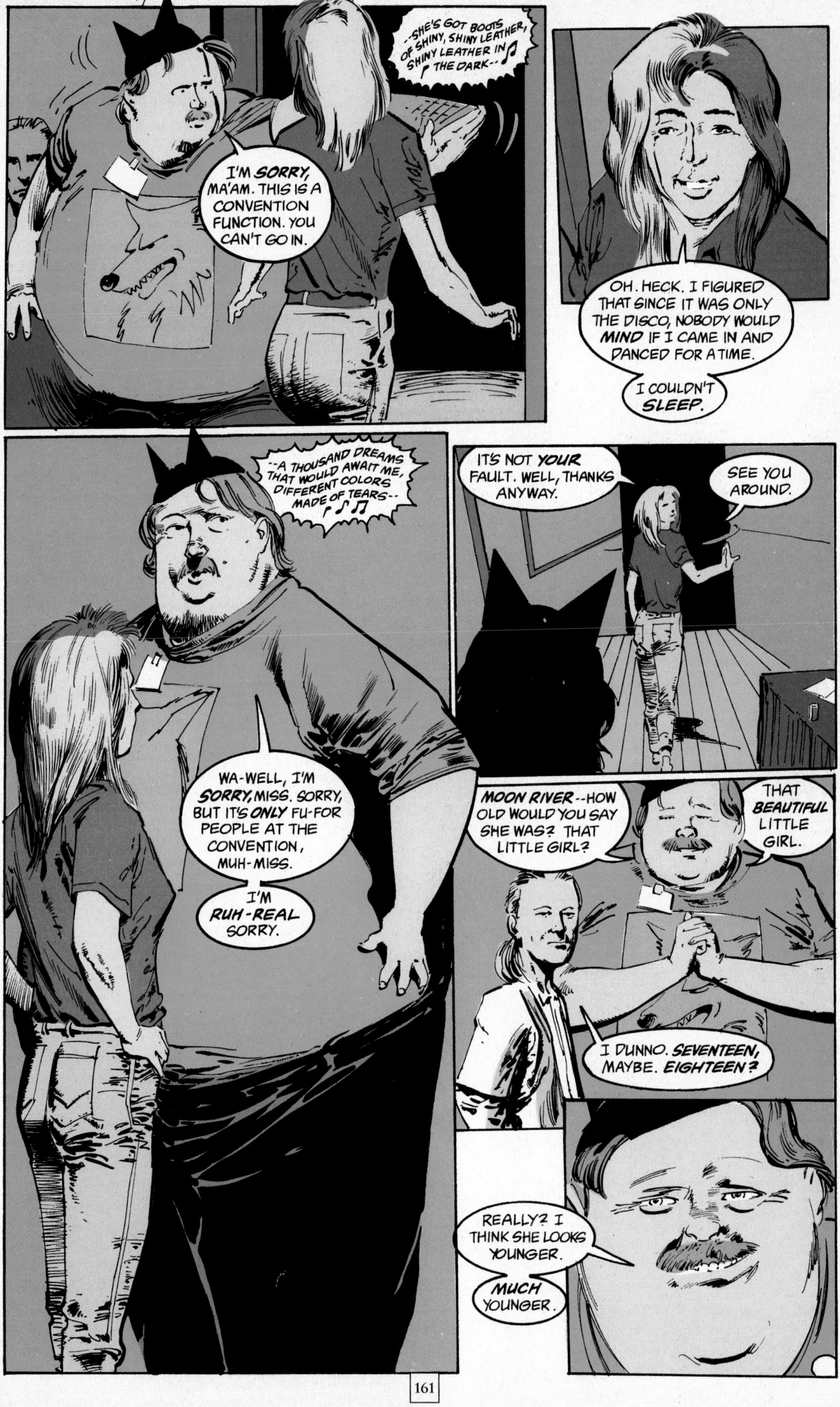
--SHE'S GOT BOOTS OF SHINY, SHINY LEATHER, SHINY LEATHER IN THE DARK--
I'M SORRY, MA'AM. THIS IS A CONVENTION FUNCTION. YOU CAN'T GO IN.
OH. HECK. I FIGURED THAT SINCE IT WAS ONLY THE DISCO, NOBODY WOULD MIND IF I CAME IN AND DANCED FOR A TIME.
I COULDN'T SLEEP.
--A THOUSAND DREAMS THAT WOULD AWAIT ME, DIFFERENT COLORS MADE OF TEARS--
WA-WELL, I'M SORRY, MISS. SORRY, BUT IT'S ONLY FU-FOR PEOPLE AT THE CONVENTION, MUH-MISS.
I'M RUH-REAL SORRY.
IT'S NOT YOUR FAULT. WELL, THANKS ANYWAY.
SEE YOU AROUND.
MOON RIVER--HOW OLD WOULD YOU SAY SHE WAS? THAT LITTLE GIRL?
THAT BEAUTIFUL LITTLE GIRL.
I DUNNO. SEVENTEEN, MAYBE. EIGHTEEN?
REALLY? I THINK SHE LOOKS YOUNGER.
MUCH YOUNGER.

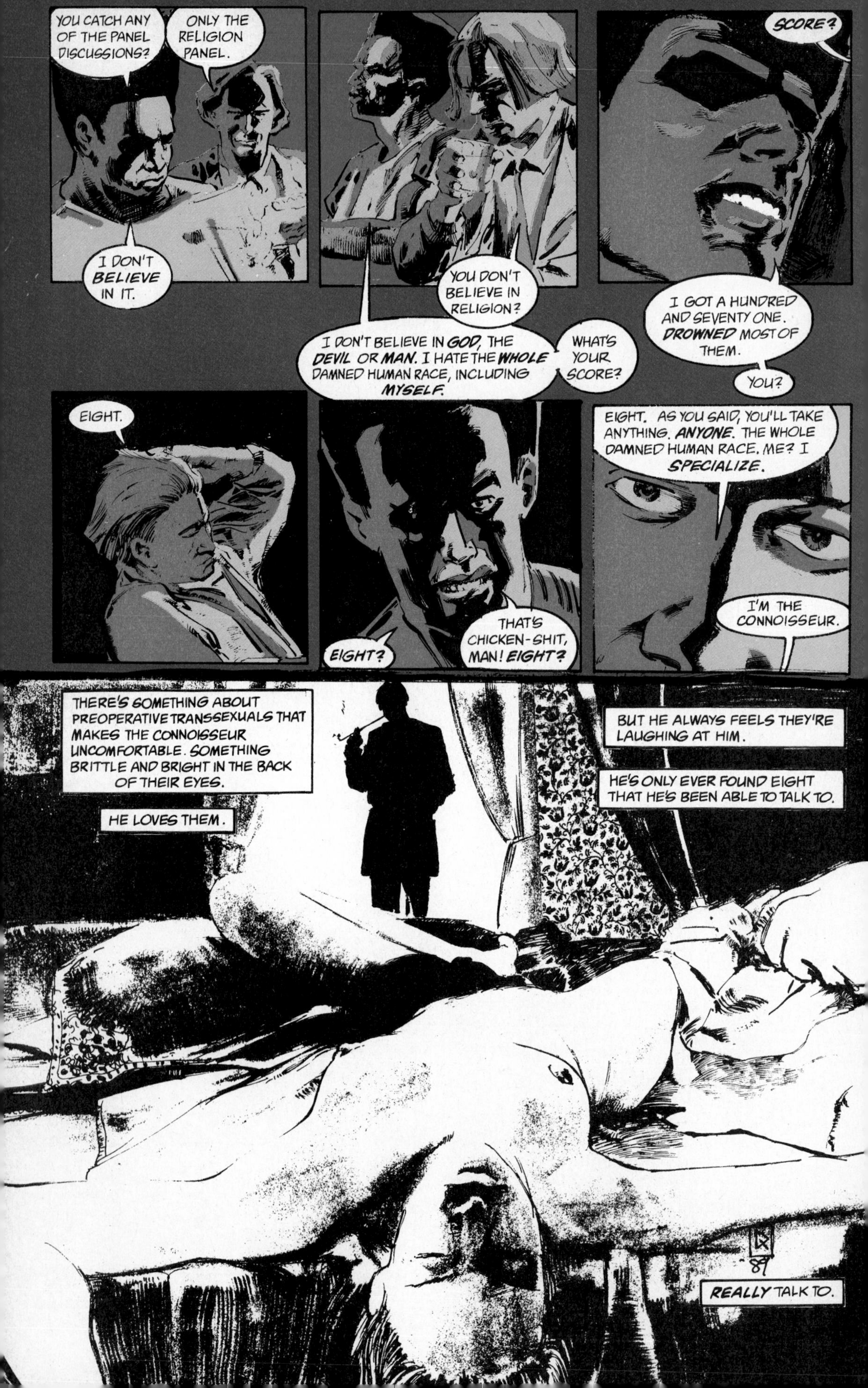
YOU CATCH ANY OF THE PANEL DISCUSSIONS?
ONLY THE RELIGION PANEL.
I DON'T BELIEVE IN IT.
YOU DON'T BELIEVE IN RELIGION?
I DON'T BELIEVE IN GOD, THE DEVIL OR MAN. I HATE THE WHOLE DAMNED HUMAN RACE, INCLUDING MYSELF.
WHAT'S YOUR SCORE?
SCORE?
I GOT A HUNDRED AND SEVENTY ONE. DROWNED MOST OF THEM.
YOU?
EIGHT.
EIGHT?
THAT'S CHICKEN-SHIT, MAN! EIGHT?
EIGHT. AS YOU SAID, YOU'LL TAKE ANYTHING. ANYONE. THE WHOLE DAMNED HUMAN RACE. ME? I SPECIALIZE.
I'M THE CONNOISSEUR.
THERE'S SOMETHING ABOUT PREOPERATIVE TRANSSEXUALS THAT MAKES THE CONNOISSEUR UNCOMFORTABLE. SOMETHING BRITTLE AND BRIGHT IN THE BACK OF THEIR EYES.
HE LOVES THEM.
BUT HE ALWAYS FEELS THEY'RE LAUGHING AT HIM.
HE'S ONLY EVER FOUND EIGHT THAT HE'S BEEN ABLE TO TALK TO.
REALLY TALK TO.

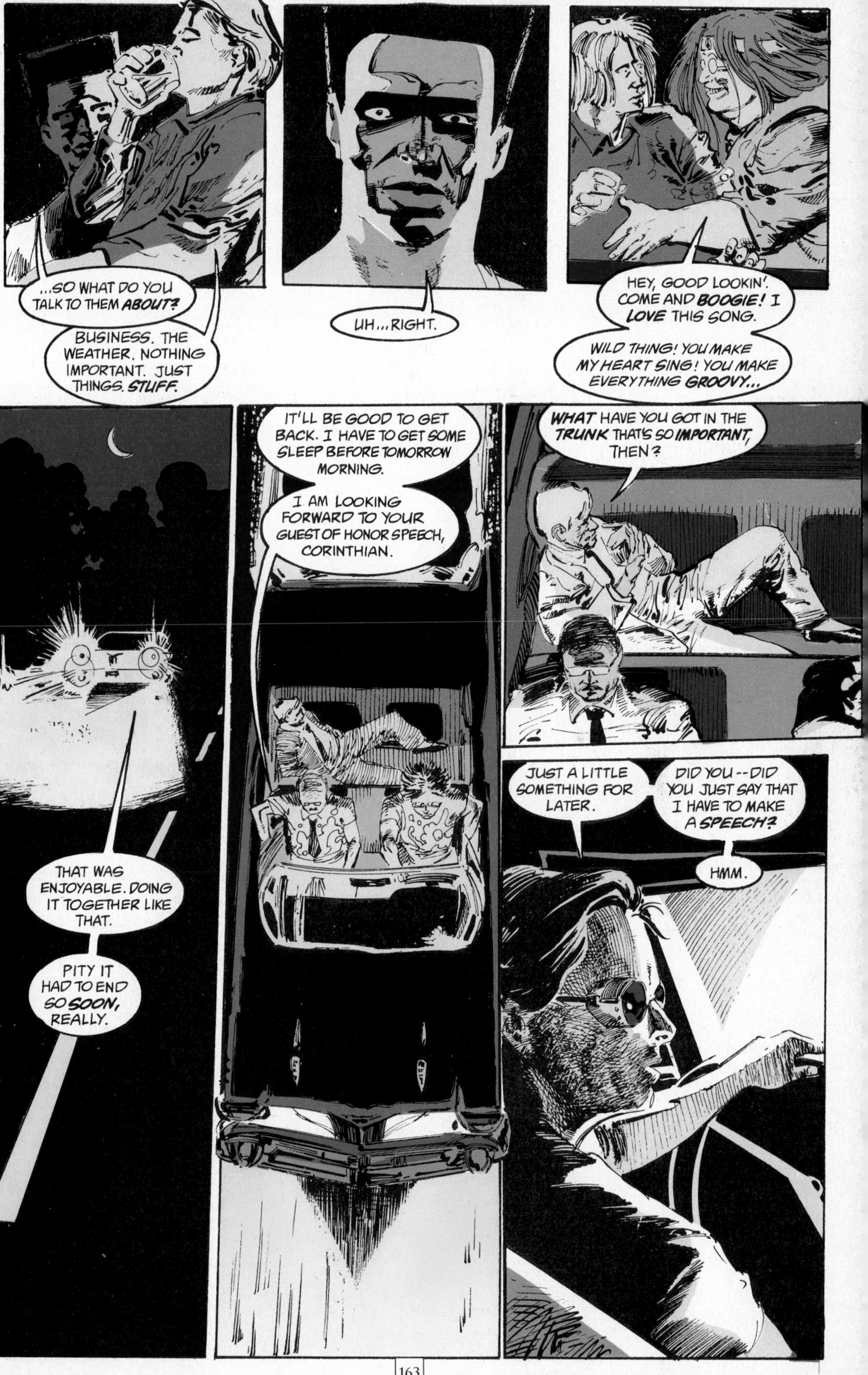
...SO WHAT DO YOU TALK TO THEM ABOUT?
BUSINESS. THE WEATHER. NOTHING IMPORTANT. JUST THINGS. STUFF.
UH... RIGHT.
HEY, GOOD LOOKIN'. COME AND BOOGIE! I LOVE THIS SONG.
WILD THING! YOU MAKE MY HEART SING! YOU MAKE EVERYTHING GROOVY...
THAT WAS ENJOYABLE. DOING IT TOGETHER LIKE THAT.
PITY IT HAD TO END SO SOON, REALLY.
IT'LL BE GOOD TO GET BACK. I HAVE TO GET SOME SLEEP BEFORE TOMORROW MORNING.
I AM LOOKING FORWARD TO YOUR GUEST OF HONOR SPEECH, CORINTHIAN.
WHAT HAVE YOU GOT IN THE TRUNK THAT'S SO IMPORTANT, THEN?
JUST A LITTLE SOMETHING FOR LATER.
DID YOU --DID YOU JUST SAY THAT I HAVE TO MAKE A SPEECH?
HMM.

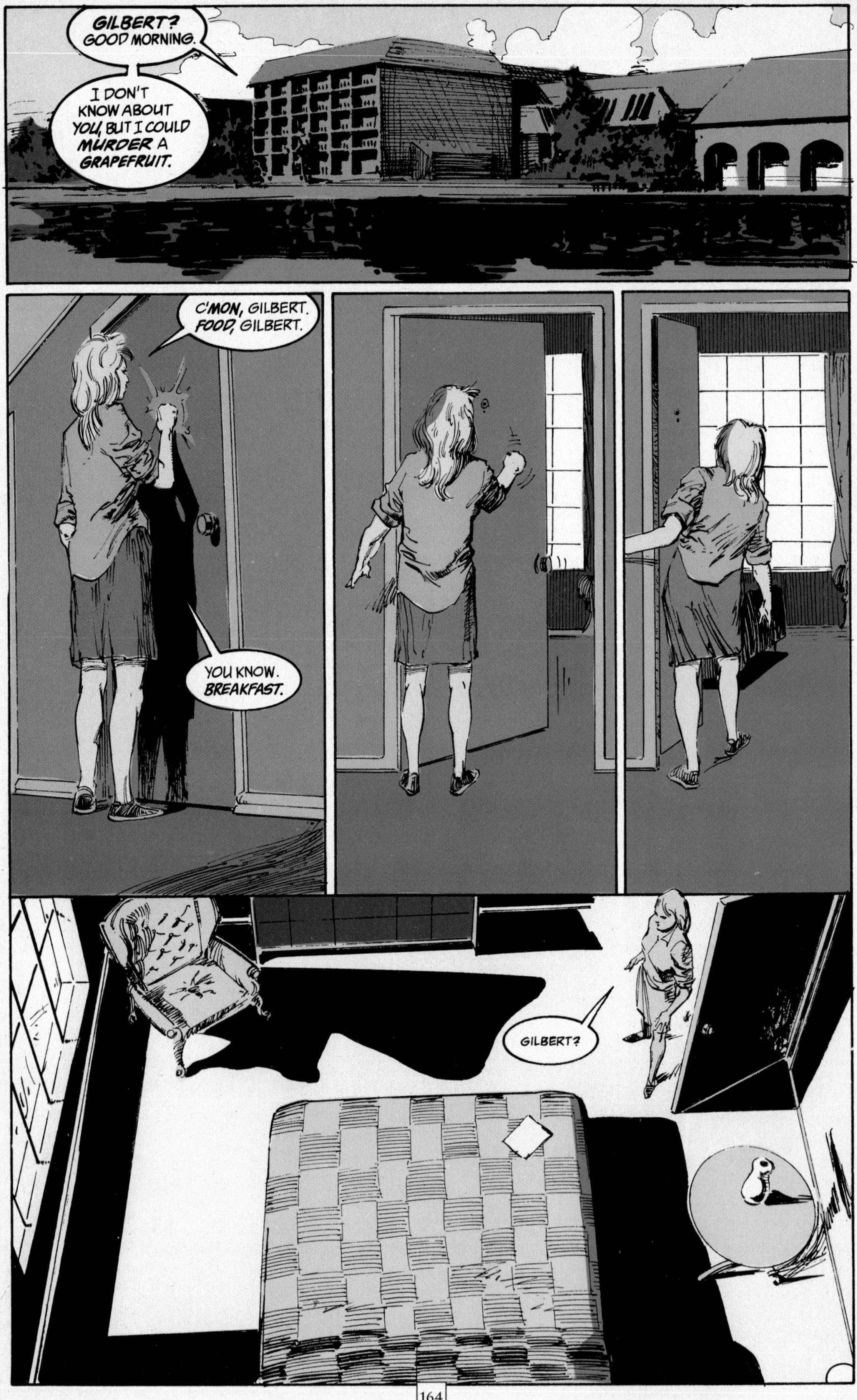
GILBERT? GOOD MORNING.
I DON'T KNOW ABOUT YOU, BUT I COULD MURDER A GRAPEFRUIT.
C'MON, GILBERT. FOOD, GILBERT.
YOU KNOW. BREAKFAST.
GILBERT?

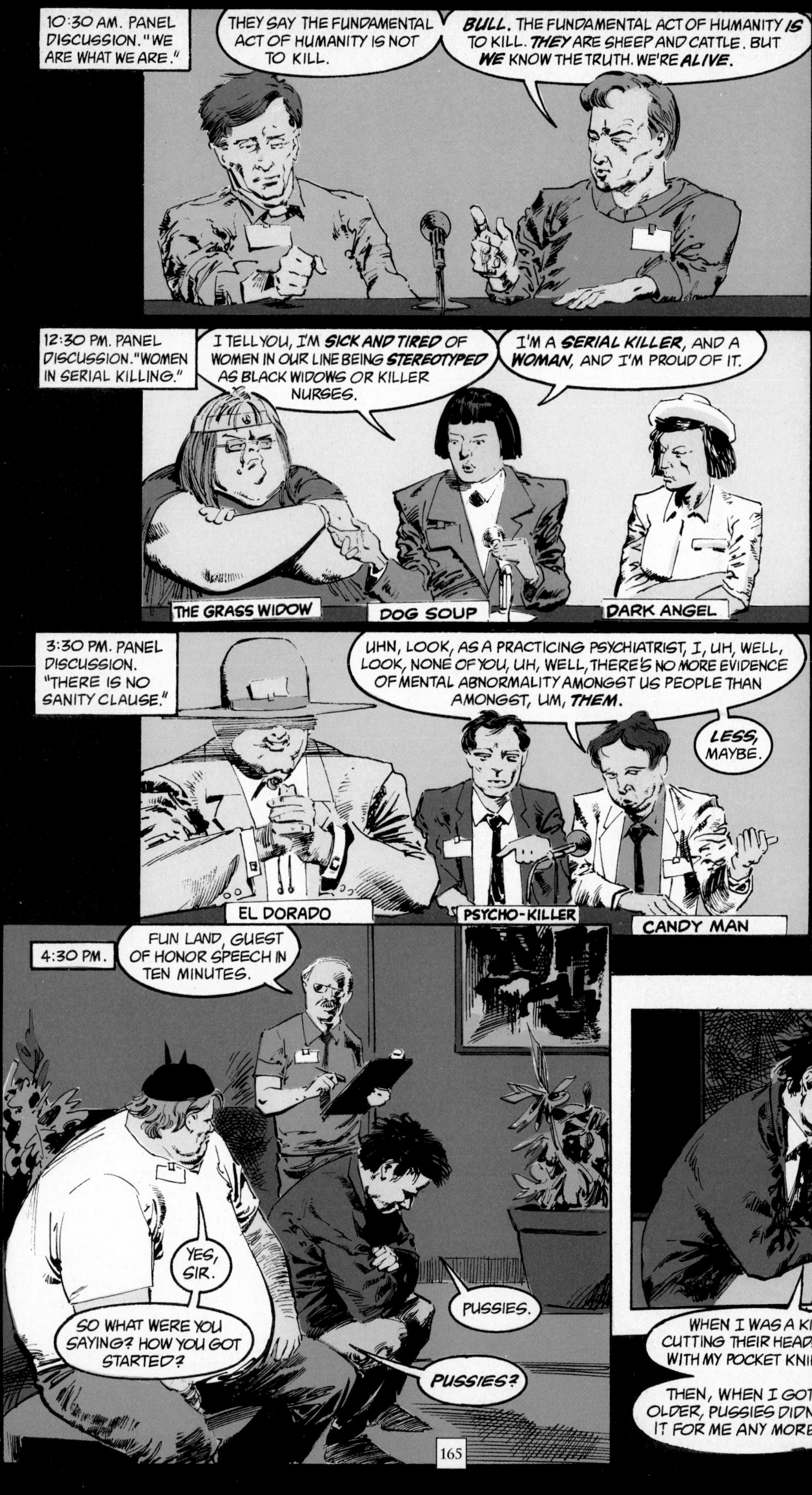

10:30 AM. PANEL DISCUSSION. "WE ARE WHAT WE ARE."
THEY SAY THE FUNDAMENTAL ACT OF HUMANITY IS NOT TO KILL.
BULL. THE FUNDAMENTAL ACT OF HUMANITY IS TO KILL. THEY ARE SHEEP AND CATTLE. BUT WE KNOW THE TRUTH. WE'RE ALIVE.
12:30 PM. PANEL DISCUSSION. "WOMEN IN SERIAL KILLING."
I TELL YOU, I'M SICK AND TIRED OF WOMEN IN OUR LINE BEING STEREOTYPED AS BLACK WIDOWS OR KILLER NURSES.
I'M A SERIAL KILLER, AND A WOMAN, AND I'M PROUD OF IT.
THE GRASS WIDOW
DOG SOUP
DARK ANGEL
3:30 PM. PANEL DISCUSSION. "THERE IS NO SANITY CLAUSE."
UHN, LOOK, AS A PRACTICING PSYCHIATRIST, I, UH, WELL, LOOK, NONE OF YOU, UH, WELL, THERE'S NO MORE EVIDENCE OF MENTAL ABNORMALITY AMONGST US PEOPLE THAN AMONGST, UM, THEM.
LESS, MAYBE.
EL DORADO
PSYCHO-KILLER
CANDY MAN
4:30 PM.
FUN LAND, GUEST OF HONOR SPEECH IN TEN MINUTES.
YES, SIR.
SO WHAT WERE YOU SAYING? HOW YOU GOT STARTED?
PUSSIES.
PUSSIES?
WHEN I WAS A KID. CUTTING THEIR HEADS OFF WITH MY POCKET KNIFE.
THEN, WHEN I GOT OLDER, PUSSIES DIDN'T DO IT FOR ME ANY MORE.

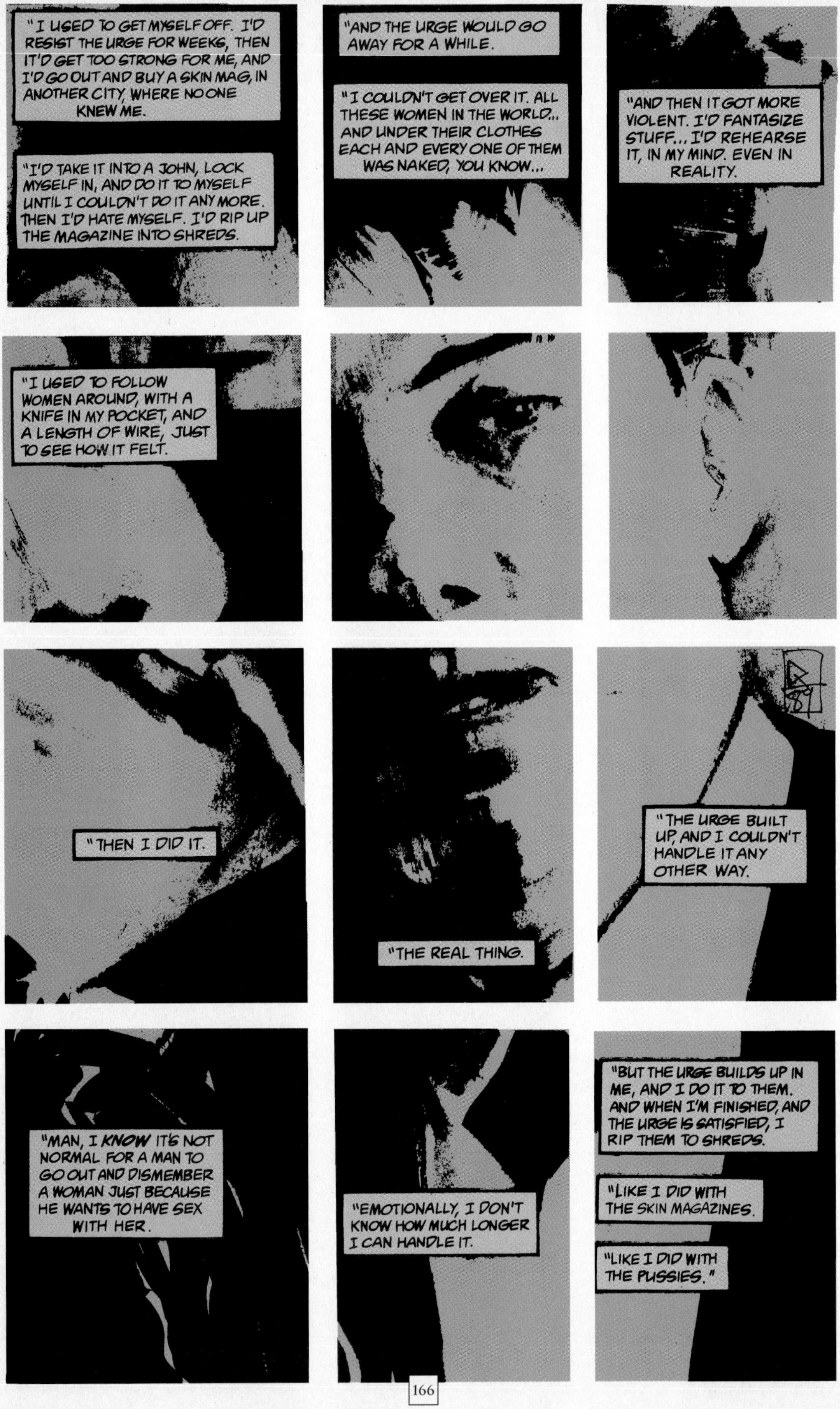
"I USED TO GET MYSELF OFF. I'D RESIST THE URGE FOR WEEKS, THEN IT'D GET TOO STRONG FOR ME, AND I'D GO OUT AND BUY A SKIN MAG, IN ANOTHER CITY, WHERE NO ONE KNEW ME.
"I'D TAKE IT INTO A JOHN, LOCK MYSELF IN, AND DO IT TO MYSELF UNTIL I COULDN'T DO IT ANY MORE. THEN I'D HATE MYSELF. I'D RIP UP THE MAGAZINE INTO SHREDS.
"AND THE URGE WOULD GO AWAY FOR A WHILE.
"I COULDN'T GET OVER IT. ALL THESE WOMEN IN THE WORLD... AND UNDER THEIR CLOTHES EACH AND EVERY ONE OF THEM WAS NAKED, YOU KNOW...
"AND THEN IT GOT MORE VIOLENT. I'D FANTASIZE STUFF... I'D REHEARSE IT, IN MY MIND. EVEN IN REALITY.
"I USED TO FOLLOW WOMEN AROUND, WITH A KNIFE IN MY POCKET, AND A LENGTH OF WIRE, JUST TO SEE HOW IT FELT.
"THEN I DID IT.
"THE REAL THING.
"THE URGE BUILT UP, AND I COULDN'T HANDLE IT ANY OTHER WAY.
"MAN, I KNOW IT'S NOT NORMAL FOR A MAN TO GO OUT AND DISMEMBER A WOMAN JUST BECAUSE HE WANTS TO HAVE SEX WITH HER.
"EMOTIONALLY, I DON'T KNOW HOW MUCH LONGER I CAN HANDLE IT.
"BUT THE URGE BUILDS UP IN ME, AND I DO IT TO THEM. AND WHEN I'M FINISHED, AND THE URGE IS SATISFIED, I RIP THEM TO SHREDS.
"LIKE I DID WITH THE SKIN MAGAZINES.
"LIKE I DID WITH THE PUSSIES."

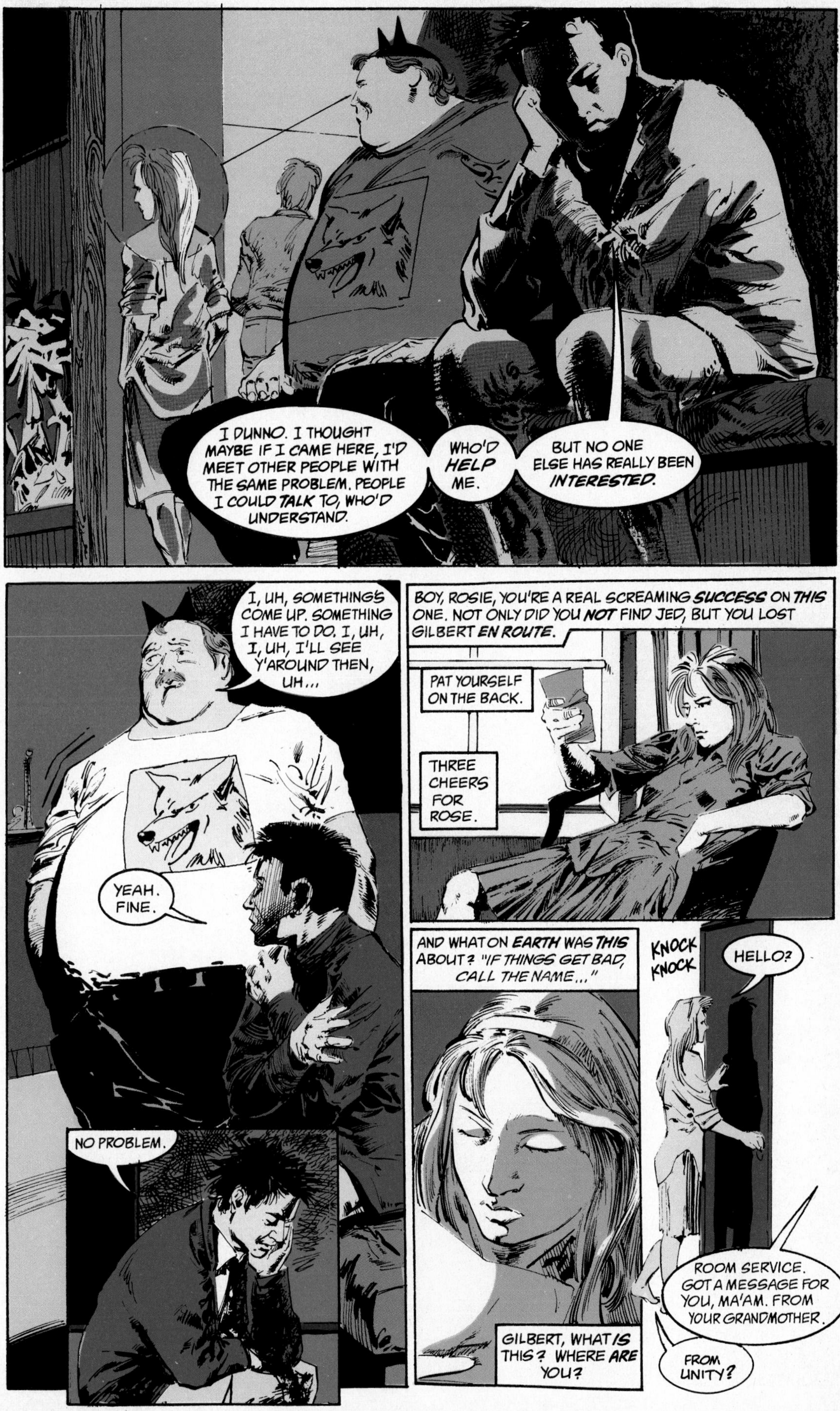
I DUNNO. I THOUGHT MAYBE IF I CAME HERE, I'D MEET OTHER PEOPLE WITH THE SAME PROBLEM. PEOPLE I COULD TALK TO, WHO'D UNDERSTAND.
WHO'D HELP ME.
BUT NO ONE ELSE HAS REALLY BEEN INTERESTED.
I, UH, SOMETHING'S COME UP. SOMETHING I HAVE TO DO. I, UH, I, UH, I'LL SEE Y'AROUND THEN, UH...
YEAH. FINE.
NO PROBLEM.
BOY, ROSIE, YOU'RE A REAL SCREAMING SUCCESS ON THIS ONE. NOT ONLY DID YOU NOT FIND JED, BUT YOU LOST GILBERT EN ROUTE.
PAT YOURSELF ON THE BACK.
THREE CHEERS FOR ROSE.
AND WHAT ON EARTH WAS THIS ABOUT? "IF THINGS GET BAD, CALL THE NAME..."
GILBERT, WHAT IS THIS? WHERE ARE YOU?
KNOCK KNOCK
HELLO?
ROOM SERVICE. GOT A MESSAGE FOR YOU, MA'AM. FROM YOUR GRANDMOTHER.
FROM UNITY?

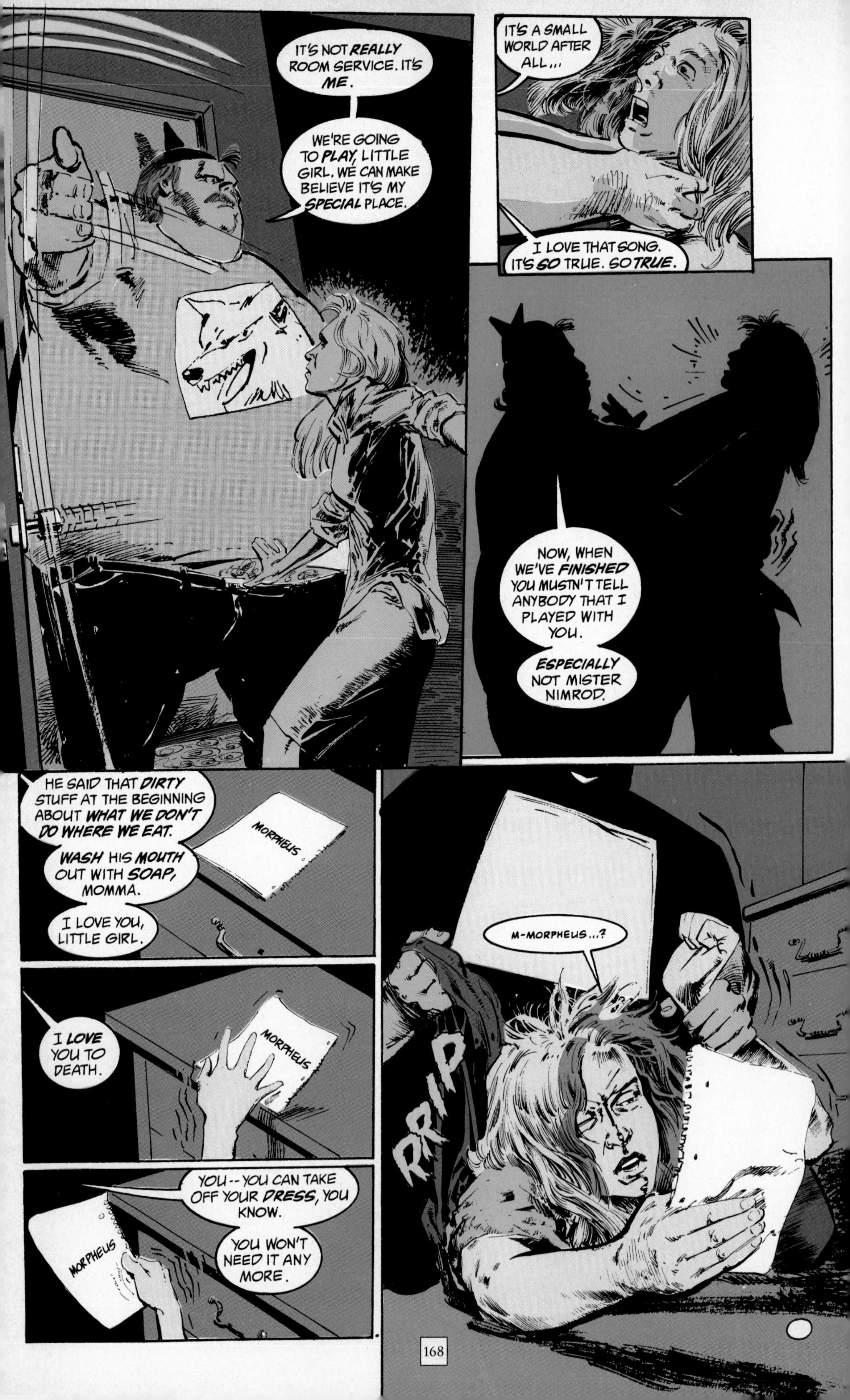

IT'S NOT REALLY ROOM SERVICE. IT'S ME.
WE'RE GOING TO PLAY, LITTLE GIRL. WE CAN MAKE BELIEVE IT'S MY SPECIAL PLACE.
IT'S A SMALL WORLD AFTER ALL...
I LOVE THAT SONG. IT'S SO TRUE. SO TRUE.
NOW, WHEN WE'VE FINISHED YOU MUSTN'T TELL ANYBODY THAT I PLAYED WITH YOU.
ESPECIALLY NOT MISTER NIMROD.
HE SAID THAT DIRTY STUFF AT THE BEGINNING ABOUT WHAT WE DON'T DO WHERE WE EAT.
WASH HIS MOUTH OUT WITH SOAP, MOMMA.
I LOVE YOU, LITTLE GIRL.
MORPHEUS
I LOVE YOU TO DEATH.
MORPHEUS
YOU--YOU CAN TAKE OFF YOUR DRESS, YOU KNOW.
YOU WON'T NEED IT ANY MORE.
MORPHEUS
M-MORPHEUS...?
RRIP

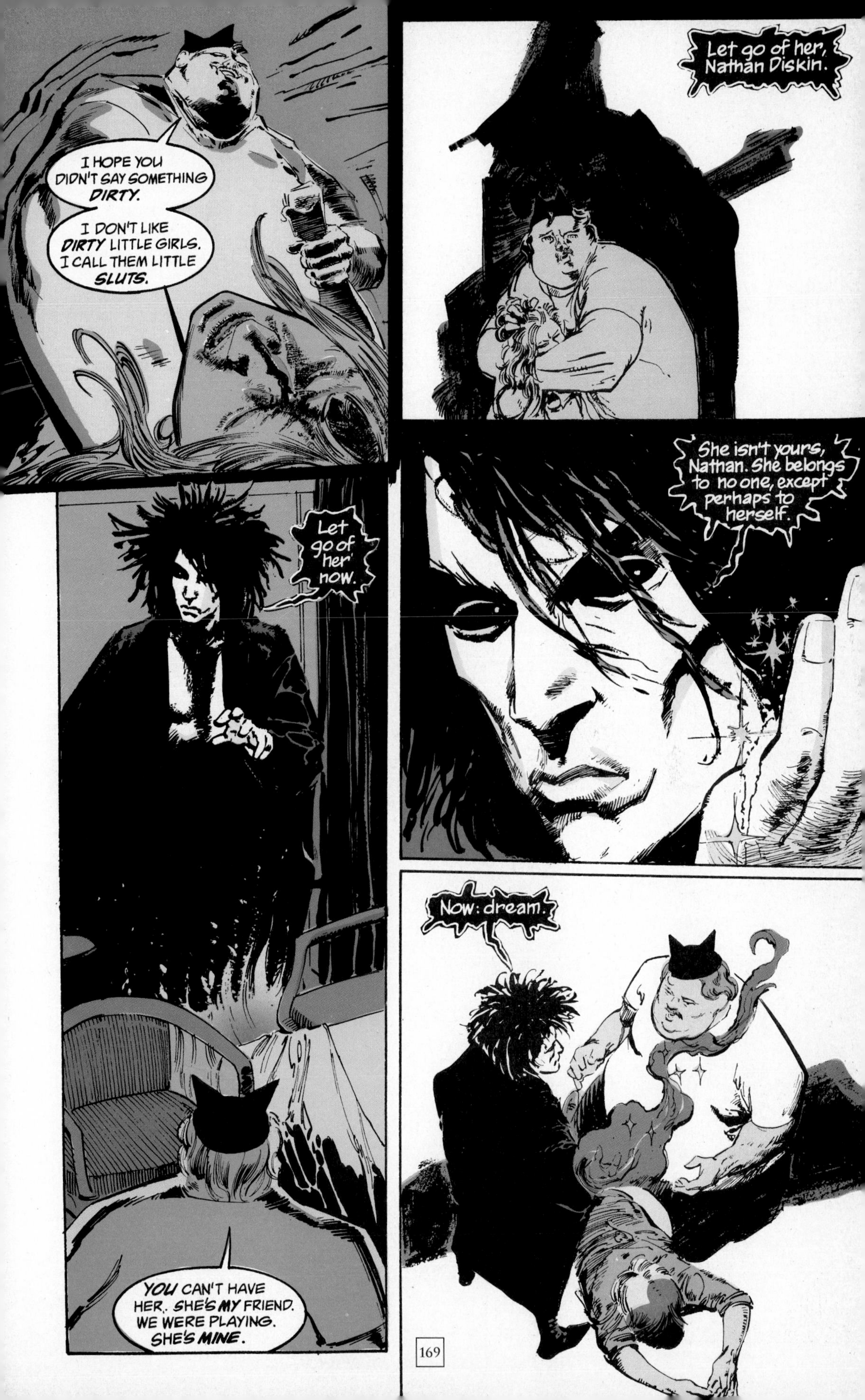

I HOPE YOU DIDN'T SAY SOMETHING DIRTY.
I DON'T LIKE DIRTY LITTLE GIRLS. I CALL THEM LITTLE SLUTS.
Let go of her, Nathan Diskin.
Let go of her now.
YOU CAN'T HAVE HER. SHE'S MY FRIEND. WE WERE PLAYING. SHE'S MINE.
She isn't yours, Nathan. She belongs to no one, except perhaps to herself.
Now: dream.

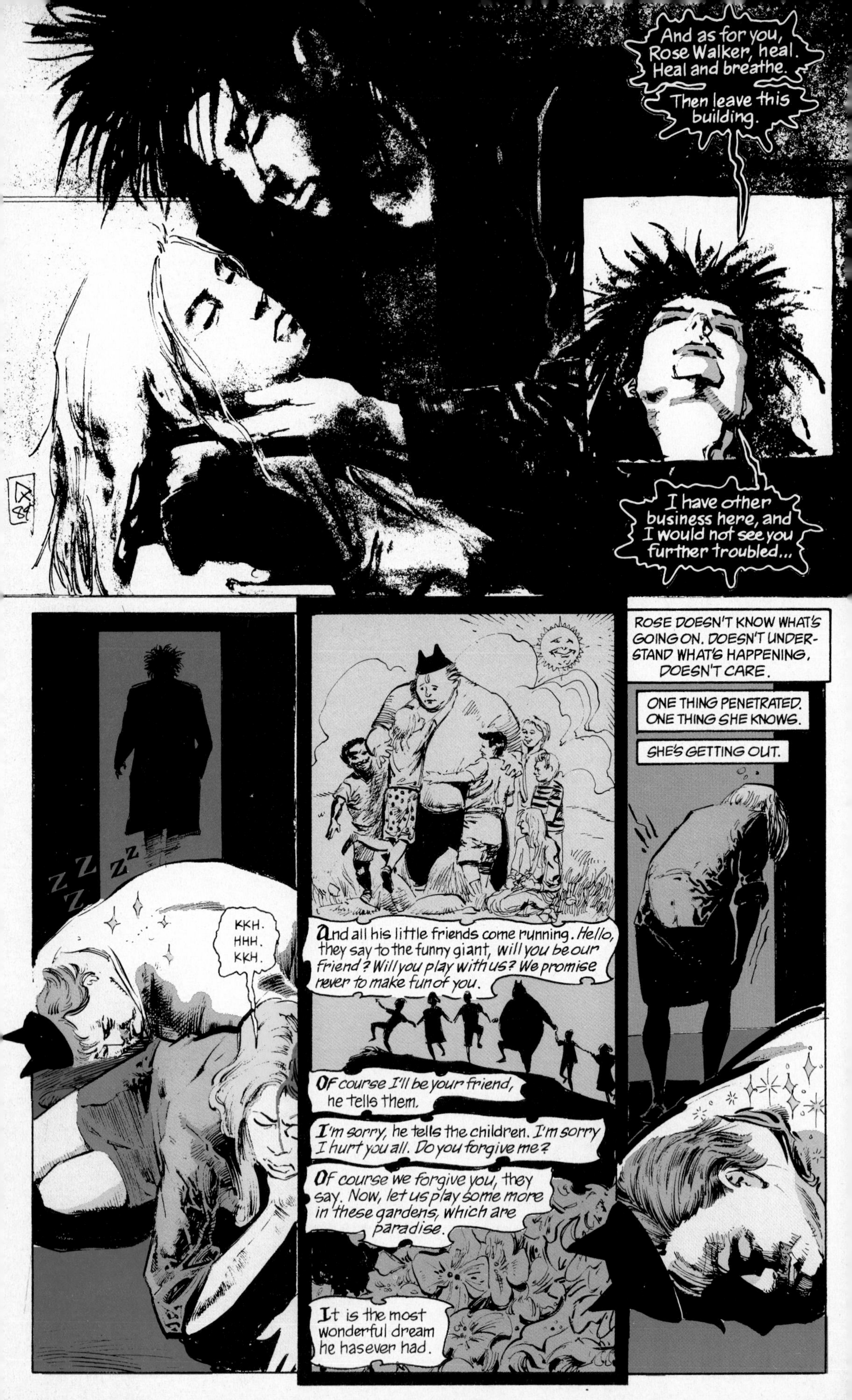
And as for you, Rose Walker, heal. Heal and breathe.
Then leave this building.
I have other business here, and I would not see you further troubled...
ROSE DOESN'T KNOW WHAT'S GOING ON. DOESN'T UNDERSTAND WHAT'S HAPPENING. DOESN'T CARE.
ONE THING PENETRATED. ONE THING SHE KNOWS.
SHE'S GETTING OUT.
ZZ ZZ
KKH. HHH. KKH.
And all his little friends come running. Hello, they say to the funny giant, will you be our friend? Will you play with us? We promise never to make fun of you.
Of course I'll be your friend, he tells them.
I'm sorry, he tells the children. I'm sorry I hurt you all. Do you forgive me?
Of course we forgive you, they say. Now, let us play some more in these gardens, which are paradise.
It is the most wonderful dream he has ever had.

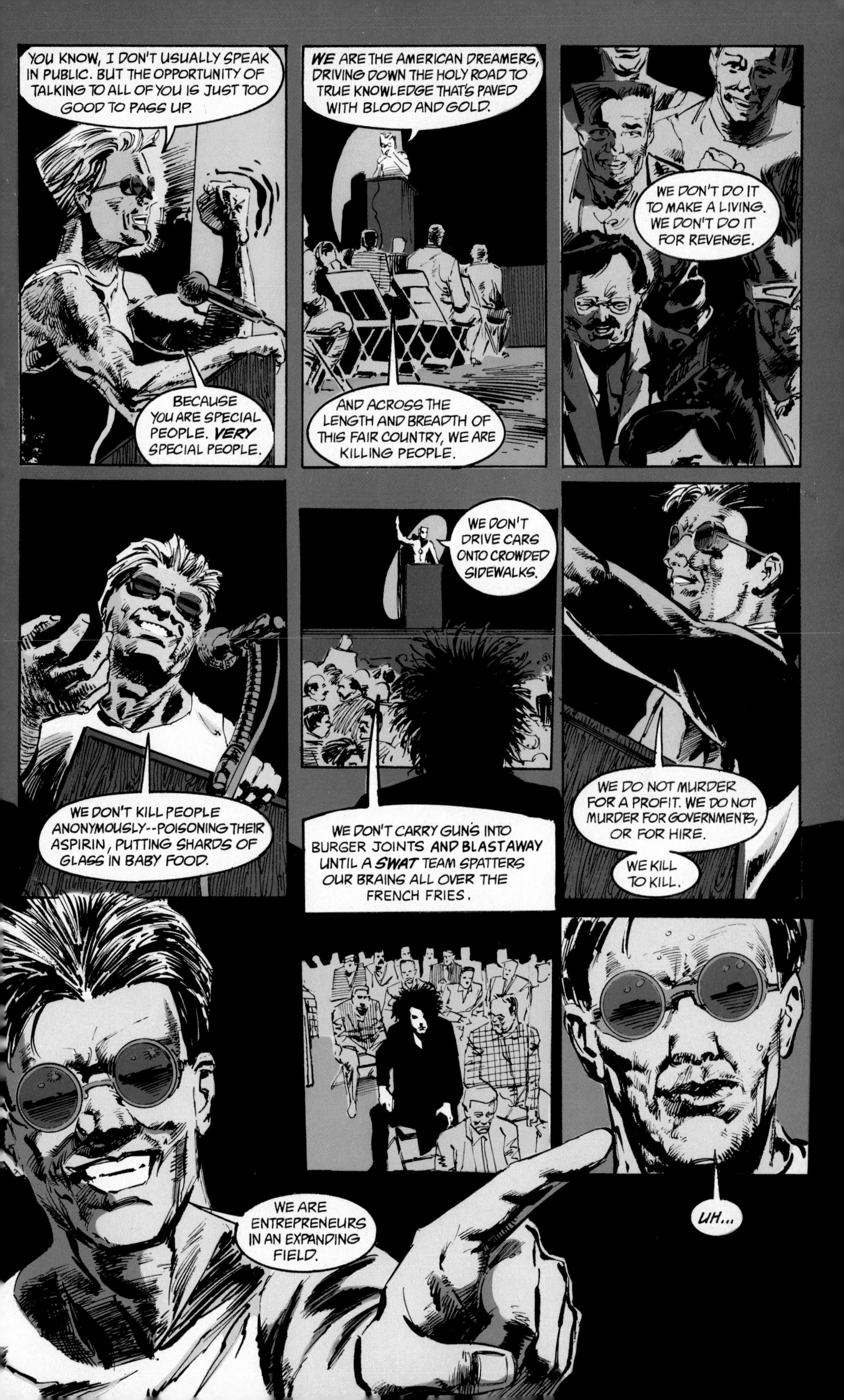
YOU KNOW, I DON'T USUALLY SPEAK IN PUBLIC. BUT THE OPPORTUNITY OF TALKING TO ALL OF YOU IS JUST TOO GOOD TO PASS UP.
BECAUSE YOU ARE SPECIAL PEOPLE. VERY SPECIAL PEOPLE.
WE ARE THE AMERICAN DREAMERS, DRIVING DOWN THE HOLY ROAD TO TRUE KNOWLEDGE THAT'S PAVED WITH BLOOD AND GOLD.
AND ACROSS THE LENGTH AND BREADTH OF THIS FAIR COUNTRY, WE ARE KILLING PEOPLE.
WE DON'T DO IT TO MAKE A LIVING. WE DON'T DO IT FOR REVENGE.
WE DON'T KILL PEOPLE ANONYMOUSLY--POISONING THEIR ASPIRIN, PUTTING SHARDS OF GLASS IN BABY FOOD.
WE DON'T DRIVE CARS ONTO CROWDED SIDEWALKS.
WE DON'T CARRY GUNS INTO BURGER JOINTS AND BLAST AWAY UNTIL A SWAT TEAM SPATTERS OUR BRAINS ALL OVER THE FRENCH FRIES.
WE DO NOT MURDER FOR A PROFIT. WE DO NOT MURDER FOR GOVERNMENTS, OR FOR HIRE.
WE KILL TO KILL.
WE ARE ENTREPRENEURS IN AN EXPANDING FIELD.
UH...

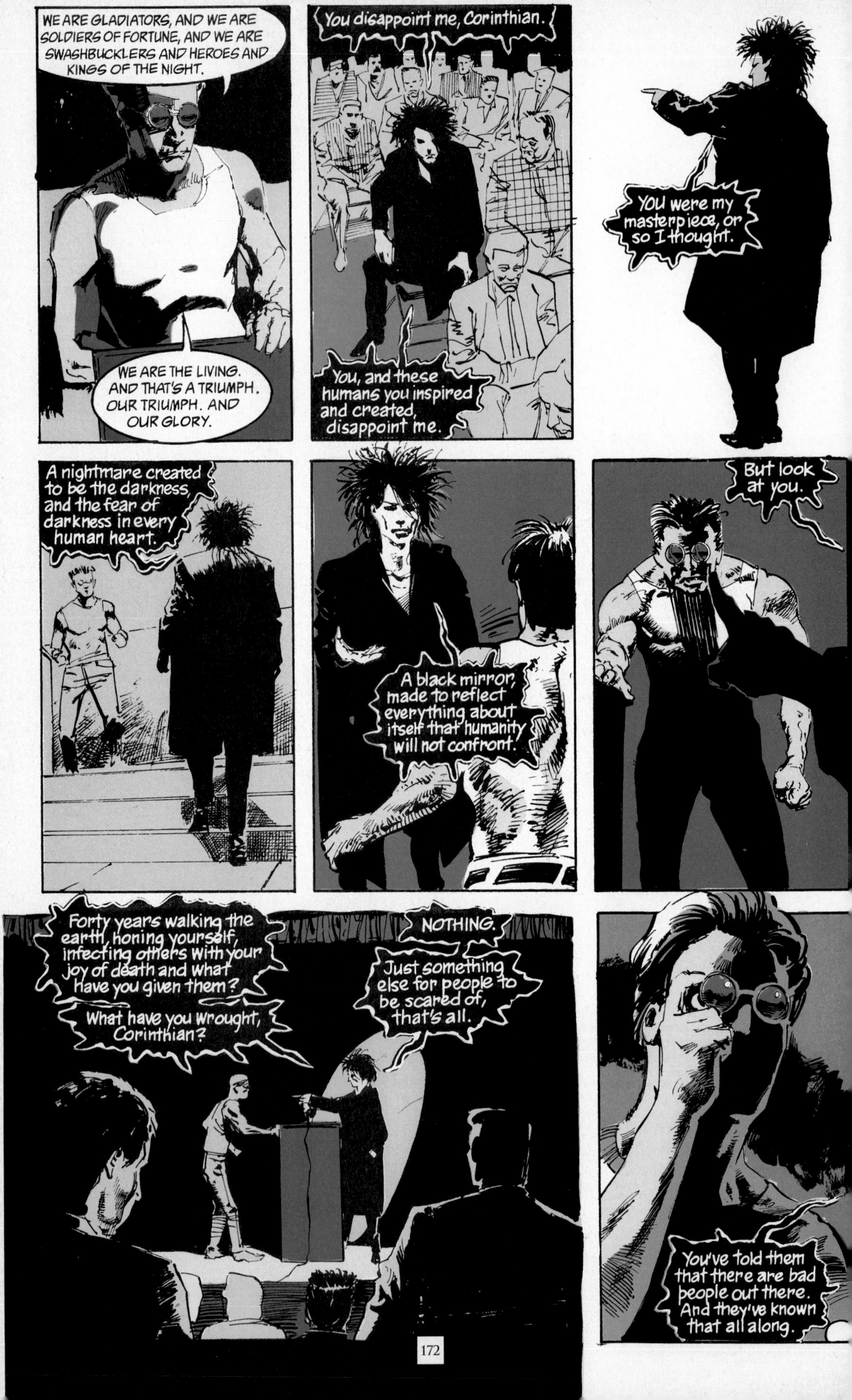
WE ARE GLADIATORS, AND WE ARE SOLDIERS OF FORTUNE, AND WE ARE SWASHBUCKLERS AND HEROES AND KINGS OF THE NIGHT.
WE ARE THE LIVING. AND THAT'S A TRIUMPH. OUR TRIUMPH. AND OUR GLORY.
You disappoint me, Corinthian.
You, and these humans you inspired and created, disappoint me.
YOU were my masterpiece, or so I thought.
A nightmare created to be the darkness, and the fear of darkness in every human heart.
A black mirror, made to reflect everything about itself that humanity will not confront.
But look at you.
Forty years walking the earth, honing yourself, infecting others with your joy of death and what have you given them?
What have you wrought, Corinthian?
NOTHING.
Just something else for people to be scared of, that's all.
You've told them that there are bad people out there. And they've known that all along.

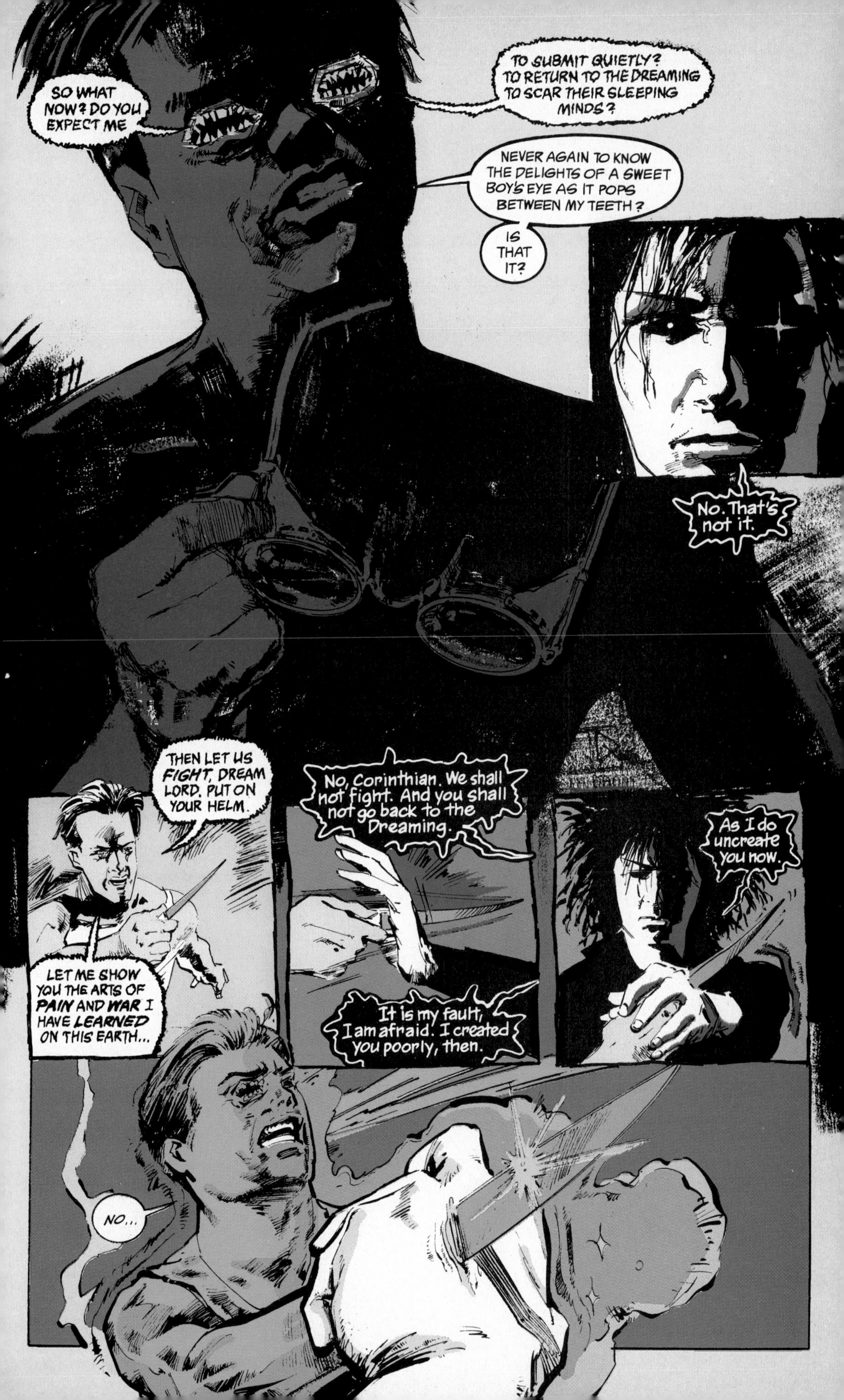
SO WHAT NOW? DO YOU EXPECT ME
TO SUBMIT QUIETLY? TO RETURN TO THE DREAMING TO SCAR THEIR SLEEPING MINDS?
NEVER AGAIN TO KNOW THE DELIGHTS OF A SWEET BOY'S EYE AS IT POPS BETWEEN MY TEETH?
IS THAT IT?
No. That's not it.
THEN LET US FIGHT, DREAM LORD. PUT ON YOUR HELM.
LET ME SHOW YOU THE ARTS OF PAIN AND WAR I HAVE LEARNED ON THIS EARTH...
No, Corinthian. We shall not fight. And you shall not go back to the Dreaming.
It is my fault, I am afraid. I created you poorly, then.
As I do uncreate you now.
NO...

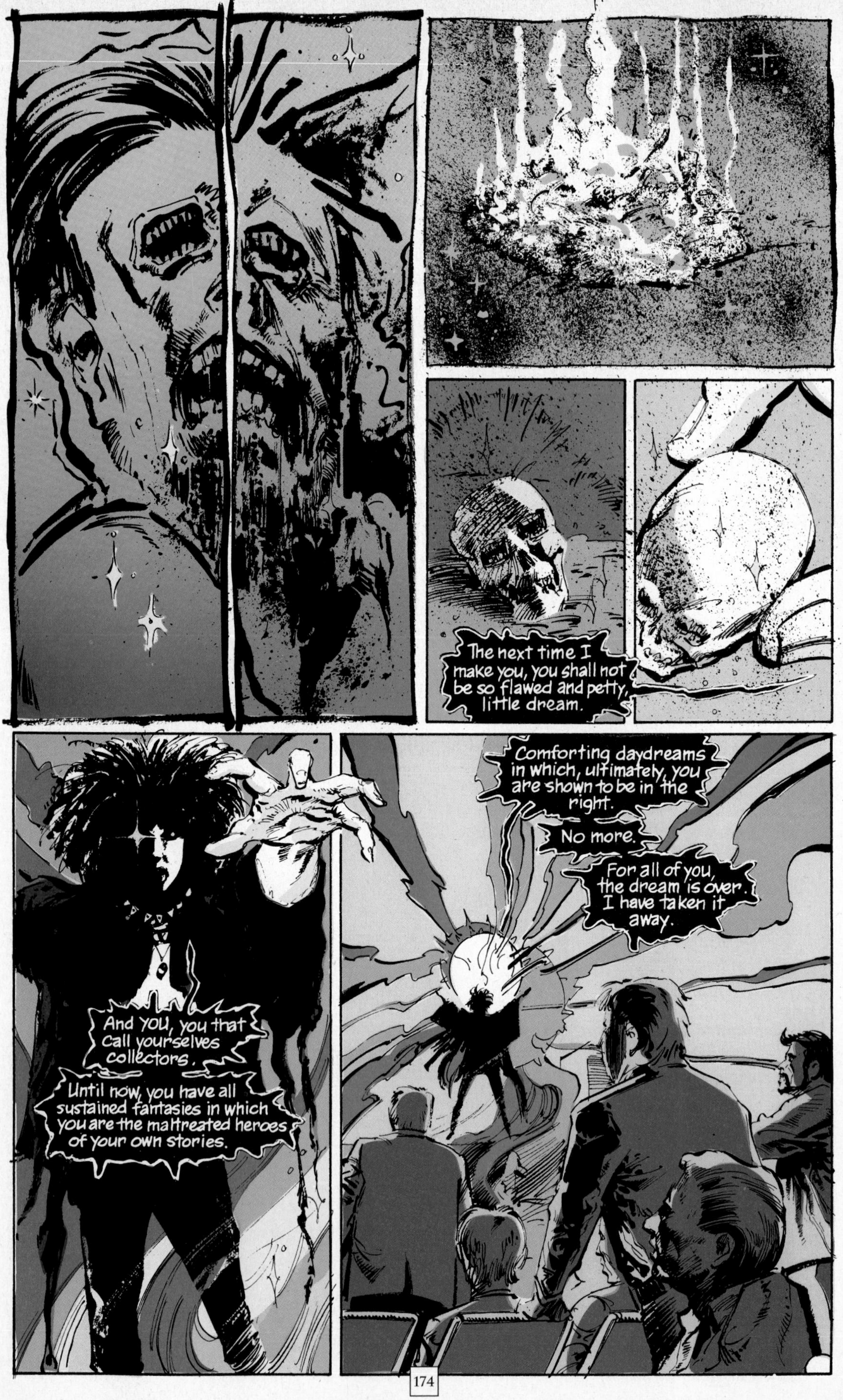

The next time I make you, you shall not be so flawed and petty, little dream.
And YOU, you that call yourselves collectors.
Until now, you have all sustained fantasies in which you are the maltreated heroes of your own stories.
Comforting daydreams in which, ultimately, you are shown to be in the right.
No more.
For all of you, the dream is over. I have taken it away.

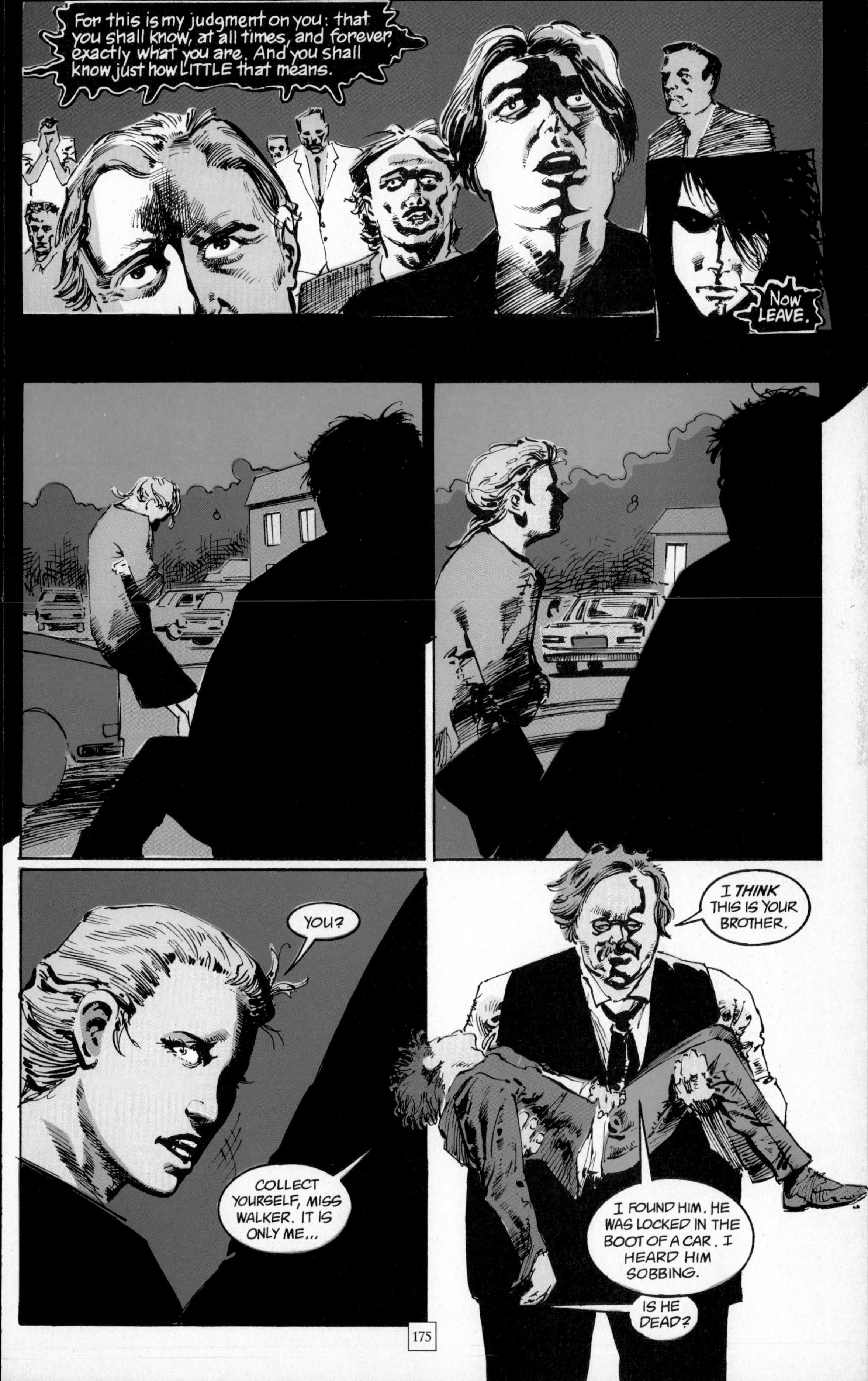
For this is my judgment on you: that you shall know, at all times, and forever, exactly what you are. And you shall know just how LITTLE that means.
NOW LEAVE.
YOU?
COLLECT YOURSELF, MISS WALKER. IT IS ONLY ME...
I THINK THIS IS YOUR BROTHER.
I FOUND HIM. HE WAS LOCKED IN THE BOOT OF A CAR. I HEARD HIM SOBBING.
IS HE DEAD?

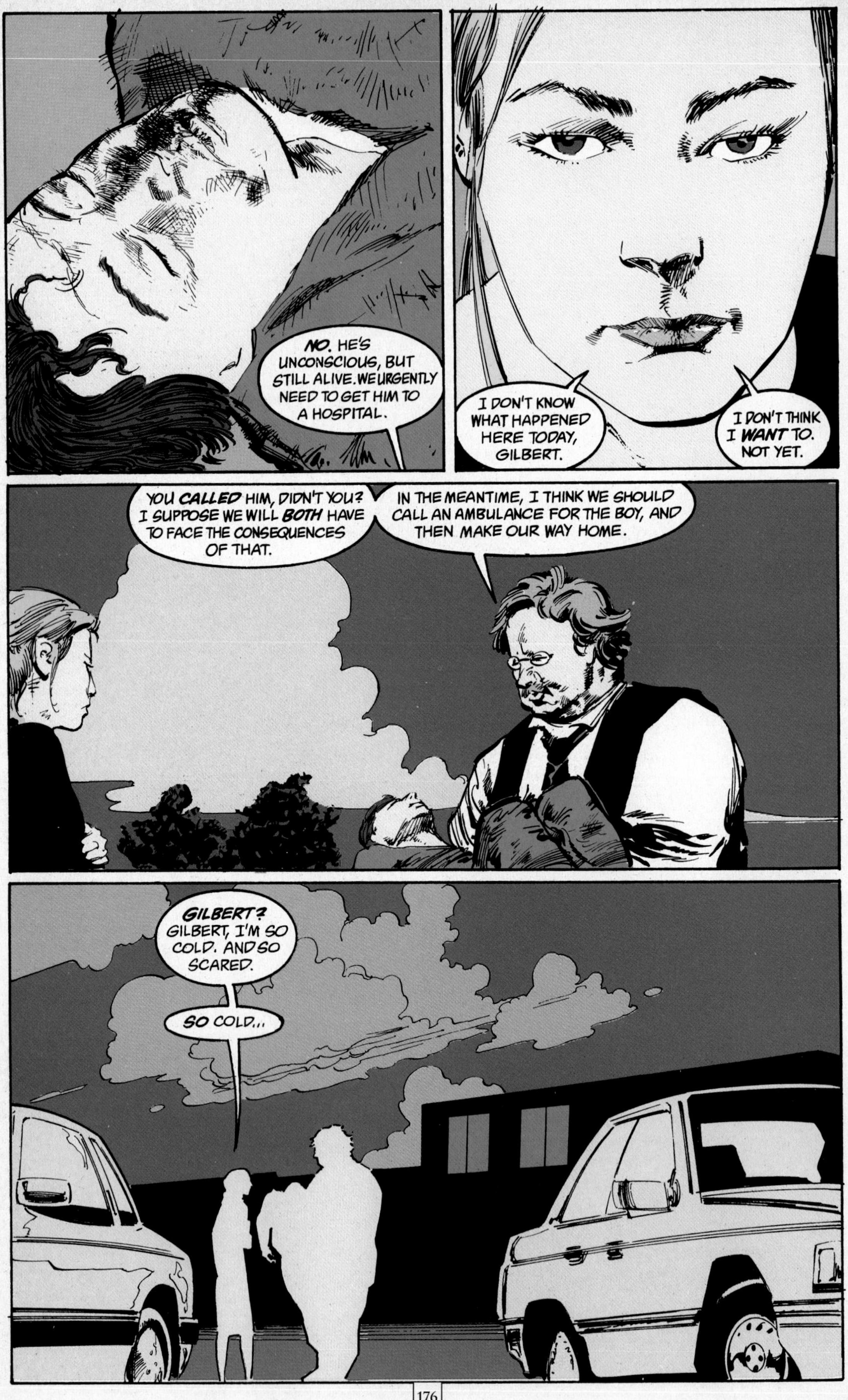
NO. HE'S UNCONSCIOUS, BUT STILL ALIVE. WE URGENTLY NEED TO GET HIM TO A HOSPITAL.
I DON'T KNOW WHAT HAPPENED HERE TODAY, GILBERT.
I DON'T THINK I WANT TO. NOT YET.
YOU CALLED HIM, DIDN'T YOU? I SUPPOSE WE WILL BOTH HAVE TO FACE THE CONSEQUENCES OF THAT.
IN THE MEANTIME, I THINK WE SHOULD CALL AN AMBULANCE FOR THE BOY, AND THEN MAKE OUR WAY HOME.
GILBERT? GILBERT, I'M SO COLD. AND SO SCARED.
SO COLD...

THE FIRST WIND OF WINTER BLEW FROM THE NORTH, AND IT HAD ICE AND RIME ON ITS BREATH.

IT WAS DIRTY AND SHARP AND IT CUT LIKE A RAZOR, AND IF IT TOUCHED YOU, YOU COULD WASH AND WASH UNTIL YOUR SKIN WAS TATTERED AND BLOODIED, BUT YOU'D NEVER BE CLEAN AGAIN.

WELCOME CEREAL CONVENTION

IT SCATTERED THEM INTO THE NIGHT, THE QUIET ONES WITH DEATH IN THEIR EYES.

BUT THEY LEFT MORE TENTATIVELY THAN THEY HAD COME, AS IF THEY HAD SEEN SOMETHING UNHOLY INSIDE THEMSELVES; SOMETHING THEY WOULD NEVER BE ABLE TO FORGET.

AND THEY LEFT, SLOWLY, ONE BY ONE, WITH RELUCTANCE, LEAVING THE SAFETY OF THE LIGHT FOR THE CHILL CERTAINTIES OF THE DARKNESS.

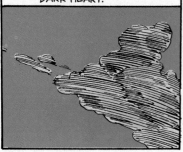

IT SEEMED LIKE THE NIGHT SUCKED THEM UP, TOOK THEM INTO ITS DARK HEART.

IT SEEMED LIKE THE DARKNESS SWALLOWED THEM...

PERHAPS IT DID.

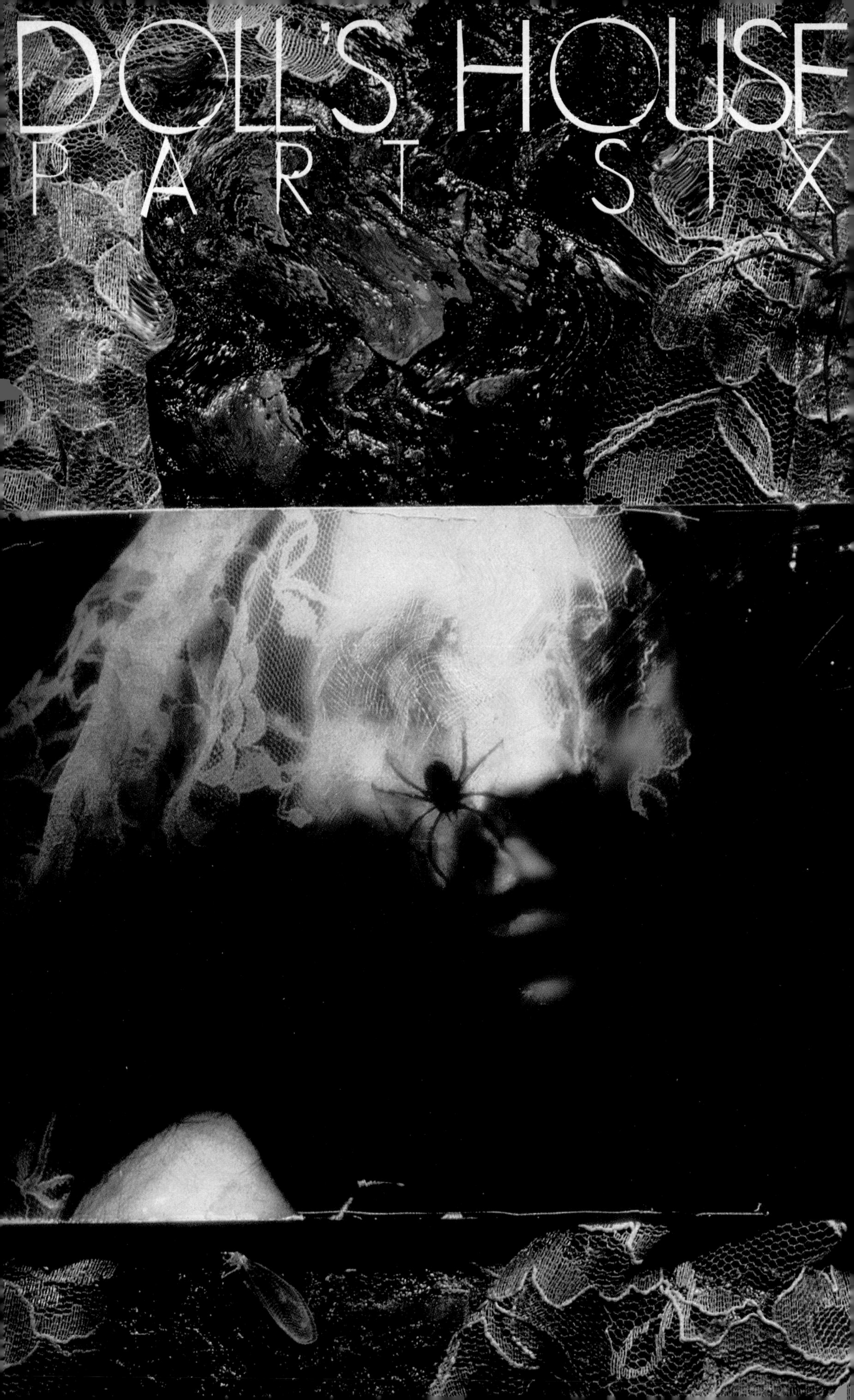
DOLL'S HOUSE
PART SIX

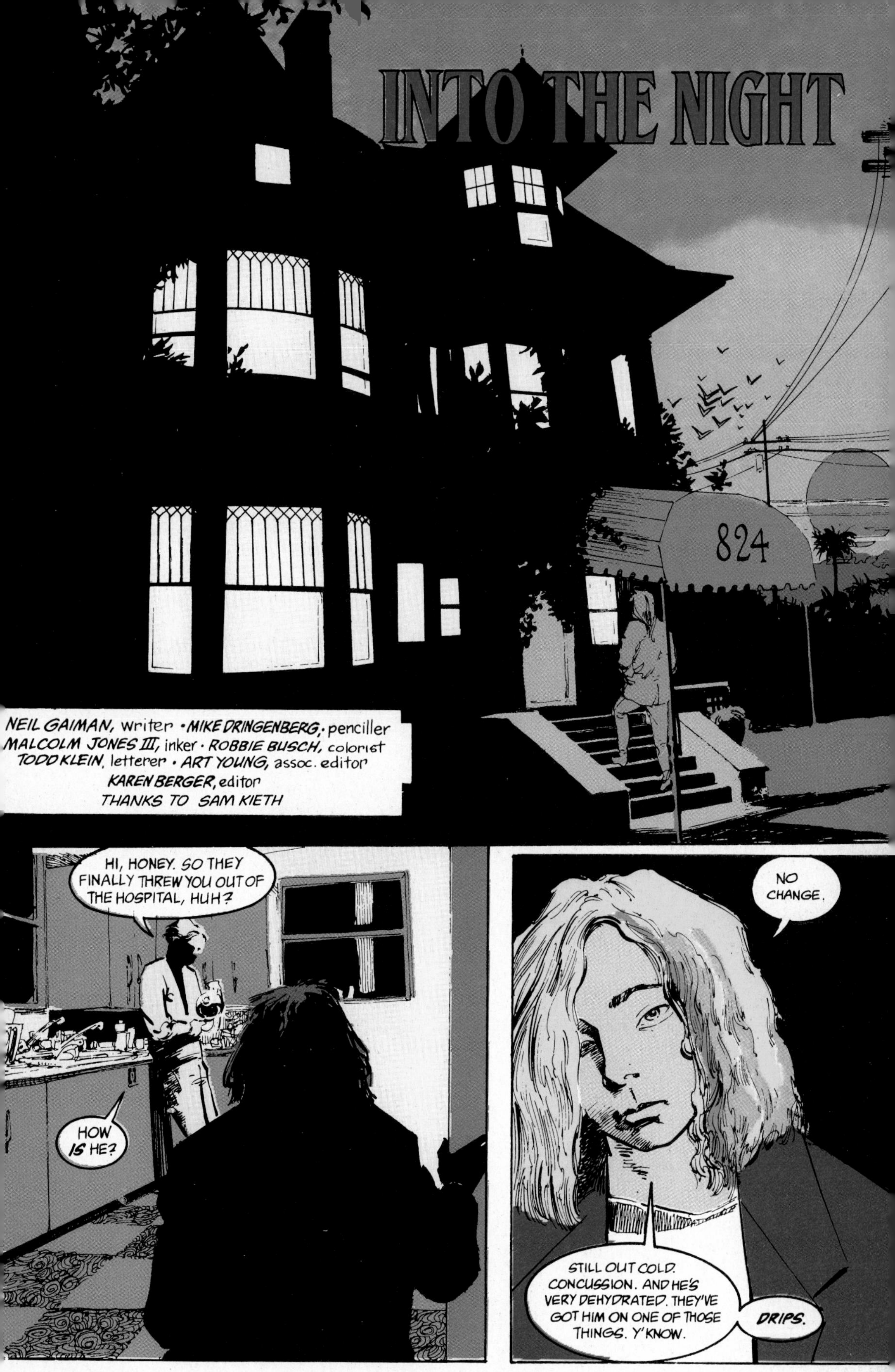
INTO THE NIGHT
824
NEIL GAIMAN, writer • MIKE DRINGENBERG, penciller
MALCOLM JONES III, inker • ROBBIE BUSCH, colorist
TODD KLEIN, letterer • ART YOUNG, assoc. editor
KAREN BERGER, editor
THANKS TO SAM KIETH
HI, HONEY. SO THEY FINALLY THREW YOU OUT OF THE HOSPITAL, HUH?
HOW IS HE?
NO CHANGE.
STILL OUT COLD. CONCUSSION. AND HE'S VERY DEHYDRATED. THEY'VE GOT HIM ON ONE OF THOSE THINGS. Y'KNOW.
DRIPS.

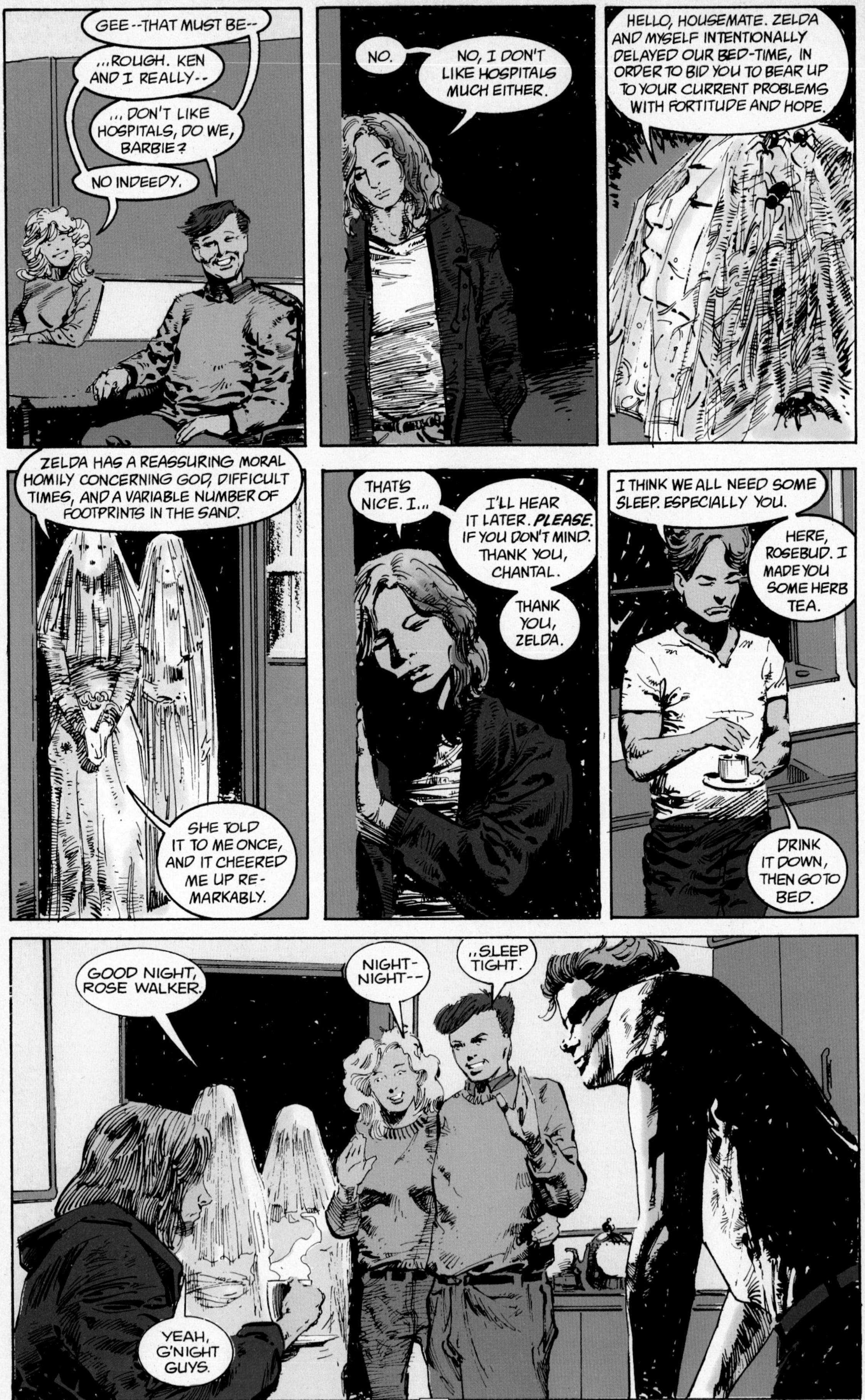
GEE--THAT MUST BE--
...ROUGH. KEN AND I REALLY--
...DON'T LIKE HOSPITALS, DO WE, BARBIE?
NO INDEEDY.
NO.
NO, I DON'T LIKE HOSPITALS MUCH EITHER.
HELLO, HOUSEMATE. ZELDA AND MYSELF INTENTIONALLY DELAYED OUR BED-TIME, IN ORDER TO BID YOU TO BEAR UP TO YOUR CURRENT PROBLEMS WITH FORTITUDE AND HOPE.
ZELDA HAS A REASSURING MORAL HOMILY CONCERNING GOD, DIFFICULT TIMES, AND A VARIABLE NUMBER OF FOOTPRINTS IN THE SAND.
SHE TOLD IT TO ME ONCE, AND IT CHEERED ME UP RE-MARKABLY.
THAT'S NICE. I...
I'LL HEAR IT LATER. PLEASE. IF YOU DON'T MIND. THANK YOU, CHANTAL.
THANK YOU, ZELDA.
I THINK WE ALL NEED SOME SLEEP. ESPECIALLY YOU.
HERE, ROSEBUD. I MADE YOU SOME HERB TEA.
DRINK IT DOWN, THEN GO TO BED.
GOOD NIGHT, ROSE WALKER.
NIGHT-NIGHT--
..SLEEP TIGHT.
YEAH, G'NIGHT GUYS.

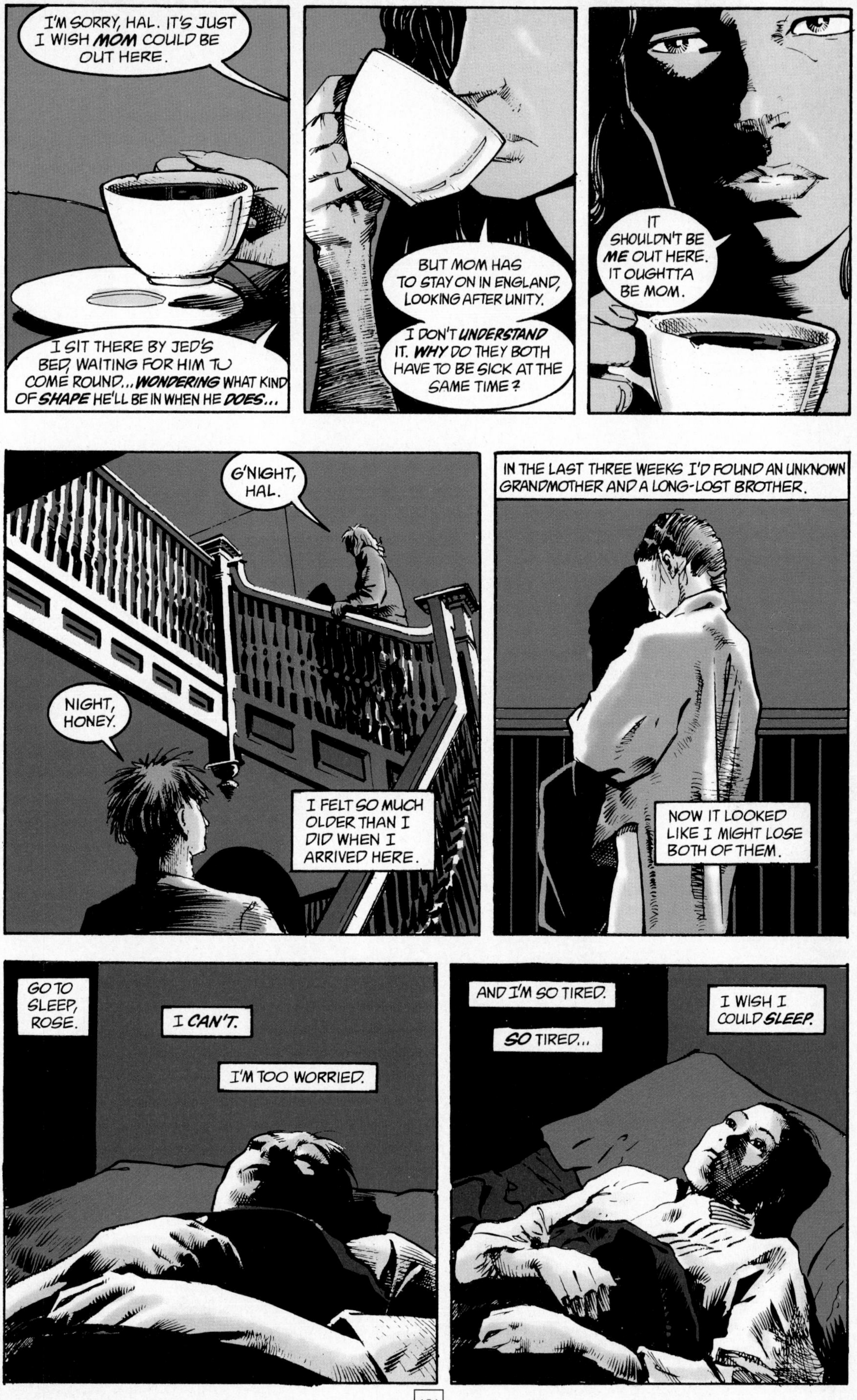

I'M SORRY, HAL. IT'S JUST I WISH **MOM** COULD BE OUT HERE.
I SIT THERE BY JED'S BED, WAITING FOR HIM TO COME ROUND... **WONDERING** WHAT KIND OF **SHAPE** HE'LL BE IN WHEN HE **DOES...**
BUT MOM HAS TO STAY ON IN ENGLAND, LOOKING AFTER UNITY.
I DON'T **UNDERSTAND** IT. **WHY** DO THEY BOTH HAVE TO BE SICK AT THE SAME TIME?
IT SHOULDN'T BE **ME** OUT HERE. IT OUGHTTA BE MOM.
G'NIGHT, HAL.
NIGHT, HONEY.
I FELT SO MUCH OLDER THAN I DID WHEN I ARRIVED HERE.
IN THE LAST THREE WEEKS I'D FOUND AN UNKNOWN GRANDMOTHER AND A LONG-LOST BROTHER.
NOW IT LOOKED LIKE I MIGHT LOSE BOTH OF THEM.
GO TO SLEEP, ROSE.
I **CAN'T.**
I'M TOO WORRIED.
AND I'M SO TIRED.
SO TIRED...
I WISH I COULD **SLEEP.**

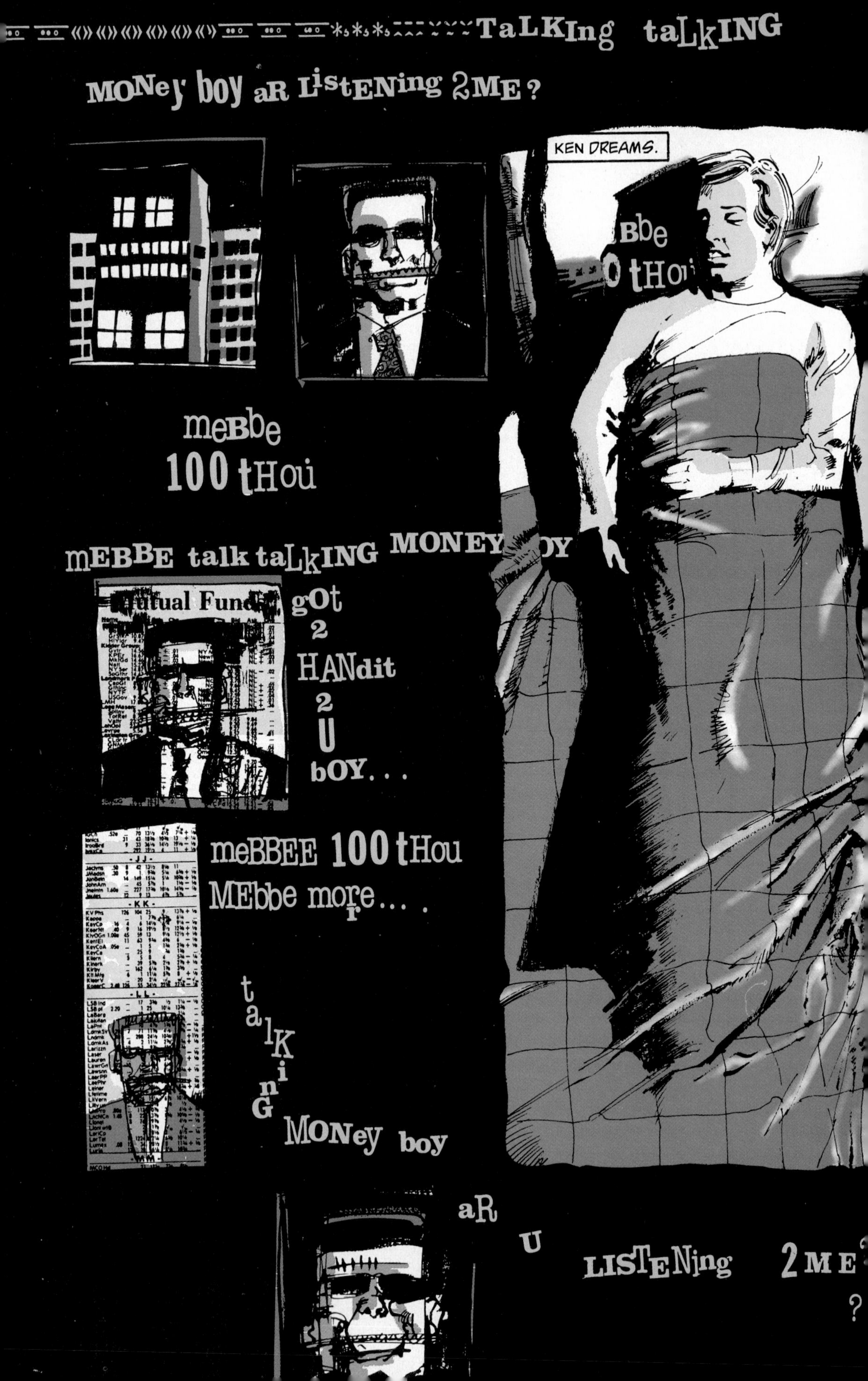
TaLKIng taLkING
MONey boy aR LIstENing 2ME?
KEN DREAMS.
mebbe 100 tHou
mEBBE talk taLkING MONEY
Mutual Funds
gOt 2 HANdit 2 U bOY...
meBBEE 100 tHou
MEbbe more....
talKing MONey boy
aR U LISTENjng 2ME?
?

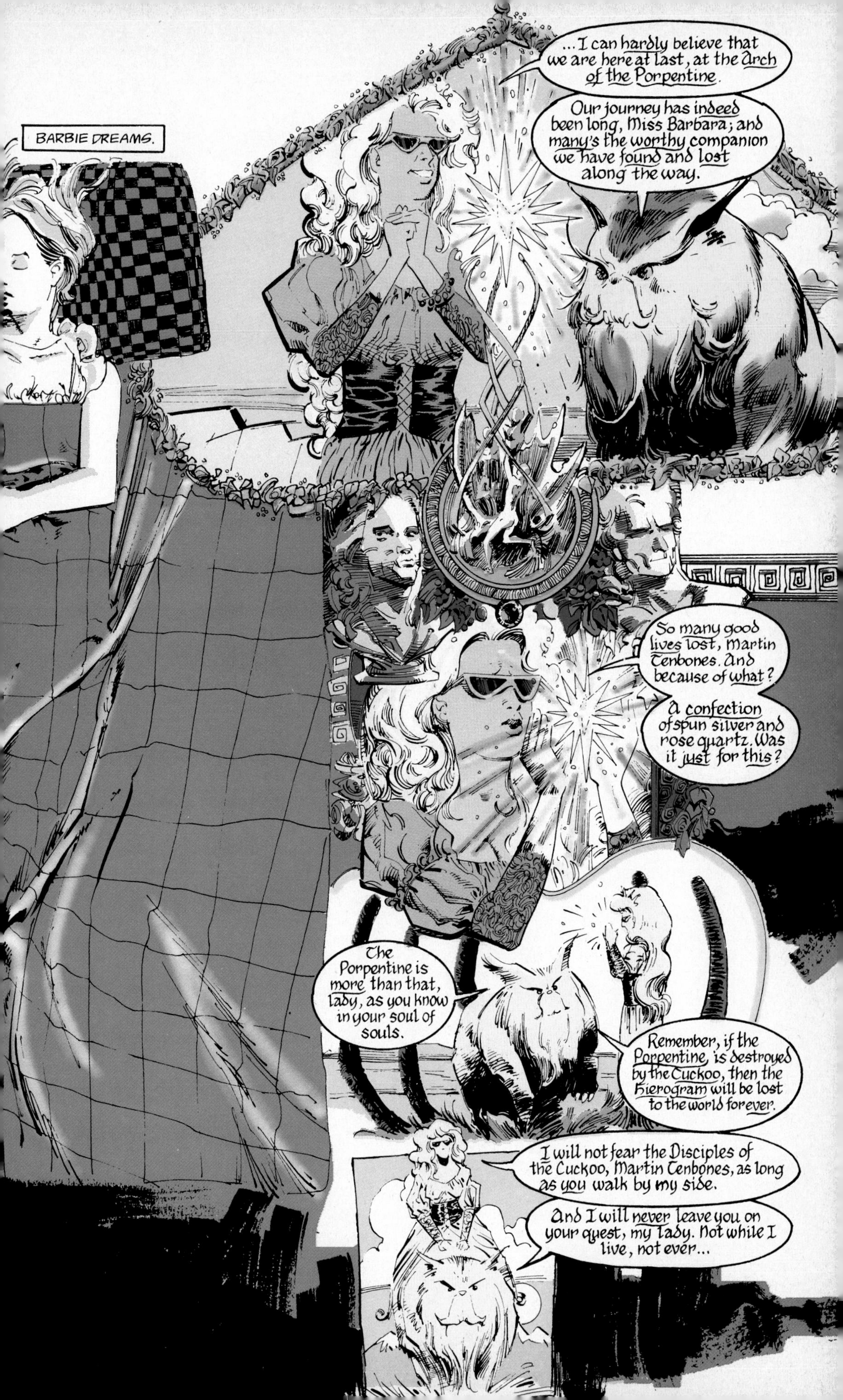
BARBIE DREAMS.
...I can hardly believe that we are here at last, at the Arch of the Porpentine.
Our journey has indeed been long, Miss Barbara; and many's the worthy companion we have found and lost along the way.
So many good lives lost, Martin Tenbones. And because of what?
A confection of spun silver and rose quartz. Was it just for this?
The Porpentine is more than that, lady, as you know in your soul of souls.
Remember, if the Porpentine is destroyed by the Cuckoo, then the Hierogram will be lost to the world forever.
I will not fear the Disciples of the Cuckoo, Martin Tenbones, as long as you walk by my side.
And I will never leave you on your quest, my lady. Not while I live, not ever...

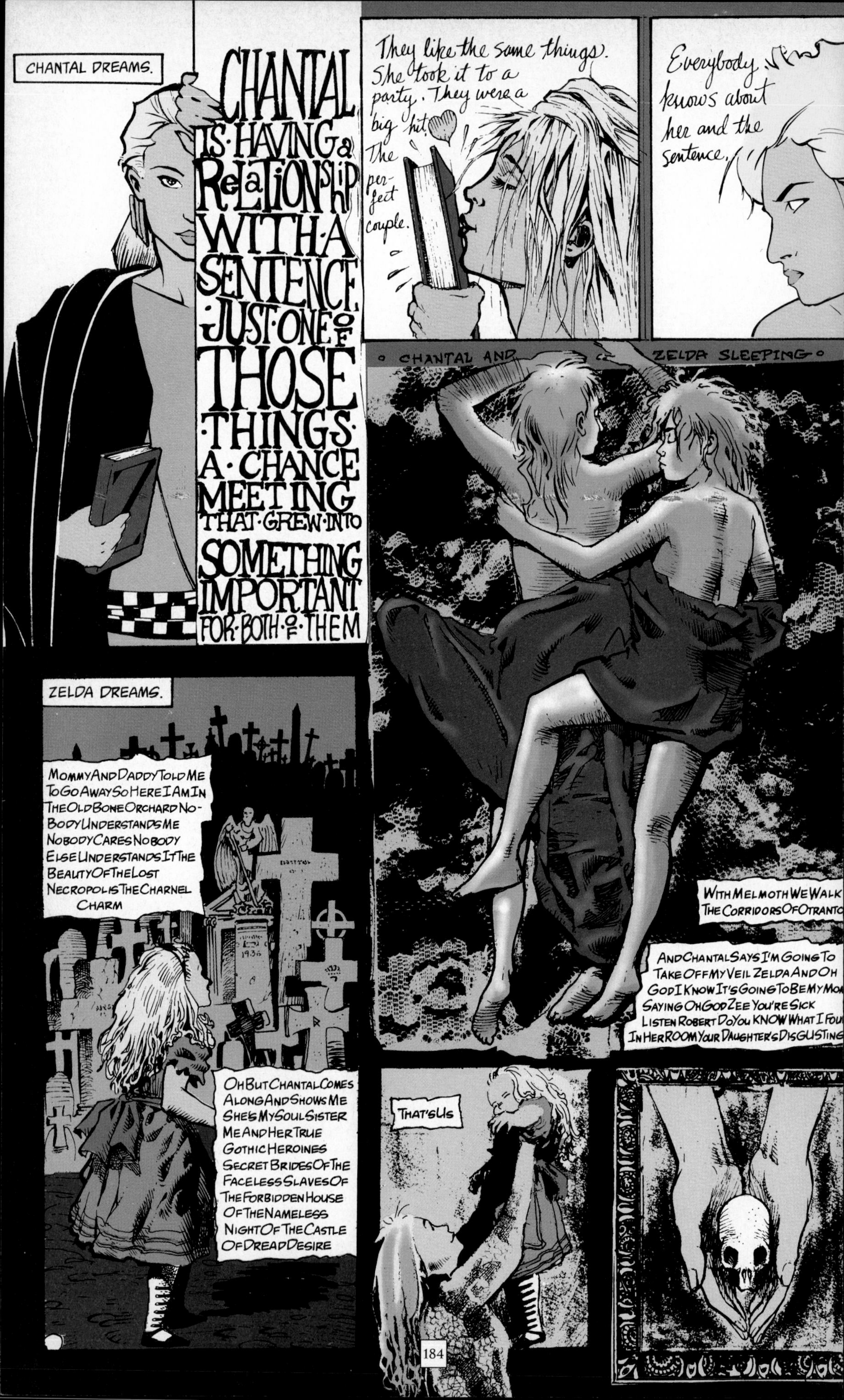
CHANTAL DREAMS.
CHANTAL IS·HAVING a RELATIONSHIP WITH·A SENTENCE. ·JUST·ONE·OF THOSE ·THINGS· A·CHANCE MEETING THAT·GREW·INTO SOMETHING IMPORTANT FOR·BOTH·OF·THEM
They like the same things. She took it to a party. They were a big hit.
The perfect couple.
Everybody knows about her and the sentence.
CHANTAL AND ZELDA SLEEPING
ZELDA DREAMS.
Mommy And Daddy Told Me To Go Away So Here I Am In The Old Bone Orchard Nobody Understands Me Nobody Cares Nobody Else Understands It The Beauty Of The Lost Necropolis The Charnel Charm
1936
Oh But Chantal Comes Along And Shows Me She's My Soul Sister Me And Her True Gothic Heroines Secret Brides Of The Faceless Slaves Of The Forbidden House Of The Nameless Night Of The Castle Of Dread Desire
With Melmoth We Walk The Corridors Of Otranto
And Chantal Says I'm Going To Take Off My Veil Zelda And Oh God I Know It's Going To Be My Mo
Saying Oh God Zee You're Sick
Listen Robert Do You KNOW What I Fou
In Her ROOM Your Daughter's DisGUSTing
That's Us

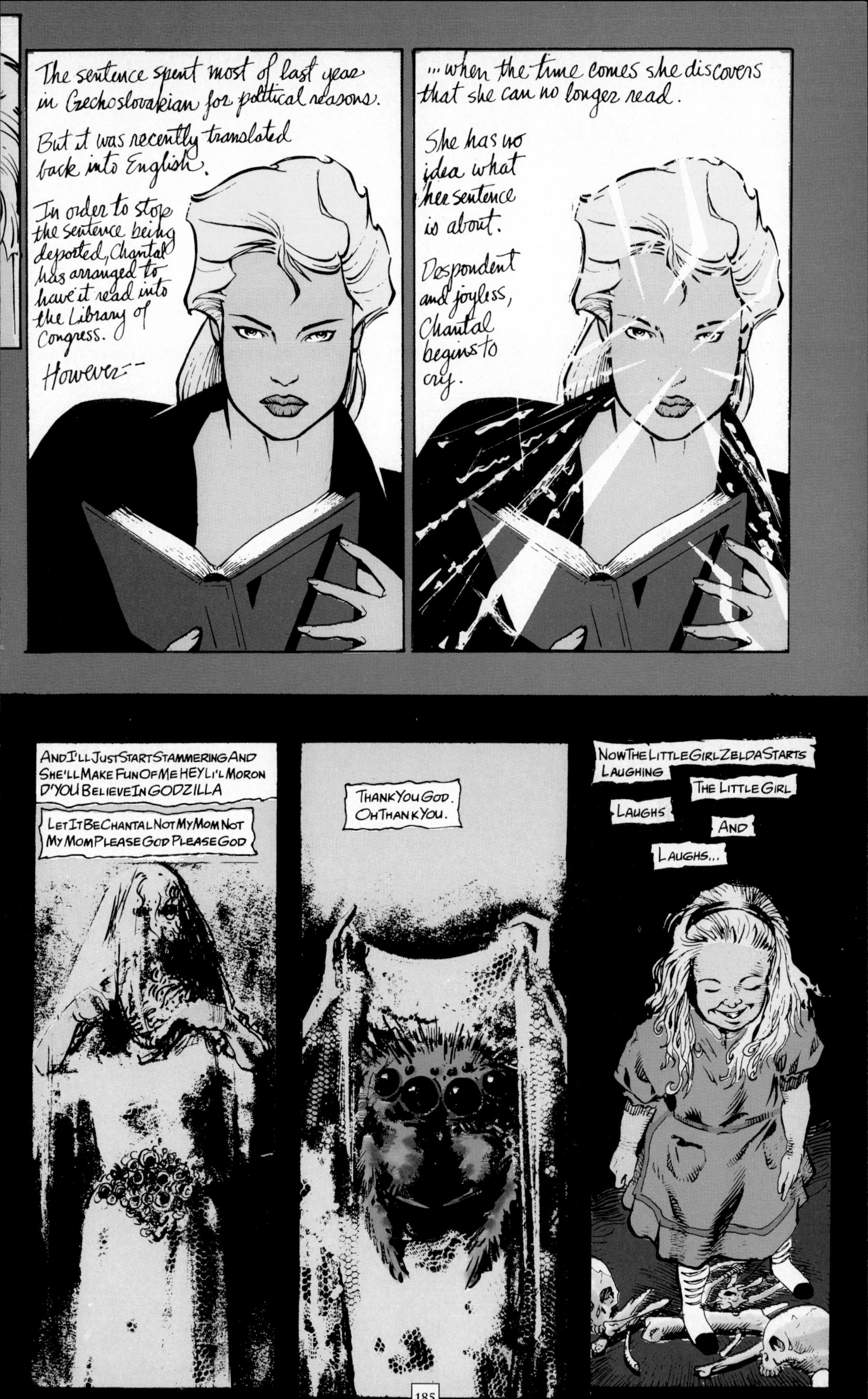

The sentence spent most of last year in Czechoslovakian for political reasons.
But it was recently translated back into English.
In order to stop the sentence being deported, Chantal has arranged to have it read into the Library of Congress.
However--
...when the time comes she discovers that she can no longer read.
She has no idea what her sentence is about.
Despondent and joyless, Chantal begins to cry.
AND I'LL JUST START STAMMERING AND SHE'LL MAKE FUN OF ME HEY LI'L MORON D'YOU BELIEVE IN GODZILLA
LET IT BE CHANTAL NOT MY MOM NOT MY MOM PLEASE GOD PLEASE GOD
THANK YOU GOD. OH THANK YOU.
NOW THE LITTLE GIRL ZELDA STARTS LAUGHING
THE LITTLE GIRL
LAUGHS
AND
LAUGHS...

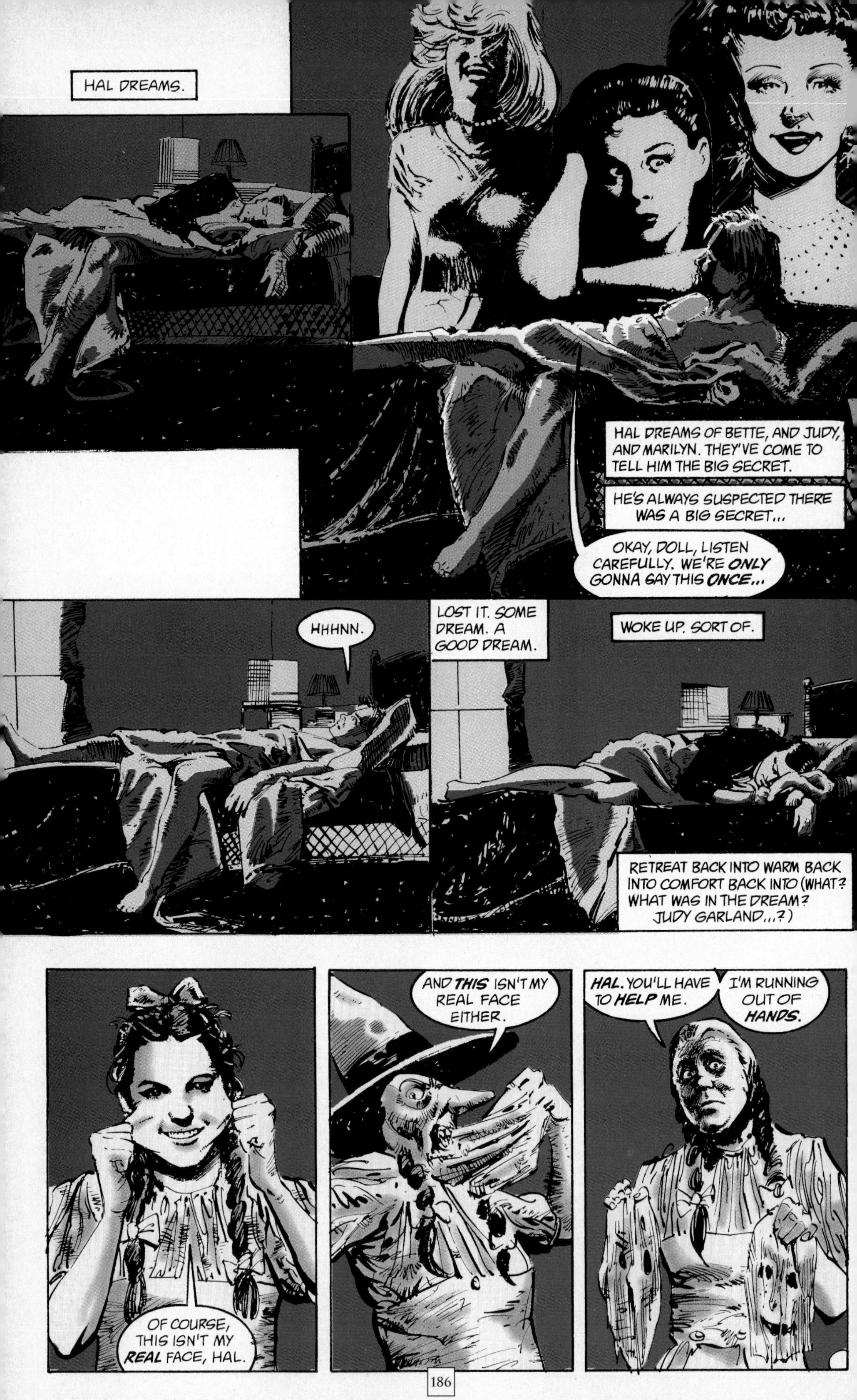

HAL DREAMS.
HAL DREAMS OF BETTE, AND JUDY, AND MARILYN. THEY'VE COME TO TELL HIM THE BIG SECRET.
HE'S ALWAYS SUSPECTED THERE WAS A BIG SECRET...
OKAY, DOLL, LISTEN CAREFULLY. WE'RE ONLY GONNA SAY THIS ONCE...
HHHNN.
LOST IT. SOME DREAM. A GOOD DREAM.
WOKE UP. SORT OF.
RETREAT BACK INTO WARM BACK INTO COMFORT BACK INTO (WHAT? WHAT WAS IN THE DREAM? JUDY GARLAND...?)
OF COURSE, THIS ISN'T MY REAL FACE, HAL.
AND THIS ISN'T MY REAL FACE EITHER.
HAL. YOU'LL HAVE TO HELP ME.
I'M RUNNING OUT OF HANDS.

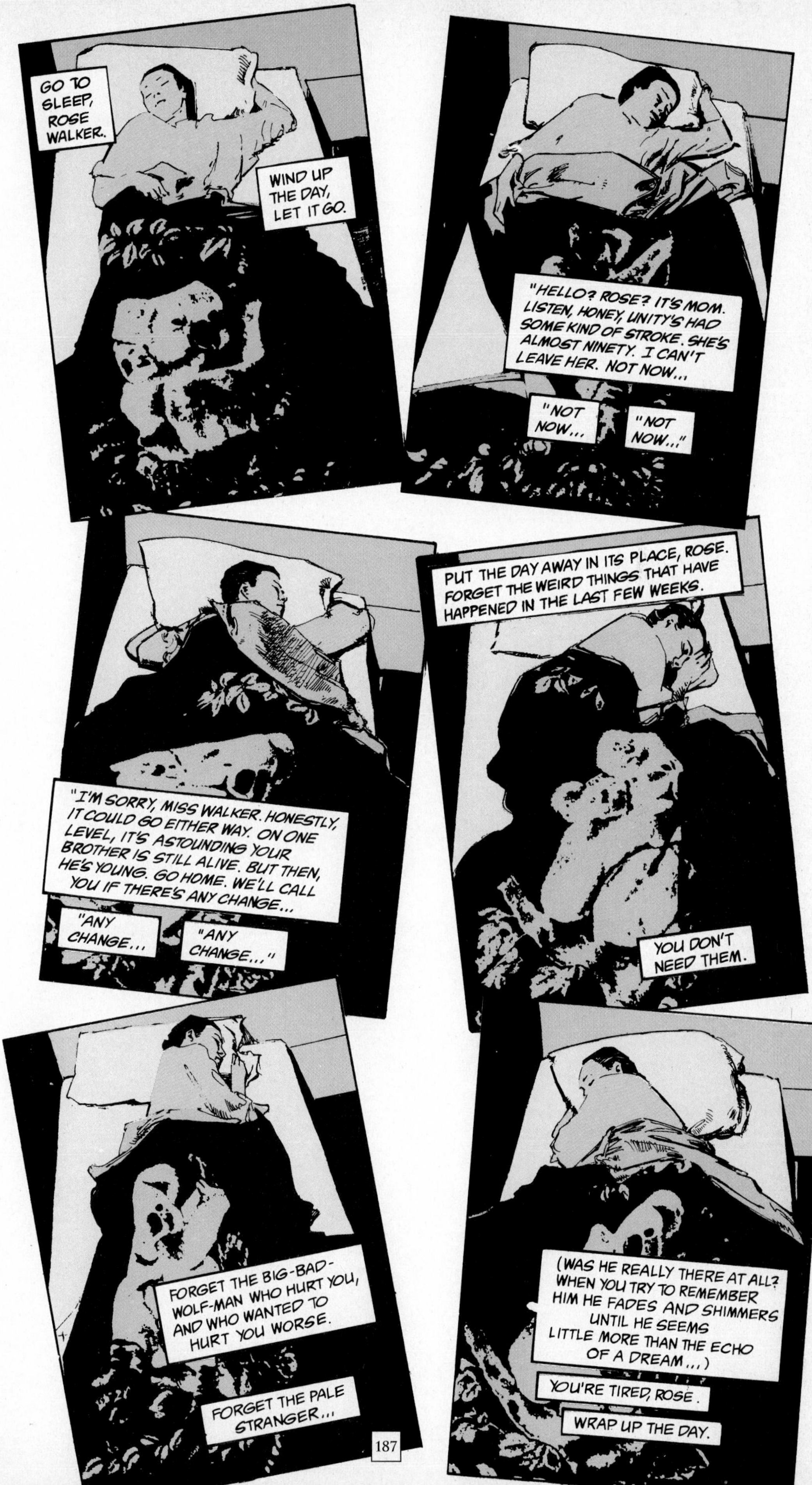

GO TO SLEEP, ROSE WALKER.
WIND UP THE DAY, LET IT GO.
"HELLO? ROSE? IT'S MOM. LISTEN, HONEY, UNITY'S HAD SOME KIND OF STROKE. SHE'S ALMOST NINETY. I CAN'T LEAVE HER. NOT NOW...
"NOT NOW...
"NOT NOW..."
"I'M SORRY, MISS WALKER. HONESTLY, IT COULD GO EITHER WAY. ON ONE LEVEL, IT'S ASTOUNDING YOUR BROTHER IS STILL ALIVE. BUT THEN, HE'S YOUNG. GO HOME. WE'LL CALL YOU IF THERE'S ANY CHANGE...
"ANY CHANGE...
"ANY CHANGE..."
PUT THE DAY AWAY IN ITS PLACE, ROSE. FORGET THE WEIRD THINGS THAT HAVE HAPPENED IN THE LAST FEW WEEKS.
YOU DON'T NEED THEM.
FORGET THE BIG-BAD-WOLF-MAN WHO HURT YOU, AND WHO WANTED TO HURT YOU WORSE.
FORGET THE PALE STRANGER...
(WAS HE REALLY THERE AT ALL? WHEN YOU TRY TO REMEMBER HIM HE FADES AND SHIMMERS UNTIL HE SEEMS LITTLE MORE THAN THE ECHO OF A DREAM...)
YOU'RE TIRED, ROSE.
WRAP UP THE DAY.

SINKING, SLOWLY, DOWNWARD AND INWARD. ENTER A WORLD WHERE EVERYTHING'S GOING TO BE JUST FINE.

UNITY WILL BE FINE.

JED WILL BE FINE.

YOU'RE SO TIRED...

JUST LET GO.

SHARP AND TUGGING: A BRIEF THOUGHT, AND YOU WONDER, **WHERE'S GILBERT?**

YOU HAVEN'T SEEN HIM FOR ALMOST A WEEK, NOW. NOT SINCE THE TWO OF YOU GOT BACK TO FLORIDA WITH JED, HALF-STARVED AND DEHYDRATED AND SCABBED AND...

LET IT GO.

IT'LL STILL BE THERE TOMORROW.

(GILBERT?)

AND SLEEP.

AND DREAM...

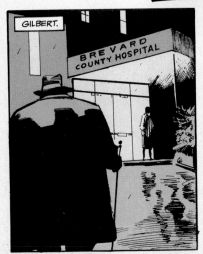

GILBERT.

BREVARD COUNTY HOSPITAL

4

HOOM.

So it begins, once more. The first vortex of this era.

Nonetheless, there is something about this one-- this time-- that I do not understand.

WROAARRKK?

TO BE HONEST, I STILL DON'T QUITE FOLLOW WHAT'S GOING ON HERE.

WHAT IS THAT THING?

It is the vortex, Matthew. It is also Rose Walker.

And it is growing.

SO, WHAT DOES THAT MEAN, CHIEF?

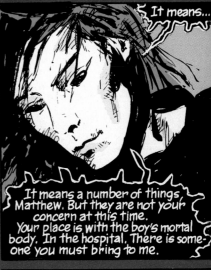

It means...

It means a number of things, Matthew. But they are not your concern at this time. Your place is with the boy's mortal body. In the hospital, there is someone you must bring to me.

I DON'T LIKE HOSPITALS.

For my part, I must deal with this vortex, as I have dealt with the others in the past. As I must deal with anything that threatens the dreaming.

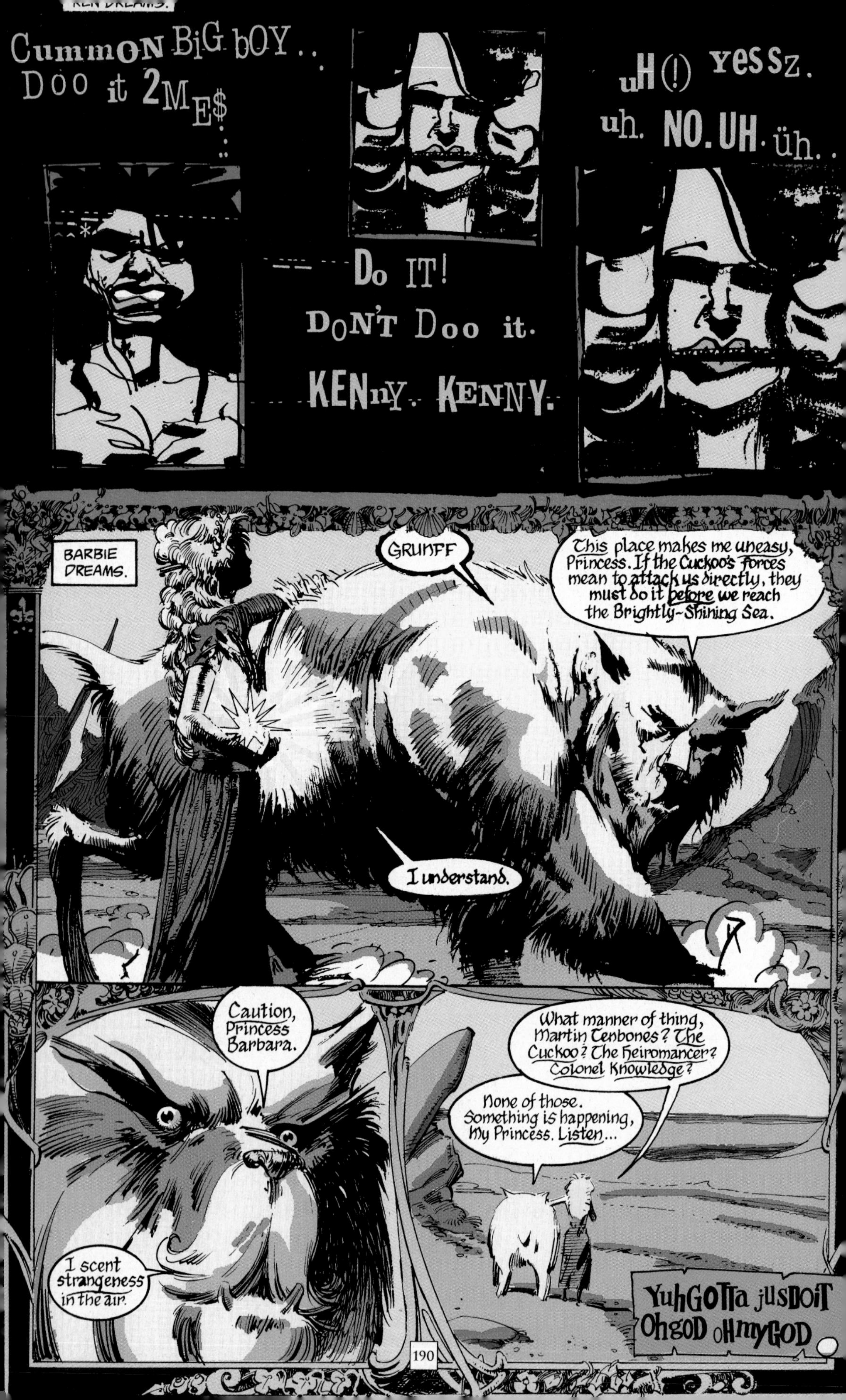

Cummon Big boy..
Doo it 2ME$
uH(!) yessz.
uh. NO.UH. üh..
Do IT!
DON'T Doo it.
KENny. KENNY.
BARBIE DREAMS.
GRUNFF
This place makes me uneasy, Princess. If the Cuckoo's Forces mean to attack us directly, they must do it before we reach the Brightly-Shining Sea.
I understand.
Caution, Princess Barbara.
What manner of thing, Martin Tenbones? The Cuckoo? The Heiromancer? Colonel Knowledge?
None of those. Something is happening, My Princess. Listen...
I scent strangeness in the air.
YuhGOTTa jusDOiT
OhgOD oHmyGOD

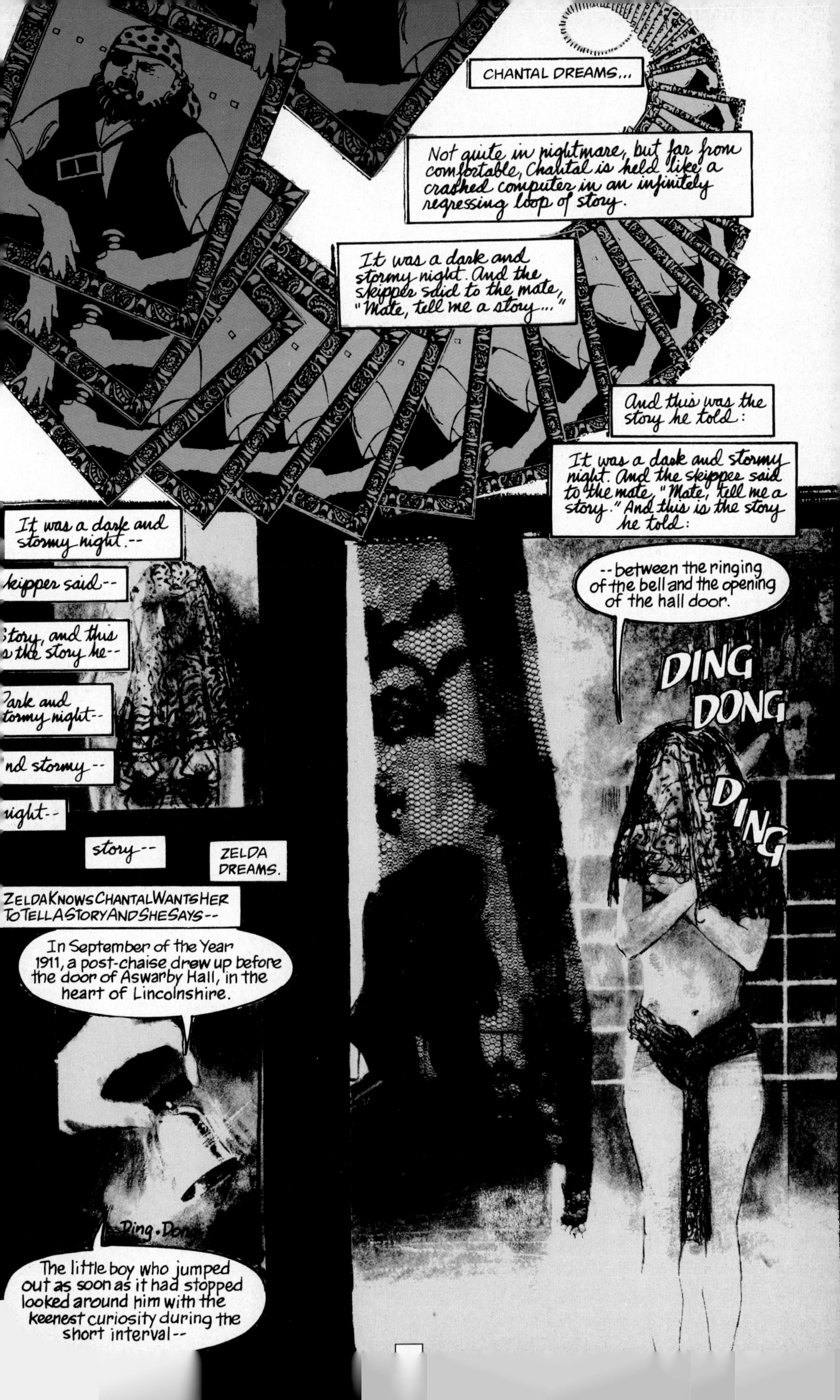

CHANTAL DREAMS...
Not quite in nightmare, but far from comfortable, Chantal is held like a crashed computer in an infinitely regressing loop of story.
It was a dark and stormy night. And the skipper said to the mate, "Mate, tell me a story...."
And this was the story he told:
It was a dark and stormy night. And the skipper said to the mate, "Mate, tell me a story." And this is the story he told:
It was a dark and stormy night.--
kipper said--
tory, and this the story he--
ark and tormy night--
nd stormy--
ight--
story--
ZELDA DREAMS.
ZELDAKNOWSCHANTALWANTSHER TOTELLASTORYANDSHESAYS--
In September of the Year 1911, a post-chaise drew up before the door of Aswarby Hall, in the heart of Lincolnshire.
Ding.Don
The little boy who jumped out as soon as it had stopped looked around him with the keenest curiosity during the short interval--
--between the ringing of the bell and the opening of the hall door.
DING DONG
DING

AND HAL SEES ROBERT AGAIN, NOT ROBERT AS HE PROVED HIMSELF TO BE-- CALLOW, SELF-CENTERED, DISHONEST...

♪...ASKED TO DESCRIBE ♪♫♩ THIS WHOLE BEAUTIFUL THING--

NO. THIS IS THE ROBERT HE HAD HOPED FOR. THE ROBERT HE HAD *DREAMED* OF. FRIENDLY, OPEN, *MAGICAL*...

♩...IF I WERE A BELL ♪♫ I'D GO DING DONG-- ♪♫

THEIR TUNE IS PLAYING IN THE BACKGROUND.

♩ DING DONG DING ♩♫ DONG DING. ♩♪♫

ROSE DREAMS.

SHE *KNOWS* SHE'S DREAMING.

SHE'S NEVER HAD A DREAM LIKE THIS BEFORE.

EVERYTHING SEEMS SO *REAL*, SO *VIVID*; MORE TRUE AND MORE VITAL THAN THE WAKING WORLD.

HER SENSE OF IDENTITY HAS NEVER BEEN SO CERTAIN.

SHE CAN FEEL HER SLEEPING BODY ON THE BED BELOW HER.

IT'S NO PART OF HER; THE ESSENTIAL HER, THE TRUE ROSE.

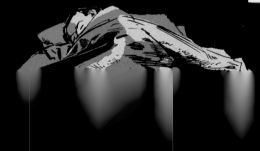

FALTERINGLY, SHE EXTENDS HER PERCEPTIONS...

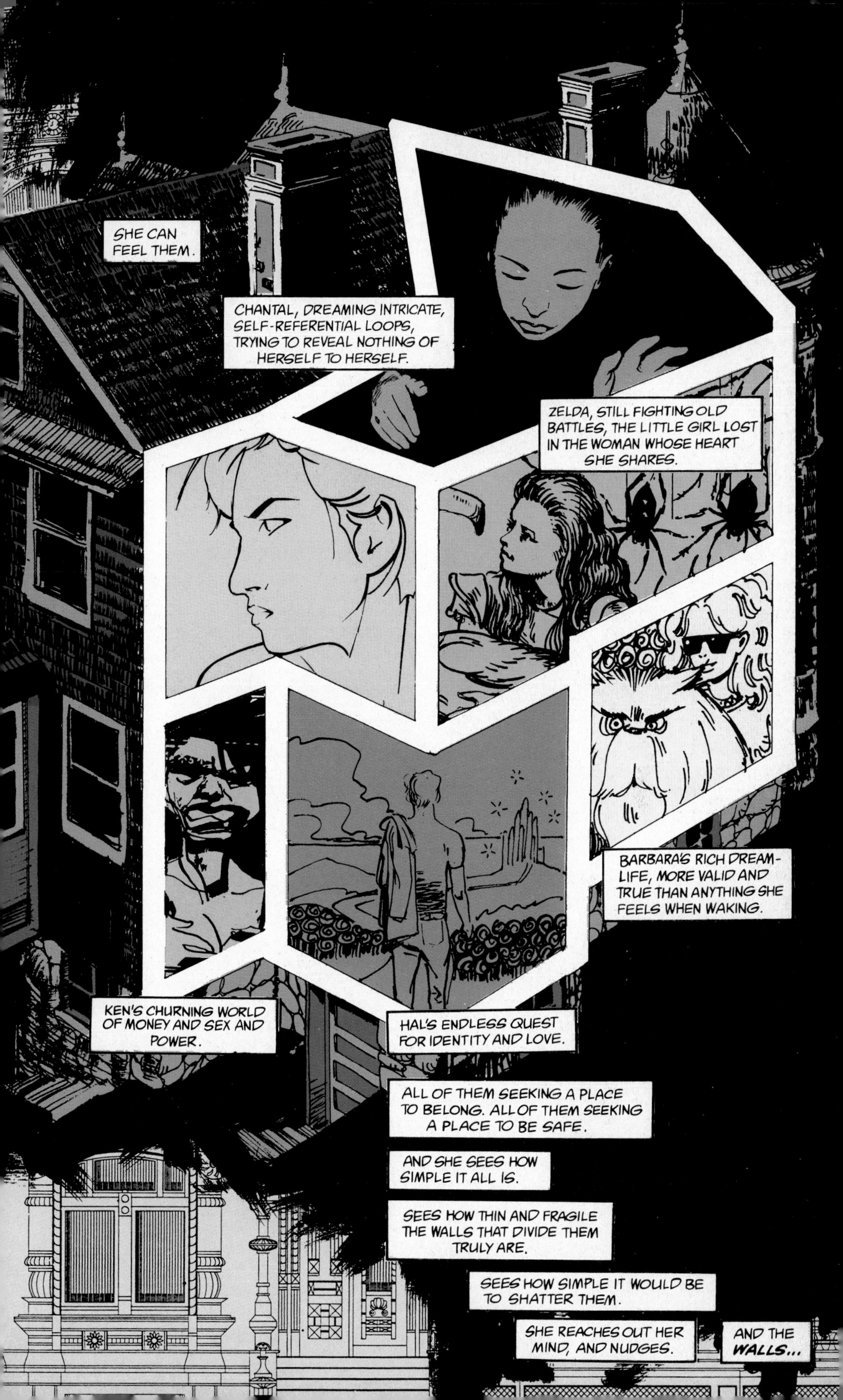
SHE CAN FEEL THEM.
CHANTAL, DREAMING INTRICATE, SELF-REFERENTIAL LOOPS, TRYING TO REVEAL NOTHING OF HERSELF TO HERSELF.
ZELDA, STILL FIGHTING OLD BATTLES, THE LITTLE GIRL LOST IN THE WOMAN WHOSE HEART SHE SHARES.
BARBARA'S RICH DREAM-LIFE, MORE VALID AND TRUE THAN ANYTHING SHE FEELS WHEN WAKING.
KEN'S CHURNING WORLD OF MONEY AND SEX AND POWER.
HAL'S ENDLESS QUEST FOR IDENTITY AND LOVE.
ALL OF THEM SEEKING A PLACE TO BELONG. ALL OF THEM SEEKING A PLACE TO BE SAFE.
AND SHE SEES HOW SIMPLE IT ALL IS.
SEES HOW THIN AND FRAGILE THE WALLS THAT DIVIDE THEM TRULY ARE.
SEES HOW SIMPLE IT WOULD BE TO SHATTER THEM.
SHE REACHES OUT HER MIND, AND NUDGES.
AND THE *WALLS...*

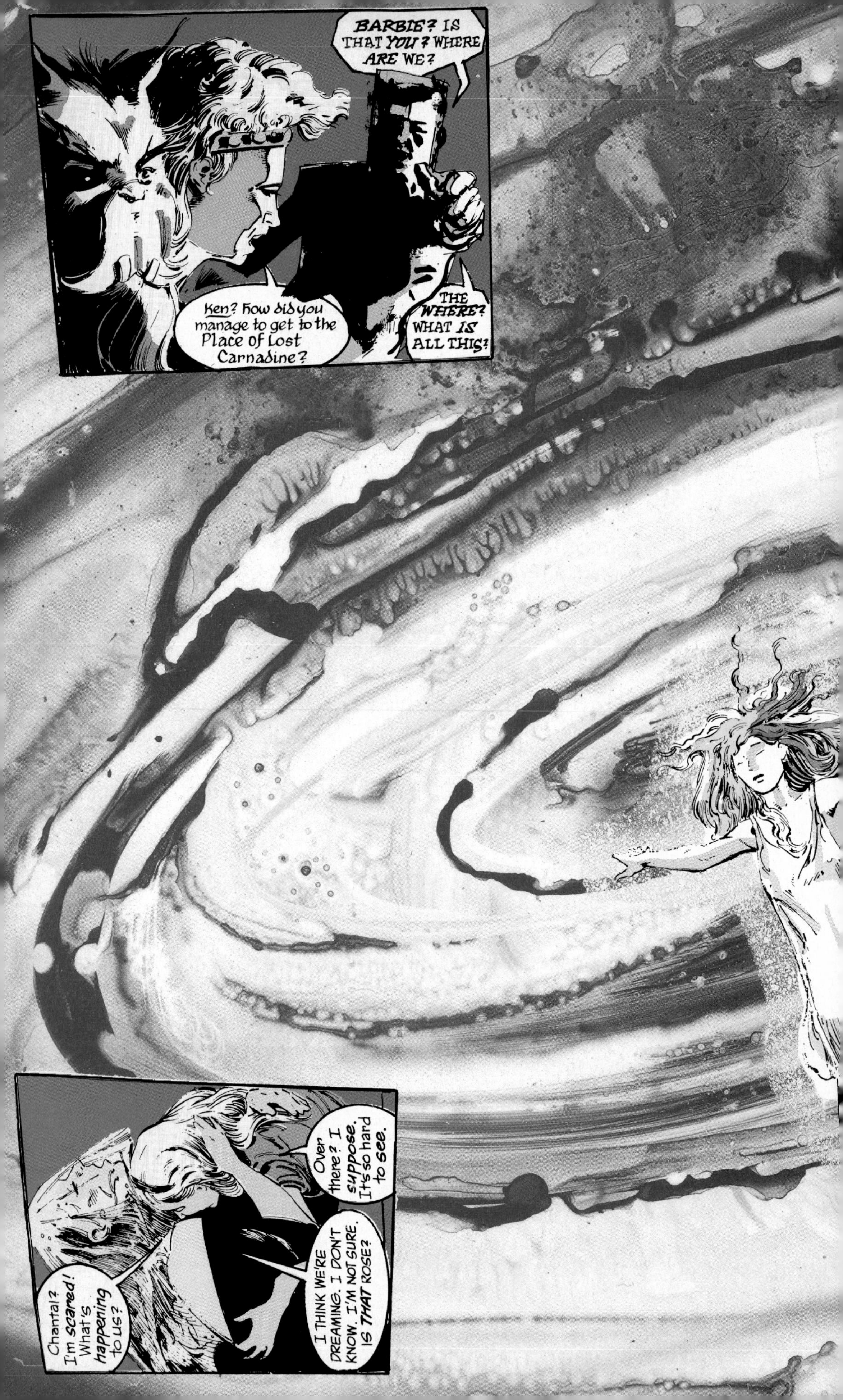
BARBIE? IS THAT YOU? WHERE ARE WE?
Ken? How did you manage to get to the Place of Lost Carnadine?
THE WHERE? WHAT IS ALL THIS?
Chantal? I'm scared! What's happening to us?
I THINK WE'RE DREAMING. I DON'T KNOW. I'M NOT SURE. IS THAT ROSE?
Over there? I suppose. It's so hard to see.

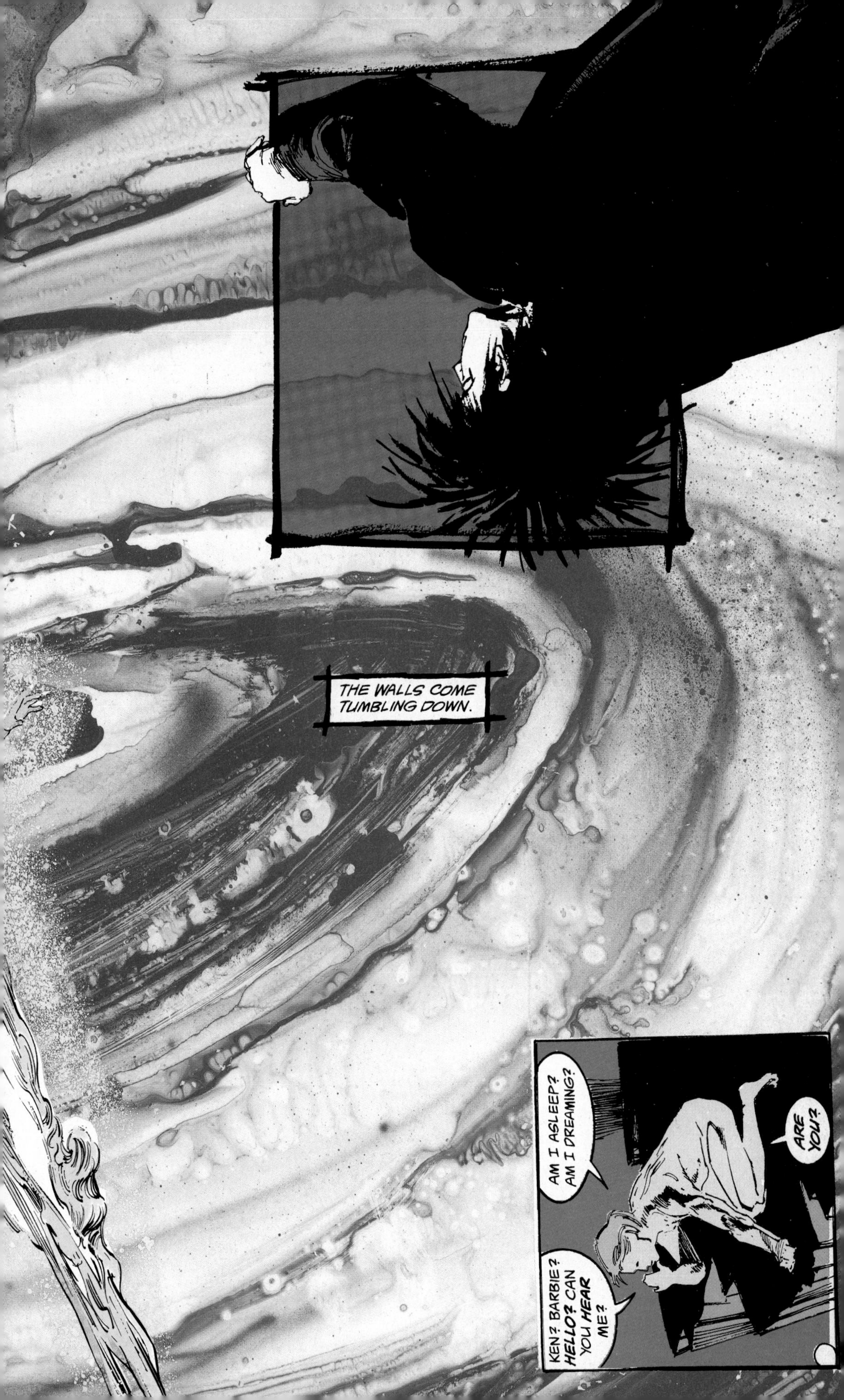
THE WALLS COME TUMBLING DOWN.
KEN? BARBIE? HELLO? CAN YOU HEAR ME?
AM I ASLEEP? AM I DREAMING?
ARE YOU?

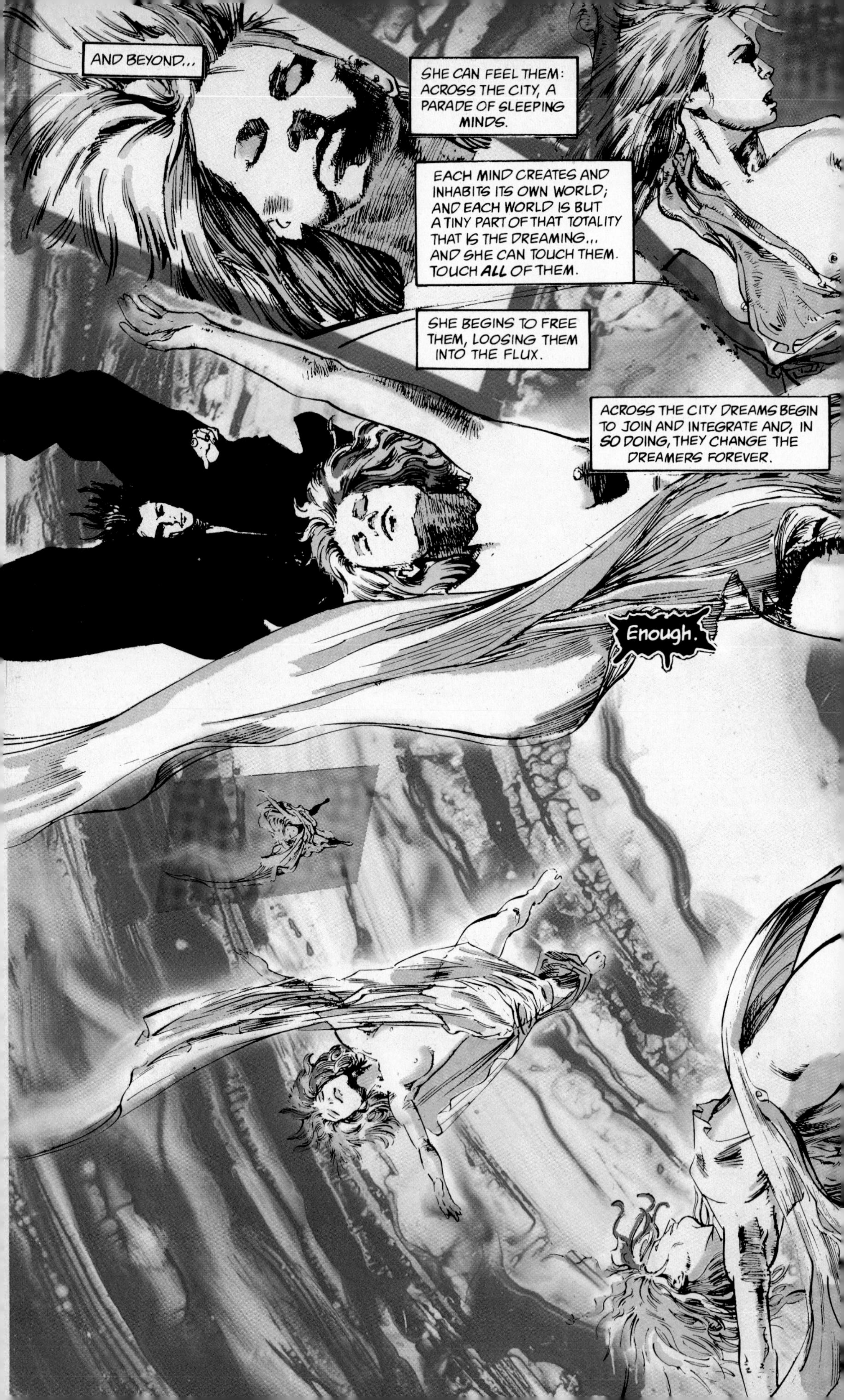
AND BEYOND...
SHE CAN FEEL THEM: ACROSS THE CITY, A PARADE OF SLEEPING MINDS.
EACH MIND CREATES AND INHABITS ITS OWN WORLD; AND EACH WORLD IS BUT A TINY PART OF THAT TOTALITY THAT IS THE DREAMING... AND SHE CAN TOUCH THEM. TOUCH ALL OF THEM.
SHE BEGINS TO FREE THEM, LOOSING THEM INTO THE FLUX.
ACROSS THE CITY DREAMS BEGIN TO JOIN AND INTEGRATE AND, IN SO DOING, THEY CHANGE THE DREAMERS FOREVER.
Enough.

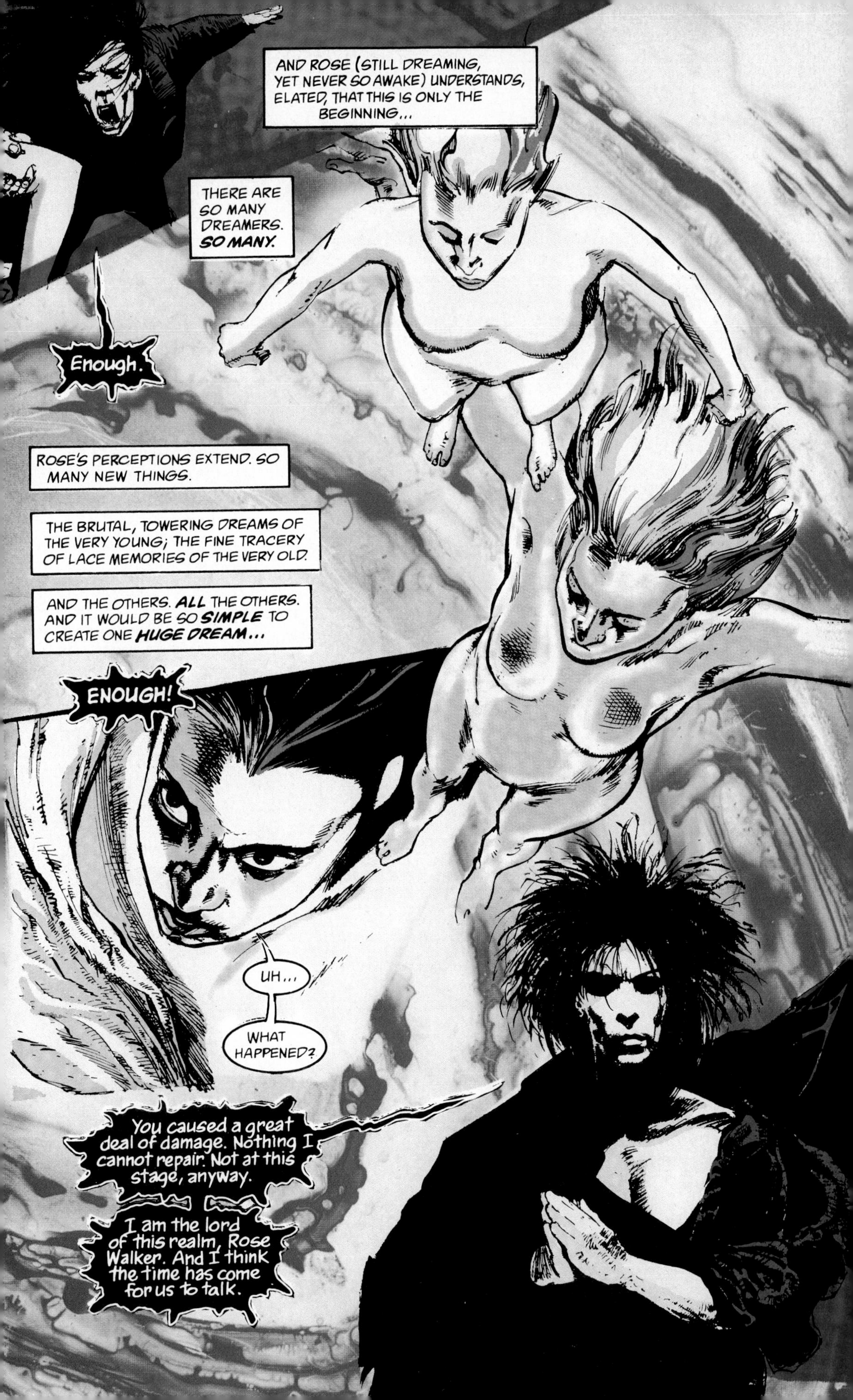

AND ROSE (STILL DREAMING, YET NEVER SO AWAKE) UNDERSTANDS, ELATED, THAT THIS IS ONLY THE BEGINNING...
THERE ARE SO MANY DREAMERS. **SO MANY.**
Enough.
ROSE'S PERCEPTIONS EXTEND. SO MANY NEW THINGS.
THE BRUTAL, TOWERING DREAMS OF THE VERY YOUNG; THE FINE TRACERY OF LACE MEMORIES OF THE VERY OLD.
AND THE OTHERS. **ALL** THE OTHERS. AND IT WOULD BE SO **SIMPLE** TO CREATE ONE **HUGE DREAM...**
ENOUGH!
UH...
WHAT HAPPENED?
You caused a great deal of damage. Nothing I cannot repair. Not at this stage, anyway.
I am the lord of this realm, Rose Walker. And I think the time has come for us to talk.

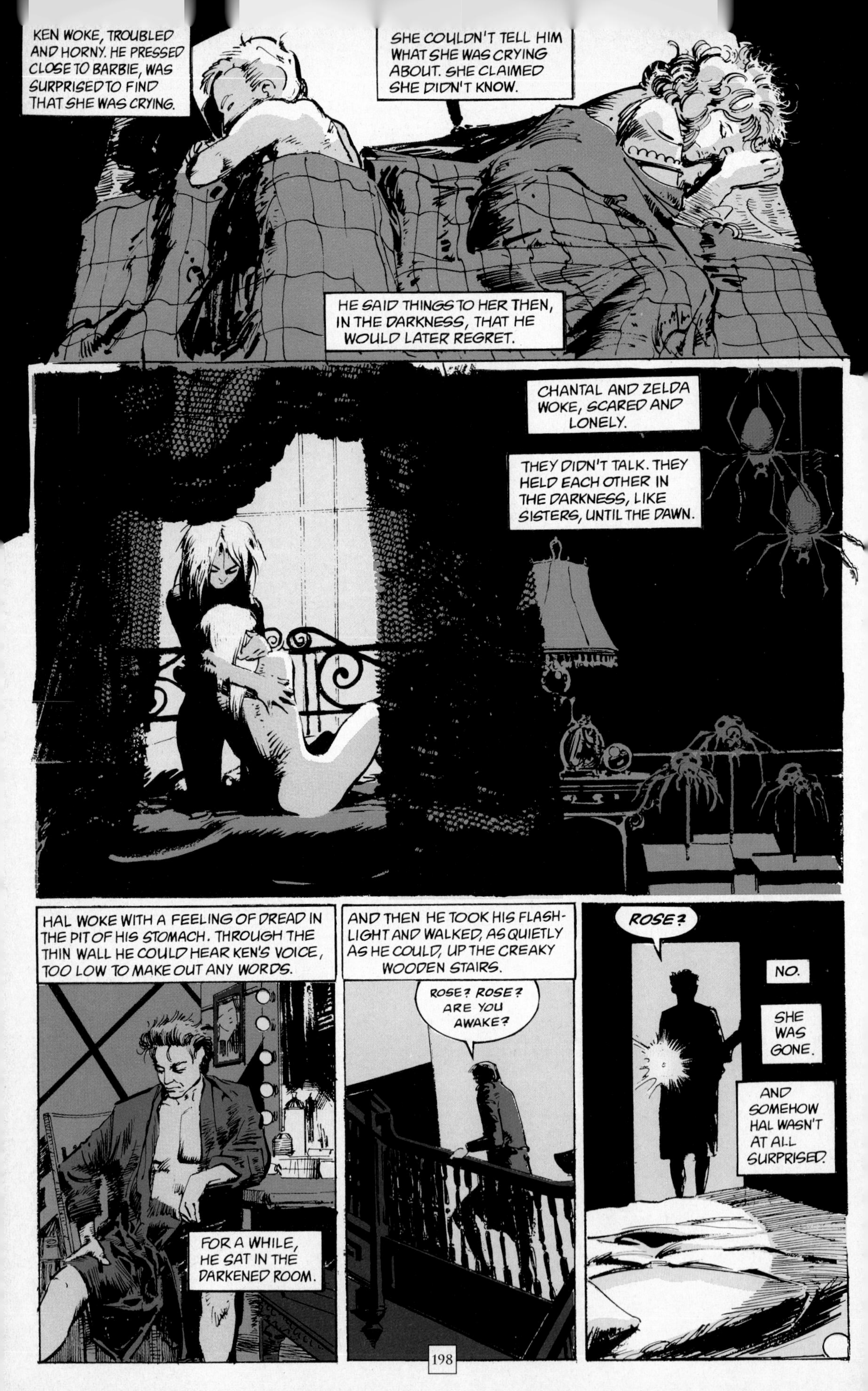

KEN WOKE, TROUBLED AND HORNY. HE PRESSED CLOSE TO BARBIE, WAS SURPRISED TO FIND THAT SHE WAS CRYING.
SHE COULDN'T TELL HIM WHAT SHE WAS CRYING ABOUT. SHE CLAIMED SHE DIDN'T KNOW.
HE SAID THINGS TO HER THEN, IN THE DARKNESS, THAT HE WOULD LATER REGRET.
CHANTAL AND ZELDA WOKE, SCARED AND LONELY.
THEY DIDN'T TALK. THEY HELD EACH OTHER IN THE DARKNESS, LIKE SISTERS, UNTIL THE DAWN.
HAL WOKE WITH A FEELING OF DREAD IN THE PIT OF HIS STOMACH. THROUGH THE THIN WALL HE COULD HEAR KEN'S VOICE, TOO LOW TO MAKE OUT ANY WORDS.
FOR A WHILE, HE SAT IN THE DARKENED ROOM.
AND THEN HE TOOK HIS FLASH-LIGHT AND WALKED, AS QUIETLY AS HE COULD, UP THE CREAKY WOODEN STAIRS.
ROSE? ROSE? ARE YOU AWAKE?
ROSE?
NO.
SHE WAS GONE.
AND SOMEHOW HAL WASN'T AT ALL SURPRISED.

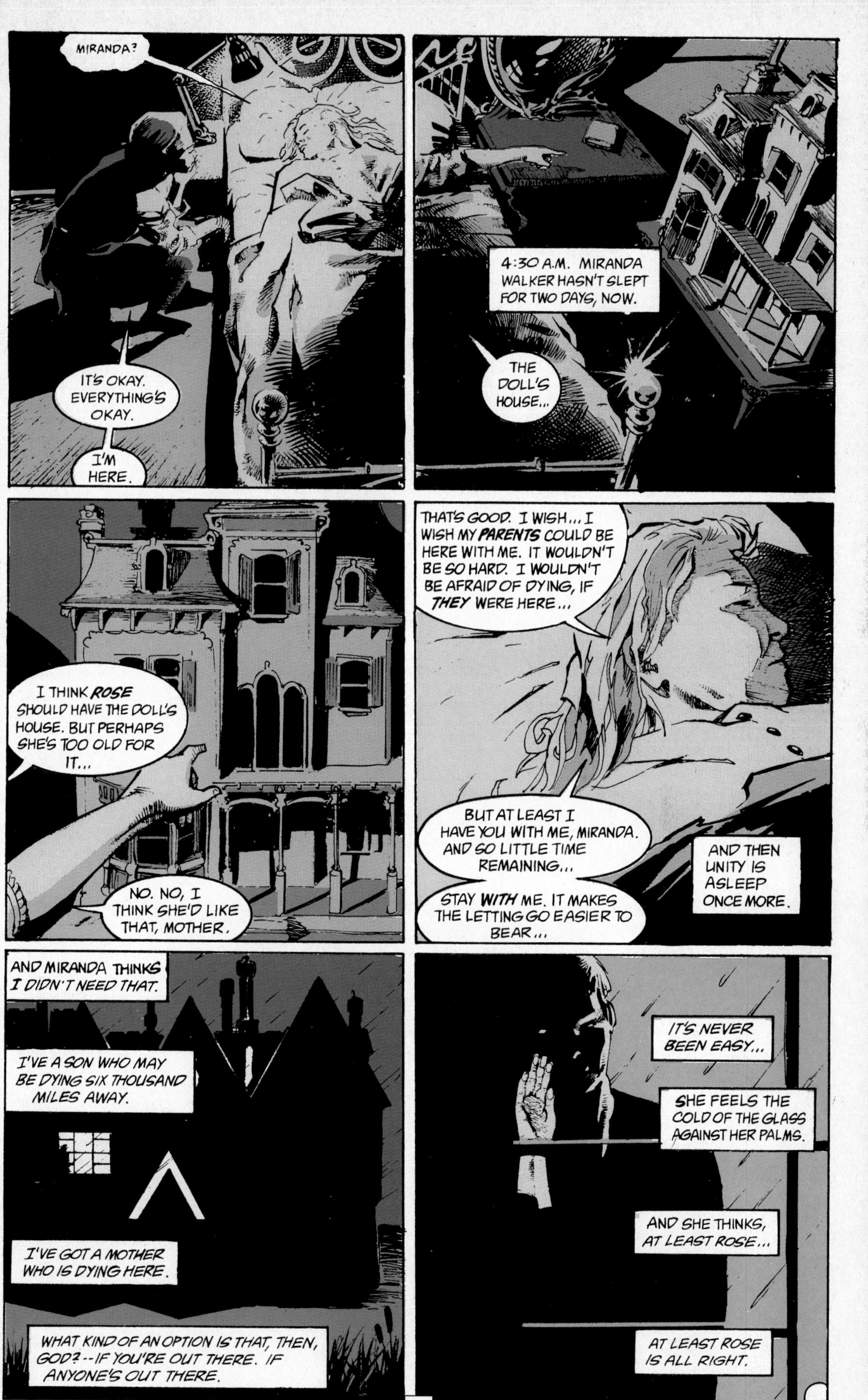
MIRANDA?
IT'S OKAY. EVERYTHING'S OKAY.
I'M HERE.
4:30 A.M. MIRANDA WALKER HASN'T SLEPT FOR TWO DAYS, NOW.
THE DOLL'S HOUSE...
I THINK ROSE SHOULD HAVE THE DOLL'S HOUSE. BUT PERHAPS SHE'S TOO OLD FOR IT...
NO. NO, I THINK SHE'D LIKE THAT, MOTHER.
THAT'S GOOD. I WISH... I WISH MY PARENTS COULD BE HERE WITH ME. IT WOULDN'T BE SO HARD. I WOULDN'T BE AFRAID OF DYING, IF THEY WERE HERE...
BUT AT LEAST I HAVE YOU WITH ME, MIRANDA. AND SO LITTLE TIME REMAINING...
STAY WITH ME. IT MAKES THE LETTING GO EASIER TO BEAR...
AND THEN UNITY IS ASLEEP ONCE MORE.
AND MIRANDA THINKS I DIDN'T NEED THAT.
I'VE A SON WHO MAY BE DYING SIX THOUSAND MILES AWAY.
I'VE GOT A MOTHER WHO IS DYING HERE.
WHAT KIND OF AN OPTION IS THAT, THEN, GOD? --IF YOU'RE OUT THERE. IF ANYONE'S OUT THERE.
IT'S NEVER BEEN EASY...
SHE FEELS THE COLD OF THE GLASS AGAINST HER PALMS.
AND SHE THINKS, AT LEAST ROSE...
AT LEAST ROSE IS ALL RIGHT.

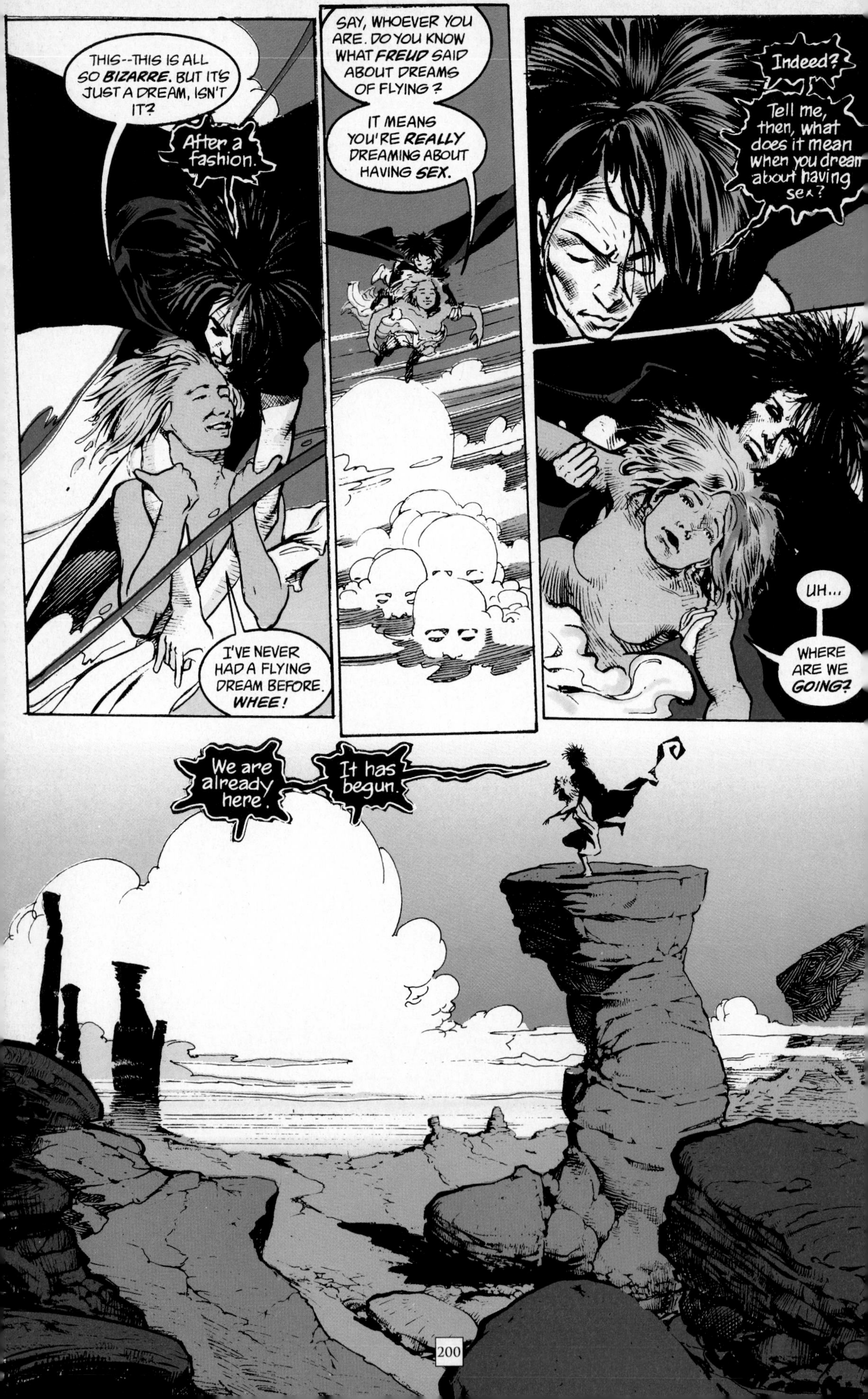
THIS--THIS IS ALL SO BIZARRE. BUT IT'S JUST A DREAM, ISN'T IT?
After a fashion.
I'VE NEVER HAD A FLYING DREAM BEFORE. WHEE!
SAY, WHOEVER YOU ARE. DO YOU KNOW WHAT FREUD SAID ABOUT DREAMS OF FLYING?
IT MEANS YOU'RE REALLY DREAMING ABOUT HAVING SEX.
Indeed?
Tell me, then, what does it mean when you dream about having sex?
UH...
WHERE ARE WE GOING?
We are already here.
It has begun.

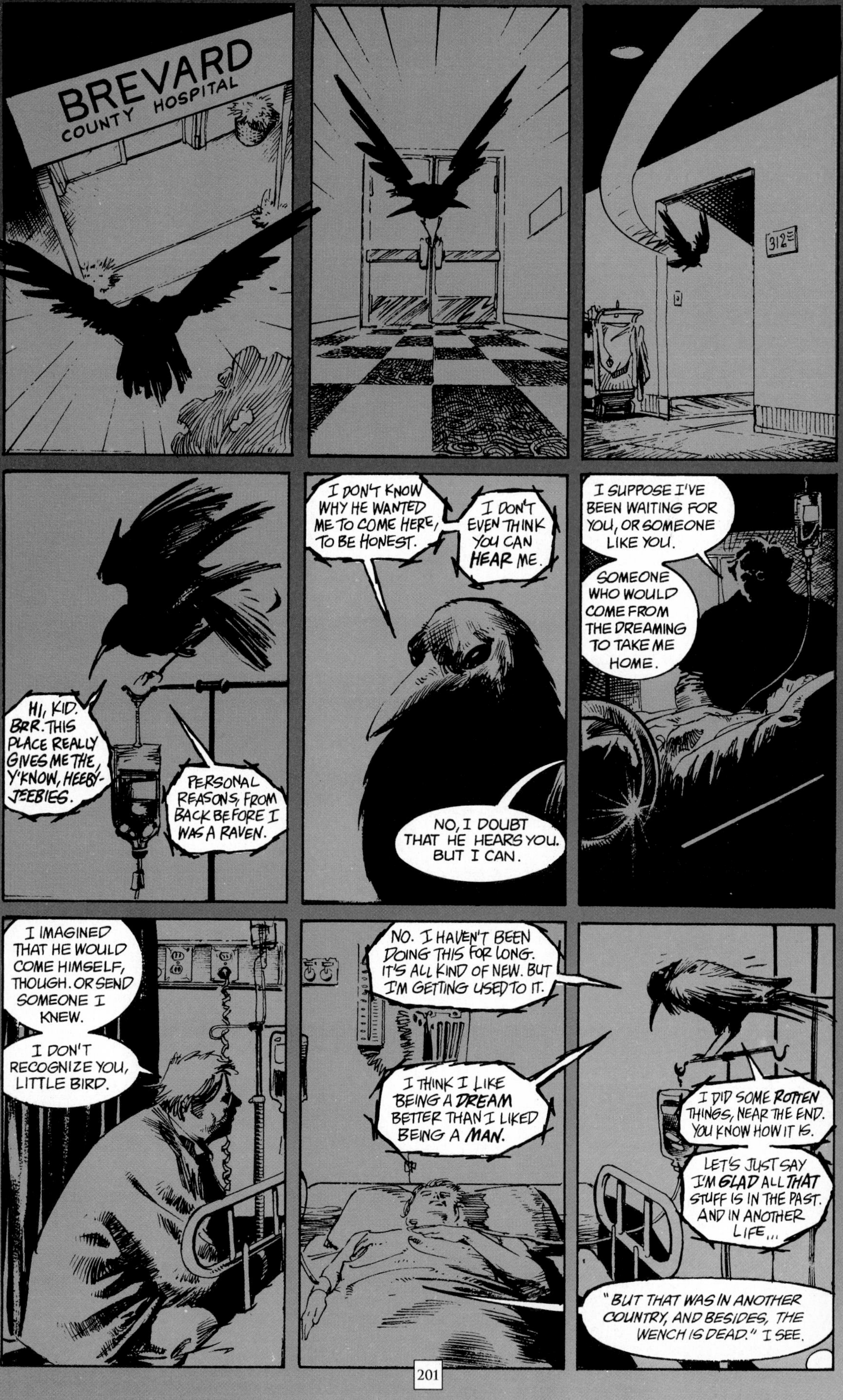
BREVARD
COUNTY HOSPITAL
312
HI, KID. BRR. THIS PLACE REALLY GIVES ME THE, Y'KNOW, HEEBY-JEEBIES.
PERSONAL REASONS, FROM BACK BEFORE I WAS A RAVEN.
I DON'T KNOW WHY HE WANTED ME TO COME HERE, TO BE HONEST.
I DON'T EVEN THINK YOU CAN HEAR ME.
NO, I DOUBT THAT HE HEARS YOU. BUT I CAN.
I SUPPOSE I'VE BEEN WAITING FOR YOU, OR SOMEONE LIKE YOU.
SOMEONE WHO WOULD COME FROM THE DREAMING TO TAKE ME HOME.
I IMAGINED THAT HE WOULD COME HIMSELF, THOUGH. OR SEND SOMEONE I KNEW.
I DON'T RECOGNIZE YOU, LITTLE BIRD.
NO. I HAVEN'T BEEN DOING THIS FOR LONG. IT'S ALL KIND OF NEW. BUT I'M GETTING USED TO IT.
I THINK I LIKE BEING A DREAM BETTER THAN I LIKED BEING A MAN.
I DID SOME ROTTEN THINGS, NEAR THE END. YOU KNOW HOW IT IS.
LET'S JUST SAY I'M GLAD ALL THAT STUFF IS IN THE PAST. AND IN ANOTHER LIFE...
"BUT THAT WAS IN ANOTHER COUNTRY, AND BESIDES, THE WENCH IS DEAD." I SEE.

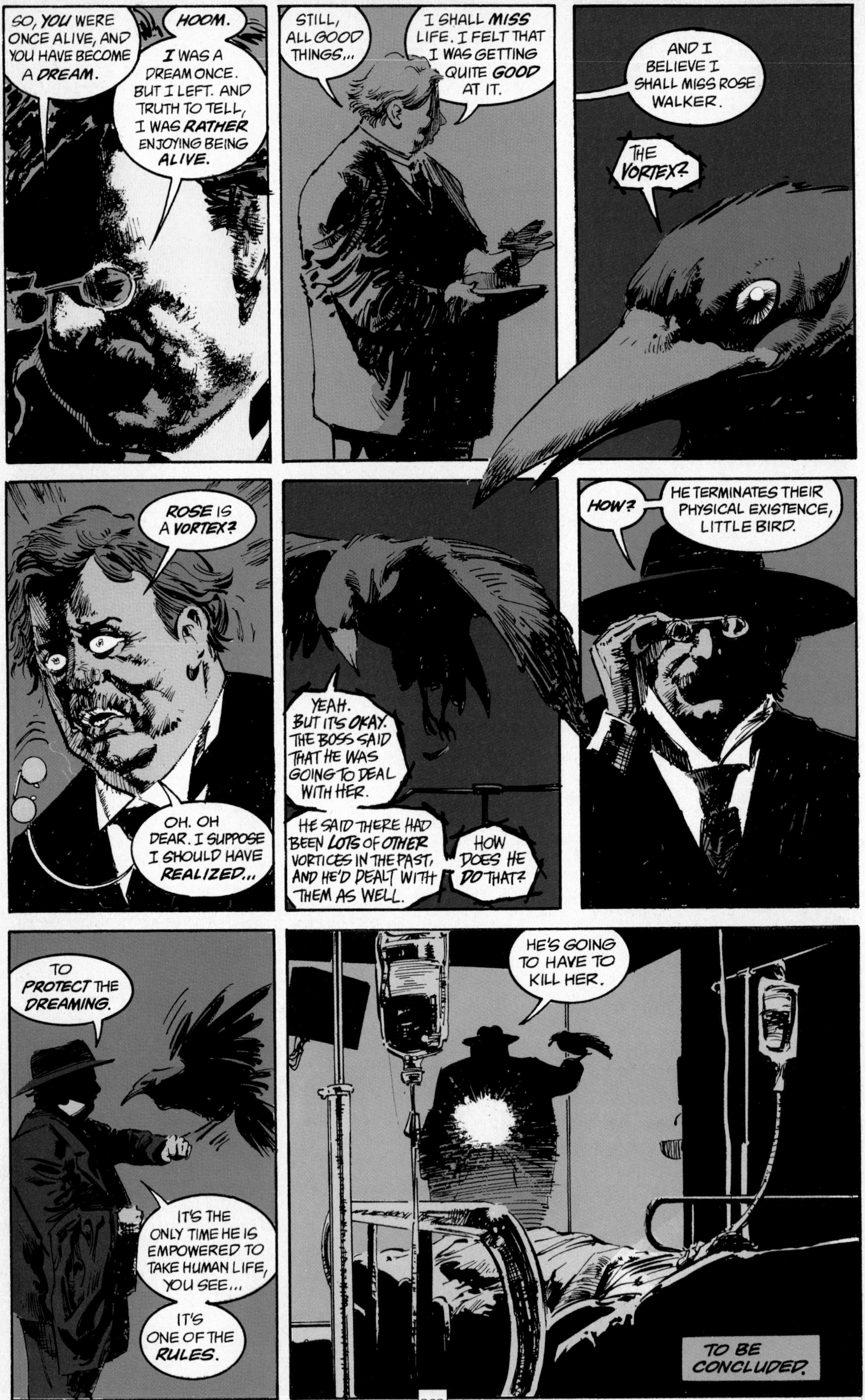
SO, YOU WERE ONCE ALIVE, AND YOU HAVE BECOME A DREAM.
HOOM.
I WAS A DREAM ONCE. BUT I LEFT. AND TRUTH TO TELL, I WAS RATHER ENJOYING BEING ALIVE.
STILL, ALL GOOD THINGS...
I SHALL MISS LIFE. I FELT THAT I WAS GETTING QUITE GOOD AT IT.
AND I BELIEVE I SHALL MISS ROSE WALKER.
THE VORTEX?
ROSE IS A VORTEX?
OH. OH DEAR. I SUPPOSE I SHOULD HAVE REALIZED...
YEAH. BUT IT'S OKAY. THE BOSS SAID THAT HE WAS GOING TO DEAL WITH HER.
HE SAID THERE HAD BEEN LOTS OF OTHER VORTICES IN THE PAST, AND HE'D DEALT WITH THEM AS WELL.
HOW DOES HE DO THAT?
HOW?
HE TERMINATES THEIR PHYSICAL EXISTENCE, LITTLE BIRD.
TO PROTECT THE DREAMING.
IT'S THE ONLY TIME HE IS EMPOWERED TO TAKE HUMAN LIFE, YOU SEE...
IT'S ONE OF THE RULES.
HE'S GOING TO HAVE TO KILL HER.
TO BE CONCLUDED.

DOLL'S HOUSE
PART SEVEN

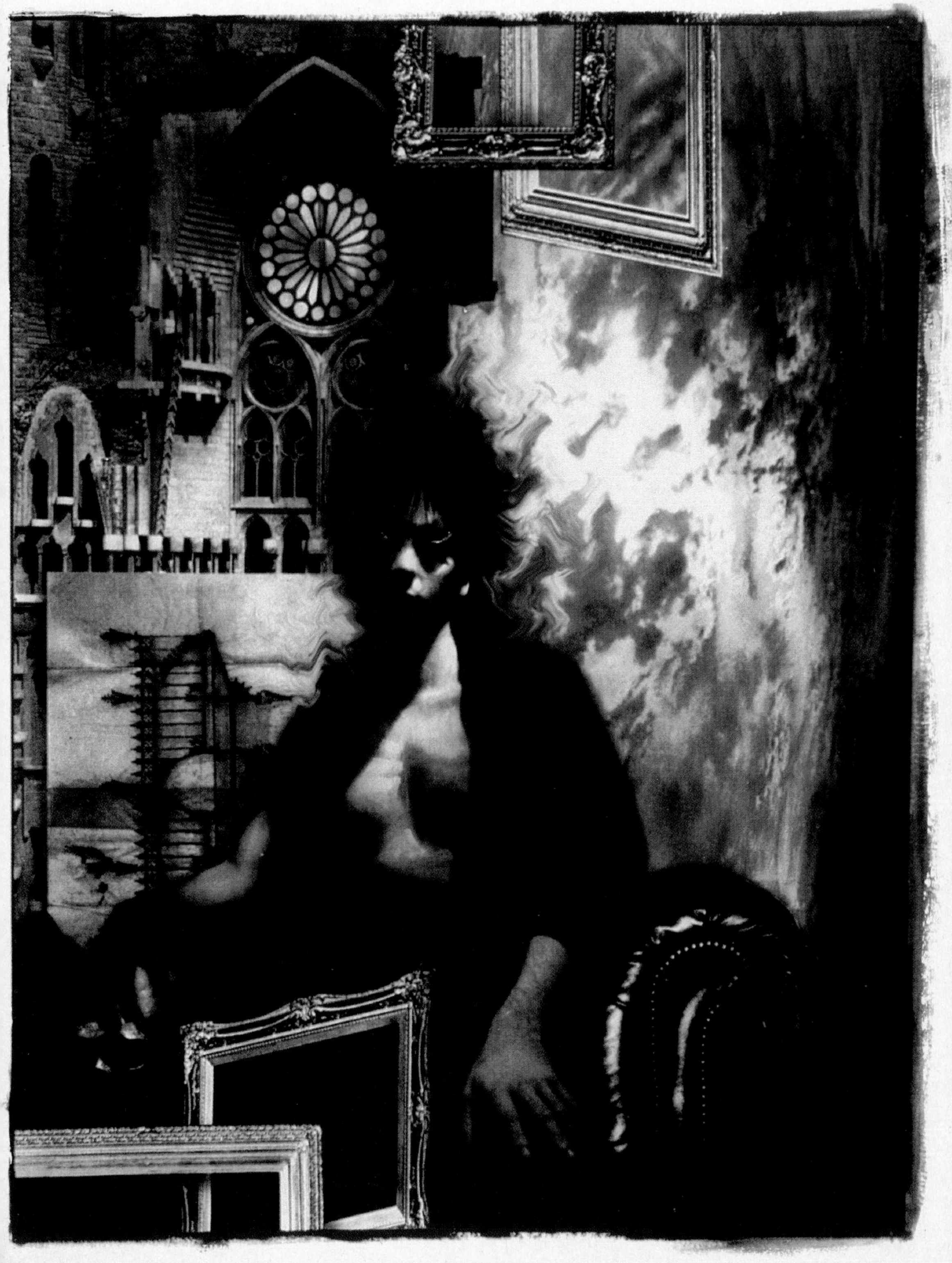

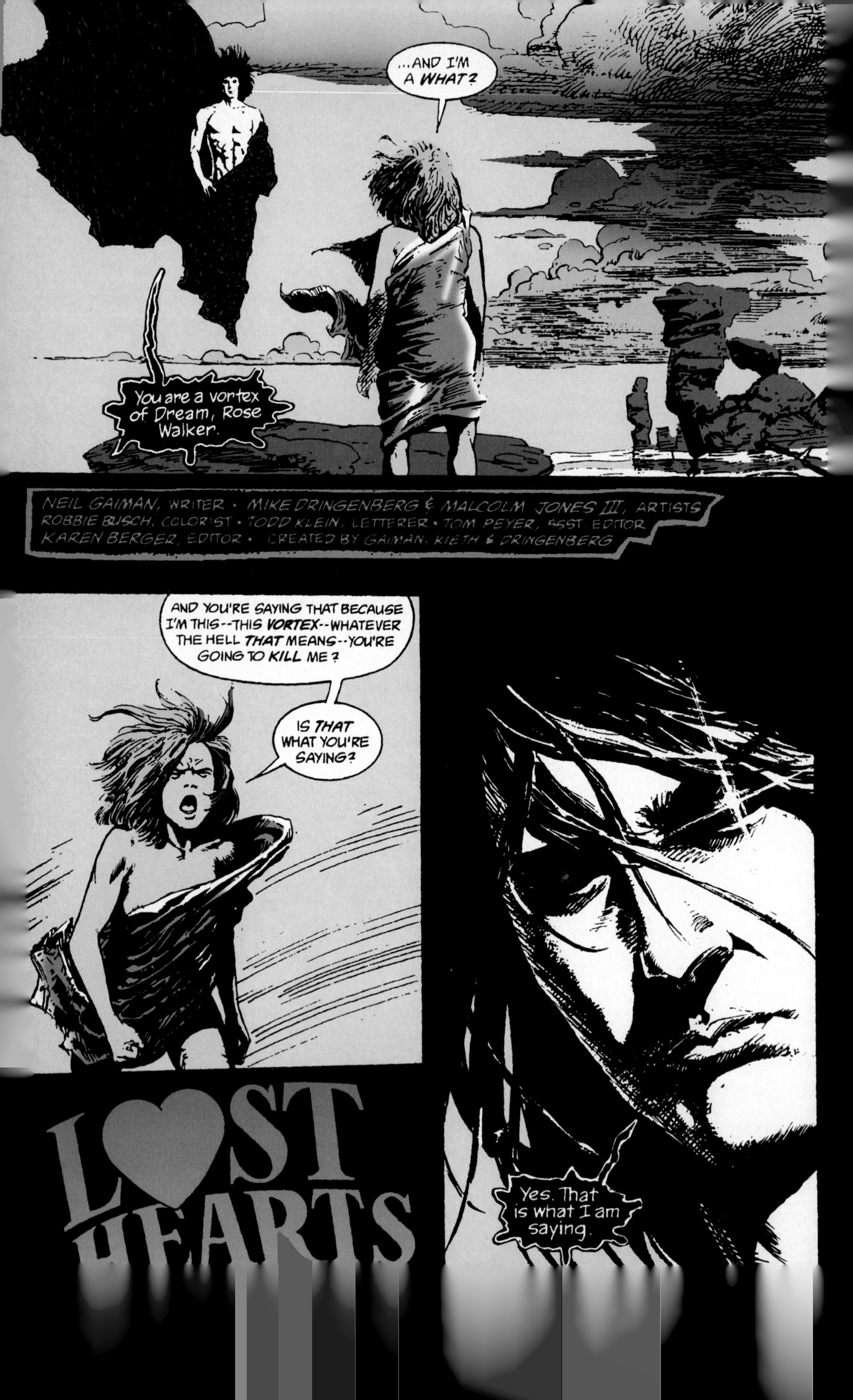
You are a vortex of Dream, Rose Walker.
...AND I'M A WHAT?
NEIL GAIMAN, WRITER • MIKE DRINGENBERG & MALCOLM JONES III, ARTISTS
ROBBIE BUSCH, COLORIST • TODD KLEIN, LETTERER • TOM PEYER, ASST. EDITOR
KAREN BERGER, EDITOR • CREATED BY GAIMAN, KIETH & DRINGENBERG
AND YOU'RE SAYING THAT BECAUSE I'M THIS--THIS VORTEX--WHATEVER THE HELL THAT MEANS--YOU'RE GOING TO KILL ME?
IS THAT WHAT YOU'RE SAYING?
LOST HEARTS
Yes. That is what I am saying.

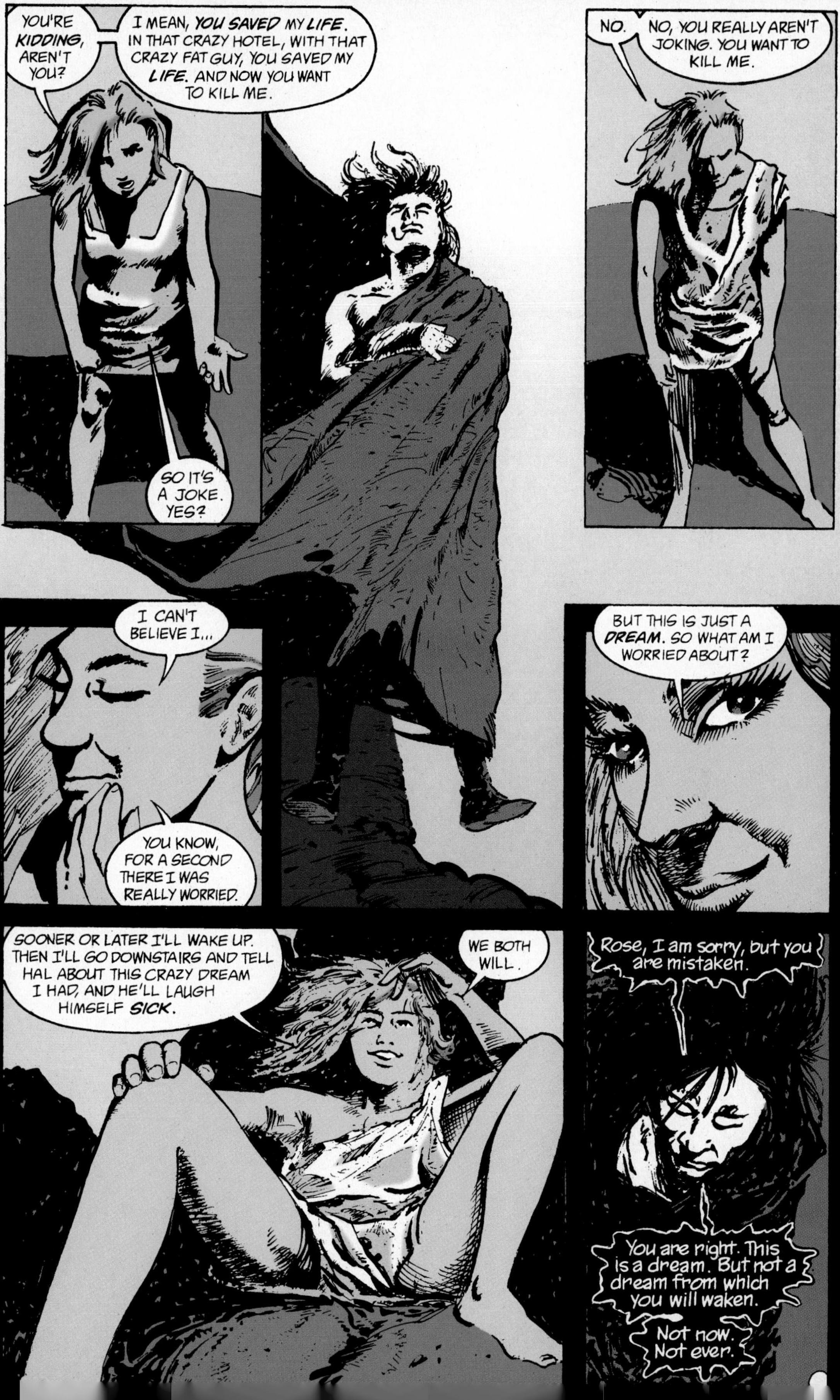
YOU'RE KIDDING, AREN'T YOU?
I MEAN, YOU SAVED MY LIFE. IN THAT CRAZY HOTEL, WITH THAT CRAZY FAT GUY, YOU SAVED MY LIFE. AND NOW YOU WANT TO KILL ME.
SO IT'S A JOKE. YES?
NO.
NO, YOU REALLY AREN'T JOKING. YOU WANT TO KILL ME.
I CAN'T BELIEVE I...
YOU KNOW, FOR A SECOND THERE I WAS REALLY WORRIED.
BUT THIS IS JUST A DREAM. SO WHAT AM I WORRIED ABOUT?
SOONER OR LATER I'LL WAKE UP. THEN I'LL GO DOWNSTAIRS AND TELL HAL ABOUT THIS CRAZY DREAM I HAD, AND HE'LL LAUGH HIMSELF SICK.
WE BOTH WILL.
Rose, I am sorry, but you are mistaken.
You are right. This is a dream. But not a dream from which you will waken.
Not now. Not ever.

Rose...

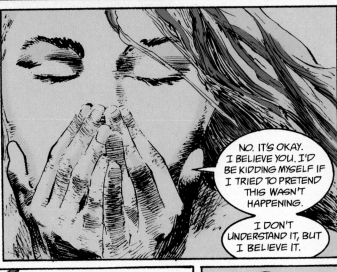

NO. IT'S OKAY. I BELIEVE YOU. I'D BE KIDDING MYSELF IF I TRIED TO PRETEND THIS WASN'T HAPPENING.

I DON'T UNDERSTAND IT, BUT I BELIEVE IT.

JUST TELL ME ONE THING.

What would that be?

WHY ME?

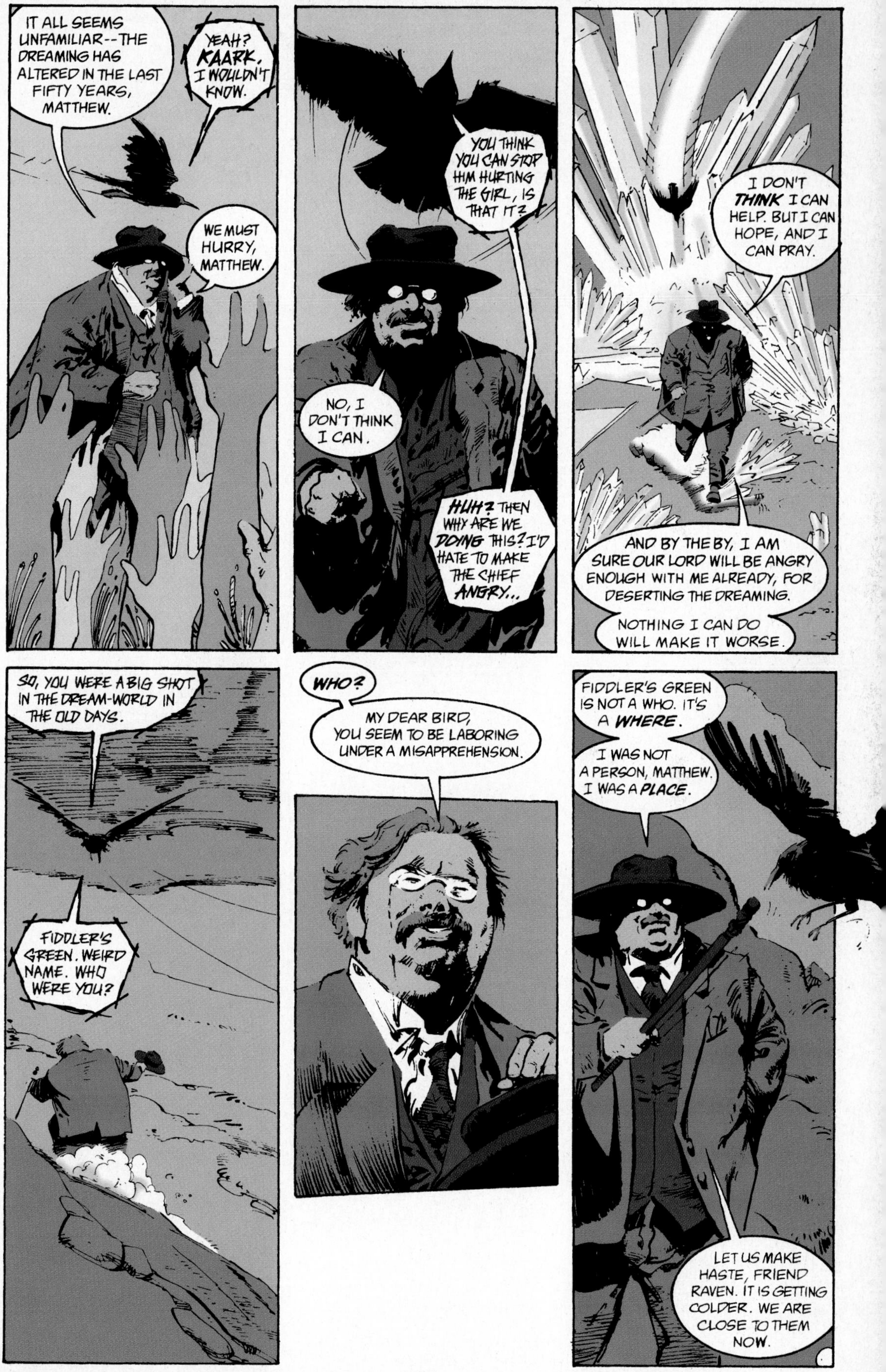
IT ALL SEEMS UNFAMILIAR--THE DREAMING HAS ALTERED IN THE LAST FIFTY YEARS, MATTHEW.
YEAH? KAARK. I WOULDN'T KNOW.
WE MUST HURRY, MATTHEW.
YOU THINK YOU CAN STOP HIM HURTING THE GIRL, IS THAT IT?
NO, I DON'T THINK I CAN.
HUH? THEN WHY ARE WE DOING THIS? I'D HATE TO MAKE THE CHIEF ANGRY...
I DON'T THINK I CAN HELP. BUT I CAN HOPE, AND I CAN PRAY.
AND BY THE BY, I AM SURE OUR LORD WILL BE ANGRY ENOUGH WITH ME ALREADY, FOR DESERTING THE DREAMING.
NOTHING I CAN DO WILL MAKE IT WORSE.
SO, YOU WERE A BIG SHOT IN THE DREAM-WORLD IN THE OLD DAYS.
FIDDLER'S GREEN. WEIRD NAME. WHO WERE YOU?
WHO?
MY DEAR BIRD, YOU SEEM TO BE LABORING UNDER A MISAPPREHENSION.
FIDDLER'S GREEN IS NOT A WHO. IT'S A WHERE.
I WAS NOT A PERSON, MATTHEW. I WAS A PLACE.
LET US MAKE HASTE, FRIEND RAVEN. IT IS GETTING COLDER. WE ARE CLOSE TO THEM NOW.

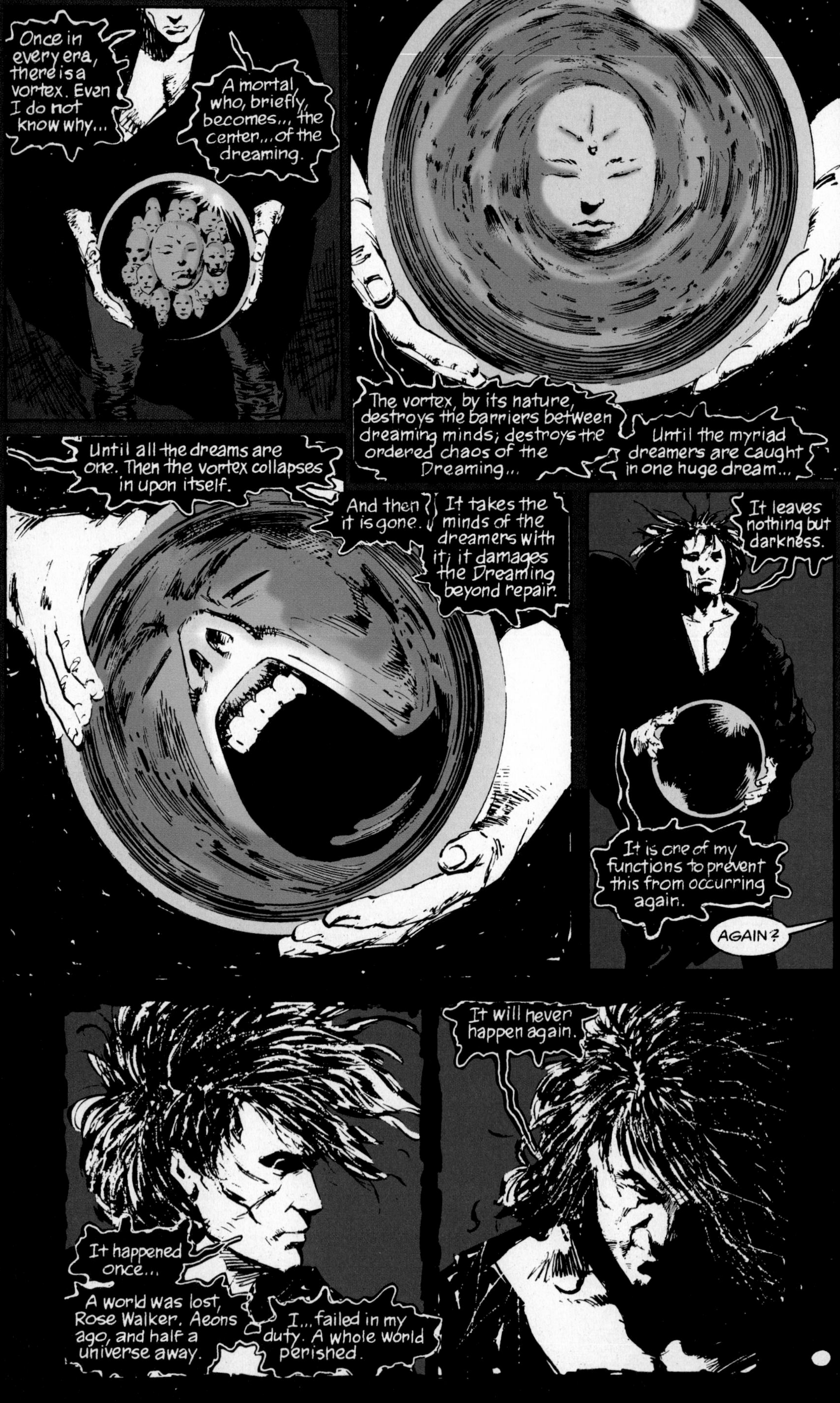
Once in every era, there is a vortex. Even I do not know why...
A mortal, who, briefly, becomes... the center... of the dreaming.
The vortex, by its nature, destroys the barriers between dreaming minds; destroys the ordered chaos of the Dreaming...
Until the myriad dreamers are caught in one huge dream...
Until all the dreams are one. Then the vortex collapses in upon itself.
And then it is gone.
It takes the minds of the dreamers with it; it damages the Dreaming beyond repair.
It leaves nothing but darkness.
It is one of my functions to prevent this from occurring again.
AGAIN?
It happened once...
A world was lost, Rose Walker. Aeons ago, and half a universe away.
I... failed in my duty. A whole world perished.
It will never happen again.

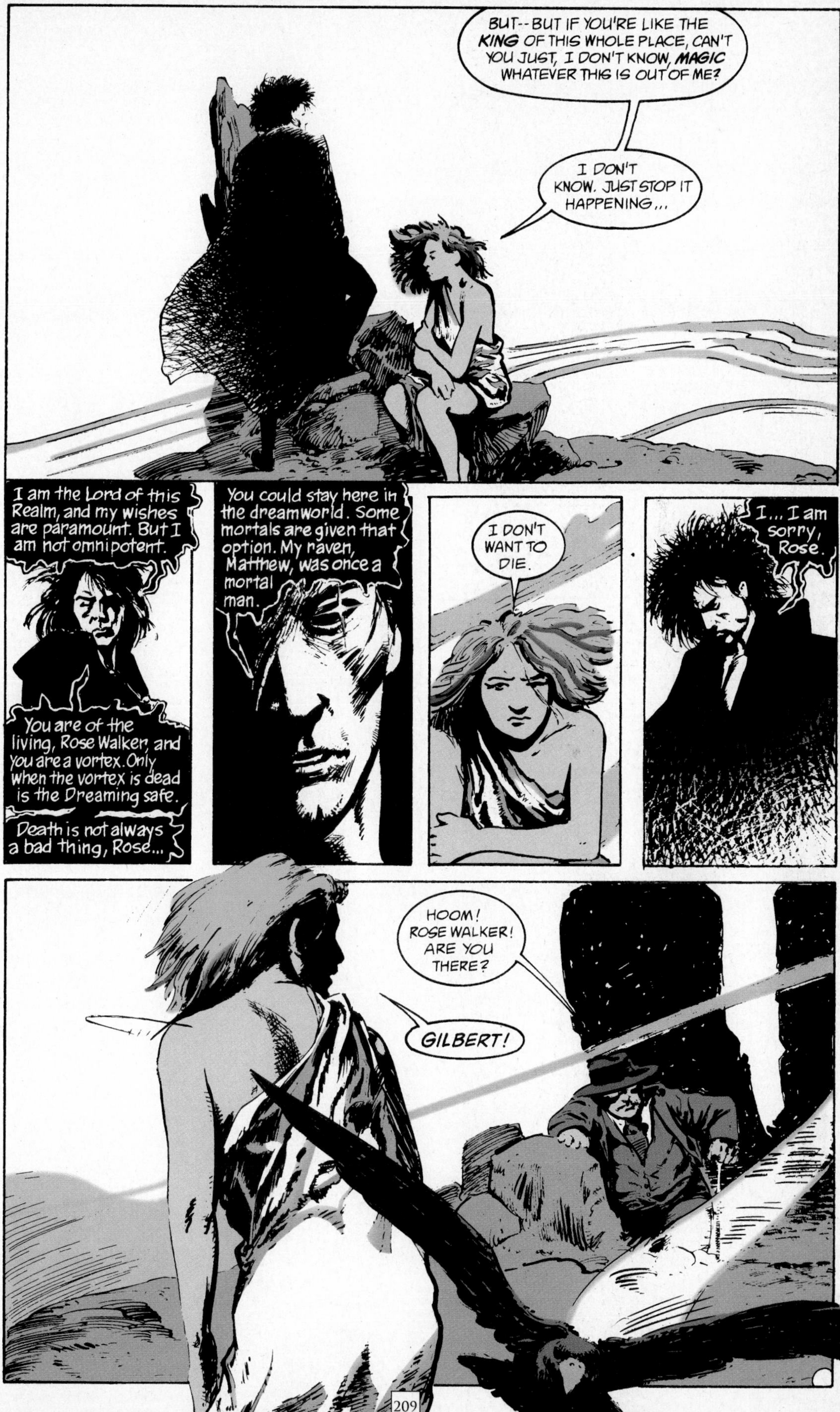
BUT-- BUT IF YOU'RE LIKE THE KING OF THIS WHOLE PLACE, CAN'T YOU JUST, I DON'T KNOW, MAGIC WHATEVER THIS IS OUT OF ME?
I DON'T KNOW. JUST STOP IT HAPPENING...
I am the Lord of this Realm, and my wishes are paramount. But I am not omnipotent.
You are of the living, Rose Walker, and you are a vortex. Only when the vortex is dead is the Dreaming safe.
Death is not always a bad thing, Rose...
You could stay here in the dreamworld. Some mortals are given that option. My raven, Matthew, was once a mortal man.
I DON'T WANT TO DIE.
I... I am sorry, Rose.
HOOM! ROSE WALKER! ARE YOU THERE?
GILBERT!

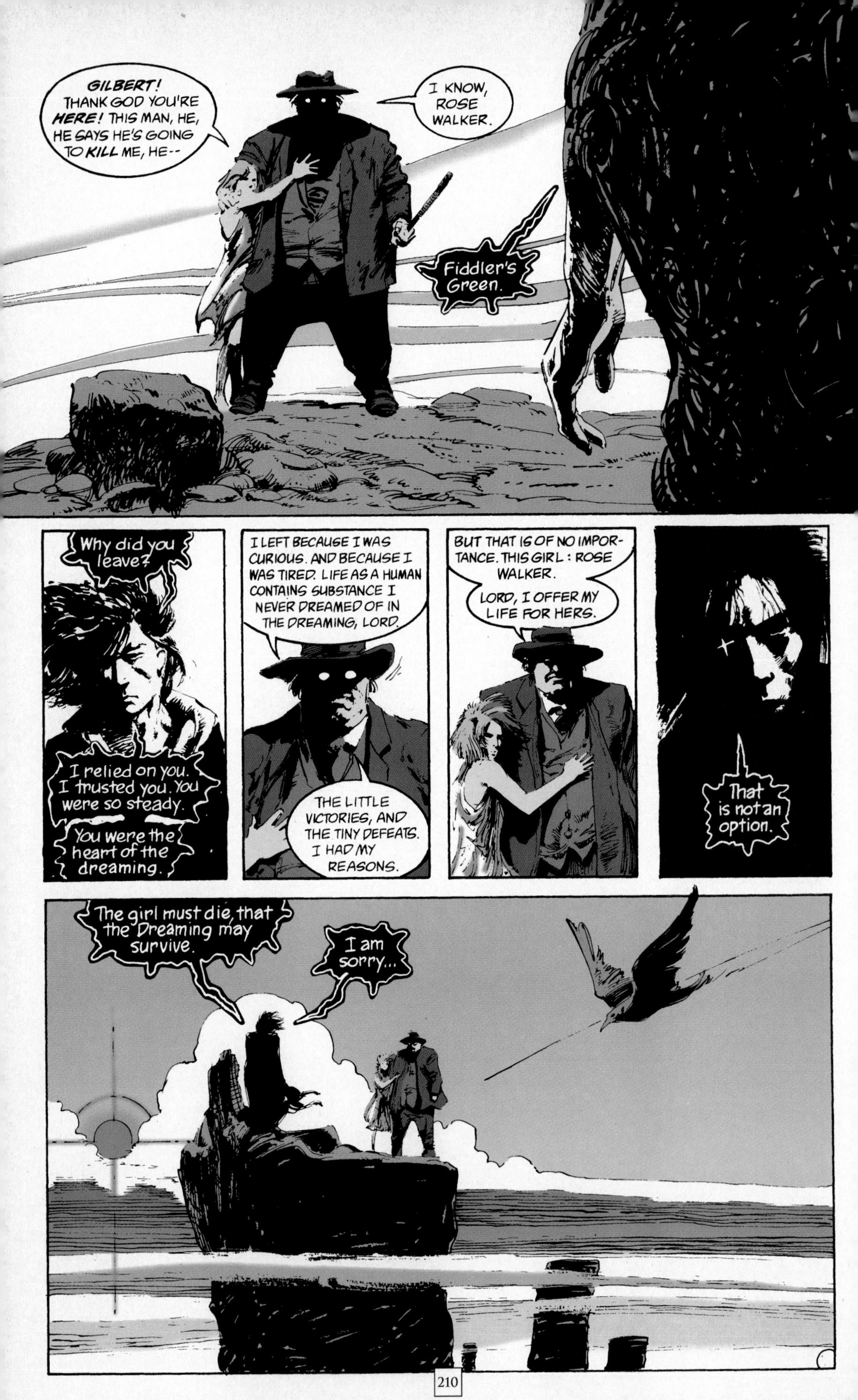
GILBERT! THANK GOD YOU'RE **HERE!** THIS MAN, HE, HE SAYS HE'S GOING TO **KILL** ME, HE--
I KNOW, ROSE WALKER.
Fiddler's Green.
Why did you leave?
I relied on you. I trusted you. You were so steady.
You were the heart of the dreaming.
I LEFT BECAUSE I WAS CURIOUS. AND BECAUSE I WAS TIRED. LIFE AS A HUMAN CONTAINS SUBSTANCE I NEVER DREAMED OF IN THE DREAMING, LORD.
THE LITTLE VICTORIES, AND THE TINY DEFEATS. I HAD MY REASONS.
BUT THAT IS OF NO IMPORTANCE. THIS GIRL : ROSE WALKER.
LORD, I OFFER MY LIFE FOR HERS.
That is not an option.
The girl must die, that the Dreaming may survive.
I am sorry...

" I'M SORRY, MIRANDA...

" I DON'T THINK I'VE BEEN A... VERY GOOD MOTHER...

DON'T THINK ABOUT IT, UNITY. MOTHER.

EVERYTHING'S GOING TO BE JUST FINE.

I... I THINK I'M GOING TO... HAVE TO SLEEP NOW.

UNITY KINKAID FINDS IT HARDER AND HARDER TO STAY ALIVE.

LIFE IS SO...

UNITY HEARS A VOICE, HER OWN VOICE, AND IT WHISPERS TO HER IN THE DARKNESS.

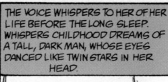

THE VOICE WHISPERS TO HER OF HER LIFE BEFORE THE LONG SLEEP. WHISPERS CHILDHOOD DREAMS OF A TALL, DARK MAN, WHOSE EYES DANCED LIKE TWIN STARS IN HER HEAD.

WHISPERS THE TRUTH.

AND THEN SHE GIVES IN TO SLEEP, HER BREATH SHALLOW AND HALT. DYING, IN A WORLD SHE FINALLY UNDERSTANDS...

UNITY DREAMS.

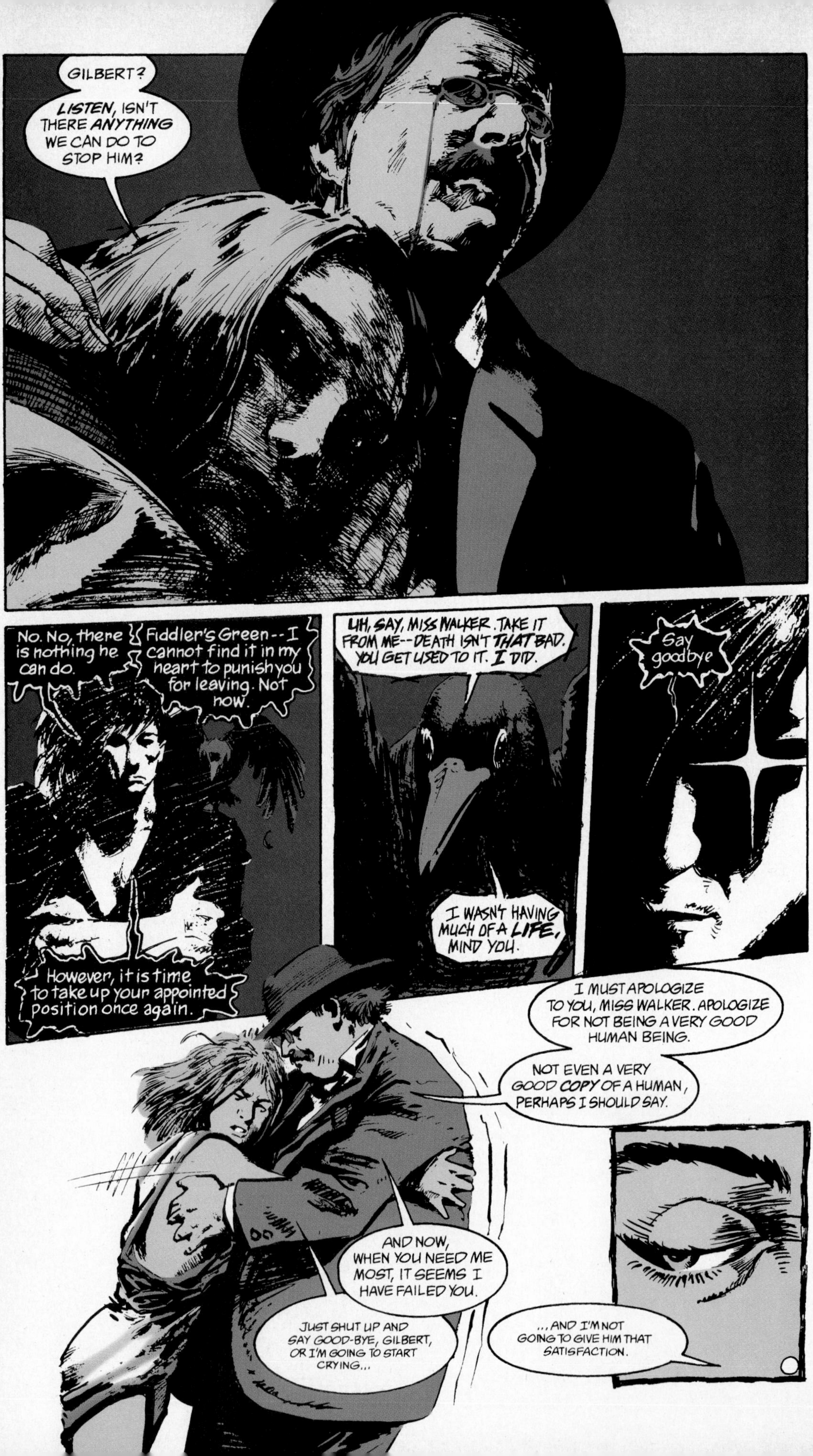

GILBERT?
LISTEN, ISN'T THERE ANYTHING WE CAN DO TO STOP HIM?
No. No, there is nothing he can do.
Fiddler's Green -- I cannot find it in my heart to punish you for leaving. Not now.
However, it is time to take up your appointed position once again.
UH, SAY, MISS WALKER. TAKE IT FROM ME--DEATH ISN'T THAT BAD. YOU GET USED TO IT. I DID.
I WASN'T HAVING MUCH OF A LIFE, MIND YOU.
Say goodbye
I MUST APOLOGIZE TO YOU, MISS WALKER. APOLOGIZE FOR NOT BEING A VERY GOOD HUMAN BEING.
NOT EVEN A VERY GOOD COPY OF A HUMAN, PERHAPS I SHOULD SAY.
AND NOW, WHEN YOU NEED ME MOST, IT SEEMS I HAVE FAILED YOU.
JUST SHUT UP AND SAY GOOD-BYE, GILBERT, OR I'M GOING TO START CRYING...
...AND I'M NOT GOING TO GIVE HIM THAT SATISFACTION.

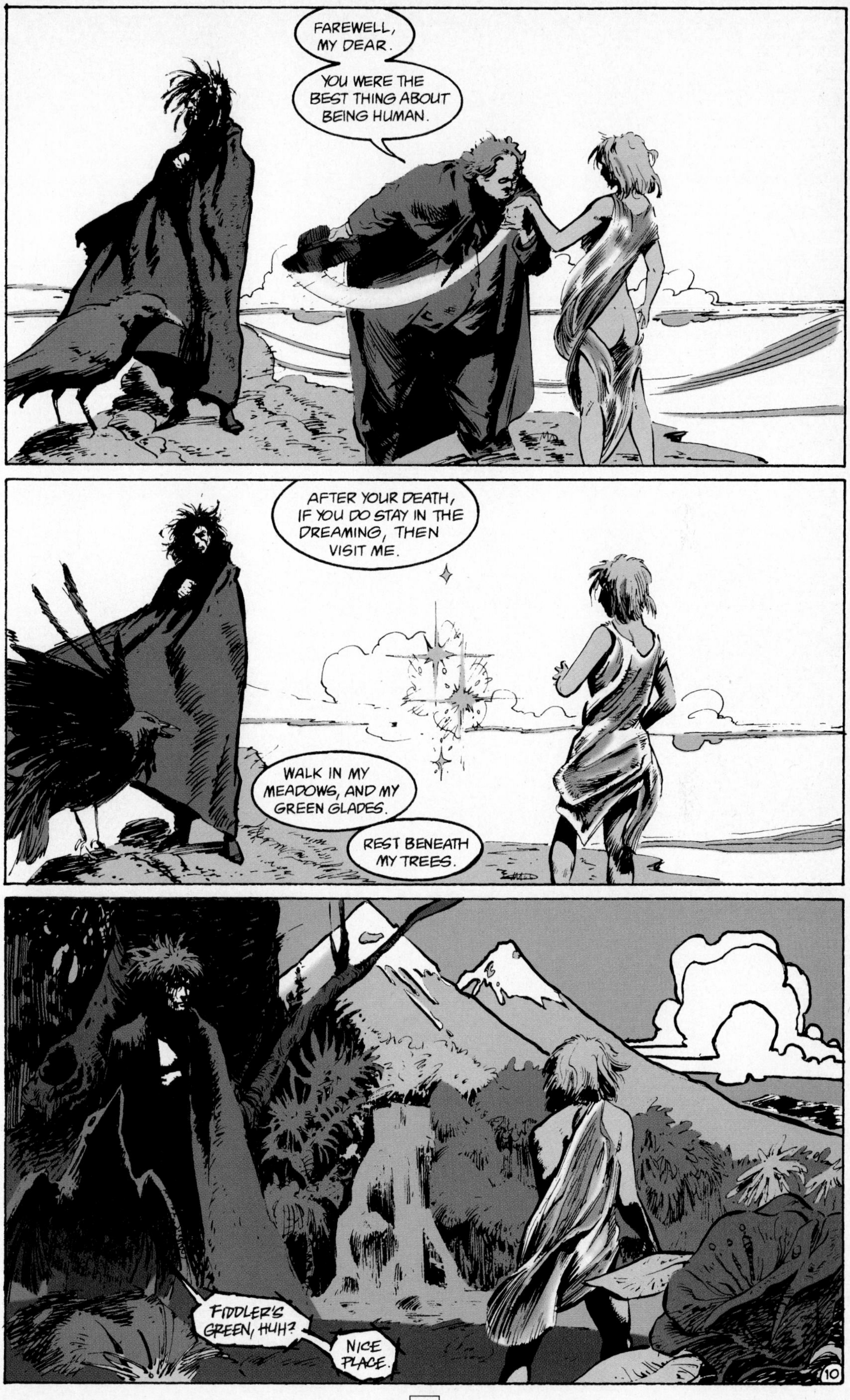
FAREWELL, MY DEAR.
YOU WERE THE BEST THING ABOUT BEING HUMAN.
AFTER YOUR DEATH, IF YOU DO STAY IN THE DREAMING, THEN VISIT ME.
WALK IN MY MEADOWS, AND MY GREEN GLADES.
REST BENEATH MY TREES.
FIDDLER'S GREEN, HUH?
NICE PLACE.
10

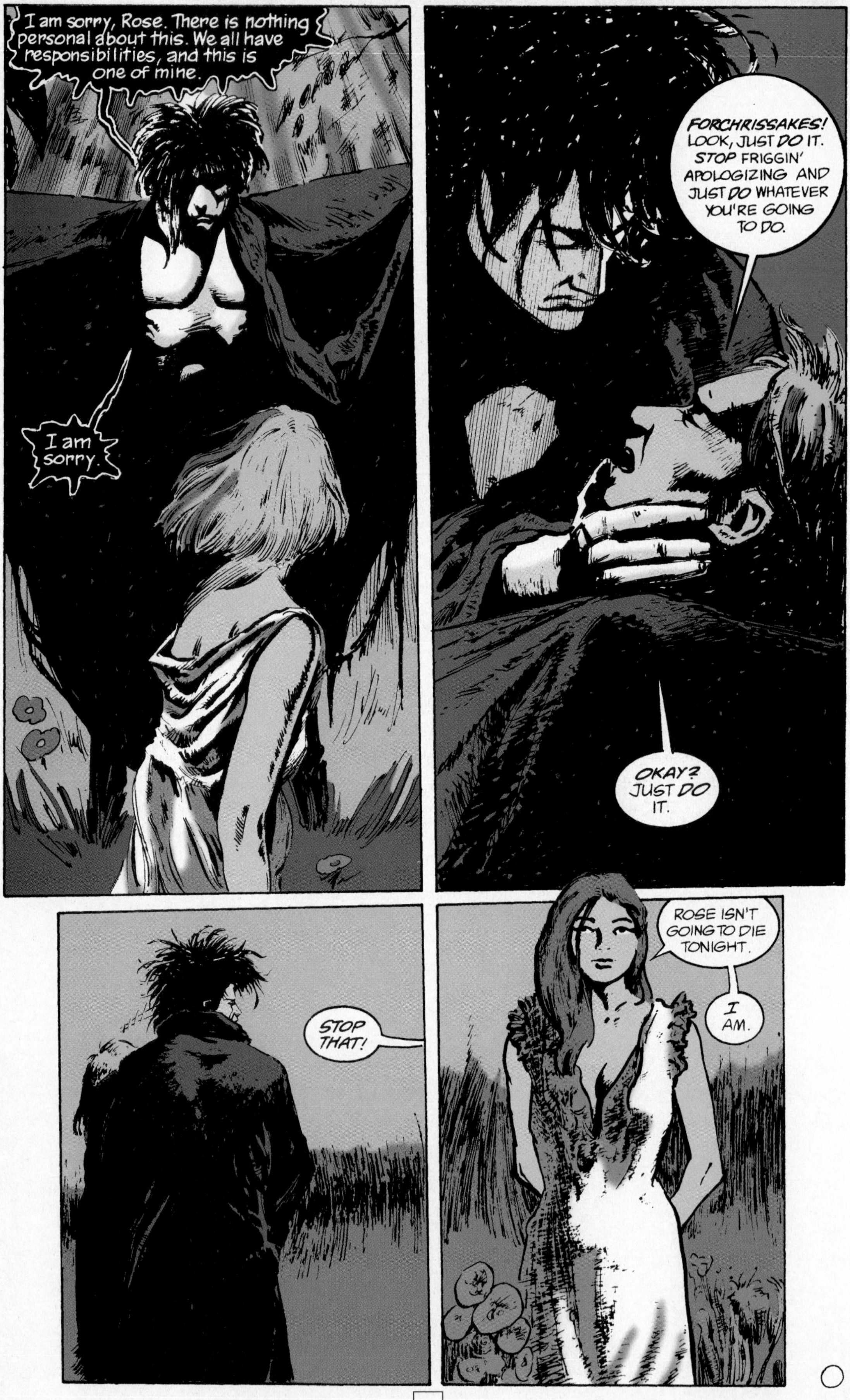

I am sorry, Rose. There is nothing personal about this. We all have responsibilities, and this is one of mine.
I am sorry.
FORCHRISSAKES! LOOK, JUST DO IT. STOP FRIGGIN' APOLOGIZING AND JUST DO WHATEVER YOU'RE GOING TO DO.
OKAY? JUST DO IT.
STOP THAT!
ROSE ISN'T GOING TO DIE TONIGHT.
I AM.

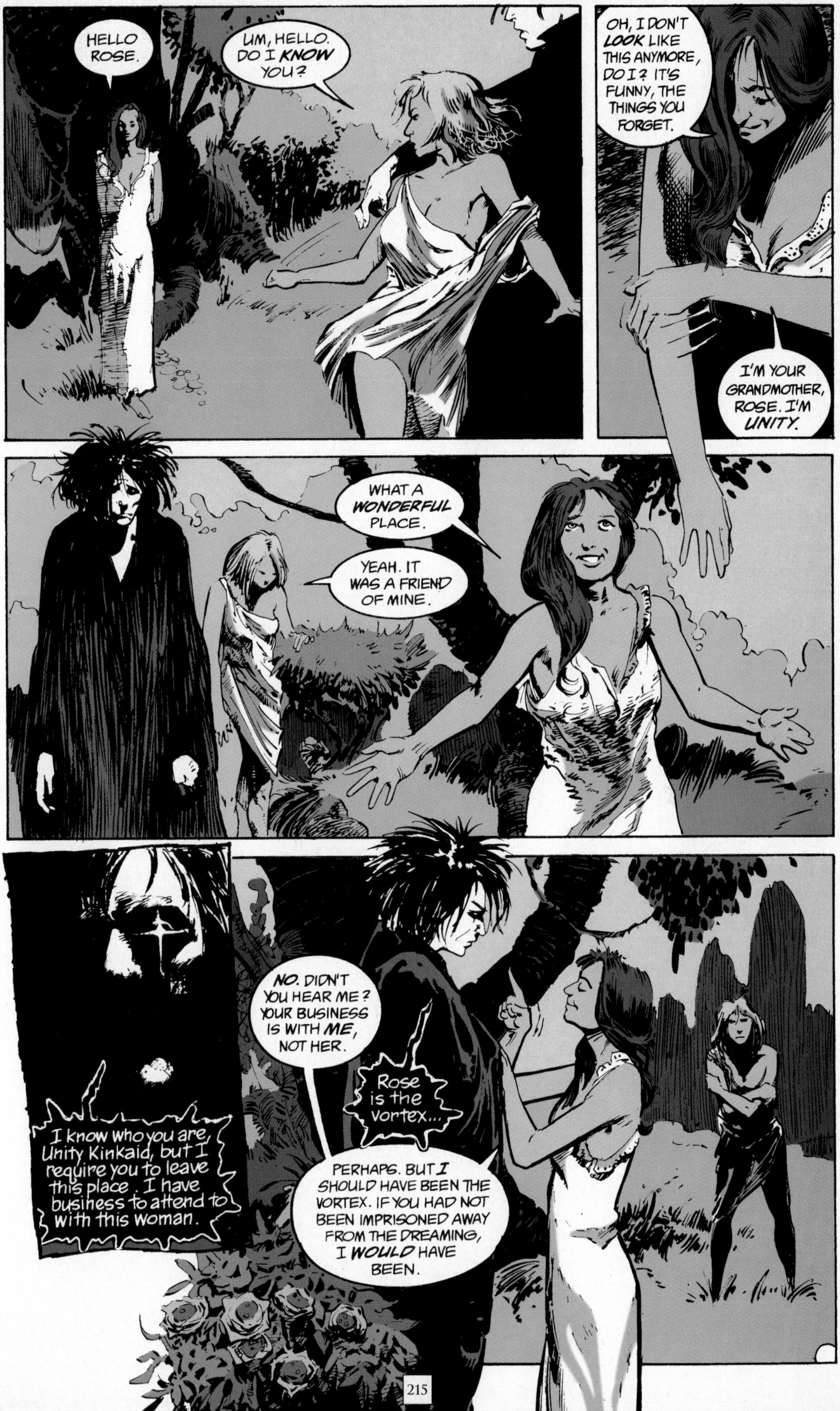
HELLO ROSE.
UM, HELLO. DO I KNOW YOU?
OH, I DON'T LOOK LIKE THIS ANYMORE, DO I? IT'S FUNNY, THE THINGS YOU FORGET.
I'M YOUR GRANDMOTHER, ROSE. I'M UNITY.
WHAT A WONDERFUL PLACE.
YEAH. IT WAS A FRIEND OF MINE.
I know who you are, Unity Kinkaid, but I require you to leave this place. I have business to attend to with this woman.
NO. DIDN'T YOU HEAR ME? YOUR BUSINESS IS WITH ME, NOT HER.
Rose is the vortex...
PERHAPS. BUT I SHOULD HAVE BEEN THE VORTEX. IF YOU HAD NOT BEEN IMPRISONED AWAY FROM THE DREAMING, I WOULD HAVE BEEN.

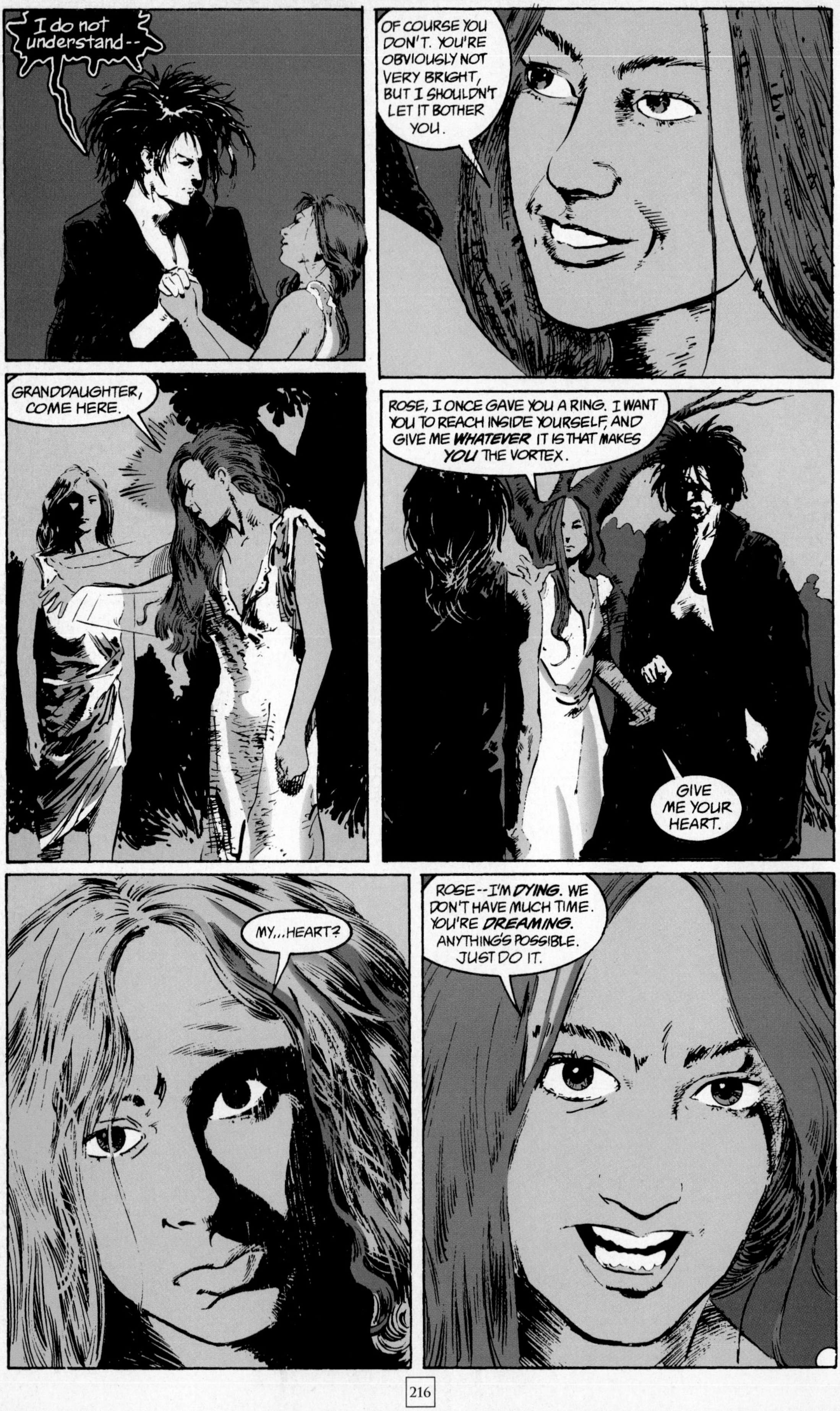
I do not understand--
OF COURSE YOU DON'T. YOU'RE OBVIOUSLY NOT VERY BRIGHT, BUT I SHOULDN'T LET IT BOTHER YOU.
GRANDDAUGHTER, COME HERE.
ROSE, I ONCE GAVE YOU A RING. I WANT YOU TO REACH INSIDE YOURSELF, AND GIVE ME WHATEVER IT IS THAT MAKES YOU THE VORTEX.
GIVE ME YOUR HEART.
MY...HEART?
ROSE--I'M DYING. WE DON'T HAVE MUCH TIME. YOU'RE DREAMING. ANYTHING'S POSSIBLE. JUST DO IT.

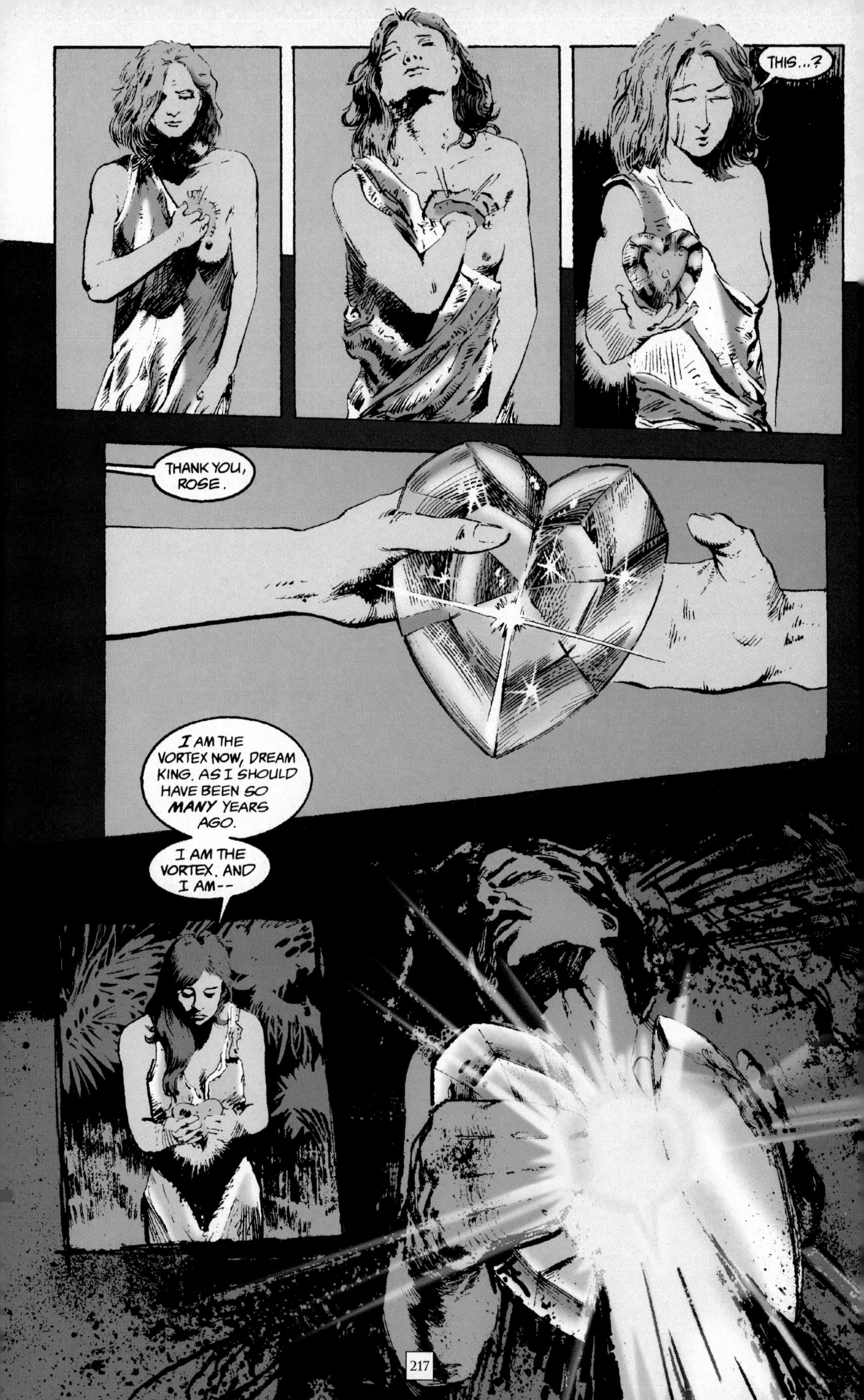
THIS...?
THANK YOU, ROSE.
I AM THE VORTEX NOW, DREAM KING. AS I SHOULD HAVE BEEN SO MANY YEARS AGO.
I AM THE VORTEX. AND I AM--

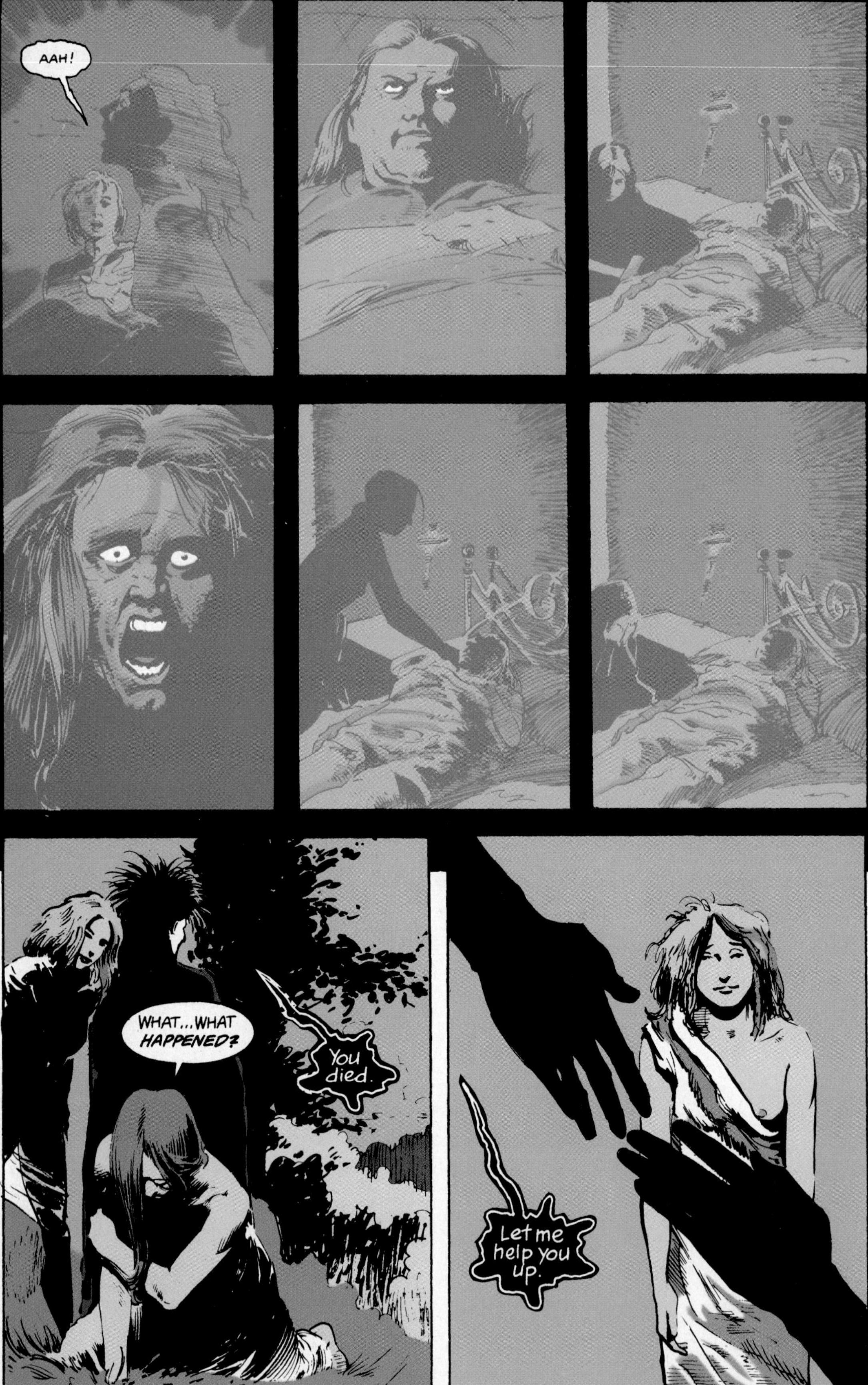
AAH!
WHAT...WHAT HAPPENED?
You died.
Let me help you up.

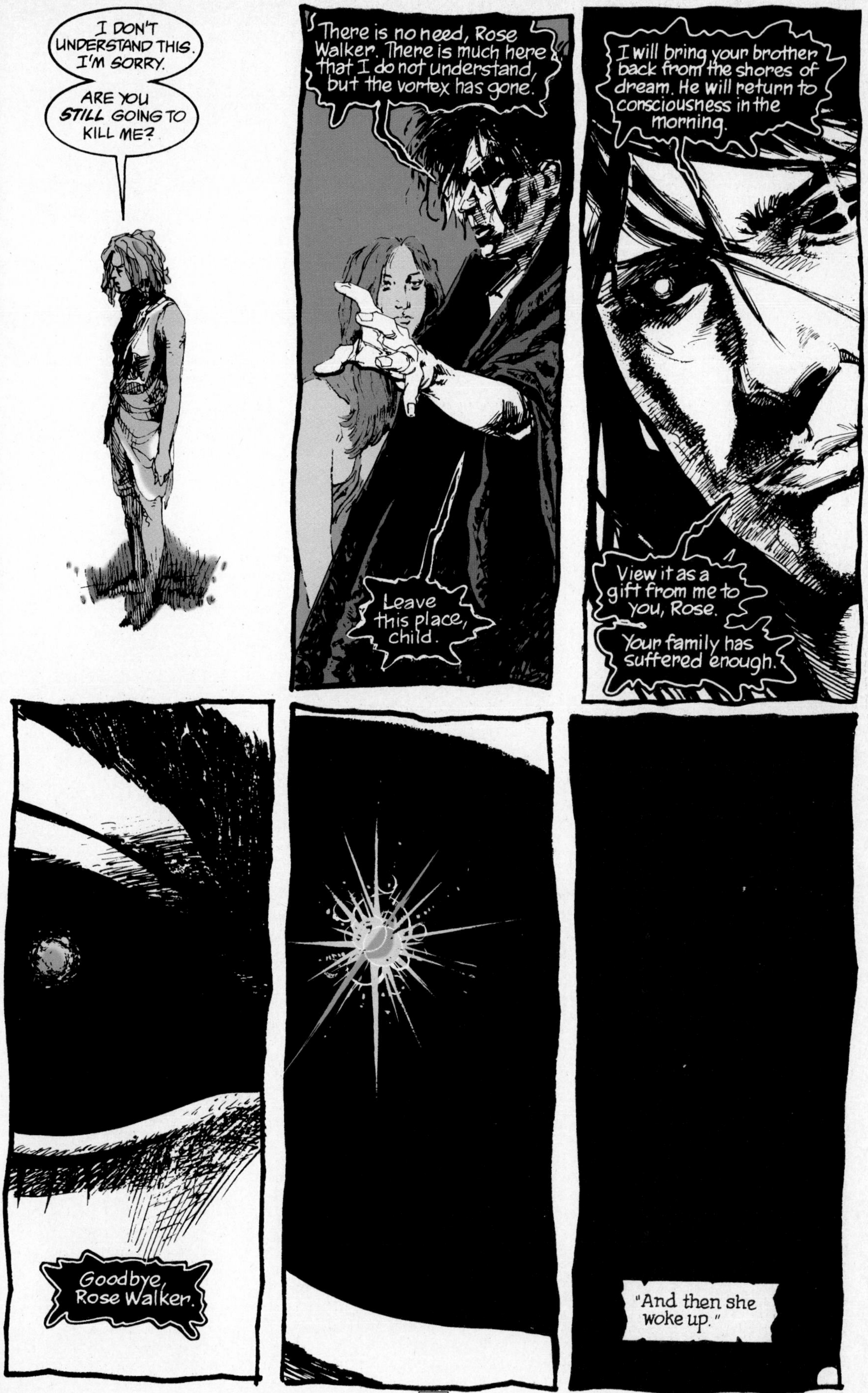
I DON'T UNDERSTAND THIS. I'M SORRY.
ARE YOU STILL GOING TO KILL ME?
There is no need, Rose Walker. There is much here that I do not understand, but the vortex has gone.
Leave this place, child.
I will bring your brother back from the shores of dream. He will return to consciousness in the morning.
View it as a gift from me to you, Rose.
Your family has suffered enough.
Goodbye, Rose Walker.
"And then she woke up."

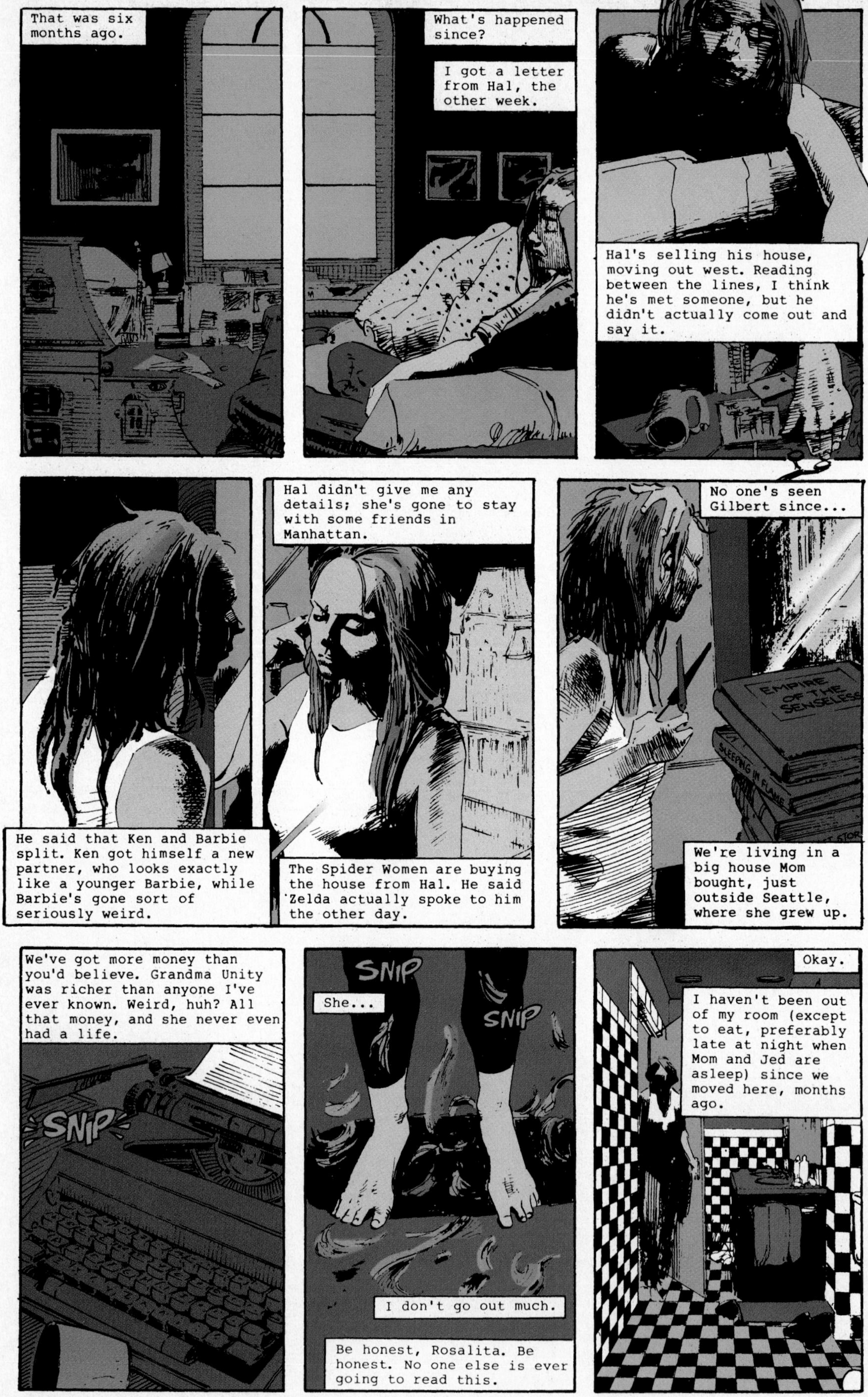
That was six months ago.
What's happened since?
I got a letter from Hal, the other week.
Hal's selling his house, moving out west. Reading between the lines, I think he's met someone, but he didn't actually come out and say it.
He said that Ken and Barbie split. Ken got himself a new partner, who looks exactly like a younger Barbie, while Barbie's gone sort of seriously weird.
Hal didn't give me any details; she's gone to stay with some friends in Manhattan.
The Spider Women are buying the house from Hal. He said Zelda actually spoke to him the other day.
No one's seen Gilbert since...
EMPIRE OF THE SENSELESS
SLEEPING IN FLAME
We're living in a big house Mom bought, just outside Seattle, where she grew up.
We've got more money than you'd believe. Grandma Unity was richer than anyone I've ever known. Weird, huh? All that money, and she never even had a life.
SNIP
SNIP
She...
SNIP
I don't go out much.
Be honest, Rosalita. Be honest. No one else is ever going to read this.
Okay.
I haven't been out of my room (except to eat, preferably late at night when Mom and Jed are asleep) since we moved here, months ago.

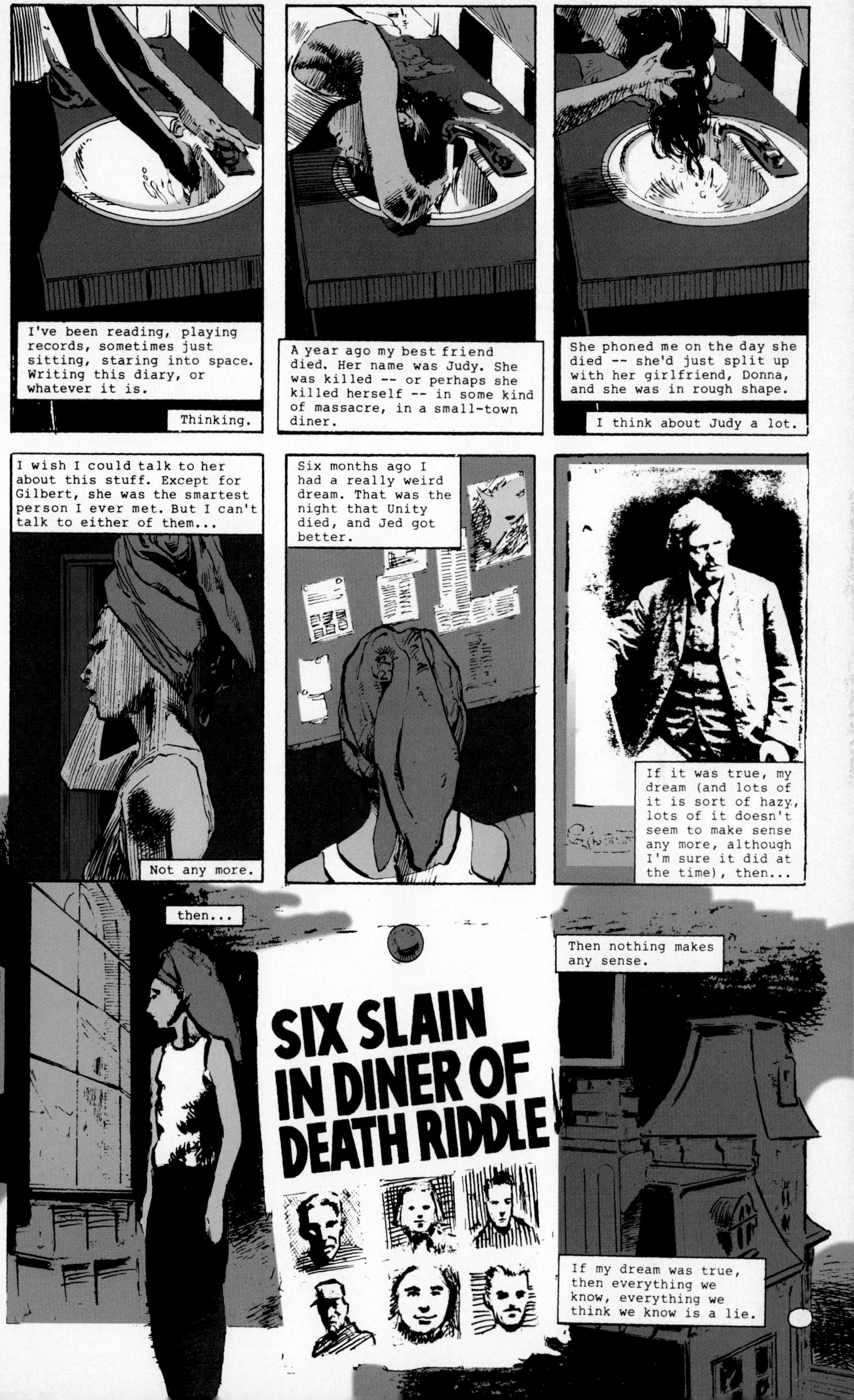
I've been reading, playing records, sometimes just sitting, staring into space. Writing this diary, or whatever it is.
Thinking.
A year ago my best friend died. Her name was Judy. She was killed -- or perhaps she killed herself -- in some kind of massacre, in a small-town diner.
She phoned me on the day she died -- she'd just split up with her girlfriend, Donna, and she was in rough shape.
I think about Judy a lot.
I wish I could talk to her about this stuff. Except for Gilbert, she was the smartest person I ever met. But I can't talk to either of them...
Not any more.
Six months ago I had a really weird dream. That was the night that Unity died, and Jed got better.
If it was true, my dream (and lots of it is sort of hazy, lots of it doesn't seem to make sense any more, although I'm sure it did at the time), then...
then...
Then nothing makes any sense.
SIX SLAIN IN DINER OF DEATH RIDDLE
If my dream was true, then everything we know, everything we think we know is a lie.

It means more than that.

It means the world's about as solid and as reliable as a layer of scum on the top of a well of black water which goes down forever, and there are things in the depths that I don't even want to think about.

It means that we're just dolls. We don't have a clue what's really going down, we just kid ourselves that we're in control of our lives while a paper's thickness away things that would drive us mad if we thought about them for too long play with us, and move us around from room to room, and put us away at night when they're tired, or bored.

In my dream, I could have destroyed everybody in the world.

In my dream, Gilbert wasn't even a person; he was a place.

In my dream, Grandma Unity gave up her life for me.

Dreams are weird and stupid and they scare me. I haven't slept properly for six months now.

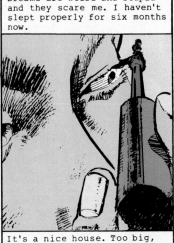

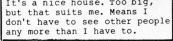

It's a nice house. Too big, but that suits me. Means I don't have to see other people any more than I have to.

That's my story.

Okay.

It's even got a happy ending: Jed and Rose and their mother were finally reunited, and they all lived together in a big old house.

I've been brooding on that night for too long now. Six months.

And I've decided.

My dream. My weird dream. It was just a dream.

That's all. Just a dream.

"And then she woke up."

You know, I always hated stories that ended like that. I always felt cheated.

Six months is long enough to feel sorry for yourself. Isn't it?

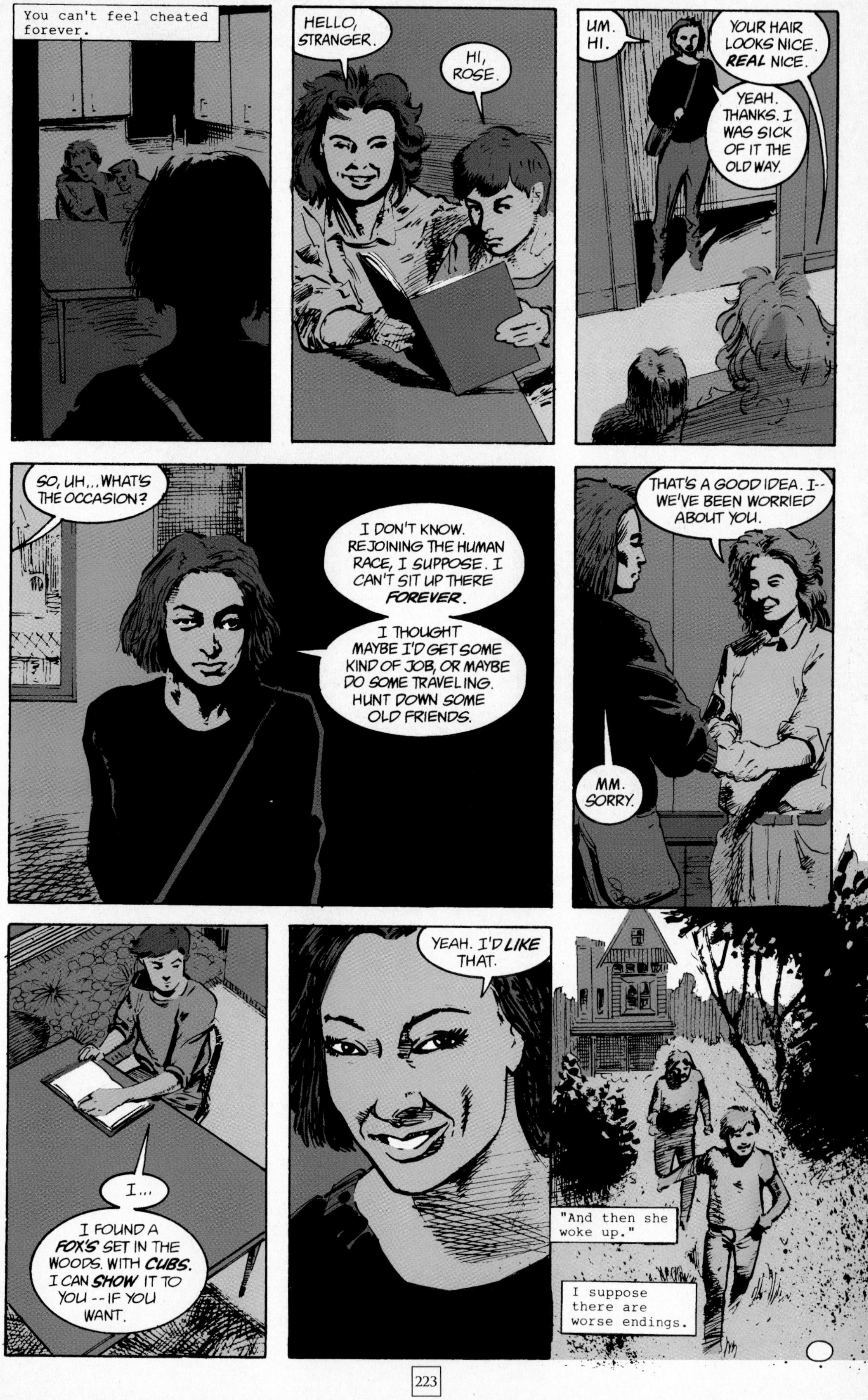
You can't feel cheated forever.
HELLO, STRANGER.
HI, ROSE.
UM. HI.
YOUR HAIR LOOKS NICE. REAL NICE.
YEAH. THANKS. I WAS SICK OF IT THE OLD WAY.
SO, UH,.. WHAT'S THE OCCASION?
I DON'T KNOW. REJOINING THE HUMAN RACE, I SUPPOSE. I CAN'T SIT UP THERE FOREVER.
I THOUGHT MAYBE I'D GET SOME KIND OF JOB, OR MAYBE DO SOME TRAVELING. HUNT DOWN SOME OLD FRIENDS.
THAT'S A GOOD IDEA. I-- WE'VE BEEN WORRIED ABOUT YOU.
MM. SORRY.
I...
I FOUND A FOX'S SET IN THE WOODS. WITH CUBS. I CAN SHOW IT TO YOU --IF YOU WANT.
YEAH. I'D LIKE THAT.
"And then she woke up."
I suppose there are worse endings.

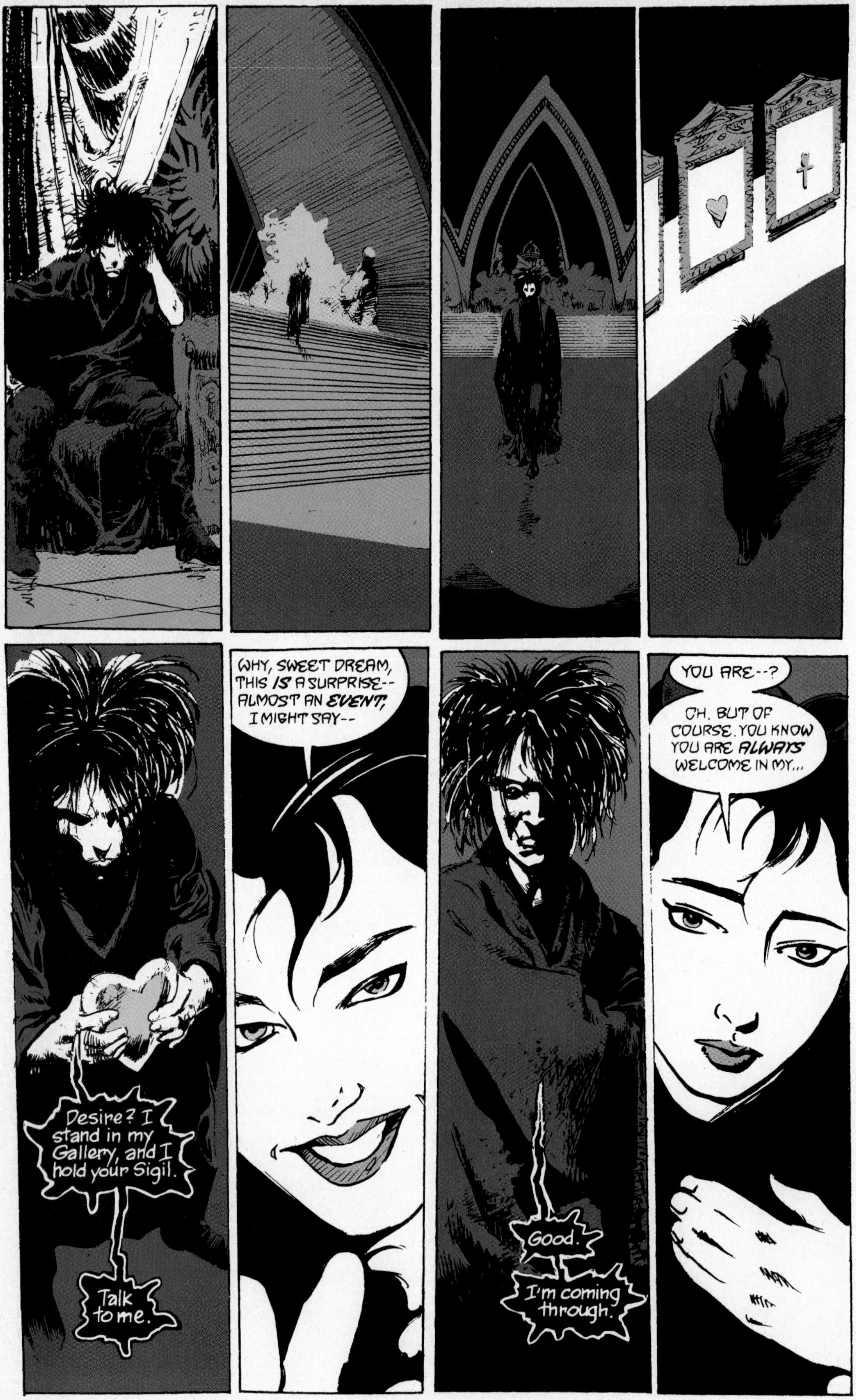
Desire? I stand in my Gallery, and I hold your Sigil.
Talk to me.
WHY, SWEET DREAM, THIS IS A SURPRISE-- ALMOST AN EVENT, I MIGHT SAY--
Good.
I'm coming through.
YOU ARE--?
OH, BUT OF COURSE. YOU KNOW YOU ARE ALWAYS WELCOME IN MY...

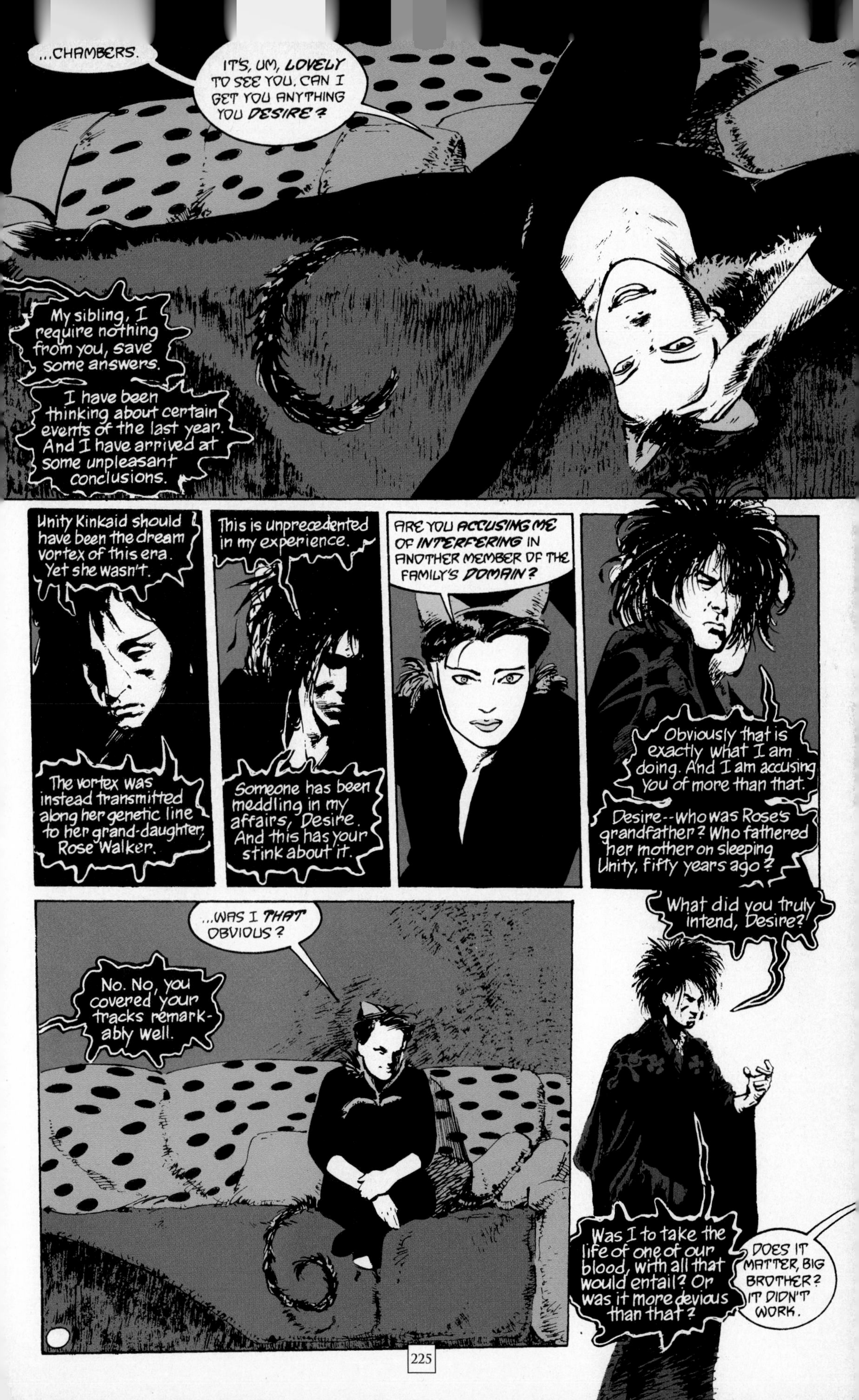
...CHAMBERS.
IT'S, UM, LOVELY TO SEE YOU. CAN I GET YOU ANYTHING YOU DESIRE?
My sibling, I require nothing from you, save some answers.
I have been thinking about certain events of the last year. And I have arrived at some unpleasant conclusions.
Unity Kinkaid should have been the dream vortex of this era. Yet she wasn't.
The vortex was instead transmitted along her genetic line to her grand-daughter, Rose Walker.
This is unprecedented in my experience.
Someone has been meddling in my affairs, Desire. And this has your stink about it.
ARE YOU ACCUSING ME OF INTERFERING IN ANOTHER MEMBER OF THE FAMILY'S DOMAIN?
Obviously that is exactly what I am doing. And I am accusing you of more than that.
Desire--who was Rose's grandfather? Who fathered her mother on sleeping Unity, fifty years ago?
...WAS I THAT OBVIOUS?
No. No, you covered your tracks remarkably well.
What did you truly intend, Desire?
Was I to take the life of one of our blood, with all that would entail? Or was it more devious than that?
DOES IT MATTER, BIG BROTHER? IT DIDN'T WORK.

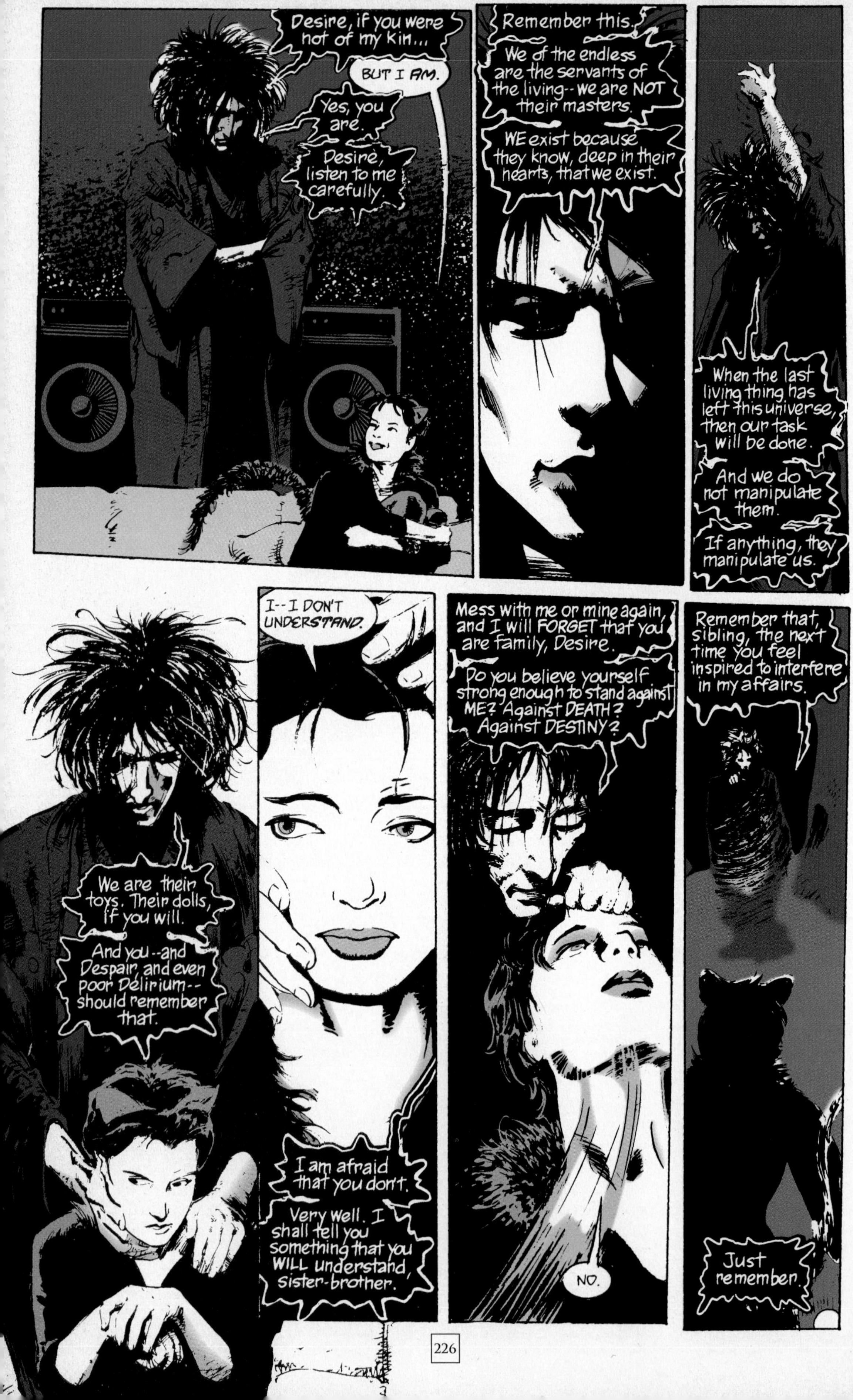
Desire, if you were not of my kin...
BUT I AM.
Yes, you are.
Desire, listen to me carefully.
Remember this.
We of the endless are the servants of the living--we are NOT their masters.
WE exist because they know, deep in their hearts, that we exist.
When the last living thing has left this universe, then our task will be done.
And we do not manipulate them.
If anything, they manipulate us.
We are their toys. Their dolls, if you will.
And you--and Despair, and even poor Délirium--should remember that.
I--I DON'T UNDERSTAND.
I am afraid that you don't.
Very well. I shall tell you something that you WILL understand, sister-brother.
Mess with me or mine again, and I will FORGET that you are family, Desire.
Do you believe yourself strong enough to stand against ME? Against DEATH? Against DESTINY?
NO.
Remember that, sibling, the next time you feel inspired to interfere in my affairs.
Just remember.

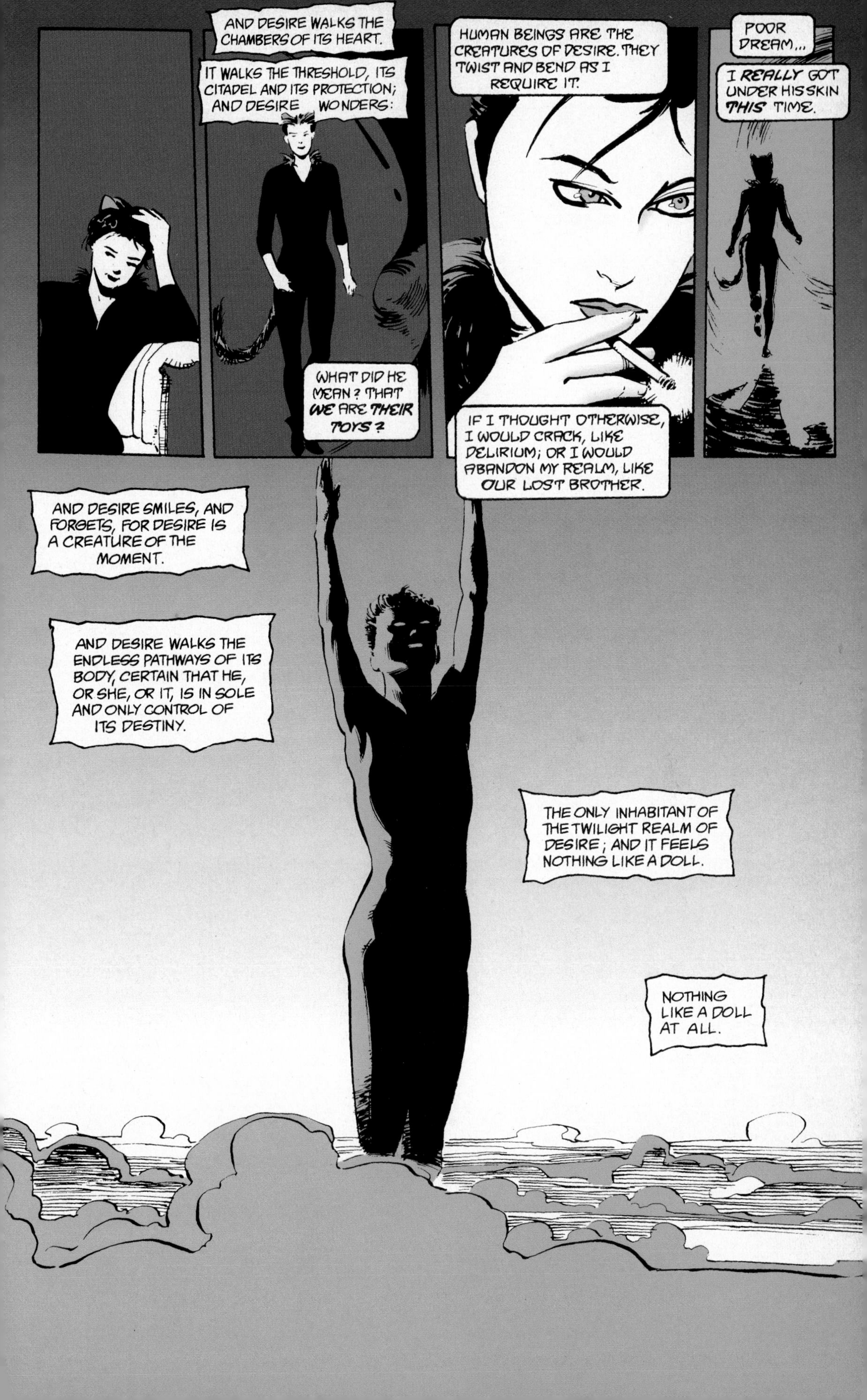
AND DESIRE WALKS THE CHAMBERS OF ITS HEART.
IT WALKS THE THRESHOLD, ITS CITADEL AND ITS PROTECTION; AND DESIRE WONDERS:
WHAT DID HE MEAN? THAT WE ARE THEIR TOYS?
HUMAN BEINGS ARE THE CREATURES OF DESIRE. THEY TWIST AND BEND AS I REQUIRE IT.
IF I THOUGHT OTHERWISE, I WOULD CRACK, LIKE DELIRIUM; OR I WOULD ABANDON MY REALM, LIKE OUR LOST BROTHER.
POOR DREAM...
I REALLY GOT UNDER HIS SKIN THIS TIME.
AND DESIRE SMILES, AND FORGETS, FOR DESIRE IS A CREATURE OF THE MOMENT.
AND DESIRE WALKS THE ENDLESS PATHWAYS OF ITS BODY, CERTAIN THAT HE, OR SHE, OR IT, IS IN SOLE AND ONLY CONTROL OF ITS DESTINY.
THE ONLY INHABITANT OF THE TWILIGHT REALM OF DESIRE; AND IT FEELS NOTHING LIKE A DOLL.
NOTHING LIKE A DOLL AT ALL.

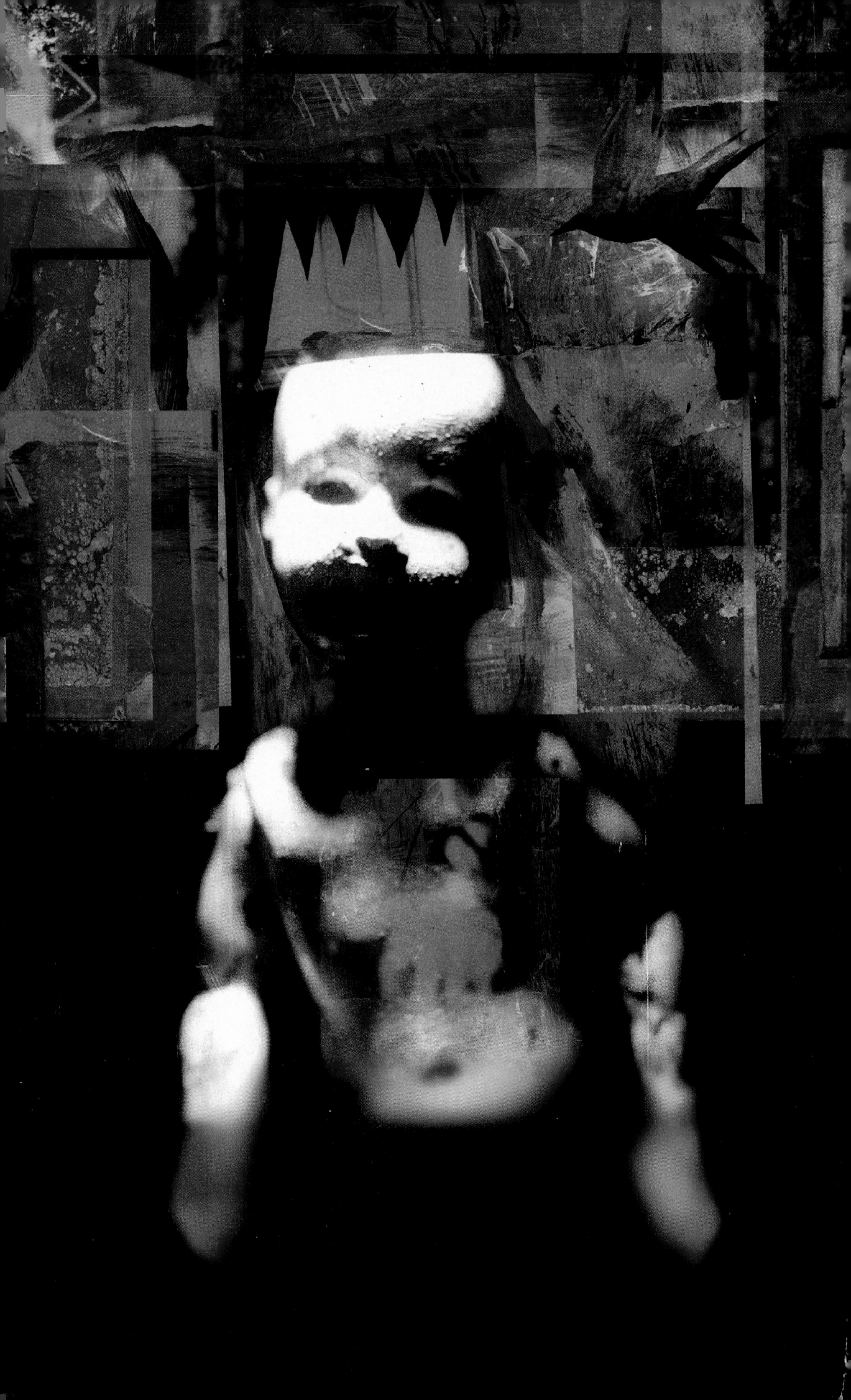

ENVOI

Never apologise. never explain.

It's not a bad two-rule maxim for life. all things considered. but it's not very helpful when it comes to writing afterwords for books. After all. the only reason people read afterwords is for some kind of explanation of what they've read. if they haven't understood it. or for some kind of apology. if they have.

So no explanations. no apologies. Instead. a few words of thanks and gratitude to the rest of the Sandman clan: thanks to Mike Dringenberg. who so beautifully turned so many ideas into people; thanks to Malcolm Jones. unsung hero of pen. brush and deadline; thanks to our guests Michael Zulli. Chris Bachalo and Steve Parkhouse. for lending their skills and unique vision to the story; heartfelt thanks to editor Karen Berger for being an embodied litany of the virtues (particularly patience. faith and hope); to Dave McKean for clearsightedness. magical covers. and friendship; and lastly grateful thanks to Todd Klein. letterer's letterer. who adds so much more to the whole than just the words.

Thanks are also due to (deep breath): Alan Moore. Clive Barker; Jack Kirby. Joe Simon. Michael Fleisher. and Roy Thomas; Winsor McCay; Persephone Longeuiel; Roz Kaveney; Mitzi and Sugar from Madame Jo-Jo's; Mary Gentle; Mikal Gilmore; Aimee and Jessie Horsting. Dave McKean and I would like to thank the cover photo models — Catherine Peters. Claire Haythornthwaite. Neil Jones. and some other guy.

And everyone who helped make the dream breathe...

NEIL GAIMAN. ENGLAND. APRIL 1990

BIOGRAPHIES | NEIL GAIMAN

Mike Dringenberg would like to thank GiGi. Shawn S.. Yann and Ivy. Bilbo. Pam. Victoria. Roland. Chandra. Sam Kieth. and A. Rimbaud. Special thanks to Cinnamon (wherever she is). the model for Death.

Malcolm Jones III would like to thank Dom Carola. Joe Rubinstein. Richard Bruning. Keith Wilson. and Dick Giordano. Special thanks to Randy DuBurke and George Pratt.

The editor would like to thank Karen Berger. Tom Peyer. KC Carlson and Ronnie Carlin for their work on the initial version of this collection.

is currently living in a big dark house in America with four cats and a great many awards from all over the world. He does not understand how he has come to be responsible for the feeding and domestic arrangements of four cats, nor, for that matter, why he lives in America. He is currently writing a television series for the BBC, called NEVERWHERE. His star-sign is Scorpio; his favorite color is black, and he likes sushi although he suspects it's secretly dead raw fish. He is married and has three children.

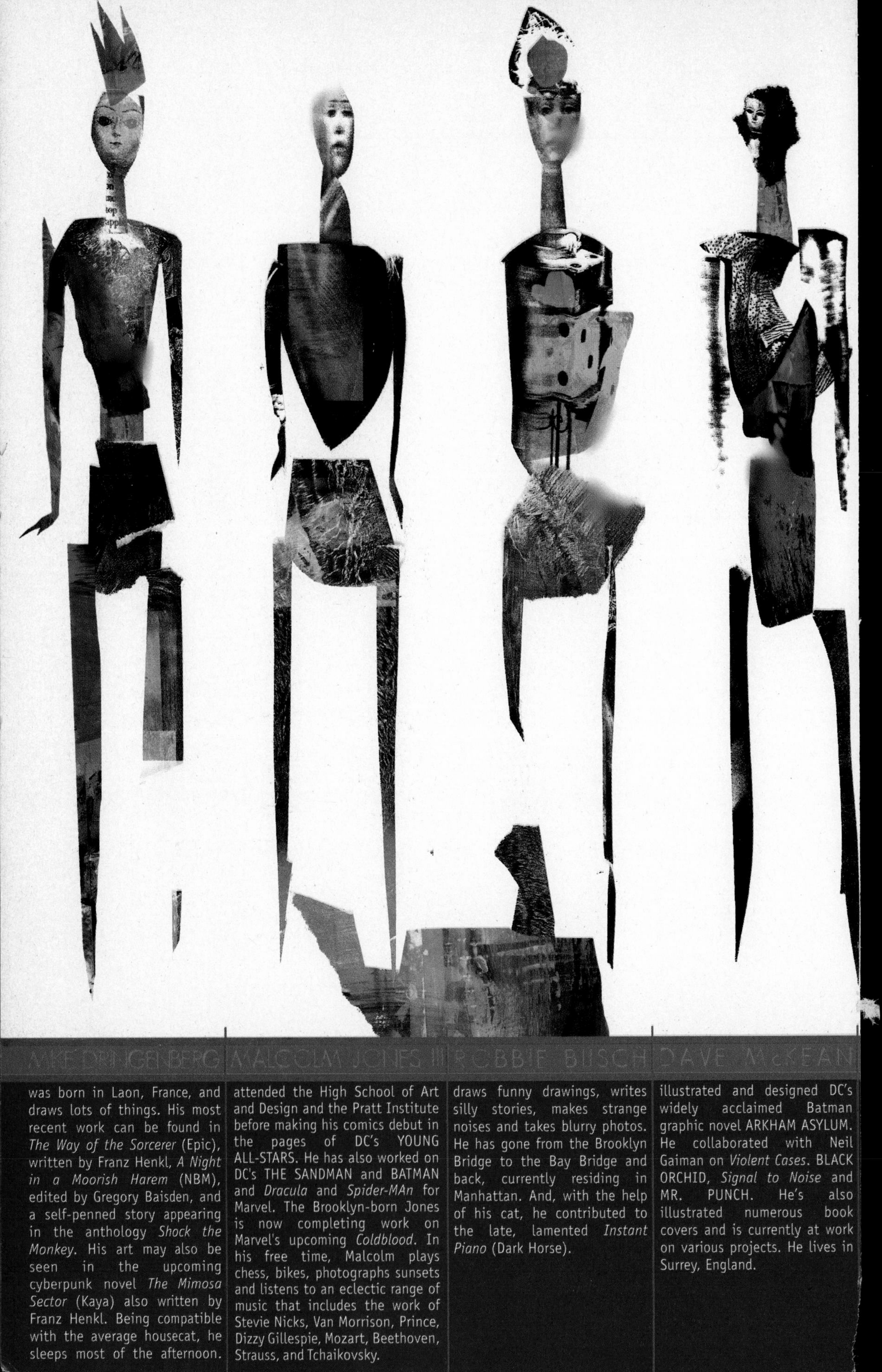

MIKE DRINGENBERG

was born in Laon, France, and draws lots of things. His most recent work can be found in *The Way of the Sorcerer* (Epic), written by Franz Henkl, *A Night in a Moorish Harem* (NBM), edited by Gregory Baisden, and a self-penned story appearing in the anthology *Shock the Monkey*. His art may also be seen in the upcoming cyberpunk novel *The Mimosa Sector* (Kaya) also written by Franz Henkl. Being compatible with the average housecat, he sleeps most of the afternoon.

MALCOLM JONES III

attended the High School of Art and Design and the Pratt Institute before making his comics debut in the pages of DC's YOUNG ALL-STARS. He has also worked on DC's THE SANDMAN and BATMAN and *Dracula* and *Spider-MAn* for Marvel. The Brooklyn-born Jones is now completing work on Marvel's upcoming *Coldblood*. In his free time, Malcolm plays chess, bikes, photographs sunsets and listens to an eclectic range of music that includes the work of Stevie Nicks, Van Morrison, Prince, Dizzy Gillespie, Mozart, Beethoven, Strauss, and Tchaikovsky.

ROBBIE BUSCH

draws funny drawings, writes silly stories, makes strange noises and takes blurry photos. He has gone from the Brooklyn Bridge to the Bay Bridge and back, currently residing in Manhattan. And, with the help of his cat, he contributed to the late, lamented *Instant Piano* (Dark Horse).

DAVE McKEAN

illustrated and designed DC's widely acclaimed Batman graphic novel ARKHAM ASYLUM. He collaborated with Neil Gaiman on *Violent Cases*. BLACK ORCHID, *Signal to Noise* and MR. PUNCH. He's also illustrated numerous book covers and is currently at work on various projects. He lives in Surrey, England.

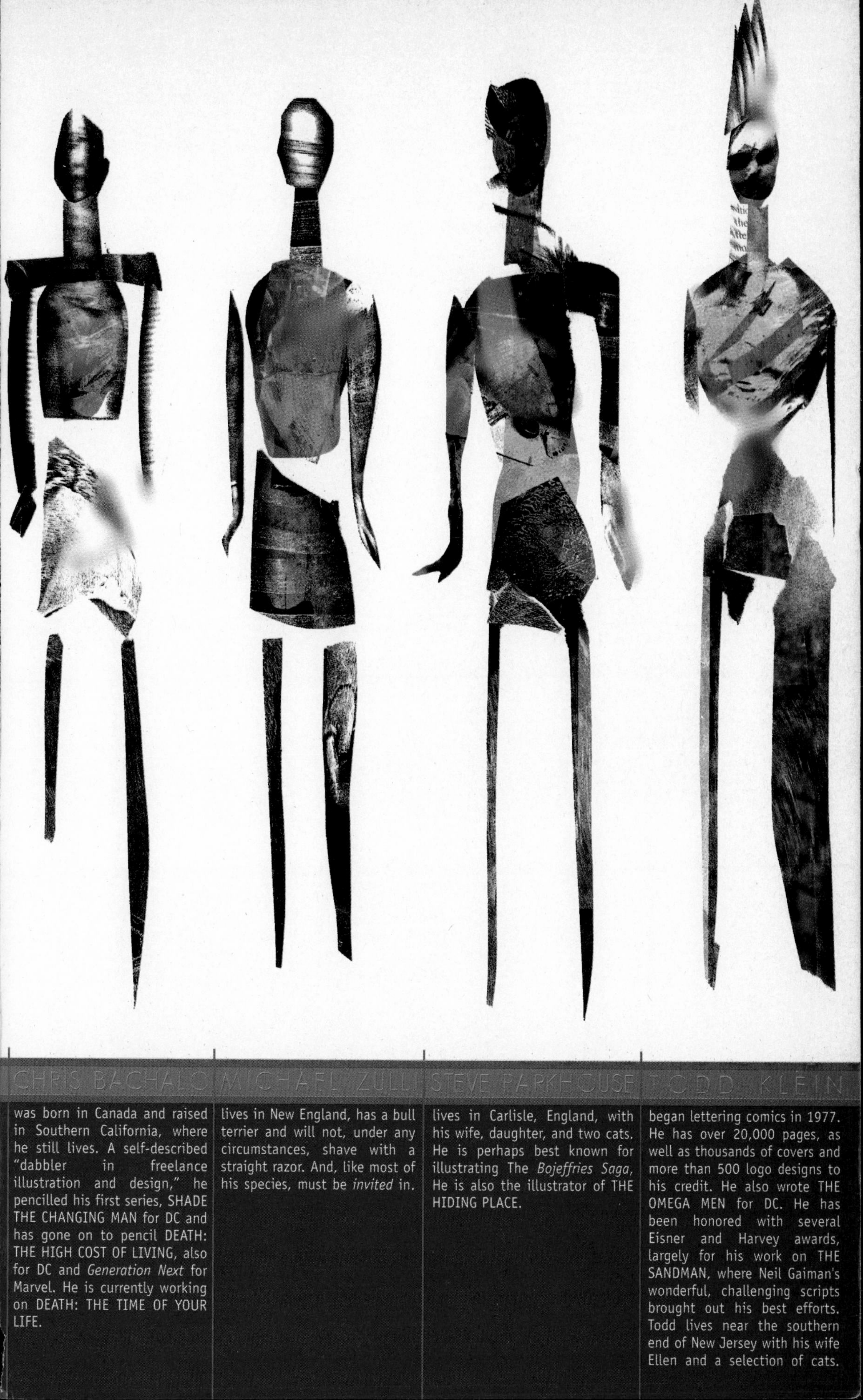

CHRIS BACHALO

was born in Canada and raised in Southern California, where he still lives. A self-described "dabbler in freelance illustration and design," he pencilled his first series, SHADE THE CHANGING MAN for DC and has gone on to pencil DEATH: THE HIGH COST OF LIVING, also for DC and *Generation Next* for Marvel. He is currently working on DEATH: THE TIME OF YOUR LIFE.

MICHAEL ZULLI

lives in New England, has a bull terrier and will not, under any circumstances, shave with a straight razor. And, like most of his species, must be *invited* in.

STEVE PARKHOUSE

lives in Carlisle, England, with his wife, daughter, and two cats. He is perhaps best known for illustrating The *Bojeffries Saga*, He is also the illustrator of THE HIDING PLACE.

TODD KLEIN

began lettering comics in 1977. He has over 20,000 pages, as well as thousands of covers and more than 500 logo designs to his credit. He also wrote THE OMEGA MEN for DC. He has been honored with several Eisner and Harvey awards, largely for his work on THE SANDMAN, where Neil Gaiman's wonderful, challenging scripts brought out his best efforts. Todd lives near the southern end of New Jersey with his wife Ellen and a selection of cats.

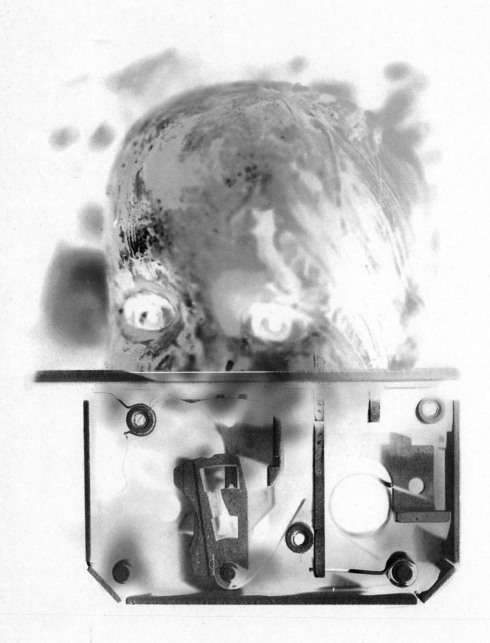